OFFICIAL
COMPANION GUIDE

Welcome, resident!

Welcome to your official companion guide to the Deserted Island Getaway Package! Whatever your goals and expectations for your personal island getaway may be, we want to help you achieve and exceed them. While putting this book together we've spent a lot of time relaxing on beaches, gathering island resources and trying on clothes in the Able Sisters' fitting room. No expense was spared, no insects were harmed and all loans have been repaid in full. We've made ourselves experts at living the island life, and now we want to share that knowledge with you. Or at least as much of it as we could fit into a reasonably-sized book. So relax, sit back and take it all in at your own pace—time is the one thing you have plenty of on a deserted island.

—The Future Press Team

What do you want to know?

Looking for something specific? Many topics in Animal Crossing: New Horizons are connected in various ways. We've aimed to cover everything in self-contained entries as much as possible (and it isn't always entirely possible), even if it sometimes means a little bit of repetition of some information. Even so, to get a complete understanding of almost any topic you'll likely need to visit various different sections of the book, so here we'll make it as clear as possible which kinds of questions each chapter is best at answering.

1 Welcome to Your Island Getaway!

2 Meet the Locals

3 The Nook Inc. Guide to Island Life

4 The Great Outdoors

⑤ The Workbench

⑥ Isabelle's Island Reviews

⑦ The Nook Collector's Catalog

The List of Lists

This book contains a whole lot of lists of the various things you can buy, collect or catch in Animal Crossing: New Horizons. Each of these lists is a valuable resource, but they aren't all in one place. Page 430, however, will give you an instant overview of all the lists in the book and what you're likely to find in them. This can make finding out about a particular subject much more convenient!

Online Calendar

To make keeping track of your island's goings on as easy as possible, we've created a handy online Animal Crossing: New Horizons calendar. To access it, head to www.future-press.com/AC, and follow the instructions there. To access this page, you can also just scan the QR code shown below or on your bookmark.

On the calendar you'll find every resident's birthday and their favorite styles, so you can prepare an appropriate present! It will also display any events that might be coming up soon, such as Fishing Tourneys and Bug-Offs, or real world events such as New Years Eve that will be celebrated in Animal Crossing: New Horizons. And you can set your calendar to match your hemisphere too!

Bookmarks

This book comes with two unique and helpful bookmarks. What makes them so helpful? Well, we've filled the back of each one with useful legends and page numbers to make finding and referencing things even easier than it hopefully already was!

Online calendar

Legend

Seasons

- Spring
- Summer
- Autumn
- Winter
- Northern Hemisphere
- Southern Hemisphere

Obtaining Items

- As an Item
- As a DIY Recipe
- In the mail
- Redeem Nook Miles
- Big sister — Personality
- 960 (240) — Price Tag: Buy (Sell)

Others

- Customization Kit
- Floor only
- Table/Platform
- Tabletop
- Table/Platform+Tabletop
- River Fish
- Pond Fish
- Sea Fish

TM & © 2020

Useful Lists

Clothes and Furnishings

Clothing Catalog	P.275
Furniture List	P.354
Rugs	P.393
DIY Recipes	P.218
Wallpaper	P.386
Flooring	P.397
Customization	P.352

Nature

Fish	P.178
Bugs	P.188
Fossils	P.194
Flowers	P.170

Island Residents

Resident List	P.82
Personality Types	P.74
Island Visitors	P.54
Photos and Posters	P.418

Online calendar

TM & © 2020 Nintendo.

Table of Contents

About Future Updates

Animal Crossing: New Horizons is an online game that will evolve as time goes by. The contents of this book, however, won't change after it's been printed. To get around this limitation, we'll be preparing PDF updates that effectively add new sections to the book whenever a major update occurs in the game. Look out for these updates at www.future-press.com/AC!

Chapter 1

Welcome to Your Island Getaway!

This chapter introduces the basic features of Animal Crossing: New Horizons.
It begins with a short overview of how Animal Crossing works, intended for players new to the series, then summarizes the goals of the game, new features and ways to play with other players.

CHAPTER HIGHLIGHTS

Getting Started in New Horizons

Animal Crossing: New Horizons brings with it some control options and menus that are new to the series. To make sure you can easily get started with the game, this section briefly explains how controlling the game works.

Controls

Let's begin by taking a look at controlling the game and learning which button does what. There are a lot of buttons, but even though each one has a use, control is simple and intuitive. You can tilt the camera's angle with the Right Stick, which is useful when you need to see behind a tree or building. You can also rotate the camera when inside houses, but not in facilities such as Resident Services. There isn't any real benefit to using a Nintendo Switch Pro Controller over the Nintendo Switch Joy-Con controllers—use whichever you find more comfortable and remember to take breaks when playing.

Game Controls

ZL NookPhone · Save and Quit · R Keyboard · ZR Reactions · Pockets · Walk/Run · Talk/Action · Tool Wheel · Sprint · Item Select · Cancel · Unequip Tool · Adjust Camera · Capture Button · HOME Menu

Touch Typing

Certain apps and features such as the bulletin board and the keyboard allow you to use the touch screen of the Nintendo Switch to do things like draw and type in a way that you may find more comfortable. Be sure to try it out and see which you prefer!

Key Actions

Other Actions

→ Digging (Shovel)
→ Climbing (Ladder)
→ Swiping (Net)
→ Swinging (Axe)
→ Fill Hole (Shovel)
→ Vaulting (Vaulting Pole)
→ Casting (Fishing Rod)
→ Shooting (Slingshot)

Here are some simple actions you'll use often that are important to get used to and remember. Once you have some tools, many other actions will be possible!

● **Further Reading**

Tools and How to Use Them	→ P.112
Gathering Materials	→ P.205

1

Sprint

Hold Ⓑ to run a little faster and get where you're going quicker! You never get tired, so sprint to your heart's content.

Push/Pull

Pressing and holding Ⓐ along with moving the Left Stick when near a placed item will let you push or pull it.

Shake

If you press Ⓐ next to a tree you'll give it a good shake, and something might fall out.

Open Doors

If a building's doors are closed, you can press Ⓐ to open them and enter the building. Unless of course it's closed to the public or the owner is sleeping.

Jump/Sit

Simply holding the Left Stick in the direction of a chair or stool will make you sit on it. Doing the same near a small gap will let you jump over it.

Pick Up

Orange

Pressing Ⓨ next to an item will pick it up and add it straight to your pockets.

Character Creator

Once you start a new game, you'll be given the chance to customize your very own resident! After choosing your skin tone, you can pick from a handful of hair styles and colors. You'll also have the chance to choose the color and shape of your eyes, as well as the shape of your nose and mouth. Finally, you'll be able to put some color in your cheeks by adding some blush. Take your time and find the combination that captures exactly what you want to look like. Once you've created a villager you're proud of, press the ⊹ Button to lock it in and begin your adventure!

● **Further Reading**

Character Customization Options   → P.266

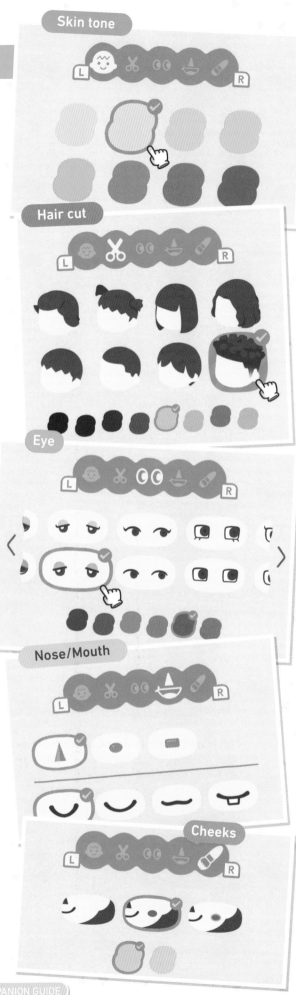

Skin tone

Hair cut

Eye

Nose/Mouth

Cheeks

Changing Your Appearance Later

As you explore the island, you'll eventually find or learn how to craft a variety of mirrors. Once you've obtained one and have placed it as furniture, a mirror can be used to freely change your character's appearance at any time by pressing Ⓐ. The menu this opens gives you access to all the options of the initial character creator, on top of new ones you can acquire by redeeming Nook Miles. If you ever change your mind about your appearance, head to the nearest mirror and try out a completely new look!

Choosing your Island

After you make your character, you'll be asked to choose from one of four potential starting islands. Each of these islands are pre-defined, and will always come with a few common features, such as a river, and a series of cliffs that block access to parts of the island. As such, while there are a wide variety of possible islands you can get, none are inherently better than any other—it all comes down to what you would like out of your island. Don't worry too much if you aren't able to get the exact island of your dreams though; you'll be able to heavily alter its geography as you progress through the game.

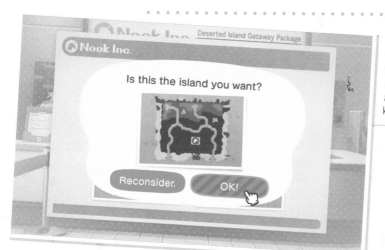

The exact island type you choose isn't very important in the long run, so don't agonize over the decision. You won't be able to move your Resident Services building later, however, and that includes the town square, so it's one thing worth keeping in mind.

● **Further Reading**

Island Types   → P.129

The Passage of Time

Many important characters and events can only been seen during the day time...

Time in the world of Animal Crossing advances at the same rate as time in the real world. The game's real-time clock is tied to the system clock of your Nintendo Switch, so the passage of time is always felt, whether you're currently playing or not. As time marches on, the island's residents will live out their lives—opening shops, wandering the wilderness, and much more. Be sure to check in with your neighbors every day, as doing so is essential for improving your relationships with them and for making sure that you don't miss out on anything. Just as in real life though, everyone needs to sleep, and the night offers its own opportunities. Certain fish and bugs are only available when it's dark, and there are even characters who will only appear after the sun has set.

Daily Growth Cycle

Although the clock moves in real-time, many things require the span of one or more days to have passed in order to happen. For instance, plants won't grow until a fresh day has begun, and you won't be able to harvest materials from trees and rocks again until the current day has ended. This daily growth cycle always occurs at precisely 5AM and is followed by an announcement if you log on past that time.

...while others only appear at night. Playing at different times of day can lead to many surprises!

● **Further Reading**

Weather   → P.159

Island Visitors   → P.54

Seasons and Events

As the days turn into weeks, the seasons will also begin to change. Depending on the time of year, you may be greeted by a shining sun or fresh layer of snow when you step outside. Much like the time of day, seasons will also play a major role in what fish and bugs are available to catch. Many creatures are only available during specific seasons and months, so be sure to check your calendar or any number of seasonal critters may pass you by.

Spring Summer Autumn Winter

● **Further Reading**

Animal Crossing's real time nature means that birthdays, contests and important dates in real life are celebrated on your island. If you have an online connection, then the game will sometimes be updated prior to these events to ensure your island will be ready for it. Events usually come with new items related to them, and characters might even dress for the occasion. A good example of this is New Year's Eve, which sees Tom Nook and Isabelle don some formal attire.

Bonus! **Online Community Calendar**

March 2020

As a bonus for anyone who owns this book, we've set up an online calendar for Animal Crossing: New Horizons. To access it, simply head to www.future-press.com/AC. The calendar will let you easily keep track of each resident's birthday and inform you of events and seasonal changes.

Mail

Who will send you letters?

→ Your Mom
→ Nook Mileage Program
→ Other Residents
→ The Happy Home Academy
→ Other Animal Crossing Players

Once you've set down your tent, you'll be able to access your very own mailbox. Whenever you receive letters or packages, a small blue flag with a tiny, blinking white letter icon will appear on the box. After receiving a letter, you can head over to your mailbox and read it by pressing Ⓐ. Your mailbox can hold up to 300 letters and packages—after it reaches this amount, the oldest letters will start to be thrown away. You'll notice that everyone who sends you mail has their own unique stationery. Most of these designs are available for your own use at the postcard stand in the airport building.

Packages

Along with letters, you will also frequently receive packages as well. Whether these be gifts from friends and family or a delivery for an online order, they can be collected from your mailbox. Once there, select the package you want and press Ⓐ to add it to your pockets. Packages count towards the limit of your mailbox, so be sure to pick them up as soon as they arrive!

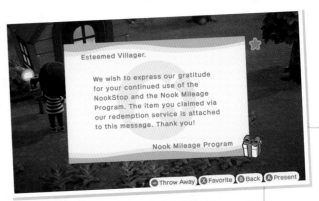

Anything you order from the Nook Mileage Program will show up in your mailbox the following day.

Sending Mail

You can also send letters and packages of your own by entering the Dodo Airlines building and pressing Ⓐ while facing the postcard stand to Orville's right. Here you can send both letters and packages to yourself or other residents for 200 Bells a piece. Once you've chosen the recipient, you will be able to pick from a wide range of postcard backgrounds to personalize your message. You can only send two letters per day to a friend, and you can add a gift to the letter by using the present icon in the bottom right. Letters to other residents will always show up the day after they've been sent, but it's possible to choose the exact date you'd like the letter to arrive if you're sending it to yourself. You can even have it delivered years later!

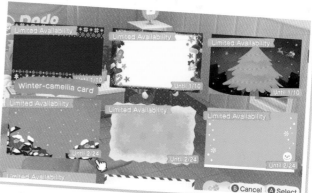

There are plenty of designs to choose from. Many are seasonal and only available for a limited time, so check in regularly!

● **Further Reading**

| Storing Items | → P.125 |
| List of Postcards | → P.414 |

The Goals of the Game

The Goals

→ Help Tom Nook
→ Improve Your House
→ Donate to the Museum
→ Complete Nook Mile Challenges
→ Build up Your Island
→ Customize Your House
→ Spend Time with Friends and Neighbors
→ Take It Easy

While Animal Crossing is often about casually living your life and going about your day, there's no shortage of more directed activities and goals. Here you'll find some of the more rewarding tasks that you can focus on. These can be completed at any pace, but there's often a significant reward for finishing many of them. If you find yourself looking for something to do, any of these are good choices.

This is the humble Resident Services tent, where you'll reliably find Tom Nook.

Help Tom Nook

Shortly after you first arrive, Tom Nook will enlist your help to turn the deserted island into a vibrant community. You'll need to complete a wide variety of tasks for him, from building specific items at a workbench, to making decisions about the future of the island. Helping him will not only teach you many of the most important things you'll need to know, but will also attract new visitors to the island. Tom Nook will also reward you with many essential upgrades, such as new apps for your NookPhone. With this in mind, it's highly recommended that you help out Tom Nook whenever you can.

● **Further Reading**

Main Storyline → P.127

Improve Your House

While Tom Nook's no-interest loans means there's no rush in paying them off, doing so will allow you to live more comfortably by upgrading your home with size increases, extra rooms, and a second floor. This will give you more freedom to decorate specialized rooms that are all your own. Upgrading your house is a long term pursuit and one of the best uses of your hard-earned Bells.

● **Further Reading**

Home Upgrades → P.34

Tent

House

Upgraded House

Donate to the Museum

As you explore the island, news of your discoveries will be passed to Tom Nook's scholarly naturalist friend, Blathers. Eventually, Blathers will establish a museum on the island, and you can bring your newly discovered wildlife or fossils to him for appraisal and donation to the museum. Once you donate a creature or item, it will permanently be put on display for all to see with a small note on its respective plaque denoting that you were the one who donated it. Visiting the museum allows you to view the creatures you've caught in all their glory. A fully equipped museum that contains every possible item is a sight to behold and would be a point of pride for any community. Not to mention it would make Blathers a very happy owl.

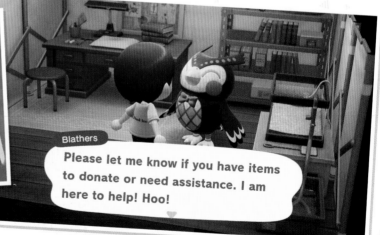

Blathers

Please let me know if you have items to donate or need assistance. I am here to help! Hoo!

Tools of the Trade

Digging up fossils requires a shovel, while catching fish and bugs requires a fishing rod and a net. These are all tools that you can craft as long as you have the right DIY recipe and some basic materials. There's nothing like being the proud owner of a good set of tools.

Blathers graciously takes on the role of the island's museum curator. Bring him anything you find and he'll give it a full appraisal.

● **Further Reading**

The Museum → P.38

Tools and How to Use Them → P.112

Complete Nook Miles Objectives

Not only are Nook Miles objectives a great way to stock up on the ever-useful Nook Miles currency, they will also unlock a wide variety of titles that can be used to customize your passport. Making the effort to check some of them off your list is always a good use of your time!

● **Further Reading**

Nook Mileage Program	→ P.146
Nook Miles+ Daily Challenges	→ P.151

Build up Your Island

Once you help Tom Nook establish the island's community, you'll find that you have a wide variety of ways to customize and improve the town. Be it creating paths, planting flower beds, building bridges, or any of the many other options available, there is no shortage of ways to shape the island to your liking. If you're in need of inspiration, you can always head to the Isabelle's Island Reviews chapter starting on P.232 for some ideas.

The further you get, the more options you'll have for improving your island and attracting more visitors.

Spend Time with Friends and Neighbors

Maybe the best part of building a community is getting to know the people and their individual quirks. Be sure to check in on your neighbors often to keep in touch and let them know that they're appreciated. You can also invite players from other islands to come visit your town. Once they've arrived, you'll be able to go fishing together, take group pictures, show off your hard work, or engage in any number of other activities. To learn more about this, check out the "Playing With Others" section later in this chapter.

● **Further Reading**

Making Friends	→ P.75
Meet the Residents	→ P.82

New faces will appear as the island takes shape, each adding more personality to your idyllic surroundings.

Decorate Your House

As you build and expand your house, you'll find yourself with plenty of personal space that you can decorate according to your tastes. These rooms can be outfitted with carpets, wallpapers, furniture, or just about anything else you can find. Take some time and design your living space into something you can be proud of. If you create something especially striking, the Happy Home Academy may even take notice!

● **Important resources for home decoration**

Upgrading Your House	→ P.136
List of Furniture	→ P.353
Nook's Cranny	→ P.42
Happy Home Academy	→ P.238

Basement Pool

Upstairs Bedroom

Bathroom

● **Further Reading**

Furniture Customization	→ P.352

Take It Easy

Just kick back and enjoy your island! There is rarely any rush to get any specific task done or loan paid back, so you're free to tackle any major challenges at whatever pace is comfortable. Be sure to take some time to relax and casually stroll your island—snap some pictures, design patterns, pick weeds, or just enjoy a sunset. Take things one day at a time and have fun!

New Features!

This section tells you all about the most important features that are new to Animal Crossing: New Horizons. We'll introduce these elements here with brief descriptions, and point to other parts of this book when there's more detail available (which there very often will be).

Resident Services

Resident Services functions as the headquarters of your island. Here you and Tom Nook will work together to begin building the island into a thriving coastal getaway. The Nook Stop can also be found here, and can be used to pay your bills, do online shopping, and deposit funds into your savings account. Lastly, you'll find the recycle box here, which sometimes contains items that have been discarded by other residents. Consult P.31 for more details!

● **Further Reading**

| Meet Tom Nook | → P.32 |

The Workbench

Want a new table in your kitchen? Head to a Workbench for a spot of DIY! The new crafting system allows you to create an impressive array of items. In fact, for a lot of items, the only way to acquire them is by building them at a workbench. Building anything requires a DIY Recipe and some basic resources. Fortunately, there are plenty of raw materials to be found from trees and rocks all over your island. We have a full chapter dedicated to DIY, starting on P.202.

Gathering materials is essential to begin your DIY activities. Once you have some, head to the Resident Services tent to use Tom Nook's workbench.

● **Further Reading**

Gathering Materials	→ P.205
Recipe List	→ P.217
DIY Basics	→ P.204

Island Bulletin Board

The Island Bulletin Board can always be found to the left of Resident Services. Here you can see any public announcements made by the other residents of the island, so checking in often is a great way to stay up to date on the latest events happening on the island. By pressing the ✛ Button, you can also create your own custom bulletin posting. Once it's been opened, you can use the keyboard to type out whatever message you like, as well as hand draw a background using either the Left Stick or the touch screen of the Nintendo Switch system. Be sure to make a welcome post to greet all your visitors!

Feel free to use the touch screen to add drawings to your messages.

Dodo Airlines

Dodo Airlines operates out of the island's very own airport, and is the gateway to endless adventure for those who want to explore. By talking to Orville, you'll be able to book a flight to a friend's island or invite other friends to come visit yours. Additionally, you can redeem a Nook Miles Ticket to go on a Mystery Tour that sends you to a randomized island. Once you arrive, you'll be able to collect extra resources, including fruit that may not be native to your home, and you can even encounter potential new residents who may be vacationing there.

● **Further Reading**

| Dodo Airlines | → P.50 |
| Mystery Tours | → P.51 |

New Tools

Animal Crossing: New Horizons brings with it lots of new tools that can enrich your island experience and make things easier. The ladder and vaulting pole are ideal for getting around an island environment, while magic wands will literally transform your wardrobe habits in an instant.

Fences

While not strictly a tool, the ability to place fences is a wonderful new addition to Animal Crossing, and acts much like a tool once you have it equipped. It lets you fence off areas, decorate paths or even create property borders, if that's your kind of thing. Creative use of this ability can have a trans formative effect on your island!

● **Further Reading**

| Tools and How to Use Them | → P.112 |
| Building Fences | → P.141 |

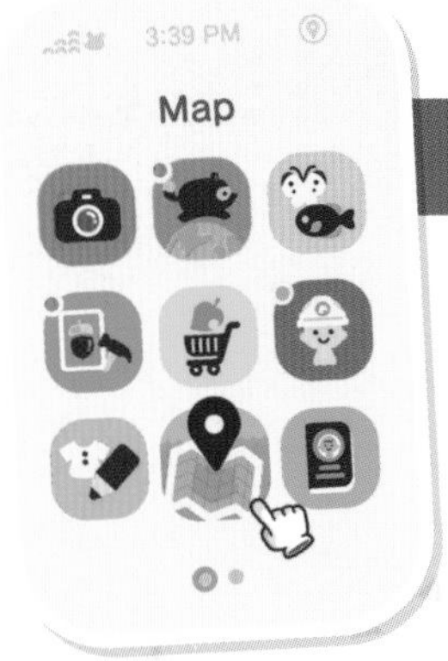

NookPhone

Your NookPhone is one of the most important items at your disposal. If you're the island's first resident, then you'll receive it immediately upon waking up after attending the founding ceremony. Players arriving later will receive their NookPhone just after landing on the island. This handy device can be accessed by pressing ZL. Together, the NookPhone's apps act as an ideal overview of the game's main activities, so we'll briefly describe each of them here to minimize spoilers, and then point you to further info on each topic.

Camera

Unlock: Default App

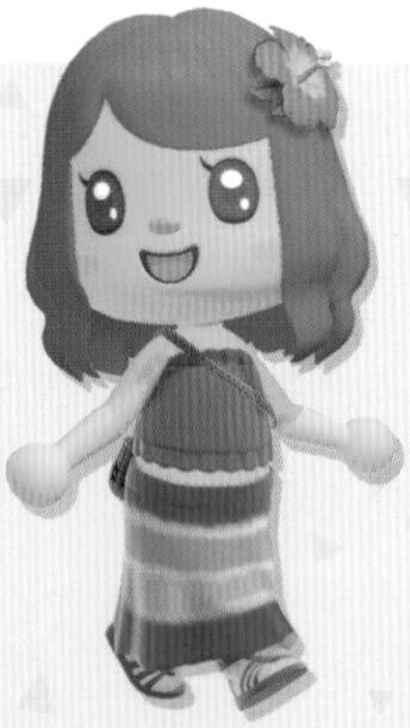

Want to capture a moment? Just pull out your phone and select the Camera app! Once you do, you'll have the ability to zoom the camera in and out using Ⓨ and Ⓧ, and you can also apply a filter over the photo to alter the color. After you've found the shot you want, press Ⓐ to snap the photo. You can then view them using the Album on the HOME Menu. Be sure to use a Reaction to strike a pose!

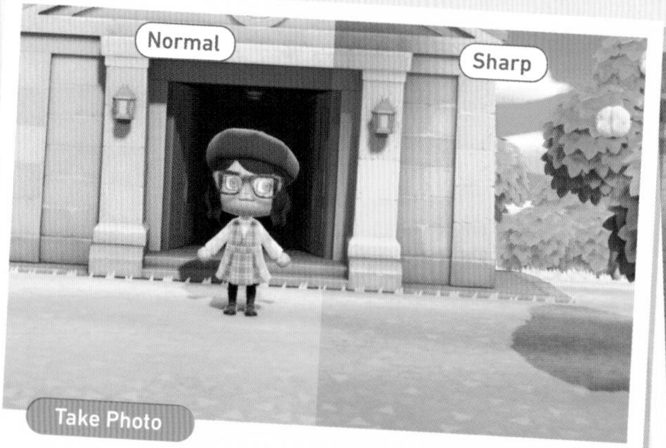

The game isn't paused while taking photos, so other residents can photobomb you!

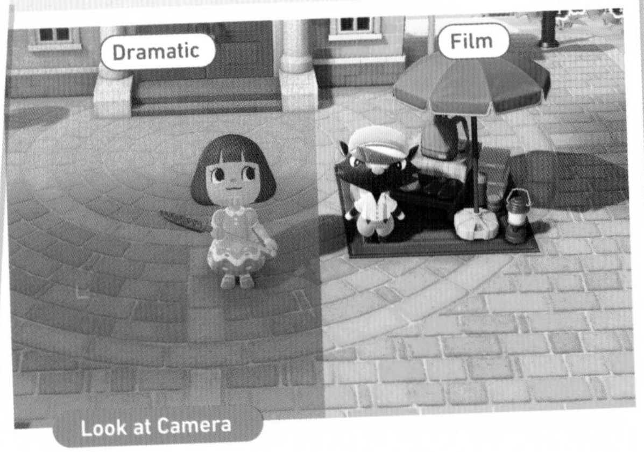

Perfect for selfies. If any residents are in the shot, they may also look at the camera!

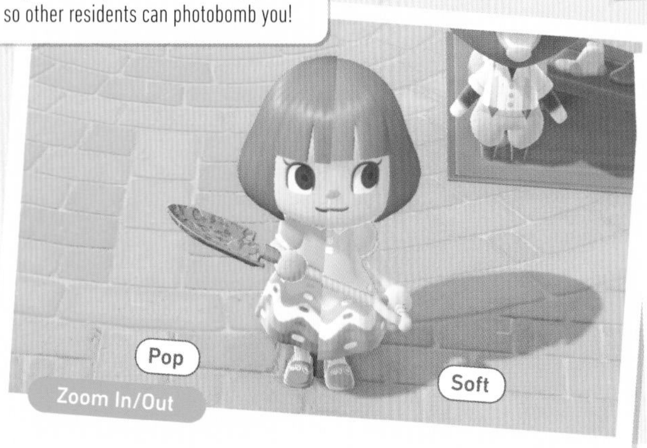

Equip tools or items before opening the app to have them appear in the shot.

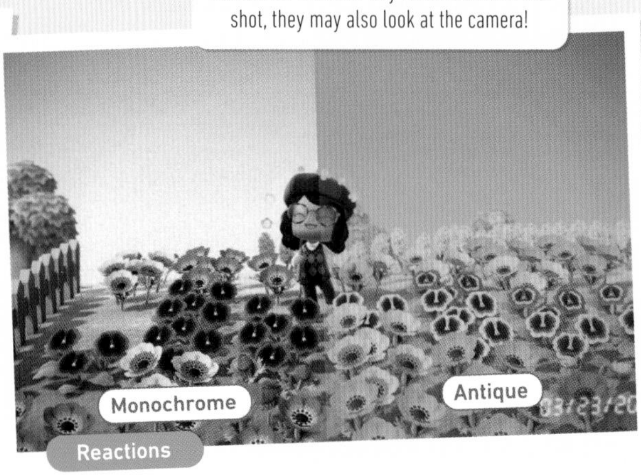

Press ZR to use Reactions to liven up your photo.

Further Reading

Visit Photopia ➜ P.69

Nook Miles — Unlock: Default App

The Nook Miles app is the main way to acquire Nook Miles for use at the Nook Stop. Initially, these can only be acquired by completing certain Nook Miles Objectives, such as First-Time Seller, which is unlocked by selling an item for the first time. The goals of these objectives can vary wildly. While many are rather straightforward, some will take a sizable amount of time and effort to unlock. Once you do, however, you'll be rewarded with Nook Miles! These Miles can be claimed by hovering over the completed card and pressing Ⓐ, and will also unlock certain exclusive titles to use on your character's passport.

Nook Mile objectives let you earn valuable Miles while doing things that benefit your island's community.

Nook Miles+ — Unlock: Pay Your Moving Fee

After upgrading your tent to a proper house, the app will be upgraded to Nook Miles+. This will grant you access to an endless rotation of small, temporary challenges that can reward you with a decent amount of Nook Miles. These challenges ensure that you'll never run out of opportunities to earn Nook Miles. The first five challenges you get each day will always feature a 2x multiplier that doubles the Nook Miles earned from completing them. On rare occasions though, you'll get a challenge with a x5 multiplier that'll give you five times as many Nook Miles for completing it! If you find yourself running short, take on some of these challenges and you'll find yourself with plenty in no time.

Good Vibrations

Not sure why your controller is shaking? Check your Nook Miles app! Whenever you complete a challenge, your phone will vibrate to let you know. Be sure to claim Nook Miles as soon as you earn them!

● **Further Reading**

Nook Mileage Program → P.146

Nook Miles+ Daily Challenges → P.151

Critterpedia — Unlock: Give Tom Nook a Creature

● **Further Reading**

Fishing → P.175

This helpful app will keep track of all the bugs and fish that you've caught. Once you catch a new species for the first time, you can use the Critterpedia to find the season and time of day during which critters you've already caught are available. Additionally, it tells you whether or not a critter has been donated to Blathers yet. Any critter that has been donated will have a small stamp in the bottom corner.

Fish/Bug Name — Koi

Time of Day it Appears

Seasonality
Jan.	Feb.	Mar.	Apr.
May	June	July	Aug.
Sept.	Oct.	Nov.	Dec.

Current Active Hours

Location Pond

Donated

When the Fish/Bug Appears

Water Type (Fish Only)

If the Fish/Bug Has Been Donated

DIY Recipes — Unlock: Complete the DIY Workshop

This app allows you to go through a complete list of the DIY Recipes you've unlocked as well as see the resources required to make them. Each Recipe belongs to a specific subcategory, such as Tools or Furniture, that you can browse through by using the Ⓛ and Ⓡ Buttons. This is especially useful for checking whether you have all the resources you need before trying to build an item at your workbench.

Once you find a recipe, use it from your pocket menu and the item you've learned to craft will permanently appear in your DIY Recipes app!

● Further Reading

Nook Shopping — Unlock: 100 purchases from Nook Shopping at Nook Stop

The Nook Shopping app works a lot like shopping at the Nook Stop found in Resident Services. You won't get this app until much later in the game, but it's worth the wait since it allows you to shop anytime and anywhere! When opening the app, you'll be able to peruse different categories that include all the wallpapers, flooring, furniture, clothes and more that you've encountered in your catalog. Special Goods are also available for purchase through this app, so you can quickly check the daily selection without needing to drop by the Nook Stop!

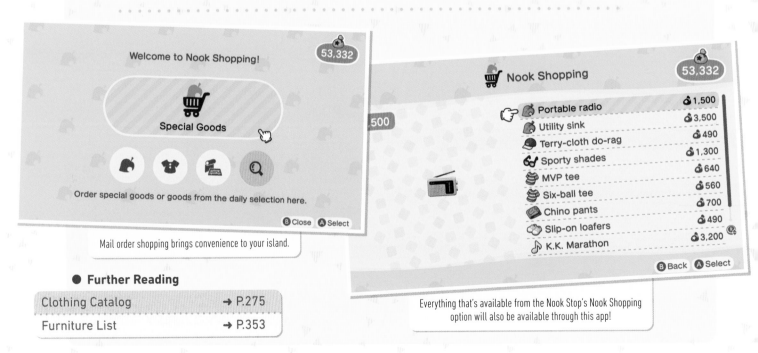

Mail order shopping brings convenience to your island.

Everything that's available from the Nook Stop's Nook Shopping option will also be available through this app!

● Further Reading

Custom Designs   Unlock: Default App

Using this app will bring you to the customs designs menu, where you can create a wide array of patterns and designs. These designs can be applied to a wide variety of items—shirts, carpets, wallpapers, phone case, or even your own face! Simply select the design you want to apply and choose whether you want to wear or display it. If you want to remove a design you chose to wear then open your pockets, select the clothing menu, and select the item to remove it.

Once you buy the Custom Design Pro Editor from the Nook Stop for 800 Nook Miles, you'll be able to access and create Pro Designs. These allow for a much higher level of detail and customizability than the standard Custom Designs. With the Pro Editor, you can design any part of a variety of shirts, dresses, and hats down to the most specific details. From the brims of hats to the hem of a robe, the Pro Editor gives you a wide array of colors and tools to bring whatever vision you have into reality. Let your imagination run wild!

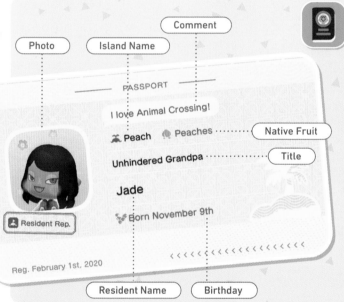

Passport   Unlock: Default App

The Passport app allows you to view and edit your own personal passport. This travel document highlights your name, title, a comment about yourself, the island you're from as well as the fruit native to your island, and your birthday (along with its respective zodiac sign). Once you've opened the app, pressing Ⓐ will allow you to change your passport photo, as well as add a short comment, up to 24 characters long. You can also give yourself a distinctive title using the keywords you've unlocked by completing any of the standard Nook Miles objectives found in the Nook Miles app.

Island Designer   Unlock: See the End Credits

The Island Designer is an app that you'll acquire after the game's credits have rolled. As you make changes to your island, you may be thinking about all the other ways you could adjust your island to truly make it yours. If so, this app might just prove that dreams can come true! Without spoiling too much, one of the app's most famed features is the landscaping tool; it really lets you give your island a unique personality. You'll need Nook Miles to unlock most of what this app can do; keep working with Tom Nook and racking up those Miles and you'll be able to do more than you've ever imagined!

● **Further Reading**

The Island Designer   → P.258

Map — Unlock: Default App

Selecting this app brings up the island's map. This map is very similar to the minimap, but far more detailed. Here you can highlight important locations such as stores and neighboring houses to help you locate them if you get lost. Additionally, its grid overlay can be incredibly useful for planning the more complicated aspects of your island's layout, particularly for things such as paths. Be sure to consult this map whenever you're starting major public projects.

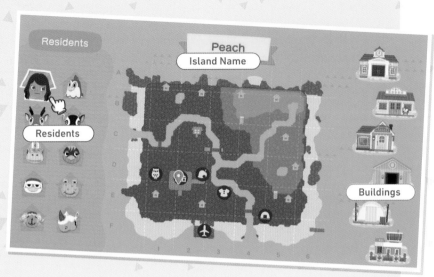

Call Resident — Unlock: Another Player Resident Joins Your Island

You'll unlock the Call Resident app once another player becomes a permanent resident on your island. Using this app, you can invite other residents from your island to spend time with you in Party Play mode. This mode is part of Animal Crossing: New Horizons' local multiplayer features, which are covered in full on the following pages.

! Rescue Service — Unlock: Default App

Selecting Rescue Service while you're outside will immediately connect you to the local Rescue Service hotline, who will offer to pick you up from wherever you currently are and return you to your home (or other locations). It costs 100 Nook Miles to use, but if you're in a jam with no Miles to spare, it might be possible to negotiate a ride regardless... This app cannot be used when other players are on your island, but if you get stranded on your own, you can count on it to get you back to safety.

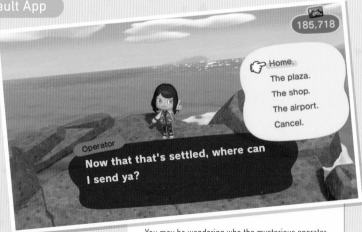

You may be wondering who the mysterious operator might be. That tune sure does seem familiar... He seems to be using some familiar phrasing too. Who could it be?

Playing With Others

There are three ways you can play Animal Crossing: New Horizons with your friends: Local Play, Party Play and Online Play. These are all different methods of inviting people to your island and vice versa, whether they're right next to you or across the globe!

Party Play

Any items that followers collect while using tools will be sent to the Recycle Box in Resident Services. You can collect these at any time, but be careful not to let it get too full or your fellow resident's work may be thrown away.

Once an island has been created, other players can move in as well by using a different profile on the same console. After you start a new game, you'll be taken straight to the island and given a NookPhone and the chance to choose where to place your tent. As soon as a second player has made their home on the island, all local residents will get a call from Tom Nook, who will install the Call Resident app. This can be used at any time to summon up to three other residents who live on the island. Once they arrive, they can be controlled by another player by connecting any Nintendo Switch controller. Keep in mind, other visitors can't be invited through Local or Online play while Party Play is active.

Followers and Leaders

As soon as another resident shows up, one player will be marked as the Leader and the rest as Followers. The Leader will get to play roughly the same as they would play alone with complete access to all standard features. This is not set in stone, though—you can change who's the Leader at any time by gently shaking the Leader's controller or by selecting the Change Leader option from the Call Resident app. Once you do, whichever player would like to take the role will need to press the Ⓐ Button to appoint themselves as Leader. The camera will always stay on the Leader first and foremost. If too much distance is put between the Leader and any of the Followers however, the Follower will be transported right next to the Leader once the distance has become too great.

Followers' options are still plentiful, but are slightly more limited than you may be used to—while you're a Follower, you will be unable to use your NookPhone, open your pockets menu, or use the chat function.

You can however still use tools, move furniture, and help the leader with a wide range of tasks.

Local Play

Using Dodo Airlines, you can really crank up the island party! If you have a friend nearby with their own Nintendo Switch, you can visit their island or open up your own for visits via Local Play. Just tell Orville at the front desk that you want to fly and visit an island via Local Play and he can scout out your friend's island for you! If multiple friends have their airport gates open at once, you can pick and choose which island you'd like to visit. You also have the option to make a secret 4-digit Dodo Code, in case you'd like to keep the riffraff out.

Starting Local Play

| Head into DAL | Talk to Orville | Select I Want Visitors | The Gates Will Open |

When Playing as a Visitor

You can't interact as much as usual with the nature of the island, whether that means excavating stones, chopping and uprooting trees, or catching fish, unless you're Best Friends with the island's owner. You can post on another islander's bulletin board, but you'll be limited to two posts. If you change your mind about something you've posted, press ⊟ to delete it.

There's tons to do on your visit. You can chat with animals, who'll tell you funny things about your friends and their islands. You may even get a sneak peak at your friend's Passport Titles. There's no need to worry about doing busywork like returning lost items, though. That's what an island's representative is for!

Orville

Wuh-oh! Looks like we're getting interference... Hang on... Someone not put their NookPhone into airplane mode again?

Make sure nobody is on their NookPhone while you're trying to fly, or it may cause some interference.

Party Time

The presence of certain special visitors can open up some great party activities since they'll still offer their services while you have guests. K.K. Slider will still gladly hold his concert for a big group, but he'll only start it once the host sits down. Fishing Contests and the Bug-Off can also accommodate guests. The Local Play session can end in a number of ways. If you're a host, you can press ⊟ to end it, or talk to Orville and have this done for you. Connection errors can also cause a trip to end. Travel is tricky business!

The Best Friends App

Once another player visits your island, Orville will give you the Best Friends List app for your Nook-Phone. When a player arrives, they'll appear on the "friends" list and the "all" list. You can then press Ⓐ to ask to be Best Friends, giving them extra privileges when they visit. To stop being Best Friends, press Ⓐ choose a player and select "Quit being best friends". This app lets you see which friends are online at the moment—you can press ⊟ to disable this feature, in case you don't want anyone to know you're online. You can also do all this from the Nintendo Switch app on your smartphone, as well as importing old designs from Animal Crossing: New Leaf and Animal Crossing: Happy Home Designer.

Facilities act differently during an island visit. Tom Nook and Isabelle won't be able to do much for the host island representative or their guests while the visit is happening. Just too much paperwork to do! The host will still be able to use the Recycle Box in the Resident Services Center, but if you happen to be the one visiting, it's rather rude to go through someone else's stuff. The Nook Stop also won't be compatible with your account on a foreign island. The host will be able to use their own Nook Stop, but you'll have to wait until you get home.

Making donations, the Drop-off Box or the postcard service, and making custom designs will all have to wait until you get home.

Online Play

Online Play requires a Nintendo Switch Online membership and uses a Wi-Fi connection to allow you to play with players across the world. You can visit their islands and they can visit yours. As usual, Dodo Airlines will facilitate bringing players to different islands, and once you're on another player's island, Online Play functions basically the same way as Local Play.

Online Etiquette

Playing with others online opens up the possibility to affect other player's islands, and not always in a positive way. If a player is doing something that you feel is offensive or particularly annoying, you can report their behavior. This can lead to consequences for the reported player, so it's best to be considerate of others and how they want their island to be.

Other Things to Consider

Trading items and Bells is a cinch if you don't mind picking things up off the ground—just drop whatever you want to trade, rather than placing it—placed furniture, fish tanks and insect tanks, both outdoors and indoors, can't be moved or picked up until the visit is over. If you're worried about how your island looks, we recommend doing your redecorating before your guests arrive.

In the Best Friends menu, you can press Ⓨ to open a keyboard menu and send a message to all of your Best Friends at once, or send individual messages by selecting a Best Friend with Ⓐ. You can use the keyboard to chat with friends (or your smartphone's keyboard if you're using the Nintendo Switch app). Usually, there's a profanity filter in place to avoid nasty words being used, but this doesn't apply to messages sent to Best Friends.

When speaking to Orville, you have the option to open your island to only your Best Friends. Be sure you trust someone when you make them a Best Friend, because they'll be able to dig up your trees and break your rocks!

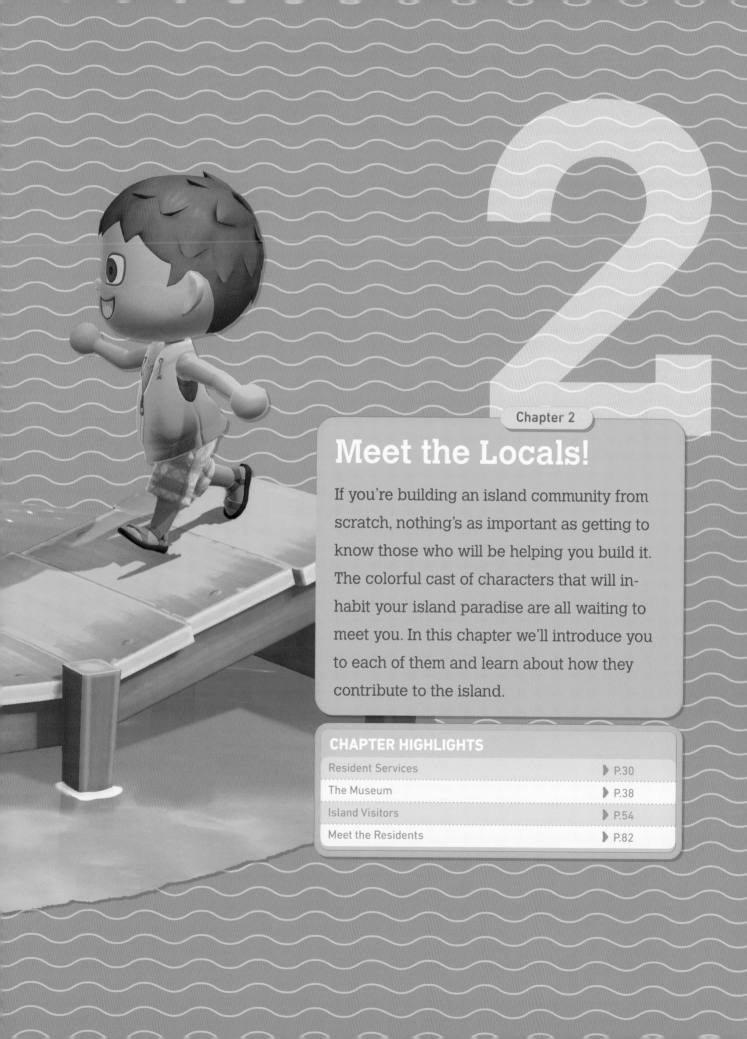

Chapter 2

Meet the Locals!

If you're building an island community from scratch, nothing's as important as getting to know those who will be helping you build it. The colorful cast of characters that will inhabit your island paradise are all waiting to meet you. In this chapter we'll introduce you to each of them and learn about how they contribute to the island.

CHAPTER HIGHLIGHTS

Resident Services

Welcome to Resident Services, the center of your island community! You'll spend much of your time shopping and crafting, and this building will act as a hub of sorts for many important gameplay features. Essential to island life, the Resident Services building will host some of the most helpful and important island residents. Let's meet them, shall we?

Workbench

Construction Consultation Counter

Isabelle's Counter

Recycle Box

Nook Stop

Upgrading Resident Services

Want to know how to move Tom Nook out of a small tent and into a residence more befitting the architect of the Deserted Island Getaway Program? It's a process that requires a lot of dedication, but we've provided a short summary in the "Island Infrastructure & Project K" section found just a few pages ahead. To see all the steps in full detail, head over to P.127 in the Nook Inc. Guide to Island Life chapter.

Island Service Providers

Tom Nook   Isabelle   Lloid

Nook Stop   This invaluable little kiosk can be found in the bottom right corner of the Resident Services building, and will quickly become a vital part of any new resident's life. Here you'll perform some of the most important tasks you'll need to take care of. Let's give its features a quick look!

ABD

The Automated Bell Dispenser, or ABD, is where you can deposit and withdraw Bells to and from your Bank of Nook savings account. At the beginning of each month, you'll gain 0.05% interest on however many Bells are in your savings account at the time. This makes the ABD easily the best place to safely store excess Bells; it keeps them from cluttering up your pockets. This is also where you'll go to pay off any outstanding debts you might have with Tom Nook.

Nook Shopping

Each day, this digital store will have a selection of special goods available for sale. Not only that, but you'll be able to purchase any standard items that you've obtained from the catalog.

Invite amiibo Camper

Have an amiibo of your favorite resident but haven't found a way to get them to move in? This is your answer! Once you've built the campsite and recruited your first new resident from it, this ability will appear at the Nook Stop. Just select the option at the Nook Stop to scan your amiibo and they'll quickly show up at your campsite. For more on amiibo functionality, turn to P.416.

Redeem Nook Miles

As soon as you've paid off your moving fees, you'll unlock the ability to redeem Nook Miles at the Nook Stop. Some of the most important items, upgrades and recipes can only be acquired using this digital store. The Nook Miles Ticket to go on Mystery Tours is the most important item you'll be coming back here for. Other vital purchases include the Tool Ring, Pocket Organization Guide, three DIY recipe packs and two hairstyle packs. Once Resident Services is upgraded, the Ultimate Pocket Stuffing upgrade item will be another essential purchase, along with some big-ticket DIY recipes. Finally, fencing recipes will be available after finishing all three house plots, and Island Designer permits will become available after seeing the end credits.

Recycle Box   See that large bin in the bottom left corner? That's the recycle box! Villagers will sometimes bring their unwanted items here, but one person's trash is another's treasure—be sure to check it from time to time in case your neighbors have thrown away an item that might be of use to you. When new residents move in they may leave their cardboard boxes here, and when they move out they're likely to leave an item of furniture behind, and maybe even some of their clothing.

If the recycle box has less than 10 items inside (after building Nook's Cranny), then each day there's a decent chance of one of the following items appearing inside it:

Items	No.	Chance
Nothing	--	55%
Clay or iron nugget	3	5%
Small Furniture (can be seasonal)	1	5%
Clothing (can be seasonal)	1	5%
Flower seed (native flowers)	1	5%
Sapling or cedar sapling	1	5%
Wallpaper or flooring	1	5%
Trash item	1	5%

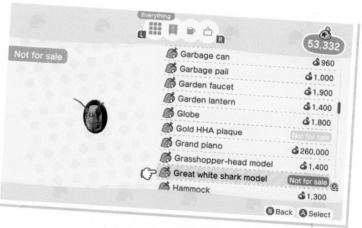

Items acquired from events or with Nook Miles can be viewed, but are not available for purchase from the catalog. Items you've acquired multiple variations of can be cycled through using the Ⓧ Button.

There are also some items that can appear in the recycle box that may not be very desirable. These items are considered trash, but sometimes even trash has its uses!

Tom Nook

> "Don't worry, anything is possible with a zero-interest loan and a generous repayment plan!"

Meet **Tom Nook**; the mastermind behind the Deserted Island Getaway Package and your partner in transforming the island into a bustling community. Tom Nook is a guy with big dreams and an even bigger heart who's here to help you make the most out of island life. He's in charge of Resident Services, where you'll spend much of your time crafting, purchasing items and using some of his many useful facilities. This guy will handle a great variety of responsibilities at the start of the game, such as taking care of any issues you may face while living on the island, helping new residents move in and adding new features and buildings to your island. You'll also need to pay off your home loans to Tom Nook.

Tom Nook is quite a resourceful businessman who makes sure to stay on top of the island's growth and development. Bells are definitely important to him, but don't be mistaken—Tom Nook cares deeply about the needs and happiness of each and every island resident. As a man of business, Tom Nook has made many connections over his lifetime and as such can introduce you to some new faces. This of course includes the esteemed Blathers, an old friend of his. Tom Nook also works very closely with Timmy and Tommy, whom you'll soon become quite familiar with!

Did You Know?

Tom Nook is commonly thought of as a raccoon, but for Japanese audiences he's a tanuki, also known as the Japanese raccoon dog. Tanukis are significant in Japanese folklore; they are masters of disguise and able to turn worthless items into valuable ones with the power of a mysterious leaf. Whether or not Tom Nook possesses these powers, however, remains a mystery.

Biography

Birthday	May 30th
First Appearance	Animal Crossing (2001)

Tom Nook first appeared in the original Animal Crossing (2001), where he would greet you as you arrived in your new town via the train. He ran the town's local store, Nook's Cranny. He was also in charge of the local real estate market, providing players with loans to buy homes as well as helping with house renovations—provided the original debt was paid, of course. In later games, Tom Nook's focus would shift more to his second love of real estate, helping players improve their homes, and working closely with the Happy Home Academy, the organization in charge of evaluating the decor of homes.

Tom Nook

Yes, yes, that's all from me for now. Sweet dreams, Villager!

Island Role Once you arrive, Tom Nook will quickly become your partner in transforming the deserted island into a vibrant getaway. While he'll fill many roles over the course of your journey, the most important one may be his ability to answer the question 'What should I do?' If you're ever in doubt about what needs to be done or how to continue improving the island, be sure to speak to Tom to receive sound advice. Tom Nook will be the one you'll come to when you want life on the island to improve and progress, and here we'll go through the different paths he'll lead you down.

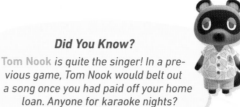

Did You Know?

Tom Nook *is quite the singer! In a previous game, Tom Nook would belt out a song once you had paid off your home loan. Anyone for karaoke nights?*

Tom Nook is often seen working on his laptop . He also drinks coffee at his desk, sorts the shelves and reads books when things aren't too busy.

In the early mornings, Tom Nook and Isabelle do some gymnastics. Isabelle seems to enjoy it more than Tom Nook does.

Opening the Museum

As you start out, you'll find yourself frequently returning to speak with Tom Nook in the Resident Services tent. Early on, he'll give you your very own NookPhone, and then he'll offer a workshop on how to build DIY items. This begins a series of events that lead to the opening of the island's very own museum. While opening the museum isn't a requirement for launching the infrastructure projects to come, it leads to rewards that greatly help to achieve those.

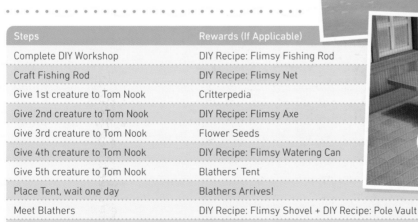

Tom Nook

With that, your move-in fees have been paid in full. This is a happy day for us both, hm?

Steps	Rewards (If Applicable)
Complete DIY Workshop	DIY Recipe: Flimsy Fishing Rod
Craft Fishing Rod	DIY Recipe: Flimsy Net
Give 1st creature to Tom Nook	Critterpedia
Give 2nd creature to Tom Nook	DIY Recipe: Flimsy Axe
Give 3rd creature to Tom Nook	Flower Seeds
Give 4th creature to Tom Nook	DIY Recipe: Flimsy Watering Can
Give 5th creature to Tom Nook	Blathers' Tent
Place Tent, wait one day	Blathers Arrives!
Meet Blathers	DIY Recipe: Flimsy Shovel + DIY Recipe: Pole Vault
Donate 15 more creatures to Blathers	Construction of Museum begins
Wait till Next Day	Museum constructed!

The path to opening the museum is completely unconnected to your loan repayments or the island infrastructure projects that owning a house leads to.

Home Renovation

Tom Nook is also in charge of home renovations. In order to make the most out of your new life, you'll need to ask him to upgrade your tent to a proper house. From there, he'll continue to offer you loans to expand your house in various ways, from extra rooms to additional floors. However, he'll only do this after you've paid any outstanding debts—even Tom's generosity has its limits.

Tom Nook

Don't worry about a thing. We can set up your getaway package to include a lovely furnished home.

As with the museum, every home upgrade after paying off your moving fees is completely unrelated to the island infrastructure projects that eventually lead to upgrading Resident Services.

- 📷 Cost in Nook Miles
- ⚪ Cost in Bells
- ⠿ Room Size
- 🗄 Storage Amount

④ Back Room
- ⚪ 348,000
- ⠿ 12x12
- 🗄 240

⑤ Left Room
- ⚪ 548,000
- ⠿ 12x12
- 🗄 320

Main Room ③ ② ①

⑥ Right Room
- ⚪ 758,000
- ⠿ 12x12
- 🗄 400

① Move-In Fees
- 📷 5000
- ⠿ 8x8
- 🗄 N/A

② Home
- ⚪ 98,000
- ⠿ 12x12
- 🗄 80

③ Expansion
- ⚪ 198,000
- ⠿ 16x16
- 🗄 120

⑧ Basement
- ⚪ 2,498,000
- ⠿ 12x20
- 🗄 1,600

⑦ Second Floor
- ⚪ 1,248,000
- ⠿ 12x20
- 🗄 800

Home Customization

Once you have a house, Tom Nook offers you the ability to customize it whenever you'd like for the humble cost of 5,000 Bells. As soon as you completely upgrade your house and pay off every single Bell of your final loan, Tom will provide this service free of charge, once per day. To see the full range of customization options you can choose from, turn to P.346.

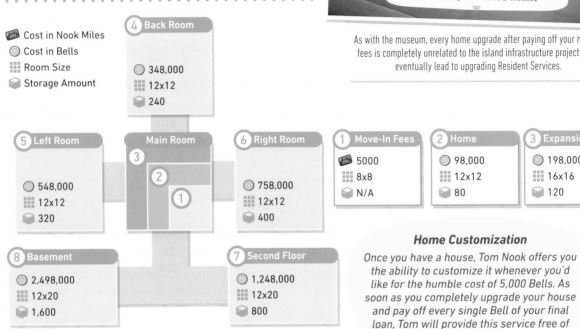

Island Infrastructure & Project K

Upgrading your tent to a real house marks the beginning of a sequence of infrastructure projects that will transform the island, all spurred on by Tom Nook's desire to create a paradise that can attract more residents (and eventually, a certain big-ticket act), a plan he calls "Project K". The Main Storyline section, starting on P.127, walks you through each of these steps in detail.

Steps	Result/Reward (If Applicable)	Page
Pay off Moving Fees (5000 Nook Miles)	Unlocks 'Redeem Nook Miles' at Nook Stop	→ 136
Take out loan to build house, wait one day	Tent upgraded to house + Mystery Tours/Nook Miles+ unlocked	→ 136
Talk to Tom Nook and Timmy	Material collection for Nook's Cranny begins	→ 138
Deliver all materials to Timmy	Shop construction kit obtained	→ 138
Choose space for Nook's Cranny, wait one day	Nook's Cranny constructed!	→ 138
Talk to Tom Nook	Craft and place bridge construction kit	→ 138
Talk to Tom Nook	Place new resident homes	→ 140
Furnish new resident homes (Need to craft 18 total items)	New residents can move in + Unlocks fences/DIY customization/Harvey	→ 141
5th Resident arrives, wait one day	New Resident Services building constructed!	→ 142
Build campsite & attract 6th resident	Unlock "Sell Land" option with Tom Nook	→ 144
Have 8 residents and raise island rating to at least 3 stars	KK Slider Concert!	→ 145

Opening Ceremonies

Tom Nook likes to celebrate any successful endeavor—after completing most projects, he'll offer you the chance to take part in an opening ceremony. Whether it be something as minor as a new bridge or as momentous as the opening of a new shop, always check in with Tom if you want to celebrate the latest addition to your community. It's guaranteed to make for a great photo op!

Construction Consultation Counter

After upgrading Resident Services into something more like a town hall, Tom Nook will move behind the construction consultation counter. Initially, the most important thing he offers here is the ability to sell land, which will be essential to allowing new residents to move in. If you're struggling to grow your community, make sure that you've spoken with Tom Nook to sell land and mark an area for your final arrivals. That's not all though—he offers everything from building and demolishing bridges and inclines, to relocating any building (other than Resident Services) for the cost of 50,000 Bells. So if your neighbor is being a bit too noisy, or you'd like a tighter knit community, you can now just reorganize your island until you've found exactly what you're looking for. Just remember that rebuilding does still take time and the cost can add up quickly.

Service	Details
Sell Land	10,000 Bells
Relocate Building	50,000 Bells
Relocate Home	30,000 Bells
Home Customization	5,000 Bells
Create Bridge	98,000-228,000 Bells
Create Incline	98,000-228,000 Bells

Isabelle

"I hope you all enjoy the loveliest of lovely days!"

Once the Resident Services building has been erected, Isabelle will start working there alongside Tom Nook. A friendly and helpful face, Isabelle is second to none when it comes to dedication and work ethic. This chipper assistant loves visiting the beach and collecting seashells, so island life will suit her well. If you want to learn more about Isabelle and how she spends her free time, pay attention to the announcements she makes every morning. She also has a brother, Digby, with whom she's especially close.

Island Role

Isabelle's job is to help you with a wide array of tasks related to the development and upkeep of the island and its residents. She can provide four distinct services, which we'll go over here.

Did You Know?

Isabelle is near-sighted. She wears contact lenses at work. If you visit her while she's taking a day off, you might find her in a pair of glasses.

Island Evaluation

Once Project K has started, her most important duty is helping manage the island's reputation through the Island Evaluation Service. After gathering feedback and comments from visitors and residents, she'll give you a tip as to how to improve your island's rating, whether that means more scenery, or cleaning up some weeds. The island can rank anywhere from one to five stars, and having a good rating is essential to making the island all that it can be and attracting big names to come visit. Keep working on getting that ranking up and there could be some special surprises and items in store for you! Head to P.234 for full details on this.

Isabelle

"This is a good island, filled with good feet that know the value of a good rug. Visitations are pleasant."

You might be able to guess who the island's reviews come from by their often... unique way of expressing their opinion.

Island Tune

Isabelle is also in charge of the official Island Tune. When you open doors, talk to villagers, or the town clock chimes, you might have noticed the same tune playing. Through Isabelle, you can change this to be whatever you'd like! This is the only place you get to make music, which makes it really special. She'll provide a menu where you can decide the notes of this song, then sing it back to you, just to make sure it sounds nice. Your tune can be a total of 16 beats. There are 13 notes ranging from a low G to a high E; you also have the option to set a beat to a random note, a rest, or to elongate a singular note. Once you're done with your song, the change takes place right away.

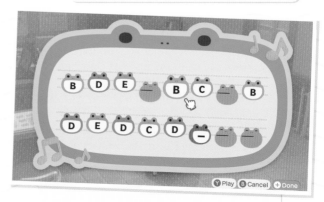

The Island Tune Maker is a powerful tool for composing music, and a good tune makes a huge difference to your island's mood.

Island Flag

Have a custom design you think would work well for the Island Flag? Isabelle will be happy to help you set it up! The Island Flag is displayed outside the Resident Services center as well as the airport. Once you submit your design, the flag will be displayed immediately.

Discussing Residents

Lastly, there's one responsibility that Isabelle holds that's a little less fun: Discussing Residents. Specifically, she's responsible for dealing with problem residents. If there's a resident that dresses inappropriately or maybe has a catchphrase you don't particularly like, you can talk to her about their clothing or the way they talk. The following day, their outfit will be changed to an Isabelle-approved default outfit, or their catchphrase will revert back to their original.

Biography

Birthday	December 20th
First Appearance	Animal Crossing: New Leaf (2012)

First appearing in Animal Crossing: New Leaf, Isabelle worked as the town mayor's assistant. She would help you set up Public Work Projects around the town, set ordinances into effect and assist with any other small changes you might like to make to the town. Since then, Isabelle has played a prominent role in Animal Crossing: Happy Home Designer, Pocket Camp and even became a fighter in Nintendo's Super Smash Bros. Ultimate!

Isabelle often takes care of the flowers on her desk. She also sometimes reads a book and even takes a short nap during quiet periods.

Lloid

Did You Know?

In previous games, Gyroids only appeared in the ground after it rained. Lloid on the other hand appears anytime you need him. Does that make him a superhero?

Lloid will act as a donation box for any projects you may start around your island, such as building a new bridge or incline. As soon as you place down the marker kit for a construction project, he'll appear in front of it and remain there until the work is complete. If you speak with him, he'll tell you how much the current project costs and how much has already been donated. Any player can then donate as many Bells as they see fit, 'till the project is paid off. Sometimes, some of the island's residents will donate as well, but gathering pocket change can take a while. How much is required depends on the specific project, but construction can't begin until it's paid in full, so don't forget to lend him a hand—after all, he doesn't have any thumbs of his own.

Biography

Birthday	August 28th
First Appearance	Animal Crossing: City Folk (2008)

This talking Gyroid first appeared in Animal Crossing: City Folk where he ran an Auction House. Players could auction off items here, or bid on items listed by others. This could be a great way to earn money or get your hands on a rare item you might not have expected. In New Leaf, Lloid became the construction foreman in charge of overseeing donations for Public Work Projects—a role he retains in New Horizons.

The Museum

Museum Curator

Blathers

Have you ever caught a bug or a fish? Perhaps you've dug up an unidentified fossil? Once you've helped Blathers set up the island's museum, any interesting specimens you find will be easily identified and can be put on display for the whole community to appreciate!

Blathers' Tent

The Museum will start off as a humble tent, which you're able to build anywhere you'd like on the island. Here you'll meet Blathers, who'll give you the DIY Recipes for the flimsy shovel and vaulting pole when you speak to him for the first time. Afterwards, you'll be able to start donating any critters you find to contribute to the Museum's collection of exhibits. Additionally, Blathers can also assess whatever fossils you may bring him and add any new ones to the collection.

The Full Museum

Once Blathers has received a combined total of 15 donations, be they fish, bugs, or fossils, construction will immediately begin on your island's new cultural hub—a fully sized, impressive Museum! It comes fully equipped with space for every fossil and critter you can find on the island, meaning no further upgrades to the building are necessary.

The Fossil Hall
Head downstairs and you'll be transported back to the island's distant past. This exhibit hosts all of the fascinating fossils you have dug up around the island.

The Insect Rooms
The left wing of the museum is where all of the bugs you've captured will be housed and on display, despite Blathers' aversion to them.

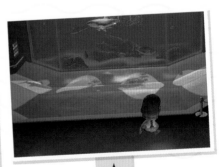

The Entrance Hall
Blathers greets you here whenever you enter the museum.

The Aquarium
The museum's right wing is dedicated to exhibiting the island's aquatic life. Any fish you've donated will appear in beautifully arranged tanks here.

Blathers

"Might I give you a short presentation on the topic? I am quite knowledgeable you know."

Expert in zoology and paleontology, **Blathers** is quite an eccentric character. Tom Nook calls him to the island once you find yourself in need of a naturalist to help identify the local fauna. You'll first meet him in his makeshift tent, but after receiving enough of your donations, he'll upgrade it to a full-sized museum.

Blathers

Hooooo... WHO?!

Blathers, being an owl, is nocturnal, so visiting the museum during the day can wake him up with a shock.

As an owl, Blathers can often be found asleep during the daytime; he's sure to wake up once you speak to him, however. Unlike most owls, he's terrified of bugs and will recoil and shudder every time you donate one to him. However, he's quite fond of fish and is fascinated by fossils. Blathers can provide you with a treasure trove of information about each specimen you donate. In fact, it's fair to say that Blathers likes to talk... a lot. You should pay attention, though; he's an expert in his field. Nobody on the island knows as much about bugs and fish as Blathers does!

Biography

Birthday	September 24th
First Appearance	Animal Crossing (2001)

We first met Blathers back in Animal Crossing (2001), where his role of assessing specimens and curating the museum was very similar. Back then, however, Blathers was not able to assess fossils by himself, as he did not have the correct qualifications. You would need to send your fossils off to the Faraway Museum to have them assessed. In the next game, Blathers had passed his exam and could assess the fossils himself. In Animal Crossing: New Leaf he dreamt up a second floor for the museum, where players could make their own exhibits, making it the biggest museum yet.

2:13 PM
July 12 Sun.

Island Role   As the local curator, Blathers is in charge of accepting donations to the museum. As soon as it's been built, you'll be able to donate any new fish or bugs that you've caught directly to Blathers. These will then be put on display for all to see in their respective wings of the museum, complete with a plaque commemorating the date it was donated and the name of the resident who donated it.

Fossil Assessment

As you explore the island, you may occasionally notice little cracks in the ground. If you dig into these cracks using a shovel, you'll often find rare fossils. Once you have one in hand, be sure to bring it to Blathers as soon as you can—he'll be able to use his robust paleontology knowledge to identify any

fossils you excavate, which can then be donated, or sold for a nice profit. While he's still in the tent, Blathers will only be able to identify one fossil at a time, but after the Museum has been built, he'll be able to assess as many fossils at you can bring him in one swift go!

As you'd expect from an academically-minded owl, Blathers can often be seen reading a book on his favorite topics: fossils, fish or er... fiction.

Ask Blathers

While Blathers may not reward you for your donations with items, he'll always be eager to offer you something even more valuable—knowledge! Whenever you donate a new critter or fossil, Blathers will offer to tell you more about the specimen you've provided. This is entirely optional of course, but who

can pass up the opportunity to learn from such a dignified educator? Additionally, if you'd like to hear his scholarly opinion on an item after it's been donated, he'll happily repeat himself if you show him a second identical specimen to jog his memory after the Museum's been built.

Blathers' knowledge of creatures is sometimes as hilarious as it is impressive.

It's easy for Blathers to get into a rhythm and recite a bit more than you necessarily need to hear.

Nook's Cranny

Nook's Cranny

Nook's Cranny

Opening Hours: 8AM - 10PM

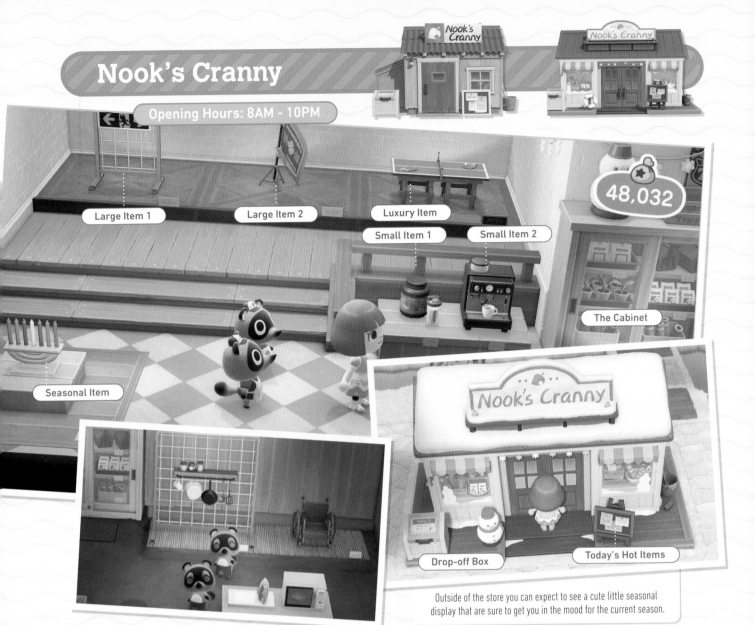

Large Item 1

Large Item 2

Luxury Item

Small Item 1

Small Item 2

48,032

The Cabinet

Seasonal Item

Nook's Cranny

Drop-off Box

Today's Hot Items

Outside of the store you can expect to see a cute little seasonal display that are sure to get you in the mood for the current season.

Need to buy or sell an item? There's no better place than Nook's Cranny! With a wide variety of unique items to purchase each day, including tools, flowers and useful accessories, Nook's Cranny is your island's one-stop shop. Run by brothers Timmy and Tommy, you'll find a variety of useful amenities here.

Nook's Cranny Shopkeepers

Timmy

Tommy

Building Nook's Cranny Think it's time Timmy and Tommy moved out of Tom Nook's tent? After paying off your moving fees, you can help them along by gathering and donating all of the materials that they ask for (30 softwood, 30 wood, 30 hardwood, and 30 iron nuggets). You'll then have the chance to decide where the new shop will go, and must only wait one day before it's open for business!

A Further Upgrade After the store has been open at least 30 days and you've made 200,000 Bells worth of transactions there (buying or selling), the twins will have the opportunity to renovate it into a much more sleek and modern store, with a further expanded inventory. Make sure to keep speaking with Timmy and Tommy and supporting their endeavors so you can help make their dreams become a reality!

Store Displays

Nook's Cranny is fully equipped with all kinds of display cases for different types of goods. Here we'll explain exactly what each one displays so you'll know what to keep your eye on while shopping.

Small Item Displays

In the front display on the blue shelf, two random items that are 1x1 block or smaller will be available for purchase each day. You can buy as many of these as you want! Really dig romantic candlelit dinners? You can buy forty candles in one go! Well, so long as you have the Bells to pay for them.

Large Item Displays

Up the staircase will be three larger furniture items, but these are in limited stock! If you see something you like, you'll need to act fast. It won't be there tomorrow and you'll only get to buy one. This is also where wall furniture may show up.

Luxury Item Display (Upgraded store only)

The furniture found on the far right of the large items display will always be a "luxury item". That means whatever's on this spot is going to cost quite the pretty penny, or Bell, in this case. This is also where you'll tend to find the biggest furniture.

Seasonal Item Display (Upgraded store only)

Near the front of the store, just left of the doorway, there's an open space that might not have anything. Keep your eyes peeled for the start of a season. There's a chance that special limited seasonal items like surfboards might show up!

After upgrading the store, the cabinet offers better tools, double the umbrellas, 30% more flowers, twice the wrapping paper and double the wallpaper and flooring!

The Cabinet

On the right-hand side of the store by the cash register, there's the cabinet, which holds all the everyday essentials. In the upgraded Nook's Cranny, there's everything from basic tools, flower seeds and even medicine. The exact items change daily, but here's a list of their basic types:

- Two types of each tool, one flimsy and one standard durability.
- Two Umbrellas (daily rotation)
- Medicine
- Nine flowers (all colors of your island's native flowers, and two random colors of a seasonal flower)
- Two saplings and your native fruit
- Nine recipes (also available in the smaller store). These never change.
- Miscellaneous tools (the Party Popper and the Timer)
- Eight wallpapers and eight floorings (daily rotation)

Drop-off Box

Nook's Cranny features a handy Drop-off Box outside the store; items you place in it will be sold overnight and you'll receive the Bells the next day. This is especially useful if you find yourself with items to sell after the pair have closed up for the day. However, it comes with two substantial drawbacks: first and foremost, all goods will sell for 20% less than they would if sold inside. Secondly, Turnips cannot be deposited into the Drop-off Box, since the twins need to check their current price before accepting them. Generally, selling to Timmy and Tommy face-to-face is the better option, unless you're in a real hurry.

Ask Timmy & Tommy or check the sign outside Nook's Cranny to find out what's in demand today. Selling a high-value item will net you double the Bells!

"Please don't hesitate to ask if you need assistance!
...assistance!"

The twins **Timmy and Tommy** are the first faces you'll meet when beginning your island adventure. Upbeat, energetic, and constantly bouncing off each other, these twins might seem like a lot to handle; don't worry though, they're strictly professional and have been working alongside Tom Nook for a long time. The pair are inseparable and even copy each other's speech at the end of a sentence, a quirk you'll come to notice the more time you spend with them.

It's almost impossible to tell Timmy and Tommy apart. Tom Nook, however, has no trouble telling the two apart. What's his secret?

Island Role Timmy and Tommy help Tom Nook around Resident Services. At the start of the game, they will help you decide your character's appearance and name, and give you a chance to pick your island. Once you arrive at your island getaway, they'll provide you with a tent to live in while the community finds its feet. After the island has been named, you can speak to Timmy inside of Resident Services to purchase and sell items at the start of the game. Tommy, meanwhile, will wander the island and offer useful tips about living there.

Timmy and Tommy look up to Tom Nook and want to impress him by working hard—they even refer to him as the island's fearless leader, a title that he's sure to embrace warmly. These young entrepreneurs are entirely devoted to their work

Timmy

President Nook! I've got Crystal here!

You might occasionally see Timmy or Tommy sip some juice or read a book while taking a break in the Resident Services tent.

Did You Know?
The twins' full names are Timothy and Thomas, and their favorite song is K.K. Paradise.

around the island and will do their absolute best to help out as much as possible. Like Tom Nook, they've also made connections with other characters in the past; this includes Mabel, who the pair will interact with when you first meet her.

Tom Nook

Welcome to Peach!

Nook's Cranny Like their mentor, the twins have great ambitions for the island: they'll want to set up their own store there once you've built your house. After you've delivered the required materials to Timmy, they'll begin construction on their own version of Nook's Cranny. With their new store, they can provide you with a greater variety of items and services to help make island life even more convenient. With each day will come a new Hot Item the pair are looking for, a random in-demand item that they'll happily pay twice the normal amount for. Additionally, they'll start keeping track of turnip prices, making them essential for playing the stalk market. Check P.70 for more information on Daisy Mae and her valuable turnips. They'll remain in the role of shop proprietors from then on, but you'll also see them attend all island events and ceremonies, no matter when or where they take place.

Timmy and Tommy can be seen wearing matching outfits. Not only do they match each other, but they also match Tom Nook. They'll even match his outfit in the colder seasons too!

Did You Know?
Timmy *has been revealed to be older than Tommy in past games. Tommy's voice is also slightly more high pitched.*

Timmy & Tommy Sign You Up

Create Your Character	Choose Your Island	Off You Go!

Timmy

Our next step will be to take a picture of you, Villager.

Timmy

Just follow your instincts and choose an island with a layout that looks appealing. That's how I'd do it!

Timmy

Ah, perfect timing! C'mon! Let's all board the plane together! ...together!

Biography

Birthday	June 7th
First Appearance	Animal Crossing (2001)

Brothers Timmy & Tommy made their first appearance in the original Animal Crossing (2001), working on the top floor of Nookington's. The pair would follow you around the store floor, assisting you in purchasing a variety of items; furniture, wallpapers, floorings and more. In later games, such as Animal Crossing: Wild World, rumors began to circulate about the connection between the twins and Tom Nook. Some residents speculated that Tom Nook had rescued them from the streets, while others thought they were his nephews. In Animal Crossing: New Leaf, Timmy and Tommy took over Nook's Cranny for Tom Nook, so he could focus on Nook's Homes and his real estate enterprises.

Able Sisters

Stall Opening hours 5AM - 10PM

Store Opening hours 9AM - 9PM

Custom Design Displays

Recommended Items

Fitting Room

Mannequins

If you need to purchase some new outfits, you'll have to speak to these lovable sisters. They can help you get the freshest looks on the island; original designs made by creative hedgehogs. Let's get to know each of them and how they fit into island life.

Shopkeepers

Mabel

Sable

Mabel's Stall

Before the Able Sisters can provide you with the ultimate fashion outlet, Mabel will be part of the weekly rotation of possible special visitors at your island (see P.55 for more on this). Her stall has less options than the full store does, only nine items to be exact, but buy from her kiosk on three different occasions and you'll unlock full access to the Able Sisters' line in no time!

Mabel can sometimes be seen arranging her apron, while Sable sometimes stretches her cloth or wipes off sweat as she's sewing.

Store Options

Here we'll take a quick run through the surprising amount of ways you can shop at the Able Sisters' store. Remember that every bit of clothing available, including Labelle's exclusive line, is listed in full detail starting on P.275.

Mannequins

Each week, the two mannequins in the shop will display two new stylish looks—each of these outfits has four items available for purchase. These mannequins will usually be dressed in recommended stylings, with items that work best when worn together.

Recommended Items

The floor display shows off the Able sisters' hottest looks! The displays change each and every day with fresh new clothes to try. Every daily selection contains a new one-piece, top, set of bottoms, pair of shoes, accessory, and hat. You can buy more than one of each item, so feel free to stock up!

Custom Design Displays

These displays are placed on the back wall of the store. When Able Sisters first opens, this wall is filled to the brim with designs you can ask to keep for yourself. There are eight available slots on the display, allowing you to show off your own designs and pro-designs, free of charge! Get creative! Who knows? Maybe one of your villagers will take a liking to one of your designs and wear it themselves!

Fitting Room

Can't decide what to buy? No problem! On the right side of the store, there's a curtain where you can walk in and try on all the hot looks that Able Sisters has to offer. This encompasses all the items available from The Able Sisters store and ones you already own, including tops, bottoms, one-pieces, hats, accessories, socks and shoes.

You can mix and match outfit pieces and even buy multiple pieces at a time once you've found your dream outfit. Select different clothes by pressing Ⓐ and then select ✛ to complete the purchase. You can even wear your new clothes right out of the fitting room. Be mindful that some garments may override others. You can't wear two sets of sunglasses at once, after all!

The Able Sisters' catalog is very extensive, and includes items from the Labelle line, exclusively designed by Label.

Mabel

"Not so fast! If you wanna buy something at THIS store, you go through ME!"

This is **Mabel**, the youngest of the three Able Sisters. She manages the Able Sisters' tailor shop and will help you purchase a variety of different clothes created by her sisters. Level-headed, confident and in charge, Mabel is very supportive of her sisters and will do whatever she possibly can to cheer them on. Mabel is especially close with Sable, although they may bicker sometimes, as sisters often do. Mabel usually has her head in the clouds and may say things that end up embarrassing Sable.

Island Role Mabel is the co-owner and clerk of the Able Sisters' tailor shop. Initially, Mabel will randomly appear on the island as a visitor from 5 AM to 10 PM. She'll set up a stall in front of Resident Services and have a limited selection of clothing to choose from. Eventually, she'll be ready to open up her own store, bringing with it access to oodles of new clothes, accessories and features to try out! She'll be in charge of all purchases as well as displaying your own designs and pro-designs.

Mabel

Aha! Something tells me that today is your lucky day!

Mabel is quite familiar with Timmy and Tommy. You can find them chatting together the first time you meet her.

Did You Know?
Mabel doesn't quite have the sewing skills that Sable does, but as the more outgoing of the two, she's the perfect fit to run the store.

Biography

| Birthday | May 22nd |
| First Appearance | Animal Crossing (2001) |

Mabel made her first appearance in Animal Crossing (2001), where her role was much the same. Back then, there were only two known Able Sisters: Mabel and Sable. In the past games, rumors would circulate about an estranged third sister; there were some clues that she had perhaps tried to get in touch with the pair.

Sable

> "Papa always told me 'Stitching overtime can save your spines!'"

This is **Sable**; the creator of all the great clothes you can purchase in the store. An expert with a sewing machine, Sable can also help you change the colors of your furniture. Before that, though, you'll need to get to know her. Sable is quite reserved; she won't open up right away. Eventually, she'll warm up to you and the two of you can expect to become great friends. Sable has been somewhat of a mother figure to her younger sister Mabel after their parents passed away. Mabel was too young to remember her parents, but for Sable it's still a very sore subject and she keeps her memories close.

 Island Role   Sable is more shy than her younger sister, but once you get to know her, she unlocks a brilliant new feature. After talking to her for eleven days in a row, she'll allow you to use some of her exquisite cloth patterns. Now that you two are friends, she'll start on a new project just to share with you! Everyday, she'll give you a new patterned fabric set to use on your customizable furniture. Not all furniture can use her patterns: you'll be able to tell when you use your customize feature and see an icon with a checkered-print square.

The large, quilted tapestry hanging on the left side of the Able Sisters' store belonged to the sisters' mother.

Each set contains 20 awesome patterns for you to choose from.

10 total pattern sets to collect	
Polka-dot print	Striped
Checkered 1	Checkered 2
Traditional 1	Traditional 2
Retro	Natural
Toys	Cool

Biography

Birthday	November 22nd
First Appearance	Animal Crossing (2001)

Like her sister Mabel, Sable first appeared in Animal Crossing (2001). Just as in New Horizons, Sable was pretty engrossed in her work and often asked you to leave her alone. With time and patience, she eventually opened up a little and shared some memories about her childhood. In Animal Crossing: Wild World, Sable also revealed that a certain month of the year makes her sad. She tells you that she and Tom Nook used to be best friends before he moved away to the city to pursue his big goals. The pair would often write to each other after this move, and Sable still thinks of Tom Nook very fondly.

Did You Know?

Sable sometimes calls her sister Mabel 'Mabes'. When she feels a little more comfortable, she even likes to tease her sister a bit over old memories too.

Dodo Airlines

Postcard Stand

Customer Service

The Gates

Seating (up to 8 players)

Aviation Crew

Orville

Wilbur

Welcome to your gateway to the skies—Dodo Airlines (or DAL) will set you on course for new horizons. At Dodo Airlines, you'll meet two new characters who can help you get where you need to go. Orville does the organizing, while Wilbur pilots the planes. Let's meet this avian pair and see what they're all about.

DAL Services The island's airport has quite a few features that are well worth knowing about and taking advantage of. We'll take a quick look at each of them here so that you're fully informed about all things DAL!

The dodos are also responsible for facilitating playing with others, either in Local Play or Online Play. For more on this, flip to P.25.

Mystery Tours

Purchase a Nook Miles Ticket from the Nook Stop in Resident Services and you'll be able to embark on a Mystery Tour to a faraway island! Take your new ticket to Orville, and he'll help set you off on your way. Wilbur will wait by his plane and can give you tools in exchange for Nook Miles, just in case any of yours break. These faraway islands are a great place to gather crafting materials when you've exhausted your own back home. Not only that, but sometimes you might run into a new animal who's camping out on the island. Talk with them and you might be able to invite them to live on your island.

Mystery Tour islands are different each time, so make sure not to leave anything behind. Any items you do leave behind will be gone the next time you visit. You may find some islands are better for certain things, such as having more rocks or more trees to get materials from. For more on this check out P.205, where we show the exact increases in mineral occurrences. These islands are also a great place to get hold of new types of fruits, fruit trees and even bamboo trees to bring back to your island. Be sure you have energy if you have plans to uproot anything!

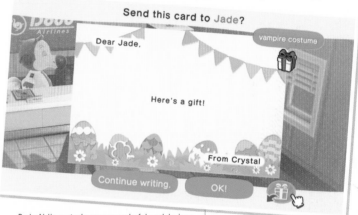

Dodo Airlines stocks many wonderful card designs. If you want to see all of them, head over to P.414.

DAL Merch! DAL rewards its most loyal frequent fliers with thank you letters in the mail. These letters come with exclusive DAL merchandise attached, so keep an eye out for them!

List of DAL merchandise	
☐ DAL apron	☐ DAL pilot jacket
☐ DAL backpack	☐ DAL slippers
☐ DAL cap	☐ DAL sunglasses
☐ DAL eye mask	☐ DAL tee
☐ DAL model plane	☐ DAL umbrella
☐ DAL mug	

Postcards

At the top right corner of the airport, next to Orville's desk, you'll find the postcard stand. Inspect it to see the current range of lovingly designed postcards. Each one is available for a cost of 200 Bells and can be mailed either to your future self, an island resident or another Animal Crossing player. Note that you can only send up to two letters to a friend each day, and that some of the card designs are seasonal items, so they'll only be available at certain times of the year. Be sure to check the postcard stand often so you don't miss some cool, unique designs.

Harv's Island

Once you've met Harvey, Dodo Airlines will offer trips to visit his island, which is home to Harv's "Photopia"! For more info on Harv's Island and Photopia, head over to Harvey's section, starting on P.68.

Orville

> "Friend, you've asked the right dodo!"

Making his first appearance in New Horizons, Orville can be found working away at the desk inside the Dodo Airlines building. This happy avian will assist you with anything you need during your visit. If you want to take a flight to another island, you'll have to talk to him first. Not only that, but Orville can also help you by giving you useful explanations about the airport. Friendly and easily approachable, no one is better suited to being the face of Dodo Airlines!

Island Role   Orville works hard at his desk 24/7 to keep Dodo Airlines running smoothly. At the front kiosk, you can ask him for the following services:

I wanna fly!

I wanna visit someone.
Use Nook Miles Ticket.
Visit Harv's Island.

I want visitors.

Via local play.
Via online play.

Most of these options lead to playing with others, either via local play or online play. If you want to know more about online and local play, head over to P.25 for a rundown of how each works.

Orville is a fast typer and a very organized dodo. He does occasionally take short breaks to drink coffee or read an exercise book, though.

Did You Know?

If you use the Apologetic Reaction toward Orville, he might get a little teary eyed. This only happens if the apology is directed toward him. It's a response to an apology that's very unique to Orville; he never wants a patron of Dodo Airlines to feel unhappy.

Biography

NEW

Birthday	October 2nd
First Appearance	Animal Crossing: New Horizons (2020)

Orville might be a new addition to Animal Crossing, but he's sure to end up a fan favorite. He's also the first of a new species to appear in the series: Dodos! Not only that but dodos are the first extinct species to appear alive and well in Animal Crossing. That's a lot of firsts! Orville and Wilbur... why does that pair of names sound familiar?

Orville

Dodo One, this is Dodo Tower—Wilbur, you copy? Got a walker who needs wings, over.

Wilbur

"Delta Oscar Delta Oscar is go!"

Also appearing for the first time in New Horizons, **Wilbur** is a bit quirkier than Orville and speaks almost entirely in aviation chatter. Though he may sometimes be a little hard to understand, Wilbur is responsible for taking you to beautiful new islands in his airplane. Once you've arrived on a new island, he may help you out by providing you with useful tools you'll need to make the most of your stay. An experienced pilot, you're bound to be in for a safe and leisurely journey in his capable hands. Or, er, wings.

Island Role   Equal parts expert aviator and stoic protector, Wilbur will be your pilot to whatever destination you fly to, including every Mystery Tour you charter. After you touch down on a mystery island, Wilbur will offer support by providing you with flimsy tools at the cost of 100 Nook Miles each. DAL's security doesn't stop you bringing your own tools with you, but this service can be helpful if you forget to pack yours before traveling. Given that you'll always find a Workbench on any island you visit, it's best to purchase these only as a last resort, when crafting isn't an option. Once you've completed your mission on the island, speak to Wilbur to return home November Oscar Whisker.

Did You Know?

Wilbur speaks in a made-up version of aviation speak. He'll use entire words to spell out other words. In aviation situations this can reduce accidents by making communication clearer, but Wilbur's approach might just have the opposite effect.

Biography

NEW

Birthday	December 17th
First Appearance	Animal Crossing: New Horizons (2020)

Wilbur is the Animal Crossing series' first registered pilot, and his unique way of speaking means he really stands out, even among the series' gigantic cast of characters. Despite having very small wings, Wilbur has no trouble reaching the controls and is already an experienced pilot by the time we meet him in Animal Crossing: New Horizons.

Wilbur

I actually burn the flight plans afterward. Security reasons. Can't explain more than that.

Wilbur makes it very clear (in his own inimitable way) that you'll never return to the same mystery island after visiting it.

Island Visitors

Island Visitors

- Gulliver
- Celeste
- Saharah
- Wisp
- Kicks
- Label
- Flick
- C.J.
- Harvey
- Daisy Mae
- K.K. Slider

As you enjoy day-to-day life on your island, visiting characters will sometimes travel from near and far just to check the place out. They can't be found on your island at all times, so make sure to talk with them when they do visit, as they may have something useful or interesting for you to do. Only one visiting character can appear at a time, so if you see one, you won't be seeing another that day. You'll want to make sure to meet each of these characters, since they all have something unique to offer that's bound to enrich your island experience!

Visitor Rotation   Every week you can expect scheduled visits from certain characters. Get used to seeing these special visitors around the island—they're sure to provide some useful wares or even an interesting quest for you to participate in.

	Name	Prerequisite	Visiting Hours	MON	TUE	WED	THU	FRI	SAT	SUN
	Daisy Mae	Nook's Cranny is built	5AM - 12PM	✗	✗	✗	✗	✗	✗	✓
	K.K. Slider	Available after K.K.'s first concert	All day, but only sings from 6PM to Midnight	✗	✗	✗	✗	✗	✓	✗
	Mabel	Nook's Cranny is built	5AM - 10PM, but is removed from rotation when shop is built	✓	✓	✓	✓	✓	✓	✓
	Saharah	Home is upgraded from a tent to a house	5AM - Midnight	✓	✓	✓	✓	✓	✓	✓
	Kicks	Able Sisters tailor shop is built	5AM - 10PM	✓	✓	✓	✓	✓	✗	✗
	Label	Able Sisters tailor shop is built	5AM - Midnight	✓	✓	✓	✓	✓	✗	✗
	Harvey	Once the "three new houses" quest is completed	5AM - 5AM next day, but only visits once per resident	✓	✓	✓	✓	✓	✓*	✓
	Flick	Resident Services is upgraded	5AM - 5AM next day	✓	✓	✓	✓	✓	✗	✗
	C.J.	Resident Services is upgraded	5AM - 5AM next day	✓	✓	✓	✓	✓	✗	✗
	Gulliver	Blathers' arrival has been announced	5AM - 5AM next day	✓	✓	✓	✓	✓	✗	✗
	Wisp	Unlocked from the beginning	8PM - 5AM next day	✓	✓	✓	✓	✓	✓	✓
	Celeste	The museum is built and it's a clear night	7PM - 5AM next day	✓	✓	✓	✓	✓	✓	✓

*Only if K.K. Slider has not yet performed on the island

Gulliver

"Ahoy there, crew! It's me, your brudder from anudder rudder!"

When taking a stroll across your beach, you may encounter **Gulliver**; a seasoned sailor who has a knack for falling overboard and being cast ashore. You can find him washed up on your shore on a weekday between 5AM and 5AM the next day. This gull might seem clueless, but he's great with technology! He even has his own communicator... ah, wait. He's damaged it. When you meet him, you may find yourself needing to lend him a hand and help him recover its pieces. Don't worry though, he's sure to reward you!

Island Role To find all of Gulliver's components, you'll need to scour your beaches. Make your way around the island and you may see a little burst of water come up from under the sand. Dig at this spot, and you'll have a chance of recovering a component. You'll need to recover a total of five components, so keep going until you find all of the pieces. Make sure to take a look far and wide—these pieces could be quite far from where you initially found Gulliver. If you don't finish this by the end of the day, Gulliver will leave and you won't be able to complete his task until he returns again.

Once you've collected all 5 components, Gulliver will thank you and reward you with an exotic souvenir that you won't be able to find anywhere else. It'll show up in your mailbox the next day, after his friends have picked him up. You can place your new item in your home or outside, so decide where it best fits and show off your new souvenir to everyone on the island. You'll also find a rusted part in the recycle box the day after helping Gulliver.

Rescue Gulliver 30 times and he'll give you the recipe for the golden shovel!

Rusted Parts

Trying to build a recipe but it requires rusted parts? Holding onto Gulliver's components for a day turns his communicator parts into rusted parts. No matter what, Gulliver's loyal crew will always be able to find him. Getting his communicator running just gets him home faster, so you don't have to feel too bad about sneaking some of these away in your pocket.

Biography

Birthday	**May 25th**
First Appearance	**Animal Crossing (2001)**

Washing up on shore in Animal Crossing (2001), Gulliver would reveal that he had fallen overboard. After speaking to him for enough time, he would reward you with a rare souvenir from a faraway land that you could place inside of your home. In later games, Gulliver could be found flying a U.F.O that you could shoot down using your Slingshot; does this make Gulliver an alien? We're not sure we want to know.

List of Gulliver's exotic souvenirs

☐ dala horse	☐ statue of liberty	☐ kaffiyeh
☐ hula doll	☐ stonehenge	☐ milkmaid hat
☐ katana	☐ tower of pisa	☐ pigtail
☐ lucky cat	**Clothing**	☐ samurai wig
☐ moai statue	☐ alpinist hat	☐ silk hat
☐ nutcracker	☐ ancient administrator hat	☐ sombrero
☐ pagoda	☐ candy-skull mask	☐ tam-o'-shanter
☐ pyramid	☐ coin headpiece	☐ tubeteika
☐ south pole	☐ elder mask	☐ turban
☐ sphinx	☐ geisha wig	☐ veil

Celeste

> "The stars above, falling all the way to earth just to hear our wishes... Isn't that a lovely, romantic idea?"

Celeste is Blathers' sister. You can often find her wandering around your island on a clear night or when a meteor shower occurs. Celeste will give you some extra information about this rare event and also give you an item to help you make the most out of it. A frequent stargazer, Celeste is obsessed with constellations. Much like her brother, Celeste does fall asleep during the daytime. Some things must run in the family.

Island Role
Celeste can only show up between 7PM and 4AM on clear nights when there's a chance of a meteor shower. When you first meet her, she'll give you a recipe for a star wand, a magic wand that can instantly change your outfit. This recipe requires a special material called 'star fragments'.

Star Fragments

'But how might you get these mysterious fragments?' you might ask. Celeste mentions that during a meteor shower, you can look up with the Right Stick and wish on a shooting star by pressing Ⓐ. Wish on a bunch of stars and the following morning you may find star fragments, large star fragments and zodiac fragments washed up on the shore. They look a little like Konpeito candy, don't they? These fragments can be used to make more than just the Star Wand.

Zodiac Furniture

The next night you see Celeste, she'll offer you a recipe for a special piece of furniture. Each month, she'll offer you the recipe for a different Zodiac-themed piece of furniture. The Zodiac set requires fragments to build, but they're definitely worth it! If Celeste has already given you the recipe for that month's Zodiac furniture, she'll give you another star related recipe, star fragments, zodiac fragments or a wand.

Zodiac Furniture

☐ Aquarius urn	☐ Gemini closet	☐ Sagittarius arrow
☐ Aries rocking chair	☐ Leo sculpture	☐ Scorpio lamp
☐ Cancer table	☐ Libra scale	☐ Taurus bathtub
☐ Capricorn ornament	☐ Pisces lamp	☐ Virgo harp

Did You Know?
Celeste can be a little mean to her brother sometimes. Once, she caught an insect and brought it to the museum. When Blathers saw it, he became so scared that he fainted.

Biography

Birthday	September 7th
First Appearance	Animal Crossing: Wild World (2005)

Celeste made her first appearance in Animal Crossing: Wild World, where she would work on the second floor of the museum, helping players create their own constellations to view in the night sky throughout the year. In Animal Crossing: New Leaf, Celeste would help players set up their own exhibits on the second floor of the museum. She could also sell you museum themed items and useful tools.

Celeste herself will sometimes wish upon a star. Flip to P.164 to learn a little more about meteor showers.

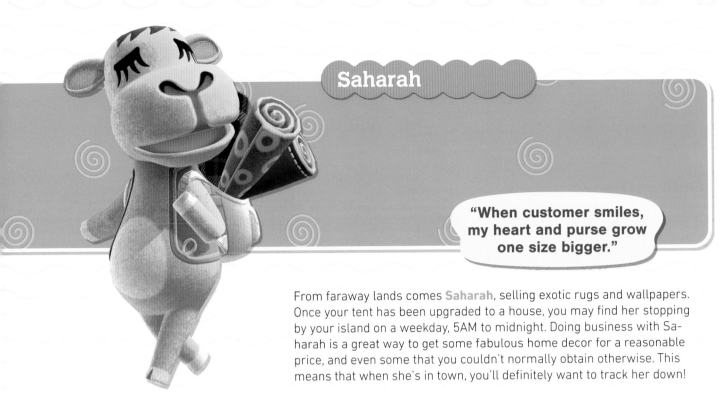

Saharah

"When customer smiles, my heart and purse grow one size bigger."

From faraway lands comes **Saharah**, selling exotic rugs and wallpapers. Once your tent has been upgraded to a house, you may find her stopping by your island on a weekday, 5AM to midnight. Doing business with Saharah is a great way to get some fabulous home decor for a reasonable price, and even some that you couldn't normally obtain otherwise. This means that when she's in town, you'll definitely want to track her down!

Island Role

Saharah sells exactly three products: flooring, wallpaper and rugs (which go on top of your flooring). You can buy a random 'mysterious' flooring or wallpaper for the price of 3000 bells. The rugs, meanwhile, come in a choice of three types:

Type	Size	Cost	Bonus Tickets
Small	2x2	1000	1
Medium	6x6	1500	2
Large	10x10	2000	3

Each of these technically-but-not-officially mysterious rugs comes with bonus 'exchange tickets'. Five of these tickets can get you a free mysterious wallpaper or flooring. Don't hesitate to come to Saharah as many times as you like while she's around. She'll accept multiple purchases in a day.

A Rug for All Floors

Saharah can sell 32 small rugs, 43 medium ones and 35 large ones. If you're aiming to acquire all of her goods, it's best to buy all rugs before buying any flooring or wallpaper; this way, you'll have loads of bonus tickets (up to 223!) This may not be too practical however; she'll only sell one type of small, medium and large rug each time she visits, so it'll take a lot of visits to grab everything.

Mysterious Redecoration

Want to collect all of Saharah's different mysterious wallpapers and flooring? The good news is that it doesn't matter if you buy them directly or exchange bonus tickets for them: both methods give you a chance of getting the same items. The bad news is that she carries a total of 39 floorings and 52 wallpapers, so if you don't use exchange tickets, it's going to take a lot of Bells (273,000) to acquire them all. The opposite page lists all of Saharah's wares.

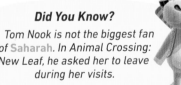

Did You Know?
Tom Nook is not the biggest fan of Saharah. In Animal Crossing: New Leaf, he asked her to leave during her visits.

Biography

Birthday	November 10th
First Appearance	Animal Crossing (2001)

Saharah made her first appearance in the original Animal Crossing. There, she would trade you a rare and exotic carpet for one of your own, in addition to a small fee. In later games, her role remained much the same, but in Animal Crossing: New Leaf she would decorate your entire home's main room for a fee of 3000 bells if you could find her wandering around the town.

Saharah

Hello. You are calling me Saharah, for it is the name I have carried for as long as I have carried these rugs.

Mysterious Wallpaper (52 Items)

- [ ] ancient wall
- [ ] backyard-fence wall
- [ ] bank-vault wall
- [ ] blackboard wall
- [ ] café-curtain wall
- [ ] chain-link fence
- [ ] circuit-board wall
- [ ] cityscape wall
- [ ] construction-site wall
- [ ] dark-chocolate wall
- [ ] desert vista
- [ ] dig-site wall
- [ ] dojo wall
- [ ] dungeon wall
- [ ] exquisite wall
- [ ] future-tech wall
- [ ] heavy-curtain wall
- [ ] imperial wall
- [ ] industrial wall
- [ ] ivy wall
- [ ] kisses wall
- [ ] laboratory wall
- [ ] magma-cavern wall
- [ ] mangrove wall
- [ ] meadow vista
- [ ] misty-garden wall
- [ ] mortar wall
- [ ] mossy-garden wall
- [ ] ocean-horizon wall
- [ ] office wall
- [ ] paintball wall
- [ ] palace wall
- [ ] ramshackle wall
- [ ] rice-paddy wall
- [ ] ringside seating
- [ ] rock-climbing wall
- [ ] ruins wall
- [ ] sea view
- [ ] security-monitors wall
- [ ] server-room wall
- [ ] shutter wall
- [ ] sky wall
- [ ] skyscraper wall
- [ ] stadium wall
- [ ] stormy-night wall
- [ ] straw wall
- [ ] strawberry-chocolate wall
- [ ] street-art wall
- [ ] summit wall
- [ ] tree-lined wall
- [ ] western vista
- [ ] white-chocolate wall

Mysterious Flooring (39 Items)

- [ ] berry-chocolates flooring
- [ ] boxing-ring mat
- [ ] circuit-board flooring
- [ ] cloud flooring
- [ ] construction-site flooring
- [ ] crop-circles flooring
- [ ] crosswalk flooring
- [ ] daisy meadow
- [ ] dark-chocolates flooring
- [ ] dig-site flooring
- [ ] dirt flooring
- [ ] field flooring
- [ ] floral rush-mat flooring
- [ ] flowing-river flooring
- [ ] future-tech flooring
- [ ] gravel flooring
- [ ] highway flooring
- [ ] imperial tile
- [ ] lava flooring
- [ ] lobby flooring
- [ ] mossy-garden flooring
- [ ] oasis flooring
- [ ] paintball flooring
- [ ] palace tile
- [ ] parking flooring
- [ ] pyramid tile
- [ ] racetrack flooring
- [ ] ramshackle flooring
- [ ] rocky-mountain flooring
- [ ] Saharah's desert
- [ ] sandlot
- [ ] scramble crosswalk
- [ ] sidewalk flooring
- [ ] sumo ring
- [ ] swamp flooring
- [ ] train-station flooring
- [ ] western desert
- [ ] white-chocolates flooring
- [ ] wildflower meadow

Rug (32 small Items)

- [ ] black-design kitchen mat
- [ ] blue kitchen mat
- [ ] blue message mat
- [ ] blue small round mat
- [ ] blue-design kitchen mat
- [ ] brown kitchen mat
- [ ] green kitchen mat
- [ ] iron entrance mat
- [ ] ivory simple bath mat
- [ ] ivory small round mat
- [ ] oval entrance mat
- [ ] red message mat
- [ ] red small round mat
- [ ] red-design kitchen mat
- [ ] rough rug
- [ ] rubber mud mat
- [ ] simple green bath mat
- [ ] simple navy bath mat
- [ ] simple pink bath mat
- [ ] simple small avocado mat
- [ ] simple small black mat
- [ ] simple small blue mat
- [ ] simple small brown mat
- [ ] simple small orange mat
- [ ] simple small purple mat
- [ ] simple small red mat
- [ ] white message mat
- [ ] white simple small mat
- [ ] yellow kitchen mat
- [ ] yellow message mat
- [ ] yellow small round mat
- [ ] yellow-design kitchen mat

Rug (43 medium Items)

- [ ] aluminum rug
- [ ] black blocks rug
- [ ] black wooden-deck rug
- [ ] blue blocks rug
- [ ] blue medium round mat
- [ ] blue vinyl sheet
- [ ] brown wooden-deck rug
- [ ] colorful vinyl sheet
- [ ] Earth rug
- [ ] fluffy rug
- [ ] fossil rug
- [ ] ivory medium round mat
- [ ] lacy rug
- [ ] magic-circle rug
- [ ] mush rug
- [ ] natural wooden-deck rug
- [ ] pink heart rug
- [ ] pink rose rug
- [ ] purple heart rug
- [ ] red blocks rug
- [ ] red carpet
- [ ] red medium round mat
- [ ] red rose rug
- [ ] red vinyl sheet
- [ ] simple medium avocado mat
- [ ] simple medium black mat
- [ ] simple medium blue mat
- [ ] simple medium brown mat
- [ ] simple medium orange mat
- [ ] simple medium purple mat
- [ ] simple medium red mat
- [ ] snowflake rug
- [ ] tatami mat
- [ ] tropical rug
- [ ] turquoise heart rug
- [ ] white heart rug
- [ ] white rose rug
- [ ] white simple medium mat
- [ ] white wooden-deck rug
- [ ] yellow blocks rug
- [ ] yellow medium round mat
- [ ] yellow rose rug
- [ ] yellow vinyl sheet

Rug (35 large Items)

- [ ] blue argyle rug
- [ ] blue dotted rug
- [ ] blue kilim-style carpet
- [ ] blue Persian rug
- [ ] blue shaggy rug
- [ ] blue stripes rug
- [ ] blue wavy rug
- [ ] botanical rug
- [ ] brown argyle rug
- [ ] brown shaggy rug
- [ ] green checked rug
- [ ] green kilim-style carpet
- [ ] green shaggy rug
- [ ] green stripes rug
- [ ] modern wavy rug
- [ ] monochromatic dotted rug
- [ ] monochromatic wavy rug
- [ ] peach checked rug
- [ ] peach stripes rug
- [ ] purple Persian rug
- [ ] purple shaggy rug
- [ ] red argyle rug
- [ ] red dotted rug
- [ ] red kilim-style carpet
- [ ] red Persian rug
- [ ] red wavy rug
- [ ] red-and-blue checked rug
- [ ] retro dotted rug
- [ ] shanty mat
- [ ] sloppy rug
- [ ] yellow argyle rug
- [ ] yellow checked rug
- [ ] yellow kilim-style carpet
- [ ] yellow Persian rug
- [ ] yellow stripes rug

2

Wisp

"N-N-NOOOOOOOOOO! A G-G-GHOOOOOOST!"

Meet **Wisp**, a somewhat spooky character you'll sometimes find roaming around the island from 8PM to 5AM. When you speak with him, five pieces of his soul will break away and spread out across your island. You'll need to go out on a hunt to find them, so take a look around and when you encounter a piece, catch it with your net.

Island Role

Wisp is quite a shy character, so you can expect him to stay away from the buildings around your island. If you're hunting for him, the best way to check if he might be around is to keep an eye out for other special visitors. If none of these characters are present on the island, then there's a good chance you'll encounter Wisp if you search the less populated portions of your island after dark.

Once you've found Wisp and caught all five pieces, head back to him; he's sure to reward you. Wisp can give you either a piece of furniture you don't yet own, or a piece of furniture that's rarer and more expensive. Your choice. After this, Wisp will disappear—where to, we don't quite know.

These pieces of Wisp's soul will emit a spooky sound when you're near them. Listen out!

Choosing "Something you don't have yet"

Wisp will pick a random item that you don't have in your Nook Shopping list with this option! This item will be worth 1500 Bells or less. If your catalog is complete, a random item at 1500 Bells or less will still be selected.

Reward Type	Furniture	Wallpaper/Flooring	Bed	Clothing
If you have a house	40%	24%	24%	12%
If you have a tent	75%	0%	0%	25%

Choosing "Something expensive"

Wisp doesn't have the best judgment of what counts as expensive. A few hundred years of being a spirit can do that. With this option, he'll pick an item with a buying price of 10,000 Bells or less. Not too shabby!

Biography

Birthday	February 26th
First Appearance	Animal Crossing (2001)

Wisp made his first appearance in the original Animal Crossing game, appearing late at night on occasion. You would need to assist Wisp in capturing some spirits he had lost. By doing so, you would be rewarded with either a rare item, a re-color of your home's roof, or he could remove all of the weeds from your town.

Did You Know?

In previous games, Wisp has had many different classifications. Once a Ghost, other times a Lamp Spirit.

Kicks

> "Welcome, chum! Have a look. No rush, no rush at all."

Kicks is a talented shoemaker who spent much of his time shining shoes outside in the city. After The Able Sisters' shop opens up, once every week, Kicks will visit your island, setting up a stall outside Resident Services to sell his goods. He's not just selling shoes either: he sells bags and socks too. His designs are unique and interesting, and they're bound to complete any look you're going for. His inventory is also completely random and will change every time he visits, so make sure to check up with him every time you see him outside of Resident Services.

Island Role

Kicks can supply shoes, socks and bags that won't show up in the Able Sisters store. He's got some rare finds in his collection, and he won't stock all color choices at one time, so it's always worth checking what he has in store. Flip to the next page to see the full selection of goods he can offer.

Did You Know?

Kicks doesn't mind bad smells! He works with a lot of shoes, socks and feet. Must be the perks of the job! Or of being a skunk...

Kicks is patient and dedicated, but he gets bored when business is slow; you might catch him playing with a coin to pass the time.

Biography

Birthday	November 30th
First Appearance	Animal Crossing: City Folk (2008)

Kicks first appears in Animal Crossing: City Folk. Players can find him in the city outside of a run-down building. For a small fee, he'll shine your shoes, which will allow you to change the color or style of what shoes you are wearing. Kicks speaks in a cockney accent and not much of his past is known. In Animal Crossing: New Leaf, Kicks will set up his own store on Main Street, where he'll provide you with a large variety of shoes and socks. Kicks will also allow you to try on the different shoes he has for sale, but not socks. Perhaps it's too stinky?

Kicks' Inventory

Kicks' selection of socks, shoes and bags on a given day is drawn from a fairly large stock of exclusive items. Here we'll show all of these items in convenient lists.

Bags

canvas backpack — 1

🪙 1300
Colors White

cloth shoulder bag — 2
🪙 1400
Colors Blue • Orange • Ivory

crossbody bag — 3
🪙 700
Colors Pink • Green • Yellow • White

crossbody boston bag — 4
🪙 1680
Colors Red • Blue

dry bag — 5
🪙 1040
Colors Yellow • Blue

evening bag — 6
🪙 1250
Colors Pink • Blue • Black

extra-large backpack — 7
🪙 2100
Colors Red • Green • Black • Blue

faux-fur bag — 8

🪙 1400
Colors Pink • Purple

foldover-top backpack — 9

🪙 1300
Colors Green • Blue • Gray • Pink

gumdrop shoulder bag — 10
🪙 2000
Colors Pop • Cool

hand-knit pouch — 11

🪙 1250
Colors Green • Purple

hard-shell backpack — 12

🪙 1680
Colors Blue • Red • Silver

knapsack — 13
🪙 630
Colors Blue • Black

messenger bag — 14

🪙 840
Colors Green • Orange • Black

mini pleather bag — 15
🪙 1600
Colors White • Black

outdoor backpack — 16
🪙 1560
Colors Avocado • Orange • Navy blue

pleather crossbody bag — 17
🪙 1120
Colors Navy blue • Black

pleather fringe bag — 18

🪙 2400
Colors Camel • White

pleather shoulder bag — 19
🪙 2400
Colors Brown • Navy blue

retro sports bag — 20
🪙 1400
Colors Blue • Red • Black

sacoche bag — 21
🪙 980
Colors Blue • Red • Black

square backpack — 22

🪙 1300
Colors Yellow • Pink • Green

straw pochette — 23

🪙 980
Colors Brown

studded backpack — 24
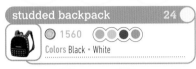
🪙 1560
Colors Black • White

tool bag — 25

🪙 910
Colors Black

town backpack — 26

🪙 1040
Colors Green • Orange • Blue • Red

travel pouch — 27

🪙 840
Colors Pink • Green • Light blue • Purple

traveler's backpack — 28

🪙 2940
Colors Orange • Blue • Brown

Shoes

babouches — 29

🪙 560
Colors Blue • Orange • Pink • Yellow • Gray • Purple • Mint • Red

ballet slippers — 30
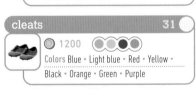
🪙 2200
Colors Pink • Mint • Blue • Purple • Black • White • Yellow • Red

cleats — 31

🪙 1200
Colors Blue • Light blue • Red • Yellow • Black • Orange • Green • Purple

embroidered shoes — 32
🪙 2100
Colors Red • White • Black • Blue

ghillie brogues — 33

🪙 2340
Colors Brown • Black • White

jester's shoes 34
1900
Colors Purple • Black • Red • Green

kiddie sneakers 35
700
Colors Red • Blue • Green • Purple • Silver • Black

kimono sandals 36
1600
Colors Black • Red • Pink • Dark blue • Gray • Purple • Yellow • Green

kung-fu shoes 37
1260
Colors Black

mage's bootie 38
1550
Colors Black • Blue • White • Red

paw slippers 39
1260
Colors Pink • Brown • White • Blue • Black

power boots 40
3150
Colors Red • Blue • Green • Black

restroom slippers 41
350
Colors Navy blue • Red • Green • Light blue • Pink

samurai greaves 42
4300
Colors Red • Black • Blue • White • Golden yellow

shiny bow platform shoes 43
2400
Colors Pink • Black • Red • Purple • Light blue • White • Light purple

ski boots 44
1800
Colors White • Orange • Red • Lime • Light blue • Purple

slip-on school shoes 45
350
Colors Red • Blue • Green • Yellow • Pink

slippers 46
350
Colors Gray • Black • White • Pink • Green • Blue • Red • Yellow

space boots 47
4300
Colors White

traditional flower shoes 48
1800
Colors Red • Pink • Blue • Yellow • Lime

visual-punk boots 49
2200
Colors Black

wooden clogs 50
1300
Colors Yellow • Blue • Red • Green • Brown

wrestling shoes 51
1080
Colors Red • Blue • Green • Pink • Black • Yellow

zap boots 52
2640
Colors White

Socks

aerobics leggings 53
700
Colors Red & pink • Emerald & lime • Purple & orange • Light blue & salmon pink • Yellow & blue

back-bow socks 54
600
Colors Pink • Yellow • Black • White • Blue • Peacock blue

color-blocked socks 55
840
Colors Purple • Green • Brown • Blue • Beige • White • Lime • Pink

compression tights 56
600
Colors Blue • Yellow • Pink • Mint • Red

frilly knee-high socks 57
840
Colors Black • Green • Red • Brown • Mint • Pink • Purple • Yellow

funny-face socks 58
600
Colors Pink • Blue • Red • Green • Black

garter socks 59
980
Colors Black • White • Purple • Red

kiddie socks 60
600
Colors Red & light blue • Blue & orange • Lime & pink • Yellow & purple • Light blue & red • Purple & green • Pink & yellow • Black & gray

sequin leggings 61
940
Colors Pink • Red • Black • Yellow • White • Blue • Purple • Green

sheer socks 62
600
Colors Blue • Berry red • Brown • Green • Olive • Gray

simple knee-high socks 63
600
Colors Pink • White • Red • Blue

soccer socks 64
800
Colors Blue • Red • Green • Light blue • Black • Orange • White

spider-web tights 65
720
Colors Black • White • Orange • Purple

wave-print socks 66
600
Colors Blue • Brown • Purple • Green • Gray

Label

"So, you know how I used to go by the name Labelle? Well, I was given that name by someone I worked with once... My mentor. "

Label (the artist formerly known as Labelle) is the third Able Sister. She's an aspiring fashion designer with big dreams. Once per week on a weekday, there's a possibility that this fashionista will appear outside of Resident Services. She's studying a large variety of styles and she can use all the help she can get: she'll ask you to dress in one specific style she's studying. Once she gives you your theme, you'll need to get to work piecing together an outfit to meet her requirements. You must be wearing at least one top and one set of bottoms for her to grade you.

Island Role Each visit, she'll have a different theme for you to dress up in. Don't worry, as Label will give you a head start by providing you with a piece of clothing that matches your assigned theme, just to give you an idea of what she's looking for.

Label

Why, hello. I'm Label...the fashion designer. I'm not sure if you've heard of me...

Label

But that's why I'm traveling to lots of different places. I want to see and learn about as many styles as I can.

Did You Know?

Label has a sweet tooth! She used to hide ice cream in the freezer behind the peas. Mabel found it and ate it anyway, much to her dismay.

Style Session Each piece of clothing you can wear belongs to one of 11 distinct fashion themes. While it's entirely possible to mix and match any

Party (PA)	Say you and your best friend were going to a fancy soiree. Just imagine the fabulous clothes you'd wear! (royal shirt)
Sporty (SP)	Try clothes that are comfortable to move around in, or maybe something an athlete would wear. (tennis sweater)
Work (WK)	Something professional, like a suit. The clothes a chef or doctor would wear works too. (worker's jacket)
Comfy (CO)	Something you'd wear if you were lounging around the house or, say, relaxing in front of the TV. (argyle sweater)
Outdoorsy (OD)	Imagine you're going for a hike or perhaps camping. What would you wear? You could also try on some casual, loose-fitting clothes. Just imagine yourself at a picnic in the park. (muscle tank)
Fairy Tale (FT)	Let knights, princesses, and storybook characters of all kinds be your inspiration. (young royal shirt, prince tunic)
Goth (GO)	Think... dark and moody! Try an outfit you might wear on Halloween...or one you might wear to scare your mother. (vampire costume)
Theatrical (TH)	Theatrical, something that shouts "I'm the star of the show!" It could be something a musician or a pop star might wear. You could also dress as if you were singing in an opera or acting in a play. (biker jacket, noble coat)
Vacation (VA)	Just think about what you'd wear on a leisurely summer trip, or to one of those big resorts. Try imagining yourself relaxing in the countryside or soaking up the sun on the beach. (top coat)
Formal (FO)	Try on the kind of super-nice clothes you'd wear to a fancy restaurant... or your cousin's graduation ceremony. (sweater-vest)
Everyday (EV)	Something you'd wear on an ordinary day. Simple-yet-stylish clothing you can wear for all sorts of occasions. (gingham picnic shirt, silk shirt)

clothes to express your own unique style, wearing an outfit that boldly showcases a fashion theme is sure to turn some heads as you parade around the island! Want to find out which fashion theme your favorite piece of clothing belongs to? Then head on over to the clothing catalog on P.275 for all the info you need!

After putting together a suitable look, Label will reward you with an appropriate gift. You'll get a coupon regardless of whether or not you pass, but you'll get more rewards with a better outfit. Your reward for 0-1 appropriate pieces is one coupon. For two matching pieces, you'll get a free piece directly from her limited edition 'Labelle' fashion line, along with a coupon. Three or more appropriate pieces in your look? You get a Labelle clothing item and two coupons! Doing better in these tests also gets Label to like you more, which is an added bonus. Plus, if you unlock a Labelle item, it will also occasionally appear in the Able Sisters' store and you can then order it in different colors through the fitting room.

Label will not grade you if you have a Wand outfit equipped.

Rewards

Now what exactly do these coupons do? These handy vouchers are redeemable at any Able Sisters' shop for 3000 Bells. You can hold 10 of these coupons in a stack, but can only use one per purchase.

Label must have a had a long journey to get here—she sometimes can be caught falling asleep standing up.

Evaluation	Items that fit the theme	Reward	Friendship Level Rise
4: Great	3 +	1 item from Labelle fashion line + Coupon x 2 (mail)	High
3: Good	2	1 item from Labelle fashion line + Coupon x 1 (mail)	Medium
2: Normal	1	Coupon x 1 (mail)	Medium
1: Not Great	0	Coupon x 1 (mail)	Low

● **Learn About Friendship**

Making Friends → P.75

Biography

Birthday	October 31st
First Appearance	Animal Crossing: City Folk (2008)

Making her first appearance in Animal Crossing: City Folk, Labelle is an employee at GracieGrace, a high end fashion and furniture store in the city. The CEO Gracie isn't keen on doing so much work, so Labelle takes charge. At this point, Labelle is not in full contact with her sisters. In Animal Crossing: New Leaf, Labelle is reunited with her two sisters and works in their store on Main Street. Labelle's role in the shop is selling accessories and hats.

Flick

> "Already I feel the all-consuming fires of the creative inferno warming my be-coldened blood!"

After you've upgraded your Resident Services tent, you may get a visit from **Flick**. Flick is an artist and bug enthusiast who hosts mini competitions around the island when he comes to visit. Nobody on the island knows as much about entomology as this cool lizard. On certain dates, he will even host a Bug-Off tournament outside of Resident Services! As a bug enthusiast, Flick will often task you with catching bugs for him in return for some unique rewards. Flick also has a partner, C.J. who happens to be his exact opposite—a lover of all things fishing.

Island Role

On non-competition days, you have the option to either sell bugs to Flick or commission an art piece from him. Selling bugs to him instead of the brothers at Nook's Cranny can be a great investment, because he'll buy your bugs for 50% more Bells than Timmy and Tommy will. If you commission him, Flick will first ask you to give him 3 of the same bug of your choice. For example, you could give him 3 common butterflies. In return, he'll mail you a gorgeous, handmade sculpture of the same insect straight to your mailbox the next day.

Flick: Scored a commission! I mean, um... AND SO OUR CONTRACT IS BOUND, HUMAN.

For more info on the Bug-Off hosted by Flick ➜ P.201

Did You Know?

Flick and C.J. are roommates and business partners. As an artist, he helps C.J. build his streaming audience by providing stellar art to dedicated anglers. However, Flick's true artistic muse is the world of entomology.

Flick: The guy who loves bugs in all their skittery, chittery, sometimes-glittery glory?

Gotta Catch 'Em All!

NEW		
Birthday	May 10th
First Appearance	Animal Crossing: New Horizons (2020)

When you order a commission from Flick. he'll give you a heartfelt letter and a model of the insect that you ordered from him. It's hard being an artist and he just so happens to make the collectibles that C.J. gives out too. These art pieces can be placed on tables or set on the ground.

C.J.

"What up, fishionista? Picked a name for your anglersona yet? Nyuk!"

This is **C.J.**—he's a seasports streamer. What does this mean? We're not quite sure... something to do with fish, maybe. Either way, C.J. is fish obsessed and will host special fishing competitions outside of Resident Services a few times a year. He'll also pop up around the island sometimes, leaving the next day at 5AM. When you meet him out and about, he'll task you with catching some fish for a reward. C.J. will also buy fish from you for a premium price. He mentions that his old man is also quite the fish enthusiast. Perhaps you may have met his father before?

Island Role If you happen to catch C.J. wandering around your island, he'll challenge you to partake in a fishing challenge. After you succeed, you'll be able to either sell fish to him at a 50% markup from the usual selling price or get a collectible from him. His partner happens to be an artist, and if you give C.J. three of the same fish, he can mail you a sweet display figurine of that fish to your mailbox the next day.

For more info on the Fishing Tourney hosted by C.J. ➡ P.200

C.J.

Anywave, ever since I started doing my seasports challenges, I've been trending in a HUGE way.

You won't get far in C.J.'s fishing challenge without a good rod. To find out how to get one, flip over to P.116.

Did You Know?

C.J. mentions that his old man is just as passionate about fishing, but he isn't all that good at it. Come to think of it, C.J.'s catchphrase sounds kind of familiar, doesn't it? Nyuk nyuk.

NEW

Gotta Catch 'Em All!

Birthday	March 7th
First Appearance	Animal Crossing: New Horizons (2020)

When ordering a collectible from C.J. he'll give you a custom letter and a life-size model of the fish that you ordered from him that matches the size of the creature's tank. These collectibles are handcrafted by his best bud and childhood friend, Flick. The models can be placed on tables or set on the ground.

Harvey

"Welcome back to Harv's Island. Or is it technically an archipelago? A Harvipelago?"

Harvey is a laid back, quirky fellow who believes in peace, love and art. If you like photos, you may have found your very best friend! A man surrounded by nature, Harvey lives peacefully on his very own island, where his biggest worry is feeding the birds.

You can find Harvey wandering your island after you build the three residential houses. When you talk to him, he mentions the lovely, neighboring island he happens to live on. He has a photo studio there that he has dubbed "Photopia". And lucky you! You get to visit Harv's Island for free via Dodo Airlines.

Island Role   Upon arriving on Harv's Island, Harvey's passion for photography becomes clear. He describes the four main features of his studio space: sets, models, wardrobe and how to take pictures, so let's go over each one here.

Harvey will sometimes drink coffee or play his tambourine.

Did You Know?
Harvey used to run a campsite back in Animal Crossing: New Leaf. He would regularly feed the birds, and even give you beans to throw for them to eat.

Biography

Birthday	August 2nd
First Appearance	Animal Crossing: New Leaf (2012)

Harvey first appeared in Animal Crossing: New Leaf, introduced as a new character in the Welcome amiibo update. Harvey was in charge of the campsite, a place where you could meet camping characters in their RVs. He was also in charge of the camp shop, and could sell you some unique items for MEOW Coupons—a special type of currency.

Harvey

Hey, you. What's happening? Any questions about the studio mixed into your mind goulash?

Sets

Harvey's studio consists of six sets where you can take photos. You can adjust the room's lighting by pressing up on the directional pad, or press down to redecorate the set to your liking. You're given access to all the items, clothing, or furniture currently logged in your catalog. When in the redecoration menu, press right on the directional pad to open up the furniture. You can also borrow these items in any customizable color. Hover over the customizable furniture (indicated by a red paintbrush icon) and press Ⓧ to view your options.

Models

Every fabulous photo needs a model, and on this island you can have up to 10! They are, however, limited to the characters that live on your island or amiibo villagers. You can invite these residents by pressing Down and on the Directional Pad and then selecting 'Residents' from the top bar, or tapping an amiibo to the NFC touchpoint. You can even pose your models with different Reactions—if you're using the Camera app on your NookPhone, press Ⓐ to signal to your models that it's time to pose. For more on which characters you can invite to Photopia, flip to P.416.

Photopia's Sets

The central room on the main floor is a fully furnished studio with the following furnishings: an imperial partition, a director's chair, two rattan armchairs, a rattan wardrobe, two studio lights, and a double sofa. It has the wooden-knot wall and the wooden-knot flooring.

Wardrobe

Nook shopping will graciously lend out clothes for both you and your models. Pick anything from your catalog to freshen up your look. Keep in mind that every villager has their tastes, and there are some clothes that a villager may refuse to wear. You also can't select anything that uses one of your Pro Designs. When you're done changing sets, press Down on the Directional Pad, select your character, and then press Ⓧ to swap their outfit.

How to Take Pictures

Here at the studio, you can take photos two ways: either with the Capture Button on your controller or the NookPhone's camera app. Be mindful that you can't use the NookPhone when you're changing studio settings, so pose your picture and set up your stage before using the NookPhone's Camera.

After you take a photo with a villager at Harvey's island for the first time, he'll make you a customized, personal portrait of your friend. These are then sold as posters through the Nook Stop. Any rooms you may have redecorated will still be as you left them the next time you visit!

North

The north room on this floor is another room with a red-brick wall and flagstone floor.

West

The left room on the main floor has the blue playroom wall and the jointed-mat flooring.

Main Room

East

The right room on the main floor has white delicate-blooms wall and simple red flooring.

Upstatrs

Upstairs there is one room with a backyard-fence wall and backyard lawn.

Downstairs

The final room downstairs has the concrete wall and a concrete flooring.

Daisy Mae

> **"Turnips, turnips! Watch 'em rise! Try to earn a nice surprise!"**

A few weeks into island life, once Nook's Cranny is built, you might see a funny girl walking around your island balancing turnips on her head. Daisy Mae is the granddaughter of Joan, a renowned turnip saleswoman who has been in the business for many, many years. Joan has decided to pass on the family business to Daisy Mae, who will visit your island every Sunday to sell you fresh turnips. Turnips might not seem too exciting from the get go, but you'll find that they may be one of your best ways to earn Bells.

Island Role

Daisy Mae is an expert turnip seller. Turnips are a special vegetable that can be purchased from Daisy Mae every Sunday morning (5AM to 12PM) for between 90 to 110 Bells for a bundle of ten. With empty pockets and a full wallet, you can buy up to 4000 turnips at once! Once you've purchased your turnips, you have one week to sell them back before they go bad—nobody wants to buy or eat a rotten turnip. If you haven't sold your turnips by Saturday, it's wise to do so regardless of the price to recover at least some of your investment.

Daisy Mae

You here to start your Sunday off with some fresh turnips?

Set your alarm for Sunday mornings so you don't miss a week of stalk market action.

Did You Know?

Daisy has a bad habit of eating turnips rather than selling them, much to her granny's dismay. Once she starts thinking about braising turnips, stewing turnips, it's hard to stop. She can't help it!

The Stalk Market

Enjoy the thrill of risking Bells for the chance of turning a huge profit? The Stalk Market is for you! Once you buy a bushel of turnips, they'll begin to fluctuate in price for the remainder of the week until they go bad. Head to Nook's Cranny, and depending on when you try to sell them, they can sell for as little as 50 Bells a piece or

Biography

NEW	Birthday	May 5th
	First Appearance	Animal Crossing: New Horizons (2020)

Daisy Mae and her family appreciate loyal customers. Up on her mountain, they grow all kinds of wonderful veggies, not just turnips. If you buy at least 100 turnips from her in a week, she'll send you bamboo shoots in the mail the following day. You can only get one of these letters per week. Bamboo shoots can be eaten or planted! This is one of the easiest ways to get bamboo shoots and bamboo trees on your island. For more information on bamboo, turn to P.167.

for as much as 800 Bells. Luckily, you can check the price of turnips every day. This means that turnips can be a powerful way to drastically increase your overall Bell count in a very short amount of time, potentially granting a staggering return on investment. However, this also means that it's possible to lose a substantial amount of money if your turnips go a full week without increasing in value. Always be sure to invest responsibly, or you may find yourself with considerably less than you started with. Never forget: Buy low, sell high!

Timmy and Tommy might be the real winners in the turnip market, since they're the ones setting the prices.

Weekly Price Fluctuations

Price fluctuation in Nook's Cranny can function in one of four ways. Turnip prices will change in the morning and afternoon every day from Monday to Saturday, for a total of 12 times throughout the week. These fluctuations will always follow one of four patterns:

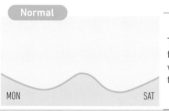

Normal

The price will rise and fall slightly, but there won't be any big changes throughout the week.

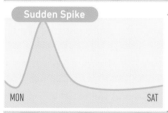

Sudden Spike

At a random point in the week, the price will suddenly rise drastically, then fall immediately after. Graph shows early week example only.

Gradual Decline

The price will not rise above the initial purchase price, and it'll fall throughout the week.

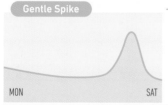

Gentle Spike

The price will rise somewhat, but not as much as the Sudden Spike pattern.

Fluctuation patterns will be decided at the start of each week. The next week's pattern will be decided based on the current week's pattern. Each of these patterns are chosen at random, but the odds of a specific pattern being chosen changes depending on what fluctuations happened this week. For instance, if this week your turnips only experienced a Gradual Decline in price, then there is a strong chance that turnips next week will experience a Sudden Spike. Note that while it's very unlikely for two weeks of Gradual Declines to occur in a row, it's not impossible—only risk what you're willing to lose.

Temporally Temperamental Turnips!

Be forewarned: turnips are especially sensitive to time paradoxes. If, for whatever reason, the time on your island travels backwards by any amount, all your turnips will instantly become rotten. If you're expecting a disruption in the natural flow of time, then proceed with extreme caution.

If you buy at least 100 turnips total from Daisy, she'll send you a special letter the following day. With it, she'll gift you three bamboo shoots inside!

Current pattern	Probability of next week's pattern			
	Normal	Sudden Spike	Gradual Decline	Gentle Spike
Normal	20%	30%	15%	35%
Sudden Spike	50%	5%	20%	25%
Gradual Decline	25%	45%	5%	25%
Gentle Spike	45%	25%	15%	15%

K.K. Slider

"I don't ask for much. A stool to sit on, a song to sing, and some folks gathered 'round to hear it."

In the world of Animal Crossing he needs no introduction—K.K. Slider is a famous musician, beloved on every shore you could visit. A renowned DJ, a master with an acoustic guitar and a well-rounded whistler, K.K. Slider has released hundreds of his own original pieces of music. You can hear him perform every Saturday at 6PM outside of Resident Services later on in the game. You'll first encounter K.K. Slider right at the end of your very first day on the island. He'll impart some wisdom upon you and disappear. Don't worry though, K.K. Slider will play a very important role in the game. What could this be?

K.K. gives some good advice at the beginning of your adventure.

Island Role

After unlocking the game's credits, K.K. will show up to your island every Saturday to hold a concert! He won't take requests until 6PM, but when he does, you have plenty of options when it comes to requesting songs. You can leave it up to him to pick for you, give him a mood ("good", "grumpy", "lazy", "a little sad' or "hard to say"), or a specific song title if you're really itching to hear your favorite! After the concert, if you speak to K.K. Slider, you can ask to hear another song. K.K. Slider will remain in the Event Plaza until 12AM.

Birthday Wishes

On your birthday, K.K. will be in front of Resident Services. Regardless of the hour, he'll be more than happy to sing you a special birthday song. As he sings, you'll get to read some heartfelt messages from your closest friends and favorite island residents on your special day!

Biography

Birthday	August 23rd
First Appearance	Animal Crossing (2001)

K.K. Slider first appeared in Animal Crossing (2001), where he would play mini concerts outside the Train Station at 8pm every Saturday night. In that game, K.K. Slider was a mysterious character, pretty much all anyone knew about him was the fact that he was one cool cat. Not literally, of course. In Animal Crossing: Wild World and also Animal Crossing: City Folk, K.K. would play concerts inside of the Roost, located at the bottom floor of the Museum. You could even bring your own friends to come see his concerts. In Animal Crossing: New Leaf, K.K. was the main attraction of Club L.O.L, where he performed as a DJ.

Did You Know?

His first appearance in the game is a callback to Animal Crossing (2001). K.K. Slider would appear similarly at the very start of the game to welcome you to the world of Animal Crossing.

Record Collecting Whenever K.K. performs, the song you ask him to sing will be added to your collection. This means you'll have access to them on your personal music-playing devices. You can only gain one song per day, even if K.K. takes more than one request at a performance. If you leave the choice of song to K.K. or only choose a mood, then the song chosen will be one that's not already in your collection. You can also request a specific song by name, which is useful for acquiring your favorites early. If you request a song by name you'd better try to spell it correctly; asking for a song that doesn't exist will lead to K.K. playing a "fake" song, that won't be added to your collection.

K.K.'s Discography K.K. has a long and celebrated history as a musician. He knows how to write a crowd pleaser and has had hits across many different styles and genres. Here we compile his currently available library for your listening pleasure. There's an additional three hidden songs that can only be heard by asking specifically for them: Animal City, Farewell, and Drivin'. These songs will be added to your collection after hearing them. If you want to see all the record covers, flip to P.408.

Mood: Good!	Mood: Grumpy	Mood: Lazy	Mood: A little sad	Mood: Hard to Say
1 Mountain Song	1 K.K. Crusin'.	1 Aloha K.K.	1 Two Days Ago	1 Hypno K.K.
2 Bubblegum K.K.	2 Lucky K.K.	2 K.K. Stroll	2 Only Me	2 K.K. Rally
3 K.K. Calypso	3 Surfin' K.K.	3 Pondering	3 K.K. Western	3 K.K. Marathon
4 K.K. Country	4 K.K. Safari	4 Soulful K.K.	4 K.K. Lament	4 Agent K.K.
5 K.K. Groove	5 K.K. Jongara	5 K.K. Jazz	5 K.K. Chorale	5 K.K. Soul
6 K.K. Salsa	6 K.K. Tango	6 K.K. Swing	6 King K.K.	6 K.K. Song
7 K.K. Samba	7 Imperial K.K.	7 Mr. K.K.	7 K.K. Etude	7 The K. Funk
8 K.K. Ska	8 Rockin' K.K.	8 K.K. Synth	8 K.K. Sonata	8 K.K. Blues
9 K.K. Dixie	9 K.K. House	9 K.K. Fusion	9 K.K. Milonga	9 K.K. Oasis
10 K.K. Disco	10 K.K. Adventure	10 K.K. Bossa	10 K.K. Ballad	10 K.K. Folk
11 Café K.K.	11 K.K. Flamenco	11 K.K. Moody	11 K.K. Lullaby	11 K.K. Technopop
12 K.K. Parade	12 K.K. Metal	12 K.K. Aria	12 K.K. Waltz	12 K.K. D & B
13 K.K. Rockabilly	13 K.K. Rock	13 K.K. Love Song	13 K.K. Dirge	13 To the Edge
14 K.K. March	14 K.K. Bazaar	14 K.K. Reggae	14 Comrade K.K.	14 K.K. Gumbo
15 K.K. Mambo	15 K.K. Steppe	15 I Love You	15 Steep Hill	15 Space K.K.
16 K.K. Mariachi	16 K.K. Casbah	16 K.K. Island	16 Stale Cupcakes	
17 Neapolitan	17 DJ K.K.	17 K.K. Faire	17 K.K. Condor	
18 Spring Blossoms	18 Go K.K. Rider!	18 Marine Song 2001		
19 K.K. Ragtime		19 Wandering		
		20 My Place		
		21 Forest Life		

Special Songs	Hidden Songs
1 K.K. Birthday	1 Animal City
2 Welcome Horizons	2 Farewell
	3 Drivin'

Island Residents

Living on an island wouldn't be the same without a community of colorful and fun animal friends to talk with. Your island can host up to 10 residents with whom you'll share your day-to-day life. As you make your way around the island, you'll no doubt run into one of these characters and you're sure to become great friends with them down the line. Each resident is unique, having their own birthdays and personality traits that sets them apart from others, just like yourself.

Personalities   Each resident can have one of eight different personality types, each with two sub-types. Each personality type will define how a resident speaks with you, as well as their interests and hobbies. A resident's personality will affect the things they talk about with you and each other, as well as the fun things you might catch them doing as they go about their day. What it won't affect, however, is how much you'll love to be their friend!

Male Personalities	Some you may know...	Things they might enjoy!
Lazy	Bob, Lucky	Daydreaming, food, superheroes, roller coasters
Jock	Jay, Bam	Jogging, working out, muscles, sports
Cranky	Wart Jr., Fang	Life advice, reliving memories, bonsai trees
Smug	Marshall, Julian	Music, travel, fashion, fame

Female Personalities	Some you may know...	Things they might enjoy!
Sweet	Merengue, Molly	Cooking, poetry, reading, knitting
Peppy	Tangy, Bunnie	Singing, dancing, fashion, pop stars
Snooty	Alli, Robin	Art, fashion, shopping, spas
Big Sis	Cherry, Charlise	Crafts, family, gardening, the countryside

Alligators

Anteaters

Bear Cubs

Bears

Making Friends

Merengue: Oh! This is a good chance to run an idea by you... How would you feel about me giving you a nickname?

Like what?
Thanks, but...

Want to become the best of friends with your fellow residents? Every day, you'll have the chance to interact with the island's residents and to strengthen your bond with them by giving them items they like. Each villager has specific types of items they prefer, and this will increase your friendship with them. Ultimately, once you've reached enough friendship points with a resident, they can potentially give you their own framed photograph!

Friendship Made Easy   The best thing you can do to increase your friendship with another islander is just to talk to them every day. The first time you talk to a villager each day, your friendship level increases. For every following uninterrupted day you talk to them, that amount increases exponentially. The amount you gain will reset if you forget a day.

Once you're friends with a resident the option to give them a gift will become available; sending a letter or giving them a gift makes your bond grow stronger. Any non-speciality item can be gifted—things like furniture or clothing or even fruit, and these can also be attached to letters you send them. Taking the extra effort to wrap a gift with some wrapping paper from Nook's Cranny can increase your friendship even more!

Making Enemies

While it's easy to make friends on this lovely island, it can be just as easy to hurt other residents' feelings. Hitting an island resident with a net multiple times, pushing them around or gifting them garbage (such as rotten turnips) can get them to like you a whole lot less.

Puck: Maybe if I went to a new place, I could meet new bugs, eat new snacks, and learn to be real cool.

No, don't go!
Good luck out there...

Raise Friendship	Lower Friendship
Talk to them (once per day)	Hit them with a tool
Send them a letter (friendship increases when they reply)	Push them around a lot
Give them a present (when friendship is already high)	Give them 'trash' items (tire, weeds, rotten turnips etc.)
Give them a wrapped birthday gift	Accept a request but fail to successfully carry it out.
Complete a request for them	--
Sell them an item they want	--

Birds

Bulls

Cats

Chickens

Birthdays

HAPPY BIRTHDAY!

Birthdays only happen once a year, so when they come around a celebration is definitely in order! You'll enter your birth date when you create your passport at the start of the game, and when the day comes your friends on the island will insist on a party. Each potential resident also has their own unique birthday (all listed later in this chapter, starting on P.82), so it's worth learning the date for any resident you care about.

Your Birthday On your special day, you'll be pulled aside by the resident you have the most friendship points with. Turns out they've been planning a surprise party for you the whole time! You'll be showered with music, friends, gifts, and cake galore! Literally! You'll also get a performance from the legendary K.K. Slider, and you'll even have a chance to play a piñata mini-game that douses you in birthday cupcakes! Sweet!

Parties in Animal Crossing don't get out of control, and no one even needs to clean up afterward. Perfect!

Islander Birthdays Birthday parties mean lots of things: friends, cake, confetti. For you, it may be the perfect opportunity to build an everlasting friendship with a special villager. One of the best ways to boost your friendship level with a villager is to attend their birthday party. The party will always be in their house, so you'll know exactly where to go when the special day is announced. You'll also get a heads up a few days in advance from other villagers and the island billboard, so keep your eyes and ears peeled so you can prepare! It's always best to bring a gift, especially one that's wrapped. Don't forget!

Cows

Deer

Dogs

Reactions

Island residents will also teach you Reactions! After Nook's Cranny is built, you might catch a resident calling out your name. They might be looking to teach you a Reaction—an emotion you can show off from your Reactions wheel. To see what each Reaction looks like, head straight to P.344.

Learning Reactions You can learn a maximum of one Reaction every day. Simply press the ZR button and your Reactions wheel will pop up. From here, you can select any Reactions you've been taught. You can use these in photos, around friends or even around fellow island residents—they may even copy your reaction!

Certain Reactions can only be learned from villagers with certain personality types. The chart here shows that many can only be learned after already learning certain others. The ones in red require you to have a high level of friendship with a villager. This means that if you want to collect all Reactions, you'll need to have all of the different personality types on your island and become good friends with each of them.

Personality	Initial Reaction	Further Reactions Learned				
SWEET		Pleased	Fearful	Sadness	Glee	Daydreaming
PEPPY		Happiness	Aggravation	Sleepy	Curiosity	Mischief
SNOOTY	Joy	Intense	Thought	Sighing	Amazed	Love
BIG SISTER	Greetings	Laughter	Cold Chill	Apologetic	Disagreement	Confident
LAZY	Delight	Bashfulness	Sorrow	Mistaken	Shyness	Pride
JOCK	Surprise!	Encouraging	Sneezing	Distress	Shocked!	Flourish
CRANKY		Agreement	Worry	Sheepish-ness	Bewilderment	Inspiration
SMUG		Smirking	Resignation	Heartbreak	Dozing	Showmanship

Letters and Presents

Sometimes, island residents will send you letters and presents in the mail. These gifts can contain a variety of interesting and useful items for you to display in your home or around the island, and the letters themselves are always an interesting read! What will your residents write to you?

Send this card to Merengue?

peaches

Dear Merengue,

Here's a gift!

From Jade

Continue writing.   OK!

Ducks   Eagles   Elephants   Frogs

The residents of your island home occasionally have their own problems or desires. Helping them out, usually by taking the time to fulfil a simple request, can really improve your relationship with them. Residents need to already be friends with you to make a request, but taking on one of these responsibilities is a great way to increase your friendship even further. If your friendship is already strong, they might reward you with a photo of themselves!

Critter Requests

Fishing or catching insects can help you increase your friendship level too! A villager might request a very specific insect or fish, or a type of fish or insect. For instance, they might ask for any kind of beetle. Another example is that they may ask you for a fish specifically from the ocean. Once you get this request, you'll have until the end of the day to finish it. If you don't, then your friendship level will go down.

Lost Items

Sometimes, you may come across a book or maybe even a bag lying randomly on the ground on your island. Pick it up and ask the island residents if it might be theirs. Even if it isn't, the first person you ask will be able to tell you who it really belongs to. After accepting this request, you'll have until the end of the day to finish it—if you don't, your friendship level will go down.

Getting Sick

Visiting your neighbors can be great, but sometimes you might enter their house and they'll be shivering and sneezing. It looks like they've got quite the nasty flu! You can craft medicine using weeds and a wasp nest, or if you have Nook's Cranny, you can buy medicine from the cabinet. Giving this poor resident medicine will not just get them feeling chipper again, but will also increase your friendship level!

Sick residents are housebound, either until they get some medicine or the illness goes away on its own.

Goats   Gorillas   Hamsters   Hippos

Delivery Requests

All the animals on your island have busy schedules. Sometimes, they just don't have the time to deliver gifts themselves, for one reason or another. There are even times where a resident might ask you to deliver a gift to help them make up with a friend they might have argued with. They'll give you an item you won't be able to sell from your inventory and it'll be your job to find the other resident and give them the gift. Delivering this gift will increase your friendship level with both the recipient and the sender, especially if you go back to the sender afterward to report a job well done! Be sure to get it done before the end of the day, or your friendship will drop with both of them.

Merengue: I said something I shouldn't have and I felt really bad about that, so I got her a gift to make up...

Someone needs help

Merengue: I'm having a hard time facing her right now though, so I was hoping maybe you could deliver it for me?

You deliver their package

Robin: So, this is from Merengue? For...me?

Everything is fine again!

Merengue: Thanks to you, I think we may be able to patch things up!

Treasure hunt

Who doesn't love a treasure hunt? One of your islanders might ask you to dig up a special hidden item somewhere on your island. You'll be given either 3 or 6 minutes in which to find the treasure, and if you succeed you'll be able to keep the treasure and also get added points toward your friendship! Fail, and they might think of you as a lesser pirate.

Agree to the game

Puck: Hey, Jade? You wanna play a treasure-hunting game?

Find the treasure

Treasure found!

Accept your praise!

Puck: Wow, Jade! You're real good at hunting for treasure!

Horses

Kangaroos

Koalas

Lions

Recruiting Residents

Want to bring some new residents to come and live on your island? Since there are so many exciting characters to potentially meet and share island life with, here are all of the ways you can do so!

Move-ins   You can get a villager to move to your island through one of three ways: using a Nook Miles ticket to go on a Mystery Tour, using the campsite or using an amiibo. A maximum of ten animal villagers can live on your island at once, and this total doesn't include your human residents. Try to populate your island with a large, diverse group of animals. Certain items, Reactions and storyline-related goals depend on having certain kinds of villagers on your island.

Mystery Tours   You can encounter potential new residents who may be vacationing on a nearby island with a Nook Miles Ticket. If you talk to them while your island can accommodate a new resident, you can convince these potential residents to permanently move there. This makes these remote islands one of the best ways to discover and recruit new residents, assuming you've been completing your Nook Miles Objectives and can afford the high cost in Nook Miles.

Plots

After you've built the campsite, you will get the option to purchase house plots from Tom Nook at Resident Services for 10,000 Bells. You can place these anywhere you would like on the island, space permitting, and any resident looking to move to the island will begin to build their home on that space. Having a plot of land purchased and available is mandatory for getting new residents to move in as your island begins to reach its capacity.

The Campsite   The campsite is a great place to recruit more residents to live on your island. Once it's been built, a potential resident is guaranteed to visit your island, though they won't arrive on the same day as a major island event. After a resident has visited, there will be a period in which you'll notice a lack of further visitors, but don't worry; another one will turn up soon, and when they do,

Mice — Monkeys — Octopuses — Ostriches

an announcement will be made. Once they arrive, your happy little tourist will set up a 4x4 tent in front of the campsite, and will stay for one day.

Days since the last camper left	1 day*	2 days	3 days	4 days	5 days	6 days+
Chance of new camper	0%	0%	5%	10%	15%	20%

*(Tent Removed)

It's important to note that visitors to the campsite are less likely to have visited or lived on the island in the past. This means you have a better chance of seeing potential residents that you haven't met before. You also have a good chance of visitors having a personality type that none of your current residents has—unless of course you already have an ideal mix of all personality types.

A Game of Chance

Like cards? Visitors you've attracted via the campsite may ask you to play a guessing game with them. They'll invite you to pick the suit or color of one out of four cards, each labeled ♡, ♦, ♧ or ♠. It's a game of pure, random chance, but if you win you might get a cool piece of furniture or clothing, or even the chance of them agreeing to live on the island! Playing games can be a great way to bond with a camper who's learning to love the beautiful nature of your island. These campers can move to your island as long as there's an available plot for them. To learn more about how to build the campsite, check out P.144.

The visiting islander isn't guaranteed to ask to move to your island, but keep pestering them and they'll eventually agree to move there.

amiibo Move-ins   Calling an amiibo to your campsite works differently than a naturally visiting islander. amiibo can be used at the Nook Stop in Resident Services to summon a specific villager to your campsite. Just like the random campsite villagers, the amiibo villagers that come to your island can be convinced to become permanent residents, but you'll need to complete a furniture quest instead of play a card game. You will have to build them one piece of furniture on three separate visits to make them eligible to move in. This will always be DIY furniture you have to make yourself, so get your hammers and workbenches ready!

If a potential resident has already visited via the campsite, then even using their amiibo won't be enough to get them to appear again.

If there isn't enough space on your island for an amiibo resident, you'll have the option to make room for them by asking someone else to leave. If you have less than 10 residents but don't have any empty homes they can occupy, then a new resident won't be able to move in. You can also only invite one resident per day using amiibo. To see the full list of compatible amiibo, flip ahead to P.416.

Penguins

Pigs

Rabbits

Rhinos

Meet the Residents

In total, there are 391 potential residents you can meet in Animal Crossing: New Horizons. These residents vary greatly in terms of personality and looks, though many will share lots in common too. For example, there are 19 cat villagers that you may meet. If you're a fan of a certain type of animal, you could try to fill your town with that one type; but generally it's good to have a variety of characters to interact with. As they say, variety is the spice of island life.

Legend Across the pages that follow you'll find details on each and every potential resident, listed alphabetically by species. If you're wondering what any particular detail means, use one of those handy bookmarks on this page to always have the answer.

Pango

- November 9

snoooooof

Orange oversized print dress

STYLE	Elegant · Cool
COLORS	Orange · Purple

Peppy

① Name
Simple: the resident's name.

② Birthday
The date on which they celebrate their birthday.

③ Catchphrase
The notable word or phrase the resident uses, often to end their sentences.

④ Default Clothing
This tag shows the resident's default clothing.

⑤ Personality
Their overall personality type. Flip back to P.74 for more on personality types.

⑥ Favorite Styles
The kind of styles they like most. This affects the clothes they'll wear and items they'll like.

⑦ Clothing Colors
This tells you which colors the resident likes most.

⑧ Room
A picture of their room.

Sheep   Squirrels   Tigers   Wolves

Alligators

Del
- May 27 -

gronk

Blue striped shirt

STYLE Cool • Simple
COLORS Blue • White

Cranky

Alfonso
- June 9 -

it's a me

Red simple parka

STYLE Simple
COLORS Red • Blue

Lazy

Drago
- February 12 -

burrrn

Yellow dragon suit

STYLE Elegant • Gorgeous
COLORS Orange • Red

Lazy

Alli
- November 8 -

graaagh

Yellow leopard tee

STYLE Gorgeous • Elegant
COLORS Yellow • Brown

Snooty

Gayle
- May 17 -

snacky

Pink lace-up dress

STYLE Cute
COLORS Pink • White

Sweet

Boots
- August 7 -

munchie

Purple & yellow jester costume

STYLE Gorgeous • Active
COLORS Colorful • Purple

Jock

Sly
- November 15 -

hoo-rah

Brown camo tee

STYLE Cool • Simple
COLORS Brown • Green

Jock

Anteaters

Anabelle
- February 16 -

snorty

Navy blue bold muumuu

STYLE Cute • Simple
COLORS Green • Blue

Peppy

Annalisa
- February 6 -

gumdrop

Pink blossoming kimono

STYLE Elegant • Gorgeous
COLORS Red • Pink

Sweet

Antonio
- October 20 -

honk

Yellow bone tee

STYLE Simple
COLORS Aqua • Blue

Jock

Cyrano
- March 9 -

ah-CHOO

White judogi

STYLE Cool • Active
COLORS Yellow • Beige

Cranky

Olaf
- May 19 -

whiffa

Black suit of lights

STYLE Elegant • Gorgeous
COLORS Red • Black

Smug

Pango
- November 9 -

snooooof

Orange oversized print dress

STYLE Elegant • Cool
COLORS Orange • Purple

Peppy

Snooty
- October 24 -

sniffff

Green misty tee

STYLE Simple
COLORS Green • Yellow

Snooty

2

Bear Cubs

Chester
• August 6 •

rookie

Yellow dragon suit

STYLE Simple
COLORS Yellow • Green

Lazy

Maple
• June 15 •

honey

Beige tree sweater

STYLE Simple • Cute
COLORS Beige • Green

Sweet

Poncho
• January 2 •

li'l bear

Yellow energetic sweater

STYLE Simple
COLORS Orange • Yellow

Jock

Barold
• March 2 •

cubby

Tiger animal-stripes tee

STYLE Simple • Cool
COLORS Yellow • Black

Lazy

Judy
• March 10 •

myohmy

Pink fairy-tale dress

STYLE Cute • Elegant
COLORS Pink • White

Snooty

Murphy
• December 29 •

malarkey

Blue puffy vest

STYLE Simple • Cool
COLORS Blue • White

Cranky

Pudge
• June 11 •

golly

Green letter jacket

STYLE Simple
COLORS Green • Blue

Lazy

Bluebear
• June 24 •

peach

White Aran-knit sweater

STYLE Cute • Simple
COLORS White • Blue

Peppy

June
• May 21 •

rainbow

Red hibiscus muumuu

STYLE Cute • Simple
COLORS White • Red

Sweet

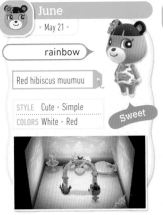

Olive
• July 12 •

sweet pea

Brown plover dress

STYLE Simple
COLORS Brown • Yellow

Sweet

Stitches
• February 10 •

stuffin'

White starry tank

STYLE Simple • Cute
COLORS Colorful • White

Lazy

Cheri
• March 17 •

tralala

Lime zigzag-print dress

STYLE Simple • Cute
COLORS Yellow • Aqua

Peppy

Kody
• September 28 •

grah grah

Pink western shirt

STYLE Active • Simple
COLORS Colorful • White

Jock

Pekoe
• May 18 •

bud

Red sleeveless silk dress

STYLE Elegant • Cute
COLORS Red • Beige

Sweet

Tammy
• June 23 •

ya heard

Red hawk jacket

STYLE Cool • Active
COLORS Red • Purple

Big sister

Vladimir
- August 2 -

nyet

Purple striped shirt

STYLE Simple • Cool
COLORS Yellow • Colorful

Cranky

Chow
- July 22 -

aiya

Black gold-print tee

STYLE Cool • Gorgeous
COLORS Black • White

Cranky

Ike
- May 16 -

roadie

Green camo bomb-er-style jacket

STYLE Cool
COLORS Green • Blue

Cranky

Paula
- March 22 -

yodelay

Purple zigzag-print dress

STYLE Cute • Active
COLORS Orange • Green

Big sister

Curt
- July 1 -

fuzzball

White MVP tee

STYLE Cool
COLORS Blue • White

Cranky

Klaus
- March 31 -

strudel

Red toga

STYLE Simple
COLORS Gray • White

Smug

Pinky
- September 9 -

wah

Pink silk floral-print shirt

STYLE Cute • Simple
COLORS Red • Pink

Peppy

Bears

Beardo
- September 27 -

whiskers

Brown tweed jacket

STYLE Elegant
COLORS Brown • Blue

Smug

Grizzly
- July 31 -

grrr

Red flannel shirt

STYLE Cool • Simple
COLORS Red • Black

Cranky

Megan
- March 13 -

sundae

Yellow dollhouse dress

STYLE Cute • Simple
COLORS Yellow • Aqua

Sweet

Teddy
- September 26 -

grooof

Yellow energetic sweater

STYLE Simple
COLORS Yellow • Orange

Jock

Charlise
- April 17 -

urgh

Red track jacket

STYLE Active • Cute
COLORS Red • Orange

Big sister

Groucho
- October 23 -

grumble

Black dragon jacket

STYLE Cool • Simple
COLORS Black • Gray

Cranky

Nate
- August 16 -

yawwwn

Green reindeer sweater

STYLE Simple
COLORS White • Green

Lazy

Tutu
- September 15 -

twinkles

Pink heart sweater

STYLE Cute • Simple
COLORS Pink • Red

Peppy

Ursala
• January 16 •

grooomph

Red striped maxi dress

STYLE Simple • Cute
COLORS Red • Orange

Big sister

Jacob
• August 24 •

ya feel

Green camo bomber-style jacket

STYLE Simple
COLORS Green • Red

Lazy

Lucha
• December 12 •

cacaw

Black track jacket

STYLE Active • Cool
COLORS Black • Gray

Smug

Robin
• December 4 •

la-di-da

Black front-tie tee

STYLE Elegant • Cool
COLORS Aqua • Purple

Snooty

Birds

Jacques
• June 22 •

zut alors

Navy blue puffy vest

STYLE Cool • Simple
COLORS Green • Black

Smug

Midge
• March 12 •

tweedledee

Blue silk shirt

STYLE Cute • Simple
COLORS Pink

Sweet

Sparro
• November 20 •

like whoa

Green earbuds combo

STYLE Active • Simple
COLORS Green • Gray

Jock

Admiral
• January 27 •

aye aye

Dark blue hanten jacket

STYLE Cool
COLORS Black • Blue

Cranky

Jay
• July 17 •

heeeeeyy

Green six-ball tee

STYLE Active
COLORS Blue • Aqua

Jock

Peck
• July 25 •

crunch

Red raglan tee

STYLE Simple • Active
COLORS Beige • Red

Jock

Twiggy
• July 13 •

cheepers

Pink striped tank

STYLE Simple • Cute
COLORS Pink • Blue

Peppy

Anchovy
• March 4 •

chuurp

Camel yodel sweater

STYLE Simple
COLORS Colorful • Orange

Lazy

Jitters
• February 2 •

bzzert

Yellow soccer-uniform top

STYLE Active
COLORS Yellow • Orange

Jock

Piper
• April 18 •

chickadee

Black lacy shirt

STYLE Elegant • Gorgeous
COLORS Black • White

Peppy

Bulls

Angus · April 30 ·
macmoo
Red flame tee
STYLE Cool
COLORS Red · Black
Cranky

T-Bone · May 20 ·
moocher
Dark blue hanten jacket
STYLE Cool · Simple
COLORS Blue · Black
Cranky

Bob · January 1 ·
pthhpth
Pink blossom tee
STYLE Simple · Cute
COLORS Colorful · Red
Lazy

Kid Cat · August 1 ·
psst
Red No. 1 shirt
STYLE Active · Simple
COLORS Red
Jock

Coach · April 29 ·
stubble
Blue relay tank
STYLE Active
COLORS Blue · Red
Jock

Vic · December 29 ·
cud
Gray viking top
STYLE Cool · Active
COLORS Aqua · Blue
Cranky

Felicity · March 30 ·
mimimi
Yellow tweed dress
STYLE Cute
COLORS Yellow · Orange
Peppy

Kiki · October 8 ·
kitty cat
Green argyle sweater
STYLE Simple
COLORS Brown · Beige
Sweet

Rodeo · October 29 ·
chaps
Red graduation gown
STYLE Simple · Cool
COLORS Black · Red
Lazy

Cats

Kabuki · November 29 ·
meooo-OH
Fuchsia kabuki-actor yukata
STYLE Simple
COLORS Purple · Red
Cranky

Kitty · February 15 ·
mrowrr
Peacock blue loose fall dress
STYLE Elegant · Gorgeous
COLORS Green · Gray
Snooty

Stu · April 20 ·
mrooooo
Light gray yodel sweater
STYLE Simple
COLORS Brown · Beige
Lazy

Ankha · September 22 ·
me meow
White palatial tank dress
STYLE Gorgeous · Simple
COLORS Colorful · Brown
Snooty

Katt · April 27 ·
purrty
Red old-school jacket
STYLE Cool
COLORS Purple · Black
Big sister

Lolly · March 27 ·
bonbon
Gray snowy sweater
STYLE Simple
COLORS Gray · Pink
Sweet

2

Merry · June 29 ·
mweee
Pink dreamy sweater
STYLE Cute
COLORS Pink · Aqua
Peppy

Olivia · February 3 ·
purrr
Navy blue sweetheart dress
STYLE Cool · Elegant
COLORS White · Black
Snooty

Rosie · February 27 ·
silly
Pink dazed dress
STYLE Cute
COLORS Pink · Red
Peppy

Tangy · June 17 ·
reeeeOWR
Green retro dress
STYLE Simple · Cute
COLORS Green · Yellow
Peppy

Mitzi · September 25 ·
mew
Pop gumdrop dress
STYLE Simple
COLORS Brown · Beige
Sweet

Punchy · April 11 ·
mrmpht
Gray madras plaid shirt
STYLE Simple
COLORS Blue · Aqua
Lazy

Rudy · December 20 ·
mush
Yellow simple parka
STYLE Active · Simple
COLORS Yellow · Beige
Jock

Tom · December 10 ·
me-YOWZA
Black bulldog jacket
STYLE Cool · Simple
COLORS Black · Gray
Cranky

Moe · January 12 ·
myawn
Black simple parka
STYLE Active · Simple
COLORS Black · Gray
Lazy

Purrl · May 29 ·
kitten
Navy blue kung-fu tee
STYLE Cool · Elegant
COLORS Gray · Blue
Snooty

Stinky · August 17 ·
GAAHHH
Red track jacket
STYLE Active · Simple
COLORS Red · Blue
Jock

Chickens

Monique · September 30 ·
pffffft
Black flapper dress
STYLE Gorgeous · Elegant
COLORS Purple · Pink
Snooty

Raymond · October 1 ·
crisp
Gray waistcoat
STYLE Elegant · Cool
COLORS Black · Gray
Smug

Tabby · August 13 ·
me-WOW
Black tee dress
STYLE Active · Cool
COLORS Black · Gray
Peppy

Ava · April 28 ·
beaker
Red checkered jumper dress
STYLE Elegant · Cute
COLORS Red · Gray
Sweet

Becky
• December 9 •

chicklet

Purple Renaissance dress

STYLE Gorgeous • Elegant
COLORS Purple • Pink

Snooty

Goose
• October 4 •

buh-kay

Navy blue bold aloha shirt

STYLE Simple • Active
COLORS Blue • White

Jock

Cows

Tipper
• August 25 •

pushy

Purple retro sweater

STYLE Gorgeous • Cute
COLORS Colorful • Pink

Snooty

Benedict
• October 10 •

uh-hoo

Blue two-ball tee

STYLE Simple
COLORS Blue • Purple

Lazy

Ken
• December 23 •

no doubt

Dark blue ninja costume

STYLE Cool • Simple
COLORS Purple • Blue

Smug

Naomi
• February 28 •

moolah

Pink marble-print dress

STYLE Elegant • Gorgeous
COLORS Colorful • Purple

Snooty

Deers

Broffina
• October 24 •

cluckadoo

Red rumba dress

STYLE Gorgeous • Elegant
COLORS Black • Red

Snooty

Knox
• November 23 •

cluckling

Red cavalier shirt

STYLE Elegant • Gorgeous
COLORS Brown • Red

Cranky

Norma
• September 20 •

hoof hoo

Fancy plaid plaid-print dress

STYLE Cute • Simple
COLORS White • Aqua

Sweet

Bam
• November 7 •

kablang

Green track jacket

STYLE Active • Simple
COLORS Green • Brown

Jock

Egbert
• October 14 •

doodle-duh

Red folk shirt

STYLE Simple
COLORS Beige • Brown

Lazy

Plucky
• October 12 •

chicky-poo

Pink bold muumuu

STYLE Cool • Simple
COLORS Aqua • Yellow

Big sister

Patty
• May 10 •

how-now

Orange orange dress

STYLE Simple • Cute
COLORS Orange • Red

Peppy

Beau
• April 5 •

saltlick

Green reindeer sweater

STYLE Simple • Cute
COLORS Beige • Orange

Lazy

Bruce
• May 26 •

gruff

Black after-school jacket

STYLE Cool • Simple
COLORS Black • Red

Cranky

Fauna
• March 26 •

dearie

Red Bohemian tunic dress

STYLE Simple • Cute
COLORS Beige • White

Sweet

Dogs

Bones
• August 4 •

yip yip

Brown printed fleece sweater

STYLE Simple • Cute
COLORS Beige • Brown

Lazy

Deirdre
• May 4 •

whatevs

Yellow flower sweater

STYLE Simple
COLORS Orange

Big sister

Fuchsia
• September 19 •

precious

Purple zigzag-print dress

STYLE Cool
COLORS Pink

Big sister

Bea
• October 15 •

bingo

Orange striped maxi dress

STYLE Simple • Cool
COLORS Aqua • Green

Sweet

Butch
• November 1 •

ROOOOOWF

Blue argyle vest

STYLE Cool • Simple
COLORS Blue • Gray

Cranky

Diana
• January 4 •

no doy

Purple mysterious dress

STYLE Elegant • Gorgeous
COLORS Purple • Pink

Snooty

Lopez
• August 20 •

badoom

Navy blue Chimayo vest

STYLE Gorgeous
COLORS Gray

Smug

Benjamin
• August 3 •

alrighty

Red striped shirt

STYLE Simple
COLORS Red • White

Lazy

Cherry
• May 11 •

what what

Black spider-web tee

STYLE Cool • Elegant
COLORS Black • Purple

Big sister

Erik
• July 27 •

chow down

Camel yodel sweater

STYLE Simple
COLORS Beige • Red

Lazy

Zell
• June 7 •

pronk

Black gilet and shirt

STYLE Cool • Gorgeous
COLORS Purple • Gray

Smug

Biskit
• May 13 •

dawg

Purple meme shirt

STYLE Gorgeous • Simple
COLORS Purple • Colorful

Lazy

Cookie
• June 18 •

arfer

Light blue retro dress

STYLE Cute
COLORS Green • Aqua

Peppy

Daisy
• November 16 •

bow-WOW

Navy, light blue & pink colorful striped sweater

STYLE Simple • Cute
COLORS Colorful • Blue

Sweet

Maddie
• January 11 •

yippee

Pink layered sleeveless dress

STYLE Simple • Cute
COLORS Purple • Pink

Peppy

Walker
• June 10 •

wuh

Orange five-ball tee

STYLE Simple
COLORS Orange • Red

Lazy

Derwin
• May 25 •

derrrr

Yellow striped tank

STYLE Simple • Elegant
COLORS Yellow • Beige

Lazy

Goldie
• December 27 •

woof

Yellow tweed dress

STYLE Simple • Cute
COLORS Yellow • Orange

Sweet

Marcel
• December 31 •

non

Dark blue sea hanten shirt

STYLE Simple • Cool
COLORS Green • Blue

Lazy

Ducks

Drake
• June 25 •

quacko

Camel yodel sweater

STYLE Cool • Simple
COLORS Brown • Red

Lazy

Lucky
• November 4 •

rrr-owch

Coral open-collar shirt

STYLE Simple
COLORS Beige • White

Lazy

Portia
• October 25 •

ruffian

Purple rad power skirt suit

STYLE Elegant • Gorgeous
COLORS Purple • Black

Snooty

Bill
• February 1 •

quacko

Purple basketball tank

STYLE Active
COLORS Blue • Purple

Jock

Freckles
• February 19 •

ducky

Green flower-print dress

STYLE Simple • Cute
COLORS Green • Colorful

Peppy

Mac
• November 11 •

woo woof

Red raglan tee

STYLE Active • Cool
COLORS Red • Black

Jock

Shep
• November 24 •

baa baa baa

Washed out denim vest

STYLE Simple • Cool
COLORS Aqua • Blue

Smug

Deena
• June 27 •

woowoo

Denim overall dress

STYLE Simple • Cute
COLORS Colorful • Blue

Sweet

Gloria
• August 12 •

quacker

Black floral lace dress

STYLE Gorgeous • Elegant
COLORS Black • Gray

Snooty

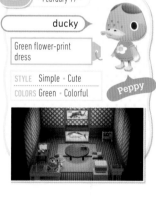

2

Joey
· January 3 ·

bleeeeeck

Green bear tee

STYLE Simple
COLORS Green · Blue

Lazy

Miranda
· April 23 ·

quackulous

Blue sleeveless shirtdress

STYLE Elegant · Gorgeous
COLORS Blue · Purple

Snooty

Quillson
· December 22 ·

ridukulous

White checkered muffler

STYLE Elegant · Cool
COLORS Beige · Orange

Smug

Amelia
· November 19 ·

cuz

Black Aran-knit sweater

STYLE Cool · Elegant
COLORS Black · White

Snooty

Ketchup
· July 27 ·

bitty

Blue lacy dress

STYLE Cute
COLORS Aqua · White

Peppy

Molly
· March 7 ·

quackidee

Lime pintuck-pleated dress

STYLE Cute · Simple
COLORS Yellow · Pink

Sweet

Scoot
· June 13 ·

zip zoom

Beige frog tee

STYLE Active · Simple
COLORS Beige · Blue

Jock

Apollo
· July 4 ·

pah

Black flight jacket

STYLE Cool · Simple
COLORS Black

Cranky

Maelle
· April 8 ·

duckling

Red flower sweater

STYLE Cool · Simple
COLORS Pink · White

Snooty

Pate
· February 23 ·

quackle

White sunflower dress

STYLE Simple · Cute
COLORS Yellow · White

Peppy

Weber
· June 30 ·

quaa

Navy blue striped shirt

STYLE Cool · Simple
COLORS Blue · Black

Lazy

Avery
· February 22 ·

skree-haw

Brown oversized shawl overshirt

STYLE Simple · Gorgeous
COLORS Orange · Brown

Cranky

Mallary
· November 17 ·

quackpth

Blue striped shirt

STYLE Cool · Gorgeous
COLORS Blue · White

Snooty

Pompom
· February 11 ·

rah rah

Pink parka dress

STYLE Cute · Simple
COLORS Pink · Aqua

Peppy

Eagles

Buzz
· December 7 ·

captain

Yellow nine-ball tee

STYLE Simple · Active
COLORS Yellow · Red

Cranky

Celia
• March 25 •

feathers

Green alpinist dress

STYLE Elegant • Cute
COLORS Pink • Green

Sweet

Sterling
• December 11 •

skraaaaw

Blue cavalier shirt

STYLE Simple • Elegant
COLORS Blue • Red

Jock

Cyd
• June 9 •

rockin'

Black dragon jacket

STYLE Cool • Active
COLORS Black • Yellow

Cranky

Margie
• January 28 •

tootie

Pink silk floral-print shirt

STYLE Elegant • Cute
COLORS Pink • Red

Sweet

Frank
• July 30 •

crushy

Blue letter jacket

STYLE Gorgeous • Cool
COLORS Brown • Yellow

Cranky

Elephants

Dizzy
• July 14 •

woo-oo

Yellow bone tee

STYLE Simple
COLORS Yellow • Blue

Lazy

Opal
• January 20 •

snoot

Black front-tie tee

STYLE Elegant • Cool
COLORS Black • Orange

Snooty

Keaton
• June 1 •

wingo

Navy blue fuzzy vest

STYLE Gorgeous • Cool
COLORS Blue • White

Smug

Axel
• March 23 •

WHONK

Green kanji tee

STYLE Active • Simple
COLORS Green • White

Jock

Ellie
• May 12 •

li'l one

Red Aran-knit sweater

STYLE Simple • Cute
COLORS Gray • Pink

Sweet

Paolo
• May 5 •

pal

Gray simple parka

STYLE Simple • Elegant
COLORS Gray • Aqua

Lazy

Pierce
• January 8 •

hawkeye

Ivory tennis sweater

STYLE Elegant • Active
COLORS Orange • Yellow

Jock

Big Top
• October 3 •

villain

Green No. 3 shirt

STYLE Simple • Active
COLORS Green

Lazy

Eloise
• December 8 •

tooooot

Lime zigzag-print dress

STYLE Elegant • Simple
COLORS Green • Orange

Snooty

Tia
• November 18 •

teacup

Black maid dress

STYLE Cute • Elegant
COLORS Black • White

Sweet

Tucker
• September 7 •

fuzzers

Yellow caveman tank

STYLE   Active • Simple
COLORS Yellow • Orange

Lazy

Croque
• July 18 •

as if

Red silk shirt

STYLE   Elegant • Cool
COLORS Red • Orange

Cranky

Gigi
• August 11 •

ribbette

Black full-length dress with pearls

STYLE   Gorgeous • Elegant
COLORS Black • White

Snooty

Jeremiah
• July 8 •

nee-deep

Orange gingham picnic shirt

STYLE   Simple
COLORS Orange • Yellow

Lazy

Frogs

Diva
• October 2 •

ya know

White palatial tank dress

STYLE   Gorgeous • Elegant
COLORS Purple • Aqua

Big sister

Henry
• September 21 •

snoozit

Blue denim jacket

STYLE   Cool • Simple
COLORS Aqua • Blue

Smug

Lily
• February 4 •

toady

White tropical muumuu

STYLE   Cute • Simple
COLORS White • Yellow

Sweet

Camofrog
• June 5 •

ten-hut

White MVP tee

STYLE   Cool • Active
COLORS Blue • White

Cranky

Drift
• October 9 •

dribbit

Green six-ball tee

STYLE   Simple • Active
COLORS Orange • Red

Jock

Huck
• July 9 •

hopper

Green striped tank

STYLE   Simple • Cool
COLORS Green • Yellow

Smug

Prince
• July 21 •

burrup

Yellow striped shirt

STYLE   Simple • Active
COLORS Yellow • White

Lazy

Cousteau
• December 17 •

oui oui

Green silk shirt

STYLE   Elegant • Gorgeous
COLORS Green • Red

Jock

Frobert
• February 8 •

fribbit

Navy blue striped tee

STYLE   Active • Simple
COLORS Blue • Colorful

Jock

Jambette
• October 27 •

croak-kay

Pink shell dress

STYLE   Cool
COLORS Brown

Sweet

Puddles
• January 13 •

splish

Green retro dress

STYLE   Cute • Gorgeous
COLORS Green • Pink

Peppy

Raddle
• June 6 •

aaach—

Black necktie doctor's coat

STYLE Elegant • Simple
COLORS White • Gray

Lazy

Kidd
• June 28 •

wut

Gray tailored jacket

STYLE Elegant • Cool
COLORS Gray • White

Smug

Velma
• January 14 •

blih

Blue prim outfit

STYLE Elegant • Gorgeous
COLORS Aqua • Purple

Snooty

Goats

Ribbot
• February 13 •

zzrrbbitt

Light blue simple parka

STYLE Simple • Active
COLORS Blue • Aqua

Jock

Billy
• March 25 •

dagnaabit

Dark blue hanten jacket

STYLE Simple • Active
COLORS Blue • Purple

Jock

Nan
• August 24 •

kid

Yellow tweed dress

STYLE Simple • Elegant
COLORS Orange • Yellow

Sweet

Gorillas

Tad
• August 3 •

sluuuurp

Yellow one-ball tee

STYLE Active • Simple
COLORS Yellow • Colorful

Jock

Chevre
• March 6 •

la baa

Red poncho coat

STYLE Cute • Elegant
COLORS Red • Pink

Sweet

Pashmina
• December 26 •

kidders

Black rainbow sweater

STYLE Cool • Elegant
COLORS Red • Colorful

Big sister

Al
• October 18 •

ayyyeee

Red track jacket

STYLE Active
COLORS Red • White

Lazy

Wart Jr.
• August 21 •

grr-ribbit

Purple hanten jacket

STYLE Simple
COLORS Blue • Purple

Cranky

Gruff
• August 29 •

bleh eh eh

Purple old-school jacket

STYLE Cool • Gorgeous
COLORS Purple • Black

Cranky

Sherb
• January 18 •

bawwww

Gray snowy sweater

STYLE Simple • Cute
COLORS Gray • Blue

Lazy

Boone
• September 12 •

baboom

Blue & white cycling shirt

STYLE Elegant • Cool
COLORS Colorful • Red

Jock

Boyd
• October 1 •
uh-oh
Red three-ball tee
STYLE Simple • Cool
COLORS Red • Black
Cranky

Peewee
• September 11 •
li'l bitty baby
Orange five-ball tee
STYLE Active • Cool
COLORS Orange • Blue
Cranky

Apple
• September 24 •
cheekers
White marble-dots tee
STYLE Cute • Simple
COLORS Colorful • Red
Peppy

Hamlet
• May 30 •
hammie
Purple big-star tee
STYLE Simple • Active
COLORS Purple • Blue
Jock

Cesar
• September 6 •
highness
Blue A tee
STYLE Cool • Elegant
COLORS Blue • Aqua
Cranky

Rocket
• April 14 •
vroom
Pink No. 4 shirt
STYLE Active • Cool
COLORS Pink • Red
Big sister

Clay
• October 19 •
thump
Orange poncho-style sweater
STYLE Elegant • Simple
COLORS Beige • Brown
Lazy

Hamphrey
• February 25 •
snort
Beige fuzzy vest
STYLE Cool • Simple
COLORS Gray • Beige
Cranky

Hans
• December 5 •
groovy
Red & yellow down ski jacket
STYLE Elegant • Gorgeous
COLORS Gray • Blue
Smug

Violet
• September 1 •
sweetie
Purple poncho-style sweater
STYLE Gorgeous • Cool
COLORS Purple • Pink
Snooty

Flurry
• January 30 •
powderpuff
Red flower sweater
STYLE Elegant • Cute
COLORS Red • Pink
Sweet

Rodney
• November 10 •
le ham
Pink striped tank
STYLE Gorgeous • Cool
COLORS Pink • Colorful
Smug

Louie
• March 26 •
hoo hoo ha
Gray muscle tank
STYLE Active • Simple
COLORS Gray • Red
Jock

Hamsters

Graham
• June 20 •
indeed
Green madras plaid shirt
STYLE Simple • Cool
COLORS Green • Orange
Smug

Soleil
• August 9 •
tarnation
Garnet sari
STYLE Cool • Gorgeous
COLORS Red • Yellow
Snooty

Hippos

Bubbles
· September 18 ·
hipster
Purple grape dress
STYLE Active · Cute
COLORS Purple · Pink
Peppy

Bertha
· April 25 ·
bloop
Pink pintuck-pleated dress
STYLE Cute · Elegant
COLORS Pink · White
Sweet

Harry
· January 7 ·
beach bum
Avocado camo tee
STYLE Cool · Simple
COLORS Green · Orange
Cranky

Biff
· March 29 ·
squirt
Black gold-print tee
STYLE Gorgeous · Active
COLORS Black · Blue
Jock

Hippeux
· October 15 ·
natch
Beige emblem blazer
STYLE Elegant · Gorgeous
COLORS Brown · Green
Smug

Bitty
· October 6 ·
my dear
Pink frilly dress
STYLE Cute · Elegant
COLORS Pink · Orange
Snooty

Rocco
· August 18 ·
hippie
Yellow danger tank
STYLE Simple · Cool
COLORS Yellow · Black
Cranky

Horses

Clyde
· May 1 ·
clip clawp
Pink madras plaid shirt
STYLE Simple · Cute
COLORS Green · White
Lazy

Annalise
· December 2 ·
nipper
Navy blue bold muumuu
STYLE Elegant · Active
COLORS Blue · Purple
Snooty

Colton
· May 22 ·
check it
Blue prince's tunic
STYLE Gorgeous · Elegant
COLORS Blue · Red
Smug

Buck
· April 4 ·
pardner
Gray sweatshirt
STYLE Active · Simple
COLORS Gray · Brown
Jock

Ed
· September 16 ·
greenhorn
Black collarless shirt
STYLE Gorgeous · Elegant
COLORS Black · Gray
Smug

Cleo
· February 9 ·
sugar
Light blue floral lace dress
STYLE Cute · Elegant
COLORS Aqua · White
Snooty

Elmer
· October 5 ·
tenderfoot
White boa fleece
STYLE Simple · Cool
COLORS Blue · White
Lazy

Julian
• March 15 •

glitter

Blue space parka

STYLE   Gorgeous • Cool
COLORS Purple • Blue

Smug

Roscoe
• June 16 •

nay

Black biker jacket

STYLE   Cool • Gorgeous
COLORS Black • Gray

Cranky

Kangaroos

Marcie
• May 31 •

pouches

Pink heart apron

STYLE   Cute • Elegant
COLORS Pink • Beige

Sweet

Papi
• January 10 •

haaay

Navy, light blue & pink colorful striped sweater

STYLE   Simple
COLORS Orange • Aqua

Lazy

Savannah
• January 25 •

y'all

Light blue top coat

STYLE   Cool • Simple
COLORS Aqua • Blue

Sweet

Astrid
• September 8 •

my pet

Black tee dress

STYLE   Cool • Active
COLORS Black • Colorful

Snooty

Mathilda
• November 12 •

wee baby

Gray sleeveless sweater dress

STYLE   Cool • Gorgeous
COLORS White • Red

Snooty

Peaches
• November 28 •

neighbor

Gray long denim cardigan

STYLE   Cute • Simple
COLORS Colorful • Aqua

Sweet

Victoria
• July 11 •

sugar cube

Yellow one-ball tee

STYLE   Active • Simple
COLORS Yellow • Orange

Peppy

Carrie
• December 5 •

little one

Red simple-dots dress

STYLE   Cute
COLORS Red • Colorful

Sweet

Rooney
• December 1 •

punches

Black sleeveless parka

STYLE   Active
COLORS Gray • Black

Cranky

Reneigh
• June 4 •

ayup yup

Purple zigzag-print dress

STYLE   Cool • Gorgeous
COLORS Black • Purple

Big sister

Winnie
• January 31 •

hay-OK

White faux-hair sweater

STYLE   Cool • Simple
COLORS White • Gray

Peppy

Kitt
• October 11 •

child

Pink striped halter dress

STYLE   Elegant • Simple
COLORS Purple • Red

Sweet

Sylvia
• May 3 •

boing

Yellow pineapple muumuu

STYLE   Simple • Gorgeous
COLORS Yellow • Green

Big sister

Walt
• April 24 •

pockets

Dark blue casual kimono

STYLE Cool
COLORS Black • Gray

Cranky

Eugene
• October 26 •

yeah buddy

Black biker jacket

STYLE Cool • Gorgeous
COLORS Black • Gray

Smug

Ozzie
• May 7 •

ol' bear

Yellow energetic sweater

STYLE Simple • Cute
COLORS Yellow • Orange

Lazy

Bud
• August 8 •

shredded

Green pineapple aloha shirt

STYLE Active • Simple
COLORS Green • Yellow

Jock

Gonzo
• October 13 •

mate

Green reindeer sweater

STYLE Simple • Cool
COLORS Black • Green

Cranky

Sydney
• June 21 •

sunshine

Beige overall dress

STYLE Cute • Simple
COLORS Beige • Yellow

Sweet

Elvis
• July 23 •

unh-hunh

Red royal shirt

STYLE Gorgeous • Elegant
COLORS Red • Black

Cranky

Koalas

Alice
• August 19 •

guvnor

Red striped maxi dress

STYLE Cute
COLORS Red • Pink

Sweet

Lyman
• October 12 •

chips

Blue vertical-stripes shirt

STYLE Simple • Active
COLORS Aqua • Yellow

Jock

Yuka
• July 20 •

tsk tsk

Orange Aran-knit sweater

STYLE Cool • Elegant
COLORS Orange • Yellow

Snooty

Leopold
• August 14 •

lion cub

Ivory tennis sweater

STYLE Elegant • Gorgeous
COLORS Purple • Green

Smug

Canberra
• May 14 •

nuh uh

Green striped tank

STYLE Active • Cool
COLORS Green • Aqua

Big sister

Melba
• April 12 •

toasty

Fancy plaid plaid-print dress

STYLE Cute
COLORS White • Green

Sweet

Lions

Lionel
• July 29 •

precisely

Green noble coat

STYLE Gorgeous • Active
COLORS Green • Gray

Smug

2

Mott
· July 10 ·
cagey
Navy blue college cardigan
STYLE Active · Elegant
COLORS Blue · Green
Jock

Anicotti
· February 24 ·
cannoli
Black, coral & pink colorful striped sweater
STYLE Simple · Elegant
COLORS Red · Pink
Peppy

Broccolo
· June 30 ·
eat it
Red raglan tee
STYLE Simple · Cute
COLORS Colorful · Yellow
Lazy

Greta
· September 5 ·
yelp
Dark blue pinafore
STYLE Elegant · Simple
COLORS Pink · Purple
Snooty

Rex
· July 24 ·
cool cat
Blue striped shirt
STYLE Simple · Cute
COLORS Blue · Aqua
Lazy

Bella
· December 28 ·
eeks
Black tee dress
STYLE Cool · Active
COLORS Black · Purple
Peppy

Candi
· April 13 ·
sweetie
Navy blue Bohemian tunic dress
STYLE Simple · Cute
COLORS Aqua · Yellow
Peppy

Limberg
· October 17 ·
squinky
Dark blue hanten jacket
STYLE Simple · Cool
COLORS Green · Blue
Cranky

Rory
· August 7 ·
capital
Blue sea hanten shirt
STYLE Simple · Active
COLORS Blue · Red
Jock

Bettina
· June 12 ·
eekers
Red chef's outfit
STYLE Simple · Elegant
COLORS White · Red
Sweet

Chadder
· December 15 ·
fromage
Black tailcoat
STYLE Elegant · Gorgeous
COLORS Black · Gray
Smug

Moose
· September 13 ·
shorty
Purple big-star tee
STYLE Cool · Gorgeous
COLORS Purple · Red
Jock

Bree
· July 7 ·
cheeseball
Navy blue sweetheart dress
STYLE Elegant · Gorgeous
COLORS Black · Blue
Snooty

Dora
· February 18 ·
squeaky
Dark blue sea hanten shirt
STYLE Simple · Elegant
COLORS Blue · Aqua
Sweet

Penelope
· February 5 ·
oh bow
Pink oversized print dress
STYLE Cute · Gorgeous
COLORS Pink · Red
Peppy

Mice

Rizzo
· January 17 ·

squee

Dark blue ninja costume

STYLE Simple · Cool
COLORS Black · Gray

Cranky

Deli
· May 24 ·

monch

Blue argyle vest

STYLE Gorgeous · Elegant
COLORS Purple · Brown

Lazy

Nana
· August 23 ·

po po

Pink pom-pom sweater

STYLE Cute
COLORS Pink · White

Sweet

Octopuses

Rod
· August 14 ·

ace

Blue striped tank

STYLE Active · Cool
COLORS Blue · Aqua

Jock

Elise
· March 21 ·

puh-lease

Purple elegant dress

STYLE Elegant · Gorgeous
COLORS Purple · Red

Snooty

Shari
· April 10 ·

cheeky

Blue garden tank

STYLE Cute · Active
COLORS Aqua · Yellow

Big sister

Marina
· June 26 ·

blurp

Pink dreamy sweater

STYLE Cute
COLORS Pink · Red

Sweet

Samson
· July 5 ·

pipsqueak

Black kanji tee

STYLE Simple · Active
COLORS Red · Yellow

Jock

Flip
· November 21 ·

rerack

Blue muscle tank

STYLE Active · Simple
COLORS Blue · Yellow

Jock

Simon
· January 19 ·

zzzook

Pink striped tank

STYLE Simple · Active
COLORS Red · Colorful

Lazy

Octavian
· September 20 ·

sucker

Black gold-print tee

STYLE Cool · Simple
COLORS Black · White

Cranky

Monkeys

Monty
· December 7 ·

g'tang

Green guayabera shirt

STYLE Cool
COLORS Yellow · Gray

Cranky

Tammi
· April 2 ·

chimpy

Purple silk floral-print shirt

STYLE Cute · Active
COLORS Purple · Green

Peppy

Zucker
· March 8 ·

bloop

Blue happi tee

STYLE Simple · Cute
COLORS Blue · Yellow

Lazy

Ostriches

Gladys
· January 15 ·

stretch

Green misty tee

STYLE Elegant · Cute
COLORS Green · Pink

Sweet

Queenie
· November 13 ·

chicken

Navy blue shirtdress

STYLE Gorgeous · Elegant
COLORS Black · Gray

Snooty

Aurora
· January 27 ·

b-b-baby

Red plover dress

STYLE Cute · Elegant
COLORS Pink · Red

Sweet

Blanche
· December 21 ·

quite so

Black butterfly visiting kimono

STYLE Elegant · Gorgeous
COLORS Black · Brown

Snooty

Julia
· July 31 ·

dahling

Coral zigzag-print dress

STYLE Elegant · Gorgeous
COLORS Purple · Red

Snooty

Sandy
· October 21 ·

speedy

Blue striped tank

STYLE Simple · Cool
COLORS Aqua · White

Sweet

Boomer
· February 7 ·

human

Brown flight jacket

STYLE Simple · Cool
COLORS Brown · Beige

Lazy

Cranston
· September 23 ·

sweatband

Brown oversized shawl overshirt

STYLE Simple · Cool
COLORS Beige · Brown

Lazy

Phil
· November 27 ·

hurk

Blue fischerhemd

STYLE Elegant · Cool
COLORS Green · Red

Smug

Sprocket
· December 1 ·

zort

Orange jumper work suit

STYLE Simple · Active
COLORS Orange · Green

Jock

Cube
· January 29 ·

brainfreeze

Yellow simple-dots tee

STYLE Simple · Cute
COLORS Yellow · Colorful

Lazy

Flora
· February 9 ·

pinky

Pop gumdrop dress

STYLE Cute · Active
COLORS Colorful · Pink

Peppy

Phoebe
· April 22 ·

sparky

Black front-tie tee

STYLE Gorgeous · Cool
COLORS Black · Red

Big sister

Penguins

Flo
· September 2 ·

cha

Red folk shirt

STYLE Cool · Gorgeous
COLORS Red · Purple

Big sister

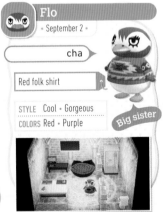

Friga
• October 16 •

brrrmph

Pink simple checkered dress

STYLE Elegant • Gorgeous
COLORS Pink • Black

Snooty

Puck
• February 21 •

brrrrrrrr

White & red ice-hockey uniform

STYLE Active • Simple
COLORS Blue • Red

Lazy

Wade
• October 30 •

so it goes

Beige frog tee

STYLE Simple • Gorgeous
COLORS Aqua • Blue

Lazy

Chops
• October 13 •

zoink

Red military uniform

STYLE Gorgeous • Elegant
COLORS Red • Green

Smug

Gwen
• January 23 •

h-h-h-hon

Green retro dress

STYLE Gorgeous • Elegant
COLORS Green • White

Snooty

Roald
• January 5 •

b-b-buddy

Red flannel shirt

STYLE Active • Simple
COLORS Red • Yellow

Jock

Pigs

Cobb
• October 7 •

hot dog

Blue flannel shirt

STYLE Simple • Active
COLORS White • Blue

Jock

Hopper
• April 6 •

slushie

Yellow dragon suit

STYLE Cool • Simple
COLORS Yellow • Red

Cranky

Sprinkle
• February 20 •

frappe

Gray snowy sweater

STYLE Cute • Elegant
COLORS Aqua • White

Peppy

Agnes
• April 21 •

snuffle

Pink striped halter dress

STYLE Simple • Elegant
COLORS Pink • White

Big sister

Curly
• July 26 •

nyoink

Yellow energetic sweater

STYLE Simple • Active
COLORS Yellow • Colorful

Jock

Iggly
• November 2 •

waddler

Red & white rugby uniform

STYLE Active • Simple
COLORS Red • Blue

Jock

Tex
• October 6 •

picante

Blue letter jacket

STYLE Cool • Elegant
COLORS Black • Gray

Smug

Boris
• November 6 •

schnort

Purple desert outfit

STYLE Cool • Gorgeous
COLORS Purple • Black

Cranky

Gala
• March 5 •

snortie

Pink flower-print dress

STYLE Cute • Elegant
COLORS Pink • White

Sweet

Hugh
• December 30 •

snortle

Brown camo tee

STYLE Simple • Active
COLORS Beige • Yellow

Lazy

Pancetti
• November 14 •

sooey

Yellow dollhouse dress

STYLE Cute • Gorgeous
COLORS Red • Yellow

Snooty

Truffles
• July 28 •

snoutie

Lime tee-parka combo

STYLE Cute • Gorgeous
COLORS Green • Red

Peppy

Carmen
• January 6 •

nougat

Sweet plaid plaid-print dress

STYLE Elegant • Cute
COLORS Green • Beige

Peppy

Kevin
• April 26 •

weeweewee

Black after-school jacket

STYLE Active • Simple
COLORS Black • Red

Jock

Peggy
• May 23 •

shweetie

Red Aran-knit sweater

STYLE Cute • Active
COLORS Blue • Red

Peppy

Rabbits

Chrissy
• August 28 •

sparkles

White marble-dots dress

STYLE Cute
COLORS Pink • White

Peppy

Lucy
• June 2 •

snoooink

Pink frilly dress

STYLE Cute • Elegant
COLORS Pink • Red

Sweet

Rasher
• April 7 •

swine

Blue pineapple aloha shirt

STYLE Cool • Simple
COLORS Blue • Black

Cranky

Bonbon
• March 3 •

deelish

Mint sleeveless tunic

STYLE Cute • Elegant
COLORS Aqua • Yellow

Peppy

Claude
• December 3 •

hopalong

Black marble-dots tee

STYLE Simple
COLORS Black • Colorful

Lazy

Maggie
• September 3 •

schep

Green pintuck-pleated dress

STYLE Cute • Elegant
COLORS Green • Yellow

Sweet

Spork
• September 3 •

snork

Green layered shirt

STYLE Simple • Active
COLORS Green • Colorful

Lazy

Bunnie
• May 9 •

tee-hee

Green lively plaid dress

STYLE Cute
COLORS Green • Pink

Peppy

Coco
• March 1 •

doyoing

Beige layered tank dress

STYLE Simple • Cute
COLORS Beige • Green

Sweet

Cole
• August 10 •

coooooool

Orange orange dress

STYLE Simple • Cute
COLORS Orange • Colorful

Lazy

Gabi
• December 16 •

honeybun

Red gingham picnic shirt

STYLE Cute • Gorgeous
COLORS Brown • Red

Peppy

Mira
• July 6 •

cottontail

Red noble zap suit

STYLE Active • Cool
COLORS Red • Yellow

Big sister

Snake
• November 3 •

bunyip

Dark blue ninja costume

STYLE Active • Simple
COLORS Black • Blue

Jock

Doc
• March 16 •

old bunny

Red flannel shirt

STYLE Simple • Elegant
COLORS Gray • Beige

Lazy

Gaston
• October 28 •

mon chou

Red color-block dress shirt

STYLE Simple • Gorgeous
COLORS Brown • Orange

Cranky

O'Hare
• July 24 •

amigo

Blue pineapple aloha shirt

STYLE Active • Cool
COLORS Blue • Aqua

Smug

Tiffany
• January 9 •

bunbun

Black chic tuxedo dress

STYLE Gorgeous • Cool
COLORS Black • Red

Snooty

Dotty
• March 14 •

wee one

Blue sleeveless tunic

STYLE Simple • Cute
COLORS Blue • Black

Peppy

Genji
• January 21 •

mochi

Green misty tee

STYLE Elegant • Simple
COLORS Green • Purple

Jock

Pippy
• June 14 •

li'l hare

Green overall dress

STYLE Cute • Simple
COLORS Green • Brown

Peppy

Francine
• January 22 •

karat

Black marble-dots dress

STYLE Elegant • Gorgeous
COLORS Blue • Black

Snooty

Hopkins
• March 11 •

thumper

Blue striped shirt

STYLE Simple • Active
COLORS Blue • Yellow

Lazy

Ruby
• December 25 •

li'l ears

Blue rabbit tee

STYLE Cute • Active
COLORS Aqua • Pink

Peppy

Hornsby
• March 20 •

schnozzle

Green argyle sweater

STYLE Simple
COLORS Green • Brown

Lazy

Rhinos

2

Merengue
• March 19 •

shortcake

Red chef's outfit

STYLE Cute • Simple
COLORS White • Red

Sweet

Tank
• May 6 •

kerPOW

Red No. 1 shirt

STYLE Active • Simple
COLORS Red • Green

Jock

Curlos
• May 8 •

shearly

Red, green & gold zigzag shirt

STYLE Active • Gorgeous
COLORS Red • Green

Smug

Muffy
• February 14 •

nightshade

Purple ruffled dress

STYLE Gorgeous • Elegant
COLORS Black • Purple

Big sister

Renée
• May 28 •

yo yo yo

Navy blue sailor's tee

STYLE Cool • Active
COLORS Purple • Yellow

Big sister

Sheep

Dom
• March 18 •

indeedaroo

Rainbow tie-dye shirt

STYLE Active • Cute
COLORS Red • Colorful

Jock

Pietro
• April 19 •

honk honk

Purple & yellow jester costume

STYLE Gorgeous • Simple
COLORS Colorful • Red

Smug

Rhonda
• January 24 •

bigfoot

Purple ruffled dress

STYLE Elegant • Gorgeous
COLORS Purple • Black

Sweet

Baabara
• March 28 •

daahling

Purple zigzag-print dress

STYLE Gorgeous • Elegant
COLORS Purple • Blue

Snooty

Eunice
• April 3 •

lambchop

Beige Aran-knit cardigan

STYLE Simple • Elegant
COLORS Beige • Orange

Sweet

Stella
• April 9 •

baa-dabing

Red flower sweater

STYLE Simple
COLORS Yellow • Beige

Sweet

Spike
• June 17 •

punk

Black gold-print tee

STYLE Cool • Gorgeous
COLORS Black • Gray

Cranky

Cashmere
• April 2 •

baaaby

Purple sleeveless tunic

STYLE Gorgeous • Elegant
COLORS Purple • Beige

Snooty

Frita
• July 16 •

oh ewe

Mustard hot-dog costume

STYLE Active • Cute
COLORS Yellow • Red

Big sister

Timbra
• October 21 •

pine nut

Red Aran-knit sweater

STYLE Elegant • Gorgeous
COLORS Green • Brown

Snooty

Vesta
• April 16 •
baaaffo
Camel hand-knit tank
STYLE Simple • Cute
COLORS Orange • Red
Sweet

Agent S
• July 2 •
sidekick
Blue No. 2 shirt
STYLE Active • Simple
COLORS Blue • Black
Peppy

Filbert
• June 3 •
bucko
Beige tree sweater
STYLE Simple • Cute
COLORS Blue • White
Lazy

Nibbles
• July 19 •
niblet
Red watermelon dress
STYLE Cute • Active
COLORS Red • Yellow
Peppy

Wendy
• August 15 •
lambkins
Red watermelon dress
STYLE Cool • Gorgeous
COLORS Red • Green
Peppy

Blaire
• July 3 •
nutlet
Berry red layered tank dress
STYLE Gorgeous • Elegant
COLORS Orange • Brown
Snooty

Hazel
• August 30 •
uni-wow
Red track jacket
STYLE Active • Cute
COLORS Red • Yellow
Big sister

Peanut
• June 8 •
slacker
Orange striped maxi dress
STYLE Cute
COLORS Red • Colorful
Peppy

Willow
• November 26 •
bo peep
Pink pom-pom sweater
STYLE Cute • Gorgeous
COLORS White • Pink
Snooty

Cally
• September 4 •
WHEE
Red fairy-tale dress
STYLE Cute • Elegant
COLORS Red • Green
Sweet

Marshal
• September 29 •
sulky
Navy blue puffy vest
STYLE Elegant • Cool
COLORS Aqua • Blue
Smug

Pecan
• September 10 •
chipmunk
Red milkmaid dress
STYLE Elegant • Gorgeous
COLORS Purple • Beige
Snooty

Caroline
• July 15 •
hulaaaa
Red striped maxi dress
STYLE Cute • Gorgeous
COLORS Colorful • White
Sweet

Mint
• May 2 •
ahhhhhh
Pop gumdrop dress
STYLE Gorgeous • Cute
COLORS Pink • Purple
Snooty

Poppy
• August 5 •
nutty
Green alpinist dress
STYLE Cute • Elegant
COLORS Green • Yellow
Sweet

Squirrels

Ricky
· September 14 ·

nutcase

Red three-ball tee

STYLE Cool · Simple
COLORS Blue · Red

Cranky

Sylvana
· October 22 ·

hubbub

Green kiwi dress

STYLE Cute · Simple
COLORS Green · Purple

Sweet

Bianca
· December 13 ·

glimmer

Pink front-tie button-down shirt

STYLE Cute
COLORS Pink · Orange

Peppy

Rowan
· August 26 ·

mango

Light blue simple-dots tee

STYLE Active · Simple
COLORS Aqua · Gray

Jock

Sally
· June 19 ·

nutmeg

Gray snowy sweater

STYLE Simple · Elegant
COLORS White · Beige

Sweet

Tasha
· November 30 ·

nice nice

Beige collarless coat

STYLE Elegant · Gorgeous
COLORS Beige · Gray

Snooty

Claudia
· November 22 ·

ooh la la

Blue lacy dress

STYLE Gorgeous · Elegant
COLORS Purple · White

Snooty

Tybalt
· August 19 ·

grrrRAH

Gray simple parka

STYLE Active · Simple
COLORS Blue · Purple

Jock

Sheldon
· February 26 ·

cardio

Green tiger jacket

STYLE Active · Cool
COLORS Green · Yellow

Jock

Leonardo
· May 15 ·

flexin'

Red hawk jacket

STYLE Active · Gorgeous
COLORS Red · Blue

Jock

Tigers

Wolves

Static
· July 9 ·

krzzt

Black dragon jacket

STYLE Cool · Active
COLORS Black · Yellow

Cranky

Bangle
· August 27 ·

growf

Mint tropical muumuu

STYLE Gorgeous · Cute
COLORS Yellow · Green

Peppy

Rolf
· August 22 ·

grrrolf

Blue down jacket

STYLE Cool · Active
COLORS Blue · Black

Cranky

Audie
· August 31 ·

foxtrot

Mint tropical muumuu

STYLE Cute · Active
COLORS Green · White

Peppy

Chief
• December 19 •

harrumph

Pink sweater on shirt

STYLE Cool • Simple
COLORS White • Gray

Cranky

Freya
• December 14 •

uff da

Green reindeer sweater

STYLE Elegant • Cool
COLORS Green • Blue

Snooty

Skye
• March 24 •

airmail

White peasant blouse

STYLE Cute
COLORS Blue • White

Sweet

Whitney
• September 17 •

snappy

Blue sleeveless shirtdress

STYLE Elegant • Cool
COLORS Blue • Aqua

Snooty

Dobie
• February 17 •

ohmmm

Navy blue fuzzy vest

STYLE Simple • Cool
COLORS Brown • Beige

Cranky

Kyle
• December 6 •

alpha

Black gilet and shirt

STYLE Gorgeous • Cool
COLORS Black • White

Smug

Vivian
• January 26 •

piffle

Blue peacoat-and-skirt combo

STYLE Gorgeous • Elegant
COLORS Gray • Purple

Snooty

Wolfgang
• November 25 •

snarrrl

Brown flight jacket

STYLE Cool • Active
COLORS Black • Green

Cranky

Fang
• December 18 •

cha-chomp

Blue snowy sweater

STYLE Simple • Cool
COLORS White • Aqua

Cranky

Lobo
• November 5 •

ah-rooooo

Avocado bomber-style jacket

STYLE Cool • Active
COLORS Black • Beige

Cranky

2

Chapter 3

The Nook Inc. Guide to Island Life!

The Deserted Island Getaway Package didn't come with a manual when you signed up, but this chapter aims to rectify that. We'll provide a series of valuable guides to help you make the most of island life. If you want to know what to focus on at a certain point, the Main Storyline walkthrough is the only resource you'll need!

CHAPTER HIGHLIGHTS

Nook Inc. Mini Guides

Welcome, resident! Very soon, we'll be walking you through island life step by step. First things first, however: there are some important things we'd like to introduce you to, to give you a handy jumpstart into island life. Animal Crossing should ultimately be a relaxing experience, but there are some things to know that'll really help you make the most out of your deserted island getaway.

Guide 1

Tools and How to Use Them

Whilst living on the island, you'll find there are few things more important to have than a collection of high-quality tools. These indispensable items can most often be found either for sale in Timmy and Tommy's store, or by crafting them at any DIY Workbench. Once you've got a tool, it can be equipped while outdoors via either the Pockets menu or the Tool Ring. Tools will allow you to interact with the world in a wide variety of ways; from catching fish to cutting down trees or jumping across rivers. Let's dig into everything tool-related.

Durability

After enough uses, most tools will eventually break, and permanently vanish from your inventory. How long this takes to happen is dependent on the durability of the tool you're using. For example, a regular shovel will always last longer than a flimsy shovel, because it has more durability. You'll often find yourself needing to replace old tools with new ones, so be sure you always have enough resources available to craft whatever you need.

If you keep hitting rocks, your shovel will eventually break. Upgrading to a tougher shovel is well worth the effort.

Tool Ring

The Tool Ring is a radial menu that allows for quick swapping between whatever tools you assign to it. You can unlock it by purchasing the "Tool Ring: It's Essential!" recipe from the Nook Stop for 800 Nook Miles once you've upgraded your tent to a house. After unlocking the Tool Ring, you'll be able to bring it up at any time (as long as you're outside) by pressing Up on the Directional Pad. To select which tool you'd like to register, highlight the slot you want and press the Ⓧ Button, and then choose the desired tool. This is especially practical for switching between the tools you'll find yourself using on a daily basis. Along with upgrading your pockets, this should be one of your first purchases once you get your hands on some Nook Miles.

This essential upgrade lets you quickly swap between a maximum of eight tools!

Energy

Need to move an entire, fully grown tree, or destroy a rock? No problem. Eating one piece of fruit will raise your Energy meter by one—this can be seen in the top left corner of your screen. The maximum amount of Energy you can store is 10. Energy only goes down when you perform an action that uses your Energy stocks, when you sit on a toilet, or when the daily cycle begins anew at 5AM. The only actions that costs Energy are hitting rocks and digging up trees, and both cost one point of Energy. It's best to only eat enough fruit to perform the actions you need to perform, however—if you need to move three trees, you should only eat three pieces of fruit for the time being.

Turnips, mushrooms and birthday cupcakes can also be eaten and can be used to quickly fill up your Energy meter if you don't mind wasting a bit of money!

WARNING!

You can destroy rocks with Energy; be careful not to destroy any by accident, because you'll have to wait until the next day for one to reappear once it's gone.

Acquiring New Tools

Your tool-using journey will begin with the humble fishing rod. Tom Nook will give you this essential tool once the island has been established and you've completed his DIY Workshop. You'll then have access to the workbench to craft more tools, including your first net. Use these new tools to catch fish and bugs, then bring your haul to Tom Nook to be rewarded with further recipes, including the flimsy axe. Soon you'll have given Tom Nook enough fish and insect specimens to warrant him calling in his friend Blathers, whose first act upon arriving will be to give you a recipe for a shovel. The chart on the following page shows how to get all of the DIY recipes for tools.

You can buy a slingshot from Timmy and Tommy as soon as the Resident Services tent opens, making it technically your first tool.

Tree branches are required to craft tools, so be sure to stock up on this useful resource when out and about!

Always having an axe on hand is essential to island life since it lets you collect materials needed to craft other tools. Keep a spare in your pockets in case it breaks!

Purchasing new tools from Timmy and Tommy is a quick and simple solution when you're out of materials needed to craft replacements. Just keep an eye on your Bell count, since this added convenience doesn't come cheap!

● Craftable Tools

Tool	Cost	Material 1	Material 2	Material 3
Flimsy axe	200	tree branch (x5)	stone (x1)	
Stone axe	560	flimsy axe (x1)	wood (x3)	
Axe	625	flimsy axe (x1)	wood (x3)	iron nugget (x1)
Golden axe	10,655	gold nugget (x1)	axe (x1)	
Flimsy fishing rod	100	tree branch (x5)		
Fishing rod	600	flimsy fishing rod (x1)	iron nugget (x1)	
Golden rod	10,400	gold nugget (x1)	fishing rod (x1)	
Ladder	1440	wood (x4)	hardwood (x4)	softwood (x4)
Flimsy net	100	tree branch (x5)		
Net	600	flimsy net (x1)	iron nugget (x1)	
Golden net	10,400	gold nugget (x1)	net (x1)	
Flimsy shovel	200	hardwood (x5)		
Shovel	600	flimsy shovel (x1)	iron nugget (x1)	
Golden shovel	10,675	gold nugget (x1)	shovel (x1)	
Slingshot	225	hardwood (x5)		
Golden slingshot	10,300	gold nugget (x1)	slingshot (x1)	
Vaulting pole	600	softwood (x5)		
Flimsy watering can	200	softwood (x5)		
Watering can	600	flimsy watering can (x1)	iron nugget (x1)	
Golden watering can	10,675	gold nugget (x1)	watering can (x1)	

Tools

Here we'll examine all the tools at your disposal and give some tips for best practice when handling them. These things can do some damage if handled without care, so it's always best to take precautions!

Shovels

Shovels are tools with several important uses, the most apparent of which is digging up buried items. This can be done by equipping the shovel, facing the patch of earth you want to dig up, and pressing Ⓐ. Digging can unearth fossils and other hidden items buried across the island. If you have Energy from eating fruit, you can also use shovels to uproot and relocate adult trees or break rocks to clear them from an area. Shovels can also be used to bury items, plant Bell trees in glowing spots, dig up water spouts on the beach and for planting fruit.

This is what expertly engineered rock hitting looks like! Digging holes like this prevents you from being pushed, making it far easier to extract the maximum amount of precious materials.

Perhaps most importantly though, the shovel can be used to hit large rocks in order to acquire mineral resources. Once you hit a rock, an invisible timer will start, giving you a limited amount of time to get in as many hits in as you can. This timer lasts 10 seconds, during which your shovel (or axe) won't take any durability damage. It's possible to hit a rock a maximum of eight times if you're quick enough at tapping the button. Doing this will require either precision or preparation, as each hit will knock you back slightly and make the next hit more difficult to land. Fortunately, this can be easily prevented by digging three holes behind yourself before you begin hitting the rock. Also note that nothing will come out if it has nowhere to land—make sure that you clear the eight spaces around the rock of holes or obstructions to maximize how many materials you extract from each rock!

If you want that golden shovel, you'll have to be extra vigilant to avoid missing any of Gulliver's appearances.

Type		Durability	Acquisition
🥄	Flimsy shovel	40	DIY recipe gifted by Blathers upon meeting him
🥄	Shovel	100	Acquired in the "Pretty Good Tools Recipes" pack at the Nook Stop (3000 Nook Miles)
🥄	Outdoorsy shovel	100	Can appear in Nook's Cranny as a large item. (2500 Bells)
🥄	Colorful shovel	100	Can appear in Nook's Cranny as a large item. (2500 Bells)
🥄	Printed-design shovel	100	Can appear in Nook's Cranny as a large item. (2500 Bells)
🥄	Gold shovel	200	Help Gulliver 30 times and he'll mail you a recipe

 **Axes**

Axes are among the most important tools you'll need on your island. This set of tools is primarily used on trees, both to gather resources from them and to permanently cut them down. Simply equip the axe near a tree and press Ⓐ. Whether or not an axe will cut down a tree or merely yield resources is determined by the quality of the axe. For instance, regular axes will always cut down trees within three swings, while flimsy axes and stone axes can't cut down trees at all.

This property can be useful, however—it makes these lower quality axes perfect for resource farming, as you won't have to worry about accidentally cutting a tree down. Unfortunately, flimsy axes are less durable and break easier than the axe, so be careful to always have enough resources to craft another. Remember to check that you've equipped a flimsy or stone axe before harvesting wood, or you might find yourself inadvertently cutting down trees you didn't intend to. Lastly, all types of axes can also be used to extract minerals from large rocks and prove to be just as effective as shovels at this task!

If you're using an axe, always be aware that they'll cut the tree down after three swings.

● **Learn About Gathering Materials**

DIY Materials → P.205

Type		Durability	Acquisition
🪓	Flimsy axe	40	Recipe acquired by donating 2 creatures to Tom Nook
🪓	Stone axe	100	Recipe acquired in the "Pretty Good Tools Recipes" pack at the Nook Stop (3000 Nook Miles)
🪓	Axe	100	Recipe acquired in the "Pretty Good Tools Recipes" pack at the Nook Stop (3000 Nook Miles)
🪓	Golden axe	200	Get the recipe in the mail after breaking 100 axes (any type)

Nets

Whether they're flying, crawling, dangling, hiding, or slithering, you'll inevitably find some bugs as you adventure across the island. Once you find something you want to catch, equip the net and slowly sneak up to it. Sneaking can be done by either tilting the Right Stick slightly or by pressing and holding Ⓐ to raise your net. Once you're close enough, release Ⓐ to bring the net down on the unsuspecting prey. All creatures cost one durability point to catch. After you've captured the critter, it can be donated to Blathers, kept as a pet, or sold for Bells at Timmy and Tommy's store (or for even more Bells if you wait for Flick to appear on your island). You can also use the net to catch leaves and snowflakes during their particular seasons. Swinging and missing with a net won't impact its durability at all, so swing with impunity!

I caught a common bluebottle!
I'll put it in a rare green jar!

Most fish and bugs will also net you a nice little pun as well. If only you could also collect those!

Type		Durability	Acquisition
	Flimsy net	10	Recipe from Tom Nook after giving him 1st fish/bug
	Net	30	Acquired in the "Pretty Good Tools Recipes" pack at the Nook Stop (3000 Nook Miles)
	Outdoorsy net	30	Can appear in Nook's Cranny as a large item. (2500 Bells)
	Colorful net	30	Can appear in Nook's Cranny as a large item. (2500 Bells)
	Star net	30	Can appear in Nook's Cranny as a large item. (2500 Bells)
	Golden net	90	Recipe arrives in mail after completing the Critterpedia's bug page

Fishing Rods

The fishing rod is a tool that can be used near ponds, rivers, and along the coast to catch fish and other marine animals. If you come across a fish's shadow in a body of water, equip the fishing rod and press Ⓐ while facing the water to cast your line. Do your best to angle your shot so that your lure lands in front of the fish, otherwise they won't take the bait. If you miss, simply press Ⓐ again to pull the lure back out and try again. Once they've taken

Sometimes it'll be almost impossible to catch a fish from where you are; moving to another spot is the easy solution.

● **Learn About Fishing and Bug Catching**

Fishing Tips	→ P.175
Bug List	→ P.188
Fish List	→ P.178

notice, the fish will swim over to the lure and begin to nibble at it. Pay close attention to the lure and keep an ear out for the sound of it being pulled under. No fish will ever nibble more than four times, so if there's already been four nibbles, get ready to bring them ashore! The moment the fish bites, press Ⓐ again to reel it in. Be careful not to reel it in before the fish bites though, or your catch will be gone for good. Stay patient and you'll be sure to land the big one!

Type		Durability	Acquisition
	Flimsy fishing rod	10	Gifted by Tom Nook when speaking to him for the first time in Resident Services tent
	Fishing rod	30	Acquired in the "Pretty Good Tools Recipes" pack at the Nook Stop (3000 Nook Miles)
	Outdoorsy fishing rod	30	Can appear in Nook's Cranny as a large item. (2500 Bells)
	Colorful fishing rod	30	Can appear in Nook's Cranny as a large item. (2500 Bells)
	Fish fishing rod	30	Can appear in Nook's Cranny as a large item. (2500 Bells)
	Golden fishing rod	90	Recipe arrives in mail after completing the Critterpedia's fish page

Bait

If you're big on fishing, you'll definitely need to craft yourself some bait. Bait can be crafted via any Workbench, and then thrown into a body of water by pressing Ⓐ once you have selected it from your inventory. Bait assists in getting more fish to appear in the water, so it's a helpful tool in allowing you to catch some of the most elusive fish—flip to P.176 for more on bait.

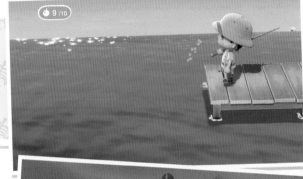

Slingshots

As you go about your day, you may sometimes encounter an unexpected sight: a balloon casually floating through the sky with an item attached to it. Where these balloons come from is a mystery, but you can claim their cargo for yourself by shooting them down with a slingshot. Line yourself up with your target and press Ⓐ to ready your shot. When you're ready, release Ⓐ to fire a pellet into the air to break the balloon. Don't worry about how many shots you take—the slingshot only takes durability damage if you actually hit a balloon, so you effectively have infinite tries to land the perfect shot. Once it pops, the item will fall to the ground; head over to where it landed and pick it up to see what's inside. What you'll find can be any number of things, from furniture to Bells or even gold nuggets, but the best prize you can hope for is one of the rare seasonal DIY Recipes. These can be hard to obtain through most other means, but will often appear in these packages. If you want to completely fill out your DIY Recipe catalog, you better keep your eyes on the sky! Just be careful not to pop balloons over the water, or you won't be able to claim your prize.

Tilting the camera like this makes hitting the balloon easier; just line yourself up carefully before shooting.

● **Learn About Balloon Contents**

DIY Materials	→ P.205
Seasonal Recipes	→ P.214

Type		Durability	Acquisition
	Slingshot	20	DIY recipe can be bought from Timmy for 300 Bells (Tent or Shop)
	Outdoorsy slingshot	20	Can appear in Nook's Cranny as a large item. (2500 Bells)
	Colorful slingshot	20	Can appear in Nook's Cranny as a large item. (2500 Bells)
	Golden slingshot	60	After shooting down a total of 300 balloons with any slingshot, a golden balloon will appear. Shoot that down to get the recipe.

Watering Can

It's never a bad idea to stop and smell the roses, or water them for that matter. Press Ⓐ while facing any planted bud, sprout or flower and watch your green thumb flex! Once you've nourished the flowers, the speed at which they'll grow for the rest of the day increases. Water your flowers consistently, and you'll find yourself in charge of a sizable field in no time. You can tell if a flower is properly watered by seeing if dew catches on the leaves and the flower sparkles afterward. If you miss your target though, don't worry—your watering can will only lose durability if it's used on an unwatered flower. Other than durability, the only difference between watering cans is their range. The flimsy watering can will only be able to water a single block in front of you. A standard watering can, however, will be able to water a 2x3 block of space (the block you're standing on, one block on either side of you, and the row of three blocks in front of you).

With the legendary golden watering can, you can enjoy watering a 3x3 block of spaces surrounding you, all at the same time.

Type		Durability	Acquisition
	Flimsy watering can	20	Recipe gifted by Tom Nook for donating 4 creatures
	Watering can	60	Acquired in the "Pretty Good Tools Recipes" pack at the Nook Stop (3000 Nook Miles)
	Outdoorsy watering can	60	Can be purchased from Nook's Cranny Cabinet after it's been upgraded for 2500 Bells
	Colorful watering can	60	Can be purchased from Nook's Cranny Cabinet after it's been upgraded for 2500 Bells
	Elephant watering can	60	Can be purchased from Nook's Cranny Cabinet after it's been upgraded for 2500 Bells
	Golden watering can	180	Recipe arrives in mail after getting a 5-Star Island Rating

Ladders

With a ladder, you'll be able to climb up any cliff. While you have the ladder equipped, you can press Ⓐ near a cliff to climb up or descend. This tool is the only way you have of reaching the top of cliffs until you gain the ability to build inclines. These cliffs are a distinct habitat from the land below, with its own plants and wildlife that can only be found at their peak. Most notably, you'll always find cedar trees and local flowers that will be essential in certain key DIY recipes. With this tool, you're really going places.

You'll need to gather flowers from atop your island's cliffs to make some of the items needed during the "three new plots" quest, so Tom Nook will send you the recipe needed to craft your very own ladder!

Tom Nook

I've already sent you a recipe for a ladder. It's the ideal tool for when you need to scale those cliffs!

Type		Durability	Acquisition
	Ladder	N/A	Recipe from Tom Nook during the "three new plots" quest

Vaulting Pole

The vaulting pole is used for crossing rivers and other narrow bodies of water. To use it, simply equip it and press Ⓐ near the water to propel yourself to the other side. It's an essential tool for exploring your island before you've gained the ability to build bridges. Although your vaulting pole can't break, be careful not to lose it once you're on the other side or you may need to use the Rescue Service app to get back home.

You don't need to perfectly line up your vaulting pole; just heading in the right general direction will get you across.

Type		Durability	Acquisition
🖊	Vaulting pole	N/A	Gifted by Blathers upon speaking to him for the first time

Wands

Wands are magical items that you can craft in a large number of styles. They function much like the Tool Ring, but for clothes—once you wave a wand by pressing Ⓐ, you'll be able to quickly swap to any outfit you've registered. To register an outfit, you'll need to visit a wardrobe of any kind and select "Edit wand outfits". Here, you can swap clothes to craft a brand new look from whatever clothing you have on you or in storage, or you can opt to register the clothes you're currently wearing as a new outfit. After you've chosen your outfit, you can also change the image representing it to make it easier to distinguish. Many normal clothing options, such as the standard wardrobe menu and the Able Sisters' fitting room, are unavailable while you're under the effects of the wand, so be sure to dispel it before you enter. You can do this by pressing Ⓐ to wave the wand and pressing Ⓧ to revert back to your original outfit.

Every time you swap to another registered outfit, the clothes you were previously wearing will be stored in the wand, allowing you to have a huge wardrobe on the fly without cluttering your inventory. If you lose a wand, don't worry about your clothes—once a set of clothing has been registered, it will be accessible with any other wand. This also means you only ever need to carry around a single wand at a time, as they'll all function the same and offer you the same set of outfits. For more on wands and to learn how to acquire all of them, head over to P.274.

Wands require star fragments to craft. Celeste will most likely give you your first wand recipe. Head to P.275 for more info on obtaining one.

Type		Durability	Acquisition
🪄	Wand	N/A	Reward: Recipe from Celeste/Fishing tourney/Bug-Off

● **Learn About Crafting Wands**

Celeste	→ P.57
DIY Recipes	→ P.212

Sub-Tools

Sub-tools act like tools, but with a much more limited use. These are generally simple and fun items that you can use to spice things up and add to your fashion repertoire.

 Umbrellas

Is the rain getting you down? No problem! You can acquire a large variety of umbrellas in this game, with many different styles to choose from. If it's raining, press the Ⓐ Button while holding an umbrella to twirl it and shake those raindrops away!

The umbrella is nice to have in the rain, but its main purpose is as a fashion item, perfect for complementing your favorite outfit.

 Pitfall Seed

Eventually, one of your jockier neighbors may gift you with the DIY recipe to craft a Pitfall Seed. These seeds can be buried in the ground and once they are, any island resident or visiting player who steps over that spot will temporarily be planted into the ground! It's a nasty bit of trickery, and it's sure to upset whoever you prank, including other residents, so please consider this before planting one! You aren't immune either, though—you can also fall into these holes! If you do, mash the Ⓐ Button to dig yourself out.

 Timer

Keep time with the handy-dandy timer! This tool shows up once you've upgraded Nook's Cranny. Simply pull it out and hit Ⓐ to begin the count, It can be a great way to have some friendly competition between players on your island. Use it to set personal records or play makeshift games with your friends!

 Fan

Sometimes, you just need to brush away the heat. Get yourself a Nook Inc. uchiwa fan and your character will have no trouble staying cool during the scorching summertime heat. Or, if you're just a big fan of... fans, use this all year around! Stay cool.

Pitfall seeds can be used to play tricks on other players, but they can be spotted if you're vigilant enough.

Musical Instruments

Got a song in your heart that you need to get out? Grab an instrument! There are three different kinds of instruments: ocarinas, pan flutes, and tambourines. After equipping one of these instruments, you'll be able to play a randomly selected note or sound by pressing Ⓐ. While composing a traditional song with these may be basically impossible, ocarinas and pan flutes will match the chord progression of the BGM from audio furniture! Try pulling one of these out the next time you're on a neighboring island—your friends will definitely appreciate the concert.

Pan Flute · Ocarina · Tambourine

 Party-popper

The need to celebrate with a bang is something that flows inside many of us. Thankfully, we have just the solution! Once Nook's Cranny opens, you'll be able to purchase party poppers, which will explode with confetti once you've pressed the Ⓐ Button! They are single use only, and you can stack 10 of them at once. Luckily, they're cheap at only 100 Bells each. Only use them on special occasions though—wouldn't want them to lose their novelty, would we?

Party-poppers are a limited use item. If you plan on using a lot of them then you'll need to stock up in advance.

A light stick isn't really any more useful if you're playing at night, but the effect is prettier.

 Light Stick

If you're wandering around in the dark, there's no better item to hold than a light stick. This colorful item can be a great way to ward away the darkness, and they can make a really nice lightshow. You can get them from special events, such as New Years, and they are unlimited in use—they don't even have a time limit. Who knows what's powering them?

Earning Bells

The main storyline walkthrough is coming soon. But first, let's talk Bells! Bells are the main form of currency in the world of Animal Crossing, and they can be used for everything from buying items at Timmy and Tommy's store to paying off Tom Nook's loans. Acquiring Bells should always be a priority, because you'll always have a use for them. Fortunately, there's a wide array of fun and interesting ways to earn plenty of them, so let's go over these methods now.

Natural Resources

Your island is full of natural resources that you can make use of in a lot of different ways, many of which will result in you earning Bells. Picking fruit, catching fish or gathering weeds are just a few examples, and there are quite a few more, so let's go over all of them here.

Fruit

The simplest way to make some quick Bells is to go and pick some fruit and then sell it. Only a single type of fruit will initially grow on your island, however, and it won't sell for much locally. If you can get your hands on more exotic fruit, then you'll be able to sell it for 500 Bells instead of 100. This can be most easily done by taking a Dodo Airlines Mystery Tour to a remote island, or by visiting the island of a friend who has different fruit. You can also get an exotic fruit from your mom in the mail, so keep an eye on your mailbox!

Weeds

You'll also notice many weeds around your island. Though these can be used for crafting (and some should definitely be kept for that), you can also sell them to turn a small profit. This is a handy way to rack up some extra Bells, as there's usually a lot more of them than there is fruit to pick.

Paleontology

While the most responsible choice is to donate any fossils you find to the local Museum, you'll inevitably come across duplicates that Blathers has no use for. Though you could display them in your own house, you can also sell them to Timmy and Tommy for sums that can be too tempting to pass up.

Helping a Friend

As the island develops into a bustling community, you'll find yourself interacting with more and more of your fellow islanders. These neighbors will occasionally ask you to help them out, often by performing some kind of errand. Doing so will always result in a grateful thank you and a reward. This reward can be a DIY Recipe, but it can also be a piece of clothing or furniture that can be sold for an easy profit.

Mystery Tour islands often have palm trees; dig some up and plant them on your island and you'll reap the rewards later! See P.165 for more on trees.

Timmy and Tommy will buy fossils you already own at a high price!

Shells

If you walk along the coast, you'll often find many seashells that have washed ashore. Some of these shells can sell for a high price, so be sure to check back often to collect what you can. Additionally, you can find marine life such as clams by digging them out of the sand; as you explore you'll come across tiny dark spots in the sand that seem to spew out water. Once you find one, equip the shovel and press Ⓐ to dig it up. Make as much bait as you need with them, and then sell the rest.

Seasonal items always fetch good prices, but make sure you have all you need before selling any.

Catching Fish and Bugs

Selling fish and bugs to Timmy and Tommy is another great way to earn Bells. The rarer the fish or bug, the more money you're likely to make. In Summer, rare bugs may start to appear on Coconut trees hosted on your beach (provided you've planted some). These bugs can be very hard to catch and will not appear often, but it's worth putting the effort in. Hold down the Ⓐ Button while holding a net to sneak towards them, and when you're close enough, let go! If your timing and precision are accurate, you may have netted yourself a bug worth a lot of Bells. Also around this time, starting in June and throughout summer, you may find sharks in the ocean. These specimens can also be sold for a large profit.

Fish are ever-present and reappear very quickly. Bugs are somewhat more difficult to farm effectively, due to their unpredictable nature, but they can sell for a substantial amount if you manage to catch the right one.

Once Resident Services is upgraded, it's best to store your fish and bugs in your house until C.J. or Flick are around to give you more Bells for them.

Money Rocks

Noticed these large rocks around the island? Each day one of them will be a Money Rock—a special rock that, once hit, will produce coins and Bell bags. This rock will be at a random location each day, and if hit correctly it can produce up to 16,100 Bells. It's important to hit the rock as quickly and as accurately as possible; just like getting minerals from rocks, once it's been hit, you don't have long before the rock will stop spewing out Bells.

They may not be amazingly lucrative, but you don't say no to free Bells.

Bell Trees

Every once in a while, you might notice a shining spot coming from underground. Use your trusty shovel to dig up a surprise 1000 Bells (or on rare occassions, 10,000 or even 30,000 Bells). But wait! Don't cover up the hole just yet. Those special magic spots can grow Bell trees. You can only harvest the Bells once per tree, but as you can see in the chart here, it can be a great way to rack up Bells. Burying 30,000 Bells is the safest bet; you can bury up to 99,000, but doing so is a big risk.

Amount Buried	Result
1000 Bells or less	100% chance of 1000 Bells x3
More than 1000, less than 10,000 Bells	30% chance of amount of Bells buried x3 70% chance of 1000 Bells x3
10,000 Bells or more	30% chance of amount of Bells buried x3 70% chance of 10,000 Bells x3

Bury money in a glowing spot, and a sapling for a Bell tree will appear. This sapling takes four days to mature—once it does, three bags of Bells will be yours for the shaking.

The amount in these bags will depend on the amount of Bells you bury. Burying 1000 Bells for instance will cultivate a total of 3000 Bells from the tree.

Usually, the maximum a Bell tree can give you is 10,000 (x3), but every once in a blue moon, you can bury more than that and get back three times that exact amount.

Converting Nook Miles to Bells

If you're in need of more Bells, you can purchase a Bell Voucher using your Nook Miles via the Nook Stop. Each voucher costs 500 Nook Miles and converts to 3000 Bells, so this is a favorable trade when you have no better use for your Nook Miles. It's crucial to save up Nook Miles during the early portion of the game, however, since large amounts are needed to purchase essential upgrades such as the Tool Ring and increased pocket size.

Letters from Mom

On certain occasions, your mom will send you a letter in the mail, such as for New Years or your birthday. These letters can potentially contain Bells or items you can sell—an extra way to get a little bit more money if you need it.

Turnips

This is the big one. If you want to make some real Bells, sell turnips. Turnips are a special vegetable that can be purchased from Daisy Mae every Sunday morning. What makes them unique is that their value goes up and down depending on the current supply conditions. This makes them a valuable commodity for a would-be market speculator to take advantage of. No other method of earning Bells comes close to the high-stakes Turnip market, so head over to Daisy Mae's section on P.70 of the Meet the Locals chapter for some insider information.

Daisy Mae

You here to start your Sunday off with some fresh turnips?

Anyone wanting to make serious Bells will need to track down Daisy Mae every Sunday.

Storage

You're almost ready for the main storyline walkthrough now, we promise! However, if you want to build an island paradise then you'll need to know how to properly manage and store your materials and items. Let's take a look at the various ways of storing all those lovely items you'll find, catch or create!

Pockets

Your Pockets are your character's primary inventory space. Here you'll find all of the items that you've collected while playing. Initially you'll only be able to carry a maximum of 20 items, but this can be increased up to 40 with the use of the Pocket Organization Guide and Ultimate Pocket Stuffing, both of which you should redeem Nook Miles for as soon as they become available. After you've opened your pockets menu, you can use the Directional Pad to move the cursor to a new item and see its name. Once you've found the item you want, press Ⓐ to view its possible uses and choose the option you'd like to use.

Pressing Left or Right on the Directional Pad will allow you to quickly scroll through whichever tools you have stored in your pockets. The order in which you'll pull out these tools is completely dependent on where they're stored in your pockets. For instance, the item kept in the leftmost slot in the top row will always come out first, while the item kept in the slot furthest to the right on the bottom row will always come last. Additionally, if you press Down on the Directional Pad to put a tool away, pressing either Right or Left will always pull out the last tool you put away first. So long as you keep your inventory neat and orderly, you'll always be able to know what tool you're going to pull out.

● **Important items**

Pocket Organization Guide	Available immediately after unlocking Nook Miles store (5000 Nook Miles)	Pockets storage +10
Ultimate Pocket Stuffing	Available immediately after upgrading to the Resident Services Building (8000 Nook Miles)	Pockets storage +10

In your pockets menu, select an item and you can set it as a favorite. This makes it appear in your quick selection roatation on the Directional Pad.

You can click the shirt icon to view all the items you're wearing and choose which ones you want to take off.

If you find yourself needing storage space early on, don't be afraid to leave things on the ground.

Home Storage

If you find yourself burdened with items that you have no immediate use for but don't want to throw away, the best option you have is to put them in storage. While not every item is able to be placed in home storage, the vast majority can be safely and permanently stored there. Once you've upgraded your tent to a proper house, you'll be able to access your storage by going inside your home and pressing Right on the Directional Pad. Here you can deposit any suitable item by selecting it in your pockets and choosing to put it in storage. You can initially store up to 80 items, but this can be upgraded to a whopping 1600 items through home renovations. If you start running out of pocket space, don't hesitate to store any items you aren't going to be using here.

● Home Storage Upgrades

Base House	80 Storage Capacity	98,000 loan
Upgrade 1	120 Storage Capacity	198,000 loan
Upgrade 2	240 Storage Capacity	348,000 loan
Upgrade 3	320 Storage Capacity	548,000 loan
Upgrade 4	400 Storage Capacity	758,000 loan
Upgrade 5	800 Storage Capacity	1,248,000 loan
Upgrade 6	1600 Storage Capacity	2,498,000 loan

● Unstorable Items

Bells

Potted Plants

Turnips

DIY Recipes

Unopened Presents

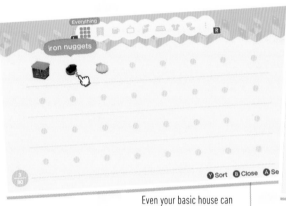

Even your basic house can store a lot of items...

...while a fully upgraded one leaves you free to hoard to your heart's desire.

Bell Wallet

Your personal Bell wallet can always be found in the bottom left corner of your pockets menu. By hovering the cursor over your Bells and pressing Ⓐ, you can pull out either 100 Bells, 1000 Bells, 10,000 Bells, or the whole sum of the wallet, and convert it into an inventory item. This bag of Bells can be buried or sent to other residents just like any other item, and can be put away back in your wallet at any time by selecting it with the cursor and pressing Ⓐ. This can be especially useful for transferring Bells between players either as a gift or as part of a trade.

The Bell wallet can hold up to 99,999 Bells at once. While this is a lot if you're just looking to do some casual shopping, it's still relatively little compared to the amount of Bells you'll be handling once your community is thriving and you're paying off the last of your debts. Any Bells you acquire beyond the maximum will become a new separate bag in your inventory that itself can con-

tain up to 99,999 Bells. This means it's possible to carry around millions of Bells at a time, but doing so will quickly clutter up your inventory. Always deposit the excess into your savings account at the Nook Stop to clear up pocket space and start gaining interest on your fortune (interest caps out at 9,999 Bells, though).

Make regular deposits at the Nook Stop's ABD to take advantage of the 0.05% interest every month.

The Main Storyline

It's finally time to start our full walkthrough of the Deserted Island Getaway Package experience. Kick back, relax and immerse yourself in the world of Animal Crossing; a place where your real world worries can be forgotten. This section aims to ensure you always know what to do next. We start with a fully-condensed rundown of how to progress through the game, which will be a useful reference if you're picking the game up again after not playing for a while. If you're just starting out and want to avoid spoilers it's best to skip this progression chart for now and flip straight to the next page.

Main Storyline Progression Chart

1

Arrive on the island, talk to Tom Nook	▶ Receive & Place Tent
Help Neighbors place tents	▶ Neighbors move in
Gather 10 tree branches and six fruit and hand them over to Tom Nook	▶ Name the island & go to sleep
Speak to Tom Nook the next day	▶ Receive NookPhone and Nook Miles app

2

Gather five branches to craft flimsy rod	▶ Receive flimsy net recipe + campfire recipe + DIY Recipes app
Craft a net and donate one creature to Tom Nook	▶ Receive Critterpedia app
Donate two creatures to Tom Nook	▶ Receive recipes for flimsy axe, bonfire, wooden stakes, tiki torch and birdhouse
Donate three creatures to Tom Nook	▶ Receive flower seeds
Donate four creatures to Tom Nook	▶ Receive flimsy watering can recipe
Donate five creatures to Tom Nook	▶ Receive and place Blathers' tent. Blathers will arrive the next day.
Talk to Blathers	▶ Receive vaulting pole and shovel recipes
Donate 15 creatures or fossils to Blathers	▶ Museum construction begins and the museum opens the next day
Talk to Tom Nook	▶ Museum opening ceremony

3

Pay off your moving fees with 5000 Nook Miles	▶ Unlock Redeem Nook Miles option at the Nook Stop
Take another loan from Tom Nook, and your house is built the next day	▶ Dodo Airlines Mystery Tours open, and Nook Miles+ is unlocked on NookPhone
Talk to Timmy and gather 30 softwood, 30 wood, 30 hardwood, and 30 iron nuggets	▶ Receive Nook's Cranny construction kit. Place it and Nook's Cranny opens the next day. Nook Shopping catalog is unlocked at Nook Stop
Talk to Tom Nook and receive bridge construction kit	▶ Build bridge
Talk to Tom Nook and receive three resident housing kits.	▶ Craft the 18 required items for the new houses
Place all crafted item in their proper places.	▶ Receive Fences, New Residents begin to move in, Tom Nook offers the DIY Customization Workshop, and Harvey arrives
Attract a fifth resident to move in	▶ Resident Services will now be upgraded

4

Talk to Tom Nook in the new Resident Services building, get campsite construction kit	▶ Place campsite, wait one day
Attract a visitor with the campsite and convince them to move in	▶ amiibo functionality is unlocked at the Nook Stop and you can now sell land when talking to Tom Nook
Talk to Tom Nook, sell some land for 10,000 Bells	▶ New resident will move in
Repeat selling land and inviting villagers until you have at least 8 animal residents	▶ More residents arrive
Raise the island rating to at least 3-Stars	▶ K.K. Slider arrives!
Watch K.K. Slider Concert	▶ See credits and unlock the Island Designer App

Pressing ⊟ while on the title screen will bring you to the Save Data Settings. Here you can speak with Tom Nook, who gives you the option to Delete Resident Registration. This can be used to permanently and completely delete your character from the island. This includes the character's house, Bells, items, and anything else associated with them. Once selected, this can not be undone, so be sure to only use this if you are absolutely certain. Additionally, you will not be able to delete the Resident Registration of whichever character has the role of Resident Representative. If you would like to delete this character, you'll also have to delete the entire island. You can do this by going to the System Settings of the Nintendo Switch, selecting Data Management, and using the Delete Save Data option to delete all save data for Animal Crossing: New Horizons. Only do this though if you are prepared to start your island adventure from the very beginning.

Title Screen

When you start the game for the very first time, you'll be greeted by the adorable Timmy and Tommy. Once you've founded your island, you'll always be brought to the title screen whenever you begin playing. Pressing Ⓐ will let you begin playing as whatever resident is linked to your current Nintendo Switch profile.

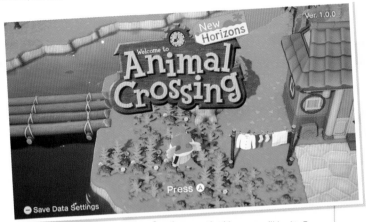

Pressing ⊟ on the title screen will lead to Tom Nook explaining how your save data works.

① Setting Up Camp

Getting Started

Timmy and Tommy will introduce you to the Deserted Island Getaway Package and ask you a few questions to start you off on your trip. Before you can go anywhere, you'll need to complete your passport. This will require giving the pair some basic information, such as your name. Afterwards, you'll be able to take a passport photo by designing your character.

After choosing your hemisphere, don't worry about any further multiple choice questions for the rest of the game; your choices won't affect your play in any way.

Designing Your Character

Choosing your character's look is one of the most important first steps in an Animal Crossing game. In Animal Crossing: New Horizons however, you can change your look completely at any given time, provided you have a Mirror to stand in front of. Still, it may take you a little bit of time to get hold of one, so consider how you want your character to look at the start of the game. Once you've designed your character, you can set your hemisphere. This will, in effect, determine what seasons appear during what time of year. Head to P.154 if you want to learn more about how this affects things.

It's best to choose an island in the hemisphere you're actually in, so the game's seasons will match your real life weather.

Next, you'll have the option to choose between four map layouts. Don't stress too much about it, though—you'll have the option to heavily customize your island later on, so you won't need to get too hung up on finding the perfect island layout.

That said, you may want to note some of the important features your island has. For example, your island is surrounded entirely by an ocean, which acts as a barrier for how far you can explore.

You also won't be able to explore all of your island right away, as progress is blocked off by rivers. As time goes by, you'll receive the appropriate tools to help navigate these obstacles. There are three main island types: A, B and C, and around 30 possible variations of each. For those who really want to get into it, we'll go through the finer points of island features here. Feel free to skip ahead if tiny consequences of almost identical choices aren't your thing.

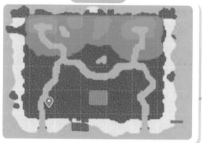
Type A

Your starting area is bordered on both sides by rivers; a centrally-focused island.

Type B

Your starting area is in the bottom left part of the island.

Type C

Your starting area is in the bottom right part of the island.

1 Beach

As you'd expect, every island has beaches. Along the beach, you can find seashells and clams, and they're good for fishing. You won't be able to change the layout of your beach later, but no beach is drastically different than any other. There are usually only small differences in where rocks and the mouths of rivers appear.

2 Rocks

Areas made up of dark grey stone can be often found along the beach, especially along your northern coast. You'll be able to place any kind of normal item on these, so long as there is room for it. However, it's worth noting that these are one of the few pieces of your island that you'll never be able to change, so make sure the rocks on your island are suitable for your needs.

3 River

The river is the first natural obstacle that you'll come across. Every island has a river that runs from one point on the coast to another, and branches at least once into a waterfall at the top of a cliff. This means you won't be able to explore your entire island before getting a vaulting pole or the ability to build a bridge.

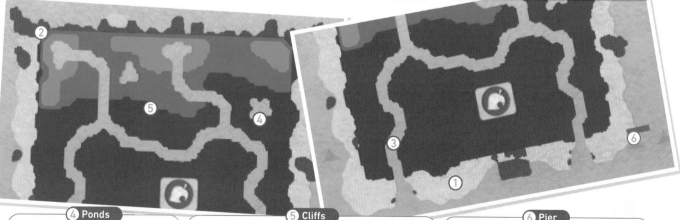

4 Ponds

All islands will have at least one pond, and these small bodies of water can be found in the middle of your island. Unique, smaller fish will often make their home in ponds, but that's not all—a handful of water-based insects can also be found here.

5 Cliffs

No matter where you decide to start, you'll always find a cliff range just beyond the river, making it the second natural barrier to your exploration. There are two levels of cliffs; one that's one level above sea level, and another above that. Fortunately, you can eventually climb them using either a Ladder or by building an incline. Just like with rivers, you can create your own cliffs (and remove existing ones) later on.

6 Pier

Each island has a small pier meant for fishing. It's always in the southeast on B Type islands, in the southwest on C Type and can be in either position on A Type islands; so you can't reach it without crossing a river. Whenever you fish here, you'll have a chance of catching huge fish that would be impossible to catch closer to shore.

Not sure what to look for in an island? There's no such thing as a bad island, but it's always worth keeping in mind what you want out of your new home. Want plenty of room to build your initial settlement? Want a river with multiple branches? Want a northern beach to watch the sunset? Have a really cool idea that will require a lot of rocky space along the coast? All the islands you'll find are more than viable, but it's up to you and your imagination to decide what's ideal for your personal getaway!

Starting Residents

When you arrive on the island, you'll be joined by two other residents who are also taking part in the Deserted Island Getaway Package. This pair is made of a male (Personality: Jock) and a female (Personality: Big Sister). It's important to get to know these two new residents, as you'll be sharing the island with them for some time. Make sure to speak to them regularly, because they may have useful information to share, and if you're lucky, items or resources to help you out.

You'll arrive with two other adventurous souls on Dodo Airlines' inaugural flight.

● Learn About Residents

Resident Personalities	→ P.74
Reactions	→ P.344

Once you get started, you'll want to make sure to speak to your fellow island residents every day, as they can continually provide you with useful tips, recipes, items, and even Reactions. Go too long without talking to a resident and they might consider moving away for good, though they won't actually do so without talking to you first. Checking in at least once a day and helping residents with anything they may need is always a good idea.

A Place to Stay

In order to stay on the island, you're going to need a place to rest your head. Tom Nook, with the help of Timmy and Tommy, will provide you with a tent at the very start of the game. Talk to Timmy or Tommy and they'll also hand you a map, which will make it much easier to navigate around your island. The map will appear as a mini-map in the bottom right corner of the screen when you stop moving.

Once you receive your tent from either of the twins, it can be placed anywhere on the island that you can currently reach. Any trees, rocks, or other items in the way will be automatically removed once you place your tent, so make sure there's nothing you want to keep around in the way. If you're unsure of where to start looking, you can check your mini-map at any time.

Did You Know?

In New Horizons, you can place your tent on the beach! This is the first time you can do this in an Animal Crossing game.

It's generally wise to place your tent near the Resident Services tent, but placing it somewhere you'll feel proud to call home is the top priority. Perhaps a nice cove for privacy, or along the coastline for easy fishing by the sea. This is completely up to you; just bear in mind there are some limitations. For example, you can't place your tent too close to the river or ocean—you wouldn't want to fall in, would you? If the tent placement is not allowed, a message will inform you and give you some tips about how to adjust your placement.

To place your tent, press the Ⓧ Button to open the menu and select the tent item to place it. You'll be given the chance to imagine what your tent will look like when it's all set up; this helps you to judge which objects it may remove. When placing your tent, some trees may be removed to make room for it. Bear in mind that you won't be able to pick items off the ground until you've placed your tent, so finding a suitable location should be your first priority.

Home Upgrades

Though you may start off small in New Horizons, Tom Nook will help you dream big by allowing you to upgrade from a tent into a cozy house. It doesn't stop there, however—Tom can assist you in making the most impressive house you've ever seen, though there are of course some fees involved in the process. You can flip ahead to P.346 if you want to see all of the house upgrade options; after you have the basic house, all further upgrades to it are entirely optional.

We'll have to do a little landscaping, but we can make this work. Should we go ahead?

Tent Location Guide

A Nice View

Why not place your tent near the water? With a nice view of the river, it will certainly make fishing a much easier task.

Convenience

Placing your tent near Resident Services could be handy if you want to be close to where the action is. Being neighbors with Tom Nook—what a treat!

Peace and Quiet

Value your own peace and quiet? Perhaps putting your tent somewhere tucked away would be nice. Enjoy nature all around you.

A Helping Hand

Of course, your fellow residents will also be in the middle of moving in and setting up their tents. After you've placed your tent and spoken with Tom Nook again, go find your new neighbors. Talk to them and they'll ask for your help with placing their tents. From here, you can either have them set up their tents right where they're standing, have them reconsider so they move somewhere else, or choose for them. If you choose for them, they'll give you their tent and you can place it just like you did with your own. Once you've helped set up both resident's tents, you'll be taken back to the Resident Services plaza.

Looks good to me!
☞ I'll find you a spot!
Maybe reconsider?

Kody
I think this spot'll do the trick, but I dunno... What do you think, Villager?

Remember that you can move buildings around later on for a cost, so the initial placement doesn't need to be perfect.

Island-warming Party

To celebrate the start of the Deserted Island Get-away Package, Tom Nook has decided it's time to host a campfire for you and the island's other residents. He'll ask you to go and collect some materials he needs. The first thing to look for is 10 tree branches; these will help you make the island's celebratory campfire.

Branches are an essential crafting material that you'll need lots of throughout your stay here. You can find them on the ground near trees, but the best way to get lots of them is to shake trees. Multiple branches can drop out if you shake the same tree repeatedly, but beware; you can also get a nasty surprise. If you're unlucky, wasps may fall out of the tree you're shaking, and unless you can find shelter indoors very quickly, or catch them with a net, you'll be stung! Don't worry, some medicine will get rid of the bruising.

Luckily, tree branches are very common; shaking any tree is likely to give you at least one.

Once you've found 10 branches, Tom Nook will ask you to find him six pieces of whichever fruit grows natively on your island. This is a fairly easy task—simply go up to any fruit-bearing tree and press Ⓐ to shake it. The fruit will then drop on the ground; press the Ⓨ Button to pick each individual piece up. It's best to gather these fruits at the same time you're collecting the branches, though it's not required. Head back to the Resident Services tent and hand them over to Tom Nook so the island celebrations can begin.

Make sure you pick a name that won't embarrass you later on!

Naming Your Island

It's now time to choose your island's name. You should think about your choice very carefully, as you won't be able to change this later. Around the campfire, you'll get to shout out your suggestion for the island's name, as will your fellow residents. Don't worry; no matter what you choose, your suggestion will be accepted and agreed upon.

Resident Representative

Tom Nook and the others will notice that you have a knack for great ideas, what with naming the entire island and all. Therefore, Tom Nook will appoint you as a Resident Representative! This means you'll be working closely alongside Resident Services to make sure the island prospers, and that all the island's residents are as happy as can be. You can also give a few words to celebrate—what will you say?

Tom Nook really knows how to start a community—he'll make sure nothing too stressful happens early on.

A Familiar Face

As you slip into sleep, someone new yet familiar will come to you in a dream: K.K. Slider. This pooch is here to introduce you to the world of Animal Crossing. He won't appear for very long, but we have a feeling you'll be seeing more of him later. Keep his advice in mind and aim to relax and enjoy the ride that island life takes you on.

Ending Your First Day

As the celebrations come to an end, it's time to wind down and head back to your tent to sleep. When you're ready to progress, talk to Tom Nook and when he asks if you'll take a rest, select "Maybe I'll go do that.", and he'll hand you your very own camping cot.

Head into your tent and open up your inventory so that you can select and place your camping cot. To move it, or any other placed furniture, hold the item by pressing Ⓐ and using the Directional Pad. You can rotate the item by tilting the Left Stick in the direction you would like the item to go.

Your NookPhone

Once you wake up, you'll find that a new day has begun and that time on the island is now synced to your Nintendo Switch's clock. This is something you'll need to get used to in the world of Animal Crossing: everything runs on a real-time clock. The moment you take a step outside of your tent, time will begin to flow just as it does in real life.

Tom Nook will be waiting outside, where he'll hand you a new device: your very own Nook-Phone! This is incredibly useful and has a variety of different apps that will assist you with island life. Tom Nook will also introduce you to the Nook Mileage Program, which rewards you with a currency called Nook Miles for completing a variety of tasks, such as fishing, pulling up weeds and

even talking to your neighbors. You can purchase a great variety of items with Nook Miles, and you can even use them to pay off your moving fees. Flip to P.20 to learn about the different NookPhone apps.

Next, Tom Nook will hand you an itemized bill. You didn't think you'd be able to live on the island free of charge, did you? Luckily, he'll let you pay it off using 5000 Nook Miles. Don't worry about it, though—you can pay off your loan in your own time and your island is full of resources to help you earn Bells, the currency used to turn your island into a thriving community. With that as your goal, the Nook Miles will easily roll in. Take it at your own pace; Tom Nook is a very understanding raccoon.

You may not need Bells to pay this fee, but they'll be very important soon enough. Head to P.122 if you want to learn about them.

Tom Nook lets you pay using the Nook Mileage Program. Head to P.146 to see why completing Nook Miles Objectives is so important.

Enjoying Your First Full Day

Your first full day on the island is a great way to get familiarized with where you'll be living. Take a look around and have a talk with some of your fellow residents. It's also a good idea to start picking up some crafting materials, such as branches and stones. These will come in handy very soon, so gather as many as you can. When you're ready to start improving the island, visit the green Resident Services tent and have a chat with Tom Nook.

Tom Nook's Announcements

As you start up the game each day, Tom Nook will announce some of the important events happening around the island. If a new resident is moving in, something new has been built or someone is visiting the island, Tom Nook is bound to let you know so you don't miss out on any of the exciting new developments that are possible each day.

Island Bulletin Board

Outside of Resident Services is the island's Bulletin Board. Important pieces of information will be shared here and players living on the island can also write on the board to share messages. If you notice a bird atop the bulletin board then there's probably something new posted. Be careful what you write; anyone visiting your island can read whatever's on the board. Think carefully before you post something!

Don't worry; Tom Nook will get over his technical difficulties. His broadcasts will soon be a source of quiet reassurance.

Unlocking Useful Tools

In order to make progress on your island, start donating fish and bugs to Tom Nook at Resident Services. First you'll need a fishing rod and a net, so go and talk to Tom Nook and take up his offer of a free DIY Workshop, which will get you a free flimsy rod recipe. Use the tree branches you've gathered to craft the rod, and Tom Nook will reward you with the recipe for the flimsy net. Use

these tools to catch a fish or a bug, and give your catch straight to Tom Nook—he'll reward you by giving you the Critterpedia app for your Nook-Phone, allowing you to keep track of every fish and bug you catch. Head to The Great Outdoors chapter, staring on P.152, to learn how to catch some of the trickier critters and start filling the Critterpedia up.

Continue catching and delivering creatures. The more you donate, the more useful items and recipes you'll unlock. Here's a handy list of what you can unlock by donating your early catches.

Tom Nook's DIY Workshop is a very generous offer, certainly frowned upon by his accountants.

● Critter Donations

Donate 1st creature	Critterpedia app
Donate 2nd creature	Flimsy axe, bonfire, tiki torch, log stakes and birdhouse recipes
Donate 3rd creature	Flower Seeds
Donate 4th creature	Flimsy watering can recipe
Donate 5th creature	Blathers calls Tom Nook
Talk to Blathers	Vaulting pole and shovel recipes
Donate 15 more creatures	Museum construction begins

Blathers Arrives

After you've shown a strong interest in the local wildlife by donating five critters, Tom Nook is able to convince his old friend Blathers that setting up his very own museum on the island would be a good idea. Once Blathers has been contacted, Tom Nook will provide you with a kit that will allow you to place down a construction plot for Blathers' museum.

Find the plot of land where you want to build the museum and place the kit from your inventory. The next day, Blathers will arrive on the island with his very own tent, where you can go and meet him. Instead of donating your bugs and fish to Tom Nook, you'll now need to donate them to Blathers.

You should think carefully about where you want your museum to be placed as it may be a while before you can move it.

Unlocking More Tools

Have a talk with Blathers and you'll be able to unlock even more useful tools. This time, the vaulting pole and the shovel are your rewards. The vaulting pole will allow you to cross over to the other side of the river at any time, and the shovel will allow you to dig up fossils and hit rocks to earn money and crafting materials. Blathers can also identify and accept donations of fossils that you may have dug up around the island to grow and eventually complete your fossil exhibit.

Upgrading Blathers' Tent

Blathers' passion for interesting new creatures is apparent from the get-go. He has a much bigger ambition, however, and that is to build a proper museum on the island. To realize his dream, you'll need to lend him a hand by donating a total of 15 more bugs, fish or fossils.

Once you've reached Blathers' donation goal, he'll go ahead and start construction work on the new museum. During this period, he won't be able to accept any donations. When you come back the next day though, the brand new museum will be complete; a much more impressive spectacle than his previous tent. The new museum will allow

room for large exhibits, perfect for hosting a large number of different specimens.

Your museum will have three different exhibits for you to explore across its many rooms. The main entrance room is where you'll always find Blathers, who, though sometimes asleep on the job, will always take donations. Downstairs is the fossil exhibit that showcases all of your brilliant paleontological wonders. To your right is the museum's aquarium, while to the left is the bug exhibit. Each section is entirely different in design and will offer a unique experience.

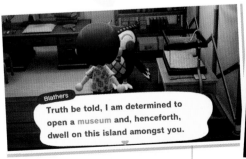

Even if you dig up all the fossils on your island, new ones will appear each day.

The museum's presence on your island will be a key factor in raising the island's rating later on.

Home Improvement

To upgrade your tent into a house, you'll first need to cough up those 5000 Nook Miles to pay off your moving fees at the Nook Stop. This might seem like a daunting task, but never fear; there are a wide variety of ways to earn Nook Miles. For example, just enrolling into the Nook Mileage Program nets you 500 Nook Miles. Even simple tasks such as fishing and catching bugs will earn you Nook Miles, as will using the Nook Stop every day, so they'll quickly come rolling in. Flip to P.146 for all the details on the Nook Mileage Program if you want to earn them as quickly as possible.

Upgrading from a tent to a house is an essential step in your journey, but all further upgrades to your house are entirely optional. The extra storage space they afford you will be very helpful as your island grows, however, so the money you invest in your home can really pay dividends in the long term. Tom Nook will eventually allow you to customize the exterior of your home, too. This will make certain that your home is the best in town; with so many options available, your home can look truly unique and suit whichever style you like the best.

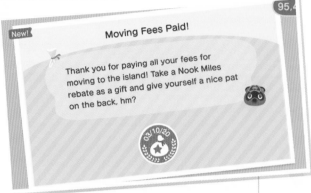

Even reading this caption gives you Nook Miles. Only kidding, but they are very generously awarded.

● **Easy Nook Miles Objectives**

Angling for Perfection!	300 Nook Miles
Island Togetherness	300 Nook Miles
Have a Nice DIY!	300 Nook Miles
Rough-hewn	300 Nook Miles
Rock-Splitting Champ	500 Nook Miles
NookPhone Life	300 Nook Miles
Active Island Resident	300 Nook Miles

Your First House Loan

Once you've paid off your moving fees, go back to Tom Nook and ask him about your house. He'll give you the option to take out another loan—this time for 98,000 Bells!—and the very next day you'll have your own house! This will also coincide with Dodo Airlines beginning to offer Mystery Tours to other islands. For more about the services Dodo Airlines offers, head to P.50. That's not all! Homeowners are automatically registered for the Nook Miles+ service, an upgrade that gives you access to a few very important redeemables: the Tool Ring (as the name says, it's essential) and the Pocket Organization Guide. Acquiring both of these should now be your priority.

To speed up development of your island, use the Nook Miles Ticket at Dodo Airlines to get some exotic fruit and gather materials.

Keep talking to the island's residents and you'll be sure to learn your first reaction around this point!

"All homeowners are automatically registered with the Happy Home Academy. The HHA, as we call it, will evaluate your home on a regular basis and send you helpful advice."

● **Learn About the HHA**

Happy Home Academy Ratings   → P.238

Earning Bells

At this point, you might begin to feel in need of serious financial aid. Fortunately, there's a number of ways to gather Bells quickly. Get Nook's Cranny built as soon as you can, because then an especially important stalk broker will start to appear on the island. Every Sunday, Daisy Mae will visit to sell her grandmother's Turnips. While these root vegetables may seem innocuous at first, make no mistake—they are easily the best way to make a massive amount of Bells in a short time. Playing the stalk market will always be inherently pricey, but can grant returns many times greater than your investment. A single good sale has the potential of earning you hundreds of thousands of Bells. Be careful though, as no investment is guaranteed a good return. Prices can, and inevitably will, go down. For more information on Daisy Mae, the stalk market, and tips on how to predict it, turn to P.70.

This is far from the only way to make Bells though—whether it be selling hot items, harvesting flowers and weeds, or gathering fruit, there's always ways to be making money. Catching bugs and fish in particular are exceptionally good ways to generate a respectable income. Also, be sure to harvest the money rock that appears on your island every day. If you prepare properly, it will grant you over 16,000 Bells for minimal effort each day. Additionally, if you find a golden spot on the ground, you can dig it up for a cool 1000 Bells and then bury however many Bells you want for a chance to grow a money tree. Like Turnips, this can be a risky gamble, but can potentially grant a massive return on investment.

With the right care, one tree can easily become many trees. Growing fruit on a large scale can really increase your income!

Once you've got your own house you're likely to get some mail from mom. She'll send you some fruit that doesn't grow on your island, which can be planted to grow profitable trees.

Building Nook's Cranny

At this point, Tom Nook will direct you to Timmy—who has decided to open a shop with his brother Tommy. They'll need some building materials to do it, though, and they're going to need your help to gather them:

| Wood x30 |
| Softwood x30 |
| Hardwood x30 |
| Iron Nuggets x30 |

Once you've gathered the right materials, you'll be able to build Nook's Cranny, an exciting new store that will allow the brothers to expand their inventory and provide you with even more items to collect. You can choose exactly where you'd like the new building to be placed, but don't worry; you'll be able to move it later on, for a fee. Building Nook's Cranny will unlock the Nook Shopping catalog, which will allow you to see all of the items you've purchased so far, and make them available to buy again at any time. Items you purchase from the catalog will be mailed to you the next day.

We'll need a lot of materials for a proper shop. And we will of course offer compensation for your efforts.

Taking a Mystery Tour is good way to speed up collecting the iron nuggets you need.

Your First Bridge

Getting around the island can be tricky at times, right? Well, fear not; Tom Nook has a solution for your problems. Have a chat with him in the Resident Services building and he'll ask you to build the island's first bridge. This little bridge will help you cross the river without the need for a vaulting pole. Residents can also use it to cross over to the other side, allowing everyone to explore more of your island.

Before you can build your bridge, you'll need some materials to build yourself a Bridge Construction Kit. Once again, if you have the Nook Miles to spare you can go on a Dodo Airlines Mystery Tour; the higher occurrence rate there will make gathering the clay a bit quicker.

| Log stakes x4 |
| Clay x4 |
| stone x4 |

Once you've got your hands on a bridge construction kit, you can make your way to a spot along the river, and place it there. Think carefully; you'll be able to remove this later on and place a new one, but having it in a convenient spot will prove useful for the time being.

Should I reserve this spot for a log bridge?

I picked a spot for a bridge! Let the land connect!

Your first bridge really expands your possibilities. If you're on a Type A island, consider placing it on the side where the pier is located.

Meet Mabel

Once the word about your island starts to get out, Mabel, one of Tom Nook's old friends, will come to visit Timmy and Tommy in their newly opened "Nook's Cranny". Afterward, she'll also bring along some of her wares; Mabel has been in the business of selling clothes for quite some time. She can appear from 5AM to 10PM outside Resident Services with a new selection of clothes to purchase every time she comes by. Mabel's arrival really opens up your wardrobe possibilities, making achieving your own individual look much easier. After you buy something from her on three separate days, Mabel will express interest in building her own shop in town.

Mabel

How about if I stop by every so often to sell some of our wares to your wonderful island dwellers?

The Able Sisters' store is another factor in raising your island's rating, so be sure to keep buying from Mabel.

● **Learn About Fashion**

| The Able Sisters | → P.46 |
| Custom Designer | → P.270 |

Island Visitors

Be sure to watch out for special island visitors. One special visitor can appear each day, and each of them offer unique items and benefits. Head to P.55 to learn who can appear when, and keep an eye on your calendar in case there's a Fishing Tourney or a Bug-Off coming up.

C.J.

Anywave, ever since I started doing my seasports challenges, I've been trending in a HUGE way.

"We'd LOVE to display your designs, of course. And if you want any of these designs... they're yours for free!"

Building the Able Sisters' Shop

Once Mabel makes her request, she'll give you a construction kit and you'll be able to build the Able Sisters' shop anywhere on your island. After construction is complete, the new clothes store will be a permanent and exciting new fixture.

The Able Sisters store will allow you to purchase more clothes and accessories than ever before. It will also house some mannequins with pre-designed looks depending on the season, giving you some great inspiration for your own outfit. As the shop is run by sisters, there's also a new character for you to meet; Sable. Sable is a little shy, but talking to her at least once a day will help her warm up to you. After 11 days, Sable will gift you her special fabric patterns for customizing furniture.

Mabel

Anyway, my sister and I would feel better opening this shop with the help of someone Tom Nook trusts.

Try not to miss Mabel appearing so that you can get access to the Able Sisters' store as soon as possible.

With the bridge built, speak to Tom Nook again, who now has a plan to improve the island and attract more residents. He'll give you three plot housing kits that you can place anywhere on your island to build houses for potential residents to move into. You can place each of them anywhere you'd like, and doing so will turn the area into a construction zone. In order to successfully build each house, you'll need to craft a designated set of six furniture items: three interior and three exterior.

Another thing that's not exactly random is which potential residents may move in. As you can see in the chart here, each plot's resident will be from a particular personality group.

To check which items are needed to build a house, inspect the numbered Construction Box attached to its scaffolding and select the "Check Interior items" or "Check Exterior items" options. Once crafted, the interior items can be submitted via the "Check Interior items" option. Exterior items must be placed in the vicinity of the plot to give potential residents a nice yard to enjoy; they can be placed in front or to either side, but make sure they're close by or they won't be counted as part of the plot. There's no need to worry, though—a handy check mark will appear next to the item's name to confirm it's been properly placed!

● Resident Personalities

Plot 1	Lazy (male)
Plot 2	Peppy (female)
Plot 3	Sweet (female)

The checkmarks in the DIY crafting menu can help you keep track of what you've crafted already: items you've crafted before but aren't currently holding in your pockets will feature a check-mark and items you're currently holding show a little bag icon.

— Wooden Simple Bed
— Wooden Chair
— Classic Pitcher

It's a good idea to use the Nintendo Switch's Capture Button to take a screen of each set of ingredients for easy access. Or just use the handy charts here.

The ladder will make it easy to get those last flowers that you need for the wreath, and a trip on a Mystery Tour can help to speed up gathering any missing materials.

To make the job of crafting all this furniture easier, Tom Nook will automatically add the necessary DIY Recipes to your DIY Recipes app when he gives you the housing kits. The required items aren't exactly random either—you can see in the charts here that each plot can have one of two possible sets of outdoor items, and only one set of indoor items. Three of the indoor items are dependent upon your island's native fruit and flowers, however: two items of furniture for Plot A require native fruit, and the flower wreath for Plot B needs your native flowers.

Regardless of the furniture you need to craft, the types of materials required can generally be gathered from trees, stones, flowers, and fruit. The flowers needed to craft the wreath for Plot B may prove elusive at first; the required flowers are native to the cliffs on your island, but you'll first need to craft a ladder to access them. You're in luck, however, since the always-one-step-ahead Tom Nook will also send you the DIY recipe for this new tool the moment you place Plot B.

● **Crafting the Items**

Wooden items	→ P.224-225
Stone items	→ P.223
Iron items	→ P.220-221
Log items	→ P.221
Fruit items	→ P.218-222
Flower Wreath	→ P.225-226

● **Outdoor Items**

	Plot 1	Plot 2	Plot 3
Set A	stone stool stone table clothesline	iron garden chair iron garden table birdhouse	log dining table log bench wooden bucket
Set B	hay bed swinging bench barrel	natural garden chair natural garden table birdbath	log garden lounge log stool water pump

● **Indoor Items**

	Plot 1	Plot 2	Plot 3
Set A	fruit furniture A* fruit furniture B** pot	wooden-block stereo wooden-block table flower wreath***	wooden simple bed wooden chair classic pitcher

● **Native Items**

	Plot 1
*Fruit furniture A	cherry speaker orange wall-mounted clock pear wardrobe peach surprise box apple chair
**Fruit furniture B	cherry lamp orange end table pear bed peach chair juicy-apple TV

	Plot 2
***Flower Wreath	cosmos wreath rose wreath tulip wreath lily wreath pansy wreath mum wreath windflower wreath hyacinth wreath

Building Fences

Have you ever wanted to make your own fences around the island to spruce things up? Once you've completed the three house plots, Tom Nook will reward you with 50 pieces of fencing to place anywhere you'd like around your island. Access these from your inventory and your character will hold a wooden hammer that allows them to put up fences. These can be good for fencing in things you would like to keep neighbors away from, or perhaps just to give yourself a nice yard. The possibilities are limitless and there are many different types of fencing you will be able to craft as time goes by. Flip over to P.349 to take a look at all of the different fences you will be able to build.

Tom Nook

Fencing should make it easier for you to create yards or parks or other outdoor areas.

Don't forget to keep up with your Nook Miles objectives! There's one for placing fencing that you can now get to work on.

A Visit From Harvey

Around this time you might find yourself getting a visit from a far out character called Harvey. Don't be alarmed though; he's as friendly as they come. Harvey will give you an invitation to his own island, which you can now visit from Dodo Airlines whenever you want. This island is a cool, relaxed place with a fully featured photography studio. To learn more about Harv's island and "Photopia", head on over to P.69.

Harvey

Wait—this ol' noodle just had a casserole of an idea! You should visit my island!

If you have any amiibo, you'll definitely want to test them out at Harv's Island...

Upgrading Resident Services

Once a total of 5 residents have moved onto the island, Tom Nook will suggest that it's time to upgrade the humble Resident Services tent into a full-sized building. This shiny new building will also mean upgrading the island plaza, by laying down some beautiful cobblestone; a perfect place to host events and perhaps even some kind of concert? Only time will tell as you take advantage of the functions of your new Resident Services building.

With the upgrade, Tom Nook will now offer some new options:

New options
Build Inclines/Bridges
Move already placed buildings
Home customization

Tom Nook

As you can imagine, I'll have my paws full today with the Resident Services construction.

Tom Nook will ensure that there's minimal interruption on the island while Resident Services is being upgraded.

All of these will grant you far more options when laying out your island, as well as allowing you to change any choices you've become less excited about. Combined with the ladder and vaulting pole, you should now be able to place buildings anywhere on the island there's space for them. Feel free to take the time to start making any major alterations you've been wanting to make to your community—as long as you have the Bells to pay for them.

Big changes are in store for the island. Now's a good time to prepare by tidying up weeds and planting trees and flowers to make the place more attractive.

● **Learn About Character Customization**

"Folks with that I'm-gonna-be-stylish-even-on-a-deserted-island mindset will want a closet or wardrobe."

DIY Customization Workshop

As soon as the new Resident Services building is ready to be built, Tom Nook will invite you to a DIY Workshop the next time you speak to him. This workshop will teach you how to customize different items you have using Customization Kits to change their color. To do this, Tom will ask you to craft a Wooden Wardrobe that he'll provide the DIY recipe for. Once you've crafted one, speak to him again and he will go through the process of customizing the dresser to be whatever color you prefer. As soon as you're done, you will gain the ability to do this with all customizable items you have using any DIY Workbench.

bunk bed

Natural

● Bedding

Need materia...

To take full advantage of furniture customization, you should befriend Sable at the Able Sisters' store; she'll give you access to lots of great pattern designs.

3

---

④ Project K

Isabelle Arrives

With the completion of your upgraded Resident Services, Isabelle will arrive to help assist Tom Nook. Though Tom Nook previously took on all responsibilities, he'll now split his work with Isabelle to lighten the load. Tom Nook will focus on home and island-related renovations, whereas Isabelle will help with administrative matters, such as resident behavior and your island's tune and flag.

Isabelle's announcements are more cheerful than Tom Nook's.

Let's take a look at the options that Isabelle can provide for you:

Options
Island Evals Learn about your island's rating.
Resident Complaint Has a resident made you uncomfortable with what they say or wear? Let Isabelle know so she can take action and inform the resident.
Change Flag Want to change your island's flag to a new design? Isabelle can help with that. Show off your artistic skills!
Island Tune If you want to change the island's jingle, this is where you can do it.

You'll be coming back to Isabelle often, especially to check your island's rating. For more on island ratings, head over to P.234.

Upon her arrival, Isabelle will also take charge of the island's announcements at the start of each day. There may not always be news for her to share, so she's likely to give you updates on her own life. What could you learn about Isabelle? Listen to her broadcasts every day to find out.

> "As long as we all work together, I'm sure we'll reach our goal of having K.K. hold a concert here!"

The materials needed to craft the campsite construction kit can easily be acquired by farming the trees and rocks around your island.

● **Learn About Residents**

| Making Friends | → P.75 |
| Resident Personalities | → P.74 |

The Campsite

Now that Resident Services has been upgraded, approach Tom Nook at the brand-new construction consultation counter and he'll inform you of his dream: to invite the famous K.K. Slider to the island! To make this a reality, you'll first need to build a campsite to attract visitors and increase the island's population. Speak to Tom again and select the "What should I do" option and he'll send you the recipe to craft a campsite construction kit. Crafting the campsite will require 15 each of the following materials: Wood, Softwood, Hardwood, Iron Nugget. Once you have the construction kit in hand, find a suitable location to place it down, then wait a day for construction to complete. This new addition to your island makes for great PR and is sure to attract some out-of-towners!

On the following day, Isabelle will announce the arrival of a visitor at the campsite. Head over there and you'll notice a tent is now pitched, indicating that someone has set up camp. Go inside and make their acquaintance!

Speak with the visitor and choose either option to invite them to become a permanent fixture of your island. This initial visitor will be excited at the prospect and won't need any prompting, but you'll need to return to Tom Nook to seal the deal. He'll be overjoyed by the news and give you a housing kit if you select the "Leave it to me!" option. All that's left now is for you to pick the perfect spot for your new friend to call home, then return to the campsite to update them on the situation. At the start of the next day, Isabelle will officially introduce the newest arrival and welcome them to the island! Do note that choosing the "I'm busy right now..." option will put this process on hold but you won't be able to make further preparations for the K.K. Slider concert until you've built a house for your new resident.

If you fail to convince subsequent campsite visitors to move to your island, you'll sometimes get one last chance that rides on the outcome of a card game.

Learn more about the campsite and recruiting new residents on P.80.

Before Tom Nook's "Project K" can come to fruition, you'll need to pique the interest of the legendary K.K. Slider by getting the word out about how amazing your island is. Inviting new residents and crafting new items to display outdoors is bound to improve your bustling community's image. As a big K.K. Slider fan, Isabelle loves the idea and will help you track the progress of your town via the "Let's talk island evals" option when you chat with her. Make sure to check up each day—you'll receive feedback on how well your island is doing and how you can improve it.

You'll need at least a 3 star island rating and a minimum of eight animal residents living on the island to make Tom Nook's dream a reality. Building homes for future residents is an essential step, so speak to him and select the "Let's talk infrastructure." option then "Sell some land." This will let you purchase up to five housing kits for 10,000 Bells each that you can then place on the island. After you've built some new houses, be sure to visit the campsite or go on mystery tours to fill them with residents! The chart shown here will help you boost your rating and avoid things that would lower it. For additional help and a detailed breakdown of island ratings, flip to P.234.

Once you've improved your island enough, K.K. Slider himself will reach out to Resident Services and express his interest in performing. From that point onwards, you're all set to host a concert from the most beloved musician in the world of Animal Crossing! Visit Resident Services the next day to enjoy the show with your fellow residents. During the concert, K.K. will perform a new song called Welcome Horizons—a fitting title. The credits will begin to roll, but don't worry; there's still plenty left to enjoy each day in Animal Crossing: New Horizons, including more concerts from K.K. Slider as well as the newly-unlocked Island Designer app that opens up a world of exciting possibilities!

● Effect on island rating

Positive	Negative
Plenty of adult trees (any type)	Lots of small items on the ground
Plenty of Flowers (any type)	Too many trees (220+)
Build the Museum	Too much clutter (can't walk around easily)
Upgrade Nook's Cranny	Too many weeds
Build the Able Sisters' shop	--
Place fences	--
Build bridges and inclines	--
Place DIY furniture (bigger are best)	--

"You've accomplished so much! I am sure you can find your own ways of having fun and living your best life."

Having items lying around, especially those that aren't placed as decoration, is bad for your island rating. Naturally occurring items like mushroom and shells won't affect it, however.

● Learn About the Island Designer

Island Designing	→ P.258

Weekly Encores

After hosting a big concert on the island, K.K. Slider will come to visit every Saturday (or on Friday of there's an event on the Saturday). He'll sit outside of Resident Services and jam. You may find some of your residents will also be sitting down, enjoying the music. K.K. won't take requests until 6pm, so sit back, relax and enjoy some of his personal favorites until then. Once 6pm hits, K.K. will take any song request you can think of. Once he's finished the song, he'll give you the Aircheck of it, which is basically an instrumental version of the song that you can play on any stereo on the island, or in your house. It helps to know all of the names of each song, so we've prepared a handy list on P.73.

The Nook Mileage Program

Welcome to the Nook Miles Rewards program! With this handy little app, you will be rewarded for completing a wide array of Objectives and Challenges. Completing these will yield Nook Miles, a special currency that will be essential to your island life. Miles will initially be used to pay off your move-in fees, after which you'll gain the ability to redeem them for any number of useful items, upgrades, or recipes from the Nook Stop. From inventory upgrades to the ability to terraform the island to exclusive furniture, the things purchasable with Nook Miles are as diverse as they are exciting. As such, you'll find yourself almost always in need of more. Luckily, a great deal of them can be acquired pretty easily—if you know where to look.

Nook Miles Objectives

Nook Miles Objectives are a series of preset tasks in the Nook Miles app that will serve as long term goals that you'll be achieving over the course of your journey. As you complete each of these, you'll be rewarded with keywords that can be used to create unique titles on your passport, as well as a sizable amount of Nook Miles. The vast majority of these Objectives have multiple tiers to unlock. For instance, the first tier of "You've got the Bug" will require you to only catch 10 bugs, while the final one will insist that you've caught a grand total of 5000! Each tier offers their own unique keywords, as well as increasing amounts of Nook Miles for your effort, making them always worth pursuing. Many of these will take a great deal of time and consistent play to fully accomplish, and are made all the more challenging by the fact that the majority of them will be hidden when you first begin. They'll gradually appear as you play, but we've listed them all here in the order found in your Nook Miles app to make things easier!

We've labeled certain objectives that we think are worth highlighting. Let's explain the two different labels we've used:

🔘 Recommended
Completing the first or second tier of objectives marked with this label is the easiest way to earn the 5000 miles needed to pay off your island moving fees.

🔘 Time Sensitive
This label is used to denote time sensitive objectives that can only be completed at specific times of the year or over lengthy periods of time. Pay attention to avoid missing your windows of opportunity!

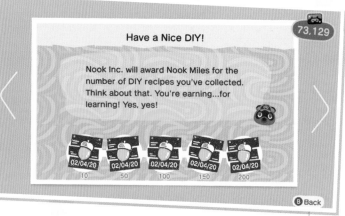

This objective lets you see how many DIY recipes you've collected in total. Some recipes can't be acquired until your total reaches certain thresholds.

Nook Stop Bonus

You'll be awarded with bonus Nook Miles just for using the Nook Stop! And this bonus goes up each consecutive day you use it. It starts at 50 Nook Miles per day, and goes up to 300 for seven or more days used in a row. Be sure to log in daily, though, or the bonus will reset to 50!

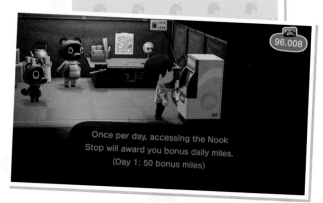

"Your Island Name"Miles!

Unlocked by moving to your island at the start of the game

	Keywords unlocked	Target	Reward
1	Nook Inc.'s • Patron	1	500

Angling for Perfection!

Catch a certain number of fish (→ P.178)

	Keywords unlocked	Target	Reward
1	Accomplished • Lad/Lass	10	300
2	Competent • Fishing Fan	100	500
3	Moderate • Beach Bum	500	1000
4	Fierce • Fisher	2000	2000
5	Battle-Tested • Catch of the Day	5000	3000

Island Ichthyologist

Fill in your Critterpedia with a number of fish entries (→ P.178)

	Keywords unlocked	Target	Reward
1	Small-Fry • Pesca Pro	10	300
2	Energetic • Angler	20	500
3	Pond-Raised • Tropical Fish	40	1000
4	Hooked • Reaction	60	2000
5	Pole-Fishing • Expert	80	3000

Island Togetherness

Chat with every resident on your island in a single day a number of times

	Keywords unlocked	Target	Reward
1	Unhindered • Wallflower	1	300
2	Unabashedly • Shy Kid	10	500
3	Respected • One	20	1000
4	Ludicrously Popular • It" Guy"	30	2000
5	Natural • Heart Stealer	50	3000

This objective requires you to speak to every single resident on your island. It does not include people like Tom Nook or Timmy & Tommy who are there in more professional capacities, but only standard residents who have homes. Doing this is naturally easier when you have fewer residents on your island, so it's best to try and keep on it as early as you can. However, so long as you check in with all your neighbors frequently, you'll get this relatively quickly.

You've Got the Bug

Catch a certain number of bugs (→ P.188)

	Keywords unlocked	Target	Reward
1	Freshly Delivered • Egg	10	300
2	Weak • Grub	100	500
3	Emerging • Pupa	500	1000
4	Soaring • Butterfly	2000	2000
5	Complete • Metamorphosis	5000	3000

Bugs Don't Bug Me

Fill in your Critterpedia with a number of bug entries (→ P.188)

	Keywords unlocked	Target	Reward
1	Hobby-Level • Bug Fan	10	300
2	Night-Owl • Insect	20	500
3	Defiant • Ant	40	1000
4	Polymorphing • Creature	60	2000
5	Scarce • Critter	80	3000

Have a Nice DIY!

Collect a number of DIY recipes (→ P.212)

	Keywords unlocked	Target	Reward
1	Trivia • Representative	10	300
2	Savvy • Intellectual	50	500
3	Understated • Authority	100	1000
4	Knowledge-Thirsty • Sidekick	150	2000
5	Clever • Father/Mother	200	3000

DIY Tools

Craft a number of DIY tools (→ P.114)

	Keywords unlocked	Target	Reward
1	Creative • Enthusiast	5	300
2	Crafty • Club Member	50	500
3	Hip • Virtuoso	200	1000
4	Bona Fide • Technician	1000	2000
5	Relentless • Meister	3000	3000

DIY Furniture

Craft a number of DIY furniture (→ P.217)

	Keywords unlocked	Target	Reward
1	Handmade • Resident	5	300
2	Emergent • Artisan	50	500
3	Picky • Crafter	200	1000
4	Humbly Begun • Master	1000	2000
5	Destructive-Creative • King/Queen	3000	3000

Furniture Freshener

Refurbish a number of pieces of furniture

	Keywords unlocked	Target	Reward
1	Unique • Eccentric	5	300
2	Change-It-Up • Challenger	20	500
3	Detail-Oriented • Engineer	50	1000
4	Mold-Breaking • Modder	100	2000
5	Remodeling • Inspiration	200	3000

After you've furnished the three homes for the second wave of residents, Tom Nook will begin to offer a workshop on how to customize items. Use this ability often and this objective will be yours. To learn more about item customization, check P.352

Rough-hewn

Hit a tree with an axe a number of times

	Keywords unlocked	Target	Reward
1	Specific • Producer	20	300
2	Aggressive • Problem Solver	100	500
3	Sharp • Guard	500	1000
4	Pointy • Tack	2000	2000
5	Productive • Superhero	5000	3000

Trashed Tools

Break a number of DIY Tools

	Keywords unlocked	Target	Reward
1	Rascally • Clown	1	300
2	Overboard • Crusher	20	500
3	Rowdy • Punk	50	1000
4	Rough-And-Tumble • Meanie	100	2000
5	Chaotic • Ruiner	200	3000

Rock-Splitting Champ

Hit a single rock eight times in a row

	Keywords unlocked	Target	Reward
1	Sports-Minded • Muscle	1	500

Dig three holes behind yourself, then repeatedly hit the rock as quickly as you can while keeping the Left Stick tilted towards it. Done properly you should get eight hits in with ease. More info on P.115

Bona Fide Bone Finder!

Dig up your first fossil (→ P.194)

	Keywords unlocked	Target	Reward
1	Discovered • Fossil	1	300

Fossil Assessment

Have a large number of fossils assessed (→ P.194)

	Keywords unlocked	Target	Reward
1	Anonymous • Something Or Other	5	300
2	Ancient • Truth	30	500
3	History-Loving • Researcher	100	1000
4	Evolving • Scatterbrain	300	2000
5	Historic • Discovery	500	3000

Greedy Weeder

Sell a large number of weeds (→ P.168)

	Keywords unlocked	Target	Reward
1	Messy • Lawn Clippings	50	300
2	Omnivorous • Custodian	200	500
3	Herbivorous • Sorter	1000	1000
4	Vigorous • Sprout	2000	2000
5	Wild • Beast	3000	3000

Flower Power

Plant a number of flowers

	Keywords unlocked	Target	Reward
1	Greenhouse • Flower	10	300
2	Thorny • Rose	50	500
3	Heavenly • Rejuvenator	100	1000
4	Sweet-Smelling • Blossom	200	2000
5	Gorgeous • Groom/Bride	300	3000

Flower Tender

Water a number of flowers

	Keywords unlocked	Target	Reward
1	Refined • Caretaker	10	300
2	Detailed • Keeper	50	500
3	Careful • Gardener	100	1000
4	Caretaking • Ringleader	500	2000
5	Flower-Loving • Boss	1000	3000

Tomorrow's Trees Today

Plant a number of tree saplings

	Keywords unlocked	Target	Reward
1	Outdoorsy • Defender	5	300
2	Organic • Dietitian	10	500
3	Hay-Feverish • Sneezer	30	1000

3

Pick of the Bunch

Sell a number of fruit

	Keywords unlocked	Target	Reward
1	Inexperienced • Observationist	20	300
2	Precocious • Bounty	100	500
3	Seasonal • Tree	500	1000
4	Mature • Kind	1000	2000
5	Rotten • Scent	3000	3000

Fruit Roots

Plant a fruit tree with non-native fruit

	Keywords unlocked	Fruit	Reward
1	Twin's • Other Half	cherry	100
2	Total • Freshman	orange	200
3	Unpearable • Pear	pear	300
4	Plucky • Star	peach	500
5	Crisp • Mr. Popular	apple	700
6	Tropically Grown • Coconut	coconut	1000

This objective will likely require you to travel to other islands, either via the Mystery Tour or by visiting a friend's island. The rewards will increase for each tree you plant, up to the maximum of 1000 Nook Miles, regardless of the order in which you plant them—always grab any foreign fruit you see.

Go Ahead. Be Shellfish!

Sell a number of seashells that wash ashore

	Keywords unlocked	Target	Reward
1	Shell-Grabbing • Shell Fan	10	300
2	Seashore • Seashell Seller	50	500
3	Shifty • Shellector	200	1000
4	Over-Shelled • Shell Master	500	2000
5	Shellfish • Shellaborator	1000	3000

Clam and Collected

Dig up a number of clams

	Keywords unlocked	Target	Reward
1	Tidal • Season	5	300
2	Ready • Coast Dweller	20	500
3	Buried • Genius	50	1000
4	Rare • Prodigy	100	2000
5	Water's Edge • Mermaid	200	3000

Trash Fishin'

Fish up a number of pieces of trash (➔ P.177)

	Keywords unlocked	Target	Reward
1	Untossable • Trash	3	300
2	Eco-Friendly • Ecologist	10	500
3	Waterway • Cleaner	20	1000

Cast Master

Consecutively reel in a large number of fish (➔ P.175)

	Keywords unlocked	Target	Reward
1	Mistakenly Caught • Fish	10	300
2	Bait-Snatching • Frenzy	50	500
3	Wave-Tossed • Life-Form	100	1000

This may prove to be the most challenging objective there is. In order to get the top tier of this objective, you'll need to catch 100 fish in a row without losing a single one. Bigger fish have a tendency to require quicker reflexes, as do sharks, so focusing on catching smaller, more common fish will be your best bet. Avoid fishing at night since the more rare, and therefore typically harder to catch fish, may show up more frequently. Stay patient, keep a level head, don't take unnecessary risks, and this objective will be yours.

Dream House

Upgrade your house a number of times (➔ P.136)

	Keywords unlocked	Target	Reward
1	One-Room • Loner	1	500
2	Single-Occupant • Beginner	2	1000
3	Homey • Sentiment	5	2000
4	Second-Floor • Landlord	6	3000
5	Basement • Backbone	7	5000

Decorated Decorator

Get an S Rank from the Happy Home Academy (➔ P.238)

	Keywords unlocked	Target	Reward
1	Happy • Overachiever	1	1000

Hoard Reward

Place number of indoor furniture items in your house.

	Keywords unlocked	Target	Reward
1	Interior • Sort	5	300
2	Tentative • Remodeler	15	1000
3	Comparative • Sundries Fan	30	2000
4	Assumed • Appliance Fan	100	3000
5	Abounding • Interior-Design Fan	150	5000

Good Things in Store!

Placed a number of items in your home storage

	Keywords unlocked	Target	Reward
1	Overstuffed • Stylist	20	300
2	Partially Obscured • Talent	50	1000
3	At-Capacity • Manager	100	2000
4	Self-Possessed • Coordinator	200	3000
5	Invulnerable • Life Hacker	300	5000

Remarkable Remodeler

Remodel your house a number of times (➔ P.346)

	Keywords unlocked	Target	Reward
1	Home • Transformer	1	500
2	Dreamy • Dreamer	3	1000
3	Quintessential • Space	5	2000

Smile Isle

Complete a number of island resident requests (➔ P.78)

	Keywords unlocked	Target	Reward
1	Kindly • Standard	1	300
2	Reliable • Ally	10	500
3	Generous • Supervisor	50	1000
4	Exalted • Savior	100	2000
5	Foolhardy • Hero/Heroine	300	3000

Reaction Ruler

Learn a number of reactions from your neighbors (➔ P.77)

	Keywords unlocked	Target	Reward
1	Overacting • Neophyte	1	300
2	Apprentice • Dancer	10	500
3	Dad-Joking • Semiprofessional	20	1000
4	Solo • Comedian	30	2000
5	Super-Popular • Mega Star	42	3000

Island Shutterbug

Take a photo with the camera app

	Keywords unlocked	Target	Reward
1	Photogenic • Photographer	1	300

Edit Credit

Edit your Passport using the Passport app in your NookPhone

	Keywords unlocked	Target	Reward
1	Future • Traveler	1	300

NookPhone Life

Use your NookPhone for the 10th time

	Keywords unlocked	Target	Reward
1	Smartphone • Savant	10	300

That's One Smart Phone

Use your NookPhone for the 1000th time

	Keywords unlocked	Target	Reward
1	Digital-Age • Child	1000	1000

Shop to It

Buy a number of things with the Nook Shopping app

	Keywords unlocked	Target	Reward
1	Internet • Surfer	1	300
2	Connected • Reviewer	20	500
3	Widely Accepted • Connector	50	1000
4	Disconnected • Worrywart	100	2000
5	Always-On • Bigwig	200	3000

Growing Collection

Catalog a large number of furniture or clothing items in the Nook Shopping app (➔ P.22)

	Keywords unlocked	Target	Reward
1	Casual • Materialist	100	300
2	Curious • Force	200	500
3	Greedy • Collector	300	1000
4	Materialistic • Avatar	400	2000
5	Legendary • Walking Dictionary	500	3000

Nook Miles for Miles!
Complete a number of Nook Miles+ Daily Challenges (→ P.151)

	Keywords unlocked	Target	Reward
1	So-Called • Ground Traveler	5	300
2	Novice • Rookie	50	500
3	Wide-Ranging • Hobbyist	200	1000
4	Perfectionist • Go-Getter	1000	2000
5	Year-Round • Dynamo	3000	3000

First-Time Buyer
Buy something from a shop for the first time.

	Keywords unlocked	Target	Reward
1	Full-Fledged • Consumer	1	300

Seller of Unwanted Stuff
Make your first sale at a shop

	Keywords unlocked	Target	Reward
1	Down-And-Out • Eventuality	1	300

Moving Fees Paid!
Repay your initial debt to Tom Nook (5000 Nook Miles)

	Keywords unlocked	Target	Reward
1	Autonomous • Life	1	500

Bell Ringer
Spend a large amount of Bells in stores

	Keywords unlocked	Target	Reward
1	Invested • Shopaholic	5000	300
2	Thrifty • Family Member	50,000	500
3	Covetous • Personality	500,000	1000
4	Wasteful • Celebrity	2,000,000	2000
5	Name-Dropping • VIP	5,000,000	3000

Miles for Stalkholders
Purchase your first Turnip from Daisy Mae

	Keywords unlocked	Target	Reward
1	Weekend • Stalkholder	1	300

Cornering the Stalk Market
Make a large amount of profit from selling turnips (→ P.70)

	Keywords unlocked	Target	Reward
1	Status-Minded • Speculator	1000	300
2	Avaricious • Moneybags	10,000	500
3	Upstart • Trader	100,000	1000
4	Worldwide • Bellionaire	1,000,000	2000
5	Shadowy • Fixer	10,000,000	3000

No More Loan Payments!
Finish paying off your house loan to Tom Nook

	Keywords unlocked	Target	Reward
1	Responsible • Bill Payer	1	1000

Bulletin-Board Benefit
Write something on your island's bulletin board for the first time

	Keywords unlocked	Target	Reward
1	Rumormongering • Influencer	1	300

Popular Pen Pal
Send a number of letters (→ P.13)

	Keywords unlocked	Target	Reward
1	Art-School • Boy/Girl	5	300
2	Science-y • Student	20	500
3	Liberal-Arts • Poet	50	1000
4	Subculture • Denizen	100	2000
5	Deadline • Writer	200	3000

Flea Flicker
Cure a number of animals of fleas

	Keywords unlocked	Target	Reward
1	Tidy • Wild Child	1	300
2	Highly Aware • Neatnik	5	500
3	Fastidious • Character	10	1000

From time to time, a flea may show up on one of your residents. If you see one bouncing around them, quickly whip out your net and hit them to catch it. They'll certainly appreciate it.

Cicada Memories
Collect a Cicada Shell in summer. (→ P.185)

	Keywords unlocked	Target	Reward
1	Shell-Less • Being	1	1000

Netting Better!
Catch five wasps in a row (→ P.187)

	Keywords unlocked	Target	Reward
1	Accurate • Deadeye	1	1000

Pit-y Party
Craft your first Pitfall

	Keywords unlocked	Target	Reward
1	Wild-Child • Troublemaker	1	300

Taking the Sting Out
Get stung by wasps twice to faint (→ P.187)

	Keywords unlocked	Target	Reward
1	Teary-Eyed • Crybaby	1	300

Faint of Heart
Get stung by a poisonous insect and faint (→ P.187)

	Keywords unlocked	Target	Reward
1	Risen • Phoenix	1	300

Overcoming Pitfalls
Fall into a pitfall trap for the first time

	Keywords unlocked	Target	Reward
1	Trapped • Reckless One	1	300

Lost Treasure
Use the slingshot tool to pop a balloon when it's flying above water. This causes the treasure to drop into the water

	Keywords unlocked	Target	Reward
1	Catchable • Klutz	1	500

It's Raining Treasure!
Shoot down a number of floating treasure balloons (→ P.214)

	Keywords unlocked	Target	Reward
1	Easy-breezy • Slingshot Ace	5	300
2	Atmospheric • Floaty Thing	20	500
3	Restless • Hunter	50	1000
4	Flying • Paradise	100	2000
5	Elusive • Vagabond	300	3000

Fun with Fences
Place at least 20 fence segments to surround your home or garden

	Keywords unlocked	Target	Reward
1	Efficient • Partitioner	20	500

Snowmaestro
Build a number of perfect Snowboys (→ P.215)

	Keywords unlocked	Target	Reward
1	Cold-Sensitive • Sprite	1	300
2	Snow • Angel	10	500
3	Cool • Imp	20	1000

Wishes Come True
Number of times you've wished upon a shooting star (→ P.164)

	Keywords unlocked	Target	Reward
1	Late-Night • Meteorite	1	300
2	Wishful • Legend	30	1000
3	Overnight • Superstar	200	2000

Exterior Decorator
Number of furniture you've placed around the island

	Keywords unlocked	Target	Reward
1	Outdoor-Loving • Decorating Fiend	10	300

"Your Island Name" Icons

Redesign both your island flag and island tune for the first time (two separate Nook Miles rewards) (→ P.30)

	Keywords unlocked	Target	Reward
1	Flapping • Flag Waver	island flag	500
2	Humming • Musician	island tune	500

Island Designer

Use the Island Designer app and get a permit for a path, river, or cliff (three separate Nook Miles rewards for each) (→ P.258)

	Keywords unlocked	Target	Reward
1	Trailblazing • Runner	Path	500
2	Swept-Away • Pioneer	River	1000
3	Cliffhanging • Creator	Cliff	1000

Wispy Island Secrets

Found Wisp a number of times
(→ P.60)

	Keywords unlocked	Target	Reward
1	Cowardly • Ghost	1	300
2	Supernatural • Soul	10	500
3	Soulful • Soul Mate	20	1000

Gulliver's Travails

Helped Gulliver a number of times
(→ P.56)

	Keywords unlocked	Target	Reward
1	Flightless • Fowl	1	300
2	Perennial • Lost One	10	500
3	Off-Season • Migratory Bird	20	1000

K.K. Mania

Attend a number of K.K. shows

	Keywords unlocked	Target	Reward
1	Fickle • Music-Lover	1	300
2	Covert • Supporter	10	500
3	Regular • Fan	30	1000
4	The Definition of • Pop Star	60	2000
5	Longtime • Follower	100	3000

True Friends

Maxed out friendship with a number
of Residents (→ P.75)

	Keywords unlocked	Target	Reward
1	Soothing • Pal	1	300
2	Friendly • Buddy	2	500
3	Friendship • Seeker	3	1000

Birthday Celebration

Celebrate a number of Residents'
birthdays with them (→ P.76)

	Keywords unlocked	Target	Reward
1	Untamed • Party Animal	1	300
2	Growing • Youth	10	500
3	Grown • Adult	20	1000

Happy Birthday!

Play the game on your birthday

	Keywords unlocked	Target	Reward
1	Celebratory • Birthday Boy/Birthday Girl	1	2000

Fishing Tourney!

Participate in the Fishing Tourney
during each season (four separate
Nook Miles rewards)

	Keywords unlocked	Target	Reward
1	Spring-Born • Free Spirit	Spring	300
2	Summer-Born • Chiller	Summer	500
3	Fall-Born • Free-Wheeler	Fall	1000
4	Winter-Born • Overheater	Winter	2000

The rewards for this Objective will increase
with each separate Fishing Tourney you
attend, up to the maximum of 2000 Nook
Miles, regardless of the order in which you
participate in them. More info on P.200.

Bug-Off!

Participate in the Bug-Off in each
of the four months that it occurs.
(→ P.201)

	Keywords unlocked	Target	Reward
1	Adolescent • Youngster	June	300
2	Rebellious • Rebel	July	500
3	Solitary • Lone Wolf	August	1000
4	Standoffish • Individual	September	2000

The rewards for this Objective will increase
with each separate Bug-Off you attend, up to
the maximum of 2000 Nook Miles, regardless of the order in which you attend them.

Countdown Celebration

Participate in the New Year Celebration for the first time

	Keywords unlocked	Target	Reward
1	Countdown • Merrymaker	1	1000

Making a Change

Get a wardrobe and use it to change
outfits for the first time

	Keywords unlocked	Target	Reward
1	Trendy • Model	1	500

First Custom Design!

Use Custom Design app to personalize your clothes for the first time
(→ P.270)

	Keywords unlocked	Target	Reward
1	Aspiring • Artist	1	500

Custom Design Pro!

Use the Pro version of the Custom
Design app for the first time

	Keywords unlocked	Target	Reward
1	Pro • Designer	1	300

Paydirt!

Use the shovel to dig out buried treasure for the first time (→ P.78)

	Keywords unlocked	Target	Reward
1	Lucky • Type	1	300

Shady Shakedown

Shake down a number of furniture
items from a tree

	Keywords unlocked	Target	Reward
1	Carefree • Figure	1	300
2	Jovial • Brute	10	1000
3	Spirited • Gifted One	20	2000
4	Factual • Outlaw	50	3000
5	Inspirational • Statement	100	5000

Furniture falling from trees has a fairly low
occurrence rate, so the higher tiers of this
objective may take some time to complete.

Golden Milestone

Acquire your first Golden tools of
each type (Net, Fishing Rod, Watering
Can, Slingshot, Axe, Shovel)

	Keywords unlocked	Target	Reward
1	Shining • Jewel	net	300
2	Top-Notch • Luminary	fishing rod	500
3	Ultimate • Miracle	watering can	1000
4	Royal • Prince/Princess	slingshot	2000
5	Glittering • Emperor/Empress	axe	3000
6	Radiant • Supreme Being	shovel	5000

The rewards for this Objective will increase
with each golden tool you acquire, up to the
maximum of 5000 Nook Miles, regardless
of the order in which you acquire the tools.
Head to P.112 to find out how to acquire
each of them. Don't miss an appearance by
Gulliver if you want the shovel; P.56 will help
ensure you always aid him. The watering
can requires you to get a 5 star island rating;
flip to P.234 for some tips on achieving that.

Island and Yourland

Visit a number of other player's
islands

	Keywords unlocked	Target	Reward
1	Traveling • Person	1	300
2	Occasional • Tourist	5	500
3	Global • Wanderer	10	1000

Host the Most

Invite a number of guests to your
island

	Keywords unlocked	Target	Reward
1	Hospitable • Friend	1	300
2	Lonely • Chum	5	500
3	Well-Known • Partier	10	1000

Active Island Resident

Spend a number of days on the
island

	Keywords unlocked	Target	Reward
1	Self-Paced • Chill Soul	3	300
2	Active • Specialist	20	500
3	Sleepless • Adventurer	50	1000
4	Nicknamed • Gamer	100	2000
5	Ready-Made • MVP	300	3000

Nook Miles+ Daily Challenges

Nook Miles+ Daily Challenges are a rotation of daily tasks introduced as part of the upgraded Nook Miles+ service that gets unlocked when you become a homeowner. Unlike the Nook Miles Objectives, completing daily challenges won't give you any keywords, but they'll always reward you with a fair amount of Nook Miles. By their very nature, these challenges are short term goals and easier to work through, but that doesn't mean they're inherently easy—while some are as simple as using your NookPhone to take a quick selfie, others will ask for more focused tasks that require a bit of time and patience, such as hunting down a specific fish or bug. Some may even ask you to do things related to the specific season you find yourself in, such as building Snowfolk or picking Mushrooms.

Regardless of how demanding they are however, it's almost always worthwhile to complete at least the first set of five Challenges you're given each day, as that initial set will always come with at least a x2 multiplier that will double the amount of Nook Miles each one is worth. The day after the Resident Services building has been completed, you'll have a huge 5x challenge multiplier on your first five challenges! On the following day, there will be a 25% chance that you'll get the 5x challenge multiplier again. This becomes a 33% chance on the next day and keeps increasing until you get the 5x challenge multiplier again. The chance then resets back down to 25% and the cycle starts over. Make sure to check your Nook Miles app every single day!

 Talk to Your Neighbors — 3x 200

 Complete Quests for Your Neighbors — 1x 250

 Catch Bugs — 5x 150

 Catch [Specific Bug] — 1x 200

 Catch Snowflakes — 3x 200

 Catch Fish — 5x 150

 Catch [Specific Fish] — 1x 200

 Sell Shells — 10x 200

 Get Fossils Assessed — 3x 150

 Sell Clumps of Weeds — 20x 100

 Tend Flowers — 8x 100

 Plant Flower Seeds — 3x 100

 Chop Wood — 10x 150

 Plant Trees — 1x 100

 Chop Down Trees — 1x 200

 Sell Fruit — 5x 150

 Grow Fruit Trees — 1x 100

 Plant Bamboo Shoots — 1x 150

 Hit Rocks — 5x 100

 Pop Balloons — 1x 200

 Pick Mushrooms — 3x 100

 Build Snowfolk — 1x 250

 Complete DIY Projects — 3x 150

 Earn Bells by Selling Items — 5000x 150

 Spend Bells to Buy Items — 5000x 200

 Redeem Nook Miles — 500x 200

 Customize Items — 2x 150

 Access Your Wardrobe and Change Your Look — 1x 150

 Sell a Hot Item for a Fortune! — 1x 200

 Capture a Memory! — 1x 100

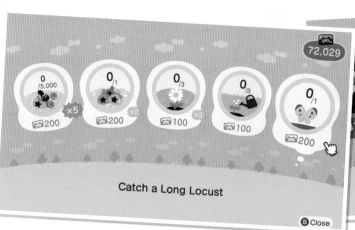

Catch a Long Locust

Every time you complete a challenge, it will be replaced by a randomly chosen new one. Only the first five will have the multiplier bonus, however.

Chop Wood

Always claim your Nook Miles+ Daily Challenge Rewards as soon as you get them so you can make space for new Challenges.

4

The Great Outdoors

Anyone signing up for a Deserted Island Getaway Package is likely to have an appreciation for nature. This chapter gets you out in the wild, cultivating plants, fishing the rivers and ponds, digging and searching for interesting bugs. Let's take in the air and get to know your island's ecosystem!

CHAPTER HIGHLIGHTS

Seasons

As the days turn into weeks, the seasons will also begin to change. Depending on the time of year, you may be greeted by a warm summer's breeze or a fresh layer of snow when you step outside. Much like the time of day, seasons also play a major role in what fish and bugs are available to catch. Many creatures are only encountered during specific seasons and months, so be sure to check your Calendar or any number of seasonal critters might pass you by.

Dates & Hemispheres

When you embark on the Deserted Island Getaway Package, you'll get to choose the preferred hemisphere for your island. The dates on which seasonal events take place will differ depending on which hemisphere you chose. The dates used in this book are all for the northern hemisphere, but working out their southern hemisphere equivalents is really simple: you just add exactly 6 months to the date. The chart here shows you the dates on which each season starts and ends in the game, and how the hemisphere calculation affects them.

Season	Northern Hemisphere	Southern Hemisphere
Spring	February 25th - May 31st	August 25th -November 30th
Summer	June 1st - August 31st	December 1st - February 29th
Autumn	September 1st - November 25th	March 1st - May 25th
Winter	November 26th - February 24th	May 26th - August 24th

Spring

February 25th - May 31st

August 25th - November 30th

As the winter snow melts and the sun begins to shine again, all kinds of critters and plants will begin to appear across the island. Not only is spring one of the most active seasons for bugs and fish, it also impacts the local plant life! As soon as spring begins, you'll be able to harvest Young Bamboo Shoots from any Bamboo stalks you've planted. This rare material can be harvested using an axe like any other bamboo or wood and is used to craft beautiful Bamboo furniture. Likewise, you may see that the leaves on many of the local trees

You only have a little over a week each year to collect these Cherry Blossom Petals, so be sure to grab as many as you can!

begin turning a light pink as the cherry blossoms begin to bloom. At the beginning of the second month of spring, these beautiful petals will begin to fall from their branches and float through the air. Should you happen to walk by one, pull out your net and grab it so you can use it in a DIY project.

● **Spring DIY Recipes**

Cherry Blossom	→ P.214
Young Spring Bamboo	→ P.214

Cherry Blossom Petals

🌸 April 1st - 10th   🍂 October 1st - 10th

Background Petals (Light)

🌸 April 7th - 9th   🍂 October 7th - 9th

Background Petals (Heavy)

🌸 April 10th   🍂 October 10th

Young Spring Bamboo

🌸 February 25th - May 31st

🍂 August 25th - November 30th

Young spring bamboo can be used to make a variety of interesting decorative items.

Summer

🌸 June 1st - August 31st

🍂 December 1st - February 29th

With the warmer days comes stronger tides along the island's coast. Once summer begins, the waves will begin to occasionally wash rare summer shells ashore. Make sure to check the beach every day to ensure that you don't miss any of these elusive seashells! There will also be a greater abundance of bugs and insects (as well as cicada shells), so summer is a great time to make progress filling out your Critterpedia. Summer is also Bug-Off season, with tourneys on the third Saturday of each summer month.

Summer is heaven for bug lovers!

Summer Shells

🌸 June 1st - August 31st

🍂 December 1st - February 29th

● **Summer DIY Recipes**

Summer Shells → P.214

Autumn

🌸 September 1st - November 25th

🍂 March 1st - May 25th

After the leaves begin to lose their color and Autumn sets in, pine cones will start to appear in cedar trees, while acorns will start to fall from hardwood trees. To collect acorns and pine cones, you'll need to shake them loose by pressing Ⓐ near trees—using an axe won't do the trick. The chances of shaking down one of these seasonal items is quite low, though, so don't get discouraged if you don't find one right away.

Mushrooms can also grow near tree stumps during the final month of Autumn!

Remember to give the trees around your island a vigorous shake once per day and your pockets will soon be filled with acorns and pine cones! Do note that burying these items won't cause any trees to start growing; they are exclusively used for cozy, Autumn-themed DIY projects.

As Autumn finally comes to a close, the old leaves will begin to fall from their branches. These Maple Leaves will drift through the air. If one happens to pass by, quickly pull out your net and snag it, because they're essential to making some of the most rustic pieces of furniture you'll find. Lastly, a variety of mushrooms will begin to appear in the season's final month. There are five kinds of mushrooms to be found in total: round, skinny, flat, elegant, and rare. These fungi can typically be found growing in the shade of mature trees, though the rare variety needs to be dug up. While eating them might be tempting, they're actually best saved for mushroom-related DIY recipes.

Maple Leaves

○ November 16th - 25th ○ April 16th - 25th

Background Leaves (Light)
○ November 7th - 9th ○ April 7th - 9th

Background Leaves (Heavy)
○ November 10th ○ April 10th

Mushrooms

○ November 1st - 30th

○ May 1st - 31st

Acorns

○ September 1st - December 10th

○ March 1st - June 10th

Pine cones

○ September 1st - December 10th

○ March 1st - June 10th

● **Autumn DIY Recipes**

Mushrooms	→ P.215
Acorns/Pine cones	→ P.215
Maple Leaves	→ P.215

● **Mushroom Appearance Rates**

			Island Rating		
		Sale Price	3 Stars or less	4 Stars	5 Stars
🍄 Skinny Mushroom		○ 300	35%	30%	25%
🍄 Flat Mushroom		○ 300	30%	30%	25%
🍄 Round Mushroom		○ 200	30%	25%	25%
🍄 Elegant Mushroom		○ 10,000	4%	10%	15%
🍄 Rare Mushroom		○ 16,000	1%	5%	10%

Keep an eye out for mushrooms in autumn—you can use them to create some fancy DIY items!

The year's last Bug-Off! will take place on the third Saturday of September.

Winter

As soon as the first snow of Winter falls, you'll begin to notice that it has a few effects on the island. First, you'll occasionally find Snowflakes floating by, which can be collected using a net. These are used to craft a variety of icy DIY Recipes that give off a chilly vibe. Starting on Dec. 11th, snow begins covering the ground; from then until the end of winter, two snowballs will appear each day at random locations on your island. When they're small, you'll be able to kick them around to roll more snow into them and increase their size. Once they grow big enough, you'll begin to roll them with your hands. If you happen to find two next to each other, you can roll the smaller ball on top of the bigger one to create a Snowboy!

During the festive period (from December 15th to January 6th), if Resident Services has been upgraded, some Cedar trees will be decked out in lovely holiday lights. Shaking these trees will cause either a Red, Blue, or Gold ornament to fall out. You can shake the same tree multiple times for more ornaments, but the drop rate will decrease exponentially until you give the poor tree a break. These delightful decorations can be used to craft special holiday DIY recipes!

Snowflakes

December 11th – February 24th

June 11th – August 24th

Ornaments

December 15th – January 6th

December 15th – January 6th

● **Winter DIY Recipes**

| Snowflakes | → P.215 |
| Ornaments | → P.215 |

● **Ornament Occurrence Rates**

Item	Chance (when shaking tree)	Sale Price
Red Ornament	7.5%	50
Blue Ornament	7.5%	50
Gold Ornament	5.0%	50
Tree Branch	80%	5

Winter is when snow begins to fall and everything on your island turns white. Look around for snowballs!

Creating the Perfect Snowboy

On top of being incredibly charming and fun to talk to, Snowboys will also reward you with seasonal DIY Recipes and other winter-themed items if you manage to build them perfectly. You'll also get a recipe the first time you make a Snowboy, regardless of quality, just as a friendly welcome to the world of snow-crafting. The determining factor when it comes to bringing a perfect Snowboy to life is the size ratio between

Handle your snowballs with care, as they are fragile and will break if pushed into water, off cliffs, or into solid objects such as furniture and buildings. If this happens, don't despair—simply enter and exit a building to spawn a fresh replacement somewhere on your island! Snowballs are typically found close to each other, so you likely won't have to search very far to find the second one.

the snowball used for its body and the one used for its head. Roll the snowball used for the body until it's reached maximum size, then start rolling the other snowball until it's grown to roughly 80 to 90% of the body's size. From there, it's simply a matter of rolling the head directly onto the body to complete your creation. Remember to stay in the vicinity of the body when rolling the snowball used for the head, or there's a risk it'll have grown too large by the time it arrives at its destination!

Ratios (Head in relation to the Body)						
Body	100%	100%	100%	100%	100%	100%
Head	~60%	~70%	~80%	~90%	~100%	~110% ~>
Rating	Worst	Not Good	Good	Perfect	Good	Not Good	Worst

Find a snowball and roll it until it stops getting any bigger.

Find a second ball and roll it near to the first one.

Snowboy

I can't believe this is your first time making me. I mean, just look at me... I'm perfect!

When it gets to around 90% of the first ball's size, roll them together to create a Snowboy!

Adjusting Snowballs

If a snowball grows beyond the desired size, rolling it onto dirt, sand, or constructed paths will cause it to shrink. No need to worry, since doing so won't cause your snowball to melt beyond its smallest possible size. Take advantage of this useful property when trying to build perfect Snowboys!

Life is Fleeting

Regardless of the quality of your craftsmanship, however, life will prove to be fleeting for all Snowboys. Though they can't be destroyed, Snowboys will begin melting the day after being born (even if it snows) and will have completely vanished by the fifth day. Thankfully, these short-lived residents have quite the sunny disposition! Be sure to make the most of your time together by speaking to your Snowboys each day. Perfect Snowboys will even reward you with a large snowflake once per day if you talk to them!

Weather

Just as in real life, weather in Animal Crossing: New Horizons can dynamically change throughout the span of a single day. This section goes over the various types of weather that you might encounter and explains when each type occurs.

Weather on the island can fluctuate and change throughout the course of a day, as each hour is assigned a basic weather condition according to the current weather pattern. You'll encounter steady and mostly unchanging weather conditions during some days, while others will come with lots of fluctuations as the day progresses. Transitions between weather conditions happen seamlessly and gradually over the span of an hour.

The chart here details the eight basic weather conditions that can be encountered as part of weather patterns. The weather patterns themselves are covered on the following page.

To ensure a pleasant atmosphere on days where special events take place, weather conditions will only ever be "Sunny". This applies to Fishing tournaments, Bug-Offs, and real world events such as New Years.

Bright & Clear

Clear sky without a hint of clouds

Rain

Light rainfall. Cannot occur during Winter.

Sunny

Clear sky with a few clouds

Heavy Rain

Heavy rainfall. Bring your umbrella! Cannot occur during Winter.

Cloudy

Lots of clouds, but still pleasant

Snow

Light snowfall. Only occurs during Winter.

Rain Clouds

Lots of clouds, gloomy atmosphere. Only occurs before or after rain.

Heavy Snow

Heavy snowfall. Only occurs during Winter.

Rain and Snow

Precipitation comes in the form of either rain or snow and will automatically water all flowers (and weeds) on the island. The presence of precipitation also has a large impact on the types of bugs you'll encounter on the island. For example, snails will only come out during rainfall, while butterflies will wait for the weather to clear before reappearing. Fish, on the other hand, are unaffected by weather conditions with the exception of the rare Coelacanth, which can only be caught while it's raining or snowing.

Most island residents that venture outside during rainy weather will seek shelter under an umbrella or opt to wear a raincoat. Frog residents appear to enjoy the rain, however, and will never be seen wearing these items. Island residents are also less likely to go shopping or fishing while it's raining.

Once Winter has settled in, rain is always replaced by snow. Snow will only be seen covering the ground and the roofs of buildings during the snowy period that lasts from Dec. 11th to Feb. 24th (northern hemisphere).

Rain brings unique bugs and the chance to make use of your collection of umbrellas!

Snow will drive away many bugs, but makes everything look nice.

Weather Patterns

The probability of encountering specific weather patterns on your island is greatly influenced by the time of year and passing of seasons. Think of weather patterns as simple guidelines for what you can expect the overall weather to be like throughout any given day where that pattern is in effect. For example, weather in a day with the Sunny pattern can still occasionally become Cloudy for a few hours, but you can be certain that there won't be any precipitation.

This page provides a brief description of each weather pattern. Note that Rain or Heavy Rain always turn to Snow or Heavy Snow during Winter period.

Sunny ①

Almost always Sunny or bright & clear with the occasional Cloudy spell that always clears up after a few hours.

Sunny then Cloudy ②

Sunny conditions that last for hours before turning Cloudy for the rest of the day with a few hours of Rain occasionally thrown into the mix.

Other ③

Slight variations of Sunny pattern that influence the appearance of sunset and sunrise throughout the year.

Rain ④

Expect Rain or Heavy Rain for the vast majority of the day with the occasional short break that lasts a few hours.

Occasional Rain ⑤

Sunny or bright & clear days with a guaranteed hour of Rain or Heavy Rain between 12PM and 3PM.

Rainy then Cloudy ⑥

Rain with occasional Heavy Rain between 6AM and 2PM followed by Cloudy conditions.

Cloudy ⑦

Mostly Cloudy conditions but it can occasionally Rain or get Sunny for a few hours.

Cloudy then Sunny ⑧

Cloudy conditions mixed with Rain between 5AM and 2PM, but Sunny or bright & clear for the rest of the day.

Cloudy then Rainy ⑨

Cloudy for hours before giving way to Rain or Heavy Rain for the remainder of the day.

Forecast

A weather pattern is randomly selected each day based on the probabilities shown in this weather forecast table. Patterns with a 0% probability cannot happen during that period of the year, while those with the highest value are the most likely to occur at that time. Using this information, we can discern that Rain is likely to be abundant during most days of the final two weeks of June, while there is a high likelihood of a dry period happening from July to September. We can also see that the chances of the Rain pattern appearing on Dec. 10th are 100%—that day marks the beginning of the snowy period so it's guaranteed to snow!

● Weather Likelihood

Measured in %	①	②	③	④	⑤	⑥	⑦	⑧	⑨
January 5th – February 23rd	60	6	0	12	0	6	4	6	6
February 24th	63	0	7	0	0	0	0	30	0
February 25th – March 31st	57	6	7	6	0	6	6	6	6
April 1st – April 10th	100	0	0	0	0	0	0	0	0
April 11th – June 15th	54	0	10	9	0	6	15	0	6
June 16th – July 5th	10	6	3	36	0	9	21	6	9
July 6th – July 31st	54	6	7	6	16	0	5	6	0
August 1st – August 31st	55	0	7	0	26	3	3	6	0
September 1st – September 15th	33	0	0	15	46	3	0	0	3
September 16th – September 30th	56	3	7	9	8	3	5	6	3
October 1st – November 14th	66	6	10	0	6	0	6	6	0
November 15th – November 24th	72	6	12	0	0	0	4	6	0
November 25th	67	0	3	0	0	0	0	30	0
November 26th – December 9th	51	6	10	9	0	6	6	6	6
December 10th	0	0	0	100	0	0	0	0	0
December 11th – December 23rd	34	6	6	24	0	9	6	6	9
December 24th – December 30th	0	0	0	40	0	30	0	0	30
December 31st – January 4th	93	0	7	0	0	0	0	0	0

TV Forecasts

If your house is furnished with a TV, you can tune in to the daily weather forecasts to check the current or upcoming weather patterns! For details on weather forecast times, check out the TV Guide on p.411. The AM forecasts show today's weather pattern, while the PM forecasts give you a heads up on what you can expect tomorrow.

Wind Patterns

Whether it's in the form of a gentle breeze or a strong gust, the presence of wind can constantly be felt while exploring your island. The wind's intensity will ebb and flow depending on the current weather conditions, but its impact is almost entirely cosmetic. Everything from flowers and leaves to your character's hair and clothing will react accordingly to the wind's intensity, creating a lovely feeling of being out in nature.

Wind can either blow from northwest to southeast or northeast to southwest. At night, its direction will reverse. Upon its creation, your island will randomly be assigned one of two wind patterns:

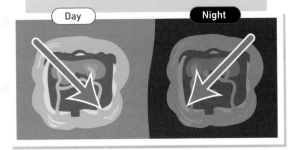

Northwestern wind during the day
Northeastern wind at night

Day   Night

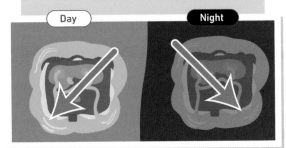

Northeastern wind during the day
Northwestern wind at night

Day   Night

Gifts From Above

Ever noticed a strange, balloon-shaped shadow on the ground and wondered what it was? Tilt your view upwards and you'll spot a balloon with a present attached to it. The direction and speed at which these mysterious balloons float by is governed by the current direction and intensity of the wind blowing across your island. Be sure to equip your slingshot and shoot them down, since the rewards are well worth the effort! Avoid popping balloons while they're floating over rivers and ponds, though, or the present they carry will plummet to a watery grave and its contents will be lost.

All special events, including opening ceremonies, will be guaranteed to have clear weather.

You'll notice the wind strength if you look carefully at your island's trees and flowers.

Special Weather

Special types of weather can occur under the right circumstances. Season, time of day and specific conditions all need to align or else you won't encounter these rare meteorological events. Let's start by looking to the skies!

Special Cloud Types

In addition to the clouds that fill the island's skies throughout the year, some special types of cloud formations can also be seen during each season if the conditions are favorable. You'll need a bit of luck to see some of these special clouds, so be sure to snap a photo whenever they're present!

Clouds can change often and will really affect the island's overall visual atmosphere.

Cumulonimbus

Summer Only
- Jul. 21st – Sept. 15th
- Jan. 21st – Mar. 15th

9AM – 9PM; Cumulonimbus clouds can appear during bright & clear or sunny weather on the day preceding poor weather.

Cirrus

Autumn Only
- Sept. 16th – Nov. 30th
- March 16th – May 31st

6AM – 4PM; Cirrus clouds can appear during bright & clear or sunny hours on a day that otherwise has poor weather.

Cirrocumulus

Autumn Only
- Sept. 16th – Nov. 30th
- March 16th – May 31st

6AM – 4PM; Cirrocumulus clouds can appear during bright & clear or sunny hours on a day that otherwise has poor weather.

Thin Clouds

Spring
- Mar. 1st – May. 31st
- Sept. 1st – Nov 30th

6AM – 4PM; Thin clouds can appear during bright & clear or sunny weather hours.

Billow Clouds

Winter
- Dec. 1st – Feb. 28th
- June 1st – August 31st

6AM – 6PM; Billow clouds can appear during bright & clear or sunny weather on the day preceding poor weather.

Plane Trails

All Year

Plane trails can be seen in the sky for 15 minutes after a DAL plane lands or departs the island. Trails are less visible during poor weather.

Turn your gaze to the skies at just the right time and you might see some truly spectacular weather phenomena. Here we'll describe them and the conditions under which they can occur.

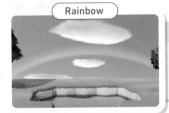

Rainbow

Dates ⏾ Feb. 25th - Nov. 25th ☀ Aug. 25th - May 25th   **Time** 7AM - 5PM

A rainbow will sometimes form in the sky in the hour following rain or heavy rain if the weather changes to bright & clear or sunny. Rainbows only appear for 45 minutes, so turn your gaze skyward once the rain has stopped if you don't want to miss it. There's even a 50% chance that you'll witness a double rainbow!

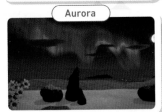

Aurora

Dates ⏾ Dec. 11th - Feb. 24th ☀ June 11th to Aug. 24th   **Time** 6PM - 4AM

The stunning aurora borealis can only be seen on bright & clear nights during Winter's snowy period. Pay attention to the daily announcements and speak to your island's residents during that time of year, since they can mention when an aurora is scheduled to appear. Spotting an aurora won't affect your play in any way, but it does make for gorgeous photos.

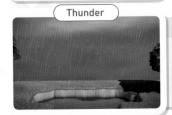

Thunder

Dates All year   **Time** All hours

Thunderstorms have a chance to form during heavy rain and last anywhere from 15 to 30 minutes before subsiding. Storms can appear all year round, but the best time to spot them is between Sept. 1st and Sept. 15th when heavy rainfall is most likely to occur. There's no danger of being struck by lightning during thunderstorms, so it's perfectly safe to remain outside and soak in the ambiance!

Fog

Heavy Fog ⏾ Sept. 21st - Feb. 24th ☀ March 21st - Aug. 24th
River & Sea Fog ⏾ Sept. 21st - March 31st ☀ March 21st - Sept. 30th   **Time** 5AM - 9AM

A thick layer of Fog can sometimes be seen blanketing the island or hanging over water for a few hours in the morning. Fog will only appear if the previous day's weather was poor and the current weather is sunny with weak winds.

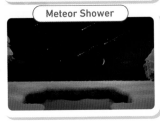

Meteor Shower

Dates All year   **Time** 7PM - 4AM

A meteor shower can only occur at night on rare occasions where the weather has been bright & clear throughout the entire day. Most meteor showers will be light, but if you're lucky it's also possible to encounter heavy showers. Celeste can appear during meteor showers and it's also possible to pray upon a star to cause unique star fragments to wash up on the island's shore the next day. Turn to P.57 for more details!

● Rainbow and Meteor Shower Occurrence

Measured in %	Rainbow	Meteors
January 5th - February 23rd	6	4
February 24th	30	2
February 25th - March 31st	6	4
April 1st - April 10th	0	0
April 11th - June 15th	0	1
June 16th - July 5th	6	0
July 6th - July 31st	16	2
August 1st - August 31st	22	2
September 1st - September 15th	16	3

Measured in %	Rainbow	Meteors
September 16th - September 30th	12	3
October 1st - November 14th	12	2
November 15th - November 24th	6	2
November 25th	30	2
November 26th - December 9th	6	2
December 10th	0	0
December 11th - December 23rd	6	3
December 24th - December 30th	0	0
December 31st - January 4th	0	4

Island Flora

Trees, fruits and flowers are a vibrant part of your island's ecosystem and are an important source of natural materials used in crafting DIY recipes. In this section, we'll be taking an in-depth look at their purpose and how you can use them to enrich your island life.

Trees

Trees are a useful resource that naturally populate your island. They're your primary source for wood and fruit, but also attract certain bugs as well. Shaking trees daily can get you wild surprises! Tree branches, hiding insects, Bells and even furniture can drop from them.

Life Cycle

Though many adult trees natively populate your island, it's also possible to grow brand-new trees by planting a sapling or fruit of the desired species. In order for a tree to grow, you'll first need to pick a suitable patch of soil to plant it in. Make sure all adjacent spaces surrounding the location you've chosen are devoid of obstacles (such as other trees, plants, rocks, items, rivers, cliffs or buildings) or else your tree will fail to thrive. No need to worry, however, as saplings and fruits planted in poor locations won't ever wither or rot regardless of how long you leave them there; it'll always be possible to uproot them using a shovel and to move them to a better spot.

Once you've picked a suitable location and planted a tree, it'll take four days for it to fully mature. Only adult trees are capable of bearing fruits or providing harvestable materials. In the case of fruit-bearing species, this cycle of life can be

Having a lot of trees on your island means you'll have plenty of crafting resources available. It will also help to improve your island rating.

perpetuated by planting the fruits collected from adult trees. When visiting other islands, always be on the lookout for types of fruits that don't currently grow on yours. Planting a single fruit will soon give you the ability to grow as many trees of that type as you wish!

Stages of Growth

Nursery

Small

Medium

Large

Adult

Cutting or Moving Trees

Feeling like there's a few too many trees crowding your island? They'll never get old or wither, so the only way to reduce their population is to cut them down using the axe tool. Keep in mind, however, that only axes other than the flimsy or stone models are sharp enough to cut through a tree's trunk. Once the deed has been done, a fallen tree will leave behind a stump that can then be uprooted using a shovel if you want to fully clear the space. Don't be so hasty to remove every stump, though, as there are a few advantages to keeping them around. Most importantly, stumps can be used to attract certain species of bugs that wouldn't appear otherwise, such as the violin beetle. And as an added bonus, their flat surface makes them the ideal place to sit down and rest whenever you get tired from all the cutting!

If you want to simply move a tree instead of permanently removing it, your trusty shovel is the tool for the job. Saplings and trees in their initial stages of growth can easily be dug out and placed in your inventory, but adult or almost fully grown trees will also require some Energy. Once the trees are safely in your pockets, just move to a suitable location and transplant them! When going on a Mystery Tour, feel free to use this method to dig out any trees you want and give them a new home on your island!

You're in control of the landscaping on your island. Plant or dig up trees to create your ideal natural environment.

Types of Trees

Hardwood

Hardwood trees are native to your island and act as your primary harvest points for wood, softwood and hardwood. Their dense foliage harbors many species of bugs, so giving these trees a good shake is bound to cause something interesting to crawl out! The leaves of hardwood trees change in color depending on the season—most notably turning a beautiful shade of pink during the cherry blossom season. During Autumn, shaking these trees might even reward you with some acorns that can be used for a few unique DIY projects!

The hardwood is the most common tree type—don't cut too many down or you'll limit your supply of resources.

Cedar

Cedar trees naturally grow atop the northern cliffs of your island, but if you're looking to bring their rustic charm closer to home, these hardy conifers are also more than capable of thriving in any patch of grass. Like most trees, cedars also yield wood, hardwood and softwood materials when struck with an axe. Cedar trees aren't affected much by the passing of seasons, but shaking them during Autumn might knock loose some pine cones that can be used in certain DIY recipes!

Planting lots of cedar trees can give your island a more rustic feel.

Fruit Trees

Most fruit-bearing trees are simply Hardwood trees capable of producing one of five types of fruits: apples, oranges, pears, peaches or cherries. Every three days, three ripe fruits will be prominently displayed in their foliage—all you need to do is shake them loose and gather up the spoils! Only a single type of fruit tree natively grows on your island, so visit other islands or exchange fruits with other players to collect them all!

Never miss a chance to plant a fruit tree for a fruit you don't currently have on your island.

Palm Trees

Palm trees are exotic trees that only grow in sand, and the cool tropical vibe they exude is sure to liven up any beach. A different kind of fruit-bearing tree, palm trees produce coconuts that can be knocked loose and harvested each day. If you're looking to add palm trees to your island, visiting another island through DAL's Mystery Tour is a guaranteed way to find them. Simply bring back a coconut from your trip, then plant it in the sand; in a few days you'll be the proud owner of a new palm tree! Beyond a bountiful supply of free coconuts, the main advantage of introducing palm trees to your island's ecosystem is their ability to attract some species of bugs and critters that you wouldn't otherwise be able to add to your museum!

Palm trees appear often on Mystery Tour islands, and you can even dig them up and replant them back home!

Bamboo Stalks

Technically considered grass, Bamboo stalks are durable plants that share a similar growth cycle to trees. If you get your hands on a bamboo sprout, plant it just like you would any tree sapling and it'll fully mature after four days. Bamboo shoots can only be harvested from adult bamboo trees once, and there's also a 30% chance to obtain young bamboo shoots during the Spring season. Both of these materials are used to craft some elegant bamboo-themed DIY recipes, so they're highly sought-after!

A reliable way to obtain bamboo sprouts is to purchase 100 or more turnips from Daisy Mae in a single day. Once these conditions have been met, this plucky entrepreneur will send you a letter containing three bamboo sprouts.

Bamboo is initially hard to come by, but it can end up covering a decent area quickly if cultivated properly.

● **Seasonal DIY Recipes**

Young Spring Bamboo → P.214

● **Bamboo plant spaces**

Once a bamboo stalk grows close to its adult size, it will produce a single bamboo sprout so long as at least one of its adjacent spaces is unobstructed. This buried bamboo sprout is completely hidden and won't grow until you dig it up and plant it elsewhere.

Fruit

Looking for a tasty snack that will fill you with enough Energy to shovel up fully-grown trees? Perhaps a resident has asked you for a certain type of fruit, or maybe you want to sell fruit to make some money? Fruits are a fantastic multi-purpose resource that's available all year round!

Not only will your island have a native fruit type, but you can grow other kinds of fruit trees too. To pick some fruit off a tree, simply shake it or hit it with an axe to loosen the fruit. Then, you can press the Ⓨ Button to collect the freshly fallen fruit. Just like other harvestable materials, when a fruit is ready to appear, it will do so at 5AM once the growth cycle occurs.

In total, there are six types of fruit that can grow on your island:

Fruit always stays fresh regardless of how long it's been sitting on the ground... or your pockets!

Fruit	Tree Type	Amount	Energy Gain
Apples	Hardwood	3	1
Oranges	Hardwood	3	1
Cherries	Hardwood	3	1
Peaches	Hardwood	3	1
Pears	Hardwood	3	1
Coconuts	Palm Tree	2	1

Weeds

An island that's properly tended to might look like a perfect getaway paradise, but unsightly clumps of weeds are bound to ruin the vibe if you don't get rid of them regularly. Each day, there's a chance that a few weeds will appear on empty patches of grass. These invasive plants will quickly grow and proliferate if left unattended, so cleaning them up on a daily basis is the best way to prevent them from lowering your island's attractiveness rating. Thankfully, removing weeds is as easy as pressing the Ⓨ Button to scoop them up and place them in your pockets. Clumps of weeds can then be used as DIY materials or sold for 10 Bells each—everything has its use!

Removing weeds can be a slow process—call in some buddies to help if you want to speed it up!

Weeds will grow and spread more easily during rainy periods.

Each patch of weeds always occupies the same 1x1 space, but they'll grow taller and be more likely to reproduce if you don't quickly remove them!

Growth Stages

Weeds feature three stages of growth. At the start of each daily growth cycle (5AM), there's a chance that some of the weeds currently on your island will grow taller. This will happen twice, with each stage having an increasing likelihood that they'll reproduce. Taller weeds are then much more likely to reproduce and spread to nearby patches of grass. To make matters worse, weather precipitation (rain, snow or your watering can) can also greatly increase the probabilities of weeds reaching the next stage of growth. Fail to remove them for a week or two and your island will almost certainly be overrun! As mentioned before, the presence of weeds will negatively impact your island's attractiveness rating, so be sure to always clean them up!

● **Growth Rate**

Growth Stage	No Water	Water
Stage 1 → Stage 2	20%	50%
Stage 2 → Stage 3	5%	10%

Stage 1	Stage 2	Stage 3
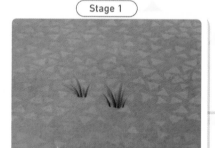		

They're Everywhere!

Weeds in their first stage of growth can't reproduce unless they've been watered, but the probability of fully-grown weeds spreading to nearby patches of grass is incredibly high. Depending on how many weeds are currently on your island, a set number of fresh weeds (outside of those that appear as a result of spreading) will also pop up during the daily growth cycle. There are no known ways of permanently ridding your island of these botanical pests, but remember that daily maintenance is an effective way of keeping them at bay!

A proliferation of weeds can ruin an otherwise lovely setting.

Probability of Spreading	No Water	Water		Current Weeds	Daily Occurrence
Stage 1	0%	5%		0 ~ 30	2
Stage 2	10%	20%		31 +	1
Stage 3	80%	100%		150 (max)	0

Flowers are one of nature's finest creations and will help transform any deserted island into an idyllic paradise. No need to worry if you have allergies—these flowers are all sneeze-free! Coming in many different shapes and colors, there are a variety of flower types to collect in Animal Crossing: New Horizons. At first, flowers are only available in the form of seed bags that can be purchased from Timmy and Tommy's store; be sure to visit their store daily to find new breeds and colors for sale! As you gain access to the ladder tool, you'll find a flower native to your island growing on higher ground. You can discover more from friends, the Mystery Tours, or through Nook's Cranny throughout the year.

Flowers can be used to decorate your island or as a crafting resource. They make great gifts and home decor too. You can also wear them as accessories! There are two ways of harvesting flowers: using a shovel to uproot an entire flower and store it in your pockets so you can transplant it elsewhere, or pressing the Ⓨ Button to pluck the flower and get a resource used for crafting. Don't worry, flowers that have been plucked will grow back within two days. If for some reason you wish to destroy a flower, the only way to go about this is to dig it out with a shovel. Running over your flowers will revert them to their budding stage, so be careful to avoid trampling your delicate flowers!

Having lots of flowers on your island can help to boost your island's ranking. Other than buying them, how else can you get more? The answer is simple: the handy dandy watering can!

There are many different types of flowers you can grow. New to Animal Crossing: New Horizons are Windflowers, Hyacinths and Mums.

Watering Flowers

Flowers have four possible stages of growth: the sprout, the stem, the bud and the fully grown flower. Flowers usually take about four days to mature, though this process can be expedited with the watering can. Watering flowers can also earn you easy Nook Miles. You'll be able to tell if a flower has already been watered if the petals sparkle. It can be hard work depending on what kind of watering can you're using, but Mother Nature can sometimes lend a hand. Rain and snow can also do the watering job for you.

For more information on the watering can itself, turn back to P.118.

Basic Types

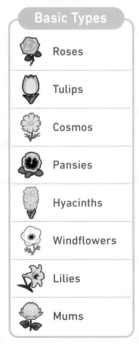

| Roses |
| Tulips |
| Cosmos |
| Pansies |
| Hyacinths |
| Windflowers |
| Lilies |
| Mums |

Breeding Flowers

Flowers typically come in up to three colors when you first arrive on your island. However, you may have noticed that while you were walking around, a whole new color flower has mysteriously appeared! Every day, there is a small chance that an adult flower will pair with another adult flower within a single block radius from them. If they pair, a flower containing hereditary information from both parents will sprout in the bud stage beside both parents. Certain colors paired together make fantastic new hybrids! For example, if you put a Red Rose and a White Rose side by side with some free space around them, and then water them each day, you might get yourself a Pink Rose.

Aside from the aesthetic appeal, rare colors of flowers will sell for a lot more than a more commonly colored one. For example...

 white rose common ⊙40

 pink rose rare ⊙80

 blue rose very rare ⊙1000

Flower Farm

Creating a flower farm can be a great way to cultivate an easy, constant income in the early game. Watering your flowers increases the chance that more flowers will naturally appear, which can save you a pretty Bell or two. This chance increases exponentially every day that you water them. If you want the highest chance of getting more flowers and more colors, you'll need to tend your flowers daily. You'll also want to keep dropped items and weeds out of the way, to give your flowers the proper room to grow.

Flowers will spread naturally given enough time and the right weather.

The Many Possible Types

Once you have yourself a variety of interesting flowers, spread them throughout your island! Perhaps you could use them to decorate the outside of a resident's house, or even in your own yard. Maybe Tom Nook would appreciate some pretty flowers outside of Resident Services?

We'll show how to get all possible types in the pages that follow, along with the price you'll get for selling each of them.

You can have fine control over your flower beds if you're careful with your watering can.

Mixing different types together isn't going result in breeding many new colors.

Roses

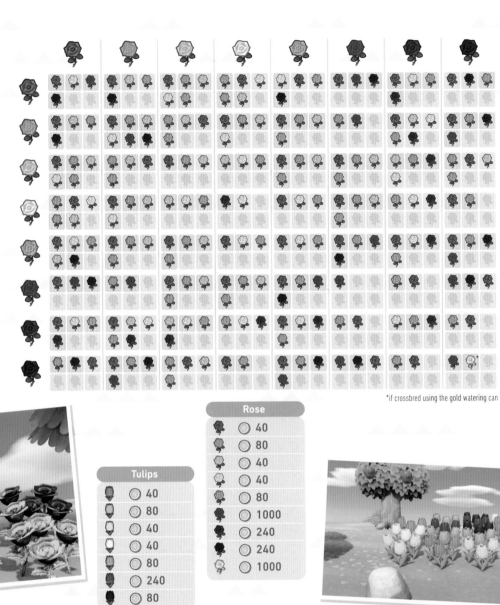

*if crossbred using the gold watering can

Rose

🌹	◯ 40
🌹	◯ 80
🌹	◯ 40
🌹	◯ 40
🌹	◯ 80
🌹	◯ 1000
🌹	◯ 240
🌹	◯ 240
🌹	◯ 1000

Tulips

🌷	◯ 40
🌷	◯ 80
🌷	◯ 40
🌷	◯ 40
🌷	◯ 80
🌷	◯ 240
🌷	◯ 80

Tulips

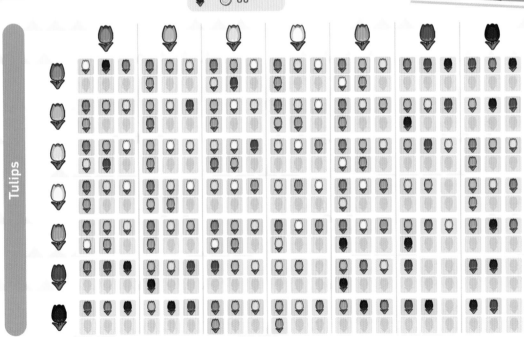

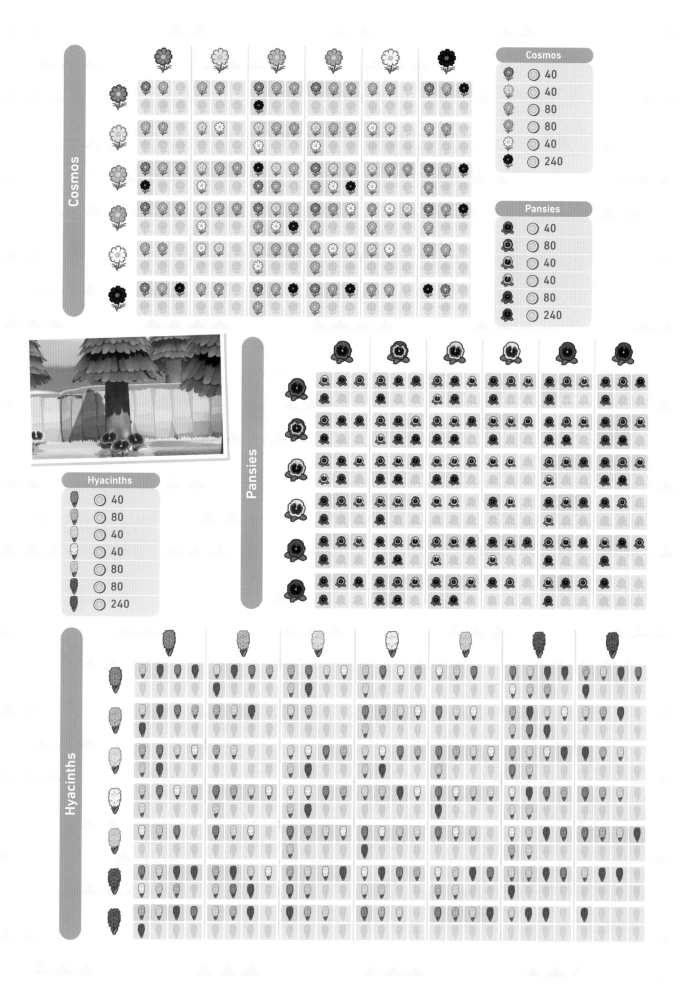

Cosmos

40	40	80	80	40	240

Pansies

40	80	40	40	80	240

Hyacinths

40	80	40	40	80	80	240

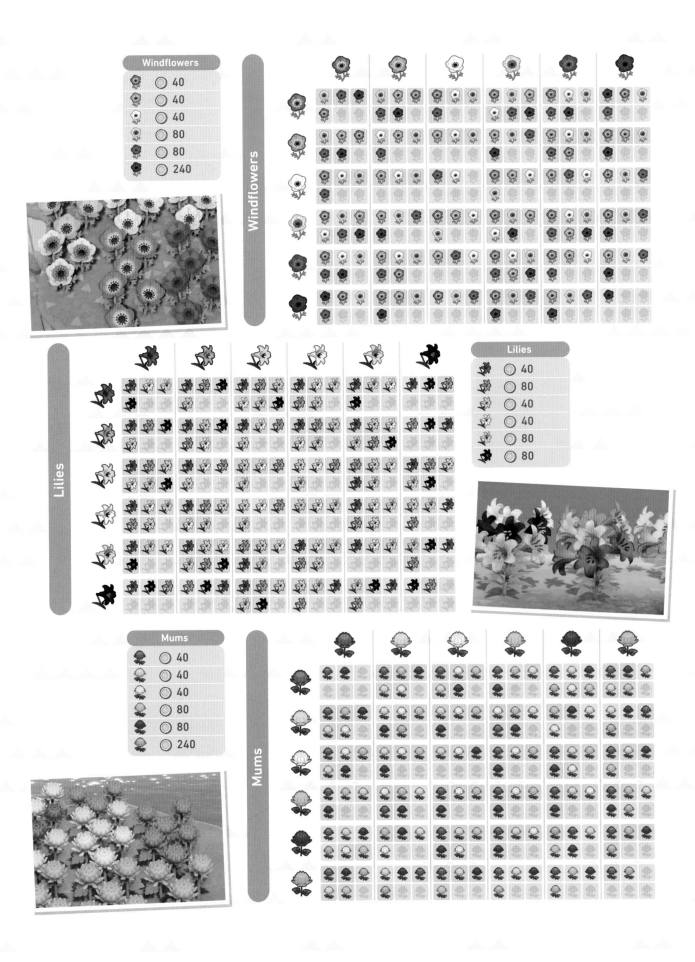

Windflowers

	◯	40
	◯	40
	◯	40
	◯	80
	◯	80
	◯	240

Windflowers

Lilies

	◯	40
	◯	80
	◯	40
	◯	40
	◯	80
	◯	80

Lilies

Mums

	◯	40
	◯	40
	◯	40
	◯	80
	◯	80
	◯	240

Mums

Fish

If you spot an oval-shaped shadow in the water, there's a good chance you've spotted a fish. Try and cast your line a little in front of where the fish is facing. It may nibble at first, but once you see a big splash and the bobber goes under, press Ⓐ to start reeling your catch in! If you're too slow, the fish will get away and you'll miss your opportunity. Remember that fish are easily startled, so yanking the line too early when one is nibbling will cause it to escape. Running or using tools too close to the water's edge should also be avoided as this will scare away nearby fish.

Fish can be found in any sizable body of water, but which species are available is dependent on various factors. Seasons, time of day, weather conditions, rarity and the location you're fishing in all play a crucial role in determining the type of fish you'll be able to reel in.

Some fish are much more common than others, usually because there are no specific conditions under which they appear.

Fishing Tips

Before a fish has a chance to bite, it'll first need to spot your bobber in the water. Some species have better vision than others (rated on a scale of 1 to 5), but it's always best to aim your line such that it lands squarely in front of a fish's head. The closer, the better! Once a fish notices your bobber, it'll immediately swim towards it and begin nibbling.

Fish can nibble on the line up to four times before finally biting. Pay attention whenever a fish begins swimming towards your line, though, since it's also possible for it to instantly bite without nibbling at all. Always be ready to yank the line the moment you see and hear the bobber go under!

Sometimes, tilting the camera upwards will make judging the bobber's position easier.

Water Current

Flowing bodies of water feature a mild current that drags both your bobber and nearby fish along its direction, while pond waters are calm and devoid of motion. Light glistening on the water's surface indicates the presence of current and can be used to ascertain its direction before throwing your line. When fishing in flowing waters, don't be so hasty to yank the line out if you aim too far ahead and miss the mark. Wait a moment instead, as the current can sometimes drag your bobber close enough for the fish to spot it and bite!

...and the current will bring it straight to the fish!

If the water current is strong, you can cast your bobber well ahead of the fish's position...

Fish Shadows

The shape and size of shadows visible from the water's surface gives a good indication of the size and nature of the fish lurking below. Fish shadows range from very small (XS), all the way up to extra, extra large (XXL). A large shadow sporting a fin (SH) is almost certainly a shark (but can also be the aptly-named suckerfish), while a large yet slightly skinnier shadow (E) is guaranteed to be an eel. The fish compendium on P.178 features the size of all fish types, so use this knowledge to quickly judge which fish shadows might belong to the catch you're after!

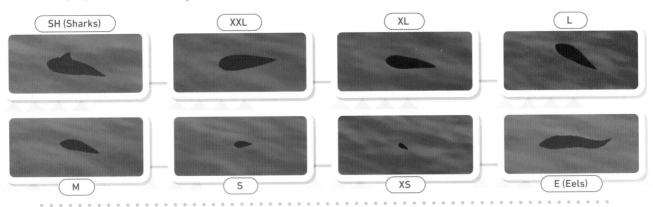

SH (Sharks)   XXL   XL   L

M   S   XS   E (Eels)

Bait

Sprinkling fish bait next to a body of water is a surefire way to lure a fish shadow to your location. Stocking up on fish bait can greatly improve your odds when angling for rare species of fish. No more waiting for fish to naturally appear when you don't land the catch you're after! An old fisherman's trick, you won't find fish bait for sale in any store. Thankfully, crafting it only requires manila clams, which can easily be found by scouring your beach for water spouts and using your shovel to extract them. One last thing—C.J. doesn't consider the use of fish bait during Fishing Tourneys to be unsportsmanlike, so don't be afraid to use this item to get an edge!

Fishing Out the Trash

Ordinary looking fish shadows can sometimes belong to an assortment of trash items buried in the depths below. Nobody knows who dumped them there, but reeling in these seemingly worthless catches does have a few surprising uses. Though unsightly (and not to mention smelly), placing trash items on the ground is the only way to attract flies that can then be caught with your net. And if you stumble upon a boot, don't be so hasty to throw it out—fishing out a second one will complete the pair and earn you the unique DIY recipe that lets you craft recycled boots! Otherwise, trash items can be safely disposed of by selling them to Timmy & Tommy or by placing them in your trash can if you've got one.

● **Trash Types**

empty can
boot
old tire
stone

Once you have the Island Designer app, you can make ponds wherever you like.

● **Trash DIY Recipes**

The Workbench	→ P.202

Hidden Requirements

Some species of fish also require you to have caught a specific amount of fish in total before they have a chance to appear. The requirement to ensure all types of fish can begin populating your waters is 100 total catches. The size and rarity of each catch doesn't matter; try to reel in as many fish as possible until you've reached this quota. Be sure to consult the fish list for each species' unlock requirements.

Fishing Spots

Trying to catch a specific type of fish but not having any luck? Then you probably aren't fishing in the right waters! Take a moment to familiarize yourself with the six different types of fishing locations, since this is essential knowledge that any up-and-coming angler should learn about!

River

Rivers are freshwater fishing spots featuring a natural current that flows towards the sea. You can catch all sorts of fish here, such as the pale chub and black bass.

River: Cliff

Rivers that reach atop the cliffs north of your island are host to unique species of fish, like the char and golden trout.

Pond

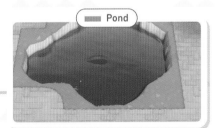

Ponds are small bodies of freshwater that are perfect for catching certain types of fish. Their motionless waters also attract insects such as the Pondskater.

River: Mouth

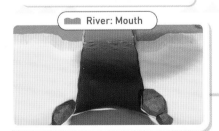

River mouths are the area where rivers connect to the sea. This is where you'll find some rare species such as the Salmon, King Salmon and Sturgeon

Sea

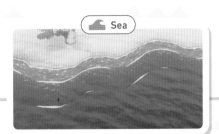

The sea surrounds your entire island and it's where you'll be able to catch most species of saltwater fish. Keep an eye out for a fin—you may catch a shark!

Sea: Pier

Fishing from your island's pier is the only way to nab some of the largest fish found in the game like the tuna and the blue marlin.

The following few pages list all fish and reveal useful information about each of them. You'll find out their shadow sizes, vision ranges and more. The huge chart here shows exactly when you can expect to find each fish by displaying their probabilities of appearing at different times of day during each month.

LEGEND
A → Morning/Evening
B → Afternoon
C → Night

Lowest Occurrence	Medium Occurrence
Small Occurrence	High Occurrence
	Very High Occurrence
	Highest Occurrence

Northern Hemisphere	JAN	FEB	MAR	APR	MAY	JUN	JUL	AUG	SEP	OCT	NOV	DEC
Southern Hemisphere	JUL	AUG	SEP	OCT	NOV	DEC	JAN	FEB	MAR	APR	MAY	JUN

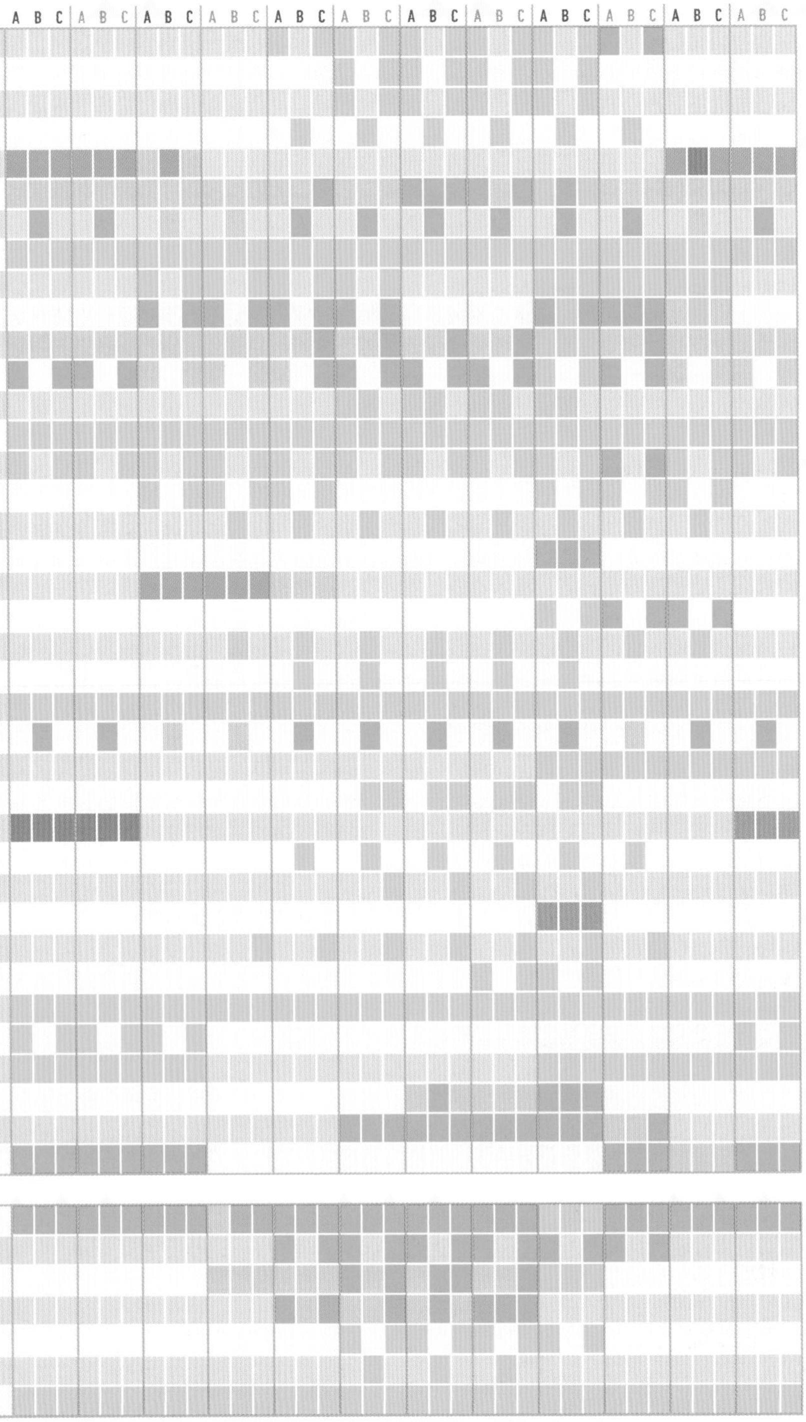

Occurances in the river

	Size	Vision	Catch
Angelfish	S	3	4
Arapaima	XXL	2	1
Arowana	L	3	1
Betta	S	2	2
Bitterling	XS	3	2
Black Bass	L	3	3
Bluegill	S	5	5
Boot	M	5	5
Char	M	2	2
Cherry Salmon	M	2	3
Crucian Carp	S	4	5
Dace	M	4	4
Dorado	XL	2	1
Empty can	S	5	5
Freshwater Goby	S	3	5
Golden Trout	M	1	1
Guppy	XS	3	4
King Salmon	XL	3	2
Loach	S	4	4
Mitten Crab	S	2	2
Neon Tetra	XS	3	4
Nibble Fish	XS	2	3
Old tire	L	5	5
Pale Chub	XS	4	4
Pike	XL	3	3
Piranha	S	5	5
Pond Smelt	S	4	4
Rainbowfish	XS	2	2
Saddled Bichir	L	2	2
Salmon	L	3	3
Snapping Turtle	L	3	2
Soft-shelled Turtle	L	2	2
Stone	XS	5	5
Stringfish	XL	1	1
Sturgeon	XXL	1	1
Sweetfish	M	3	2
Tilapia	M	3	2
Yellow Perch	M	2	3

Occurances in the pond

	Size	Vision	Catch
Carp	L	3	5
Catfish	L	3	3
Crawfish	S	5	5
Frog	S	5	4
Gar	XL	4	2
Giant Snakehead	L	3	2
Goldfish	XS	3	4

| Northern Hemisphere | JAN | FEB | MAR | APR | MAY | JUN | JUL | AUG | SEP | OCT | NOV | DEC |
| Southern Hemisphere | JUL | AUG | SEP | OCT | NOV | DEC | JAN | FEB | MAR | APR | MAY | JUN |

	Size	Vision	Catch
Killifish	XS	3	3
Koi	L	3	4
Pop-eyed Goldfish	XS	3	4
Ranchu Goldfish	S	2	2
Tadpole	XS	5	4

Occurances in the sea

	Size	Vision	Catch
Anchovy	S	5	5
Barred Knifejaw	M	3	2
Barreleye	S	1	1
Blowfish	M	1	3
Blue Marlin	XXL	2	1
Boot	M	5	5
Butterfly Fish	S	3	4
Clown Fish	XS	3	3
Coelacanth	XXL	1	1
Dab	M	3	4
Empty can	S	5	5
Football Fish	L	4	5
Giant Trevally	XL	1	1
Great White Shark	SH	2	1
Hammerhead Shark	SH	2	2
Horse Mackerel	S	4	5
Mahi-mahi	XL	1	1
Moray Eel	E	3	4
Napoleonfish	XXL	3	2
Oarfish	XXL	1	2
Ocean Sunfish	SH	1	2
Old tire	L	5	5
Olive Flounder	XL	2	3
Puffer Fish	M	3	4
Ray	XL	3	4
Red Snapper	L	3	2
Ribbon Eel	E	1	2
Saw Shark	SH	1	2
Sea Bass	XL	4	4
Sea Butterfly	XS	1	4
Sea Horse	XS	2	3
Squid	M	4	4
Stone	XS	5	5
Suckerfish	SH	5	5
Surgeonfish	S	3	4
Tuna	XXL	2	1
Whale Shark	SH	1	1
Zebra Turkeyfish	M	4	5

Fish List

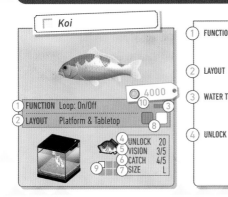

Koi

① FUNCTION Loop: On/Off
② LAYOUT Platform & Tabletop
⑩ 4000
③ (Sea)
⑧
④ UNLOCK 20
⑤ VISION 3/5
⑥ CATCH 4/5
⑦ SIZE L
⑨

①	FUNCTION	Points out any special animations or functions when the fish is placed as a furniture object.
②	LAYOUT	Describes the rules for placing the fish as an item of furniture.
③	WATER TYPE	This symbol shows the type of water the fish can be found in. River / Pond / Sea
④	UNLOCK	Some fishes will only appear once a certain total number have been caught. This tells you how many you'll need to have caught for them to appear.

⑤	VISION	Rates the distance at which the fish can see your bobber in the water.
⑥	CATCH	Rates the difficulty of successfully catching the fish, since some are more erratic at biting than others. 1 means hardest to catch, and 5 means easiest to catch.
⑦	SIZE	Shows the size of the fish's shadow in a range from XS to XXL. See P.176.
⑧	COLORS	The fish's system colors are shown here.
⑨	OBJECT SIZE	This shows how much space the fish takes up when placed as an object.
⑩	SELL PRICE	This shows how much you'll get when selling the fish to Timmy and Tommy.

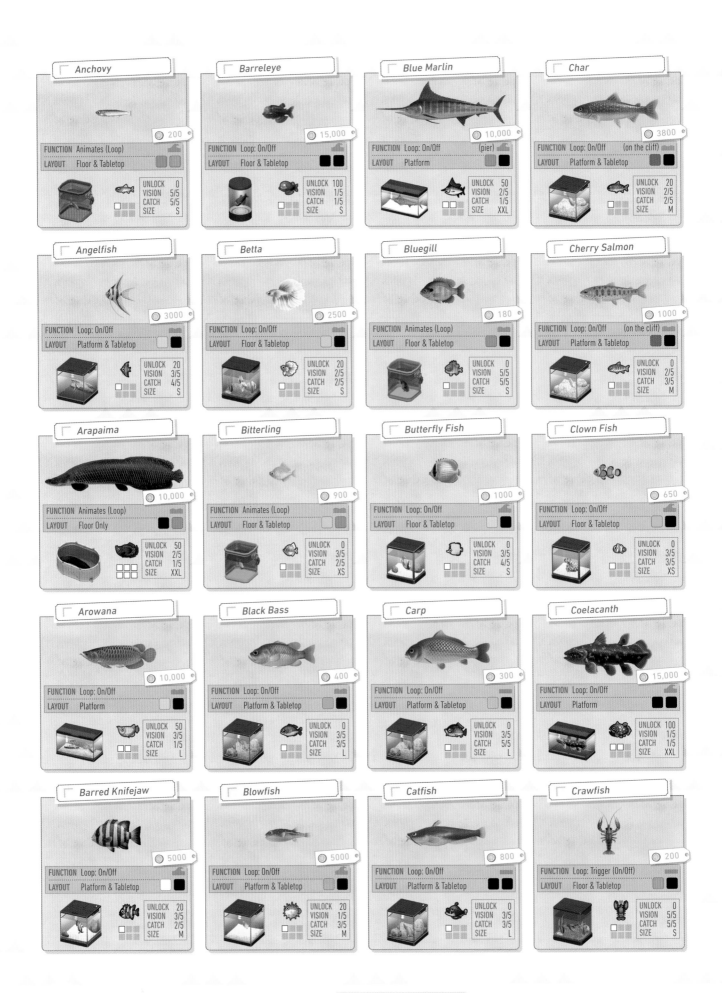

Anchovy
- 200
- FUNCTION: Animates (Loop)
- LAYOUT: Floor & Tabletop
- UNLOCK 0
- VISION 5/5
- CATCH 5/5
- SIZE S

Barreleye
- 15,000
- FUNCTION: Loop: On/Off
- LAYOUT: Floor & Tabletop
- UNLOCK 100
- VISION 1/5
- CATCH 1/5
- SIZE S

Blue Marlin
- 10,000
- FUNCTION: Loop: On/Off (pier)
- LAYOUT: Platform
- UNLOCK 50
- VISION 2/5
- CATCH 1/5
- SIZE XXL

Char
- 3800
- FUNCTION: Loop: On/Off (on the cliff)
- LAYOUT: Platform & Tabletop
- UNLOCK 20
- VISION 2/5
- CATCH 2/5
- SIZE M

Angelfish
- 3000
- FUNCTION: Loop: On/Off
- LAYOUT: Platform & Tabletop
- UNLOCK 20
- VISION 3/5
- CATCH 4/5
- SIZE S

Betta
- 2500
- FUNCTION: Loop: On/Off
- LAYOUT: Floor & Tabletop
- UNLOCK 20
- VISION 2/5
- CATCH 2/5
- SIZE S

Bluegill
- 180
- FUNCTION: Animates (Loop)
- LAYOUT: Floor & Tabletop
- UNLOCK 0
- VISION 5/5
- CATCH 5/5
- SIZE S

Cherry Salmon
- 1000
- FUNCTION: Loop: On/Off (on the cliff)
- LAYOUT: Platform & Tabletop
- UNLOCK 0
- VISION 2/5
- CATCH 3/5
- SIZE M

Arapaima
- 10,000
- FUNCTION: Animates (Loop)
- LAYOUT: Floor Only
- UNLOCK 50
- VISION 2/5
- CATCH 1/5
- SIZE XXL

Bitterling
- 900
- FUNCTION: Animates (Loop)
- LAYOUT: Floor & Tabletop
- UNLOCK 0
- VISION 3/5
- CATCH 2/5
- SIZE XS

Butterfly Fish
- 1000
- FUNCTION: Loop: On/Off
- LAYOUT: Floor & Tabletop
- UNLOCK 0
- VISION 3/5
- CATCH 4/5
- SIZE S

Clown Fish
- 650
- FUNCTION: Loop: On/Off
- LAYOUT: Floor & Tabletop
- UNLOCK 0
- VISION 3/5
- CATCH 3/5
- SIZE XS

Arowana
- 10,000
- FUNCTION: Loop: On/Off
- LAYOUT: Platform
- UNLOCK 50
- VISION 3/5
- CATCH 1/5
- SIZE L

Black Bass
- 400
- FUNCTION: Loop: On/Off
- LAYOUT: Platform & Tabletop
- UNLOCK 0
- VISION 3/5
- CATCH 3/5
- SIZE L

Carp
- 300
- FUNCTION: Loop: On/Off
- LAYOUT: Platform & Tabletop
- UNLOCK 0
- VISION 3/5
- CATCH 5/5
- SIZE L

Coelacanth
- 15,000
- FUNCTION: Loop: On/Off
- LAYOUT: Platform
- UNLOCK 100
- VISION 1/5
- CATCH 1/5
- SIZE XXL

Barred Knifejaw
- 5000
- FUNCTION: Loop: On/Off
- LAYOUT: Platform & Tabletop
- UNLOCK 20
- VISION 3/5
- CATCH 2/5
- SIZE M

Blowfish
- 5000
- FUNCTION: Loop: On/Off
- LAYOUT: Platform & Tabletop
- UNLOCK 20
- VISION 1/5
- CATCH 1/5
- SIZE M

Catfish
- 800
- FUNCTION: Loop: On/Off
- LAYOUT: Platform & Tabletop
- UNLOCK 0
- VISION 3/5
- CATCH 3/5
- SIZE L

Crawfish
- 200
- FUNCTION: Loop: Trigger (On/Off)
- LAYOUT: Floor & Tabletop
- UNLOCK 0
- VISION 5/5
- CATCH 5/5
- SIZE S

Crucian Carp
FUNCTION	Loop: On/Off
LAYOUT	Platform & Tabletop

UNLOCK 0
VISION 4/5
CATCH 5/5
SIZE S

Freshwater Goby
FUNCTION	Loop: On/Off
LAYOUT	Platform & Tabletop

UNLOCK 0
VISION 3/5
CATCH 5/5
SIZE S

Golden Trout
FUNCTION	Loop: On/Off (on the cliff)
LAYOUT	Platform & Tabletop

UNLOCK 100
VISION 1/5
CATCH 1/5
SIZE M

Horse Mackerel
FUNCTION	Loop: On/Off
LAYOUT	Platform & Tabletop

UNLOCK 0
VISION 4/5
CATCH 5/5
SIZE S

Dab
FUNCTION	Loop: On/Off
LAYOUT	Platform & Tabletop

UNLOCK 0
VISION 3/5
CATCH 4/5
SIZE M

Frog
FUNCTION	Loop: On/Off
LAYOUT	Floor & Tabletop

UNLOCK 0
VISION 5/5
CATCH 4/5
SIZE S

Goldfish
FUNCTION	Animates (Loop)
LAYOUT	Floor & Tabletop

UNLOCK 0
VISION 3/5
CATCH 4/5
SIZE XS

Killifish
FUNCTION	Loop: On/Off
LAYOUT	Floor & Tabletop

UNLOCK 0
VISION 3/5
CATCH 3/5
SIZE XS

Dace
FUNCTION	Loop: On/Off
LAYOUT	Platform & Tabletop

UNLOCK 0
VISION 4/5
CATCH 4/5
SIZE M

Gar
FUNCTION	Loop: On/Off
LAYOUT	Platform

UNLOCK 50
VISION 4/5
CATCH 2/5
SIZE XL

Great White Shark
FUNCTION	Animates (Loop)
LAYOUT	Floor Only

UNLOCK 50
VISION 2/5
CATCH 1/5
SIZE SH

King Salmon
FUNCTION	Loop: On/Off (mouth)
LAYOUT	Platform

UNLOCK 20
VISION 3/5
CATCH 2/5
SIZE XL

Dorado
FUNCTION	Loop: On/Off
LAYOUT	Platform

UNLOCK 100
VISION 2/5
CATCH 1/5
SIZE XL

Giant Snakehead
FUNCTION	Loop: On/Off
LAYOUT	Platform

UNLOCK 50
VISION 3/5
CATCH 2/5
SIZE L

Guppy
FUNCTION	Loop: On/Off
LAYOUT	Floor & Tabletop

UNLOCK 0
VISION 3/5
CATCH 4/5
SIZE XS

Koi
FUNCTION	Loop: On/Off
LAYOUT	Platform & Tabletop

UNLOCK 20
VISION 3/5
CATCH 4/5
SIZE L

Football Fish
FUNCTION	Loop: On/Off
LAYOUT	Platform

UNLOCK 20
VISION 4/5
CATCH 5/5
SIZE L

Giant Trevally
FUNCTION	Loop: On/Off (pier)
LAYOUT	Platform

UNLOCK 20
VISION 1/5
CATCH 1/5
SIZE XL

Hammerhead Shark
FUNCTION	Loop: On/Off
LAYOUT	Platform

UNLOCK 20
VISION 2/5
CATCH 2/5
SIZE SH

Loach
FUNCTION	Animates (Loop)
LAYOUT	Floor & Tabletop

UNLOCK 0
VISION 4/5
CATCH 4/5
SIZE S

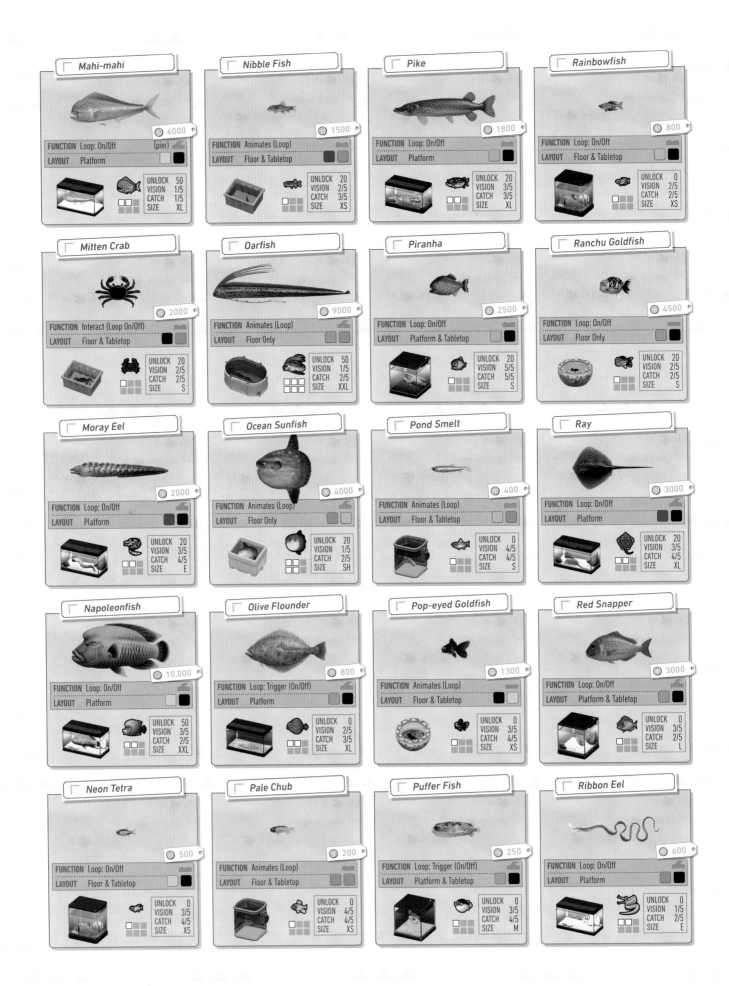

Mahi-mahi
🔘 6000
FUNCTION Loop: On/Off   (pier) 🐟
LAYOUT   Platform
UNLOCK 50
VISION 1/5
CATCH   1/5
SIZE   XL

Nibble Fish
🔘 1500
FUNCTION Animates (Loop)
LAYOUT   Floor & Tabletop
UNLOCK 20
VISION 2/5
CATCH   3/5
SIZE   XS

Pike
🔘 1800
FUNCTION Loop: On/Off
LAYOUT   Platform
UNLOCK 20
VISION 3/5
CATCH   3/5
SIZE   XL

Rainbowfish
🔘 800
FUNCTION Loop: On/Off
LAYOUT   Floor & Tabletop
UNLOCK 0
VISION 2/5
CATCH   2/5
SIZE   XS

Mitten Crab
🔘 2000
FUNCTION Interact (Loop On/Off)
LAYOUT   Floor & Tabletop
UNLOCK 20
VISION 2/5
CATCH   2/5
SIZE   S

Oarfish
🔘 9000
FUNCTION Animates (Loop)
LAYOUT   Floor Only
UNLOCK 50
VISION 1/5
CATCH   2/5
SIZE   XXL

Piranha
🔘 2500
FUNCTION Loop: On/Off
LAYOUT   Platform & Tabletop
UNLOCK 20
VISION 5/5
CATCH   5/5
SIZE   S

Ranchu Goldfish
🔘 4500
FUNCTION Loop: On/Off
LAYOUT   Floor Only
UNLOCK 20
VISION 2/5
CATCH   2/5
SIZE   S

Moray Eel
🔘 2000
FUNCTION Loop: On/Off
LAYOUT   Platform
UNLOCK 20
VISION 3/5
CATCH   4/5
SIZE   E

Ocean Sunfish
🔘 4000
FUNCTION Animates (Loop)
LAYOUT   Floor Only
UNLOCK 20
VISION 1/5
CATCH   2/5
SIZE   SH

Pond Smelt
🔘 400
FUNCTION Animates (Loop)
LAYOUT   Floor & Tabletop
UNLOCK 0
VISION 4/5
CATCH   4/5
SIZE   S

Ray
🔘 3000
FUNCTION Loop: On/Off
LAYOUT   Platform
UNLOCK 20
VISION 3/5
CATCH   4/5
SIZE   XL

Napoleonfish
🔘 10,000
FUNCTION Loop: On/Off
LAYOUT   Platform
UNLOCK 50
VISION 3/5
CATCH   2/5
SIZE   XXL

Olive Flounder
🔘 800
FUNCTION Loop: Trigger (On/Off)
LAYOUT   Platform
UNLOCK 0
VISION 2/5
CATCH   3/5
SIZE   XL

Pop-eyed Goldfish
🔘 1300
FUNCTION Animates (Loop)
LAYOUT   Floor & Tabletop
UNLOCK 0
VISION 3/5
CATCH   4/5
SIZE   XS

Red Snapper
🔘 3000
FUNCTION Loop: On/Off
LAYOUT   Platform & Tabletop
UNLOCK 0
VISION 3/5
CATCH   2/5
SIZE   L

Neon Tetra
🔘 500
FUNCTION Loop: On/Off
LAYOUT   Floor & Tabletop
UNLOCK 0
VISION 3/5
CATCH   4/5
SIZE   XS

Pale Chub
🔘 200
FUNCTION Animates (Loop)
LAYOUT   Floor & Tabletop
UNLOCK 0
VISION 4/5
CATCH   4/5
SIZE   XS

Puffer Fish
🔘 250
FUNCTION Loop: Trigger (On/Off)
LAYOUT   Platform & Tabletop
UNLOCK 0
VISION 3/5
CATCH   4/5
SIZE   M

Ribbon Eel
🔘 600
FUNCTION Loop: On/Off
LAYOUT   Platform
UNLOCK 0
VISION 1/5
CATCH   2/5
SIZE   E

Saddled Bichir

💿 4000

FUNCTION	Loop: On/Off	
LAYOUT	Platform	

UNLOCK 20
VISION 2/5
CATCH 2/5
SIZE L

Sea Horse

💿 1100

FUNCTION	Loop: On/Off	
LAYOUT	Floor & Tabletop	

UNLOCK 0
VISION 2/5
CATCH 3/5
SIZE XS

Sturgeon

💿 10,000

FUNCTION	Loop: On/Off	(mouth)
LAYOUT	Platform	

UNLOCK 20
VISION 1/5
CATCH 1/5
SIZE XXL

Tilapia

💿 800

FUNCTION	Loop: On/Off	
LAYOUT	Platform & Tabletop	

UNLOCK 0
VISION 3/5
CATCH 2/5
SIZE M

Salmon

💿 700

FUNCTION	Loop: On/Off	(mouth)
LAYOUT	Platform	

UNLOCK 0
VISION 3/5
CATCH 3/5
SIZE L

Snapping Turtle

💿 5000

FUNCTION	Interact (Loop On/Off)	
LAYOUT	Floor & Tabletop	

UNLOCK 0
VISION 3/5
CATCH 2/5
SIZE L

Suckerfish

💿 1500

FUNCTION	Loop: On/Off	
LAYOUT	Platform & Tabletop	

UNLOCK 20
VISION 5/5
CATCH 5/5
SIZE SH

Tuna

💿 7000

FUNCTION	Loop: On/Off	(pier)
LAYOUT	Platform	

UNLOCK 50
VISION 2/5
CATCH 1/5
SIZE XXL

Saw Shark

💿 12,000

FUNCTION	Loop: On/Off	
LAYOUT	Platform	

UNLOCK 50
VISION 1/5
CATCH 2/5
SIZE SH

Soft-shelled Turtle

💿 3750

FUNCTION	Animates (Loop)	
LAYOUT	Floor & Tabletop	

UNLOCK 20
VISION 2/5
CATCH 2/5
SIZE L

Surgeonfish

💿 1000

FUNCTION	Loop: On/Off	
LAYOUT	Floor & Tabletop	

UNLOCK 0
VISION 3/5
CATCH 4/5
SIZE S

Whale Shark

💿 13,000

FUNCTION	Animates (Loop)	
LAYOUT	Floor Only	

UNLOCK 50
VISION 1/5
CATCH 1/5
SIZE SH

Sea Bass

💿 400

FUNCTION	Loop: On/Off	
LAYOUT	Platform	

UNLOCK 0
VISION 4/5
CATCH 4/5
SIZE XL

Squid

💿 500

FUNCTION	Loop: On/Off	
LAYOUT	Platform & Tabletop	

UNLOCK 0
VISION 4/5
CATCH 4/5
SIZE M

Sweetfish

💿 900

FUNCTION	Loop: On/Off	
LAYOUT	Platform & Tabletop	

UNLOCK 0
VISION 3/5
CATCH 2/5
SIZE M

Yellow Perch

💿 300

FUNCTION	Loop: On/Off	
LAYOUT	Platform & Tabletop	

UNLOCK 0
VISION 2/5
CATCH 3/5
SIZE M

Sea Butterfly

💿 1000

FUNCTION	Loop: Trigger (On/Off)	
LAYOUT	Floor & Tabletop	

UNLOCK 0
VISION 1/5
CATCH 4/5
SIZE XS

Stringfish

💿 15,000

FUNCTION	Loop: On/Off	(on the cliff)
LAYOUT	Platform	

UNLOCK 100
VISION 1/5
CATCH 1/5
SIZE XL

Tadpole

💿 100

FUNCTION	Animates (Loop)	
LAYOUT	Floor & Tabletop	

UNLOCK 0
VISION 5/5
CATCH 4/5
SIZE XS

Zebra Turkeyfish

💿 500

FUNCTION	Loop: On/Off	
LAYOUT	Platform & Tabletop	

UNLOCK 0
VISION 4/5
CATCH 5/5
SIZE M

4

Bugs

I caught a common bluebottle! I'll put it in a rare green jar!

As with fish, some insects are less fussy about where and when they'll appear.

You'll find a wide range of bugs all around the island. The species you'll encounter will vary heavily depending on the season, time of day, rarity and weather. Knowing where to look is also important: many types of bugs will be out in the open, either flying through the air or skittering along the ground, while others can only be found by checking under rocks, or by shaking them from tree branches. Savvy bug hunters know that searching near flowers of a specific color, or even placing rotten turnips on the ground, can sometimes be the key to finding particularly elusive species!

No matter where you find them, these critters can all be caught using your trusty net tool. Some bugs will flee if they sense your presence, so a stealthy approach is often advisable. Be sure to hunt down all seasonal specimens whenever the opportunity presents itself, or it could be quite a while before you get another chance!

Bug Ban

Just like fish, certain types of bugs won't begin appearing until you've caught a fixed total amount during your bug-hunting career. The type and rarity isn't important, but you'll need to successfully meet the quota before some species can spawn. Once you've reached 100 catches total, every species will be unlocked, so we recommend that you nab any bug you come across if you've just started playing! For more details, consult the Bug Compendium table on P.188.

Bug Sightings

Can't find a specific type of bug even when you're sure the season, weather and time of day are all favorable for it to appear? Then you probably aren't hunting in the right spot! This section will teach you about all the possible bug hiding spots and show you just where to look in order to add each specimen to your collection.

Fluttering Freely

🦋 Common Butterfly		🦋 Tiger Butterfly
🦋 Yellow Butterfly		🦟 Mosquito

These bugs can be seen fluttering freely out in the open. Look around your island when all other conditions line up and you're sure to spot one of them soon enough. Mosquitoes will show up at night and might even bite you if you stand still! There's no penalty for being bitten, but you'll want to catch them with your net as they make their approach.

Near Flowers (all colors)

🦋 Monarch Butterfly		🐞 Stinkbug
🦋 Emperor Butterfly		🐞 Ladybug
🦋 Agrias Butterfly		🦋 Paper Kite Butterfly
🦋 Rajah Brooke's Birdwing		🦋 Great Purple Emperor
🦋 Queen Alexandra's Birdwing		🐞 Man-Faced Stink Bug
🐝 Honeybee		🦋 Madagascan Sunset Moth
🦗 Mantis		

Near Flowers (special colors)

🦋 Peacock Butterfly (Blue/Black/Purple flowers)
🦗 Orchid Mantis (White flowers)

The bugs listed here are all attracted to flowers. The breed of flower isn't important, but you'll need to seek out the right kind of color before you can hope to catch them. This means you might have to do a bit of flower breeding to get the color needed to attract a particular specimen to your island. Check the complete insect list starting on P.190 to see exactly which colors you'll need for each bug!

Near Lamps

 Moth

The nocturnal Moths are helplessly drawn to the light produced by the lamps attached to certain buildings on the island. Look for them in the middle of the night near Resident Services, Nook's Cranny, Able Sisters or any of the island resident's houses.

Near Trees

 Walking Leaf

If you spot a leaf icon representing a dropped item near a tree, there's a high probability that you're in the presence of a Walking Leaf! These masters of disguise will remain camouflaged until you get close enough, at which point they'll reveal their true nature and attempt to flee. Ready your net in advance and grab 'em before they have time to escape!

Tree Stumps

Violin Beetle	Jewel Beetle
Citrus Long-Horned Beetle	Rosalia Batesi Beetle

The beetles listed here can only be found on tree stumps left behind after cutting Hardwood, Cedar, or Palm trees. Get your hands dirty and chop down a few trees to attract these specimens to your island!

On Grass, Dirt or Sand

Long Locust	Grasshopper
Migratory Locust	Mole Cricket
Rice Grasshopper	Tiger Beetle
Cricket	Tarantula
Bell Cricket	Scorpion

These bugs can all be found crawling on the ground and shouldn't be too difficult to spot if you're walking around in the right type of soil. Watch out for both the Tarantula and Scorpion if you're hunting during nighttime, though! For more details on these poisonous terrors, visit P.187.

On Tree Trunks

Atlas Moth	Giant Stag
Brown Cicada	Rainbow Stag
Robust Cicada	Horned Dynastid
Giant Cicada	Drone Beetle
Walker Cicada	Cyclommatus Stag
Evening Cicada	Golden Stag
Cicada Shell	Horned Atlas
Walking Stick	Horned Elephant
Earth-boring Dung Beetle	Horned Hercules
Scarab Beetle	Goliath Beetle
Miyama Stag	Giraffe Stag
Saw Stag	Blue Weevil Beetle

These critters can all be found clinging to the trunks of either Hardwood, Cedar or Palm trees. If all other conditions are favorable, look around for the right type of tree and with a bit of patience you'll eventually spot the specimen you're looking for.

Shaking Trees

Spider	Bagworm

Give either Hardwood or Cedar trees a vigorous shake and there's a possibility that a spider or bagworm will briefly drop down from a thread. Quickly equip your net and catch them before they hide back in the tree's foliage!

Wasp Nest

 Wasp

Spiders and bagworms aren't the only bugs you might encounter when shaking down Hardwood or Cedar trees. Watch out when a wasp nest hits the ground, since an angry swarm of wasps will soon be heading directly for you! For tips on how to catch these nasty customers, turn to P.187.

Near Water

 Red Dragonfly   Firefly

 Darner Dragonfly   Damselfly

 Banded Dragonfly

Search for these species near bodies of freshwater water such as ponds and rivers when all other conditions are favorable. With a bit of luck the specimen you're looking will be flying in the vicinity.

Skimming on Water

 Giant Water Bug   Diving Beetle

 Pondskater

These aquatic bugs love nothing more than to swim on the surface of pond or river water. Wait for these pond-dwellers to swim near the edge and snatch them up with your net when they get close enough! True to its name, the Diving Beetle can even submerge itself, where it'll temporarily appear as a fish shadow. It'll eventually resurface, and that's when you should also snatch it with your net!

Near Trash

 Fly

Another reliable means of attracting Flies consists of placing down trash items such as Boots, Old Tires or Empty Cans on the ground. They won't be able to resist the bait and you'll soon be able to swipe one up using your net!

Under Rocks

 Pill Bug   Centipede

Pill Bugs and Centipedes prefer to hide in the moist soil found directly under rocks. To forcefully evict these critters from their homes, you'll need to bust out your trusty shovel and hit the rock to jostle them out. Be careful not to step on them as they attempt to scurry away or they'll disappear!

On Seaside Rocks

 Wharf Roach

Wharf Roaches like to hang out atop the flat rock formations that can be found along your island's coastline. These bugs are quite a rare find, however, so stay on the lookout and you'll be able to catch one sooner or later!

On Rotten Turnips

 Ant   Fly

Ants and Flies are both drawn to the pungent aroma of rotten turnips. To ensure that your turnips are well past their expiration date, leave some on the ground and simply wait for a week to pass by. If all other conditions are favorable, you'll soon find a bunch of Ants swarming over the turnip or some Flies buzzing around it.

On Rocks

 Snail

Snails can be seen slowly crawling atop one of the grey rocks used for harvesting materials. There's a maximum of six of these rocks on your island, so make sure the conditions are favorable and check each of them. When it rains, snails can also be found on shrubs, if you've bought some from Leif. Remember you can head to www.future-press.com/AC for updated content, including deatails on Leif.

Rolling Snowballs

 Dung Beetle

These unique beetles are obsessed with pushing snowballs around using their powerful hind legs. When the ground is covered with a layer of snow, look around your island and there's a good chance you'll spot one of these critters happily rolling a snowball!

On Beach

 Hermit Crab

The Hermit Crab will first appear as an ordinary shell on the beach. The big tip-off to this little disguise is that the shell will wiggle a little when you get close. Get too close and it'll get scared and attempt to flee. Be quick and catch it with your net before it has a chance to disappear!

On Residents

 Flea

Unfortunate residents can sometimes become infested by these pests. They're small and hard to see, but you'll spot little black dots bouncing off an islander. To catch a Flea, raise your net and swing it right down on the islander's head. Don't worry! They won't be upset about being whacked. They'll be pretty thankful for the pest control, so long as you keep it a secret.

Hazardous Critters

Tarantulas and scorpions are dangerous nocturnal critters that can show up on grass, dirt, or sand between 7PM to 4AM. Tarantulas are only active during spring and winter, while scorpions only come out during summer and autumn. Encounters with these poisonous terrors are quite rare, but don't let them sting you or you'll instantly faint and be sent back home. There's no real penalty for fainting, though your assailant will have left the scene of the crime and you'll miss out on the opportunity to add it to your collection.

Thankfully, tarantulas and scorpions won't behave aggressively unless they see you holding a net. Try to stealthily approach one of these critters from behind, then quickly equip your net and hold Ⓐ to sneak into range and catch it. Don't dilly-dally for too long, though, since tarantulas and scorpions will disappear if you don't quickly make your move!

Tarantulas know when you're trying to catch them, and will react accordingly.

If you get spotted, you'll have a brief window of opportunity to swipe with your net and catch these bad bugs before they get a chance to attack. If a tarantula or scorpion begins chasing you, your best bet is to run away as fast as you can. The maintained distance between yourself and your pursuer should give you just enough time to perform a quick 180-degree turn followed by a swipe of your net to turn the tables and nab them.

Wasps

Be careful when you're chopping wood or shaking trees—wasps do not appreciate having their home knocked to the ground. Unlike bees, wasps will chase you and leave you with a nasty sting unless you manage to get indoors quickly. If you're stung twice in a day, they'll even knock you out! Wasps can't sting you while you're in your inventory menu. If you're quick and accurate, you can bust out your net using the menu and instantly swipe in the swarm's direction to catch it. Let the hunter become the hunted!

I caught a wasp!
That's gotta sting...

Ow! Ow ow ow...
I got stung by wasps!

Insect Occurrences

The following pages list all bugs and compile the most useful information about each of them, such as where and when to look for them, how much they are worth and how they work when placed as a decorative object. Their size when placed as an object is always 1x1, so it's not shown in their separate entries. The huge chart here shows when you can expect to find each bug—it lists their chances of appearing at different times of day during each month of the year.

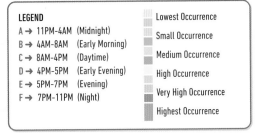

LEGEND
A → 11PM-4AM (Midnight)
B → 4AM-8AM (Early Morning)
C → 8AM-4PM (Daytime)
D → 4PM-5PM (Early Evening)
E → 5PM-7PM (Evening)
F → 7PM-11PM (Night)

Lowest Occurrence
Small Occurrence
Medium Occurrence
High Occurrence
Very High Occurrence
Highest Occurrence

| Northern Hemisphere | JAN | FEB | MAR | APR | MAY | JUN | JUL | AUG | SEP | OCT | NOV | DEC |
| Southern Hemisphere | JUL | AUG | SEP | OCT | NOV | DEC | JAN | FEB | MAR | APR | MAY | JUN |

Agrias Butterfly
Ant → P.186
Atlas Moth
Bagworm
Banded Dragonfly
Bell Cricket
Blue Weevil Beetle
Brown Cicada
Centipede
Cicada Shell
Citrus Long-horned Beetle
Common Bluebottle
Common Butterfly
Cricket
Cyclommatus Stag
Damselfly
Darner Dragonfly
Diving Beetle
Drone Beetle
Dung Beetle
Earth-boring Dung Beetle
Emperor Butterfly
Evening Cicada
Firefly
Flea
Fly → P.186
Giant Cicada
Giant Stag
Giant Water Bug
Giraffe Stag
Golden Stag
Goliath Beetle
Grasshopper
Great Purple Emperor
Hermit Crab
Honeybee
Horned Atlas
Horned Dynastid
Horned Elephant
Horned Hercules

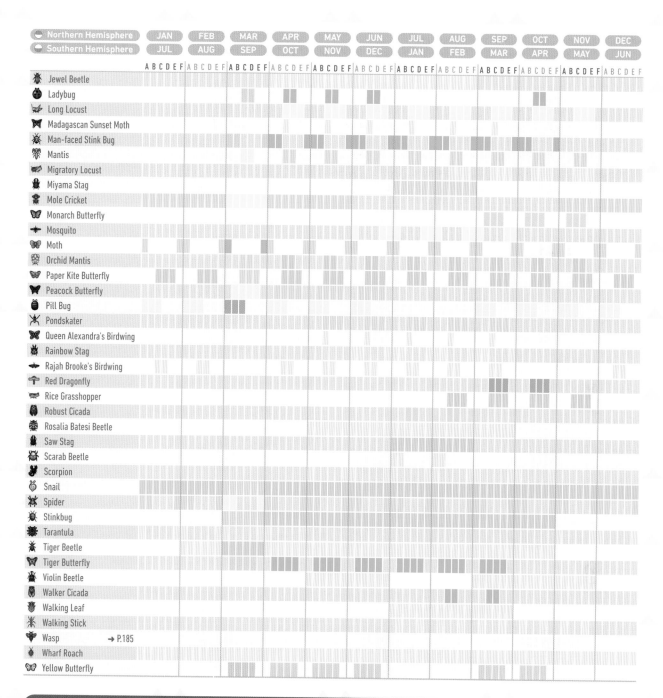

Jewel Beetle
Ladybug
Long Locust
Madagascan Sunset Moth
Man-faced Stink Bug
Mantis
Migratory Locust
Miyama Stag
Mole Cricket
Monarch Butterfly
Mosquito
Moth
Orchid Mantis
Paper Kite Butterfly
Peacock Butterfly
Pill Bug
Pondskater
Queen Alexandra's Birdwing
Rainbow Stag
Rajah Brooke's Birdwing
Red Dragonfly
Rice Grasshopper
Robust Cicada
Rosalia Batesi Beetle
Saw Stag
Scarab Beetle
Scorpion
Snail
Spider
Stinkbug
Tarantula
Tiger Beetle
Tiger Butterfly
Violin Beetle
Walker Cicada
Walking Leaf
Walking Stick
Wasp → P.185
Wharf Roach
Yellow Butterfly

Insect List

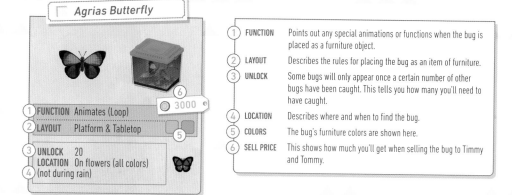

Agrias Butterfly

1. FUNCTION Animates (Loop)
2. LAYOUT Platform & Tabletop
3. UNLOCK 20
   LOCATION On flowers (all colors)
4. (not during rain)
6. ● 3000 ●

1. FUNCTION Points out any special animations or functions when the bug is placed as a furniture object.
2. LAYOUT Describes the rules for placing the bug as an item of furniture.
3. UNLOCK Some bugs will only appear once a certain number of other bugs have been caught. This tells you how many you'll need to have caught.
4. LOCATION Describes where and when to find the bug.
5. COLORS The bug's furniture colors are shown here.
6. SELL PRICE This shows how much you'll get when selling the bug to Timmy and Tommy.

Agrias Butterfly
FUNCTION Animates (Loop)
LAYOUT Platform & Tabletop
3000
UNLOCK 20
LOCATION On flowers (all colors) (not during rain)

Bell Cricket
FUNCTION Audio: Chirps
LAYOUT Floor & Tabletop
430
UNLOCK 0
LOCATION On Grass (not during rain)

Citrus Long-horned Beetle
FUNCTION Animates (Loop)
LAYOUT Floor & Tabletop
350
UNLOCK 0
LOCATION Trees stumps (Hardwood/Cedar/Palm) (not during rain)

Damselfly
FUNCTION Animates (Loop)
LAYOUT Platform & Tabletop
500
UNLOCK 0
LOCATION Near Water (not during rain)

Ant
FUNCTION Animates (Loop)
LAYOUT Floor & Tabletop
80
UNLOCK 0
LOCATION Rotten Turnips (any weather)

Blue Weevil Beetle
FUNCTION Animates (Loop)
LAYOUT Floor & Tabletop
800
UNLOCK 0
LOCATION Adult Trees (Palm) (any weather)

Common Bluebottle
FUNCTION Animates (Loop)
LAYOUT Platform & Tabletop
300
UNLOCK 0
LOCATION Any (not during rain)

Darner Dragonfly
FUNCTION Animates (Loop)
LAYOUT Platform & Tabletop
230
UNLOCK 0
LOCATION Near Water (not during rain)

Atlas Moth
FUNCTION Animates (Loop)
LAYOUT Platform & Tabletop
3000
UNLOCK 20
LOCATION Adult Trees (Hardwood/Cedar/Palm) (any weather)

Brown Cicada
FUNCTION Audio: Chirps
LAYOUT Platform & Tabletop
250
UNLOCK 0
LOCATION Adult Trees (Hardwood/Cedar) (any weather)

Common Butterfly
FUNCTION Animates (Loop)
LAYOUT Floor & Tabletop
160
UNLOCK 0
LOCATION Any (not during rain)

Diving Beetle
FUNCTION Interact (Loop On/Off)
LAYOUT Floor & Tabletop
800
UNLOCK 0
LOCATION Skimming on Water (any weather)

Bagworm
FUNCTION Animates (Loop)
LAYOUT Platform & Tabletop
600
UNLOCK 0
LOCATION Adult Trees (Hardwood/Cedar) (any weather)

Centipede
FUNCTION Animates (Loop)
LAYOUT Floor & Tabletop
300
UNLOCK 0
LOCATION Rocks (any weather)

Cricket
FUNCTION Audio: Chirps
LAYOUT Floor & Tabletop
130
UNLOCK 0
LOCATION On Grass (not during rain)

Drone Beetle
FUNCTION Animates (Loop)
LAYOUT Floor & Tabletop
200
UNLOCK 0
LOCATION Adult Trees (Hardwood/Cedar/Palm) (any weather)

Banded Dragonfly
FUNCTION Animates (Loop)
LAYOUT Platform & Tabletop
4500
UNLOCK 50
LOCATION Near Water (not during rain)

Cicada Shell
FUNCTION Animates (Loop)
LAYOUT Floor & Tabletop
10
UNLOCK 50
LOCATION Adult Trees (Hardwood/Cedar) (any weather)

Cyclommatus Stag
FUNCTION Animates (Loop)
LAYOUT Platform & Tabletop
8000
UNLOCK 100
LOCATION Adult Trees (Palm) (any weather)

Dung Beetle
FUNCTION Animates (Loop)
LAYOUT Platform & Tabletop
3000
UNLOCK 0
LOCATION Snowballs (any weather)

Earth-boring Dung Beetle
FUNCTION	Animates (Loop)
LAYOUT	Floor & Tabletop

UNLOCK 0
LOCATION Adult Trees (Hardwood/Cedar/Palm) (any weather)
💰 300

Fly
FUNCTION	Interact (Loop On/Off)
LAYOUT	Floor & Tabletop

UNLOCK 0
LOCATION Trash/Rotten Tunips (any weather)
💰 60

Golden Stag
FUNCTION	Animates (Loop)
LAYOUT	Platform & Tabletop

UNLOCK 100
LOCATION Adult Trees (Palm) (any weather)
💰 12,000

Honeybee
FUNCTION	Animates (Loop)
LAYOUT	Floor & Tabletop

UNLOCK 0
LOCATION On flowers (all colors) (not during rain)
💰 200

Emperor Butterfly
FUNCTION	Animates (Loop)
LAYOUT	Platform & Tabletop

UNLOCK 20
LOCATION On flowers (all colors) (not during rain)
💰 4000

Giant Cicada
FUNCTION	Audio: Chirps
LAYOUT	Platform & Tabletop

UNLOCK 20
LOCATION Adult Trees (Hardwood/Cedar) (any weather)
💰 500

Goliath Beetle
FUNCTION	Animates (Loop)
LAYOUT	Platform & Tabletop

UNLOCK 100
LOCATION Adult Trees (Palm) (any weather)
💰 8000

Horned Atlas
FUNCTION	Animates (Loop)
LAYOUT	Platform & Tabletop

UNLOCK 100
LOCATION Adult Trees (Palm) (any weather)
💰 8000

Evening Cicada
FUNCTION	Audio: Chirps
LAYOUT	Platform & Tabletop

UNLOCK 0
LOCATION Adult Trees (Hardwood/Cedar) (any weather)
💰 550

Giant Stag
FUNCTION	Animates (Loop)
LAYOUT	Platform & Tabletop

UNLOCK 50
LOCATION Adult Trees (Hardwood/Cedar/Palm) (any weather)
💰 10,000

Grasshopper
FUNCTION	Audio: Chirps
LAYOUT	Floor & Tabletop

UNLOCK 0
LOCATION On Grass (not during rain)
💰 160

Horned Dynastid
FUNCTION	Animates (Loop)
LAYOUT	Platform & Tabletop

UNLOCK 0
LOCATION Adult Trees (Hardwood/Cedar/Palm) (any weather)
💰 1350

Firefly
FUNCTION	Animates (Loop)
LAYOUT	Floor & Tabletop

UNLOCK 0
LOCATION Near Water (not during rain)
💰 300

Giant Water Bug
FUNCTION	Interact (Loop On/Off)
LAYOUT	Floor & Tabletop

UNLOCK 50
LOCATION Skimming on Water (any weather)
💰 2000

Great Purple Emperor
FUNCTION	Animates (Loop)
LAYOUT	Platform & Tabletop

UNLOCK 50
LOCATION On flowers (all colors) (not during rain)
💰 3000

Horned Elephant
FUNCTION	Animates (Loop)
LAYOUT	Platform & Tabletop

UNLOCK 100
LOCATION Adult Trees (Palm) (any weather)
💰 8000

Flea
FUNCTION	Interact (Loop On/Off)
LAYOUT	Floor & Tabletop

UNLOCK 0
LOCATION On Villagers (any weather)
💰 70

Giraffe Stag
FUNCTION	Animates (Loop)
LAYOUT	Platform & Tabletop

UNLOCK 100
LOCATION Adult Trees (Palm) (any weather)
💰 12,000

Hermit Crab
FUNCTION	Animates (Loop)
LAYOUT	Platform & Tabletop

UNLOCK 0
LOCATION Beach (any weather)
💰 1000

Horned Hercules
FUNCTION	Animates (Loop)
LAYOUT	Platform & Tabletop

UNLOCK 100
LOCATION Adult Trees (Palm) (any weather)
💰 12,000

4

Jewel Beetle
FUNCTION	Animates (Loop)
LAYOUT	Platform & Tabletop

UNLOCK 20
LOCATION Trees stumps (Hardwood/Cedar/Palm) (not during rain)

2400

Mantis
FUNCTION	Animates (Loop)
LAYOUT	Platform & Tabletop

UNLOCK 0
LOCATION On flowers (all colors) (not during rain)

430

Mosquito
FUNCTION	Interact (Loop On/Off)
LAYOUT	Floor & Tabletop

UNLOCK 0
LOCATION Any (not during rain)

130

Pill Bug
FUNCTION	Animates (Loop)
LAYOUT	Floor & Tabletop

UNLOCK 0
LOCATION Rocks (any weather)

250

Ladybug
FUNCTION	Animates (Loop)
LAYOUT	Floor & Tabletop

UNLOCK 0
LOCATION On flowers (all colors) (not during rain)

200

Migratory Locust
FUNCTION	Animates (Loop)
LAYOUT	Platform & Tabletop

UNLOCK 20
LOCATION On Grass (any weather)

600

Moth
FUNCTION	Animates (Loop)
LAYOUT	Floor & Tabletop

UNLOCK 0
LOCATION Near lamps (not during rain)

130

Pondskater
FUNCTION	Interact (Loop On/Off)
LAYOUT	Floor & Tabletop

UNLOCK 0
LOCATION Skimming on Water (any weather)

130

Long Locust
FUNCTION	Animates (Loop)
LAYOUT	Platform & Tabletop

UNLOCK 0
LOCATION On Grass (any weather)

200

Miyama Stag
FUNCTION	Animates (Loop)
LAYOUT	Platform & Tabletop

UNLOCK 0
LOCATION Adult Trees (Hardwood/Cedar/Palm) (any weather)

1000

Orchid Mantis
FUNCTION	Animates (Loop)
LAYOUT	Platform & Tabletop

UNLOCK 20
LOCATION On flowers (White) (not during rain)

2400

Queen Alexandra's Birdwing
FUNCTION	Animates (Loop)
LAYOUT	Platform & Tabletop

UNLOCK 50
LOCATION On flowers (all colors) (not during rain)

4000

Madagascan Sunset Moth
FUNCTION	Animates (Loop)
LAYOUT	Platform & Tabletop

UNLOCK 20
LOCATION On flowers (all colors) (not during rain)

2500

Mole Cricket
FUNCTION	Interact (Loop On/Off)
LAYOUT	Platform & Tabletop

UNLOCK 0
LOCATION On Grass, Dirt, or Sand (any weather)

500

Paper Kite Butterfly
FUNCTION	Animates (Loop)
LAYOUT	Platform & Tabletop

UNLOCK 0
LOCATION On flowers (all colors) (not during rain)

1000

Rainbow Stag
FUNCTION	Animates (Loop)
LAYOUT	Platform & Tabletop

UNLOCK 50
LOCATION Adult Trees (Hardwood/Cedar/Palm) (any weather)

6000

Man-faced Stink Bug
FUNCTION	Animates (Loop)
LAYOUT	Platform & Tabletop

UNLOCK 20
LOCATION On flowers (all colors) (not during rain)

1000

Monarch Butterfly
FUNCTION	Animates (Loop)
LAYOUT	Platform & Tabletop

UNLOCK 0
LOCATION On flowers (all colors) (not during rain)

140

Peacock Butterfly
FUNCTION	Animates (Loop)
LAYOUT	Platform & Tabletop

UNLOCK 20
LOCATION On flowers (Blue/Black/Purple) (not during rain)

2500

Rajah Brooke's Birdwing
FUNCTION	Animates (Loop)
LAYOUT	Platform & Tabletop

UNLOCK 20
LOCATION On flowers (all colors) (not during rain)

2500

Red Dragonfly
FUNCTION	Animates (Loop)
LAYOUT	Platform & Tabletop

UNLOCK 0
LOCATION Near Water (not during rain)
180

Scarab Beetle
FUNCTION	Animates (Loop)
LAYOUT	Platform & Tabletop

UNLOCK 50
LOCATION Adult Trees (Hardwood/Cedar/Palm) (any weather)
10,000

Tarantula
FUNCTION	Animates (Loop)
LAYOUT	Platform & Tabletop

UNLOCK 0
LOCATION On Grass, Dirt or Sand (any weather)
8000

Walking Leaf
FUNCTION	Animates (Loop)
LAYOUT	Platform & Tabletop

UNLOCK 20
LOCATION Near Trees (any weather)
600

Rice Grasshopper
FUNCTION	Animates (Loop)
LAYOUT	Floor & Tabletop

UNLOCK 0
LOCATION On Grass (any weather)
400

Scorpion
FUNCTION	Animates (Loop)
LAYOUT	Platform & Tabletop

UNLOCK 0
LOCATION On Grass, Dirt or Sand (any weather)
8000

Tiger Beetle
FUNCTION	Animates (Loop)
LAYOUT	Floor & Tabletop

UNLOCK 20
LOCATION On Grass (not during rain)
1500

Walking Stick
FUNCTION	Interact (Loop On/Off)
LAYOUT	Platform & Tabletop

UNLOCK 20
LOCATION Adult Trees (Hardwood/Cedar/Palm) (any weather)
600

Robust Cicada
FUNCTION	Audio: Chirps
LAYOUT	Platform & Tabletop

UNLOCK 0
LOCATION Adult Trees (Hardwood/Cedar) (any weather)
300

Snail
FUNCTION	Animates (Loop)
LAYOUT	Floor & Tabletop

UNLOCK 0
LOCATION On Rocks (rain only)
250

Tiger Butterfly
FUNCTION	Animates (Loop)
LAYOUT	Platform & Tabletop

UNLOCK 0
LOCATION Any (not during rain)
240

Wasp
FUNCTION	Animates (Loop)
LAYOUT	Platform & Tabletop

UNLOCK 0
LOCATION Wasp Nest (any weather)
2500

Rosalia Batesi Beetle
FUNCTION	Animates (Loop)
LAYOUT	Platform & Tabletop

UNLOCK 20
LOCATION Trees stumps (Hardwood/Cedar/Palm) (not during rain)
3000

Spider
FUNCTION	Animates (Loop)
LAYOUT	Platform & Tabletop

UNLOCK 0
LOCATION Adult Trees (Hardwood/Cedar) (any weather)
600

Violin Beetle
FUNCTION	Animates (Loop)
LAYOUT	Platform & Tabletop

UNLOCK 0
LOCATION Trees stumps (Hardwood/Cedar/Palm) (not during rain)
450

Wharf Roach
FUNCTION	Animates (Loop)
LAYOUT	Floor & Tabletop

UNLOCK 0
LOCATION Coastal Rocks (any weather)
200

Saw Stag
FUNCTION	Animates (Loop)
LAYOUT	Platform & Tabletop

UNLOCK 0
LOCATION Adult Trees (Hardwood/Cedar/Palm) (any weather)
2000

Stinkbug
FUNCTION	Animates (Loop)
LAYOUT	Floor & Tabletop

UNLOCK 0
LOCATION On flowers (all colors) (not during rain)
120

Walker Cicada
FUNCTION	Audio: Chirps
LAYOUT	Platform & Tabletop

UNLOCK 0
LOCATION Adult Trees (Hardwood/Cedar) (any weather)
400

Yellow Butterfly
FUNCTION	Animates (Loop)
LAYOUT	Floor & Tabletop

UNLOCK 0
LOCATION Any (not during rain)
160

4

Fossils

As you explore the island, you might notice small, star-shaped cracks in the ground. If you use a shovel to dig beneath them, you will often unearth fossils belonging to all kinds of prehistoric life.

Before these ancient remains can be properly identified, however, you'll first need to seek out the keen eye of an expert paleontologist. Bring any fossils you find to Blathers and he'll give you the lowdown on what you've discovered. Once he's appraised a fossil, you'll have the choice of either holding on to it or donating it to the museum for all to admire. Fossils are often worth quite a few Bells, but we recommend donating every new find to the museum before selling any duplicates.

> "Empty display cases will not do, I'm told. Display cases with something to display— THAT is another matter!"

When Do Fossils Appear?

Every day at 5AM, between two and four newly-generated fossils can appear somewhere on your island. If you don't collect them all, you'll end up with a maximum of six fossils waiting to be dug up. Want to quickly kickstart your collection? More buried fossils can also be unearthed by visiting other islands via the Mystery Tour—even if you've already dug up all of those available on yours. Remember that seeking out buried fossils every day is the most efficient way to work towards completing your museum collection!

Fossil List

Fossils are classified into two distinct categories: standalone or part of a set. Standalone fossils typically depict a smaller lifeform and take up only one exhibit slot, while fossils belonging to a set will be assembled together to form an entire dinosaur skeleton. Here we'll show all of them along with some useful information about each one. Standalone fossils are always 1x1 when placed as furniture, while dinosaur skeleton pieces are always 2x2. The only exception to this is the dunkleosteus skeleton, which is 2x2 despite only being one piece.

dunkleosteus	
	④ 3500
① FUNCTION	None
② LAYOUT	Floor only ③

①	FUNCTION	Points out any special animations or functions when the fossil is placed as a furniture object.
②	LAYOUT	Describes the rules for placing the fossil as an item of furniture.
③	COLORS	The fossil's furniture colors are shown here.
④	SELL PRICE	This shows how much you'll get when selling the appraised fossil to Timmy and Tommy.

● **Donating Fossils**

The Museum → P.38

acanthostega
FUNCTION None
LAYOUT Platform & Tabletop
2000

anomalocaris
FUNCTION None
LAYOUT Platform & Tabletop
2000

coprolite
FUNCTION None
LAYOUT Platform & Tabletop
1100

juramaia
FUNCTION None
LAYOUT Platform & Tabletop
1500

amber
FUNCTION None
LAYOUT Platform & Tabletop
1200

archaeopteryx
FUNCTION None
LAYOUT Platform & Tabletop
1300

dinosaur track
FUNCTION None
LAYOUT Platform & Tabletop
1000

myllokunmingia
FUNCTION None
LAYOUT Platform & Tabletop
1500

ammonite
FUNCTION None
LAYOUT Platform & Tabletop
1100

australopith
FUNCTION None
LAYOUT Platform & Tabletop
1100

eusthenopteron
FUNCTION None
LAYOUT Platform & Tabletop
2000

shark-tooth pattern
FUNCTION None
LAYOUT Platform & Tabletop
1000

trilobite
FUNCTION None
LAYOUT Platform & Tabletop
1300

ankylosaurus
ankylo skull   ankylo torso   ankylo tail
3500   3000   2500
FUNCTION None
LAYOUT Floor only

archelon
archelon skull   archelon tail
4000   3500
FUNCTION None
LAYOUT Floor only

dunkleosteus
FUNCTION None
LAYOUT Floor only
3500

brachiosaurus
brachio skull   brachio chest   brachio pelvis   brachio tail
6000   5500   5000   5500
FUNCTION None
LAYOUT Floor only

deinonychus
deinony torso   deinony tail
3000   2500
FUNCTION None
LAYOUT Floor only

4

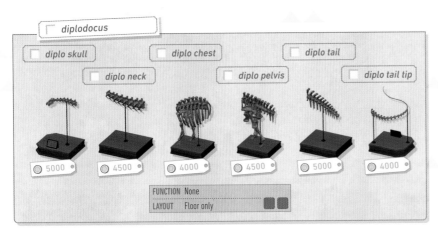

☐ diplodocus

☐ diplo skull   ☐ diplo chest   ☐ diplo tail

☐ diplo neck   ☐ diplo pelvis   ☐ diplo tail tip

● 5000 ● 4500 ● 4000 ● 4500 ● 5000 ● 4000

FUNCTION	None
LAYOUT	Floor only

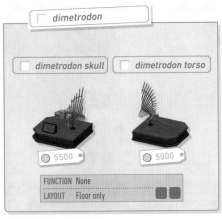

☐ dimetrodon

☐ dimetrodon skull   ☐ dimetrodon torso

● 5500   ● 5000

FUNCTION	None
LAYOUT	Floor only

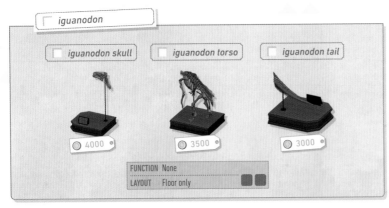

☐ iguanodon

☐ iguanodon skull ☐ iguanodon torso ☐ iguanodon tail

● 4000   ● 3500   ● 3000

FUNCTION	None
LAYOUT	Floor only

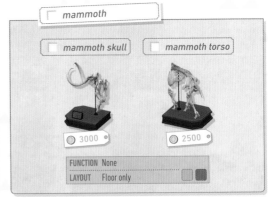

☐ mammoth

☐ mammoth skull   ☐ mammoth torso

● 3000   ● 2500

FUNCTION	None
LAYOUT	Floor only

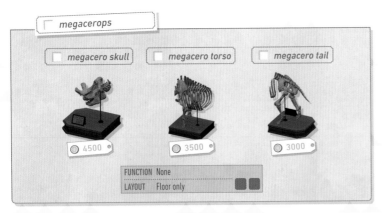

☐ megacerops

☐ megacero skull ☐ megacero torso ☐ megacero tail

● 4500   ● 3500   ● 3000

FUNCTION	None
LAYOUT	Floor only

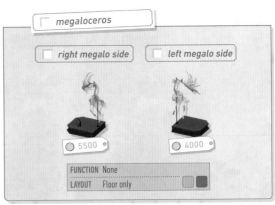

☐ megaloceros

☐ right megalo side   ☐ left megalo side

● 5500   ● 4000

FUNCTION	None
LAYOUT	Floor only

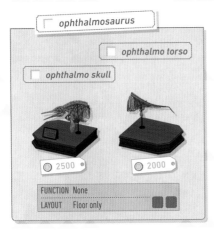

☐ ophthalmosaurus

☐ ophthalmo torso

☐ ophthalmo skull

● 2500   ● 2000

FUNCTION	None
LAYOUT	Floor only

☐ pachycephalosaurus

☐ pachy tail

☐ pachy skull

● 4000   ● 3500

FUNCTION	Skull: Interact (On/Off)
LAYOUT	Floor only

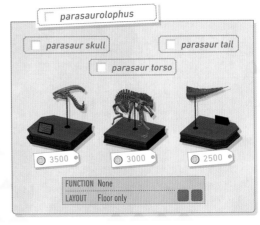

☐ parasaurolophus

☐ parasaur skull   ☐ parasaur tail

☐ parasaur torso

● 3500   ● 3000   ● 2500

FUNCTION	None
LAYOUT	Floor only

plesiosaurus

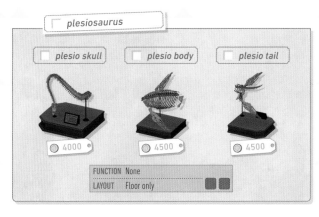

☐ plesio skull	☐ plesio body	☐ plesio tail
4000	4500	4500

FUNCTION None
LAYOUT Floor only

quetzalcoatlus

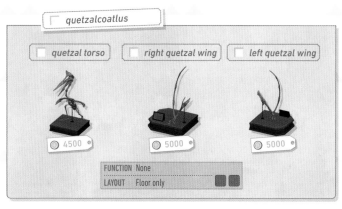

☐ quetzal torso	☐ right quetzal wing	☐ left quetzal wing
4500	5000	5000

FUNCTION None
LAYOUT Floor only

pteranodon

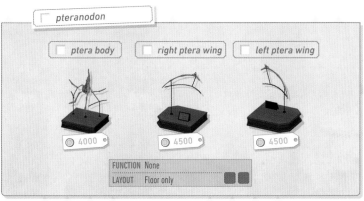

☐ ptera body	☐ right ptera wing	☐ left ptera wing
4000	4500	4500

FUNCTION None
LAYOUT Floor only

sabertooth Tiger

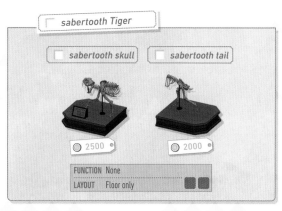

☐ sabertooth skull	☐ sabertooth tail
2500	2000

FUNCTION None
LAYOUT Floor only

spinosaurus

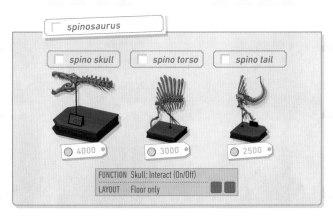

☐ spino skull	☐ spino torso	☐ spino tail
4000	3000	2500

FUNCTION Skull: Interact (On/Off)
LAYOUT Floor only

stegosaurus

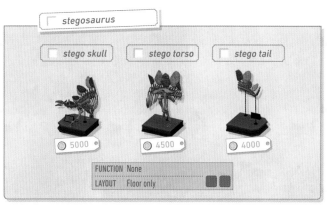

☐ stego skull	☐ stego torso	☐ stego tail
5000	4500	4000

FUNCTION None
LAYOUT Floor only

T. rex

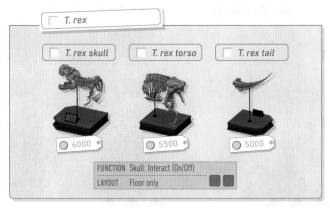

☐ T. rex skull	☐ T. rex torso	☐ T. rex tail
6000	5500	5000

FUNCTION Skull: Interact (On/Off)
LAYOUT Floor only

triceratops

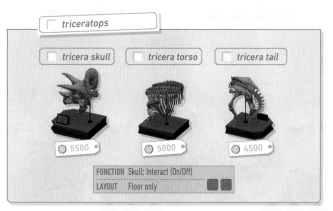

☐ tricera skull	☐ tricera torso	☐ tricera tail
5500	5000	4500

FUNCTION Skull: Interact (On/Off)
LAYOUT Floor only

4

Seasonal Tournaments

Once the Resident Services tent has been up-graded to a fully fledged building, C.J and Flick will start to visit your island. These two characters are fish and bug fanatics respectively, and they are responsible for hosting the seasonal Fishing Tourneys and Bug-Off tournaments around the island. These competitions are open to yourself, island residents and any visiting players, so every-body can participate!

The goal of the tournaments is to reel in as many fish or catch as many bugs as possible before the 3 minute time limit ex-pires. Each fish or bug you catch before the timer runs out will give you points that can then be swapped for unique prizes you won't find anywhere else. Be sure to try your hand at these fun optional events whenever they're available!

Entry Fees

Your first entry of the day is always free, but solo players will need to cough up 500 Bells for any subsequent rounds. Entry fees are waived if any players are currently visiting your island, so everybody gets to participate as long as they have a Fishing Rod or Net in their pockets!

Friendly Competition

Invite your friends to join in on the fun! While these tour-naments can certainly spark some friendly competition, there are no losers here—everybody racks up points regardless of who caught the most fish or bugs. And the more participants there are, the easier it becomes to unlock co-op score bonuses! Any player who talks to C.J. or Flick can decide to host a round, at which point every other player currently on the island will automatically participate. If you're currently busy with some other activity and would prefer not to join in, simply ignore the timer and continue going about your business. You'll even get some free points if the group manages to reach the co-op score bonuses!

Flick always seems like he wants to join in the tourney.

Fish Cooler & Bug Cage

The specimens you've caught during a Fishing Tourney or Bug-Off will be temporarily stored in a fish cooler or bug cage located next to the event's stall. These containers can hold a total of 20 spec-imens each, and interacting with them will present you with two options: transferring individual catches to your pockets, or selling them at a staggering 50% markup. Take a brief moment to inspect your haul once a round has ended, since you'll want to avoid selling any species that haven't been donated to the museum yet! Lastly, it's important to remember that every participant will need to empty their cooler or bug cage before another round can begin.

> OK, wanna get your feet wet in the Fishing Tourney? There's no entry fee if off-island visitors are around.

If you know there's a tourney coming up, invite some friends to get rid of the entry fees!

Earning Points

Each fish or bug you catch while the timer is active will reward you with 1 point. Every species is worth the same amount of points, so always aim for quantity instead of quality! A solo bonus is reached once you've personally caught three critters, netting you two additional points once the round ends. It's still possible to obtain this solo bonus even when other players are participating, so always try to catch at least three critters before the timer runs out. When other players are visiting your island, co-op bonuses also become available if a certain number of critters are caught by the group as a whole.

C.J.

OK, so it looks like the total haul for everyone was...7 fish, with a co-op bonus wadin' in at 5 or more fish.

Luckily, C.J.'s maths are up to the job of keeping score.

Total Number of Critters Caught (Solo)	Bonus Pts.
3 +	2
Total Number of Critters Caught (Co-op)	Bonus Pts.
5 ~ 9	5
10 ~ 14	7
15 +	10

Counting Score

The score is tallied once the round ends and you return to Flick or C.J. Let's look at an example scenario to illustrate how points are calculated. Three players participated in this event: a resident and two visitors. The resident player caught 7 fish before the timer ran out, while the group as a whole caught 14 fish total.

Now let's breakdown how many points the resident player has earned:

	Calculation example	Pts
	7 fish caught solo =	7 Pts
	Solo bonus for catching at least 3 fish =	2 Pts
	Co-op bonus for the group catching a total of 14 fish =	7 Pts

I caught a
Rajah Brooke's birdwing!
Gotta keep this up!

Don't panic if your friends are ahead, just look for more bugs!

Doing the math is as simple as adding all three categories together (7+2+7 = 16), which means in this scenario the result would be a total of 16 points! Once you've earned more than 10 points, you can swap them for prizes while the event is active by talking to either Flick or C.J. Both of them will also stick around until 8PM to give you a chance to spend your points after the event concludes at 6PM. Do note that points earned during Fishing Tourneys and Bug-Offs are completely separate and non-interchangeable.

Exchanging 10 points will earn you a randomly chosen reward from a selection of unique bug- or fish-themed items that are only available here. Once you've obtained everything on the list, you'll get a completely random item instead. Try to collect as many unique items as possible before the event ends!

If you play multiple rounds and manage to score lots of points over the course of these events, you might even be eligible to receive a special trophy in the mail based on your performance! Consult the reward section of both the Fishing Tourney and Bug-Off entries on the following pages for a complete list of possible prizes.

Fishing Tourneys

Fishing Tourneys are hosted by C.J and will involve you catching a whole bunch of fish! On specific dates, C.J will set his stall up outside of Resident Services and this is where you'll be able to register for his seasonal Fishing Tourney. To participate in this event, you'll need a Fishing Rod, so make sure you've crafted one of those first. Some great fish-themed prizes are available to be won, so let's get to the rules.

"Way to wreck that seasports challenge! What a haul!"

C.J. is always a gracious and fair tourney organizer.

Rules

Catch as many fish as possible within three minutes! To start, talk to C.J. and select the "Sign me up!" option. The timer will begin counting down as soon as you finish talking and will appear at the top of the screen for all players to see. Fish will spawn as they normally would while the timer is active, but you won't have to worry about reeling in trash or your Fishing Rod breaking until the round is over. The use of fish bait is authorized, so stocking up beforehand can allow you to score a ton of points! Once time is up, a bell will ring to signal the end of the round. Each fish caught will net you some points that can then be traded in for some items by selecting the "Swap my points for swag!" option when talking to C.J.

Event Dates

Fishing Tourneys are held once per season between 9AM and 6PM. Both hemispheres share the same dates:

- 2nd Saturday of April
- 2nd Saturday of July
- 2nd Saturday of October
- 2nd Saturday of January

The forecast will always be bright and sunny during these events, so there's no need to worry about bad weather spoiling the mood!

Reward List (10 points each)

fish-drying rack
fishing-rod stand
anchor statue
fish print
fish rug
fish doorplate
tackle bag (blue)

fresh cooler
fish-print tee
fish wand
fish pochette
fishing bag
fish umbrella
marine pop wall

Trophies

100 Pts.
Bronze fish trophy

200 Pts.
Silver fish trophy

300 Pts.
Gold fish trophy

Have your bait at the ready if you want to good chance at earning lots of points.

Bug-Off

This is the Bug-Off, an event hosted by Flick. As you've probably guessed, the goal of this competition will be to catch lots of bugs that can then be exchanged for unique prizes. On these special occasions, Flick will set his stall up in the plaza outside of Resident Services, where you'll be able to sign up by talking to him. A net is always required to participate in this event, so make sure everybody has crafted one of those first.

"If for some reason you don't want to keep your bugs, I'm happy to libera—BUY them all from you!"

Bug-Off competitions are held four times a year during the span of a four month window. The dates vary depending on which hemisphere your island is located in, but registrations will always be open between 9AM and 6PM. It's possible for a Bug-Off event to be pushed forward to the 3rd Saturday of the month if it interferes with K.K. Slider's appearance. To avoid missing out on the action, check your local bulletin board regularly and pay attention to Isabelle's announcements during scheduled Bug-Off months!

You'll need to empty your bug cage before a new round can begin.

Rules

This event works the same as the Fishing Tourney, with the exception that you will need to catch bugs instead of fish. Catch as many as you can within the 3 minute time limit to earn yourself some fantastic bug-themed prizes. Bugs can still be found in their usual hiding spots throughout the island while the timer is active. You also don't have to be concerned about your net breaking, since that can't happen until the round is over! A bell will ring once the round has come to an end. Every bug you've caught will reward you with points that can be exchanged for prizes by choosing "Swap my points for swag!" at Flick's stall.

Reward List (10 points each)

Termite mound
Toy cockroach
Spider web
Toy centipede
Butterflies wall
Ladybug rug
Spider doorplate

Artisanal bug cage
Bug wand
Bug aloha shirt
Bug cage (green)
Butterfly backpack (pink)
Ladybug umbrella

Trophies

| 100 Pts. | 200 Pts. | 300 Pts. |
| Bronze bug trophy | Silver bug trophy | Gold bug trophy |

Event Dates

Northern Hemisphere		Southern Hemisphere	
Summer	4th Saturday of June	Summer	3rd Saturday of December
Summer	4th Saturday of July	Summer	3rd Saturday of January
Summer	4th Saturday of August	Summer	3rd Saturday of February
Autumn	4th Saturday of September	Autumn	3rd Saturday of March

As with other events, you can expect the weather to always be clear and sunny on the dates where Bug-Off tournaments take place.

4

5

Chapter 5

The Workbench

Having a do-it-yourself mindset is a perfect complement to island living. Deserted islands are well known for their abundance of natural resources, just waiting to be put to use in aid of a fledgling community. The real beauty of your island is that the more lovely trees and flowers you cultivate on it, the more resources you'll be able to gather for DIY projects!

CHAPTER HIGHLIGHTS

Introduction to DIY

Need an item made? Do it yourself! The new crafting system allows you to create an impressive array of items that you can use for various purposes around your island. This even includes creating your own tools, which will be infinitely useful. Many items can only be acquired by building them at a workbench after acquiring their DIY Recipes, but building anything requires resources. Fortunately, there are plenty to be found from trees and rocks all over your island.

> "The basic idea is to gather materials, follow a recipe, and then craft using a workbench like this one!"

The Basics

The Workbench is where the magic happens—where a recipe and some basic resources turn into actual, usable items and tools! To find the Workbench, simply pay a visit to Resident Services. Later on you'll be able to craft your own Workbench and place it wherever you'd like, making the process slightly more convenient.

You can receive DIY recipes either as data, sent directly to your phone, or as recipe cards, which you must use to learn the recipe. You can sell recipe cards for 200 Bells each, but we strongly recommend never selling a recipe that you haven't already learned. Cards can also be dropped on the ground, which means they can be traded with other players.

If you stand in front of a Workbench and press Ⓐ you'll see all the recipes you've collected. These recipes are sorted into their own general categories, such as Furniture and Accessories, that you can browse through using the Ⓛ and Ⓡ buttons. Any time you obtain a new recipe, it will appear here and you'll be able to see if you can craft it or not, depending on which resources you have in your inventory.

Get Recipe

SWEET! I learned a DIY recipe for a simple DIY workbench!

Recipes come from many sources. Once you have one, use it from your pockets menu to learn it!

Use Workbench

Should I craft something using Tom Nook's workbench?

Next, head to Tom Nook's workbench to see which resources you need to craft the recipe.

Create New Item!

I made some log stakes!

Gather the resources, then head back to the workbench. Crafting your item will then be basically instant!

Unlocking Recipes

Some recipes are given to you by residents of specific personality types. You will often get these by talking to them while they are crafting a recipe in their home or from bottles that wash up on the beach, sent by potential residents. To be able to get some of these, the player on your island with most unlocked recipes must have reached certain totals: 50, 100 or 200. The higher the total required, the harder the recipe will be to craft.

Let's craft!
Not right now.

Should I craft something?

Resources

Resources are the primary materials that you'll be using in your DIY crafting. Broadly speaking, resources fall into three categories—wood, mineral and shell—though there are plenty of others besides. Wood resources can be acquired from trees, mineral resources can only be received from the large rocks you'll find around your island, and shell resources can be found on the beach. It's also well worth visiting a friend's island to gather resources, especially those not native to yours.

If you plant some Bamboo it will grow on your island and be a valuable source of resources.

Mystery Tour Islands

Your island's trees, rocks and beaches can only provide a limited amount of resources each day. You can get around this limit, however, by using a Nook Miles Ticket to visit a random island with an abundance of extra resources.

This is not the first time we've recommended taking a Mystery Tour to gather important resources, but as you can see in the chart here it really is a great way to get mineral resources. Some islands will be better than others in terms of gathering minerals; most only have four rocks in total, but some rare ones can have up to seven. There is also a rare island with a rock that only provides gold nuggets! May luck be on your side.

Similarly, most mystery islands have trees that grow your island's native fruit, but some rarer ones will have different fruit growing. Some will even be filled with bamboo plants, regardless of the time of year! Mystery islands are also great for finding rare fish and bugs—if you see one with a large pond or covered in hardwood trees, be

sure to have your fishing rod or net at the ready! Each island also has a basic DIY workbench that you can make use of in case you forget an important tool.

The charts on the following pages will show you exactly how many recipes each resource is used in, and how many you'll need in total to craft every recipe once.

You need some clay? Get yourself a Nook Miles Ticket and Wilbur will drop you on an island where it's quite a bit easier to find.

● Mineral Occurrence Rate

Item	Probability (Main Island)	Probability (Mystery Tour)	Sell Price
Stone	50%	8%	75
Iron Nugget	34%	50%	375
Clay	15%	41%	100
Gold Nugget	1%	1%	10,000

Trees will always be natively plentiful on your island and will provide you with perhaps the most vital resources you'll need to survive. Sometimes the most basic resources are the most important, such as tree branches, which can often be found on the ground near trees, or by shaking them loose by pressing Ⓐ near a tree. Don't underestimate this humble resource—it's used in a lot of crucial recipes, so always keep some on hand.

bamboo piece		80	RECIPES 19	TOTAL 117
bamboo shoot		250	RECIPES 2	TOTAL 8
hardwood		60	RECIPES 50	TOTAL 344
softwood		60	RECIPES 48	TOTAL 273
tree branch		5	RECIPES 19	TOTAL 109
wood		60	RECIPES 94	TOTAL 620

Once you have an axe of any kind, you can use it to farm wood, hardwood and softwood; hitting a tree with an axe by pressing Ⓐ near it will yield up to three pieces of wood, after which the tree will no longer provide any resources until the next day. Any kind of tree can produce these wood variants, so if you're in need of a specific kind of wood, your best bet is to just keep harvesting from any untapped trees—just beware of wasps!

Trees in the museum's atrium can't be shook for resources or cut down.

Bamboo trees are rare, but essential for building certain recipes. You can receive bamboo sprouts courtesy of Daisy Mae once you've bought 100 turnips from her in a single day. Bamboo can also show up on a Mystery Tour island, though its occurrence is fairly rare. If you see one while abroad, be sure to dig it up!

Speaking of Mystery Tours, they can actually be a great way for you to discover and acquire new kinds of trees. You'll need to use an axe to get the most of these resources, and a basic wooden axe is recommended to yield more materials, as an iron axe will chop the tree down after three hits. Thankfully, wooden axes are easy to craft and require only very basic resources.

If something looks like it's made out of wood... it's probably made out of wood!

Bamboo

Bamboo is used a in a great deal of recipes, so you'll want to focus on gathering a lot of it at once. You can't get it as early as you can other types of wood, but once you so, be sure to plant at least a few bamboo plants to have access to it regularly.

Mineral Resources

For constructing some of the sturdier DIY items, you'll need to collect materials from one of the large rocks you'll find scattered across the island. Let's go over some rock-related rules: each island can have a maximum of six rocks. If one or more rocks are destroyed, a new rock will appear each day until you've returned to maximum capacity. Rocks can be hit with either a shovel or an axe to acquire stones, clay, iron nuggets, and gold nuggets, and it's also not uncommon to find a stray stone or two naturally nearby.

clay		100	RECIPES 39	TOTAL 178
gold nugget		10,000	RECIPES 37	TOTAL 104
iron nugget		375	RECIPES 102	TOTAL 567
stone		75	RECIPES 48	TOTAL 585

Unlike trees, you're not guaranteed to always get the same amount of resources from a rock. Instead, once you first hit a rock, an invisible, 10-second timer will begin, and hitting the rock again before it runs out will result in a new material emerging. This means that if you aren't efficient, it's possible to get only a single item from a rock. If you're fast, though, it's possible to be rewarded with as many as eight items before you'll need to wait for the rock's minerals to replenish the next day. Your island's rocks will remain in the same places until you destroy one of them; if that happens, a new rock will appear the following day in a random location. If one of your rocks is in a hard to reach place it's worth destroying it to speed up your daily mineral gathering. Always be sure to clear out the space around the rock before starting though—no items will appear from the rock if there's no space for them to land in.

Remember that your shovel will shatter rocks to pieces if you have even a single point of Energy. This can be incredibly useful for clearing out space and getting rocks to appear in more convenient places the next day, but you probably don't want to destroy them by accident!

Try to leave some space for your rocks when planning your island's ideal structure. Remember you need space around them for minerals to land.

Striking Gold

Gold may be a soft metal, but it's the hardest material there is to find. You'll only get it very rarely from hitting rocks, even on a Mystery Tour island. Balloons, however, can also yield gold, and they can do so at a slightly higher rate than rocks (around an 8% chance). So when you're in need of gold, take aim for the skies!

● **Get More Minerals**

Dodo Airlines → P.50

You'll find it best to make one pass around your island every day, exhausting each of your rocks as you come to them—combine this with fossil hunting for efficiency!

Flower Resources

Flowers are only used in some recipes for items like decorative headwear. When they are required, however, you'll often need to acquire a bunch of different types, each in specific colors. Some colors will take some real effort to breed, so if you want to craft these recipes then head over to our flower breeding guide on P.171. Flower breeding is a fairly long term endeavor; given all of the plant tending that's required, it can take a while before you'll craft all flower-related recipes.

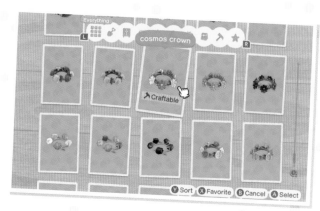

Flower	Cost	Recipes	Total
red roses	40	RECIPES 5	TOTAL 17
yellow roses	40	RECIPES 4	TOTAL 11
orange roses	80	RECIPES 3	TOTAL 8
white roses	40	RECIPES 2	TOTAL 5
pink roses	80	RECIPES 4	TOTAL 9
blue roses	1000	RECIPES 2	TOTAL 16
purple roses	240	RECIPES 2	TOTAL 9
black roses	240	RECIPES 2	TOTAL 6
gold roses	1000	RECIPES 2	TOTAL 16
red tulips	40	RECIPES 4	TOTAL 11
orange tulips	40	RECIPES 2	TOTAL 4
yellow tulips	40	RECIPES 2	TOTAL 5
white tulips	40	RECIPES 2	TOTAL 4
pink tulips	80	RECIPES 2	TOTAL 5
purple tulips	240	RECIPES 2	TOTAL 5
black tulips	80	RECIPES 2	TOTAL 15
red cosmos	40	RECIPES 4	TOTAL 11
yellow cosmos	40	RECIPES 2	TOTAL 5
orange cosmos	80	RECIPES 2	TOTAL 6
white cosmos	40	RECIPES 3	TOTAL 6
pink cosmos	80	RECIPES 3	TOTAL 12
black cosmos	240	RECIPES 2	TOTAL 17

Flower	Cost	Recipes	Total
red pansies	40	RECIPES 2	TOTAL 5
orange pansies	80	RECIPES 2	TOTAL 6
yellow pansies	40	RECIPES 5	TOTAL 14
white pansies	40	RECIPES 2	TOTAL 5
blue pansies	80	RECIPES 2	TOTAL 6
purple pansies	240	RECIPES 2	TOTAL 16
red hyacinths	40	RECIPES 2	TOTAL 7
orange hyacinths	80	RECIPES 2	TOTAL 5
yellow hyacinths	40	RECIPES 2	TOTAL 5
white hyacinths	40	RECIPES 3	TOTAL 8
pink hyacinths	80	RECIPES 3	TOTAL 6
blue hyacinths	80	RECIPES 2	TOTAL 7
purple hyacinths	240	RECIPES 3	TOTAL 21
red windflowers	40	RECIPES 3	TOTAL 8
orange windflowers	80	RECIPES 3	TOTAL 6
white windflowers	40	RECIPES 3	TOTAL 8
pink windflowers	80	RECIPES 2	TOTAL 6
blue windflowers	80	RECIPES 2	TOTAL 6
purple windflowers	240	RECIPES 3	TOTAL 20
red lilies	40	RECIPES 2	TOTAL 5
orange lilies	80	RECIPES 2	TOTAL 5
yellow lilies	40	RECIPES 4	TOTAL 9
white lilies	40	RECIPES 6	TOTAL 15
pink lilies	80	RECIPES 2	TOTAL 5
black lilies	80	RECIPES 2	TOTAL 16
red mums	40	RECIPES 3	TOTAL 8
yellow mums	40	RECIPES 4	TOTAL 9
white mums	40	RECIPES 2	TOTAL 5
pink mums	80	RECIPES 2	TOTAL 6
purple mums	80	RECIPES 2	TOTAL 6
green mums	240	RECIPES 2	TOTAL 16

Shell Resources

Shells are useful resources that can be found on your island's beaches. Although they are not used in very many DIY recipes, you'll undoubtedly find yourself needing them to craft some useful and cool items along the way. Generally, recipes that use shells tend to use a few different types at once. Try to be diligent with your daily beach-combing to build up a stockpile of as many varieties as possible because whenever you need one shell, you'll often need multiple different types.

conch	700	RECIPES 2	TOTAL 7
coral	500	RECIPES 5	TOTAL 13
cowrie	60	RECIPES 4	TOTAL 10
giant clam	900	RECIPES 8	TOTAL 22
manila clam*	100	RECIPES 1	TOTAL 1
sand dollar	120	RECIPES 4	TOTAL 12
sea snail	180	RECIPES 3	TOTAL 5
venus comb	300	RECIPES 3	TOTAL 8

* **manila clam** Inspiration: fish bait

Fruit Resources

Fruit is used in recipes from a lot of different categories, from furniture to clothing, so regardless of what aspect of your island you're looking to improve, theres a good chance that some kind of fruit will be needed. Each type of fruit is usually associated with craftable items that follow the theme of that fruit. So you can have a pear-themed house to walk around in while wearing your pear-themed clothing if you want, but you'll probably need to gather a lot of pears. This does have the advantage of allowing you to focus on growing and harvesting a specific fruit first, if there's one you really prefer.

apple	500	RECIPES 10	TOTAL 71
cherry	500	RECIPES 10	TOTAL 72
coconut	250	RECIPES 4	TOTAL 8
orange	500	RECIPES 10	TOTAL 72
peach	500	RECIPES 10	TOTAL 70
pear	500	RECIPES 10	TOTAL 70

Look at all those juicy apple products!

Once harvested, fruit takes three full days to grow back again.

Seasonal Resources

Some precious resources can only be acquired during certain times of the year. You'll need to collect as many of these as you can while they're available, or you'll be waiting a full year to get another chance. They're often used in recipes that are also only available in the same period. If you're missing one of these and the season has passed, you can ask a visiting friend if they have any to spare.

Cherry blossom petals, maple leaves and snowflakes can all be caught with your net as they float through the air during their seasonal periods. Pine cones and ornaments are acquired by shaking them free from cedar trees, while acorns can be shaken from hardwood trees and young spring bamboo from bamboo plants. Summer shells, meanwhile, are found on the beach. Mushrooms come in five varieties and can be found near trees, at a rate of a few per day. Finally, the large snowflake can only be acquired by building a perfect Snowboy. To learn more about doing that, flip over to P.157.

This cherry-blossom petal is so lovely! Pink is really its color!

Spring is all about growing your trees and plants—take care of your bamboo while you catch cherry blossom petals and breed flowers.

Spring

cherry-blossom petal	200	RECIPES 14	TOTAL 89
young spring bamboo	200	RECIPES 10	TOTAL 56

Young Spring Bamboo is especially important to acquire while it's available, because it's used in recipes for tools that you might like to own, such as the pan flute and wand.

Summer

summer shell	600	RECIPES 8	TOTAL 30

Summer shells might be summer's only rare material, but they're used to make some great flooring and wallpapers for your house, so don't miss out on them.

Autumn

acorn	200	RECIPES 8	TOTAL 35
elegant mushroom	10,000	RECIPES 2	TOTAL 3
flat mushroom	200	RECIPES 7	TOTAL 14
maple leaf	200	RECIPES 9	TOTAL 51
pine cone	200	RECIPES 7	TOTAL 31
rare mushroom	16,000	RECIPES 1	TOTAL 1
round mushroom	200	RECIPES 5	TOTAL 8
skinny mushroom	300	RECIPES 8	TOTAL 15

The total amount of mushrooms you'll need isn't that great, especially compared to some other materials. Some recipes, such as the wallpapers for instance, require quite a few different varieties at once, however, so getting all of the mushroom themed recipes might not be as easy as it first seems. Go for variety over quantity when gathering them.

The maple leaf season overlaps with the acorn and pine cone season, so you'll have some extra gathering to do in autumn.

Winter

blue ornament	50	RECIPES 7	TOTAL 38
gold ornament	50	RECIPES 10	TOTAL 37
large snowflake	2500	RECIPES 15	TOTAL 15
red ornament	50	RECIPES 7	TOTAL 31
snowflake	200	RECIPES 21	TOTAL 143

Ornaments are easily gathered during the festive season. Gold ones are used in more recipes and are a little harder to come by, so make sure you collect enough of them before the season ends. You'll also notice that a large amount of snowflakes are needed to craft all possible recipes, so never miss a chance to grab one.

Ornaments come in three colors and are used to make a variety of festive-themed items.

You can really make your island a festive delight by crafting these items.

Other Resources

Sometimes you'll come across other resources that can be used to craft items. These resources might not be used in as many recipes, but they will still be useful and we recommend holding on to them when you come across them. You'll sometimes fish up some trash when hoping to catch a fish—these items may seem worthless, but don't throw them away if you're looking to collect everything, because they'll inspire new DIY recipes that make use of them.

Star fragments, including the unique ones for each zodiac period, can be collected from the beach on the morning after seeing a meteor shower, providing you wished upon some stars. The number that wash up correlates to the number of stars you wish upon. These are used to craft wands, flooring and wallpapers as well as unique zodiac decorative items. The zodiac recipes always require two gold nuggets, but since you can only acquire one zodiac recipe per month, this needn't be a problem.

Aquarius fragment	500	RECIPES 1	TOTAL 2
Aries fragment	500	RECIPES 1	TOTAL 2
boot*1	10	RECIPES 4	TOTAL 7
campfire	--	RECIPES 4	TOTAL 3
Cancer fragment	500	RECIPES 1	TOTAL 2
Capricorn fragment	500	RECIPES 1	TOTAL 2
cardboard box	30	RECIPES 7	TOTAL 22
clump of weeds*2	10	RECIPES 38	TOTAL 373
empty can*3	10	RECIPES 5	TOTAL 7
Gemini fragment	500	RECIPES 1	TOTAL 2
large star fragment	2500	RECIPES 9	TOTAL 9
Leo fragment	500	RECIPES 1	TOTAL 2

Libra fragment	500	RECIPES 1	TOTAL 2
log stakes	360	RECIPES 2	TOTAL 4
old tire*4	10	RECIPES 6	TOTAL 13
Pisces fragment	500	RECIPES 1	TOTAL 2
rusted part	10	RECIPES 1	TOTAL 30
Sagittarius fragment	500	RECIPES 1	TOTAL 2
Scorpius fragment	500	RECIPES 1	TOTAL 2
star fragment	250	RECIPES 52	TOTAL 250
Taurus fragment	500	RECIPES 1	TOTAL 2
Virgo fragment	500	RECIPES 1	TOTAL 2
wasp nest*5	300	RECIPES 4	TOTAL 15
wooden-block toy	360	RECIPES 10	TOTAL 9

*1 **boot** Inspiration: trash bags, recycled boots
*2 **clump of weeds** Inspiration: succulent plant
*3 **empty can** Inspiration: garbage-heap wall, garbage-heap flooring, recycled-can thumb piano, trash bags

*4 **old tire** Inspiration: tire stack, tire toy
*5 **wasp nest** Inspiration: medicine (talk to a resident after being stung)

DIY Recipes

DIY recipes can be obtained in a variety of ways, from buying them in stores, to receiving them as gifts from other villagers, or simply finding them in bottles that have washed ashore. Once you have a recipe, it can be used to permanently learn how to build its respective item. Recipes will most often use crafting resources such as wood or stone, but can also call for any other item as well. For instance, you'll need to have crafted a wood block before you can craft a wood block table. Here we'll go through all of the ways you can earn DIY Recipes.

Recipe Sources

Island Residents

Sometimes you can earn DIY recipes just by chatting with a fellow island resident. It's important to chat with your neighbors often, as these recipes will be a big help in crafting useful items!

You can get different recipes depending on the personality type of the resident you're talking to, so it's best to have residents of differing personalities on your island. Some of these recipes will only become possible to acquire once your total recipe count is over a certain number. In these cases, the unlock number will be shown in the recipe lists later in this chapter.

You'll also acquire quite a lot of the most essential recipes by talking to important island figures such as Tom Nook and Blathers. They will, for example, provide you with your earliest recipes for tools, which are needed in order to gather any materials. Tom Nook will provide you with the recipe for your first ladder, and will provide you with a free wardrobe recipe before you can complete his DIY Customization Workshop. Blathers, meanwhile, will give you the vaulting pole recipe, providing you with an ingenious means of crossing rivers and allowing you to access new parts of your island for the first time. You can sell recipes for 200 Bells each, but we highly recommend not selling any recipe you haven't already learned!

"But the river!" you say. "It cannot be crossed!" you say. Hoo! Silly you! I have a solution as audacious as trying to populate an entirely deserted island.

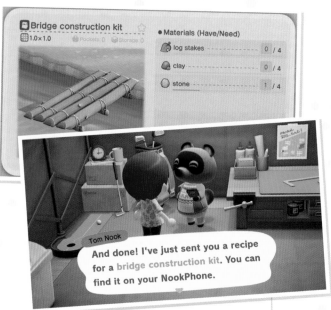

And done! I've just sent you a recipe for a bridge construction kit. You can find it on your NookPhone.

Not all items can be crafted more than once—the bridge construction kit from Tom Nook is a one-time-use recipe!

This manila clam could be used as fishing bait... I've got an idea for a DIY recipe!

Message Bottles

Sometimes when you're roaming the beach, you might find a bottle that has washed ashore. After picking it up, access this bottle via your inventory and open it up—you'll find a note inside from a potential resident who might eventually move to your island. Most importantly, the note will come with a useful DIY recipe. Score! The bottle will appear at a rate of roughly one per day, but sadly the recipes they contain can't be seasonal ones.

Summer is perfect for walks along the beach—you never know what you might find.

Celeste

Celeste is Blathers' adorable sister. She sometimes shows up at night, and always on nights when a meteor shower occurs. If you find her and talk to her, Celeste will offer you a star wand recipe. On subsequent meetings, she'll give you a new recipe based on the current zodiac sign; since there are 12 zodiac signs, that means there are 12 recipes in total that you can collect over the course of a year. If you've already received the zodiac DIY recipe for the current period, then she's likely to give you a lot of star fragments or a wand recipe instead. If you show her a zodiac star fragment, she'll identify it for you and tell a little about its constellation.

"Oh, hootie-toot! I happened upon this just the other night when the stars twinkled ever so beautifully."

The zodiac recipes have high crafting requirements, but result in some very unique furniture.

If you want to know more about Celeste, head over to P.57 in the Meet the Locals chapter.

Seasonal Recipes

Some recipes can only be acquired at specific times of the year. Most of these will be obtainable only by shooting down balloons during these periods. We'll list all of them here for convenience.

Balloons

At random times throughout the day, balloons will float over your island, and you can shoot them down using your slingshot. It's always worth aiming for these when you see one. Although balloons can contain a number of different items, such as furniture and Bells, the most highly coveted among them are the seasonal recipes. They'll only contain these at particular times of the year, and in these cases, the recipes they provide are the only source for some truly spectacular items, so be sure to have your slingshot at the ready!

Never miss a chance to shoot down a balloon. It could very well contain a seasonal recipe!

Cherry Blossom recipes	Young Spring Bamboo	Summer Shell	Acorn/Pine cone recipes
◐ Apr. 1st - 10th	◐ Feb. 25th - May. 31st	◐ Jun. 1st - Aug. 31st	◐ Sept. 1st - Dec. 10th
◑ Oct. 1st - 10th	◑ Aug. 25th - Nov. 30th	◑ Dec. 1st - Feb. 29th	◑ Mar. 1st - Jun. 10th

Cherry Blossom recipes	Young Spring Bamboo	Summer Shell	Acorn/Pine cone recipes
sakura-wood wall	bamboo doll	shell wreath	traditional balancing toy
cherry-blossom bonsai	bamboo-grove wall	shell wand	tree's bounty mobile
cherry-blossom-petal pile	steamer-basket set	underwater flooring	tree's bounty lamp
cherry-blossom branches	bamboo-shoot lamp	water flooring	tree's bounty little tree
outdoor picnic set	pan flute	shellfish pochette	leaf campfire
cherry-blossom clock	bamboo noodle slide	underwater wall	pile of leaves
blossom-viewing lantern	bamboo wand	tropical vista	yellow-leaf pile
cherry-blossom flooring	green-leaf pile	starry-sands flooring	pine bonsai tree
cherry-blossom-trees wall	basket pack		acorn pochette
cherry-blossom pond stone	light bamboo rug		tree's bounty big tree
cherry-blossom wand			tree's bounty arch
cherry-blossom umbrella			
Pink cherry-blossom pochette			
pink wood flooring			

Summer shell

Mushroom recipes	Maple Leaf recipes	Snowflake recipes	Ornament recipes
◐ Nov. 1st– Nov. 30th	◐ Oct. 1st –10th	◐ 11th Dec. – 24th Feb.	◐ Dec. 15th – Jan. 6th
◑ May 1st – May 31st	◑ Apr. 1st – 10th	◑ 11th Jun. – 24th Aug.	◑ Dec. 15th – Jan. 6th
mush table	autumn wall	snowflake wreath	illuminated tree
mush lamp	tree's bounty big tree	iceberg flooring	ornament wreath
mush log	tree's bounty arch	ski-slope wall	big festive tree
mush partition	colored-leaves flooring	iceberg wall	festive tree
mush parasol	maple-leaf pond stone	snowflake wall	Jingle wall
mush low stool	leaf stool	ski-slope flooring	holiday candle
mushroom wreath	maple-leaf umbrella	snowflake pochette	tabletop festive tree
mush wall	red-leaf pile		illuminated reindeer
forest wall	maple-leaf pochette		illuminated present
forest flooring			illuminated snowflakes
mushroom wand			ornament mobile
mush umbrella			festive top set

Snowboy

It's winter time and you've just made yourself a Snowboy. If he's a happy, perfect Snowboy, he'll give you a DIY recipe for one of the furniture pieces in the frozen set, and a large snowflake to craft them with. He will in fact give you one large snowflake every day until he melts. For more information on building Snowboy, turn to P.157.

turn to P.157.

◐ Dec 11th - Feb. 24th ◑ June 11th - Aug. 24th

frozen arch	frozen bed
frozen sculpture	frozen-treat set
frozen chair	ice flooring
frozen counter	ice wall
frozen tree	three-tiered snowman
frozen table	ice wand
frozen partition	snowman head
frozen pillar	

Snowboy

Please, take it! It's an awesome large snowflake!

Snowboy

Now listen, to thank you for making me, I want to share some knowledge about how to craft a special item.

Building a Snowboy can really pay off— he's full of great recipes to try out!

Buying Recipes

While Timmy is still in the Resident Services tent, he'll sell you the flimsy axe, flimsy watering can and slingshot recipes, along with the DIY for Beginners recipe pack. Once you've helped Timmy and Tommy to build Nook's Cranny, a larger selection is available. They'll stock recipes for all of the flimsy tools as well as the slingshot, and they'll sell recipes for the ladder and vaulting pole once you've acquired those tools from Tom Nook and Blathers, respectively. They'll also sell three recipe packs, each of which contain a selection of mostly decorative items.

"Curious about what's in the cabinet? Here's what we have today! ...today!"

Recipe Packs

There are four recipe packs available to purchase; three from Nook's Cranny and one from redeeming Nook Miles. These will show up for purchase as Nook's Cranny and the Redeem Nook Miles service are available, so watch out for them!

"DIY for Beginners" is a digital DIY recipe book! ...book!

Pretty Good Tools Recipes

This is the only recipe pack that you can exchange Nook Miles for at the Nook Stop (at a cost of 3000 Nook Miles). It contains recipes for more sturdy versions of the basic tools that you're likely to already have.

3000

axe
watering can
shovel
fishing rod
net
stone axe

DIY For Beginners

This is the first of three recipe packs you can buy from the cabinet at Nook's Cranny once it opens. It contains some simple recipes for furniture along with the ocarina musical instrument.

480

wooden-block toy
stone stool
hay bed
wooden washtub
frying pan
ocarina

Test Your DIY Skills

The second pack you can acquire from Nook's Cranny's cabinet, this one contains eight more fairly simple recipes. The mini DIY workbench and wooden-block stereo require some iron nuggets, which might take a few days to gather. The stereo lets you listen to any K.K. Slider songs you've already heard.

2680

ringtoss
rocking chair
swinging bench
wooden-block bookshelf
mini DIY workbench
wooden-block stereo
wooden-block chair
potted ivy

Wildest Dreams

This is the final recipe pack from Nook's Cranny's cabinet. It will take a bit more effort to gather all the materials required, especially for the ironwood kitchenette, since it requires some pre-crafted items.

6980

brick oven
ironwood kitchenette
iron wall lamp
plain sink
wooden fish
hearth

Gather Nook Miles and you can purchase DIY Recipes from the Nook Stop in Resident Services. As well as the Pretty Good Tools recipe pack, the Nook Miles shop will stock recipes for fencing and some single, big ticket items. These recipes will allow you to build many interesting pieces of furniture and novelty items, such as fountains, archways and even a giant robot sculpture.

stone fence
iron fence
country fence
corral fence
manhole cover
destinations signpost
brick well
outdoor bath
rope fence
imperial fence
straw fence
spiky fence
iron-and-stone fence
zen fence
barbed-wire fence
robot hero
stall
silo
fountain
stone tablet
stone arch
simple wooden fence
lattice fence

5000 Nook Miles seems a bit steep for a giant robot recipe...

...but that's nothing compared to the materials required to craft the robot.

"Thanks to you, we've gained a lot of customers on this island who can't wait for me to come here peddlin'."

It'll be a real status symbol for your island if you manage to craft it, though!

Recipe List

The following pages list every single DIY recipe in the game. For each one, you'll find the exact number and type of materials needed, and how to acquire the recipe.

	MATERIALS	The materials needed to craft the item are shown here. The number in parenthesis is how many of the material is required.
②	OBTAIN	This tells you how to get the recipe. Some have multiple sources, usually including talking to a resident of a specific personality type. This is often the way other players will get a recipe, since they won't get it from Tom Nook.
③	UNLOCK	This number tells you if you'll need to have obtained a certain number of recipes to have a chance of getting this one from a resident.
④	SELL PRICE	This shows you how much the item you'll craft will sell for to Timmy and Tommy. All recipes sell for 200 Bells.

Furniture Recipes

acoustic guitar
880 3210
- softwood x8
- iron nugget x3

OBTAIN Resident: Smug

angled signpost
600
- hardwood x2
- softwood x3

OBTAIN Resident: Lazy
UNLOCK 100

apple chair
2480
- apple x10
- wood x4

OBTAIN Tom Nook ("Three New Plots" quest) •
Resident: Big sister • UNLOCK 100

Aquarius urn
22,125
- star fragment x3
- Aquarius fragment x2
- gold nugget x2
- stone x5

OBTAIN Zodiac recipe (Reward: Celeste)

Aries rocking chair
12,125
- star fragment x3
- Aries fragment x2
- gold nugget x1
- stone x5

OBTAIN Zodiac recipe (Reward: Celeste)

aroma pot
600
- clay x3

OBTAIN Resident: Snooty

asteroid
4000
- star fragment x5
- stone x10

OBTAIN Star fragment recipe (Reward: Celeste)

astronaut suit
6250
- star fragment x5
- iron nugget x5

OBTAIN Star fragment recipe (Reward: Celeste)

bamboo basket
1120
- bamboo piece x7

OBTAIN Resident: Snooty
UNLOCK 50

bamboo bench
1280
- bamboo piece x8

OBTAIN Resident: Sweet
UNLOCK 50

bamboo candleholder
880
- bamboo piece x3
- clay x2

OBTAIN Resident: Snooty
UNLOCK 50

bamboo doll
2400
- young sp. bamboo x6

OBTAIN Seasonal recipe: Bamboo

bamboo drum
720
- bamboo piece x3
- softwood x2

OBTAIN Resident: Jock
UNLOCK 50

bamboo floor lamp
1280
- bamboo piece x8

OBTAIN Resident: Sweet
UNLOCK 50

bamboo lunch box
640
- bamboo piece x4

OBTAIN Resident: Snooty
UNLOCK 50

bamboo noodle slide
3160
- young sp. bamboo x7
- wood x3

OBTAIN Seasonal recipe: Bamboo

bamboo partition
2020
- bamboo piece x7
- stone x6

OBTAIN Resident: Cranky
UNLOCK 50

bamboo shelf
2400
- bamboo piece x15

OBTAIN Resident: Snooty
UNLOCK 50

bamboo speaker
1230
- bamboo piece x3
- iron nugget x1

OBTAIN Resident: Snooty
UNLOCK 50

bamboo sphere
480
- bamboo piece x3

OBTAIN Resident: Sweet
UNLOCK 50

bamboo stool
800
- bamboo piece x5

OBTAIN Resident: Snooty
UNLOCK 50

bamboo stopblock
480
- bamboo piece x3

OBTAIN Resident: Jock
UNLOCK 50

bamboo wall decoration
160
- bamboo piece x1

OBTAIN Resident: Jock
UNLOCK 50

bamboo-shoot lamp
4900
- young sp. bamboo x4
- bamboo shoot x5
- clay x4

OBTAIN Seasonal recipe: Bamboo

barbell
7500
- iron nugget x10

OBTAIN Resident: Jock

barrel
2100
- wood x5
- iron nugget x2

OBTAIN Tom Nook ("Three New Plots" quest) •
Resident: Cranky

beekeeper's hive
2400
- wasp nest x3
- wood x5

OBTAIN Resident: Jock

big festive tree
3200
- red ornament x6
- blue ornament x6
- gold ornament x4
- wood x5
- clay x5

OBTAIN Seasonal recipe: Ornament

birdbath
900
- stone x6

OBTAIN Tom Nook ("Three New Plots" quest) •
Resident: Snooty

birdcage
960
- wood x8

OBTAIN Resident: Big sister

birdhouse
840
- wood x2
- softwood x5

OBTAIN Tom Nook ("Three New Plots" quest) • Reward:
Give him 2nd creature • Resident: Peppy
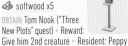

blossom-viewing lantern
2880
- cherry-bloss. petal x6
- hardwood x4

OBTAIN Seasonal recipe: Cherry blossom

bonfire
1230
- campfire x1
- wood x10

OBTAIN Reward: Give Tom Nook 2nd creature
Resident: Cranky

bonsai shelf
8460
- cherry-bloss. bonsai x1
- pine bonsai tree x1
- wood x8

OBTAIN Resident: Cranky
UNLOCK 100

boomerang
360
- hardwood x3

OBTAIN Resident: Lazy
UNLOCK 50

brick oven
3820
- clay x8
- iron nugget x2
- wood x6

OBTAIN Wildest Dreams DIY: Shop (Cabinet)

brick well
2800
- clay x8
- wood x5
- flimsy shovel x1

OBTAIN Redeem Nook Miles

butter churn
1980
- wood x4
- iron nugget x2

OBTAIN Resident: Snooty

campfire
30
- tree branch x3

OBTAIN Reward: DIY Workshop

Cancer table
21,975
- star fragment x3
- Cancer fragment x2
- gold nugget x2
- stone x3

OBTAIN Zodiac recipe (Reward: Celeste)

Capricorn ornament
⭐ star fragment x3 — 22,650
🍂 Capricorn fragment x2
🪨 gold nugget x2
🪨 stone x12
OBTAIN Zodiac recipe (Reward: Celeste)

cardboard bed
📦 cardboard box x4 — 240
OBTAIN Resident: Lazy

cardboard chair
📦 cardboard box x1 — 60
OBTAIN Resident: Lazy

cardboard sofa
📦 cardboard box x2 — 120
OBTAIN Resident: Peppy

cardboard table
📦 cardboard box x4 — 240
OBTAIN Resident: Peppy

cherry lamp
🍒 cherry x10 — 2400
🪨 clay x2
OBTAIN Resident: Peppy • Tom Nook ("Three New Plots" quest) • UNLOCK 100

cherry speakers
🍒 cherry x10 — 3500
iron nugget x2
OBTAIN Resident: Peppy • Tom Nook ("Three New Plots" quest) • UNLOCK 100

cherry-blossom bonsai
🌸 cherry-bloss. petal x6 — 3300
hardwood x2
clump of weeds x3
🪨 clay x3
OBTAIN Seasonal recipe: Cherry blossom

cherry-blossom branches
🌸 cherry-bloss. petal x8 — 4240
🪵 tree branch x4
🪨 clay x5
OBTAIN Seasonal recipe: Cherry blossom

cherry-blossom clock
🌸 cherry-bloss. petal x5 — 2750
iron nugget x1
OBTAIN Seasonal recipe: Cherry blossom

---

cherry-blossom pond stone
🪨 stone x10 — 2700
🌸 cherry-bloss. petal x3
OBTAIN Seasonal recipe: Cherry blossom

cherry-blossom-petal pile
🌸 cherry-bloss. petal x5 — 2000
OBTAIN Seasonal recipe: Cherry blossom

clackercart
hardwood x2 — 960
softwood x6
OBTAIN Resident: Lazy

classic pitcher
🪨 clay x4 — 800
OBTAIN Tom Nook ("Three New Plots" quest) • Resident: Snooty

clothesline
🪵 tree branch x10 — 100
OBTAIN Tom Nook ("Three New Plots" quest) • Resident: Cranky

coconut juice
🥥 coconut x1 — 500
OBTAIN Resident: Snooty

coconut wall planter
🥥 coconut x1 — 600
clump of weeds x5
OBTAIN Resident: Snooty UNLOCK 50

cosmos shower
pink cosmos x5 — 3050
iron nugget x3
OBTAIN Resident: Snooty UNLOCK 50

crescent-moon chair
⭐ star fragment x7 — 8500
⭐ large star fragment x1
OBTAIN Star fragment recipe (Reward: Celeste)

crewed spaceship
⭐ star fragment x10 — 20,000
iron nugget x20
OBTAIN Star fragment recipe (Reward: Celeste)

cutting board
hardwood x2 — 990
iron nugget x1
OBTAIN Resident: Sweet

---

decoy duck
softwood x4 — 480
OBTAIN Resident: Smug

deer decoration
softwood x8 — 960
OBTAIN Resident: Lazy
UNLOCK 50

deer scare
bamboo piece x3 — 1740
🪨 stone x8
clump of weeds x3
OBTAIN Resident: Cranky
UNLOCK 50

destinations signpost
hardwood x4 — 1440
softwood x8
OBTAIN Redeem Nook Miles

DIY workbench
wood x5 — 6630
hardwood x5
softwood x5
iron nugget x3
mini DIY workbench x1
OBTAIN Resident: Big sister • UNLOCK 100

document stack
scattered papers x1 — 400
OBTAIN Resident: Smug
UNLOCK 100

doghouse
wood x10 — 2040
hardwood x7
OBTAIN Resident: Jock

drinking fountain
🪨 stone x8 — 2700
iron nugget x2
OBTAIN Redeem Nook Miles

festive top set
gold ornament x2 — 320
hardwood x1
OBTAIN Seasonal recipe: Ornament

festive tree
red ornament x3 — 1400
blue ornament x3
gold ornament x2
wood x5
OBTAIN Seasonal recipe: Ornament

---

firewood
wood x8 — 960
OBTAIN Resident: Jock

flat garden rock
🪨 stone x20 — 3000
OBTAIN Resident: Snooty

floral swag
clump of weeds x10 — 200
OBTAIN Resident: Sweet
UNLOCK 50

flower stand
red roses x1 — 2880
pink roses x2
orange roses x2
white lilies x2
yellow lilies x1
purple windflowers x4
OBTAIN Resident: Big sister • UNLOCK 100

flying saucer
⭐ star fragment x15 — 15,000
iron nugget x10
OBTAIN Star fragment recipe (Reward: Celeste)

fountain
drinking fountain x1 — 11,700
🪨 stone x20
iron nugget x8
OBTAIN Redeem Nook Miles

frozen arch
❄️ large snowflake x1 — 9000
❄️ snowflake x10
OBTAIN Reward: Snowboy

frozen bed
❄️ large snowflake x1 — 9000
❄️ snowflake x10
OBTAIN Reward: Snowboy

frozen chair
❄️ large snowflake x1 — 6200
❄️ snowflake x3
OBTAIN Reward: Snowboy

frozen counter
❄️ large snowflake x1 — 7000
❄️ snowflake x5
OBTAIN Reward: Snowboy

frozen partition
❄️ large snowflake x1 — 7400
❄️ snowflake x6
OBTAIN Reward: Snowboy

5

frozen pillar ⓑ6200
- ❄ large snowflake x1
- ❄ snowflake x3

OBTAIN Reward: Snowboy

frozen sculpture ⓑ6600
- ❄ large snowflake x1
- ❄ snowflake x4

OBTAIN Reward: Snowboy

frozen table ⓑ8200
- ❄ large snowflake x1
- ❄ snowflake x8

OBTAIN Reward: Snowboy

frozen tree ⓑ8200
- ❄ large snowflake x1
- ❄ snowflake x8

OBTAIN Reward: Snowboy

frozen-treat set ⓑ5400
- ❄ large snowflake x1
- ❄ snowflake x1

OBTAIN Reward: Snowboy

fruit basket ⓑ1000
- 🍎 apple x1
- 🍐 pear x1
- 🍒 cherry x1
- 🍊 orange x1
- 🍑 peach x1

OBTAIN Resident: Cranky • UNLOCK 100

frying pan ⓑ1500
- 🔩 iron nugget x2

OBTAIN DIY for Beginners: Shop (Cabinet)

garden bench ⓑ4440
- 🪵 wood x12
- 🔩 iron nugget x4

OBTAIN Resident: Snooty

garden rock ⓑ2250
- ⚪ stone x15

OBTAIN Resident: Lazy

garden wagon ⓑ3180
- 🌼 white hyacinths x3
- 🌸 red cosmos x3
- 🌹 yellow roses x3
- 🪵 wood x8
- 🔩 iron nugget x2

OBTAIN Resident: Peppy

Gemini closet ⓑ22,200
- ✦ star fragment x3
- ✦ Gemini fragment x2
- 🪙 gold nugget x2
- ⚪ stone x6

OBTAIN Zodiac recipe (Reward: Celeste)

giant teddy bear ⓑ6300
- 🐻 Papa bear x1
- 🐻 Mama bear x1
- 🐻 Baby bear x1

OBTAIN Resident: Peppy
UNLOCK 100

gold bars ⓑ30,000
- 🪙 gold nugget x3

OBTAIN Resident: Snooty
UNLOCK 100

golden arowana model ⓑ30,000
- 🪙 gold nugget x3

OBTAIN Resident: Lazy
UNLOCK 100

golden candlestick ⓑ20,000
- 🪙 gold nugget x2

OBTAIN Resident: Smug

golden casket ⓑ80,000
- 🪙 gold nugget x8

OBTAIN Resident: Smug
UNLOCK 200

golden dishes ⓑ10,000
- 🪙 gold nugget x1

OBTAIN Resident: Snooty

golden dung beetle ⓑ30,000
- 🪙 gold nugget x3

OBTAIN Resident: Lazy
UNLOCK 100

golden gears ⓑ11,125
- 🪙 gold nugget x1
- 🔩 iron nugget x3

OBTAIN Resident: Smug
UNLOCK 50

golden seat ⓑ50,000
- 🪙 gold nugget x5

OBTAIN Resident: Snooty
UNLOCK 200

golden toilet ⓑ60,000
- 🪙 gold nugget x6

OBTAIN Resident: Snooty
UNLOCK 200

---

gong ⓑ5100
- 🔩 iron nugget x6
- 🪵 wood x5

OBTAIN Resident: Cranky

grass standee ⓑ480
- 🪵 wood x2
- 🪵 softwood x2

OBTAIN Resident: Sweet

green-leaf pile ⓑ600
- 🎋 young sp. bamboo x1
- 🌿 clump of weeds x10

OBTAIN Seasonal recipe: Bamboo

hanging terrarium ⓑ3240
- 🌿 clump of weeds x12
- 🔩 iron nugget x4

OBTAIN Resident: Peppy
UNLOCK 50

hay bed ⓑ400
- 🌿 clump of weeds x20

OBTAIN DIY for Beginners: Shop (Cabinet) • Tom Nook ("Three New Plots" quest)

hearth ⓑ5470
- 🎋 bamboo piece x2
- 🔩 iron nugget x5
- 🟤 clay x4
- 🪵 hardwood x5

OBTAIN Wildest Dreams DIY: Shop (Cabinet)

hedge standee ⓑ600
- 🪵 wood x2
- 🪵 softwood x3

OBTAIN Resident: Sweet

holiday candle ⓑ600
- 🔴 red ornament x5
- 🌿 clump of weeds x5

OBTAIN Seasonal recipe: Ornament

hyacinth lamp ⓑ3000
- 🌷 purple hyacinths x5
- 🟤 clay x3

OBTAIN Resident: Big sister
UNLOCK 50

illuminated present ⓑ2950
- 🔴 red ornament x3
- 🟡 gold ornament x4
- 🔩 iron nugget x3

OBTAIN Seasonal recipe: Ornament

illuminated reindeer ⓑ4350
- 🟡 gold ornament x6
- 🔩 iron nugget x5

OBTAIN Seasonal recipe: Ornament

---

illuminated snowflakes ⓑ3150
- 🔵 blue ornament x9
- 🔩 iron nugget x3

OBTAIN Seasonal recipe: Ornament

illuminated tree ⓑ6700
- 🔴 red ornament x8
- 🔵 blue ornament x8
- 🟡 gold ornament x6
- 🔩 iron nugget x6

OBTAIN Seasonal recipe: Ornament

infused-waterdispenser ⓑ3000
- 🍎 apple x2
- 🍐 pear x2
- 🍒 cherry x2
- 🍊 orange x2
- 🍑 peach x2
- 🥥 coconut x2

OBTAIN Resident: Cranky • UNLOCK 100

iron closet ⓑ9000
- 🔩 iron nugget x12

OBTAIN Resident: Big sister

iron frame ⓑ15,000
- 🔩 iron nugget x20

OBTAIN Resident: Jock

iron garden bench ⓑ6000
- 🔩 iron nugget x8

OBTAIN Resident: Big sister

iron garden chair ⓑ2250
- 🔩 iron nugget x3

OBTAIN Tom Nook ("Three New Plots" quest) • Resident: Big sister

iron garden table ⓑ3750
- 🔩 iron nugget x5

OBTAIN Tom Nook ("Three New Plots" quest) • Resident: Big sister

iron hanger stand ⓑ2250
- 🔩 iron nugget x3

OBTAIN Resident: Cranky

iron shelf ⓑ10,500
- 🔩 iron nugget x14

OBTAIN Resident: Big sister

---

iron wall lamp ⊙3400
- iron nugget x4
- clay x2

OBTAIN Wildest Dreams DIY: Shop (Cabinet)

iron wall rack ⊙2450
- iron nugget x3
- clay x1

OBTAIN Resident: Smug
UNLOCK 50

iron worktable ⊙7500
- iron nugget x10

OBTAIN Resident: Big sister

ironwood bed ⊙9900
- wood x20
- iron nugget x10

OBTAIN Resident: Smug

ironwood cart ⊙3720
- wood x6
- iron nugget x4

OBTAIN Resident: Smug

ironwood chair ⊙1860
- wood x3
- iron nugget x2

OBTAIN Resident: Smug

ironwood clock ⊙1740
- wood x2
- iron nugget x2

OBTAIN Resident: Smug
UNLOCK 50

ironwood cupboard ⊙9780
- wood x12
- iron nugget x6
- ironwood dresser x1

OBTAIN Resident: Snooty
UNLOCK 100

ironwood DIY workbench ⊙8520
- wood x12
- iron nugget x6
- mini DIY workbench x1

OBTAIN Resident: Cranky
UNLOCK 100

ironwood dresser ⊙3840
- wood x7
- iron nugget x4

OBTAIN Resident: Snooty

---

ironwood kitchenette ⊙7560
- wood x4
- iron nugget x3
- ironwood dresser x1
- cutting board x1

OBTAIN Wildest Dreams DIY: Shop (Cabinet)

ironwood low table ⊙3720
- wood x6
- iron nugget x4

OBTAIN Resident: Snooty

ironwood table ⊙5940
- wood x12
- iron nugget x6

OBTAIN Resident: Cranky

jail bars ⊙3750
- iron nugget x5

OBTAIN Resident: Cranky

juicy-apple TV ⊙3500
- apple x10
- iron nugget x2

OBTAIN Tom Nook ("Three New Plots" quest) • Resident: Big sister • UNLOCK 100

kettle bathtub ⊙6270
- iron nugget x8
- wood x2
- campfire x1

OBTAIN Resident: Cranky

kettlebell ⊙3750
- iron nugget x5

OBTAIN Resident: Jock

key holder ⊙1110
- wood x3
- iron nugget x1

OBTAIN Resident: Big sister
UNLOCK 50

large cardboard boxes ⊙300
- cardboard box x5

OBTAIN Resident: Lazy

leaf campfire ⊙1330
- pinecone x3
- clump of weeds x5
- tree branch x3

OBTAIN Seasonal recipe: Acorn/Pinecone

leaf stool ⊙1560
- maple leaf x3
- wood x3

OBTAIN Seasonal recipe: Maple Leaf

Leo sculpture ⊙21,975
- star fragment x3
- Leo fragment x2
- gold nugget x2
- stone x3

OBTAIN Zodiac recipe (Reward: Celeste)

Libra scale ⊙21,750
- star fragment x3
- Libra fragment x2
- gold nugget x2

OBTAIN Zodiac recipe (Reward: Celeste)

lily record player ⊙3010
- white lilies x5
- iron nugget x3
- wood x3

OBTAIN Resident: Cranky
UNLOCK 50

log bed ⊙3600
- hardwood x30

OBTAIN Tom Nook ("Three New Plots" quest) • Resident: Peppy

log bench ⊙600
- hardwood x5

OBTAIN Tom Nook ("Three New Plots" quest) • Resident: Sweet

log decorative shelves ⊙1560
- log bench x2
- hardwood x3

OBTAIN Resident: Sweet
UNLOCK 100

log dining table ⊙1800
- hardwood x15

OBTAIN Tom Nook ("Three New Plots" quest) • Resident: Cranky

log extra-long sofa ⊙1920
- log sofa x2

OBTAIN Resident: Sweet
UNLOCK 100

log garden lounge ⊙1440
- hardwood x12

OBTAIN Tom Nook ("Three New Plots" quest) • Resident: Peppy

log round table ⊙1800
- hardwood x15

OBTAIN Resident: Peppy

log chair ⊙960
- hardwood x8

OBTAIN Resident: Sweet

---

log stakes ⊙360
- wood x3

OBTAIN Reward: Give Tom Nook 2nd creature • Resident: Smug

log stool ⊙480
- hardwood x4

OBTAIN Tom Nook ("Three New Plots" quest) • Resident: Peppy

log wall-mounted clock ⊙990
- hardwood x2
- iron nugget x1

OBTAIN Resident: Lazy
UNLOCK 50

lucky gold cat ⊙21,675
- gold nugget x2
- lucky cat x1

OBTAIN Resident: Snooty
UNLOCK 100

lunar lander ⊙16,250
- star fragment x10
- iron nugget x15

OBTAIN Star fragment recipe (Reward: Celeste)

lunar rover ⊙12,580
- star fragment x10
- iron nugget x10
- old tire x4

OBTAIN Star fragment recipe (Reward: Celeste)

magazine rack ⊙690
- magazine x2
- wood x4

OBTAIN Resident: Peppy
UNLOCK 100

manhole cover ⊙2250
- iron nugget x3

OBTAIN Redeem Nook Miles

maple-leaf pond stone ⊙2700
- stone x10
- maple leaf x3

OBTAIN Seasonal recipe: Maple Leaf

matryoshka ⊙600
- softwood x5

OBTAIN Resident: Lazy

medium cardboard boxes ⊙240
- cardboard box x4

OBTAIN Resident: Lazy

mini DIY workbench ⬤2580
- wood x3
- hardwood x3
- softwood x3
- iron nugget x2

OBTAIN Test Your DIY Skills: Shop (Cabinet)

modeling clay ⬤400
- clay x2

OBTAIN Resident: Cranky

moon ⬤12,500
- star fragment x15
- large star fragment x1

OBTAIN Star fragment recipe (Reward: Celeste)

mossy garden rock ⬤2550
- stone x15
- clump of weeds x15

OBTAIN Resident: Lazy

mountain standee ⬤1080
- wood x4
- softwood x5

OBTAIN Resident: Jock

mum cushion ⬤440
- yellow mums x3
- clump of weeds x10

OBTAIN Resident: Peppy
UNLOCK 50

mush lamp ⬤1600
- skinny mushroom x1
- clay x5

OBTAIN Seasonal recipe: Mushroom

mush log ⬤1680
- skinny mushroom x2
- log stool x1

OBTAIN Seasonal recipe: Mushroom

mush low stool ⬤800
- round mushroom x2

OBTAIN Seasonal recipe: Mushroom

mush parasol ⬤1200
- flat mushroom x3

OBTAIN Seasonal recipe: Mushroom

mush partition ⬤1800
- skinny mushroom x3

OBTAIN Seasonal recipe: Mushroom

mush table ⬤1520
- flat mushroom x2
- wood x6

OBTAIN Seasonal recipe: Mushroom

music stand ⬤960
- hardwood x8

OBTAIN Resident: Lazy

natural garden chair ⬤2220
- hardwood x6
- iron nugget x2

OBTAIN Tom Nook ("Three New Plots" quest) • Resident: Peppy

natural garden table ⬤3330
- hardwood x9
- iron nugget x3

OBTAIN Tom Nook ("Three New Plots" quest) • Resident: Sweet

natural square table ⬤1980
- hardwood x4
- iron nugget x2

OBTAIN Resident: Sweet

nova light ⬤2500
- star fragment x5

OBTAIN Star fragment recipe (Reward: Celeste)

oil-barrel bathtub ⬤655
- oil barrel x1
- campfire x1
- stone x2

OBTAIN Resident: Jock
UNLOCK 100

old-fashioned washtub ⬤360
- softwood x3

OBTAIN DIY for Beginners: Shop (Cabinet)

orange end table ⬤2480
- orange x10
- wood x4

OBTAIN Tom Nook ("Three New Plots" quest) • Resident: Lazy • UNLOCK 100

orange wall-mounted clock ⬤2240
- orange x10
- wood x2

OBTAIN Tom Nook ("Three New Plots" quest) • Resident: Lazy • UNLOCK 100

ornament mobile ⬤340
- red ornament x1
- blue ornament x1
- gold ornament x1
- tree branch x4

OBTAIN Seasonal recipe: Ornament

outdoor bath ⬤4350
- stone x20
- shovel x1

OBTAIN Redeem Nook Miles

outdoor picnic set ⬤4000
- cherry-bloss. petal x10

OBTAIN Seasonal recipe: Cherry blossom

palm-tree lamp ⬤3280
- coconut x4
- wood x4
- clay x4

OBTAIN Resident: Snooty

pansy table ⬤760
- yellow pansies x5
- hardwood x3

OBTAIN Resident: Sweet
UNLOCK 50

peach chair ⬤2600
- peach x10
- wood x5

OBTAIN Tom Nook ("Three New Plots" quest) • Resident: Sweet • UNLOCK 100

peach surprise box ⬤2480
- peach x10
- softwood x4

OBTAIN Tom Nook ("Three New Plots" quest) • Resident: Sweet • UNLOCK 100

pear bed ⬤2720
- pear x10
- softwood x6

OBTAIN Tom Nook ("Three New Plots" quest) • Resident: Jock • UNLOCK 100

pear wardrobe ⬤2600
- pear x10
- wood x5

OBTAIN Tom Nook ("Three New Plots" quest) • Resident: Jock • UNLOCK 100

pile of leaves ⬤1300
- pinecone x3
- clump of weeds x5

OBTAIN Seasonal recipe: Acorn/Pinecone

pile of zen cushions ⬤750
- zen cushion x3

OBTAIN Resident: Cranky
UNLOCK 100

pine bonsai tree ⬤4200
- pinecone x8
- clay x5

OBTAIN Seasonal recipe: Acorn/Pinecone

Pisces lamp ⬤22,050
- star fragment x3
- Pisces fragment x2
- gold nugget x2
- stone x4

OBTAIN Zodiac recipe (Reward: Celeste)

plain sink ⬤2270
- wood x6
- clay x4
- iron nugget x1

OBTAIN Wildest Dreams DIY: Shop (Cabinet)

plain wooden shop sign ⬤720
- wood x6

OBTAIN Resident: Jock

pond stone ⬤1500
- stone x10

OBTAIN Resident: Snooty

pot ⬤1000
- clay x5

OBTAIN Tom Nook ("Three New Plots" quest) • Resident: Cranky

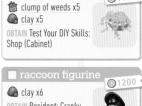

potted ivy ⬤1100
- clump of weeds x5
- clay x5

OBTAIN Test Your DIY Skills: Shop (Cabinet)

raccoon figurine ⬤1200
- clay x6

OBTAIN Resident: Cranky

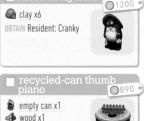

recycled-can thumb piano ⬤890
- empty can x1
- wood x1
- iron nugget x1

OBTAIN Inspiration: Empty can

red-leaf pile ⬤1280
- maple leaf x3
- clump of weeds x4

OBTAIN Seasonal recipe: Maple Leaf

ringtoss ○480
- wood x2
- softwood x2

OBTAIN Test Your DIY Skills: Shop (Cabinet)

robot hero ○250,000
- rocket x1
- gold armor x1
- rusted part x30
- iron nugget x90
- gold nugget x10

OBTAIN Redeem Nook Miles

rocket ○20,000
- star fragment x10
- iron nugget x20

OBTAIN Star fragment recipe (Reward: Celeste)

rocking chair ○960
- wood x3
- softwood x5

OBTAIN Test Your DIY Skills: Shop (Cabinet)

rocking horse ○600
- softwood x5

OBTAIN Resident: Sweet

rose bed ○1400
- red roses x10
- wood x5

OBTAIN Resident: Smug
UNLOCK 50

Sagittarius arrow ○21,750
- star fragment x3
- Sagittarius fragment x2
- gold nugget x2

OBTAIN Zodiac recipe (Reward: Celeste)

satellite ○16,250
- star fragment x10
- iron nugget x15

OBTAIN Star fragment recipe (Reward: Celeste)

sauna heater ○3510
- stone x6
- iron nugget x3
- wood x3

OBTAIN Resident: Lazy

scarecrow ○130
- tree branch x3
- clump of weeds x5

OBTAIN Resident: Cranky

scattered papers ○400
- document stack x1

OBTAIN Resident: Smug
UNLOCK 100

Scorpio lamp ○22,125
- star fragment x3
- Scorpius fragment x2
- gold nugget x2
- stone x5

OBTAIN Zodiac recipe (Reward: Celeste)

shell arch ○12,360
- sea snail x3
- venus comb x3
- sand dollar x3
- coral x3
- giant clam x3
- cowrie x3

OBTAIN Resident: Lazy • UNLOCK 100

shell bed ○10,200
- giant clam x5
- clay x3
- stone x4

OBTAIN Resident: Peppy

shell fountain ○9450
- giant clam x5
- stone x3

OBTAIN Resident: Lazy

shell lamp ○4200
- giant clam x2
- clay x3

OBTAIN Resident: Big sister

shell partition ○8000
- venus comb x4
- conch x4

OBTAIN Resident: Big sister

shell speaker ○5700
- conch x3
- iron nugget x2

OBTAIN Resident: Big sister

shell stool ○600
- cowrie x5

OBTAIN Resident: Big sister

shell table ○2280
- sand dollar x7
- clay x3

OBTAIN Resident: Peppy

signpost ○600
- hardwood x2
- softwood x3

OBTAIN Resident: Lazy
UNLOCK 100

silo ○13,920
- iron nugget x12
- hardwood x6
- clay x12
- stone x12

OBTAIN Redeem Nook Miles

simple DIY workbench ○1350
- hardwood x5
- iron nugget x1

OBTAIN Resident: Jock • Letter from Nintendo

simple well ○2850
- stone x15
- flimsy shovel x1

OBTAIN Redeem Nook Miles

sleigh ○960
- wood x8

OBTAIN Resident: Cranky

small cardboard boxes ○120
- cardboard box x2

OBTAIN Resident: Peppy

space shuttle ○10,000
- star fragment x5
- iron nugget x10

OBTAIN Star fragment recipe (Reward: Celeste)

stack of books ○725
- book x5

OBTAIN Resident: Lazy
UNLOCK 100

stacked magazines ○630
- magazine x6

OBTAIN Resident: Peppy
UNLOCK 100

stall ○1440
- wood x12

OBTAIN Redeem Nook Miles

standard umbrella stand ○2250
- iron nugget x3

OBTAIN Resident: Cranky

star clock ○2250
- star fragment x3
- iron nugget x1

OBTAIN Star fragment recipe (Reward: Celeste)

starry garland ○5000
- star fragment x10

OBTAIN Star fragment recipe (Reward: Celeste)

steamer-basket set ○2400
- young sp. bamboo x6

OBTAIN Seasonal recipe: Bamboo

stone arch ○13,500
- stone x90

OBTAIN Redeem Nook Miles

stone lion-dog ○3600
- stone x24

OBTAIN Resident: Smug
UNLOCK 100

stone stool ○450
- stone x3

OBTAIN DIY for Beginners: Shop (Cabinet) • Tom Nook ("Three New Plots" quest)

stone table ○1200
- stone x8

OBTAIN Tom Nook ("Three New Plots" quest) • Resident: Lazy

stone tablet ○1800
- stone x12

OBTAIN Redeem Nook Miles

street piano ○26,755
- upright piano x1
- painting set x1

OBTAIN Resident: Big sister
UNLOCK 100

succulent plant ○220
- clump of weeds x10
- empty can x1

OBTAIN Inspiration: Clump of weeds

swinging bench ○1440
- wood x5
- softwood x7

OBTAIN Test Your DIY Skills: Shop (Cabinet) • Tom Nook ("Three New Plots" quest)

tabletop festive tree ○930
- gold ornament x5
- tree branch x3
- clay x2

OBTAIN Seasonal recipe: Ornament

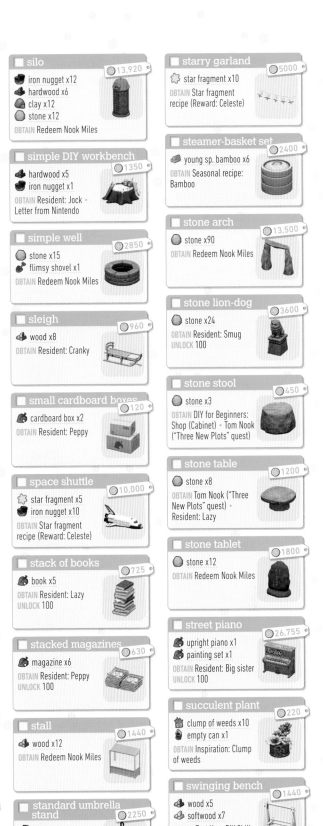

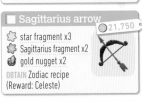

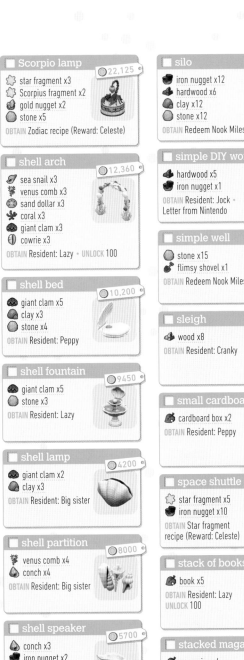

tall garden rock
- stone x60
- ⊙9000
- OBTAIN Resident: Snooty

tall lantern
- stone x18
- ⊙2700
- OBTAIN Resident: Smug
- UNLOCK 100

Taurus bathtub
- star fragment x3
- Taurus fragment x2
- gold nugget x1
- stone x8
- ⊙12,350
- OBTAIN Zodiac recipe (Reward: Celeste)

tea table
- hardwood x12
- ⊙1440
- OBTAIN Resident: Cranky

terrarium
- clump of weeds x12
- iron nugget x2
- ⊙1740
- OBTAIN Resident: Sweet

three-tiered snowperson
- large snowflake x1
- snowflake x6
- tree branch x2
- ⊙7420
- OBTAIN Reward: Snowboy

tiki torch
- tree branch x5
- wood x5
- ⊙650
- OBTAIN Reward: Give Tom Nook 2nd creature •
- Resident: Cranky

tiny library
- book x3
- wood x5
- ⊙1035
- OBTAIN Resident: Sweet
- UNLOCK 100

tire stack
- old tire x3
- ⊙60
- OBTAIN Inspiration: Old tire

tire toy
- old tire x1
- ⊙20
- OBTAIN Inspiration: Old tire

traditional balancing toy
- acorn x4
- hardwood x2
- ⊙1840
- OBTAIN Seasonal recipe: Acorn/Pinecone

trash bags
- empty can x1
- boot x1
- old tire x1
- ⊙60
- OBTAIN Inspiration: Empty can, boot

tree standee
- wood x5
- softwood x8
- ⊙1560
- OBTAIN Resident: Jock

tree's bounty arch
- pinecone x4
- acorn x5
- maple leaf x5
- tree branch x15
- ⊙5750
- OBTAIN Seasonal recipe: Maple Leaf

tree's bounty big tree
- pinecone x5
- acorn x4
- maple leaf x4
- tree branch x8
- clay x4
- ⊙6080
- OBTAIN Seasonal recipe: Maple Leaf

tree's bounty lamp
- acorn x6
- clay x4
- ⊙3200
- OBTAIN Seasonal recipe: Acorn/Pinecone

tree's bounty little tree
- pinecone x6
- acorn x4
- hardwood x1
- ⊙4120
- OBTAIN Seasonal recipe: Acorn/Pinecone

tree's bounty mobile
- pinecone x2
- acorn x3
- tree branch x3
- ⊙2030
- OBTAIN Seasonal recipe: Acorn/Pinecone

trophy case
- hardwood x24
- gold nugget x3
- iron nugget x6
- ⊙33,690
- OBTAIN Resident: Jock
- UNLOCK 100

tulip surprise box
- red tulips x5
- softwood x3
- ⊙760
- OBTAIN Resident: Jock
- UNLOCK 50

ukulele
- hardwood x5
- ⊙600
- OBTAIN Resident: Smug

unglazed dish set
- clay x3
- ⊙600
- OBTAIN Resident: Snooty

Virgo harp
- star fragment x3
- Virgo fragment x2
- gold nugget x2
- stone x4
- ⊙22,050
- OBTAIN Zodiac recipe (Reward: Celeste)

water pump
- iron nugget x2
- clay x6
- ⊙2700
- OBTAIN Tom Nook ("Three New Plots" quest) •
- Resident: Lazy

wave breaker
- stone x10
- clay x10
- ⊙3500
- OBTAIN Redeem Nook Miles

western-style stone
- stone x30
- ⊙4500
- OBTAIN Resident: Sweet
- UNLOCK 100

wild log bench
- hardwood x8
- ⊙960
- OBTAIN Resident: Jock

windflower fan
- red windflowers x3
- iron nugget x2
- ⊙1740
- OBTAIN Resident: Lazy
- UNLOCK 50

wooden bookshelf
- book x5
- wood x10
- ⊙1925
- OBTAIN Resident: Lazy
- UNLOCK 100

wooden bucket
- wood x3
- iron nugget x1
- ⊙1110
- OBTAIN Tom Nook ("Three New Plots" quest) •
- Resident: Smug

wooden chair
- wood x6
- ⊙720
- OBTAIN Tom Nook ("Three New Plots" quest) •
- Resident: Snooty

wooden chest
- wood x16
- ⊙1920
- OBTAIN Resident: Lazy

wooden double bed
- wood x30
- ⊙3600
- OBTAIN Resident: Smug

wooden end table
- wood x8
- ⊙960
- OBTAIN Resident: Snooty

wooden fish
- wood x3
- ⊙360
- OBTAIN Wildest Dreams DIY: Shop (Cabinet)

wooden full-length mirror
- wood x5
- iron nugget x1
- ⊙1350
- OBTAIN Resident: Peppy

wooden low table
- wood x10
- ⊙1200
- OBTAIN Resident: Smug

wooden mini table
- wood x6
- ⊙720
- OBTAIN Resident: Big sister

wooden simple bed
- wood x18
- ⊙2160
- OBTAIN Tom Nook ("Three New Plots" quest) •
- Resident: Lazy

wooden stool
- wood x4
- ⊙480
- OBTAIN Resident: Peppy

wooden table
- wood x15
- ⊙1800
- OBTAIN Resident: Big sister

wooden table mirror
- wood x3
- iron nugget x1
- ⊙1110
- OBTAIN Resident: Big sister

wooden toolbox
- softwood x4
- iron nugget x2
- ⊙1980
- OBTAIN Resident: Sweet

wooden wardrobe ⊙1440
🪵 wood x12
OBTAIN Reward: Customization Workshop

wooden-block bookshelf ⊙720
🪵 wooden-block toy x1
🪵 softwood x3
OBTAIN Test Your DIY Skills: Shop (Cabinet)

wooden-block stool ⊙600
🪵 wooden-block toy x1
🪵 softwood x2
OBTAIN Resident: Peppy

wooden-plank sign ⊙600
🪵 hardwood x5
OBTAIN Resident: Cranky
UNLOCK 50

wooden waste bin ⊙480
🪵 wood x4
OBTAIN Resident: Big sister

wooden-block chair ⊙720
🪵 wooden-block toy x1
🪵 softwood x3
OBTAIN Test Your DIY Skills: Shop (Cabinet)

wooden-block table ⊙1320
🪵 wooden-block toy x1
🪵 softwood x8
OBTAIN Tom Nook ("Three New Plots" quest) • Resident: Big sister

yellow-leaf pile ⊙1300
🌰 acorn x3
🌿 clump of weeds x5
OBTAIN Seasonal recipe: Acorn/Pinecone

wooden-block bed ⊙2400
🪵 wooden-block toy x1
🪵 softwood x17
OBTAIN Resident: Sweet

wooden-block chest ⊙1800
🪵 wooden-block toy x1
🪵 softwood x12
OBTAIN Resident: Sweet

wooden-block toy ⊙360
🪵 softwood x3
OBTAIN DIY for Beginners: Shop (Cabinet)

zen-style stone ⊙4500
⚪ stone x30
OBTAIN Resident: Lazy
UNLOCK 100

wooden-block bench ⊙840
🪵 wooden-block toy x1
🪵 softwood x4
OBTAIN Resident: Big sister

wooden-block stereo ⊙2460
🪵 wooden-block toy x1
🪵 softwood x5
⛏ iron nugget x2
OBTAIN Test Your DIY Skills: Shop (Cabinet) • Tom Nook ("Three New Plots" quest)

wooden-block wall clock ⊙1350
🪵 wooden-block toy x1
🪵 softwood x2
⛏ iron nugget x1
OBTAIN Resident: Peppy
UNLOCK 50

Door Decoration Recipes

blue rose wreath ⊙20,000
🌹 blue roses x10
OBTAIN Resident: Any Type
UNLOCK 200

cool windflower wreath ⊙1200
🌼 blue windflowers x3
🌼 pink windflowers x3
🌼 white windflowers x3
OBTAIN Resident: Any Type
UNLOCK 100

dark tulip wreath ⊙1600
🌷 black tulips x10
OBTAIN Resident: Any Type
UNLOCK 200

fruit wreath ⊙2000
🍎 apple x2
🍐 pear x1
🍒 cherry x3
🍊 orange x3
🍑 peach x1
OBTAIN Resident: Cranky • UNLOCK 100

bone doorplate ⊙360
🪵 softwood x3
OBTAIN Resident: Lazy
UNLOCK 50

cosmos wreath ⊙720
🌼 yellow cosmos x3
🌼 white cosmos x3
🌼 red cosmos x3
OBTAIN Tom Nook ("Three New Plots" quest) • Resident: Any Type
UNLOCK 50

fancy lily wreath ⊙1200
🌸 orange lilies x3
🌸 pink lilies x3
🌸 yellow lilies x3
OBTAIN Resident: Any Type
UNLOCK 100

gold rose wreath ⊙20,000
🌹 gold roses x10
OBTAIN Resident: Any Type
UNLOCK 200

chic cosmos wreath ⊙4800
🌼 black cosmos x10
OBTAIN Resident: Any Type
UNLOCK 200

fancy mum wreath ⊙1200
🌸 pink mums x3
🌸 purple mums x3
🌸 red mums x3
OBTAIN Resident: Any Type
UNLOCK 100

hyacinth wreath ⊙720
🌷 white hyacinths x3
🌷 red hyacinths x3
🌷 yellow hyacinths x3
OBTAIN Tom Nook ("Three New Plots" quest) • Resident: Any Type
UNLOCK 50

chic windflower wreath ⊙4800
🌼 purple windflowers x10
OBTAIN Resident: Any Type
UNLOCK 200

crest doorplate ⊙3000
⛏ iron nugget x4
OBTAIN Resident: Smug
UNLOCK 50

fancy rose wreath ⊙1200
🌹 orange roses x3
🌹 pink roses x3
🌹 yellow roses x3
OBTAIN Resident: Any Type
UNLOCK 100

iron doorplate ⊙1500
⛏ iron nugget x2
OBTAIN Resident: Big sister
UNLOCK 50

cool hyacinth wreath ⊙1440
🌷 orange hyacinths x3
🌷 blue hyacinths x3
🌷 pink hyacinths x3
OBTAIN Resident: Any Type
UNLOCK 100

dark lily wreath ⊙1600
🌸 black lilies x10
OBTAIN Resident: Any Type
UNLOCK 200

lily wreath ⊙720
🌸 white lilies x3
🌸 red lilies x3
🌸 yellow lilies x3
OBTAIN Tom Nook ("Three New Plots" quest) • Resident: Any Type • UNLOCK 50

cool pansy wreath ⊙4800
🌸 purple pansies x10
OBTAIN Resident: Any Type
UNLOCK 200

dark rose wreath ⊙4320
🌹 black roses x3
🌹 purple roses x6
OBTAIN Resident: Any Type
UNLOCK 200

fossil doorplate ⊙500
🦴 fossil x1
⚪ stone x2
OBTAIN Resident: Jock
UNLOCK 50

mum wreath ⊘720
- 🌼 white mums x3
- 🌼 yellow mums x3
- 🌼 red mums x3

OBTAIN Tom Nook ("Three New Plots" quest) • Resident: Any Type • UNLOCK 50

pansy wreath ⊘720
- 🌸 yellow pansies x3
- 🌸 white pansies x3
- 🌸 red pansies x3

OBTAIN Tom Nook ("Three New Plots" quest) • Resident: Any Type • UNLOCK 50

purple hyacinth wreath ⊘4800
- 🌷 purple hyacinths x10

OBTAIN Resident: Any Type UNLOCK 200

snowflake wreath ⊘1600
- ❄ snowflake x4

OBTAIN Seasonal recipe: Snowflake

mushroom wreath ⊘1500
- 🌿 tree branch x10
- ⚪ round mushroom x1
- 🍄 skinny mushroom x1
- 🍄 flat mushroom x1

OBTAIN Seasonal recipe: Mushroom

paw-print doorplate ⊘360
- 🪵 wood x3

OBTAIN Resident: Peppy UNLOCK 50

rose wreath ⊘720
- 🌹 red roses x3
- 🌹 white roses x3
- 🌹 yellow roses x3

OBTAIN Tom Nook ("Three New Plots" quest) • Resident: Any Type • UNLOCK 50

timber doorplate ⊘400
- 🪵 wood x2
- 🌹 pink roses x1

OBTAIN Resident: Snooty UNLOCK 50

natural mum wreath ⊘4800
- 🌼 green mums x10

OBTAIN Resident: Any Type UNLOCK 200

pretty cosmos wreath ⊘1200
- 🌼 orange cosmos x3
- 🌼 pink cosmos x3
- 🌼 red cosmos x3

OBTAIN Resident: Any Type UNLOCK 100

shell wreath ⊘4720
- 🐚 summer shell x1
- 🐚 sea snail x1
- 🐚 sand dollar x1
- 🪸 coral x1
- 🐚 giant clam x1
- 🐚 cowrie x1

OBTAIN Seasonal recipe: Summer shell

tree branch wreath ⊘100
- 🌿 tree branch x10

OBTAIN Resident: Big sister UNLOCK 50

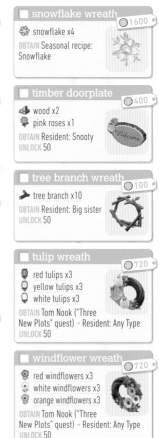

tulip wreath ⊘720
- 🌷 red tulips x3
- 🌷 yellow tulips x3
- 🌷 white tulips x3

OBTAIN Tom Nook ("Three New Plots" quest) • Resident: Any Type UNLOCK 50

ornament wreath ⊘800
- 🔵 blue ornament x6
- 🟡 gold ornament x2

OBTAIN Seasonal recipe: Ornament

pretty tulip wreath ⊘2400
- 🌷 orange tulips x3
- 🌷 pink tulips x3
- 🌷 purple tulips x3

OBTAIN Resident: Any Type UNLOCK 100

snazzy pansy wreath ⊘1200
- 🌸 orange pansies x3
- 🌸 blue pansies x3
- 🌸 yellow pansies x3

OBTAIN Resident: Any Type UNLOCK 100

windflower wreath ⊘720
- 🌼 red windflowers x3
- 🌼 white windflowers x3
- 🌼 orange windflowers x3

OBTAIN Tom Nook ("Three New Plots" quest) • Resident: Any Type UNLOCK 50

Fence Recipes

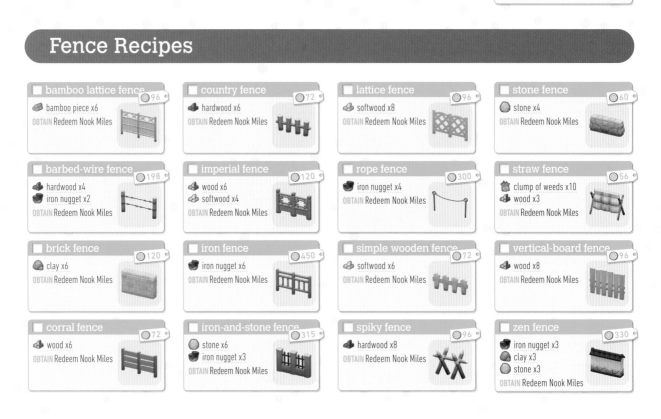

bamboo lattice fence ⊘96
- 🎋 bamboo piece x6

OBTAIN Redeem Nook Miles

country fence ⊘72
- 🪵 hardwood x6

OBTAIN Redeem Nook Miles

lattice fence ⊘96
- 🪵 softwood x8

OBTAIN Redeem Nook Miles

stone fence ⊘60
- 🪨 stone x4

OBTAIN Redeem Nook Miles

barbed-wire fence ⊘198
- 🪵 hardwood x4
- ⛏ iron nugget x2

OBTAIN Redeem Nook Miles

imperial fence ⊘120
- 🪵 wood x6
- 🪵 softwood x4

OBTAIN Redeem Nook Miles

rope fence ⊘300
- ⛏ iron nugget x4

OBTAIN Redeem Nook Miles

straw fence ⊘56
- 🌾 clump of weeds x10
- 🪵 wood x3

OBTAIN Redeem Nook Miles

brick fence ⊘120
- 🟤 clay x6

OBTAIN Redeem Nook Miles

iron fence ⊘450
- ⛏ iron nugget x6

OBTAIN Redeem Nook Miles

simple wooden fence ⊘72
- 🪵 softwood x6

OBTAIN Redeem Nook Miles

vertical-board fence ⊘96
- 🪵 wood x8

OBTAIN Redeem Nook Miles

corral fence ⊘72
- 🪵 wood x6

OBTAIN Redeem Nook Miles

iron-and-stone fence ⊘315
- 🪨 stone x6
- ⛏ iron nugget x3

OBTAIN Redeem Nook Miles

spiky fence ⊘96
- 🪵 hardwood x8

OBTAIN Redeem Nook Miles

zen fence ⊘330
- ⛏ iron nugget x3
- 🟤 clay x3
- 🪨 stone x3

OBTAIN Redeem Nook Miles

Flooring Recipes

backyard lawn 〇600

🌿 clump of weeds x30
OBTAIN Resident: Peppy

bamboo flooring 〇2400

🪵 bamboo piece x15
OBTAIN Resident: Cranky
UNLOCK 50

basement flooring 〇1500

🪨 stone x10
OBTAIN Resident: Smug

cherry-blossom flooring 〇4400

🌸 cherry-bloss. petal x10
🌿 clump of weeds x20
OBTAIN Seasonal recipe: Cherry blossom

colored-leaves flooring 〇4300

🍁 maple leaf x10
🌿 clump of weeds x15
OBTAIN Seasonal recipe: Maple Leaf

forest flooring 〇35,000

🍄 rare mushroom x1
🍄 round mushroom x2
🍄 skinny mushroom x2
🍄 flat mushroom x2
🌿 clump of weeds x10
OBTAIN Seasonal recipe: Mushroom

galaxy flooring 〇7500
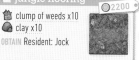
⭐ star fragment x5
✨ large star fragment x1
OBTAIN Star fragment recipe (Reward: Celeste)

garbage-heap flooring 〇120

🥫 empty can x2
👢 boot x2
⚫ old tire x2
OBTAIN Inspiration: Empty can

golden flooring 〇40,000

🪙 gold nugget x4
OBTAIN Resident: Smug
UNLOCK 100

honeycomb flooring 〇3000

🐝 wasp nest x5
OBTAIN Resident: Jock

ice flooring 〇8200

❄️ large snowflake x1
❄️ snowflake x8
OBTAIN Reward: Snowboy

iceberg flooring 〇4000

❄️ snowflake x10
OBTAIN Seasonal recipe: Snowflake

jungle flooring 〇2200

🌿 clump of weeds x10
🪨 clay x10
OBTAIN Resident: Jock

lunar surface 〇7500

⭐ star fragment x5
✨ large star fragment x1
OBTAIN Star fragment recipe (Reward: Celeste)

money flooring 〇25,000

🪙 50,000 bells x1
OBTAIN Resident: Snooty
UNLOCK 100

sakura-wood flooring 〇3200

🌸 cherry-bloss. petal x5
🪵 wood x10
OBTAIN Seasonal recipe: Cherry blossom

sandy-beach flooring 〇4120

🐚 sea snail x1
🌸 venus comb x1
🟤 sand dollar x1
🪸 coral x1
🐚 giant clam x1
🐚 cowrie x1
OBTAIN Resident: Jock

sci-fi flooring 〇7500

⭐ star fragment x5
✨ large star fragment x1
OBTAIN Star fragment recipe (Reward: Celeste)

ski-slope flooring 〇3200
❄️ snowflake x8
OBTAIN Seasonal recipe: Snowflake

starry-sands flooring 〇7720

🐚 summer shell x3
🪨 sandy-beach flooring x1
OBTAIN Seasonal recipe: Summer shell

steel flooring 〇5250

⬛ iron nugget x7
OBTAIN Resident: Smug

underwater flooring 〇6600

🍂 summer shell x3
🪸 coral x3
OBTAIN Seasonal recipe: Summer shell

water flooring 〇7200

🍂 summer shell x6
OBTAIN Seasonal recipe: Summer shell

Wallpaper Recipes

apple wall 〇4000
🍎 apple x20
OBTAIN Resident: Big sister
UNLOCK 100

autumn wall 〇4700
🍁 maple leaf x10
🪵 wood x5
🌿 clump of weeds x5
OBTAIN Seasonal recipe: Maple Leaf

bamboo wall 〇2400

🪵 bamboo piece x15
OBTAIN Resident: Cranky
UNLOCK 50

bamboo-grove wall 〇4300

🪨 young sp. bamboo x7
🟤 bamboo shoot x3
OBTAIN Seasonal recipe: Bamboo

brown herringbone wall 〇1800

🪵 softwood x15
OBTAIN Resident: Big sister

cabin wall 〇1800
🪵 hardwood x15
OBTAIN Resident: Peppy

cherry wall 〇4000
🍒 cherry x20
OBTAIN Resident: Peppy
UNLOCK 100

cherry-blossom-trees wall 〇4600
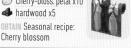
🌸 cherry-bloss. petal x10
🪵 hardwood x5
OBTAIN Seasonal recipe: Cherry blossom

chocolate herringbone wall 〇1800
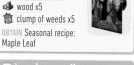
🪵 softwood x15
OBTAIN Resident: Smug

classic-library wall 〇1450

📕 book x10
OBTAIN Resident: Sweet
UNLOCK 100

dark wooden-mosaic wall 〇1800

🪵 wood x15
OBTAIN Resident: Big sister

forest wall 〇44,000
🍄 elegant mushroom x2
🍄 round mushroom x2
🍄 skinny mushroom x2
🍄 flat mushroom x2
🪵 wood x10
OBTAIN Seasonal recipe: Mushroom

garbage-heap wall — 120
- empty can x2
- boot x2
- old tire x2

OBTAIN Inspiration: Empty can

gold-screen wall — 20,750
- gold nugget x2
- screen wall x1

OBTAIN Resident: Smug
UNLOCK 100

golden wall — 40,000
- gold nugget x4

OBTAIN Resident: Smug
UNLOCK 100

honeycomb wall — 3600
- wasp nest x6

OBTAIN Resident: Jock

ice wall — 8200
- large snowflake x1
- snowflake x8

OBTAIN Reward: Snowboy

iceberg wall — 4000
- snowflake x10

OBTAIN Seasonal recipe: Snowflake

Jingle wall — 2500
- red ornament x5
- blue ornament x5
- gold ornament x5
- clay x5

OBTAIN Seasonal recipe: Ornament

jungle wall — 1380
- clump of weeds x15
- wood x3
- hardwood x3
- softwood x3

OBTAIN Resident: Jock

manga-library wall — 1050
- magazine x10

OBTAIN Resident: Peppy
UNLOCK 100

modern wood wall — 1800
- wood x5
- softwood x5
- hardwood x5

OBTAIN Resident: Snooty

mush wall — 21,400
- elegant mushroom x1
- round mushroom x1
- skinny mushroom x1
- flat mushroom x1

OBTAIN Seasonal recipe: Mushroom

orange wall — 4000
- orange x20

OBTAIN Resident: Lazy
UNLOCK 100

peach wall — 4000
- peach x20

OBTAIN Resident: Sweet
UNLOCK 100

pear wall — 4000
- pear x20

OBTAIN Resident: Jock
UNLOCK 100

rustic-stone wall — 1750
- stone x5
- clay x5

OBTAIN Resident: Snooty

sakura-wood wall — 3200
- cherry-bloss. petal x5
- wood x10

OBTAIN Seasonal recipe: Cherry blossom

sci-fi wall — 7500
- star fragment x5
- large star fragment x1

OBTAIN Star fragment recipe (Reward: Celeste)

ski-slope wall — 3200
- snowflake x8

OBTAIN Seasonal recipe: Snowflake

snowflake wall — 4800
- snowflake x12

OBTAIN Seasonal recipe: Snowflake

stacked-wood wall — 1800
- hardwood x15

OBTAIN Resident: Jock

starry wall — 7500
- star fragment x5
- large star fragment x1

OBTAIN Star fragment recipe (Reward: Celeste)

starry-sky wall — 7500
- star fragment x5
- large star fragment x1

OBTAIN Star fragment recipe (Reward: Celeste)

steel-frame wall — 6000
- iron nugget x8

OBTAIN Resident: Smug

stone wall — 1500
- stone x10

OBTAIN Resident: Smug

tropical vista — 6000
- summer shell x5

OBTAIN Seasonal recipe: Summer shell

underwater wall — 8600
- summer shell x3
- coral x5

OBTAIN Seasonal recipe: Summer shell

wild-wood wall — 1800
- wood x15

OBTAIN Resident: Cranky

wooden-knot wall — 1800
- hardwood x15

OBTAIN Resident: Smug

wooden-mosaic wall — 1800
- wood x15

OBTAIN Resident: Sweet

woodland wall — 1380
- clump of weeds x15
- softwood x9

OBTAIN Resident: Sweet

Rug Recipes

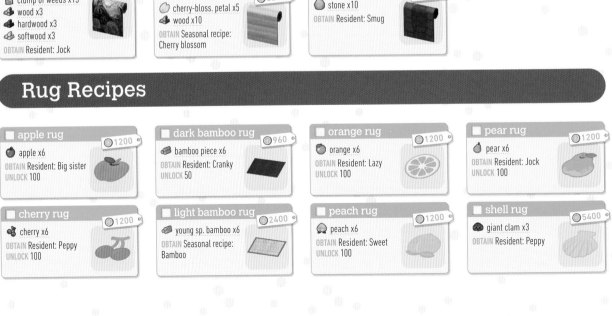

apple rug — 1200
- apple x6

OBTAIN Resident: Big sister
UNLOCK 100

cherry rug — 1200
- cherry x6

OBTAIN Resident: Peppy
UNLOCK 100

dark bamboo rug — 960
- bamboo piece x6

OBTAIN Resident: Cranky
UNLOCK 50

light bamboo rug — 2400
- young sp. bamboo x6

OBTAIN Seasonal recipe: Bamboo

orange rug — 1200
- orange x6

OBTAIN Resident: Lazy
UNLOCK 100

peach rug — 1200
- peach x6

OBTAIN Resident: Sweet
UNLOCK 100

pear rug — 1200
- pear x6

OBTAIN Resident: Jock
UNLOCK 100

shell rug — 5400
- giant clam x3

OBTAIN Resident: Peppy

Tool Recipes

axe
 ⊘625
- flimsy axe x1
- wood x3
- iron nugget x1

OBTAIN Pretty Good Tools Recipes (Redeem Nook Miles)

bamboo wand
 ⊘3900
- young sp. bamboo x6
- star fragment x3

OBTAIN Seasonal recipe: Bamboo

cherry-blossom wand
 ⊘2700
- cherry-bloss. petal x3
- star fragment x3

OBTAIN Seasonal recipe: Cherry blossom

cosmos wand
 ⊘1580
- white cosmos x1
- star fragment x3

OBTAIN Star fragment recipe (Reward: Celeste)

fishing rod
 ⊘600
- flimsy fishing rod x1
- iron nugget x1

OBTAIN Pretty Good Tools Recipes (Redeem Nook Miles)

flimsy axe
 ⊘200
- tree branch x5
- stone x1

OBTAIN Reward: Give Tom Nook 2nd creature

flimsy fishing rod
 ⊘100
- tree branch x5

OBTAIN Reward: DIY Workshop

flimsy net
 ⊘100
- tree branch x5

OBTAIN Reward: DIY Workshop

flimsy shovel
 ⊘200
- hardwood x5

OBTAIN Reward: Talk to Blathers 1st time

flimsy watering can
 ⊘200
- softwood x5

OBTAIN Reward: Give Tom Nook 4th creature

golden axe
 ⊘10,655
- gold nugget x1
- axe x1

OBTAIN Inspiration: Break 100 axes (any type)

golden net
 ⊘10,400
- gold nugget x1
- net x1

OBTAIN Complete all bugs in Critterpedia (Mail)

golden rod
 ⊘10,400
- gold nugget x1
- fishing rod x1

OBTAIN Complete all fish in Critterpedia (Mail)

golden shovel
 ⊘10,675
- gold nugget x1
- shovel x1

OBTAIN Help Gulliver 30 times and he'll mail you a recipe

golden slingshot
 ⊘10,300
- gold nugget x1
- slingshot x1

OBTAIN Shoot down 300 balloons with a slingshot (any type)

golden wand
 ⊘20,750
- gold nugget x2
- star fragment x3

OBTAIN Star fragment recipe (Reward: Celeste)

golden watering can
 ⊘10,675
- gold nugget x1
- watering can x1

OBTAIN Get a 5-star Island Rating

hyacinth wand
 ⊘1660
- pink hyacinths x1
- star fragment x3

OBTAIN Star fragment recipe (Reward: Celeste)

ice wand
 ⊘6500
- large snowflake x1
- star fragment x3

OBTAIN Reward: Snowboy

iron wand
 ⊘3750
- iron nugget x3
- star fragment x3

OBTAIN Star fragment recipe (Reward: Celeste)

ladder
 ⊘1440
- wood x4
- hardwood x4
- softwood x4

OBTAIN Tom Nook ("Three New Plots" quest)

lily wand
 ⊘1580
- white lilies x1
- star fragment x3

OBTAIN Star fragment recipe (Reward: Celeste)

mums wand
 ⊘1580
- yellow mums x1
- star fragment x3

OBTAIN Star fragment recipe (Reward: Celeste)

mushroom wand
 ⊘3300
- skinny mushroom x3
- star fragment x3

OBTAIN Seasonal recipe: Mushroom

net
 ⊘600
- flimsy net x1
- iron nugget x1

OBTAIN Pretty Good Tools Recipes (Redeem Nook Miles)

ocarina
 ⊘1000
- clay x5

OBTAIN DIY for Beginners: Shop (Cabinet)

pan flute
 ⊘2800
- young sp. bamboo x7

OBTAIN Seasonal recipe: Bamboo

pansy wand
 ⊘1580
- yellow pansies x1
- star fragment x3

OBTAIN Star fragment recipe (Reward: Celeste)

rose wand
 ⊘1580
- red roses x1
- star fragment x3

OBTAIN Star fragment recipe (Reward: Celeste)

shell wand
 ⊘5100
- summer shell x3
- star fragment x3

OBTAIN Seasonal recipe: Summer shell

shovel
 ⊘600
- flimsy shovel x1
- iron nugget x1

OBTAIN Pretty Good Tools Recipes (Redeem Nook Miles)

slingshot
 ⊘225
- hardwood x5

OBTAIN Shop (Tent/Cabinet)

star wand
 ⊘6500
- large star fragment x1
- star fragment x3

OBTAIN Star fragment recipe (Reward: Celeste)

stone axe
 ⊘560
- flimsy axe x1
- wood x3

OBTAIN Pretty Good Tools Recipes (Redeem Nook Miles)

tree-branch wand
 ⊘1550
- tree branch x5
- star fragment x3

OBTAIN Star fragment recipe (Reward: Celeste)

tulip wand
 ⊘1580
- red tulips x1
- star fragment x3

OBTAIN Star fragment recipe (Reward: Celeste)

vaulting pole
 ⊘600
- softwood x5

OBTAIN Reward: Talk to Blathers 1st time

wand
 ⊘1000
- star fragment x2

OBTAIN Star fragment recipe (Reward: Celeste)

watering can
 ⊘600
- flimsy water. can x1
- iron nugget x1

OBTAIN Pretty Good Tools Recipes (Redeem Nook Miles)

windflower wand
⊘1580
- orange windflowers x1
- star fragment x3

OBTAIN Star fragment recipe (Reward: Celeste)

Clothing Recipes

Tops

traditional straw coat
- clump of weeds x8
- OBTAIN Resident: Sweet

Bottoms

grass skirt
- clump of weeds x7
- OBTAIN Resident: Sweet

green grass skirt
- clump of weeds x7
- OBTAIN Resident: Peppy

One piece

apple dress
- apple x8
- OBTAIN Resident: Big sister
- UNLOCK 100

cherry dress
- cherry x8
- OBTAIN Resident: Peppy
- UNLOCK 100

gold armor
- gold nugget x8
- OBTAIN Resident: Smug
- UNLOCK 100

iron armor
- iron nugget x8
- OBTAIN Resident: Cranky
- UNLOCK 100

orange dress
- orange x8
- OBTAIN Resident: Lazy
- UNLOCK 100

peach dress
- peach x8
- OBTAIN Resident: Sweet
- UNLOCK 100

pear dress
- pear x8
- OBTAIN Resident: Jock
- UNLOCK 100

Headwear

apple hat
- apple x5
- OBTAIN Resident: Big sister
- UNLOCK 100

bamboo hat
- clump of weeds x10
- OBTAIN Resident: Cranky

blue rose crown
- blue roses x6
- OBTAIN Resident: Any Type
- UNLOCK 200

cherry hat
- cherry x5
- OBTAIN Resident: Peppy
- UNLOCK 100

chic mum crown
- purple mums x3
- pink mums x3
- OBTAIN Resident: Any Type
- UNLOCK 100

chic rose crown
- purple roses x3
- black roses x3
- OBTAIN Resident: Any Type
- UNLOCK 200

chic tulip crown
- purple tulips x2
- pink tulips x2
- orange tulips x1
- OBTAIN Resident: Any Type
- UNLOCK 100

cool hyacinth crown
- blue hyacinths x4
- pink hyacinths x2
- orange hyacinths x2
- OBTAIN Resident: Any Type
- UNLOCK 100

cool pansy crown
- orange pansies x3
- blue pansies x3
- OBTAIN Resident: Any Type
- UNLOCK 100

cool windflower crown
- blue windflowers x3
- pink windflowers x3
- OBTAIN Resident: Any Type
- UNLOCK 100

cosmos crown
- red cosmos x2
- yellow cosmos x2
- white cosmos x3
- OBTAIN Resident: Any Type

cute lily crown
- pink lilies x2
- orange lilies x2
- white lilies x2
- OBTAIN Resident: Any Type
- UNLOCK 100

cute rose crown
- pink roses x3
- orange roses x3
- OBTAIN Resident: Any Type
- UNLOCK 100

dark cosmos crown
- black cosmos x7
- OBTAIN Resident: Any Type
- UNLOCK 200

dark lily crown
- black lilies x6
- OBTAIN Resident: Any Type
- UNLOCK 200

dark tulip crown
- black tulips x5
- OBTAIN Resident: Any Type
- UNLOCK 200

gold helmet
- gold nugget x5
- OBTAIN Resident: Smug
- UNLOCK 200

gold rose crown
- gold roses x6
- OBTAIN Resident: Any Type
- UNLOCK 200

hyacinth crown
- red hyacinths x4
- yellow hyacinths x2
- white hyacinths x2
- OBTAIN Resident: Any Type

knight's helmet
- iron nugget x5
- OBTAIN Resident: Cranky
- UNLOCK 100

leaf mask
- clump of weeds x10
- OBTAIN Resident: Peppy

lily crown
- red lilies x2
- yellow lilies x2
- white lilies x2
- OBTAIN Resident: Any Type

lovely cosmos crown
- pink cosmos x4
- orange cosmos x3
- OBTAIN Resident: Any Type
- UNLOCK 100

mum crown
- red mums x2
- yellow mums x2
- white mums x2
- OBTAIN Resident: Any Type

orange hat
- orange x5
- OBTAIN Resident: Lazy
- UNLOCK 100

pansy crown
- red pansies x2
- yellow pansies x2
- white pansies x2
- OBTAIN Resident: Any Type

peach hat
- peach x5
- OBTAIN Resident: Sweet
- UNLOCK 100

pear hat
- pear x5
- OBTAIN Resident: Jock
- UNLOCK 100

purple hyacinth crown
- purple hyacinths x6
- OBTAIN Resident: Any Type
- UNLOCK 200

purple pansy crown ⚬2880
- purple pansies x6
- OBTAIN Resident: Any Type
- UNLOCK 200

purple windflower crown ⚬2880
- purple windflowers x6
- OBTAIN Resident: Any Type
- UNLOCK 200

rose crown ⚬480
- red roses x2
- yellow roses x2
- white roses x2
- OBTAIN Resident: Any Type

simple mum crown ⚬2880
- green mums x6
- OBTAIN Resident: Any Type
- UNLOCK 200

snowperson head ⚬7000
- large snowflake x1
- snowflake x5
- OBTAIN Reward: Snowboy

star head ⚬2500
- star fragment x5
- OBTAIN Star fragment recipe (Reward: Celeste)

straw umbrella hat ⚬200
- clump of weeds x10
- OBTAIN Resident: Smug

tulip crown ⚬400
- red tulips x2
- yellow tulips x2
- white tulips x1
- OBTAIN Resident: Any Type

windflower crown ⚬480
- red windflowers x2
- orange windflowers x2
- white windflowers x2
- OBTAIN Resident: Any Type

Accessories

leaf ⚬100
- clump of weeds x5
- OBTAIN Resident: Jock

Shoes

armor shoes ⚬3000
- iron nugget x4
- OBTAIN Resident: Cranky
- UNLOCK 100

gold-armor shoes ⚬40,000
- gold nugget x4
- OBTAIN Resident: Smug
- UNLOCK 200

recycled boots ⚬40
- boot x2
- OBTAIN Inspiration: Boot

Bags

acorn pochette ⚬2400
- acorn x6
- OBTAIN Seasonal recipe: Acorn/Pinecone

basket pack ⚬2400
- young sp. bamboo x6
- OBTAIN Seasonal recipe: Bamboo

cherry-blossom pochette ⚬2400
- cherry-bloss. petal x6
- OBTAIN Seasonal recipe: Cherry blossom

knitted-grass backpack ⚬400
- clump of weeds x20
- OBTAIN Resident: Sweet

log pack ⚬960
- wood x3
- hardwood x5
- OBTAIN Resident: Jock

maple-leaf pochette ⚬2400
- maple leaf x6
- OBTAIN Seasonal recipe: Maple Leaf

shellfish pochette ⚬10,800
- giant clam x2
- summer shell x6
- OBTAIN Seasonal recipe: Summer shell

---

snowflake pochette ⚬2400
- snowflake x6
- OBTAIN Seasonal recipe: Snowflake

star pochette ⚬3000
- star fragment x6
- OBTAIN Star fragment recipe (Reward: Celeste)

Umbrellas

apple umbrella ⚬1400
- apple x7
- OBTAIN Resident: Big sister
- UNLOCK 100

cherry umbrella ⚬1400
- cherry x7
- OBTAIN Resident: Peppy
- UNLOCK 100

cherry-blossom umbrella ⚬2800
- cherry-bloss. petal x7
- OBTAIN Seasonal recipe: Cherry blossom

Miscellaneous Recipes

bridge construction kit
- log stakes x4
- clay x4
- stone x4
- OBTAIN Tom Nook ("Build the Log Bridge"

campsite construct. kit
- wood x15
- softwood x15
- hardwood x15
- iron nugget x15
- OBTAIN Tom Nook ("Build the Campsite")

fish bait ⚬200
- manila clam x1
- OBTAIN Inspiration: Manila clam

---

leaf umbrella ⚬300
- clump of weeds x15
- OBTAIN Resident: Big sister

maple-leaf umbrella ⚬2800
- maple leaf x7
- OBTAIN Seasonal recipe: Maple Leaf

mush umbrella ⚬1200
- flat mushroom x3
- OBTAIN Seasonal recipe: Mushroom

orange umbrella ⚬1400
- orange x7
- OBTAIN Resident: Lazy
- UNLOCK 100

peach umbrella ⚬1400
- peach x7
- OBTAIN Resident: Sweet
- UNLOCK 100

pear umbrella ⚬1400
- pear x7
- OBTAIN Resident: Jock
- UNLOCK 100

medicine ⚬100
- wasp nest x1
- clump of weeds x3
- OBTAIN Inspiration: Wasp nest

pitfall seed ⚬140
- clump of weeds x4
- tree branch x6
- OBTAIN Resident: Jock
- UNLOCK 100

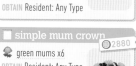

5

Chapter 6

Isabelle's Island Reviews

Even on a deserted island getaway, it's good to have long term goals, right? This chapter covers the things you can strive toward once you've got a populated, developed island and helps you to get the whole place, indoors and out, looking its absolute best!

CHAPTER HIGHLIGHTS

Island Rating

One of Isabelle's many tasks in the Resident Services office involves managing your island's PR. She'll collect notes and comments from island residents and visitors, and keep tabs on your island's reputation. You can find out what people think of your island by talking to her in the Resident Services building and selecting "Let's talk island evals."

Isabelle
Hello there, everyone!

Isabelle's Evaluations

Isabelle will do her best to provide helpful advice on how to improve your island. Your island will be ranked on a scale of 1 to 5 stars—if it reaches 5 stars, Isabelle will reward you with the recipe for the golden watering can, and you'll also get an exciting new flower called a lily-of-the-valley. This flower will grow naturally somewhere on your island and cannot be bought.

There are two main categories on which your island is rated, which Isabelle will mention during evals: "Island Scenery" and "Island Development". Scenery points are concerned with DIY furniture and the plantlife growing on your island, while Island Development points involve the buildings other attractions your island is home to. After mentioning one of these factors, she'll sometimes say if there's been a positive change since the last rating, and will then give some tips for further improvements. Your final rating is calculated based on the chart here—your Development and Scenery scores are checked, and the rating as decided based on the lower of the two (along with total number of residents, which must be eight or more to get above 2 stars).

Star Rating Values

Development	Scenery	Rating
Less than 80	Less than 200	▸ 1 Star
80 to 159	200 to 269	▸ 2 Star
160 to 399	270 to 349	▸ 3 Star
400 to 664	350 to 449	▸ 4 Star
665+	450+	▸ 5 Star

"How excellent! I'm so pleased that you've taken an interest in the image of our island! Well, allow me to explain how the task force—that's me—collects and analyzes data for my reports."

Positive Conditions

There are plenty of ways to rack up points for your island: here we'll explain the subcategories for grading, and the tile system it's based on. Every island is divided into 9216 uniformly-sized tiles that form a 96x96 square. Within that, furniture placed on the island is graded on an 8x8 tile basis—each tile is approximately the size of the space that your character can stand or sit on. On your NookPhone's map, the island is split into 16x16 blocks, which can help you to visualize the smaller 8x8 blocks. It also helps to use your shovel to dig lots of holes, or place custom designs on the ground to visualize these blocks. Furniture can be moved a half block and may overlap into an adjacent block. Each block is scored on its own, however, and the overlapping piece of furniture will count for both blocks. Plantlife scoring doesn't take this grid into account. You'll simply receive points for each tree or flower growing on your island.

Scenery

Plantlife	Added points
Trees (including bamboo) ▸	+ 1 point for each fully grown tree (up to a maximum of 190 points)
Flower Sprout ▸	+0.5 points
Flower Stem ▸	+0.7 points
Flower Bud ▸	+0.7 points
Adult Flower ▸	+1 point

Development

Condition	Added Points
The Museum is built ▸	+15
Nook's Cranny has been upgraded ▸	+15
Able Sisters is built ▸	+15
Your island has a bridge ▸	+(Number of bridges) x 15
Your island has an incline ▸	+(Number of slopes) x 15

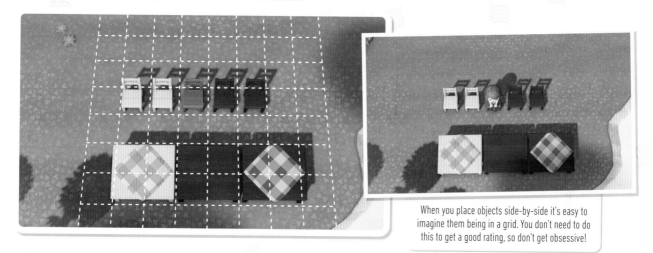

When you place objects side-by-side it's easy to imagine them being in a grid. You don't need to do this to get a good rating, so don't get obsessive!

DIY Furniture

DIY furniture adds to your Scenery points, and variety is key here! You'll get more points for placing down different pieces of furniture, rather than the same thing over and over. Some furniture will count as being the same "type" but will still count as a unique piece. A type is a category such as chairs, tables, wardrobes, etc. For instance, placing down a wooden chair and an office chair will only count as one type, but will count as two unique pieces. Even color variants of the same item count as unique types of furniture that will gain you more bonuses, so keep that in mind.

DIY Furniture Points

Furniture within a block	Added points to Scenery
For each unique piece of DIY furniture that is 3x1, 3x2 or 3x3 tile size ▸	+1 point
4 or less different types of furniture ▸	+The number of furniture placed × 0.25 points
5 - 10 different types of furniture ▸	+The number of furniture placed × 0.25 points
10 or more different types of furniture ▸	+The number of furniture placed x 0.25 +The number of types x 0.75

Example A	20 unique pieces of furniture (all chairs) ▸	20x1 = 20 points
Example B	20 unique pieces of furniture, 4 different types. ▸	(20x1)+(20x0.25) = 20+5 = 25 points
Example C	20 unique pieces of furniture, 5 different types. ▸	(20x1)+(20x0.5)+(5X0.25) = 20+10+1.25 = 31.25 points

Non-DIY Furniture

Furniture that doesn't fit under the 'Scenery' category can still earn you points for 'Development'. The system works slightly differently, though. These furnishings will still be graded on an 8x8 tile basis.

Example A	4 unique pieces of furniture, regardless of type.	▷	4x1 = 4 points
Example B	8 pieces of furniture, 4 types.	▷	(8x0.5)+(4x0.5) = 4+2 = 6 points
Example C	10 pieces of furniture, 5 types.	▷	(10x0.25)+5(x0.75) = 2.5+3.75 = 6.25 points

Bonus Points

There are some other tasks that can boost your 'Development' score, such as removing weeds and placing fences. Some extra bonuses can be gotten by placing expensive furniture outdoors, especially pieces that work best in outdoor situations.

Non-DIY Furniture Points

Furniture within a block	Added Points
If there are less than 5 unique types of furniture placed	+The number of placed furniture × 1
If there are 5 to 10 unique types of furniture placed	+The number of placed furniture × 0.5 +The number of types × 0.5
If there are 10 unique types of furniture or more	+The number of furniture placed x 0.25 +The number of types x 0.75

Furniture Type

Bonus	Added points
The placed furniture is recommended for the outdoors	+The number of outdoor furniture x 0.5 additional points
The placed furniture costs 2000 - 20,000 Bells	+The number of applicable furniture x 1
The placed furniture costs over 20,000 Bells	+The number of applicable furniture x 2

Other Bonuses

Bonus	Added points
Placed Fences	▷ The number of fences x 0.2

Negative Conditions

Certain conditions can cause your fuzzy friends to enjoy your island less, and these will subtract points from your Island Rating score. If any of the following conditions are met, you will not be able to get a 5 star island.

Clutter

It's possible to have too much of a good thing. Too much furniture can make it hard to walk around and navigate your island. Clutter is gauged in the same 8x8 tile division as furniture grading. There are a total of 64 spaces available in every 8x8 block, and if 45 or more tiles are covered, the block will be considered cluttered. Buildings, bridges, buried items, rocks, cliffs, rivers and inclines will not count toward clutter.

Littering

If there are more than 15 small items dropped on the ground (not placed as furniture), your island will be deemed messy. Sea shells, tree branches, stones, mushrooms, and star fragments don't count toward your island's messiness, since these occur naturally in the wild.

Example Islands

Now that you know how grading works, you should have no problem building an attractive, highly rated island. We've created a few highly rated islands and taken some choice shots to help inspire you. The arrangements seen here all score favorably in Isabelle's various points calculations. Enjoy!

"Keep contributing however you can and soon this island will be decorated to perfection!"

Lily-of-the-Valley

In addition to the golden watering can recipe, owners of 5 star islands will find a nice surprise popping up around their island. The Lily-of-the-Valley flower will only grow on an island with a current 5 star rating, and has a chance of appearing every day. You can dig it up, and then you'll have a chance for another to appear—keep doing this and you may eventually have enough for a real flower bed.

The Happy Home Academy

Once you've moved into your very own house, the Happy Home Academy (HHA for short) will begin evaluating your interior decoration skills. There's no pressure to participate, but HHA provides a fun incentive to spend time decorating and arranging your home's interior. Check your mailbox each week on Sunday and you'll find a letter detailing your weekly HHA evaluation report. These letters will give you general tips on how to improve your home decor, as well as occasional rewards for achieving certain milestones or better grades. The whole island is abuzz with talk about HHA on Saturdays, since all residents who own a house are also excited to receive their evaluation letters the next day!

HHA Letters

Every Sunday, the HHA will send you a letter with your house score and a friendly house decorating tip. Even after your house has ranked at an S, the HHA will still be there to advise you and give you even more helpful hints, in case you feel like redecorating.

The HHA will also congratulate you with a letter and a gift for every upgrade of your house. Even just redecorating your house a little might end up in a surprise from the HHA. Certain decorating milestones, like putting up wall furniture for the first time, can also get you a pleasant letter and gift.

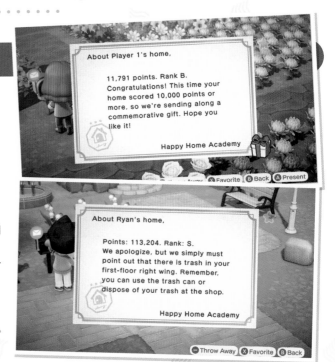

Evaluation

Now let's go over the basics of home evaluation. The main goal is to arrange furniture items in ways that conform with the various rules used by the HHA committee to evaluate the quality of your home's interior design. How well you've arranged your furniture according to each of these rules will dictate the amount of HHA points you're awarded on a per rule basis. From there, simply add together the points you've earned under each rule to determine your final HHA rating. In addition to the numerical score seen in previous Animal Crossing titles, you'll now also receive one of three Evaluation Ranks (B -> A -> S) to help you better gauge your interior decorating skills.

To compensate for the increase in scoring potential that comes with having more space to decorate, the score threshold used to determine your Rank will also increase each time you upgrade the size of your house. The larger the house, the more points you'll need!

● Rank Requirements by House Level

Increase in Room Space	Points per Rank
① Starter Tent (8x8)	N/A
② House (12x12)	S = 15,000+ A = 10,000 - 14,999 B = 0 - 9999
③ Upgraded House (16x16)	S = 23,000 A = 17,000 - 22,999 B = 0 - 16,999
④ Back Room (12x12)	S = 35,000 A = 25,000 - 34,999 B = 0 - 24,999
⑤ Left Room (12x12)	S = 47,000 A = 38,000 - 46,999 B = 0 - 37,999
⑥ Right Room(12x12)	S = 60,000 A = 50,000 - 59,999 B = 0 - 49,999
⑦ Second Floor (12x20)	S = 75,000 A = 64,000 - 74,999 B = 0 - 63,999
⑧ Basement (12x20)	S = 90,000 A = 80,000 - 89,999 B = 0 - 79,999

Tips for Better Ratings

🍃 Placing a chair, a table, a dresser or wardrobe and a bed somewhere in your house will unlock the Type bonus and earn you an easy 2500 points!

🍃 Make sure that each room is filled with enough furniture to meet the Basic Interior Design requirements. Placing a minimum of 20 furniture items in each room will net you a quick 4000 points per room!

🍃 Hang at least three pieces of wall-hanging furniture in each of your rooms to score an additional 1200 points per room!

🍃 If you have four pieces of furniture belonging to the same theme, place them in the same room!

🍃 Replacing your standard wallpaper and flooring with some that's been purchased from Nook's Cranny or Saharah will net you some extra points. Don't worry about how the new wallpaper and flooring matches with your furniture since it won't affect your color or feng shui bonuses.

🍃 Build DIY furniture. The easiest and cheapest way to get a Theme Bonus is to build all the pieces yourself. The cardboard, ironwood and woodblock recipes are easy to get in the early game and don't require too many materials to craft.

🍃 Making perfect snowmen is the fastest way to get an entire collection of themed, seasonal furniture. The seasonal bonus from the frozen themed furniture can really help during winter.

🍃 Potted flowers make for an easy extra category filler, since they count as a houseplant!

🍃 Avoid any penalties. Be sure to stomp out all cockroaches if you haven't played for a while!

● Scoring Rules

Base Points
The base point values for each furniture item

Theme Bonus
Bonus Points for displaying multiple items from the same Theme

Set Completion Bonus
Bonus Points for displaying all items from a Set in the same room

Type Bonus
Bonus Points for displaying all daily life necessities (chair, table, bed, wardrobe or dresser)within the house

Feng Shui Bonus
Bonus Points for displaying items of a certain color in the appropriate area of the room.

Color Bonus
Bonus Points for color uniformity among items in the room

Category
Bonus Points for displaying items of various Categories within the same room (3 or more)

Lucky/Season Bonus
Bonus points for items which match the current season, or items which are "Lucky Furniture"

Basic Interior Design Bonus
Various criteria based on the ability to arrange a well-designed room and follow basic interior design principles.

Situation Bonus
Bonus points for displaying more than a set number of items from the same "Situation"

Penalties
Points deducted for rooms in poor condition (cockroaches, trash, furniture facing wall, etc)

6

In-Depth Scoring

This section gives you an in-depth break-down of all the different scoring rules that are taken into account when calculating your final HHA score. We'll explain how each rule works and list any items that it applies to.

Filling rooms with high value items can work if you can a afford it, but the HHA's grading can equally reward more minimal setups.

Base Points

Every furniture item is assigned a base point value that's immediately added to your overall score when that item is placed in your house. Each item's base value is determined by how the item can be obtained. As a general rule, items acquired through events or those that can be sold for large amounts of Bells are worth more base points.

Event Items: *Highly prized items that can only be obtained by participating in events or as reward for accomplishing special tasks. They're few in numbers, but these items are worth a ton of Base points!*

High Value Furniture: *Valuable furniture that can be purchased from the luxury or seasonal displays in the upgraded Nook's Cranny. DIY furniture crafted from seasonal materials also falls in this category, as well as certain items obtained from special visitors.*

Normal Furniture: *A large variety of basic furniture items are included here, as well as fish, bugs, fossils and clothes placed as furniture. Wallpaper and flooring purchased from Nook's Cranny will also award you with some Base points when assigned to a room.*

Normal Items: *Small and large umbrellas that have been bought from Nook's Cranny are worth 3 Base points when placed in your house.*

Non-furniture Items: *Basic non-furniture items such as fruits, DIY materials, recipes and tools will not award you any Base points when dropped on the ground (leaf icon).*

Range of Base point values

Item Type	Base Points
Umbrellas	3
Kicks' items	23
New Years items	33
Clothing	51
Recycle Box items	53
Bugs	64
Fish	71
Nook Miles furniture (800)	83
Fossils/Flowers	87
K.K. Slider songs/Small furniture	103
Nook Miles furniture (1500)	121
Regular furniture/Wallpaper/Flooring (Shop)	151
Nook Miles furniture (2000)	171
Large furniture/Seasonal Items (DIY or Shop)	201
Nook Miles furniture (3000)	221
DAL Souvenirs/Bug/Fish models/Posters/High Quality furniture	251
Saharah Rugs	253
Zodiac Items	301
Resident Photos/Label Rewards	351
Mom's Art	365
Giant Robot	403
Snowman	444
Gulliver Rewards/Saharah Mystery Flooring/Wallpaper	451
Fishing Tournament/Bug-Off trophy	501
HHA rewards & Trophies	573

Theme Bonus

Some groups of furniture items share a theme. You'll be awarded a bonus when at least four items belonging to the same theme are placed in the same room, with additional items increasing the bonus. If your house has multiple rooms, each room's theme bonus will be calculated separately. It's important to note that only the theme with the most furniture items will be used to determine the room's bonus. Focus on a single theme per room and maximize your bonus by collecting every item in that group!

Getting fully themed room isn't easy, but it's rewarding both in terms of HHA points and in how neatly consistent your room looks.

antique

antique bed	antique mini table
antique bureau	antique phone
antique chair	antique table
antique clock	antique vanity
antique console table	antique wardrobe

Theme Scoring

Criteria	Scoring
4 or more Theme items displayed ▶	Number of Theme items x1000

bamboo

bamboo basket	bamboo shelf
bamboo bench	bamboo speaker
bamboo candleholder	bamboo sphere
bamboo doll	bamboo stool
bamboo drum	bamboo stopblock
bamboo floor lamp	bamboo wall
bamboo flooring	bamboo wall decoration
bamboo lunch box	bamboo-grove wall
bamboo noodle slide	bamboo-shoot lamp
bamboo partition	deer scare

flowers

blue rose wreath	fancy rose wreath	pretty tulip wreath
chic cosmos wreath	garden wagon	purple hyacinth wreath
chic windflower wreath	gold rose wreath	red rose rug
cool hyacinth wreath	hyacinth lamp	rose bed
cool pansy wreath	hyacinth wreath	rose wreath
cool windflower wreath	lily record player	snazzy pansy wreath
cosmos shower	lily wreath	tulip surprise box
cosmos wreath	mum cushion	tulip wreath
dark lily wreath	mum wreath	white rose rug
dark rose wreath	natural mum wreath	windflower fan
dark tulip wreath	pansy table	windflower wreath
fancy lily wreath	pansy wreath	yellow rose rug
fancy mum wreath	pretty cosmos wreath	

cardboard

cardboard bed	cardboard table
cardboard box	large cardboard boxes
cardboard chair	medium cardboard boxes
cardboard sofa	small cardboard boxes

cherry blossoms

blossom-viewing lantern
cherry-blossom bonsai
cherry-blossom branches
cherry-blossom clock
cherry-blossom flooring
cherry-blossom pond stone
cherry-blossom-petal pile
cherry-blossom-trees wall
outdoor picnic set
sakura-wood wall

diner

diner chair
diner counter chair
diner counter table
diner dining table
diner mini table
diner neon clock
diner neon sign
diner sofa
jukebox
retro gas pump

festive

big festive tree
festive top set
festive tree
holiday candle
illuminated present
illuminated reindeer
illuminated snowflakes
illuminated tree
Jingle wall
ornament mobile
ornament wreath
sleigh
tabletop festive tree

frozen

frozen arch	frozen table
frozen bed	frozen tree
frozen chair	frozen-treat set
frozen counter	ice flooring
frozen partition	ice wall
frozen pillar	three-tiered snowperson
frozen sculpture	

fruits

apple chair	fruit wreath	peach rug
apple rug	infused-water dispenser	peach surprise box
apple wall	juicy-apple TV	peach wall
cherry lamp	orange end table	pear bed
cherry rug	orange rug	pear rug
cherry speakers	orange wall	pear wall
cherry wall	orange wall-mounted clock	pear wardrobe
fruit basket	peach chair	

cute

cute bed
cute chair
cute DIY table
cute floor lamp
cute music player
cute sofa
cute tea table
cute vanity
cute wall-mounted clock
cute wardrobe

golden

gold bars	golden gears
golden candlestick	golden seat
golden casket	golden toilet
golden dishes	golden wall
golden flooring	

iron

iron closet	iron hanger stand
iron doorplate	iron shelf
iron entrance mat	iron wall lamp
iron garden bench	iron wall rack
iron garden chair	iron worktable
iron garden table	

ironwood

ironwood bed	ironwood DIY workbench
ironwood cart	ironwood dresser
ironwood chair	ironwood kitchenette
ironwood clock	ironwood low table
ironwood cupboard	ironwood table

log

log bed	log round table
log bench	log sofa
log decorative shelves	log stakes
log dining table	log stool
log extra-long sofa	log wall-mounted clock
log garden lounge	wild log bench

mush

forest flooring	mush partition
forest wall	mush rug
mush lamp	mush table
mush log	mush wall
mush low stool	mushroom wreath
mush parasol	

motherly

Mom's art	Mom's pen stand
Mom's candle set	Mom's playful kitchen mat
Mom's cool kitchen mat	Mom's plushie
Mom's cushion	Mom's reliable kitchen mat
Mom's embroidery	Mom's tea cozy
Mom's homemade cake	Mom's tissue box
Mom's lively kitchen mat	

rattan

rattan armchair	rattan table lamp
rattan bed	rattan towel basket
rattan end table	rattan vanity
rattan flooring	rattan wardrobe
rattan low table	rattan waste bin
rattan stool	

shell

shell arch	shell rug
shell bed	shell speaker
shell fountain	shell stool
shell lamp	shell table
shell partition	shell wreath

stars

Aquarius urn	nova light
Aries rocking chair	Pisces lamp
Cancer table	Sagittarius arrow
Capricorn ornament	Scorpio lamp
crescent-moon chair	star clock
Gemini closet	starry garland
Leo sculpture	starry-sky wall
Libra scale	Taurus bathtub
lunar surface	Virgo harp

toy

throwback container	throwback race-car bed
throwback dino screen	throwback rocket
throwback gothic mirror	throwback skull radio
throwback hat table	throwback wall clock
throwback mitt chair	throwback wrestling figure

tree's bounty/leaves

autumn wall	traditional balancing toy
colored-leaves flooring	tree's bounty arch
leaf campfire	tree's bounty big tree
leaf stool	tree's bounty lamp
maple-leaf pond stone	tree's bounty little tree
pile of leaves	tree's bounty mobile
red-leaf pile	yellow-leaf pile

wooden

wooden bookshelf	wooden mini table
wooden bucket	wooden simple bed
wooden chair	wooden stool
wooden chest	wooden table
wooden double bed	wooden table mirror
wooden end table	wooden toolbox
wooden full-length mirror	wooden wardrobe
wooden low table	wooden waste bin

wooden-block

wooden-block bed	wooden-block stereo
wooden-block bench	wooden-block stool
wooden-block bookshelf	wooden-block table
wooden-block chair	wooden-block toy
wooden-block chest	wooden-block wall clock

imperial

imperial bed	imperial low table
imperial chest	imperial partition
imperial decorative shelves	

Set Completion Bonus

Sets are smaller groups of matching furniture items that can add a bit of flair to your room. The set completion bonus is only awarded when every item belonging to that set is placed in the same room. If your house has multiple rooms, each room's set completion bonus will be calculated separately. Placing multiple completed sets in the same room is encouraged since they'll each count towards the bonus. Make sure that each set is unique, though, since duplicates won't be counted!

Items in a given set tend to match very well, since they're generally made of the same materials.

Set Scoring

Criteria	Scoring
Entire Set displayed ▶	Number of Set items x800

apple

juicy-apple TV	apple chair

bear

Papa bear	Baby bear
Mama bear	giant teddy bear

birthday

birthday candles	birthday table
birthday cake	birthday sign

cherry

cherry speakers	cherry lamp

den

den desk	den chair

imperial dining

imperial dining table	imperial dining lantern
imperial dining chair	

lecture hall

lecture-hall bench	lecture-hall desk

natural

natural garden chair	natural square table
natural garden table	

office

modern office chair	office desk

orange

orange end table	orange wall-mounted clock

panda

Baby panda	Papa panda
Mama panda	

peach

peach chair	peach surprise box

pear

pear wardrobe	pear bed

pet

pet food bowl	kitty litter box
pet bed	

school

school chair	school desk

sports ring

blue corner	neutral corner
red corner	

standee

grass standee	mountain standee
hedge standee	tree standee

stone

stone table	stone stool

writing

writing poster	writing chair
writing desk	

Type Bonus

Four types of furniture items are considered essential to daily life:

- **Chairs**
- **Dressers or Wardrobes**
- **Tables**
- **Beds**

You'll be awarded the Type bonus when your house is furnished with at least one chair, one table, one dresser or wardrobe and one bed. All models are valid. They don't need to be placed in the same room either—just make sure that at least one of each type is in your house. The Type bonus can only be counted once for the entire house.

Bed		
antique bed	imperial bed	rose bed
bunk bed	inflatable sofa	shell bed
camping cot	ironwood bed	tatami bed
cardboard bed	log bed	throwback race-car bed
cute bed	log garden lounge	wooden double bed
frozen bed	pear bed	wooden simple bed
futon	rattan bed	wooden-block bed

Criteria	Scoring
All 4 Types of furniture displayed ▸	2500

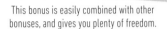

This bonus is easily combined with other bonuses, and gives you plenty of freedom.

Table		
antique console table	ironwood low table	rattan low table
antique mini table	ironwood table	school desk
antique table	kotatsu	shell table
Cancer table	lecture-hall desk	stone table
cardboard table	loft bed with desk	table with cloth
cute tea table	log dining table	tea table
den desk	log round table	throwback hat table
diner counter table	mush table	vintage TV tray
diner dining table	natural garden table	wooden end table
diner mini table	natural square table	wooden low table
frozen counter	office desk	wooden mini table
frozen table	orange end table	wooden table
imperial low table	outdoor table	wooden-block table
iron garden table	pansy table	
iron worktable	rattan end table	

Chair		
antique chair	folding chair	peach chair
apple chair	frozen chair	piano bench
arcade seat	garden bench	pile of zen cushions
baby chair	golden seat	public bench
bamboo bench	imperial dining chair	rattan armchair
bamboo stool	iron garden bench	rattan stool
box corner sofa	iron garden chair	rocking chair
box sofa	ironwood chair	school chair
cardboard chair	lawn chair	shell stool
cardboard sofa	leaf chair	stone stool
crescent-moon chair	lecture-hall bench	throwback mitt chair
cushion	log bench	velvet stool
cute chair	log extra-long sofa	wild log bench
cute sofa	log sofa	wooden chair
den chair	log stool	wooden stool
diner chair	modern office chair	wooden-block bench
diner counter chair	Mom's cushion	wooden-block chair
diner sofa	mum cushion	wooden-block stool
director's chair	mush low stool	writing chair
double sofa	natural garden chair	zen cushion
floor seat	outdoor bench	

Closet		
antique wardrobe	imperial chest	throwback rocket
Capricorn ornament	iron closet	upright locker
clothes closet	ironwood dresser	wooden chest
cute wardrobe	pear wardrobe	wooden wardrobe
Gemini closet	rattan wardrobe	wooden-block chest

Color Bonus

Most furniture items are assigned their two most prominent colors by default. These are known as "system colors" and are used to determine the room's color and Feng Shui bonuses. You'll be awarded the color bonus if over 70% of the furniture placed in a room matches in at least one system color. Some furniture items don't have any system colors, but these can still be matched with other colorless furniture to get the color bonus. Keep in mind that custom designs, wallpaper and flooring won't be counted for any color-related bonuses. If your house has multiple rooms, each room's color bonus will be calculated separately. Every furniture item must also be unique, so duplicates won't be counted. The color bonus triples per item if over 90% of the room is a match, so removing any items that don't fit in can be a great way to boost your score! To see each item's system colors, check out the full furniture list, starting on P.353.

Criteria		Scoring
At least 8 items in the room, of which at least 70% contain the same color.	▶	Number of unique items displayed ×200
At least 8 items in the room, of which at least 90% contain the same color.	▶	Number of unique items displayed ×600

*Percentage calculated by number of same colored furniture divided by total number of items

Working towards color bonuses can lead to some striking results.

Feng Shui Bonus

The Feng Shui bonus is based on an ancient principle that believes the placement of furniture according to cardinal direction and color is essential to a room's harmony. The only colors that matter in Animal Crossing: New Horizons' simplified version of Feng Shui are green, red and yellow. Each of these colors corresponds to the cardinal directions south, east and west respectively.

To receive points, you'll need to place furniture of green, red or yellow system colors on the two rows of floor tiles adjacent to the matching side of the room. Wall-hanging items placed on the matching walls also count, but wallpaper and flooring will not. Larger furniture items, even partially placed in the effective area, will be valid and will be counted for the bonus even if they're not completely resting on top of the Feng Shui tiles.

You can get feng shui bonus points while having a very natural looking room.

Scoring

The Feng Shui bonus is determined by the presence of one matching furniture item in each of the valid cardinal directions. Placing additional furniture within a section of the room won't increase the bonus, so just focus on including one matching item for each direction. This means the maximum Feng Shui bonus for a room is 1500 points. If your house has multiple rooms, each room's Feng Shui bonus will be calculated separately.

Feng Shui Scoring

Criteria		Scoring
Items are placed in the corresponding Feng Shui areas of the room	▶	Number of valid sections per room ×500

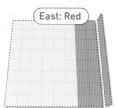

East: Red

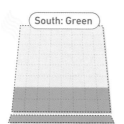

South: Green

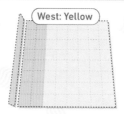

West: Yellow

Season Bonus

A few seasonal furniture items can net you a season bonus if placed in your house during the appropriate time of year. For example, a bamboo shelf will give you a bonus when placed in your house during Spring, but that bonus will disappear once Spring has ended. Remember to replace these seasonal furniture items whenever a new season rolls around. Where you place these items in your house doesn't matter, but keep in mind that duplicates won't add to your score.

Spring
bamboo shelf
cherry-blossom bonsai

Summer
anchor statue
artisanal bug cage
horned hercules
Napoleonfish
palm-tree lamp
scorpion
shell wreath

Autumn
cricket
mush parasol
tree's bounty big tree

Winter
big festive tree
frozen tree
stringfish
tarantula

Season	Northern Hemisphere	Southern Hemisphere
Spring	March ~ May	September ~ November
Summer	June ~ August	December ~ February
Autumn	September ~ November	March ~ May
Winter	December ~ February	June ~ August

To take real advantage of the seasonal bonuses you'll need to put some work in collecting seasonal recipes and materials.

You could keep one room of your house that changes with the seasons.

Lucky Bonus

Some furniture is said to bring good fortune all year round. Each piece of lucky furniture placed in your home will give you a score bonus, regardless of the current season. Like seasonal furniture, where you place lucky items in your house isn't important. Make sure they're all unique, though, since duplicates won't be counted.

Lucky
crescent-moon chair
gold bug trophy
gold fish trophy
gold HHA trophy
gold rose wreath
golden candlestick
katana
koi
lucky gold cat
pop-eyed goldfish
ring
robot hero
resident's photo

Certain items have their own innate luck, and that can equal points!

Season & Lucky Bonus Scoring

Criteria	Bonus
Total number of unique Season & Lucky items displayed ▸	x777

Category Bonus

You'll be awarded the category bonus when furniture items from at least three different categories are placed in the same room. These items are all useful to daily life, and range from TVs and stereos, to clocks and garbage cans. The number of items belonging to each category isn't important, so focus instead on a single item per category to increase your score. The more categories represented by at least one item, the higher the bonus! If your house has multiple rooms, each room's category bonus will be calculated separately.

This is another bonus that is easy to combine with others while achieving some very pleasant results.

Category Bonus Scoring

Criteria		Bonus
Furniture of at least 3 different categories displayed	▸	Number of categories x777

Air Conditioning

air circulator	fire pit	round space heater
air conditioner	fireplace	sauna heater
bonfire	outdoor air conditioner	wall fan
campfire	retro fan	windflower fan
fan	retro radiator	wood-burning stove

Appliances

antique phone	humidifier	refrigerator
automatic washer	intercom monitor	rice cooker
breaker	ironing board	rotary phone
cordless phone	ironing set	sewing machine
deluxe washer	microwave	stand mixer
digital scale	mini fridge	upright vacuum
double-door refrigerator	mixer	vacuum cleaner
fragrance diffuser	pants press	video camera
freezer	pop-up toaster	wall-mounted phone

Clock

antique clock	old-fashioned alarm clock
cherry-blossom clock	orange wall-mounted clock
cuckoo clock	park clock
cute wall-mounted clock	pendulum clock
digital alarm clock	star clock
diner neon clock	throwback wall clock
double-sided wall clock	wall clock
ironwood clock	wooden-block wall clock
log wall-mounted clock	

Vanity

antique vanity	rattan vanity	wooden table mirror
cute vanity	throwback gothic mirror	
desk mirror	wooden full-length mirror	

Creatures

All fish	All bugs

Odds and Ends

birdcage	hamster cage	public bench

Lights

bamboo candleholder	golden candlestick	rocket lamp
bamboo floor lamp	holiday candle	Scorpio lamp
bamboo-shoot lamp	hyacinth lamp	shaded floor lamp
birthday candles	imperial dining lantern	shell lamp
blossom-viewing lantern	iron wall lamp	soft-serve lamp
candle	lantern	streetlamp
celebratory candles	Mom's candle set	studio spotlight
cherry lamp	mush lamp	studio wall spotlight
cute floor lamp	nova light	table lamp
floor lamp	palm-tree lamp	tree's bounty lamp
floor light	paper lantern	wall-mounted candle
folding floor lamp	Pisces lamp	
garden lantern	rattan table lamp	

Mannequins

Baby bear	matryoshka
Baby panda	Mr. Flamingo
decoy duck	Mrs. Flamingo
dolly	nutcracker
giant teddy bear	Papa bear
hula doll	Papa panda
lucky cat	paper tiger
lucky gold cat	raccoon figurine
Mama bear	throwback wrestling figure
Mama panda	

Music Players		
bamboo speaker	high-end stereo	retro stereo
cassette player	jukebox	shell speaker
cherry speakers	lily record player	tape deck
cute music player	phonograph	throwback skull radio
DJ's turntable	portable record player	wooden-block stereo
hi-fi stereo	pro tape recorder	

Musical Instruments		
acoustic guitar	fancy violin	rock guitar
alto saxophone	grand piano	street piano
bamboo drum	harp	synthesizer
cello	marimba	ukulele
drum set	metronome	upright piano
electric bass	record box	Virgo harp
electric guitar	recycled-can thumb piano	

Plants		
anthurium plant	cypress plant	moss ball
bamboo wall decoration	fan palm	pine bonsai tree
bonsai shelf	floating-biotope planter	potted ivy
cacao tree	floral swag	succulent plant
cat grass	flower stand	terrarium
cherry-blossom bonsai	hanging terrarium	yucca
cherry-blossom branches	mini-cactus set	
coconut wall planter	monstera	

Trash Can		
garbage bin	garbage pail	wooden waste bin
garbage can	rattan waste bin	

Trinkets		
accessories stand	festive top set	nail-art set
aroma pot	firewood	oil lamp
bamboo sphere	fortune-telling set	painting set
bingo wheel	fragrance sticks	plasma ball
board game	frozen-treat set	portable radio
book	glass holder with candle	revolving spice rack
book stands	globe	ring
bottled ship	homework set	sea globe
brine-shrimp aquarium	hourglass	sewing project
cartoonist's set	incense burner	snow globe
chessboard	magazine	stack of books
coconut juice	magic kit	stovetop espresso maker
coffee cup	modeling clay	sturdy sewing box
cream and sugar	Mom's pen stand	tea set
DAL model plane	Mom's plushie	throwback race-car bed
DAL mug	Mom's tea cozy	tissue box
electronics kit	Mom's tissue box	tree's bounty little tree
essay set	mug	unfinished puzzle

TV		
juicy-apple TV	LCD TV (50 in.)	wall-mounted TV (50 in.)
LCD TV (20 in.)	wall-mounted TV (20 in.)	

Basic Interior Design Bonus

A bonus will be awarded for meeting each of the basic interior design requirements listed in this table. If your house has multiple rooms, each room's basic
interior design bonus will be calculated separately. The rules are simple: just
fill each of your rooms with at least 20 furniture items and hang three items
on the walls to greatly boost your score!

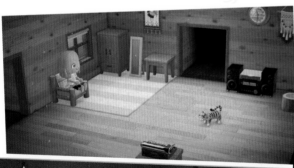

It's quite possible to meet the requirements for this bonus
without having cluttered rooms. Make use of the walls!

Interior Design

Requirement	Scoring
① Place at least 6 pieces of furniture	▸ 1000
② Place at least 10 pieces of furniture	▸ 1000 Stacks with ① (Total 2000 points)
③ Place at least 15 pieces of furniture	▸ 1000 Stacks with ② (Total 3000 points)
④ Place at least 20 pieces of furniture	▸ 1000 Stacks with ③ (Total 4000 points)
⑤ Hang furniture items on wall	▸ 400 per item Maximum 3 items per room Therefore, 1 wall item = 400 points, 2 wall items = 800 points, 3 items = 1200 points. (The bonus will remain at 1200 points even if 4 or more items are placed in the room)

Situation Bonus

Every single piece of furniture fits into either one or two situations. A bonus will be awarded when at least five furniture items of the same situation are placed in the same room. If your house has multiple rooms, each room's point total will be calculated separately. When furniture from more than one situation is present in the same room, the situation with the most items will be used to calculate the room's situation bonus. It's important to note that each item doesn't need to be unique for it to count towards the situation bonus, so duplicates can be a great way to increase your score!

Situations

Outdoors	School	Den	Fitness
Music	Child's Room	Bathroom	Concert
Ocean	Facility	Fancy	Expensive
Office	Freezing Cold	Garden	Folk Art
Shop	Garage	Party	Horror
Space	Kitchen	Zen-Style	Living Room

Situation Bonus

Criteria	Bonus
5 or more items with the same Situation displayed in one room ▸	Number of items from that situation ×400

bathroom

aqua tile wall	blue desert-tile wall	cosmos shower	kettle bathtub	purple desert-tile flooring	standing toilet
Aquarius urn	blue honeycomb tile	cypress bathtub	long bathtub	purple desert-tile wall	tankless toilet
argyle tile flooring	blue honeycomb-tile wall	deluxe washer	monochromatic-tile wall	rattan towel basket	Taurus bathtub
automatic washer	blue mosaic-tile flooring	digital scale	mosaic-tile wall	red two-toned tile wall	toilet
bathroom sink	blue tile wall	drying rack	oil-barrel bathtub	sauna heater	toilet-cleaning set
bathroom towel rack	blue two-toned tile wall	floral mosaic-tile flooring	old-fashioned washtub	shower booth	whirlpool bath
beige desert-tile flooring	brown honeycomb tile	golden toilet	olive desert-tile flooring	shower set	white honeycomb tile
beige desert-tile wall	claw-foot tub	green honeycomb tile	olive desert-tile wall	simple green bath mat	white honeycomb-tile wall
bidet	clothesline pole	green honeycomb-tile wall	peach two-toned tile wall	simple navy bath mat	white mosaic-tile flooring
black two-toned tile wall	colorful mosaic-tile flooring	honeycomb-tile wall	plain sink	simple pink bath mat	
blue desert-tile flooring	colorful-tile wall	ivory simple bath mat	portable toilet	squat toilet	

child's room

ant farm	blue quilt wall	cherry wall	cute yellow-tile flooring	fortune-telling set	leaf stool
apple rug	blue simple-cloth wall	clackercart	cute-paint flooring	fossil rug	loft bed with desk
apple wall	blue small round mat	colorful puzzle flooring	DAL model plane	frozen-treat set	magazine
Baby bear	blue stripes rug	colorful puzzle wall	decoy duck	giant teddy bear	magic kit
baby chair	blue wavy rug	colorful tile flooring	desk mirror	globe	magic-circle rug
Baby panda	blue-paint flooring	cool-paint flooring	digital alarm clock	gray-striped wall	Mama bear
beige art-deco wall	blue-striped wall	cubic parquet flooring	dolly	green checked rug	Mama panda
birch flooring	board game	cuckoo clock	Earth rug	green molded-panel wall	marine pop flooring
blue camo flooring	bone doorplate	cushion	electric kick scooter	green painted-wood wall	marine pop wall
blue camo wall	boomerang	cute blue wall	elephant slide	green playroom wall	mint dot flooring
blue dot flooring	book stands	cute blue-tile flooring	fan	green stripes rug	mobile
blue dotted rug	brine-shrimp aquarium	cute red wall	fish doorplate	green-paint flooring	modeling clay
blue heart-pattern wall	camo flooring	cute red-tile flooring	fish rug	ivory medium round mat	modern wavy rug
blue medium round mat	camo wall	cute white wall	floor seat	ivory small round mat	modern wood flooring
blue message mat	cartoonist's set	cute white-tile flooring	fluffy rug	jointed-mat flooring	modern wood wall
blue playroom wall	cherry rug	cute yellow wall	folding floor lamp	ladybug rug	monochromatic dot flooring

continue child's room

monochromatic dotted rug	peach surprise box	red dotted rug	stripe flooring	white message mat	wooden-block stereo
monochromatic dotted wall	peach wall	red dotted wall	table lamp	white painted-wood wall	wooden-block stool
monochromatic wavy rug	pear rug	red heart-pattern wall	throwback container	white simple-cloth wall	wooden-block table
monster statue	pear wall	red medium round mat	throwback dino screen	white-paint flooring	wooden-block toy
mush rug	pennant	red message mat	throwback gothic mirror	wooden bookshelf	wooden-block wall clock
nail-art set	pine-board flooring	red small round mat	throwback hat table	wooden chair	wooden-knot flooring
Nook Inc. rug	pink heart rug	red wavy rug	throwback mitt chair	wooden chest	wooden-knot wall
old-fashioned alarm clock	pink heart-pattern wall	red-and-blue checked rug	throwback race-car bed	wooden double bed	writing chair
orange camo flooring	pink painted-wood wall	retro dotted rug	throwback rocket	wooden end table	writing desk
orange camo wall	pink playroom wall	ringtoss	throwback skull radio	wooden full-length mirror	writing poster
orange molded-panel wall	pink quilt wall	robot hero	throwback wall clock	wooden low table	yellow checked rug
orange rug	pink simple-cloth wall	rocking horse	throwback wrestling figure	wooden mini table	yellow heart-pattern wall
orange wall	pink-paint flooring	sakura-wood flooring	timber doorplate	wooden simple bed	yellow medium round mat
orange-paint wall	pink-striped wall	sakura-wood wall	toy box	wooden stool	yellow message mat
painting set	plasma ball	sepia puzzle flooring	toy centipede	wooden table	yellow playroom wall
Papa bear	playground gym	sepia puzzle wall	toy cockroach	wooden table mirror	yellow quilt wall
Papa panda	purple camo flooring	skull wall	traditional balancing toy	wooden wardrobe	yellow simple-cloth wall
pastel dotted wall	purple camo wall	skull-print flooring	train set	wooden waste bin	yellow small round mat
pastel puzzle flooring	purple dotted wall	sloppy rug	tricycle	wooden-block bed	yellow stripes rug
pastel puzzle wall	purple heart rug	spider doorplate	tulip surprise box	wooden-block bench	yellow-paint wall
peach checked rug	purple quilt wall	stacked magazines	turquoise heart rug	wooden-block bookshelf	yellow-striped wall
peach rug	red art-deco wall	starry wall	unfinished puzzle	wooden-block chair	
peach stripes rug	red dot flooring	street organ	white heart rug	wooden-block chest	

concert

amp	floor light	street piano
DJ's turntable	pedal board	studio spotlight
drum set	record box	studio wall spotlight
effects rack	recycled-can thumb piano	synthesizer
electric bass	rock guitar	TV camera
electric guitar	silver mic	

den

book	scattered papers	document stack
book stands	simple blue flooring	formal paper
classic-library wall	simple purple flooring	homework set
den chair	simple red flooring	manga-library wall
den desk	stack of books	typewriter
essay set	table lamp	
monochromatic tile flooring	autograph cards	

expensive

aluminum briefcase	blue Persian rug	elaborate kimono stand	gray molded-panel wall	pool	simple purple flooring
anatomical model	blue-crown wall	fancy violin	gray vinyl flooring	poolside bed	simple red flooring
antique bed	botanical-tile wall	fireplace	green delicate-blooms wall	purple Persian rug	skyscraper wall
antique bureau	bronze bug trophy	Gemini closet	green vinyl flooring	red argyle rug	stately wall
antique chair	bronze fish trophy	gold bars	hanging scroll	red carpet	Statue of Liberty
antique clock	bronze HHA plaque	gold bug trophy	HHA pennant	red delicate-blooms wall	stone tile
antique console table	bronze HHA trophy	gold fish trophy	hi-fi stereo	red Persian rug	system kitchen
antique mini table	brown argyle rug	gold HHA plaque	imperial tile	red rose rug	table setting
antique phone	brown argyle-tile flooring	gold HHA trophy	imperial wall	red-and-black vinyl flooring	Taurus bathtub
antique table	brown botanical-tile wall	gold iron-parquet flooring	iron entrance mat	ring	trophy case
antique vanity	brown iron-parquet flooring	gold rose wreath	kitchen island	rose flooring	upright piano
antique wardrobe	brown-crown wall	gold-screen wall	lacy rug	rosewood flooring	Virgo harp
Aquarius urn	café-curtain wall	golden candlestick	Leo sculpture	safe	whirlpool bath
arabesque flooring	Cancer table	golden casket	Libra scale	Sagittarius arrow	white botanical-tile wall
arched-window wall	Capricorn ornament	golden dishes	lucky gold cat	Scorpio lamp	white delicate-blooms wall
Aries rocking chair	cello	golden dung beetle	money flooring	screen	white iron-parquet flooring
bank-vault wall	chessboard	golden flooring	palace tile	shell arch	white rose rug
black botanical-tile wall	chic wall	golden gears	palace wall	shell bed	yellow Persian rug
black iron-parquet flooring	cityscape wall	golden seat	patchwork-tile flooring	shell fountain	yellow rose rug
black-crown wall	claw-foot tub	golden toilet	phonograph	silver bug trophy	
blue argyle rug	cool vinyl flooring	golden wall	pink rose rug	silver fish trophy	
blue delicate-blooms wall	crest doorplate	grand piano	pink-crown wall	silver HHA plaque	
blue molded-panel wall	double-door refrigerator	gray argyle-tile flooring	Pisces lamp	silver HHA trophy	

abstract wall	box corner sofa	film projector	microscope	rocket lamp	steel flooring
air conditioner	box sofa	flagstone flooring	mini fridge	rough rug	steel-frame wall
ant farm	breaker	floor light	monochromatic-tile wall	rubber-tile flooring	stone tile
aqua tile flooring	brine-shrimp aquarium	floor sign	mosaic-tile wall	rustic-stone wall	stone wall
aqua tile wall	brown argyle-tile flooring	floral mosaic-tile flooring	mounted black bass	safe	studio spotlight
arcade combat game	brown botanical-tile wall	folding chair	mounted blue marlin	sci-fi flooring	studio wall spotlight
arcade fighting game	brown hallway wall	foosball table	mush log	sci-fi wall	surveillance camera
arcade mahjong game	brown honeycomb tile	fossil doorplate	Newton's cradle	scramble crosswalk	switch
arcade seat	brown-brick flooring	fountain	oil lamp	screen wall	teacup ride
arched-brick flooring	brown-brick wall	garbage bin	olive desert-tile flooring	security-monitors wall	termite mound
argyle tile flooring	bunk bed	gears	olive desert-tile wall	server	terra-cotta flooring
artisanal bug cage	butter churn	golden arowana model	outdoor air conditioner	server-room wall	tool shelf
artsy parquet flooring	butterflies wall	grasshopper-head model	paintball flooring	shutter wall	tourist telescope
asteroid	butterfly-fish model	gravel flooring	paintball wall	sidewalk flooring	train-station flooring
bank-vault wall	cabin wall	gray argyle-tile flooring	pants press	simple medium avocado mat	TV camera
basement flooring	candy machine	green honeycomb tile	parabolic antenna	simple medium black mat	upright locker
basic wall	changing room	green honeycomb-tile wall	parking flooring	simple medium blue mat	video camera
beige desert-tile flooring	chocolate hallway wall	highway flooring	peach two-toned tile wall	simple medium brown mat	wasp-head model
beige desert-tile wall	circuit-board flooring	honeycomb flooring	pedal board	simple medium orange mat	wavy-tile wall
billiard table	circuit-board wall	honeycomb wall	perforated-board wall	simple medium purple mat	wheelchair
black botanical-tile wall	colorful mosaic-tile flooring	honeycomb-tile wall	phone box	simple medium red mat	white botanical-tile wall
black hallway wall	colorful-tile wall	ice flooring	pinball machine	simple panel	white hallway wall
black perforated-board wall	concrete flooring	ice wall	popcorn machine	simple small avocado mat	white honeycomb tile
black two-toned tile wall	concrete wall	industrial wall	portable toilet	simple small black mat	white honeycomb-tile wall
black-brick flooring	cone	intercom monitor	pro tape recorder	simple small blue mat	white mosaic-tile flooring
black-brick wall	construction sign	ivy wall	public bench	simple small brown mat	white perforated-board wall
blue desert-tile flooring	construction-site flooring	jail bars	purple desert-tile flooring	simple small orange mat	white simple medium mat
blue desert-tile wall	construction-site wall	jukebox	purple desert-tile wall	simple small purple mat	white simple small mat
blue honeycomb tile	crosswalk flooring	jungle flooring	random-square-tile flooring	simple small red mat	white subway-tile wall
blue honeycomb-tile wall	dartboard	jungle wall	rattan flooring	slate flooring	white-brick flooring
blue mosaic-tile flooring	double-sided wall clock	lab-experiments set	red perforated-board wall	snack machine	white-brick wall
blue subway-tile wall	drink machine	laboratory wall	red two-toned tile wall	spider web	woodland wall
blue tile wall	effects rack	lobby flooring	red-brick flooring	springy ride-on	
blue two-toned tile wall	electronics kit	manga-library wall	red-brick wall	stacked-wood wall	
botanical-tile wall	exit sign	mantis-head model	robot hero	stadiometer	

accessories stand	blue-striped wall	cute chair	floral rush-mat flooring	illuminated tree	Mom's tissue box
apple chair	brown diner wall	cute DIY table	fluffy rug	Jingle wall	monochromatic dot flooring
apple rug	butterflies wall	cute floor lamp	fossil rug	juicy-apple TV	monochromatic dotted rug
apple wall	cherry lamp	cute music player	fragrance sticks	kisses wall	monochromatic dotted wall
Aries rocking chair	cherry rug	cute red wall	fruit basket	lacy rug	Mr. Flamingo
Baby bear	cherry speakers	cute red-tile flooring	fruit wreath	ladybug rug	Mrs. Flamingo
Baby panda	cherry wall	cute sofa	garden wagon	leaf stool	mum cushion
beige blossoming wall	cherry-blossom bonsai	cute tea table	giant teddy bear	leopard-print flooring	mum wreath
berry-chocolates flooring	cherry-blossom branches	cute vanity	giraffe-print flooring	lily record player	mush rug
big festive tree	cherry-blossom clock	cute wall-mounted clock	gray diner wall	lily wreath	mush wall
birthday cake	cherry-blossom flooring	cute wardrobe	gray-striped wall	Mama bear	nail-art set
birthday candles	cherry-blossom-petal pile	cute white wall	green blossoming wall	Mama panda	natural mum wreath
birthday sign	chic cosmos wreath	cute white-tile flooring	green flower-print wall	marine pop flooring	Nook Inc. rug
birthday table	chic windflower wreath	cute yellow wall	green molded-panel wall	matryoshka	Nook Inc. wall
blue blossoming wall	cloud flooring	cute yellow-tile flooring	green painted-wood wall	mint dot flooring	nova light
blue diner wall	colorful puzzle flooring	cute-paint flooring	green playroom wall	mobile	orange end table
blue dot flooring	colorful puzzle wall	dark lily wreath	green stripes rug	Mom's art	orange molded-panel wall
blue dotted rug	cool hyacinth wreath	dark rose wreath	green-paint flooring	Mom's candle set	orange rug
blue flower-print wall	cool pansy wreath	dark tulip wreath	green-paint wall	Mom's cool kitchen mat	orange wall
blue heart-pattern wall	cool windflower wreath	dark-chocolate wall	heart doorplate	Mom's cushion	orange wall-mounted clock
blue painted-wood wall	cosmos shower	dark-chocolates flooring	holiday candle	Mom's embroidery	orange-paint wall
blue playroom wall	cosmos wreath	dolly	honeycomb flooring	Mom's homemade cake	ornament mobile
blue quilt wall	cotton-candy stall	fancy lily wreath	honeycomb wall	Mom's lively kitchen mat	ornament wreath
blue rose wreath	crescent-moon chair	fancy mum wreath	hyacinth lamp	Mom's pen stand	pansy table
blue stripes rug	cute bed	fancy rose wreath	hyacinth wreath	Mom's playful kitchen mat	pansy wreath
blue-paint flooring	cute blue wall	festive top set	illuminated present	Mom's plushie	Papa bear
blue-paint wall	cute blue-tile flooring	festive tree	illuminated reindeer	Mom's reliable kitchen mat	Papa panda
blue-rose wall		fish doorplate	illuminated snowflakes	Mom's tea cozy	party flooring

fancy (continued)

party garland	pink flower-print wall	purple-rose wall	sepia puzzle flooring	tiger-print flooring	windflower fan
party wall	pink heart rug	red dot flooring	sepia puzzle wall	toy box	windflower wreath
pastel dotted wall	pink heart-pattern wall	red dotted rug	shell rug	traditional balancing toy	yellow argyle rug
pastel puzzle flooring	pink painted-wood wall	red dotted wall	sky wall	tree's bounty arch	yellow flower-print wall
pastel puzzle wall	pink playroom wall	red heart-pattern wall	snazzy pansy wreath	tree's bounty big tree	yellow heart-pattern wall
paw-print doorplate	pink quilt wall	red rose rug	snowflake rug	tree's bounty lamp	yellow playroom wall
peach chair	pink rose rug	retro dotted rug	snowflake wreath	tree's bounty little tree	yellow quilt wall
peach rug	pink-crown wall	retro flower-print wall	soft-serve lamp	tree's bounty mobile	yellow rose rug
peach stripes rug	pink-paint flooring	ring	springy ride-on	tulip surprise box	yellow stripes rug
peach surprise box	pink-striped wall	ringtoss	star clock	tulip wreath	yellow-paint wall
peach wall	purple dotted wall	rocking horse	starry garland	turquoise heart rug	yellow-striped wall
pear bed	pretty cosmos wreath	rose bed	starry wall	white heart rug	zebra-print flooring
pear rug	pretty tulip wreath	rose flooring	starry-sands flooring	white rose rug	
pear wall	purple heart rug	rose wall	strawberry-chocolate wall	white-chocolate wall	
pear wardrobe	purple hyacinth wreath	rose wreath	street organ	white-chocolates flooring	
pink blossoming wall	purple puzzle flooring	sakura-wood flooring	tabletop festive tree	white-rose wall	
pink diner wall	purple quilt wall	sakura-wood wall	teacup ride	wildflower meadow	

fitness

ball	climbing wall	green rubber flooring	pool	ringside seating	throwback hat table
barbell	dojo wall	handy water cooler	protein shaker bottle	rock-climbing wall	throwback mitt chair
basketball hoop	exercise ball	judge's bell	pull-up-bar stand	soccer goal	treadmill
blue corner	exercise bike	kettlebell	punching bag	speed bag	weight bench
blue rubber flooring	football	mountain bike	racetrack flooring	stadium wall	
boxing-ring mat	golf bag	neutral corner	red corner	sumo ring	

folk art

ancient wall	future-tech wall	moai statue	palace wall	Saharah's desert	Stonehenge
bottled ship	hula doll	nutcracker	pyramid	South Pole	straw wall
Dala horse	katana	oasis flooring	pyramid tile	sphinx	Tower of Pisa
desert vista	lucky cat	pagoda	rammed-earth wall	Statue of Liberty	western desert
future-tech flooring	matryoshka	palace tile	ruins wall	stone lion-dog	western vista

freezing cold

frozen arch	frozen partition	frozen tree	iceberg flooring	ski-slope wall	snowflake wreath
frozen bed	frozen pillar	frozen-treat set	iceberg wall	snow globe	three-tiered snowperson
frozen chair	frozen sculpture	ice flooring	illuminated snowflakes	snowflake rug	
frozen counter	frozen table	ice wall	ski-slope flooring	snowflake wall	

garage

barrel	concrete flooring	garbage can	ironwood DIY workbench	plastic canister	tool cart
blue shanty wall	concrete wall	garbage pail	key holder	pot	tool shelf
breaker	cone	garbage-heap flooring	large cardboard boxes	small cardboard boxes	toolbox
brown shanty wall	construction sign	garbage-heap wall	medium cardboard boxes	stacked magazines	trash bags
cardboard bed	construction-site flooring	gears	metal can	stacked-wood wall	wall-mounted tool board
cardboard box	construction-site wall	gray shanty wall	mini DIY workbench	steel flooring	wooden toolbox
cardboard chair	DIY workbench	iron frame	oil barrel	steel-frame wall	
cardboard sofa	firewood	iron wall lamp	paintball flooring	street-art wall	
cardboard table	floor sign	iron wall rack	paintball wall	tin bucket	
chain-link fence	garbage bin	iron worktable	pink shanty wall	tire stack	

garden

aluminum rug	dig-site flooring	handcart	meadow vista	plastic pool	summit wall
angled signpost	dig-site wall	hay bed	misty-garden wall	playground gym	swamp flooring
artisanal bug cage	dirt flooring	hose reel	mossy garden rock	pond stone	swinging bench
autumn wall	doghouse	iron garden bench	mossy-garden flooring	red vinyl sheet	tall garden rock
backyard lawn	drinking fountain	iron garden chair	mountain bike	red-leaf pile	termite mound
backyard-fence wall	drying rack	iron garden table	Mr. Flamingo	retro gas pump	three-tiered snowperson
beekeeper's hive	electric kick scooter	jungle flooring	Mrs. Flamingo	rice-paddy wall	tiki torch
birdbath	elephant slide	jungle wall	mush lamp	rocky-mountain flooring	tiny library
birdhouse	field flooring	lawn mower	mush log	sand castle	tire stack
blue vinyl sheet	firewood	leaf campfire	mush low stool	sandbox	tire toy
bonsai shelf	fish-drying rack	lighthouse	mush parasol	sandlot	tree-lined wall
brick well	flat garden rock	log bed	mush partition	scarecrow	tree's bounty arch
butter churn	floating-biotope planter	log bench	mush table	signpost	tricycle
chain-link fence	flowing-river flooring	log decorative shelves	mushroom wreath	silo	utility pole
cherry-blossom flooring	forest flooring	log dining table	natural garden chair	simple DIY workbench	water pump
cherry-blossom pond stone	forest wall	log extra-long sofa	natural garden table	simple well	western-style stone
cherry-blossom-trees wall	fountain	log garden lounge	natural square table	sleigh	wild log bench
clothesline	garden bench	log round table	oasis flooring	South Pole	wildflower meadow
clothesline pole	garden faucet	log sofa	outdoor air conditioner	stone arch	wind turbine
colored-leaves flooring	garden gnome	log stakes	outdoor bath	stone lion-dog	wooden bucket
colorful vinyl sheet	garden lantern	log stool	outdoor picnic set	stone stool	yellow vinyl sheet
crop-circles flooring	garden rock	log wall-mounted clock	park clock	stone table	yellow-leaf pile
daisy meadow	garden wagon	mangrove wall	pile of leaves	stone tablet	
deer scare	gravel flooring	manhole cover	plain wooden shop sign	Stonehenge	
destinations signpost	green-leaf pile	maple-leaf pond stone	plastic canister	streetlamp	

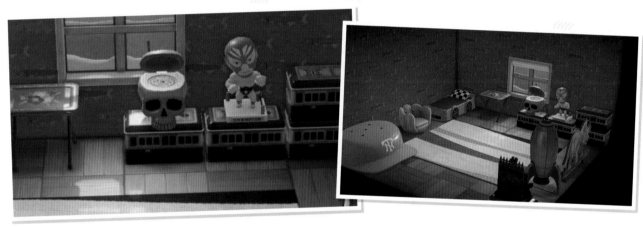

horror

ancient wall	dirt-clod wall	golden casket	ramshackle flooring	skull-print flooring	toy centipede
basement flooring	dungeon wall	golden flooring	ramshackle wall	spider doorplate	toy cockroach
candle	forest flooring	golden wall	ruins wall	spider web	wall-mounted candle
celebratory candles	fortune-telling set	jail bars	scarecrow	stone tablet	western desert
dark lily wreath	future-tech flooring	lava flooring	Scorpio lamp	stone wall	western vista
dark rose wreath	future-tech wall	magic-circle rug	simple well	stormy-night wall	western-style stone
dark tulip wreath	garbage-heap flooring	magma-cavern wall	skeleton	swamp flooring	woodland wall
dig-site flooring	garbage-heap wall	monster statue	skull doorplate	throwback gothic mirror	zen-style stone
dig-site wall	golden candlestick	old wallpaper	skull wall	throwback skull radio	

kitchen

analog kitchen scale	cream and sugar	golden dishes	microwave	protein shaker bottle	system kitchen
beaded-curtain wall	cutting board	green kitchen mat	mixer	red-design kitchen mat	tea set
black-design kitchen mat	DAL mug	green retro flooring	Mom's cool kitchen mat	refrigerator	unglazed dish set
blue kitchen mat	dinnerware	hourglass	Mom's lively kitchen mat	revolving spice rack	ventilation fan
blue-design kitchen mat	dish-drying rack	infused-water dispenser	Mom's playful kitchen mat	rice cooker	yellow kitchen mat
brick oven	double-door refrigerator	ironwood cupboard	Mom's reliable kitchen mat	serving cart	yellow-design kitchen mat
brown kitchen mat	espresso maker	ironwood kitchenette	mug	shaved-ice maker	
classic pitcher	freezer	kettle	open-frame kitchen	simple kettle	
clay furnace	fruit basket	kitchen island	orange retro flooring	soup kettle	
coffee cup	frying pan	knife block	pop-up toaster	stand mixer	
coffee grinder	gas range	magnetic knife rack	pot rack	stovetop espresso maker	

living room

air circulator	cat grass	hamster cage	Mom's candle set	red small round mat	tree branch wreath
anthurium plant	cat tower	hanging terrarium	Mom's cushion	red wavy rug	trophy case
antique bed	chessboard	HHA pennant	Mom's embroidery	red-and-blue checked rug	upright vacuum
antique bureau	chic wall	hi-fi stereo	Mom's homemade cake	retro fan	vacuum cleaner
antique chair	chocolate herringbone wall	high-end stereo	Mom's pen stand	retro flower-print wall	vintage TV tray
antique clock	clothes closet	hourglass	Mom's plushie	retro radiator	wall-mounted phone
antique console table	coconut wall planter	humidifier	Mom's tea cozy	retro stereo	wall-mounted TV (20 in.)
antique mini table	colorful tile flooring	incense burner	Mom's tissue box	rocking chair	wall-mounted TV (50 in.)
antique phone	common flooring	intercom monitor	monochromatic tile flooring	rosewood flooring	water cooler
antique table	common wall	iron closet	monochromatic wavy rug	rotary phone	white delicate-blooms wall
antique vanity	cordless phone	iron doorplate	monstera	round space heater	white iron-parquet flooring
antique wardrobe	cubic parquet flooring	iron hanger stand	old sewing machine	rush tatami	white painted-wood wall
arabesque flooring	cuckoo clock	iron shelf	old-fashioned alarm clock	rush tatami flooring	white simple medium mat
aroma pot	cushion	iron wall lamp	oval entrance mat	sea globe	white simple small mat
beige art-deco wall	cypress plant	iron wall rack	paw-print doorplate	sewing machine	white simple-cloth wall
beige blossoming wall	DAL model plane	ironing board	peach checked rug	sewing project	white-paint flooring
birch flooring	DAL mug	ironing set	pendulum clock	shaded floor lamp	wild-wood wall
birdcage	dark herringbone flooring	ironwood bed	pet bed	silver HHA plaque	wooden bookshelf
black blocks rug	dark parquet flooring	ironwood cart	pet food bowl	simple blue flooring	wooden chair
black iron-parquet flooring	dark wood-pattern flooring	ironwood chair	pile of zen cushions	simple medium avocado mat	wooden chest
blue argyle rug	dark wooden-mosaic wall	ironwood clock	pine-board flooring	simple medium black mat	wooden double bed
blue blocks rug	deer decoration	ironwood dresser	pink blossoming wall	simple medium blue mat	wooden end table
blue blossoming wall	desktop computer	ironwood low table	pink flower-print wall	simple medium brown mat	wooden full-length mirror
blue delicate-blooms wall	digital alarm clock	ironwood table	pink simple-cloth wall	simple medium orange mat	wooden low table
blue floral flooring	double sofa	ivory medium round mat	plasma ball	simple medium purple mat	wooden mini table
blue flower-print wall	fan	ivory small round mat	portable record player	simple medium red mat	wooden simple bed
blue intricate wall	fan palm	key holder	potted ivy	simple small avocado mat	wooden stool
blue kilim-style carpet	fireplace	kitty litter box	pro tape recorder	simple small black mat	wooden table
blue medium round mat	fish print	laptop	purple Persian rug	simple small blue mat	wooden table mirror
blue painted-wood wall	fishing-rod stand	LCD TV (20 in.)	purple shaggy rug	simple small brown mat	wooden wardrobe
blue Persian rug	floating-biotope planter	LCD TV (50 in.)	rattan armchair	simple small orange mat	wooden waste bin
blue shaggy rug	floor lamp	light herringbone flooring	rattan bed	simple small purple mat	wooden-knot flooring
blue simple-cloth wall	floral swag	light parquet flooring	rattan end table	simple small red mat	wooden-knot wall
blue small round mat	folding floor lamp	light wood-pattern flooring	rattan low table	simple white flooring	wooden-mosaic wall
blue wavy rug	fragrance diffuser	log bed	rattan stool	sloppy rug	yellow argyle rug
blue-paint wall	fragrance sticks	log decorative shelves	rattan table lamp	snow globe	yellow blocks rug
blue-rose wall	glass holder with candle	log dining table	rattan towel basket	stack of books	yellow checked rug
board game	go board	log extra-long sofa	rattan vanity	stripe flooring	yellow floral flooring
bone doorplate	gold HHA plaque	log round table	rattan wardrobe	sturdy sewing box	yellow flower-print wall
botanical rug	gold iron-parquet flooring	log sofa	rattan waste bin	succulent plant	yellow intricate wall
bronze HHA plaque	green blossoming wall	log wall-mounted clock	record box	switch	yellow kilim-style carpet
brown argyle rug	green checked rug	macrame tapestry	red argyle rug	tape deck	yellow medium round mat
brown floral flooring	green delicate-blooms wall	magazine	red art-deco wall	tapestry	yellow Persian rug
brown herringbone wall	green floral flooring	magazine rack	red blocks rug	tatami	yellow simple-cloth wall
brown iron-parquet flooring	green flower-print wall	mini-cactus set	red delicate-blooms wall	tatami flooring	yellow small round mat
brown shaggy rug	green intricate wall	modern wavy rug	red intricate wall	tea table	yucca
cabin wall	green kilim-style carpet	modern wood flooring	red kilim-style carpet	terrarium	zen cushion
cacao tree	green shaggy rug	modern wood wall	red medium round mat	timber doorplate	
cassette player	green-paint wall	Mom's art	red Persian rug	tissue box	

music

acoustic guitar	brown hallway wall	fancy violin	marimba	perforated-board wall	velvet stool
alto saxophone	cello	grand piano	metronome	piano bench	Virgo harp
black hallway wall	chocolate hallway wall	harp	mic stand	red perforated-board wall	white hallway wall
black perforated-board wall	cork flooring	heavy-curtain wall	music stand	upright piano	white perforated-board wall

ocean

anchor statue	fish rug	lifeguard chair	sandy-beach flooring	shell rug	tropical vista
beach ball	fish-drying rack	lighthouse	sea globe	shell speaker	ukulele
beach chair	fishing-boat flag	marine pop wall	sea view	shell stool	underwater flooring
beach towel	fishing-rod stand	mounted black bass	shaved-ice maker	shell table	underwater wall
bottled ship	fresh cooler	mounted blue marlin	shell arch	shell wreath	water flooring
butterfly-fish model	golden arowana model	ocean-horizon wall	shell bed	ship deck	wave breaker
coconut juice	hula doll	palm-tree lamp	shell fountain	starry-sands flooring	
coconut wall planter	lawn chair	poolside bed	shell lamp	surfboard	
fish print	life ring	sand castle	shell partition	tropical rug	

office

air circulator	corkboard	fax machine	office wall	typewriter
air conditioner	desktop computer	humidifier	scattered papers	wall clock
aluminum briefcase	document stack	laptop	server	wall fan
basic wall	exercise ball	modern office chair	standard umbrella stand	water cooler
cordless phone	exit sign	office desk	tissue box	whiteboard

outdoors

aluminum rug	camp stove	director's chair	lantern	picnic basket	tiki torch
barbecue	campfire	dirt flooring	natural wooden-deck rug	portable radio	white wooden-deck rug
black wooden-deck rug	campfire cookware	fire pit	outdoor bench	simple DIY workbench	
bonfire	camping cot	hammock	outdoor generator	sleeping bag	
brown wooden-deck rug	cooler box	inflatable sofa	outdoor table	smoker	

party

big festive tree	camo flooring	flower stand	Jingle wall	orange camo wall	silver mic
bingo wheel	camo wall	giraffe-print flooring	kisses wall	ornament mobile	stall
birthday cake	colorful wheel	groovy wall	kitschy tile	party flooring	table with cloth
birthday candles	cotton-candy stall	heavy-curtain wall	leopard-print flooring	party garland	tabletop festive tree
birthday sign	DJ's turntable	holiday candle	lobby flooring	party wall	tiger-print flooring
birthday table	festive top set	illuminated present	mic stand	popcorn machine	tree's bounty big tree
blue camo flooring	festive tree	illuminated reindeer	mod wall	purple camo flooring	tree's bounty little tree
blue camo wall	flashy-flower sign	illuminated tree	orange camo flooring	purple camo wall	zebra-print flooring

school

anatomical model	champion's pennant	grass standee	microscope	racetrack flooring	tennis table
autograph cards	common flooring	green rubber flooring	modeling clay	retro radiator	tree standee
ball	common wall	handy water cooler	mountain standee	rough rug	upright locker
basic teacher's desk	cork flooring	hedge standee	natural-block flooring	round space heater	utility sink
basketball hoop	corkboard	homework set	Newton's cradle	rubber mud mat	wall clock
blackboard wall	dark-block flooring	jointed-mat flooring	Nook Inc. flooring	school chair	wall fan
blue rubber flooring	electronics kit	lab-experiments set	oil lamp	school desk	writing poster
book	football	lecture-hall bench	painting set	skeleton	
broom and dustpan	formal paper	lecture-hall desk	phone box	stadiometer	
chalkboard	globe	marimba	podium	standard umbrella stand	

shop

abstract wall	brown herringbone wall	diner mini table	infused-water dispenser	pop-up toaster	stand mixer
accessories stand	brown-brick flooring	diner neon clock	iron entrance mat	portable record player	steamer-basket set
analog kitchen scale	brown-brick wall	diner neon sign	ivy wall	pot rack	stovetop espresso maker
arcade combat game	café-curtain wall	diner sofa	jukebox	random-square-tile flooring	table setting
arcade fighting game	candy machine	dinnerware	kettle	rattan flooring	table with cloth
arcade mahjong game	changing room	dish-drying rack	knife block	red intricate wall	tea set
arcade seat	chic tearoom wall	drink machine	lattice wall	red-brick flooring	tennis table
arched-brick flooring	chocolate herringbone wall	espresso maker	light herringbone flooring	red-brick wall	terra-cotta flooring
arched-window wall	cityscape wall	exquisite wall	light parquet flooring	refrigerator	traditional tea set
artsy parquet flooring	classic pitcher	flagstone flooring	light wood-pattern flooring	retro gas pump	unglazed dish set
beaded-curtain wall	coconut juice	foosball table	magazine rack	revolving spice rack	utility sink
billiard table	coffee cup	freezer	magnetic knife rack	rice cooker	ventilation fan
black-brick flooring	coffee grinder	fresh cooler	menu chalkboard	rubber-tile flooring	wavy-tile wall
black-brick wall	cooler box	frying pan	microwave	rustic-stone wall	white subway-tile wall
blackboard wall	cream and sugar	gas range	modern shoji-screen wall	serving cart	white-brick flooring
blue diner wall	cutting board	gray diner wall	modern tearoom wall	shutter wall	white-brick wall
blue floral flooring	dark herringbone flooring	gray molded-panel wall	mug	sidewalk flooring	wild-wood wall
blue intricate wall	dark wood-pattern flooring	green floral flooring	Nook Inc. flooring	simple kettle	wood-burning stove
blue molded-panel wall	dark wooden-mosaic wall	green intricate wall	Nook Inc. wall	simple white flooring	wooden-mosaic wall
blue subway-tile wall	dartboard	green retro flooring	open-frame kitchen	slate flooring	yellow floral flooring
box corner sofa	desk mirror	harmonious wall	orange retro flooring	snack machine	yellow intricate wall
box sofa	diner chair	hexagonal floral flooring	patchwork-tile flooring	soft-serve lamp	
brick oven	diner counter chair	imperial dining chair	pennant	soothing tearoom wall	
brown diner wall	diner counter table	imperial dining lantern	pinball machine	soup kettle	
brown floral flooring	diner dining table	imperial dining table	pink diner wall	stall	

space

asteroid	Earth rug	lunar rover	rocket	solar panel	starry-sky wall
astronaut suit	flying saucer	lunar surface	satellite	space shuttle	telescope
crescent-moon chair	galaxy flooring	moon	sci-fi flooring	star clock	throwback rocket
crewed spaceship	lunar lander	nova light	sci-fi wall	starry garland	tourist telescope

zen-style

bamboo basket	bamboo-screen wall	futon	kettle bathtub	pagoda	steamer-basket set
bamboo bench	bamboo-shoot lamp	go board	kimono stand	paper lantern	sumo ring
bamboo candleholder	blossom-viewing lantern	gold-screen wall	kotatsu	paper tiger	tall lantern
bamboo doll	bonsai shelf	gong	lattice wall	pile of zen cushions	tatami
bamboo drum	cherry-blossom bonsai	hanging scroll	light bamboo rug	pine bonsai tree	tatami bed
bamboo floor lamp	cherry-blossom branches	harmonious wall	loom	pond stone	tatami flooring
bamboo flooring	cherry-blossom pond stone	hearth	low screen	pot	tatami mat
bamboo lunch box	cherry-blossom-petal pile	hexagonal floral flooring	lucky cat	raccoon figurine	tea table
bamboo noodle slide	chic tearoom wall	imperial bed	maple-leaf pond stone	rush tatami	traditional tea set
bamboo partition	clay furnace	imperial chest	modern shoji-screen wall	rush tatami flooring	wooden fish
bamboo shelf	crepe-design wall	imperial decorative shelves	modern tearoom wall	screen	wooden-plank sign
bamboo speaker	dark bamboo rug	imperial dining chair	mortar wall	screen wall	zen cushion
bamboo sphere	deer scare	imperial dining lantern	moss ball	shanty mat	zen-style stone
bamboo stool	dojo wall	imperial dining table	mossy garden rock	shoji screen	
bamboo stopblock	elaborate kimono stand	imperial low table	mossy-garden flooring	soothing tearoom wall	
bamboo wall	exquisite wall	imperial partition	mossy-garden wall	spinning wheel	
bamboo wall decoration	floor seat	incense burner	outdoor bath	squat toilet	
bamboo-grove wall	floral rush-mat flooring	katana	outdoor picnic set	standard tearoom wall	

Penalties

Failing to keep your house clean and well organized will result in penalties to your overall score. If your house has more than one room, penalties can be applied for each offending room. Check to make sure that no furniture items, such as couches and chairs, are facing the walls and don't forget to pick up any items or trash dropped on the floor. The biggest penalty comes from cockroaches that infest your house if you haven't played in a while, however, so always remember to stomp them out!

Penalties

Criteria	Points Deducted
Items other than furniture are placed on the floor	-1(× # of non-furniture items)
Items that can be rotated are facing the wall	-300 (× # of improperly placed items)
Cockroaches in the room	-2500 (× # of cockroaches)
Trash in room	-500 (× # of pieces of trash)

Cockroaches

Walking into a house infested with cockroaches can be a real bummer. These nasty critters show up if you haven't come back to play Animal Crossing: New Horizons in over 30 days, and up to two can show up in each room for a total of 12 in the house. Some might even be hiding underneath your furniture, so look out! You can get rid of cockroaches by running over them or dragging furniture over them.

Make sure furniture items like couches and chairs haven't been rotated to directly face a wall, since that will result in a scoring penalty.

HHA Prizes

All you hard work perfectly arranging your various rooms will eventually lead to some rewards! The HHA will send out rewards in the mail once you reach certain point totals, which are all shown in the chart here. Aim for the gold trophy!

HHA Prizes

Rank	Reward
150,000	gold HHA trophy
100,000	silver HHA trophy
70,000	bronze HHA trophy
50,000	gold HHA plaque
30,000	silver HHA plaque
20,000	bronze HHA plaque
10,000	HHA pennant

The Island Designer

As a reward for being a stellar Island Representative, Tom Nook has one last app to give you after the credits roll. The Island Designer app allows you to change the very landscape of your island and build entirely new structures—with the right permits, of course. You can unlock different features on your Island Designer app by purchasing permits at the Nook Stop. These features include various path types that must be purchased individually, waterscaping and the cliff-construction permit. After purchasing a new permit, the Island Designer app will be updated. A permit only needs to be purchased once to be used forever. Here, we'll explain the many amazing things you can do with this app.

How it Works

When you select the app, your NookPhone will ask you if you would like to start constructing. If you select 'yes', you will don a special construction helmet (for safety) and a new menu will appear on your screen. You can open this menu by pressing the ✛ Button and access all the features of your purchased permits. You also have the option to 'Request Cleanup' which can pickup certain items around you like fences, or 'Check the Manual'

which can help you refresh your memory on how to use your toolsets.

You won't be able to do any construction work while inside buildings (though you can still wear your helmet), but just about everywhere else is fair game. While in construction mode, you can still use your other tools as well. To quit using the Island Designer app, open your NookPhone again and select the Island Designer to get the prompt to leave the application.

Landscaping

The landscaping tool will fill up with different pathway permits as you purchase them. Using this tool, you'll be able to place down pathways a single 1x1 tile at a time. These pathways replace any patch of grass, and cannot be picked up the way a placed custom design can. You also won't be able to use your shovel on these pathways.

Pressing Ⓐ over an existing patch of pathway will

erase it, unless the tile is attached to more pathway. If the spot you're aiming at is connected to more path, paving over it once will round out the corners. This can be great if you prefer pathways with smooth, rounded corners. If you really want to erase the tile, pressing Ⓐ again will do the job. There are three default paths, and seven more available by exchanging Nook Miles. These paths have different properties depending on what category they belong to; paths that don't match won't connect together, so keep that in mind when designing your island. Finally, it's worth remembering that custom designs with transparency can be placed on top of the paths you lay down.

Two different types of path won't connect to each other.

Landscaping Types

Type	Paths	Properties
Hard	Stone Path, Brick Path, Arch Tile Path, Terra-cota Tiles, Wooden Path, Custom Path	Flowers and trees cannot grow on this type of path.
Soft	Grass, Dirt Path, Dark Dirt Path, Sand Path,	Flowers can grow on this type of path. Fossils can also spawn on soft paths.

Landscaping Permit Costs

Path	Cost (Nook Miles)
Arch Tile Path	2000
Brick Path	2000
Dark Dirt Path	2000
Sand Path	2000
Terra-cotta Tile	2000
Wooden Path	2000
Custom Design Path	2300

Sometimes residents will get in the way of your landscaping work.

Cliffs

The cliff-construction permit gives you a special shovel that allows you to build or destroy cliffs, a single 1x1 tile at a time. There are three levels of altitude for your island: sea-level, a low cliff and a high cliff. Cliffs need to be built up from the level below where the cliff will be and can't be built from the top down.

Cliff-Construction Permit ▶ **6000 Nook Miles**

Cliffs must be destroyed from beneath, not while standing atop them. If you want more natural looking cliffs, use the tool to hit any sharp right angles once to round them out. Cliffs that have items on them or are too close to trees can't be broken down. Cliffs also need to be broken down one level at a time; a high cliff block cannot be removed from sea level. Tunnels can't be made using the cliff constructing tool, nor can bridge building kits be used to connect cliff areas.

Clear out an area before you begin any large-scale cliff work.

All sorts of paths and mazes are suddenly possible!

Waterscaping

Once you have the permit, waterscaping is done using a shovel tool that allows you to make ponds, lakes and rivers. Each press of Ⓐ will replace a single 1x1 tile of ground with water. Sharp corners can be rounded out for a more natural look by pressing Ⓐ again over a hard angle. Creating water next to the edge of a cliff will create waterfalls. You can also use bridge building kits over man made bodies of water. If a body of water is big enough, fish will also spawn there.

Waterscaping Permit	▶ 6000 Nook Miles

Water and paths will be naturally separated.

You can't destroy items with the waterscaping tool equipped, so remove things like flowers beforehand.

Example Builds

Our friendly team of animals have put together some of the ways in which your Island Designer can enrich your island. Don't be afraid to experiment with all the tools at your disposal. The possibilities are endless!

Lake Loves-A-Lot

You have the power to shape your island. Lakes and rivers don't have to be in natural shapes. The easiest way to make fun shapes using the waterscaping tool is to plot out the general shape first. Decide the perimeter of what you're building and then round out the corners afterward.

Make the shape roughly, then round out the corners!

While symmetrical shapes are easier to make, don't be afraid to get creative.

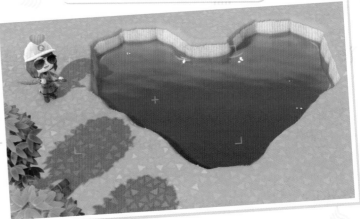

If you're looking for a bit more privacy during your getaway, you can use the waterscaping tool to create islands within your island. Make sure you place down all the things you want on your private island first before you start building the moat, lest you don't give yourself enough room and have to start over. If you don't want to drop the Bells for a fancy bridge or use your vaulting pole, you can make natural land bridges as well. You can jump across a single tile of water, so making smaller islands can make your private space just a hop, skip and jump away!

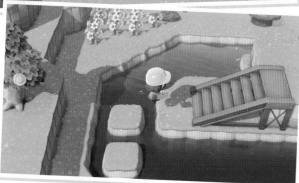

Make sure to build a way in and out!

We recommend building inclines before enclosing your island to avoid running out of space!

Extreme Waterfalls

Make waterfalls even more grandiose and breathtaking by stacking them on top of each other! Using your cliff construction tool first, create an area where a river can flow down twice into itself.

We recommend making sure that this space has plenty of room for you to walk around it so you don't get stuck.

Pre-existing water doesn't need to be below the falls in order to make them.

For the best results, make sure there is a decent amount of cliff on either side of the falls.

Spice up a Plaza

Combining your Island Designer tools with your DIY crafting skills can make for beautiful scenery. These things go hand in hand and look even better together. A fountain can turn into a gorgeous plaza with just a little help from the path tool.

Fountains are generally an inexpensive recipe that can really add to your island.

Grass will always separate two types of path.

Life's a Playground

Making fun areas on your island also works with non-DIY furniture. Check out the Nook Shopping catalog and the Nook Mileage Program—there are plenty of furniture pieces designed for the outdoors for purchase. Just look at what you can make!

Fencing and floral arrangements can help to further define spaces where you've placed pathways.

Use different colored paths to create borders and fields.

"Well I think there's only one way to respond to this information... Decorate the entire island head to toe... or stream to sea!"

"There's some positive buzz floating around about our island. Folks are starting to take notice!"

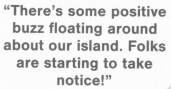

Chapter 7

The Nook Collector's Catalogue

If you're a collector, hoarder or serious shopper, this is the chapter for you. There's an almost unending supply of things to fill your island with, and the pro designer provides practically infinite ways to customize your character's appearance. Here we'll display all of them for your perusing pleasure.

CHAPTER HIGHLIGHTS

Character Customization

Want to get a really particular, absolutely perfect look for your character? Fashionistas, you're in luck. Animal Crossing: New Horizons provides many different options for getting your character exactly the way you want it! From hairstyles to skin color to every item of clothing you can think of, everything can be made to fit your own desired look. Here we'll show you everything about customizing your character. Before you go clothes shopping, though, let's be sure your hair's in order and you're looking your absolute best.

1 Character Building

Choosing your character's look is a critical step in any Animal Crossing game. In Animal Crossing: New Horizons, however, you can change your look completely at any time, provided you have a Mirror to stand in front of. Still, it may take you a little bit of time to get hold of one, so consider how you want your character to look at the start of the game.

You can customize your look any time you like once you have any piece of furniture with a mirror.

Skin Tone

On the first customization page, you can select your character's skin tone. There are a total of eight different options.

Nose/Mouth

Want to get the perfect mouth or nose type for your character? Look no further. In total, there are three nose types and four mouth types to choose from.

Cheeks

You can also decide whether you would like to have blushy cheeks on your character. There are three options here, and two colors to choose between.

266 Animal Crossing: New Horizons OFFICIAL COMPANION GUIDE

Eyes

There are 26 different eye types and shapes to choose from, along with six eye colors.

Hairstyles

You'll start off with eight diverse hairstyles when you make your passport at the beginning of the game. You'll then unlock six more once you find or craft your first piece of furniture with a mirror. Finally, you'll gain access to 16 more hairstyles by exchanging Nook Miles for the hairstyle packs "Top 8 Pop Hairstyles" and "Top 8 Cool Hairstyles" at the Nook Stop in Resident Services (once you've unlocked Nook Miles+). Let's take a look at every single possible hairstyle in the game!

Extra hair colors can also be unlocked by purchasing the "Top 8 Stylish Hair Colors" pack with Nook Miles at the Nook Stop.

You can change your character type to boy or girl, but this setting makes no difference to their visual options at all—all hairstyles and face parts can be used either way.

Face Paint

None   Custom Design

Choose your setting.

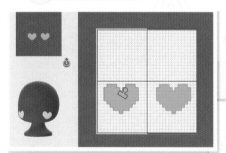

Bed Head

Have you not had time to play in the last 30 days? If so, you'll probably be surprised to find that the next time you turn the game on, you won't be looking like your usual self. You'll emerge from your house looking tired and with your hair in a mess! It's no big deal, though—a quick shake and everything is back to normal. This carefree hairstyle will even be added to your character customization options afterwards!

Face Paint

Your NookPhone's Custom Designs app can be used to paint a custom pattern on your character's face. Select from one of your patterns and apply the look! Generally speaking, transparent patterns will look a lot better on your character, but you can use any type of pattern you would like! Adding some unique designs to your character's face is a great way to make you stand out. Here are a few examples to get your creative juices flowing!

Lovely Cheeks

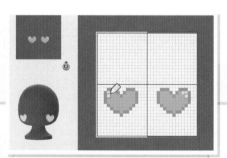

With this design, we've used the heart stamp tool to make custom blush marks that add a bit of extra cuteness to any look!

The midpoint of the canvas, where the top two quadrants meet the bottom two, is where the bottom of your character's nose rests.

Putting designs on the cheeks will actually be closer to this midpoint line than the center of the bottom two quadrants. Keep this in mind as you make designs specifically for the cheeks.

Struck by Lightning

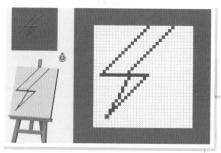

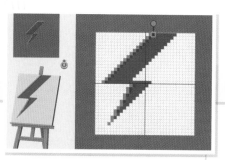

This look features a lightning bolt across the face, inspired by radical rock stars. Use the line tool to easily draw the shape.

Face paint doesn't cover your character's eye and will set approximately one pixel above the eye and continue beneath the nose.

Keep this in mind when figuring out where a design may end and where it will continue.

Tiara Time

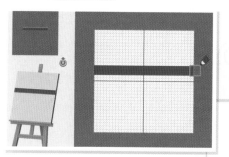

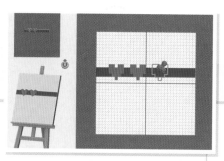

Take advantage of face paint by making your own accessories that rest beneath the hair!

In this example, we've used the stamp tool to make a cute but simple tiara that bands across the forehead.

You can use this area to make anything from sweatbands, forehead protectors, bindis and even cool scars.

Anime Tears

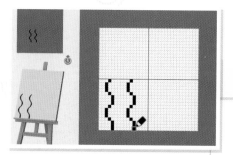

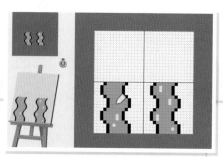

The eyes won't be affected by face paint, but there are still funny face paint designs you can make around them.

Here, we've designed comical running tears that can add to your sad or sobbing Reactions. You will need three colors, white, a light blue and then either black or a dark blue.

Make small lines with the white to create the illusion of light reflecting off the tears. Try to center the design within each of the lower quadrants, since that's where your eyes will be.

② Custom Designs

If you're itching to get creative yourself, then the Custom Designs app has you covered. The app comes with your NookPhone, but the Pro add-on can be unlocked by exchanging 800 Nook Miles at the Nook Stop in Resident Services (after you've unlocked Nook Miles+). This upgrade allows you to make complex clothing designs like never before.

Select a slot and get started creating a custom design that can be applied to a wide variety of clothing. This includes tanks, tees, dress shirts, sweaters, hoodies, coats, six types of dresses and three different hats.

Don't be scared by all the tools at your disposal. Making a fashion masterpiece is a cinch! We'll give you a brief explanation of each and then provide some examples of how to use them.

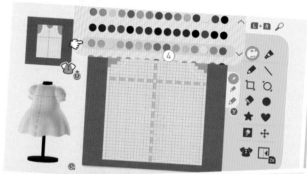

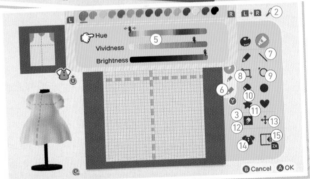

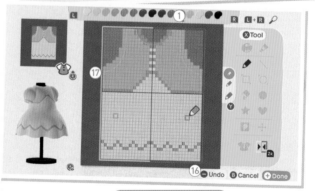

Button	Function
① Color Palette	Shuffles through all 15 colors in the palette (Ⓛ/Ⓡ Buttons)
② Eyedropper Tool	Selects the color the cursor is currently on (Ⓛ/Ⓡ Buttons simultaneously)
③ Tools	Swap tools (Ⓧ)
④ Swap Palette	Change the palette of colors you have to work with (Ⓐ)
⑤ Change Color	You can shift the hue, vividness or brightness of the last placed color (Ⓐ)
⑥ Pen	A free draw tool that comes in 1-, 2- and 3-pixel sizes (Press Ⓐ and hold to drag. Ⓨ to swap between 3 sizes.)
⑦ Line Tool	Create straight lines, 1 pixel thick (Ⓐ to select starting point and press again to select the end point)
⑧ Rectangle Tool	Makes boxes of various sizes with a 1 pixel border (Ⓐ to select starting point and press again to select the end point)
⑨ Circle Tool	Makes circles of various sized with a 1 pixel border (Ⓐ to select starting point and press again to select the end point)
⑩ Fill	This will fill enclosed spaces placed on the design with one color (Ⓐ)
⑪ Stamps	Will stamp an image in 3 sizes. It comes in circle, heart or star shapes (Ⓐ, Ⓨ to shuffle through sizes)
⑫ Fill All	This will fill the entire design with one color, deleting everything else (Ⓐ)
⑬ Drag Design	This can move everything you've placed (Press Ⓐ and hold to drag)
⑭ Swap/Copy	Switches which part of the garment you're working on and lets you copy designs between parts (Ⓐ over icon or press down on the Right Stick)
⑮ Mirror Mode	This will make every action you take on one side also happen on the other, so the design is symmetrical (Ⓩⓡ)
⑯ Undo/Redo	Can erase the last action you did, but only the last action and nothing prior! Pressing it again will make it reappear. (⊝)
⑰ Rotate	This will shift the view of the preview display on the left. (Rotate Right Stick)

Floor Designs

Custom designs can also be placed as floor tiles straight from your NookPhone's Custom Design app. Choose a design and select "Display on Ground" and you'll have the option to either place it down as a mannequin, a painting on a canvas stand or as a single tile directly on the floor. You can pick up these designs by pressing Ⓨ while you're near them, and you won't be able to place items on top of them. They can be great for temporary usage, or for piecing together larger art pieces.

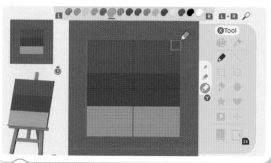

① Place down your base colors first. For this example, we'll use 3 colors.

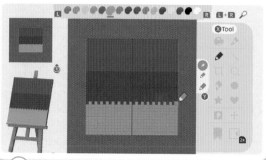

② Using the pencil tool, pick your first color and place singular dots against the edge of where this first color ends. Be sure to skip every other pixel.

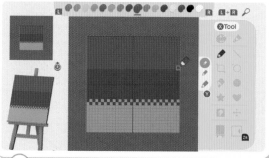

③ Then, with the pencil tool still selected, move one pixel beyond that line and use that same color to make another line of dots, but alternating which pixels you leave clear, like a checkerboard.

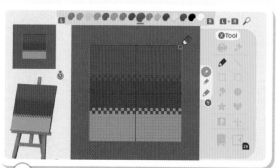

④ Repeat this pattern with the other colors on your design.

How to Make Plaid

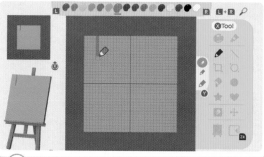

① For this project, you will need to pick three colors. One base color, one darker shade, and one even darker shade. Keep these in your palette, then fill the canvas with your base color.

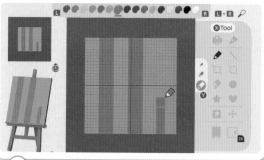

② Using the line or pencil tool, map out equally spaced lines with your darker shade. We suggest making these sections at least 3 pixels wide and an odd number. Fill these out using your fill bucket.

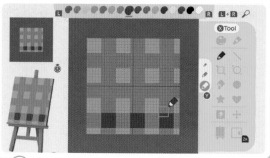

③ With the rectangle tool or a large pencil, create boxes where these lines intersect with your darkest color. Fill these in too.

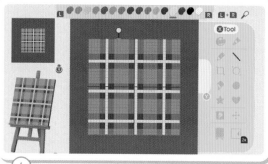

④ If you want some extra flair to your plaid, use the line tool to take a bright shade and create intersecting lines between the darkest boxes.

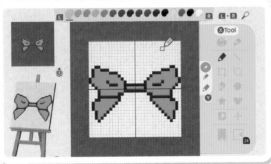

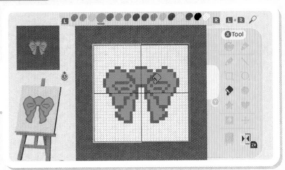

Here you'll find templates for various ribbons that you can easily copy! We recommend starting from the center and using the mirror tool to much more easily and quickly create bows and ribbons.

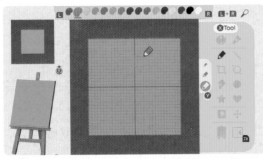

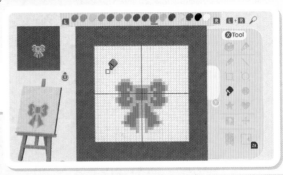

3-D Buttons

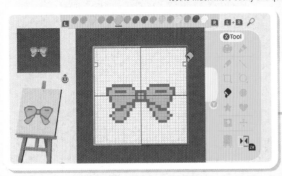

① Pick a color for your button, but also pick one much lighter shade and one darker shade.

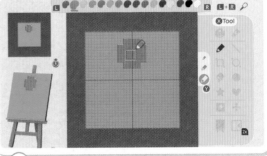

② Pick a size for your buttons using the circle stamp.

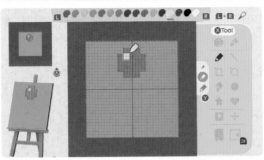

③ Using the pencil tool, use your lighter color to make a smaller shape in one of the top corners of the button. This mimics the look of light reflecting off of a shiny button.

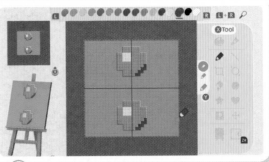

④ In the opposing corner, line part of the button with your darker color. This shadow gives extra depth to the button and makes it really feel three-dimensional. Repeat this for all your buttons!

Repeating Designs

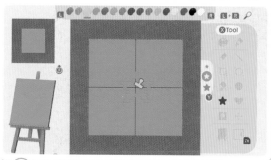

① For this design, start off with one of the stamp tools. For this example, we'll be using the star.

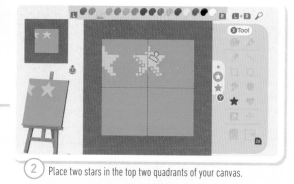

② Place two stars in the top two quadrants of your canvas.

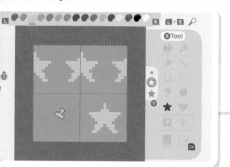

③ With the drag tool, move this design to the left until half of the first star is cut off and is moved to the right of the canvas. Use the stamp tool again to place two more stars in the bottom two quadrants.

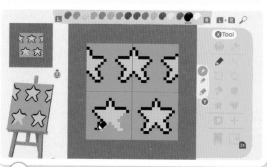

④ This will create a pattern that can seamlessly blend together with other parts of your garment that have the same pattern.

Selling Your Designs

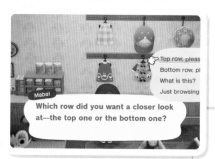

Go to the back wall in the Able Sisters' store; inspect it and choose a row.

Select "Display my work here", and choose the design you want to showcase from the list that comes up.

You'll get to decide whether to keep the design that was in the spot before, or throw it away, and then yours will instantly replace it!

Wrapping Paper

In Nook's Cranny, the cabinet offers a daily rotation of different wrapping papers that can be used to wrap all kinds of items that you can then gift to other residents on the island. Putting in the extra effort to wrap your gifts will give you an extra friendship level boost. For more information on friendship, turn to P.75. There are sixteen possible colors to pick from, though your animal friends will be just as pleased regardless of the color you've chosen. It's the thought that counts!

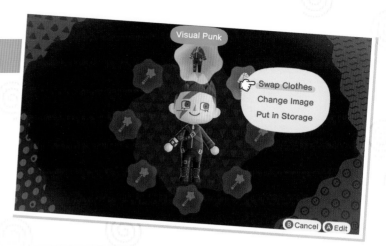

③ Using Wands

Another way to personalize your everyday island life is with the wand tool. Once you've obtained a wand, opening any wardrobe or dresser you come across will allow you to edit your wand outfits. This feature gives you eight slots to assign to various outfits, that you can then change into instantly using your wands. Open the menu, and three options will be available when hovering over an outfit slot: Swap Clothes, Change Image and Put in Storage.

Swap Clothes

This function is what allows you to assign clothes to a wand outfit, or edit a previous outfit. Handily, the menu is almost identical to your typical wardrobe, where you can sort through your collection with the Ⓛ/Ⓡ triggers and select the piece you want to assign to this outfit by pressing Ⓐ over the item. Pressing Ⓧ will remove the item currently selected. In the top right, you'll also be able to assign Pro-design clothing to your wand outfit. A wand outfit must have at least one clothing item included in order to be assigned to a slot. When you're done, press ✛, and you'll be taken to a keyboard menu, where you can name your outfit.

Assigning clothing pieces to an outfit will take them out of your storage, but will not take up pocket space. In order to access these items individually, however, you'll have to go back to your wardrobe, edit your wand outfits and manually remove the item from the slot before putting it back into your storage.

It doesn't matter which type of wardrobe you use; all types let you edit your outfits.

Change Image

This opens a mini menu, where you can select one of the individual garments from an outfit to act as the display image for this outfit. This will not change the outfit in the slot in any way, but might make it easier for you to pick what you're looking for while you're swapping clothes.

Put in Storage

Selecting this will return whatever clothes were assigned to this outfit slot back into your storage. This action can't be undone without manually reassigning the same clothes to this outfit slot, so be careful when using this option!

bamboo wand
15,600 (3900)
OBTAIN Seasonal recipe: Young Spring Bamboo

golden wand
83,000 (20,750)
OBTAIN Star fragment recipe (Reward: Celeste)

mums wand
6320 (1580)
OBTAIN Star fragment recipe (Reward: Celeste)

star wand
26,000 (6500)
OBTAIN Star fragment recipe (Reward: Celeste)

bug wand
6000 (1500)
OBTAIN Reward: Bug-Off!

hyacinth wand
6640 (1660)
OBTAIN Star fragment recipe (Reward: Celeste)

mushroom wand
13,200 (3300)
OBTAIN Seasonal recipe: Mushroom

tree-branch wand
6200 (1550)
OBTAIN Star fragment recipe (Reward: Celeste)

cherry-blossom wand
10,800 (2700)
OBTAIN Seasonal recipe: Cherry blossom

ice wand
26,000 (6500)
OBTAIN Reward: Snowboy

pansy wand
6320 (1580)
OBTAIN Star fragment recipe (Reward: Celeste)

tulip wand
6320 (1580)
OBTAIN Star fragment recipe (Reward: Celeste)

cosmos wand
6320 (1580)
OBTAIN Star fragment recipe (Reward: Celeste)

iron wand
15,000 (3750)
OBTAIN Star fragment recipe (Reward: Celeste)

rose wand
6320 (1580)
OBTAIN Star fragment recipe (Reward: Celeste)

wand
4000 (1000)
OBTAIN Star fragment recipe (Reward: Celeste)

fish wand
6000 (1500)
OBTAIN Reward: Fishing Tourney

lily wand
6320 (1580)
OBTAIN Star fragment recipe (Reward: Celeste)

shell wand
20,400 (5100)
OBTAIN Seasonal recipe: Summer shell

windflower wand
6320 (1580)
OBTAIN Star fragment recipe (Reward: Celeste)

(4) Clothing Catalog

It's time to step into the fitting room and try on some new styles. The following pages display every piece of clothing and accessory in the game, listed in alphabetical order within the various clothing categories. Each entry comes with some useful information about the item, and we'll go through what all this information means here. You can also refer to the back of your bookmarks if you're ever unsure. Items obtained as DIY recipes only show the sell price of the finished item.

open-collar shirt
OBTAIN The Able Sisters (Stall) ① ⑥ ②
STYLE Simple • Elegant • CO • EV ③ 960 (240) ⑦
④
⑤

① OBTAIN This tells you how to acquire the item. Depending on how you receive the item, at least one of the following icons will be shown:
🌰 This means you'll receive it as an item.
📋 This means you'll receive it as a DIY recipe and must then craft it.
📦 This means you'll receive it via mail.
💳 This means you'll need to acquire it by redeeming Nook Miles at the Nook Stop.

② SEASON This describes seasonality. A circle will be highlighted for each season the item is available during:
● Spring ● Summer ● Autumn ● Winter

③ STYLE This tells you the styles the item counts as. Each resident has their own preferred styles.
The short abbreviations are for the item's fashion themes, used in Label's grading:

PA = party	SP = sporty	WK = work
CO = comfy	OD = outdoorsy	FT = fairy tale
GO = goth	TH = theatrical	VA = vacation
FO = formal	EV = everyday	

④ IMAGE Pictures of all color variations of the item are shown here.

⑤ COLORS These are the item's system colors, which can affect Label's outfit grading, resident conversations, and even HHA grading (if you place the item in your house as furniture).

⑥ PERSONALITY This appears when the item **Big sister** can be obtained as a DIY recipe by talking to a resident, and means that the resident must be of the listed personality type. If there's a number in parenthesis before this label, it means you must have that many DIY recipes unlocked in order for a resident to give you this one.

⑦ PRICE This is the price tag. It shows how many Bells the item costs to buy. If it can't be bought, this will say "N/A". The value in parenthesis is how much you'll get when selling the item.

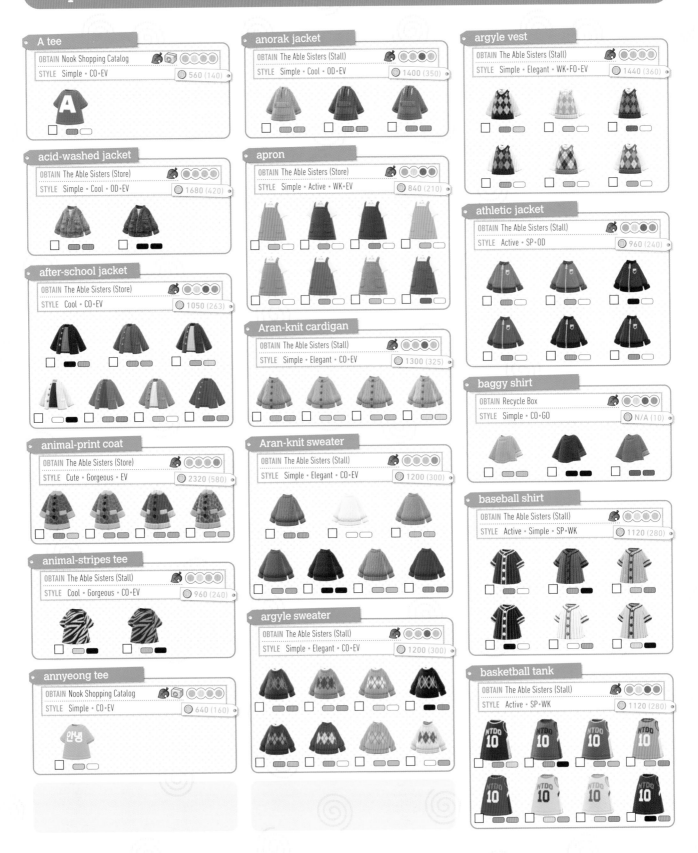

A tee
OBTAIN	Nook Shopping Catalog
STYLE	Simple • CO•EV

560 (140)

acid-washed jacket
OBTAIN	The Able Sisters (Store)
STYLE	Simple • Cool • OD•EV

1680 (420)

after-school jacket
OBTAIN	The Able Sisters (Store)
STYLE	Cool • CO•EV

1050 (263)

animal-print coat
OBTAIN	The Able Sisters (Store)
STYLE	Cute • Gorgeous • EV

2320 (580)

animal-stripes tee
OBTAIN	The Able Sisters (Stall)
STYLE	Cool • Gorgeous • CO•EV

960 (240)

annyeong tee
OBTAIN	Nook Shopping Catalog
STYLE	Simple • CO•EV

640 (160)

anorak jacket
OBTAIN	The Able Sisters (Stall)
STYLE	Simple • Cool • OD•EV

1400 (350)

apron
OBTAIN	The Able Sisters (Store)
STYLE	Simple • Active • WK•EV

840 (210)

Aran-knit cardigan
OBTAIN	The Able Sisters (Stall)
STYLE	Simple • Elegant • CO•EV

1300 (325)

Aran-knit sweater
OBTAIN	The Able Sisters (Stall)
STYLE	Simple • Elegant • CO•EV

1200 (300)

argyle sweater
OBTAIN	The Able Sisters (Stall)
STYLE	Simple • Elegant • CO•EV

1200 (300)

argyle vest
OBTAIN	The Able Sisters (Stall)
STYLE	Simple • Elegant • WK•FO•EV

1440 (360)

athletic jacket
OBTAIN	The Able Sisters (Stall)
STYLE	Active • SP•OD

960 (240)

baggy shirt
OBTAIN	Recycle Box
STYLE	Simple • CO•GO

N/A (10)

baseball shirt
OBTAIN	The Able Sisters (Stall)
STYLE	Active • Simple • SP•WK

1120 (280)

basketball tank
OBTAIN	The Able Sisters (Stall)
STYLE	Active • SP•WK

1120 (280)

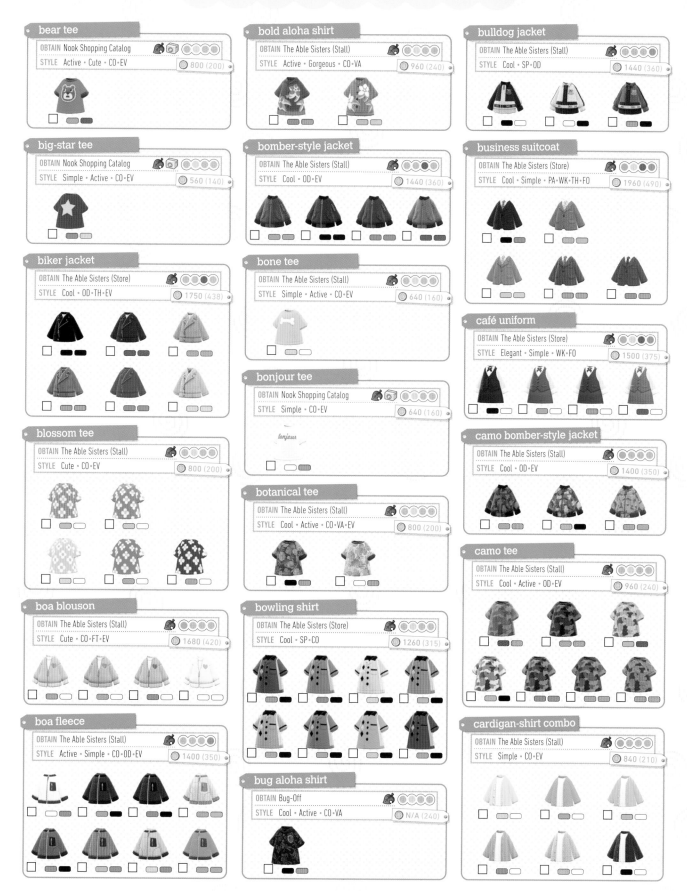

bear tee
OBTAIN Nook Shopping Catalog
STYLE Active • Cute • CO • EV
800 (200)

big-star tee
OBTAIN Nook Shopping Catalog
STYLE Simple • Active • CO • EV
560 (140)

biker jacket
OBTAIN The Able Sisters (Store)
STYLE Cool • OD • TH • EV
1750 (438)

blossom tee
OBTAIN The Able Sisters (Stall)
STYLE Cute • CO • EV
800 (200)

boa blouson
OBTAIN The Able Sisters (Stall)
STYLE Cute • CO • FT • EV
1680 (420)

boa fleece
OBTAIN The Able Sisters (Stall)
STYLE Active • Simple • CO • OD • EV
1400 (350)

bold aloha shirt
OBTAIN The Able Sisters (Stall)
STYLE Active • Gorgeous • CO • VA
960 (240)

bomber-style jacket
OBTAIN The Able Sisters (Stall)
STYLE Cool • OD • EV
1440 (360)

bone tee
OBTAIN The Able Sisters (Stall)
STYLE Simple • Active • CO • EV
640 (160)

bonjour tee
OBTAIN Nook Shopping Catalog
STYLE Simple • CO • EV
640 (160)

botanical tee
OBTAIN The Able Sisters (Stall)
STYLE Cool • Active • CO • VA • EV
800 (200)

bowling shirt
OBTAIN The Able Sisters (Store)
STYLE Cool • SP • CO
1260 (315)

bug aloha shirt
OBTAIN Bug-Off
STYLE Cool • Active • CO • VA
N/A (240)

bulldog jacket
OBTAIN The Able Sisters (Stall)
STYLE Cool • SP • OD
1440 (360)

business suitcoat
OBTAIN The Able Sisters (Store)
STYLE Cool • Simple • PA • WK • TH • FO
1960 (490)

café uniform
OBTAIN The Able Sisters (Store)
STYLE Elegant • Simple • WK • FO
1500 (375)

camo bomber-style jacket
OBTAIN The Able Sisters (Stall)
STYLE Cool • OD • EV
1400 (350)

camo tee
OBTAIN The Able Sisters (Stall)
STYLE Cool • Active • OD • EV
960 (240)

cardigan-shirt combo
OBTAIN The Able Sisters (Stall)
STYLE Simple • CO • EV
840 (210)

7

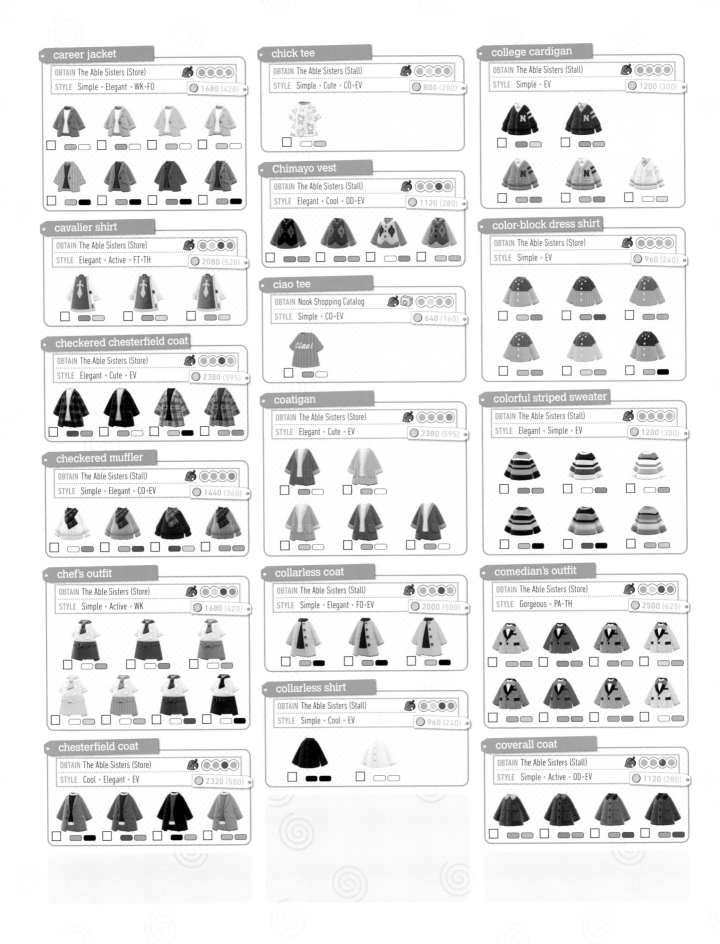

career jacket
OBTAIN The Able Sisters (Store)
STYLE Simple • Elegant • WK•FO   1680 (420)

cavalier shirt
OBTAIN The Able Sisters (Store)
STYLE Elegant • Active • FT•TH   2080 (520)

checkered chesterfield coat
OBTAIN The Able Sisters (Store)
STYLE Elegant • Cute • EV   2380 (595)

checkered muffler
OBTAIN The Able Sisters (Stall)
STYLE Simple • Elegant • CO•EV   1440 (360)

chef's outfit
OBTAIN The Able Sisters (Store)
STYLE Simple • Active • WK   1680 (420)

chesterfield coat
OBTAIN The Able Sisters (Store)
STYLE Cool • Elegant • EV   2320 (580)

chick tee
OBTAIN The Able Sisters (Stall)
STYLE Simple • Cute • CO•EV   800 (200)

Chimayo vest
OBTAIN The Able Sisters (Stall)
STYLE Elegant • Cool • OD•EV   1120 (280)

ciao tee
OBTAIN Nook Shopping Catalog
STYLE Simple • CO•EV   640 (160)

coatigan
OBTAIN The Able Sisters (Store)
STYLE Elegant • Cute • EV   2380 (595)

collarless coat
OBTAIN The Able Sisters (Stall)
STYLE Simple • Elegant • FO•EV   2000 (500)

collarless shirt
OBTAIN The Able Sisters (Stall)
STYLE Simple • Cool • EV   960 (240)

college cardigan
OBTAIN The Able Sisters (Stall)
STYLE Simple • EV   1200 (300)

color-block dress shirt
OBTAIN The Able Sisters (Store)
STYLE Simple • EV   960 (240)

colorful striped sweater
OBTAIN The Able Sisters (Stall)
STYLE Elegant • Simple • EV   1200 (300)

comedian's outfit
OBTAIN The Able Sisters (Store)
STYLE Gorgeous • PA•TH   2500 (625)

coverall coat
OBTAIN The Able Sisters (Stall)
STYLE Simple • Active • OD•EV   1120 (280)

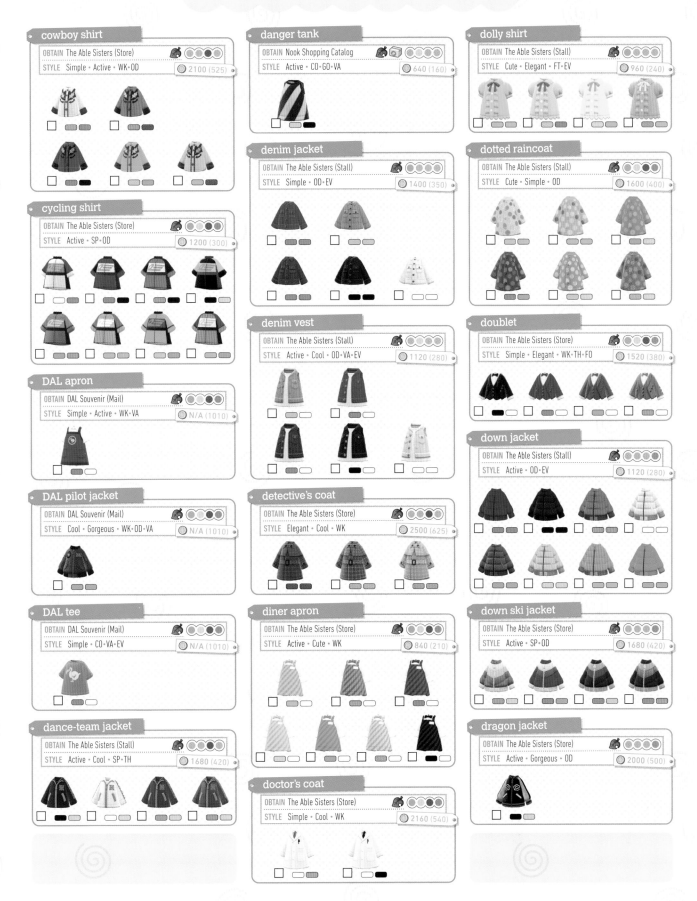

cowboy shirt

OBTAIN The Able Sisters (Store)
STYLE Simple • Active • WK•OD
2100 (525)

cycling shirt

OBTAIN The Able Sisters (Store)
STYLE Active • SP•OD
1200 (300)

DAL apron

OBTAIN DAL Souvenir (Mail)
STYLE Simple • Active • WK•VA
N/A (1010)

DAL pilot jacket

OBTAIN DAL Souvenir (Mail)
STYLE Cool • Gorgeous • WK•OD•VA
N/A (1010)

DAL tee

OBTAIN DAL Souvenir (Mail)
STYLE Simple • CO•VA•EV
N/A (1010)

dance-team jacket

OBTAIN The Able Sisters (Stall)
STYLE Active • Cool • SP•TH
1680 (420)

danger tank

OBTAIN Nook Shopping Catalog
STYLE Active • CO•GO•VA
640 (160)

denim jacket

OBTAIN The Able Sisters (Stall)
STYLE Simple • OD•EV
1400 (350)

denim vest

OBTAIN The Able Sisters (Stall)
STYLE Active • Cool • OD•VA•EV
1120 (280)

detective's coat

OBTAIN The Able Sisters (Store)
STYLE Elegant • Cool • WK
2500 (625)

diner apron

OBTAIN The Able Sisters (Store)
STYLE Active • Cute • WK
840 (210)

doctor's coat

OBTAIN The Able Sisters (Store)
STYLE Simple • Cool • WK
2160 (540)

dolly shirt

OBTAIN The Able Sisters (Stall)
STYLE Cute • Elegant • FT•EV
960 (240)

dotted raincoat

OBTAIN The Able Sisters (Stall)
STYLE Cute • Simple • OD
1600 (400)

doublet

OBTAIN The Able Sisters (Store)
STYLE Simple • Elegant • WK•TH•FO
1520 (380)

down jacket

OBTAIN The Able Sisters (Stall)
STYLE Active • OD•EV
1120 (280)

down ski jacket

OBTAIN The Able Sisters (Store)
STYLE Active • SP•OD
1680 (420)

dragon jacket

OBTAIN The Able Sisters (Store)
STYLE Active • Gorgeous • OD
2000 (500)

7

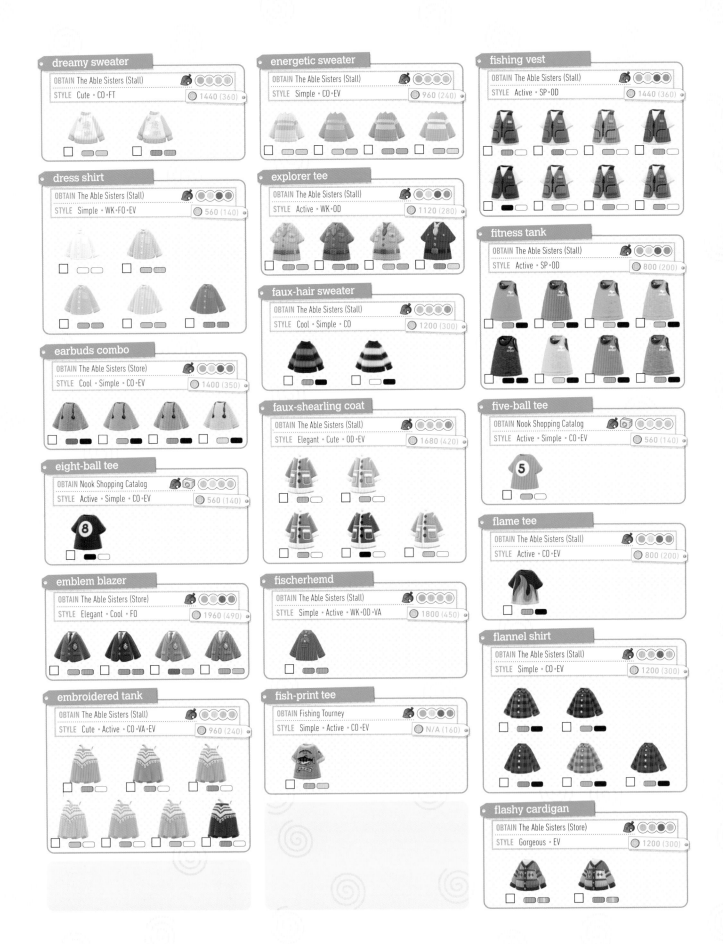

dreamy sweater

OBTAIN The Able Sisters (Stall)
STYLE Cute · CO·FT
1440 (360)

dress shirt

OBTAIN The Able Sisters (Stall)
STYLE Simple · WK·FO·EV
560 (140)

earbuds combo

OBTAIN The Able Sisters (Store)
STYLE Cool · Simple · CO·EV
1400 (350)

eight-ball tee

OBTAIN Nook Shopping Catalog
STYLE Active · Simple · CO·EV
560 (140)

emblem blazer

OBTAIN The Able Sisters (Store)
STYLE Elegant · Cool · FO
1960 (490)

embroidered tank

OBTAIN The Able Sisters (Stall)
STYLE Cute · Active · CO·VA·EV
960 (240)

energetic sweater

OBTAIN The Able Sisters (Stall)
STYLE Simple · CO·EV
960 (240)

explorer tee

OBTAIN The Able Sisters (Stall)
STYLE Active · WK·OD
1120 (280)

faux-hair sweater

OBTAIN The Able Sisters (Stall)
STYLE Cool · Simple · CO
1200 (300)

faux-shearling coat

OBTAIN The Able Sisters (Stall)
STYLE Elegant · Cute · OD·EV
1680 (420)

fischerhemd

OBTAIN The Able Sisters (Stall)
STYLE Simple · Active · WK·OD·VA
1800 (450)

fish-print tee

OBTAIN Fishing Tourney
STYLE Simple · Active · CO·EV
N/A (160)

fishing vest

OBTAIN The Able Sisters (Stall)
STYLE Active · SP·OD
1440 (360)

fitness tank

OBTAIN The Able Sisters (Stall)
STYLE Active · SP·OD
800 (200)

five-ball tee

OBTAIN Nook Shopping Catalog
STYLE Active · Simple · CO·EV
560 (140)

flame tee

OBTAIN The Able Sisters (Stall)
STYLE Active · CO·EV
800 (200)

flannel shirt

OBTAIN The Able Sisters (Stall)
STYLE Simple · CO·EV
1200 (300)

flashy cardigan

OBTAIN The Able Sisters (Store)
STYLE Gorgeous · EV
1200 (300)

flashy jacket
OBTAIN The Able Sisters (Store)
STYLE Gorgeous • PA•TH•FO
1960 (490)

flight jacket
OBTAIN The Able Sisters (Store)
STYLE Cool • WK•OD
1680 (420)

flower sweater
OBTAIN The Able Sisters (Stall)
STYLE Cute • CO•EV
1200 (300)

folk shirt
OBTAIN The Able Sisters (Stall)
STYLE Simple • Active • CO•EV
1300 (325)

football shirt
OBTAIN The Able Sisters (Store)
STYLE Active • SP•WK
1120 (280)

four-ball tee
OBTAIN Nook Shopping Catalog
STYLE Active • Simple • CO•EV
560 (140)

frog tee
OBTAIN Nook Shopping Catalog
STYLE Active • Cute • CO•EV
640 (160)

front-tie button-down shirt
OBTAIN The Able Sisters (Stall)
STYLE Active • Elegant • VA•EV
800 (200)

front-tie tee
OBTAIN The Able Sisters (Stall)
STYLE Active • Cool • CO•VA•EV
640 (160)

fuzzy vest
OBTAIN The Able Sisters (Stall)
STYLE Simple • Active • OD•EV
1300 (325)

garden tank
OBTAIN The Able Sisters (Stall)
STYLE Cute • CO•FT•VA•EV
1120 (280)

gilet and shirt
OBTAIN The Able Sisters (Store)
STYLE Cool • Simple • CO•VA•EV
1120 (280)

gingham picnic shirt
OBTAIN The Able Sisters (Store)
STYLE Simple • EV
960 (240)

gold-print tee
OBTAIN The Able Sisters (Stall)
STYLE Cool • Gorgeous • PA•CO
1120 (280)

gown coat
OBTAIN The Able Sisters (Store)
STYLE Elegant • Gorgeous • EV
2000 (500)

graduation gown
OBTAIN The Able Sisters (Store)
STYLE Simple • Elegant • WK•FO
3360 (840)

groovy shirt
OBTAIN The Able Sisters (Stall)
STYLE Cool • Gorgeous • CO•VA•EV
1440 (360)

groovy tunic
OBTAIN The Able Sisters (Stall)
STYLE Active • Gorgeous • TH•EV
1680 (420)

guayabera shirt
OBTAIN The Able Sisters (Stall)
STYLE Cool • Elegant • CO•OD•VA•EV
1120 (280)

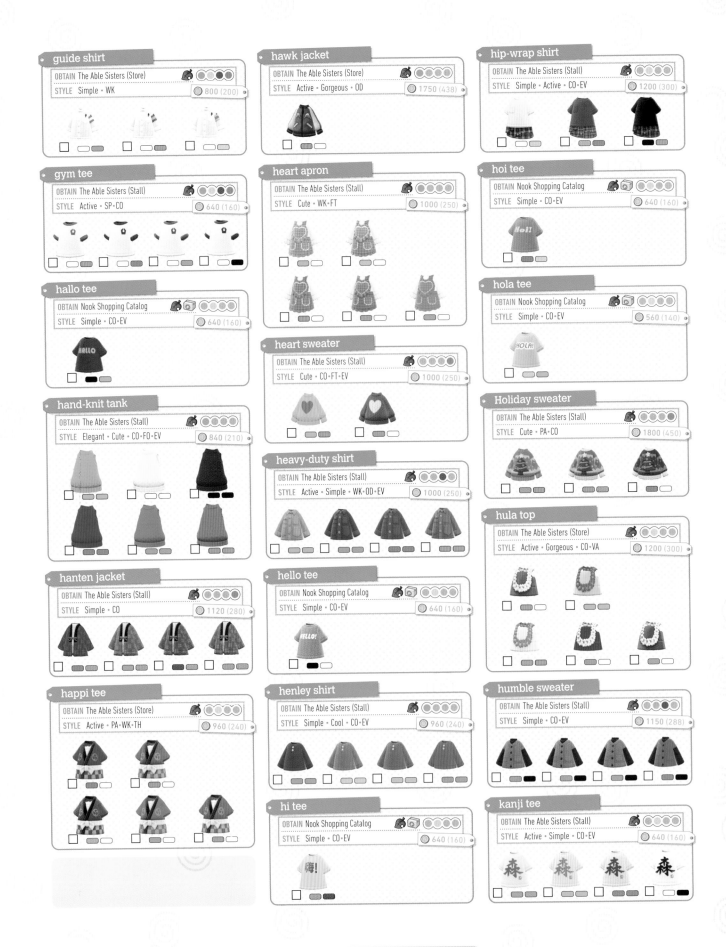

guide shirt
OBTAIN The Able Sisters (Store)
STYLE Simple • WK
800 (200)

gym tee
OBTAIN The Able Sisters (Stall)
STYLE Active • SP•CO
640 (160)

hallo tee
OBTAIN Nook Shopping Catalog
STYLE Simple • CO•EV
640 (160)

hand-knit tank
OBTAIN The Able Sisters (Stall)
STYLE Elegant • Cute • CO•FO•EV
840 (210)

hanten jacket
OBTAIN The Able Sisters (Stall)
STYLE Simple • CO
1120 (280)

happi tee
OBTAIN The Able Sisters (Store)
STYLE Active • PA•WK•TH
960 (240)

hawk jacket
OBTAIN The Able Sisters (Store)
STYLE Active • Gorgeous • OD
1750 (438)

heart apron
OBTAIN The Able Sisters (Stall)
STYLE Cute • WK•FT
1000 (250)

heart sweater
OBTAIN The Able Sisters (Stall)
STYLE Cute • CO•FT•EV
1000 (250)

heavy-duty shirt
OBTAIN The Able Sisters (Stall)
STYLE Active • Simple • WK•OD•EV
1000 (250)

hello tee
OBTAIN Nook Shopping Catalog
STYLE Simple • CO•EV
640 (160)

henley shirt
OBTAIN The Able Sisters (Stall)
STYLE Simple • Cool • CO•EV
960 (240)

hi tee
OBTAIN Nook Shopping Catalog
STYLE Simple • CO•EV
640 (160)

hip-wrap shirt
OBTAIN The Able Sisters (Stall)
STYLE Simple • Active • CO•EV
1200 (300)

hoi tee
OBTAIN Nook Shopping Catalog
STYLE Simple • CO•EV
640 (160)

hola tee
OBTAIN Nook Shopping Catalog
STYLE Simple • CO•EV
560 (140)

Holiday sweater
OBTAIN The Able Sisters (Stall)
STYLE Cute • PA•CO
1800 (450)

hula top
OBTAIN The Able Sisters (Store)
STYLE Active • Gorgeous • CO•VA
1200 (300)

humble sweater
OBTAIN The Able Sisters (Stall)
STYLE Simple • CO•EV
1150 (288)

kanji tee
OBTAIN The Able Sisters (Stall)
STYLE Active • Simple • CO•EV
640 (160)

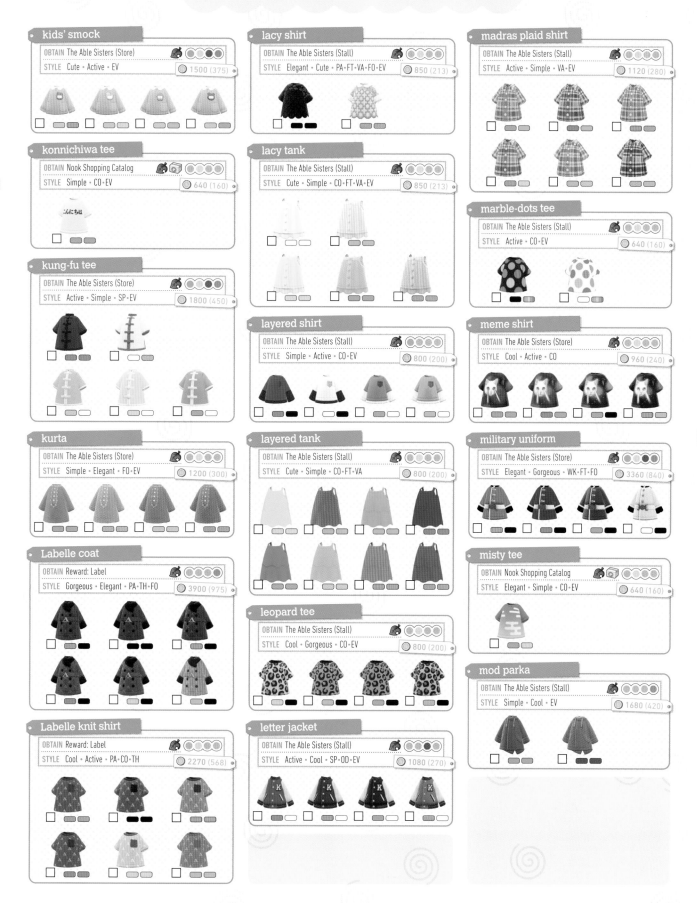

kids' smock
OBTAIN The Able Sisters (Store)
STYLE Cute · Active · EV
1500 (375)

konnichiwa tee
OBTAIN Nook Shopping Catalog
STYLE Simple · CO·EV
640 (160)

kung-fu tee
OBTAIN The Able Sisters (Store)
STYLE Active · Simple · SP·EV
1800 (450)

kurta
OBTAIN The Able Sisters (Store)
STYLE Simple · Elegant · FO·EV
1200 (300)

Labelle coat
OBTAIN Reward: Label
STYLE Gorgeous · Elegant · PA·TH·FO
3900 (975)

Labelle knit shirt
OBTAIN Reward: Label
STYLE Cool · Active · PA·CO·TH
2270 (568)

lacy shirt
OBTAIN The Able Sisters (Stall)
STYLE Elegant · Cute · PA·FT·VA·FO·EV
850 (213)

lacy tank
OBTAIN The Able Sisters (Stall)
STYLE Cute · Simple · CO·FT·VA·EV
850 (213)

layered shirt
OBTAIN The Able Sisters (Stall)
STYLE Simple · Active · CO·EV
800 (200)

layered tank
OBTAIN The Able Sisters (Stall)
STYLE Cute · Simple · CO·FT·VA
800 (200)

leopard tee
OBTAIN The Able Sisters (Stall)
STYLE Cool · Gorgeous · CO·EV
800 (200)

letter jacket
OBTAIN The Able Sisters (Stall)
STYLE Active · Cool · SP·OD·EV
1080 (270)

madras plaid shirt
OBTAIN The Able Sisters (Stall)
STYLE Active · Simple · VA·EV
1120 (280)

marble-dots tee
OBTAIN The Able Sisters (Stall)
STYLE Active · CO·EV
640 (160)

meme shirt
OBTAIN The Able Sisters (Store)
STYLE Cool · Active · CO
960 (240)

military uniform
OBTAIN The Able Sisters (Store)
STYLE Elegant · Gorgeous · WK·FT·FO
3360 (840)

misty tee
OBTAIN Nook Shopping Catalog
STYLE Elegant · Simple · CO·EV
640 (160)

mod parka
OBTAIN The Able Sisters (Stall)
STYLE Simple · Cool · EV
1680 (420)

7

Mom's hand-knit sweater

OBTAIN Mom (Mail)

STYLE Cute • Active • CO

N/A (88)

Mom's handmade apron

OBTAIN Mom (Mail)

STYLE Cute • Active • CO

N/A (88)

morning coat

OBTAIN The Able Sisters (Store)

STYLE Elegant • PA • WK • TH • FO

2500 (625)

mountain parka

OBTAIN The Able Sisters (Stall)

STYLE Active • SP • OD

1400 (350)

multipurpose vest

OBTAIN The Able Sisters (Store)

STYLE Simple • OD

1680 (420)

muscle tank

OBTAIN The Able Sisters (Stall)

STYLE Active • SP • OD

640 (160)

music-fest shirt

OBTAIN The Able Sisters (Store)

STYLE Active • OD • TH

1200 (300)

MVP tee

OBTAIN Nook Shopping Catalog

STYLE Simple • Active • CO • EV

640 (160)

ni hao tee

OBTAIN Nook Shopping Catalog

STYLE Simple • CO • EV

640 (160)

nine-ball tee

OBTAIN Nook Shopping Catalog

STYLE Active • Simple • CO • EV

560 (140)

No. 1 shirt

OBTAIN Nook Shopping Catalog

STYLE Simple • Active • CO • EV

560 (140)

No. 2 shirt

OBTAIN Nook Shopping Catalog

STYLE Simple • CO • EV

560 (140)

No. 3 shirt

OBTAIN Nook Shopping Catalog

STYLE Simple • CO • EV

560 (140)

No. 4 shirt

OBTAIN Nook Shopping Catalog

STYLE Simple • CO • EV

560 (140)

noble coat

OBTAIN The Able Sisters (Store)

STYLE Gorgeous • PA • FT • TH • FO

4800 (1200)

Nook Inc. aloha shirt

OBTAIN Redeem Nook Miles

STYLE Simple • Active • CO • VA

N/A (3000)

Nook Inc. blouson

OBTAIN Redeem Nook Miles

STYLE Simple • Active • WK • OD

N/A (4000)

Nook Inc. tee

OBTAIN Redeem Nook Miles

STYLE Simple • CO • EV

N/A (3000)

nurse's jacket

OBTAIN The Able Sisters (Store)

STYLE Simple • Active • WK

1500 (375)

nylon jacket

OBTAIN The Able Sisters (Stall)

STYLE Cool • SP • OD

1120 (280)

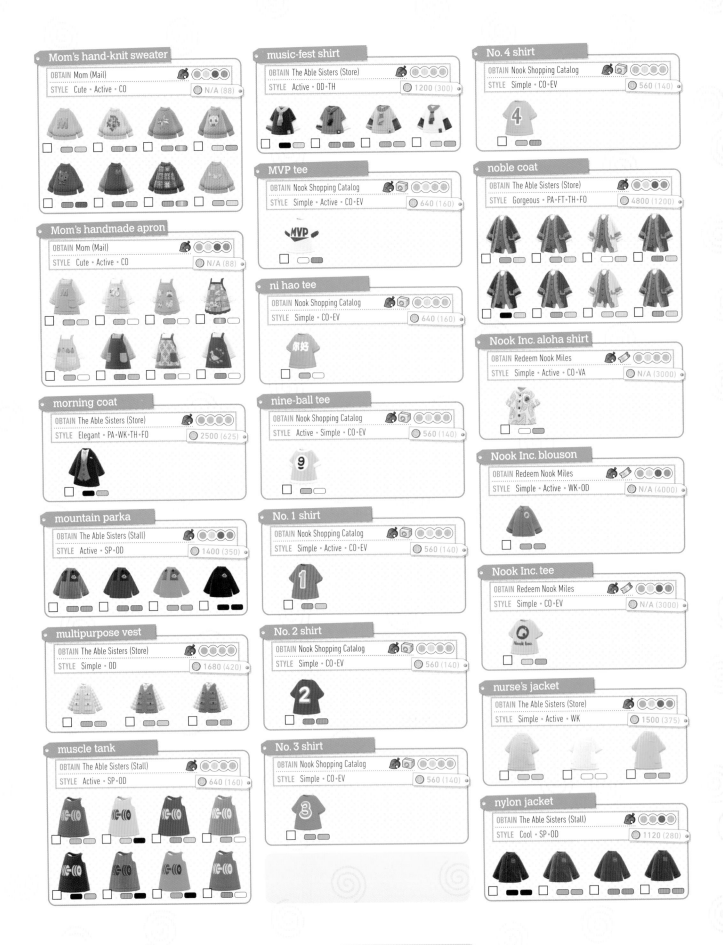

oilskin coat

OBTAIN The Able Sisters (Stall)
STYLE Active • Cool • WK•OD
1400 (350)

old-school jacket

OBTAIN The Able Sisters (Store)
STYLE Gorgeous • Active • TH
1800 (450)

one-ball tee

OBTAIN Nook Shopping Catalog
STYLE Active • Simple • CO•EV
560 (140)

open-collar shirt

OBTAIN The Able Sisters (Stall)
STYLE Simple • Elegant • CO•EV
960 (240)

oversized shawl overshirt

OBTAIN The Able Sisters (Stall)
STYLE Cool • CO•OD•EV
1120 (280)

parka undercoat

OBTAIN The Able Sisters (Store)
STYLE Cool • Simple • EV
2320 (580)

patchwork coat

OBTAIN The Able Sisters (Store)
STYLE Cute • Elegant • EV
2380 (595)

peacoat

OBTAIN The Able Sisters (Store)
STYLE Simple • EV
1960 (490)

peasant blouse

OBTAIN The Able Sisters (Stall)
STYLE Elegant • VA•EV
1680 (420)

pineapple aloha shirt

OBTAIN The Able Sisters (Stall)
STYLE Active • CO•VA
960 (240)

plaid puffed-sleeve shirt

OBTAIN The Able Sisters (Stall)
STYLE Cute • Simple • FT•VA•EV
1200 (300)

pleather trench coat

OBTAIN The Able Sisters (Store)
STYLE Elegant • Gorgeous • FO•EV
1680 (420)

plover cardigan

OBTAIN The Able Sisters (Stall)
STYLE Cute • Elegant • PA•WK•FO•EV
1440 (360)

plushie-muffler coat

OBTAIN The Able Sisters (Store)
STYLE Cute • Elegant • EV
1960 (490)

pocket tee

OBTAIN The Able Sisters (Stall)
STYLE Simple • CO•EV
560 (140)

polo shirt

OBTAIN The Able Sisters (Stall)
STYLE Simple • WK•VA•EV
720 (180)

pom-pom sweater

OBTAIN The Able Sisters (Store)
STYLE Cute • CO•FT•EV
1440 (360)

poncho coat

OBTAIN The Able Sisters (Store)
STYLE Cute • FT•EV
2320 (580)

poncho-style sweater

OBTAIN The Able Sisters (Stall)
STYLE Elegant • Active • OD•EV
1500 (375)

7

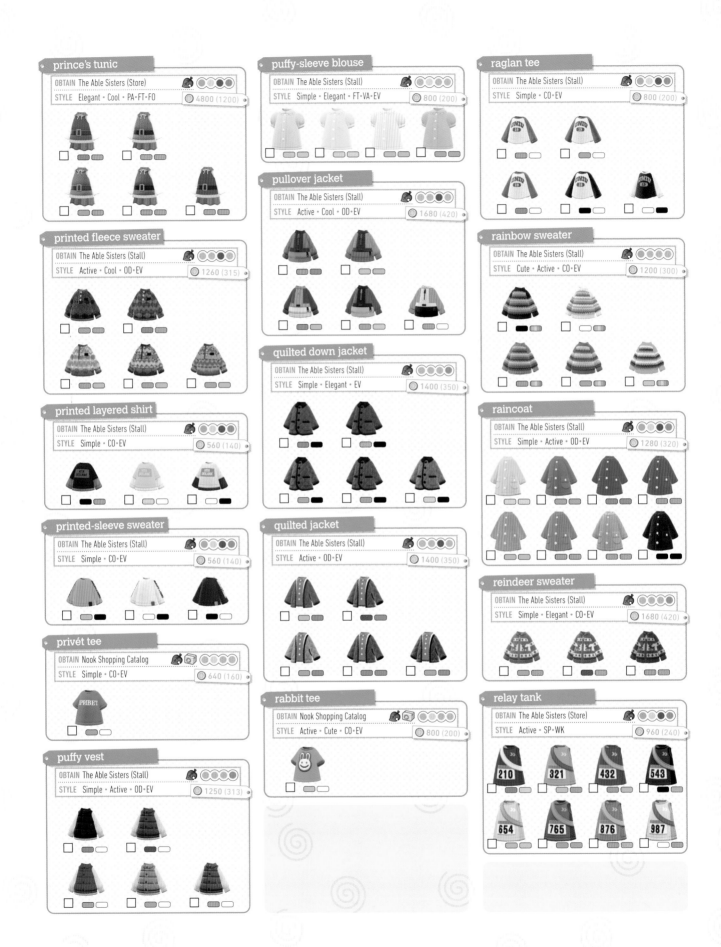

prince's tunic
OBTAIN The Able Sisters (Store)
STYLE Elegant • Cool • PA•FT•FO
4800 (1200)

printed fleece sweater
OBTAIN The Able Sisters (Stall)
STYLE Active • Cool • OD•EV
1260 (315)

printed layered shirt
OBTAIN The Able Sisters (Stall)
STYLE Simple • CO•EV
560 (140)

printed-sleeve sweater
OBTAIN The Able Sisters (Stall)
STYLE Simple • CO•EV
560 (140)

privét tee
OBTAIN Nook Shopping Catalog
STYLE Simple • CO•EV
640 (160)

puffy vest
OBTAIN The Able Sisters (Stall)
STYLE Simple • Active • OD•EV
1250 (313)

puffy-sleeve blouse
OBTAIN The Able Sisters (Stall)
STYLE Simple • Elegant • FT•VA•EV
800 (200)

pullover jacket
OBTAIN The Able Sisters (Stall)
STYLE Active • Cool • OD•EV
1680 (420)

quilted down jacket
OBTAIN The Able Sisters (Stall)
STYLE Simple • Elegant • EV
1400 (350)

quilted jacket
OBTAIN The Able Sisters (Stall)
STYLE Active • OD•EV
1400 (350)

rabbit tee
OBTAIN Nook Shopping Catalog
STYLE Active • Cute • CO•EV
800 (200)

raglan tee
OBTAIN The Able Sisters (Stall)
STYLE Simple • CO•EV
800 (200)

rainbow sweater
OBTAIN The Able Sisters (Stall)
STYLE Cute • Active • CO•EV
1200 (300)

raincoat
OBTAIN The Able Sisters (Stall)
STYLE Simple • Active • OD•EV
1280 (320)

reindeer sweater
OBTAIN The Able Sisters (Stall)
STYLE Simple • Elegant • CO•EV
1680 (420)

relay tank
OBTAIN The Able Sisters (Store)
STYLE Active • SP•WK
960 (240)

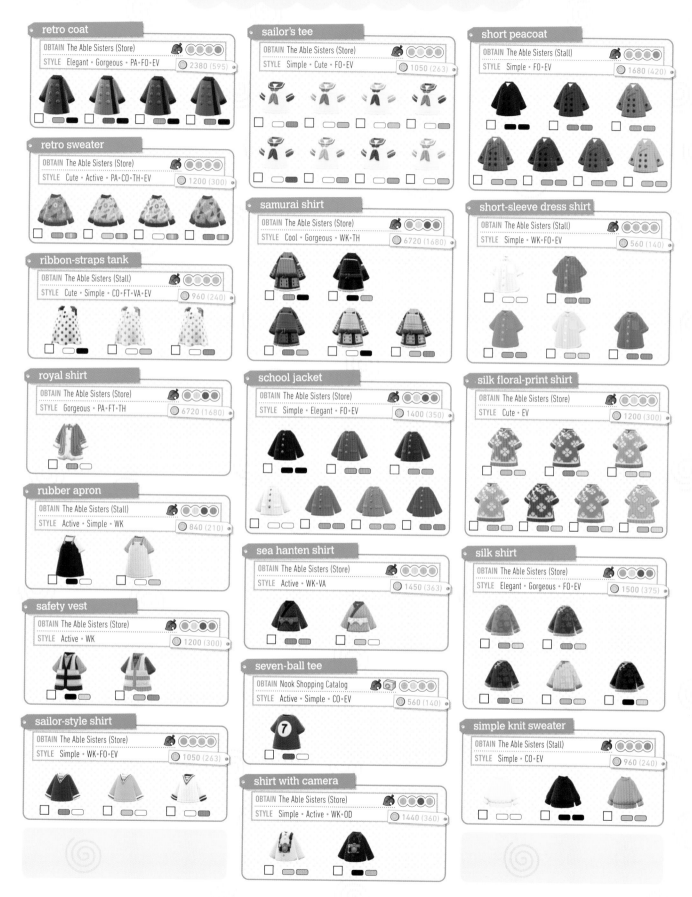

retro coat
OBTAIN The Able Sisters (Store)
STYLE Elegant · Gorgeous · PA·FO·EV
2380 (595)

retro sweater
OBTAIN The Able Sisters (Store)
STYLE Cute · Active · PA·CO·TH·EV
1200 (300)

ribbon-straps tank
OBTAIN The Able Sisters (Stall)
STYLE Cute · Simple · CO·FT·VA·EV
960 (240)

royal shirt
OBTAIN The Able Sisters (Store)
STYLE Gorgeous · PA·FT·TH
6720 (1680)

rubber apron
OBTAIN The Able Sisters (Stall)
STYLE Active · Simple · WK
840 (210)

safety vest
OBTAIN The Able Sisters (Store)
STYLE Active · WK
1200 (300)

sailor-style shirt
OBTAIN The Able Sisters (Store)
STYLE Simple · WK·FO·EV
1050 (263)

sailor's tee
OBTAIN The Able Sisters (Store)
STYLE Simple · Cute · FO·EV
1050 (263)

samurai shirt
OBTAIN The Able Sisters (Store)
STYLE Cool · Gorgeous · WK·TH
6720 (1680)

school jacket
OBTAIN The Able Sisters (Store)
STYLE Simple · Elegant · FO·EV
1400 (350)

sea hanten shirt
OBTAIN The Able Sisters (Store)
STYLE Active · WK·VA
1450 (363)

seven-ball tee
OBTAIN Nook Shopping Catalog
STYLE Active · Simple · CO·EV
560 (140)

shirt with camera
OBTAIN The Able Sisters (Store)
STYLE Simple · Active · WK·OD
1440 (360)

short peacoat
OBTAIN The Able Sisters (Stall)
STYLE Simple · FO·EV
1680 (420)

short-sleeve dress shirt
OBTAIN The Able Sisters (Stall)
STYLE Simple · WK·FO·EV
560 (140)

silk floral-print shirt
OBTAIN The Able Sisters (Store)
STYLE Cute · EV
1200 (300)

silk shirt
OBTAIN The Able Sisters (Store)
STYLE Elegant · Gorgeous · FO·EV
1500 (375)

simple knit sweater
OBTAIN The Able Sisters (Stall)
STYLE Simple · CO·EV
960 (240)

7

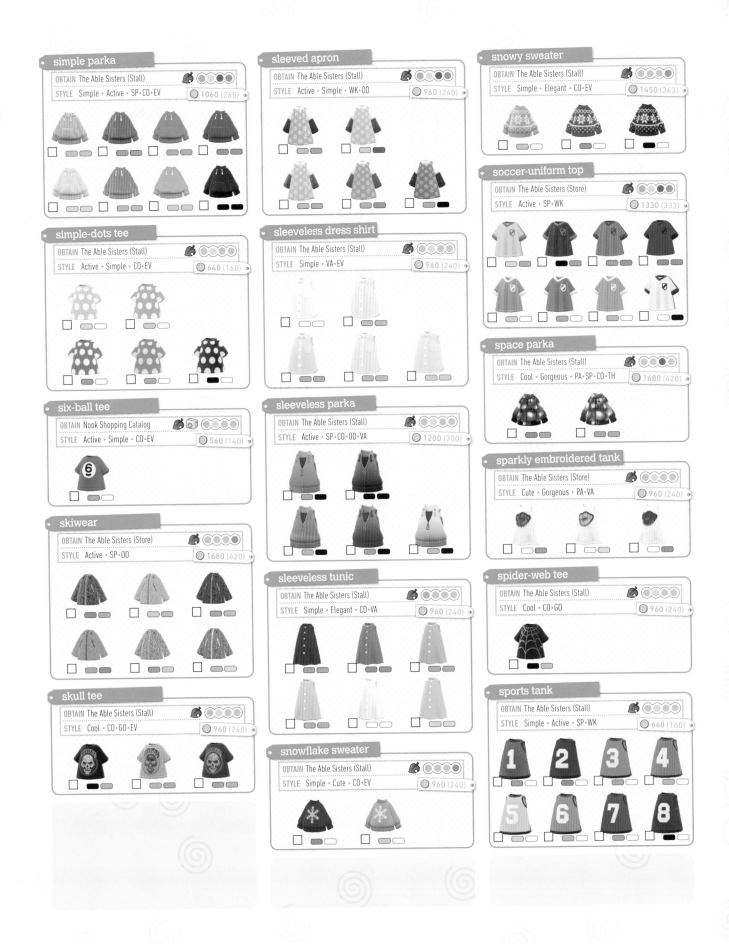

simple parka
OBTAIN The Able Sisters (Stall)
STYLE Simple • Active • SP•CO•EV
1060 (265)

simple-dots tee
OBTAIN The Able Sisters (Stall)
STYLE Active • Simple • CO•EV
640 (160)

six-ball tee
OBTAIN Nook Shopping Catalog
STYLE Active • Simple • CO•EV
560 (140)

skiwear
OBTAIN The Able Sisters (Store)
STYLE Active • SP•OD
1680 (420)

skull tee
OBTAIN The Able Sisters (Stall)
STYLE Cool • CO•GO•EV
960 (240)

sleeved apron
OBTAIN The Able Sisters (Stall)
STYLE Active • Simple • WK•OD
960 (240)

sleeveless dress shirt
OBTAIN The Able Sisters (Stall)
STYLE Simple • VA•EV
960 (240)

sleeveless parka
OBTAIN The Able Sisters (Stall)
STYLE Active • SP•CO•OD•VA
1200 (300)

sleeveless tunic
OBTAIN The Able Sisters (Stall)
STYLE Simple • Elegant • CO•VA
960 (240)

snowflake sweater
OBTAIN The Able Sisters (Stall)
STYLE Simple • Cute • CO•EV
960 (240)

snowy sweater
OBTAIN The Able Sisters (Stall)
STYLE Simple • Elegant • CO•EV
1450 (363)

soccer-uniform top
OBTAIN The Able Sisters (Store)
STYLE Active • SP•WK
1330 (333)

space parka
OBTAIN The Able Sisters (Stall)
STYLE Cool • Gorgeous • PA•SP•CO•TH
1680 (420)

sparkly embroidered tank
OBTAIN The Able Sisters (Store)
STYLE Cute • Gorgeous • PA•VA
960 (240)

spider-web tee
OBTAIN The Able Sisters (Stall)
STYLE Cool • CO•GO
960 (240)

sports tank
OBTAIN The Able Sisters (Stall)
STYLE Simple • Active • SP•WK
640 (160)

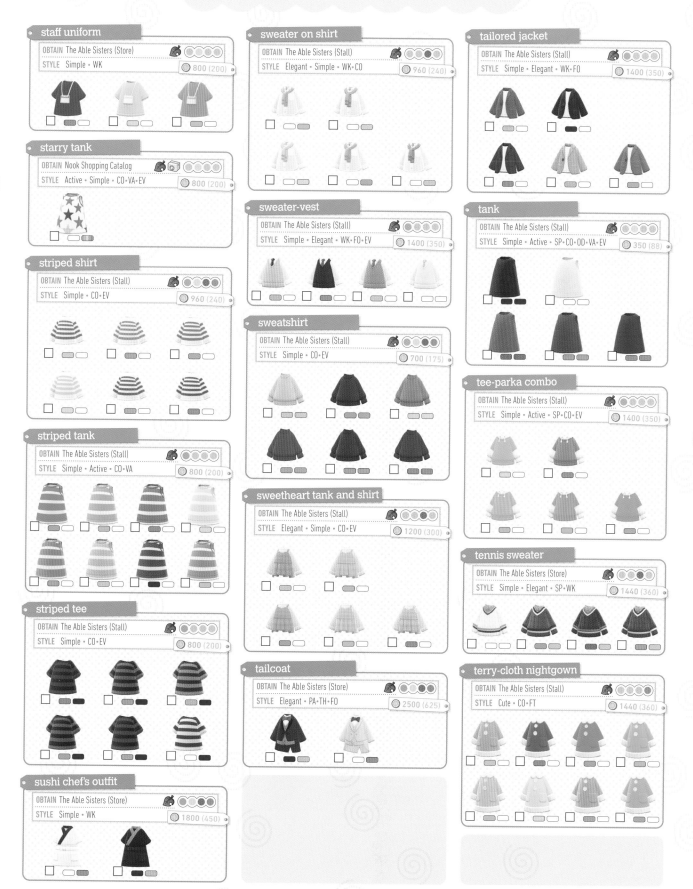

staff uniform

OBTAIN The Able Sisters (Store)
STYLE Simple • WK
800 (200)

starry tank

OBTAIN Nook Shopping Catalog
STYLE Active • Simple • CO•VA•EV
800 (200)

striped shirt

OBTAIN The Able Sisters (Stall)
STYLE Simple • CO•EV
960 (240)

striped tank

OBTAIN The Able Sisters (Stall)
STYLE Simple • Active • CO•VA
800 (200)

striped tee

OBTAIN The Able Sisters (Stall)
STYLE Simple • CO•EV
800 (200)

sushi chef's outfit

OBTAIN The Able Sisters (Store)
STYLE Simple • WK
1800 (450)

sweater on shirt

OBTAIN The Able Sisters (Stall)
STYLE Elegant • Simple • WK•CO
960 (240)

sweater-vest

OBTAIN The Able Sisters (Stall)
STYLE Simple • Elegant • WK•FO•EV
1400 (350)

sweatshirt

OBTAIN The Able Sisters (Stall)
STYLE Simple • CO•EV
700 (175)

sweetheart tank and shirt

OBTAIN The Able Sisters (Stall)
STYLE Elegant • Simple • CO•EV
1200 (300)

tailcoat

OBTAIN The Able Sisters (Store)
STYLE Elegant • PA•TH•FO
2500 (625)

tailored jacket

OBTAIN The Able Sisters (Stall)
STYLE Simple • Elegant • WK•FO
1400 (350)

tank

OBTAIN The Able Sisters (Stall)
STYLE Simple • Active • SP•CO•OD•VA•EV
350 (88)

tee-parka combo

OBTAIN The Able Sisters (Stall)
STYLE Simple • Active • SP•CO•EV
1400 (350)

tennis sweater

OBTAIN The Able Sisters (Store)
STYLE Simple • Elegant • SP•WK
1440 (360)

terry-cloth nightgown

OBTAIN The Able Sisters (Stall)
STYLE Cute • CO•FT
1440 (360)

7

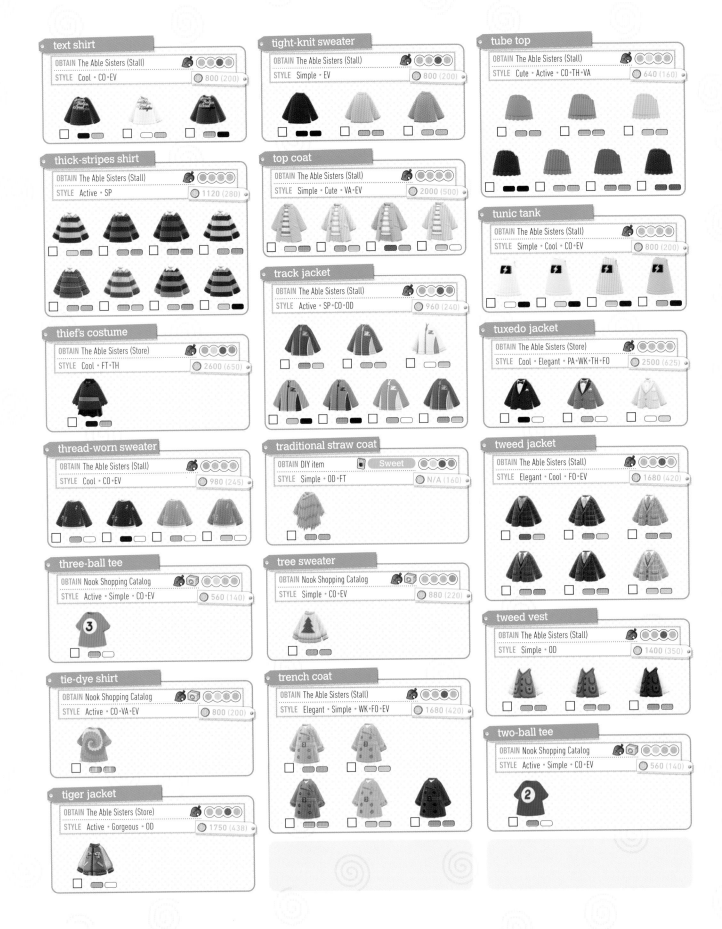

text shirt
OBTAIN The Able Sisters (Stall)
STYLE Cool • CO•EV
800 (200)

thick-stripes shirt
OBTAIN The Able Sisters (Stall)
STYLE Active • SP
1120 (280)

thief's costume
OBTAIN The Able Sisters (Store)
STYLE Cool • FT•TH
2600 (650)

thread-worn sweater
OBTAIN The Able Sisters (Stall)
STYLE Cool • CO•EV
980 (245)

three-ball tee
OBTAIN Nook Shopping Catalog
STYLE Active • Simple • CO•EV
560 (140)

tie-dye shirt
OBTAIN Nook Shopping Catalog
STYLE Active • CO•VA•EV
800 (200)

tiger jacket
OBTAIN The Able Sisters (Store)
STYLE Active • Gorgeous • OD
1750 (438)

tight-knit sweater
OBTAIN The Able Sisters (Stall)
STYLE Simple • EV
800 (200)

top coat
OBTAIN The Able Sisters (Stall)
STYLE Simple • Cute • VA•EV
2000 (500)

track jacket
OBTAIN The Able Sisters (Stall)
STYLE Active • SP•CO•OD
960 (240)

traditional straw coat
OBTAIN DIY item   Sweet
STYLE Simple • OD•FT
N/A (160)

tree sweater
OBTAIN Nook Shopping Catalog
STYLE Simple • CO•EV
880 (220)

trench coat
OBTAIN The Able Sisters (Stall)
STYLE Elegant • Simple • WK•FO•EV
1680 (420)

tube top
OBTAIN The Able Sisters (Stall)
STYLE Cute • Active • CO•TH•VA
640 (160)

tunic tank
OBTAIN The Able Sisters (Stall)
STYLE Simple • Cool • CO•EV
800 (200)

tuxedo jacket
OBTAIN The Able Sisters (Store)
STYLE Cool • Elegant • PA•WK•TH•FO
2500 (625)

tweed jacket
OBTAIN The Able Sisters (Stall)
STYLE Elegant • Cool • FO•EV
1680 (420)

tweed vest
OBTAIN The Able Sisters (Stall)
STYLE Simple • OD
1400 (350)

two-ball tee
OBTAIN Nook Shopping Catalog
STYLE Active • Simple • CO•EV
560 (140)

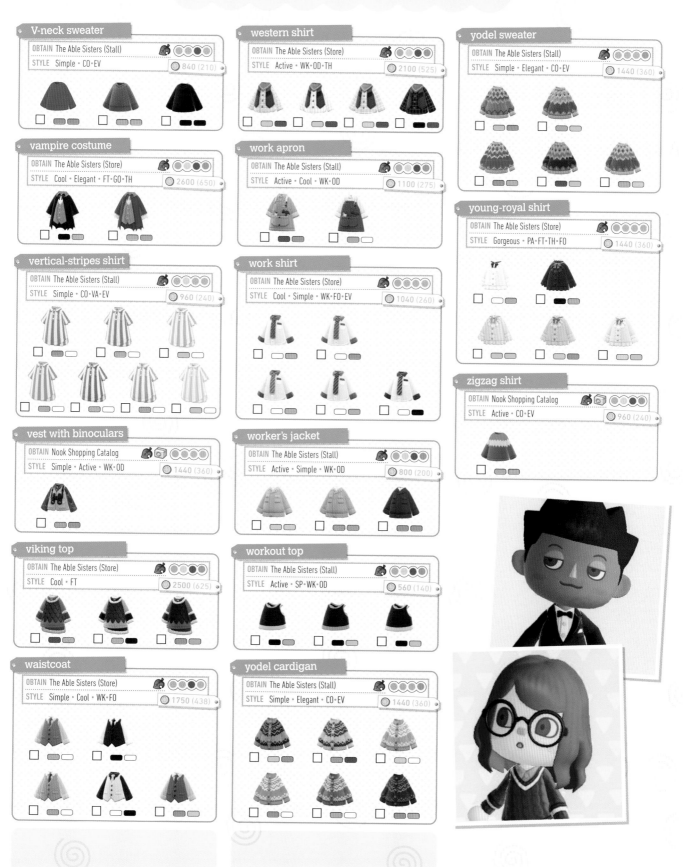

V-neck sweater

OBTAIN The Able Sisters (Stall)
STYLE Simple · CO·EV
840 (210)

vampire costume

OBTAIN The Able Sisters (Store)
STYLE Cool · Elegant · FT·GO·TH
2600 (650)

vertical-stripes shirt

OBTAIN The Able Sisters (Stall)
STYLE Simple · CO·VA·EV
960 (240)

vest with binoculars

OBTAIN Nook Shopping Catalog
STYLE Simple · Active · WK·OD
1440 (360)

viking top

OBTAIN The Able Sisters (Store)
STYLE Cool · FT
2500 (625)

waistcoat

OBTAIN The Able Sisters (Store)
STYLE Simple · Cool · WK·FO
1750 (438)

western shirt

OBTAIN The Able Sisters (Store)
STYLE Active · WK·OD·TH
2100 (525)

work apron

OBTAIN The Able Sisters (Stall)
STYLE Active · Cool · WK·OD
1100 (275)

work shirt

OBTAIN The Able Sisters (Store)
STYLE Cool · Simple · WK·FO·EV
1040 (260)

worker's jacket

OBTAIN The Able Sisters (Stall)
STYLE Active · Simple · WK·OD
800 (200)

workout top

OBTAIN The Able Sisters (Stall)
STYLE Active · SP·WK·OD
560 (140)

yodel cardigan

OBTAIN The Able Sisters (Stall)
STYLE Simple · Elegant · CO·EV
1440 (360)

yodel sweater

OBTAIN The Able Sisters (Stall)
STYLE Simple · Elegant · CO·EV
1440 (360)

young-royal shirt

OBTAIN The Able Sisters (Store)
STYLE Gorgeous · PA·FT·TH·FO
1440 (360)

zigzag shirt

OBTAIN Nook Shopping Catalog
STYLE Active · CO·EV
960 (240)

7

Bottoms

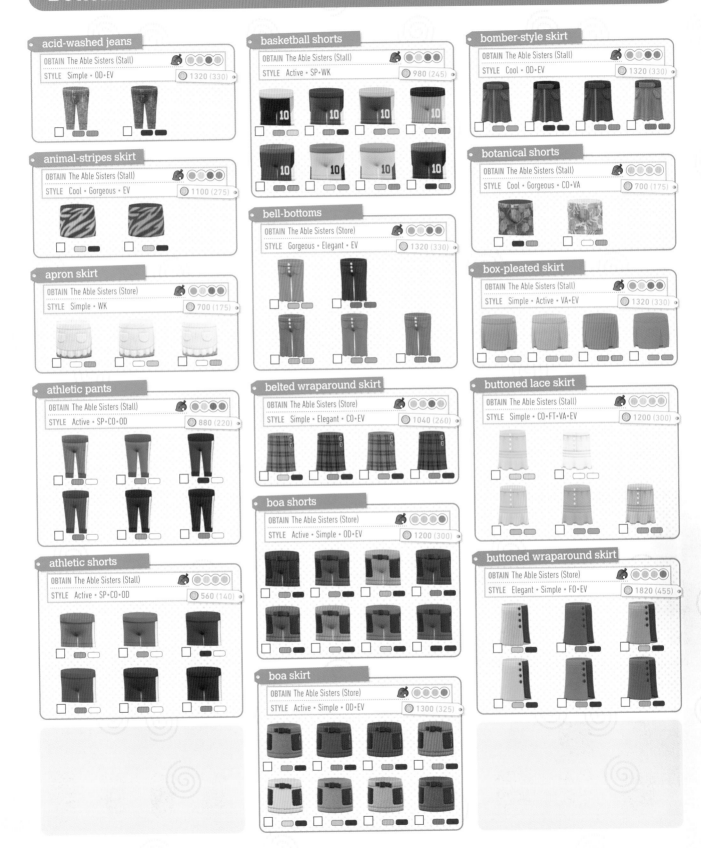

acid-washed jeans
OBTAIN The Able Sisters (Stall)
STYLE Simple • OD•EV
1320 (330)

animal-stripes skirt
OBTAIN The Able Sisters (Stall)
STYLE Cool • Gorgeous • EV
1100 (275)

apron skirt
OBTAIN The Able Sisters (Store)
STYLE Simple • WK
700 (175)

athletic pants
OBTAIN The Able Sisters (Stall)
STYLE Active • SP•CO•OD
880 (220)

athletic shorts
OBTAIN The Able Sisters (Stall)
STYLE Active • SP•CO•OD
560 (140)

basketball shorts
OBTAIN The Able Sisters (Stall)
STYLE Active • SP•WK
980 (245)

bell-bottoms
OBTAIN The Able Sisters (Store)
STYLE Gorgeous • Elegant • EV
1320 (330)

belted wraparound skirt
OBTAIN The Able Sisters (Store)
STYLE Simple • Elegant • CO•EV
1040 (260)

boa shorts
OBTAIN The Able Sisters (Store)
STYLE Active • Simple • OD•EV
1200 (300)

boa skirt
OBTAIN The Able Sisters (Store)
STYLE Active • Simple • OD•EV
1300 (325)

bomber-style skirt
OBTAIN The Able Sisters (Stall)
STYLE Cool • OD•EV
1320 (330)

botanical shorts
OBTAIN The Able Sisters (Stall)
STYLE Cool • Gorgeous • CO•VA
700 (175)

box-pleated skirt
OBTAIN The Able Sisters (Stall)
STYLE Simple • Active • VA•EV
1320 (330)

buttoned lace skirt
OBTAIN The Able Sisters (Stall)
STYLE Simple • CO•FT•VA•EV
1200 (300)

buttoned wraparound skirt
OBTAIN The Able Sisters (Store)
STYLE Elegant • Simple • FO•EV
1820 (455)

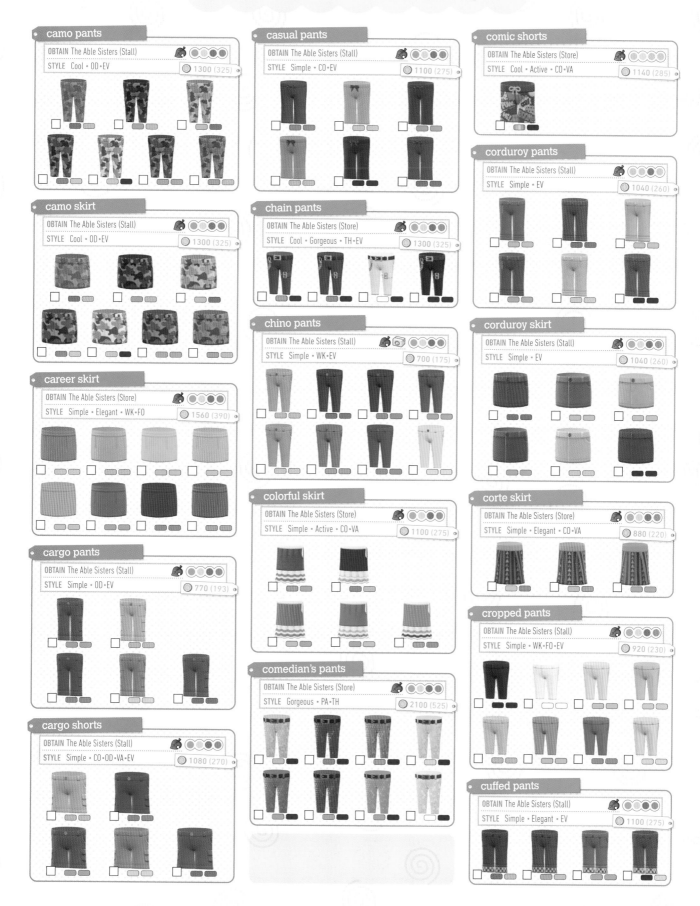

camo pants
OBTAIN The Able Sisters (Stall)
STYLE Cool · OD·EV
1300 (325)

camo skirt
OBTAIN The Able Sisters (Stall)
STYLE Cool · OD·EV
1300 (325)

career skirt
OBTAIN The Able Sisters (Store)
STYLE Simple · Elegant · WK·FO
1560 (390)

cargo pants
OBTAIN The Able Sisters (Stall)
STYLE Simple · OD·EV
770 (193)

cargo shorts
OBTAIN The Able Sisters (Stall)
STYLE Simple · CO·OD·VA·EV
1080 (270)

casual pants
OBTAIN The Able Sisters (Stall)
STYLE Simple · CO·EV
1100 (275)

chain pants
OBTAIN The Able Sisters (Store)
STYLE Cool · Gorgeous · TH·EV
1300 (325)

chino pants
OBTAIN The Able Sisters (Stall)
STYLE Simple · WK·EV
700 (175)

colorful skirt
OBTAIN The Able Sisters (Store)
STYLE Simple · Active · CO·VA
1100 (275)

comedian's pants
OBTAIN The Able Sisters (Store)
STYLE Gorgeous · PA·TH
2100 (525)

comic shorts
OBTAIN The Able Sisters (Store)
STYLE Cool · Active · CO·VA
1140 (285)

corduroy pants
OBTAIN The Able Sisters (Stall)
STYLE Simple · EV
1040 (260)

corduroy skirt
OBTAIN The Able Sisters (Stall)
STYLE Simple · EV
1040 (260)

corte skirt
OBTAIN The Able Sisters (Store)
STYLE Simple · Elegant · CO·VA
880 (220)

cropped pants
OBTAIN The Able Sisters (Stall)
STYLE Simple · WK·FO·EV
920 (230)

cuffed pants
OBTAIN The Able Sisters (Stall)
STYLE Simple · Elegant · EV
1100 (275)

7

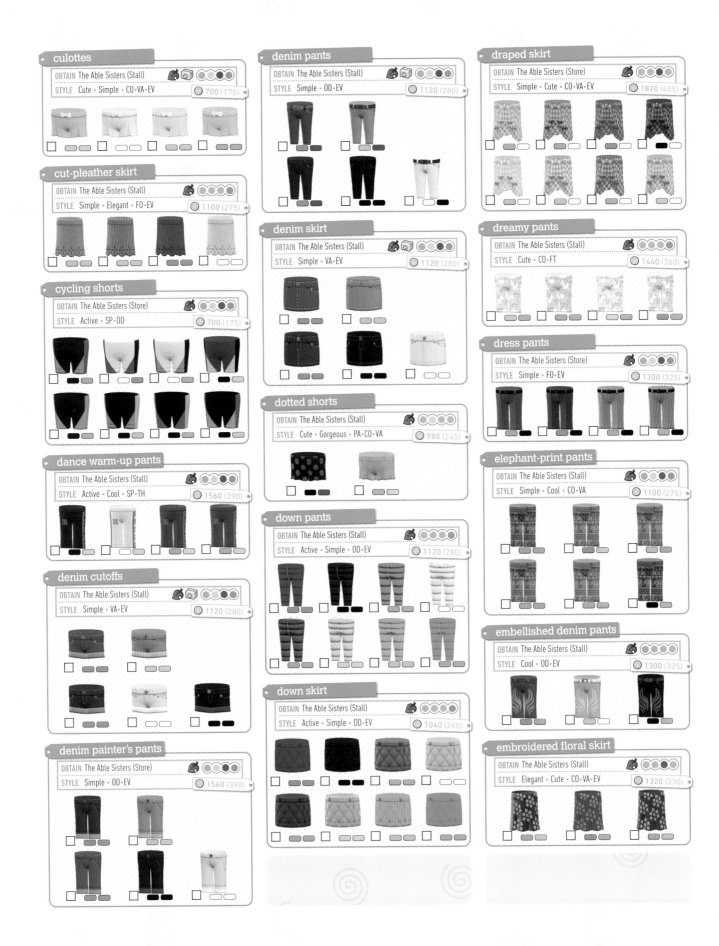

culottes

OBTAIN The Able Sisters (Stall)
STYLE Cute · Simple · CO·VA·EV
700 (175)

cut-pleather skirt

OBTAIN The Able Sisters (Stall)
STYLE Simple · Elegant · FO·EV
1100 (275)

cycling shorts

OBTAIN The Able Sisters (Store)
STYLE Active · SP·OD
700 (175)

dance warm-up pants

OBTAIN The Able Sisters (Stall)
STYLE Active · Cool · SP·TH
1560 (390)

denim cutoffs

OBTAIN The Able Sisters (Stall)
STYLE Simple · VA·EV
1120 (280)

denim painter's pants

OBTAIN The Able Sisters (Store)
STYLE Simple · OD·EV
1560 (390)

denim pants

OBTAIN The Able Sisters (Stall)
STYLE Simple · OD·EV
1120 (280)

denim skirt

OBTAIN The Able Sisters (Stall)
STYLE Simple · VA·EV
1120 (280)

dotted shorts

OBTAIN The Able Sisters (Stall)
STYLE Cute · Gorgeous · PA·CO·VA
980 (245)

down pants

OBTAIN The Able Sisters (Stall)
STYLE Active · Simple · OD·EV
1120 (280)

down skirt

OBTAIN The Able Sisters (Stall)
STYLE Active · Simple · OD·EV
1040 (260)

draped skirt

OBTAIN The Able Sisters (Store)
STYLE Simple · Cute · CO·VA·EV
1820 (455)

dreamy pants

OBTAIN The Able Sisters (Stall)
STYLE Cute · CO·FT
1440 (360)

dress pants

OBTAIN The Able Sisters (Store)
STYLE Simple · FO·EV
1300 (325)

elephant-print pants

OBTAIN The Able Sisters (Stall)
STYLE Simple · Cool · CO·VA
1100 (275)

embellished denim pants

OBTAIN The Able Sisters (Stall)
STYLE Cool · OD·EV
1300 (325)

embroidered floral skirt

OBTAIN The Able Sisters (Stall)
STYLE Elegant · Cute · CO·VA·EV
1320 (330)

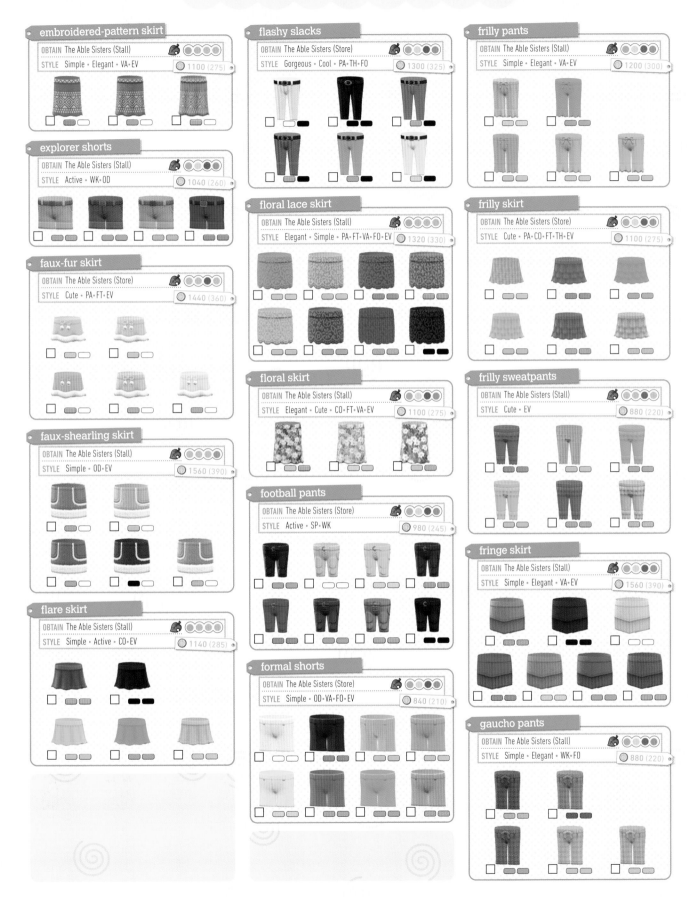

embroidered-pattern skirt

OBTAIN The Able Sisters (Stall)
STYLE Simple • Elegant • VA•EV
1100 (275)

explorer shorts

OBTAIN The Able Sisters (Stall)
STYLE Active • WK•OD
1040 (260)

faux-fur skirt

OBTAIN The Able Sisters (Store)
STYLE Cute • PA•FT•EV
1440 (360)

faux-shearling skirt

OBTAIN The Able Sisters (Stall)
STYLE Simple • OD•EV
1560 (390)

flare skirt

OBTAIN The Able Sisters (Stall)
STYLE Simple • Active • CO•EV
1140 (285)

flashy slacks

OBTAIN The Able Sisters (Store)
STYLE Gorgeous • Cool • PA•TH•FO
1300 (325)

floral lace skirt

OBTAIN The Able Sisters (Stall)
STYLE Elegant • Simple • PA•FT•VA•FO•EV
1320 (330)

floral skirt

OBTAIN The Able Sisters (Stall)
STYLE Elegant • Cute • CO•FT•VA•EV
1100 (275)

football pants

OBTAIN The Able Sisters (Store)
STYLE Active • SP•WK
980 (245)

formal shorts

OBTAIN The Able Sisters (Store)
STYLE Simple • OD•VA•FO•EV
840 (210)

frilly pants

OBTAIN The Able Sisters (Stall)
STYLE Simple • Elegant • VA•EV
1200 (300)

frilly skirt

OBTAIN The Able Sisters (Store)
STYLE Cute • PA•CO•FT•TH•EV
1100 (275)

frilly sweatpants

OBTAIN The Able Sisters (Stall)
STYLE Cute • EV
880 (220)

fringe skirt

OBTAIN The Able Sisters (Stall)
STYLE Simple • Elegant • VA•EV
1560 (390)

gaucho pants

OBTAIN The Able Sisters (Stall)
STYLE Simple • Elegant • WK•FO
880 (220)

7

geometric-print pants

OBTAIN The Able Sisters (Stall)
STYLE Simple • Gorgeous • CO•VA•EV   1040 (260)

gingham picnic skirt

OBTAIN The Able Sisters (Stall)
STYLE Simple • EV   880 (220)

gobelin shorts

OBTAIN The Able Sisters (Store)
STYLE Elegant • Gorgeous • VA•EV   840 (210)

grass skirt

OBTAIN DIY item   Sweet
STYLE Active • OD•VA   N/A (140)

green grass skirt

OBTAIN DIY item   Peppy
STYLE Active • OD•VA   N/A (140)

hickory-stripe pants

OBTAIN The Able Sisters (Store)
STYLE Simple • SP•OD•EV   1560 (390)

jogging shorts

OBTAIN The Able Sisters (Stall)
STYLE Active • SP•CO•OD   700 (175)

kilt

OBTAIN The Able Sisters (Store)
STYLE Simple • Elegant • WK•FO•EV   1000 (250)

knit pants

OBTAIN The Able Sisters (Stall)
STYLE Simple • Elegant • CO•EV   910 (228)

knit skirt

OBTAIN The Able Sisters (Stall)
STYLE Simple • Elegant • CO•EV   910 (228)

kung-fu pants

OBTAIN The Able Sisters (Store)
STYLE Simple • Active • SP•EV   1680 (420)

Labelle shorts

OBTAIN Reward: Label
STYLE Cool • Active • PA•TH•FO   2540 (635)

Labelle skirt

OBTAIN Reward: Label
STYLE Elegant • Cute • PA•TH•FO   3100 (775)

lace shorts

OBTAIN The Able Sisters (Stall)
STYLE Cute • FT•VA•EV   840 (210)

lace skirt

OBTAIN The Able Sisters (Stall)
STYLE Cute • Simple • FT•VA•EV   920 (230)

lemon skirt

OBTAIN The Able Sisters (Stall)
STYLE Elegant • Cute • CO•VA•EV   880 (220)

leopard miniskirt

OBTAIN The Able Sisters (Store)
STYLE Cool • Gorgeous • EV   1820 (455)

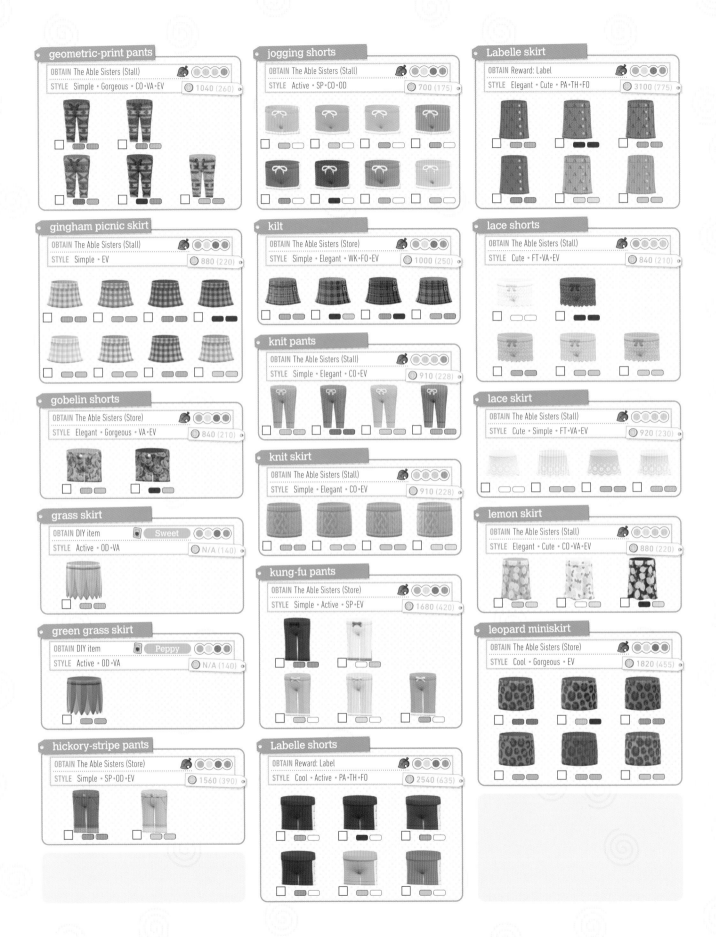

long chino skirt
OBTAIN The Able Sisters (Stall)
STYLE Simple • CO•EV
1560 (390)

long denim skirt
OBTAIN The Able Sisters (Stall)
STYLE Simple • EV
1560 (390)

long plaid skirt
OBTAIN The Able Sisters (Stall)
STYLE Simple • Elegant • CO•EV
1450 (363)

long pleated skirt
OBTAIN The Able Sisters (Store)
STYLE Simple • Elegant • EV
1560 (390)

long polka skirt
OBTAIN The Able Sisters (Stall)
STYLE Simple • VA•EV
1300 (325)

long sailor skirt
OBTAIN The Able Sisters (Store)
STYLE Simple • FO•EV
1560 (390)

long sweatskirt
OBTAIN The Able Sisters (Stall)
STYLE Active • Simple • CO•EV
1000 (250)

muay-thai shorts
OBTAIN The Able Sisters (Store)
STYLE Active • SP•CO
980 (245)

multicolor shorts
OBTAIN The Able Sisters (Stall)
STYLE Active • Simple • OD•VA•EV
1100 (275)

noble pants
OBTAIN The Able Sisters (Store)
STYLE Gorgeous • Elegant • PA•FT•TH•FO
4300 (1075)

outdoor shorts
OBTAIN The Able Sisters (Stall)
STYLE Active • Simple • SP•OD
700 (175)

patched-knee pants
OBTAIN The Able Sisters (Stall)
STYLE Simple • SP•WK•VA•EV
880 (220)

patchwork skirt
OBTAIN The Able Sisters (Stall)
STYLE Cute • Active • CO•VA•EV
2100 (525)

pearl skirt
OBTAIN The Able Sisters (Store)
STYLE Cute • Elegant • PA•FT•TH•FO
1680 (420)

petal skirt
OBTAIN The Able Sisters (Store)
STYLE Gorgeous • Active • PA•TH
1540 (385)

pineapple aloha shorts
OBTAIN The Able Sisters (Stall)
STYLE Active • Cool • CO•VA
840 (210)

plaid shorts
OBTAIN The Able Sisters (Stall)
STYLE Simple • VA•EV
980 (245)

7

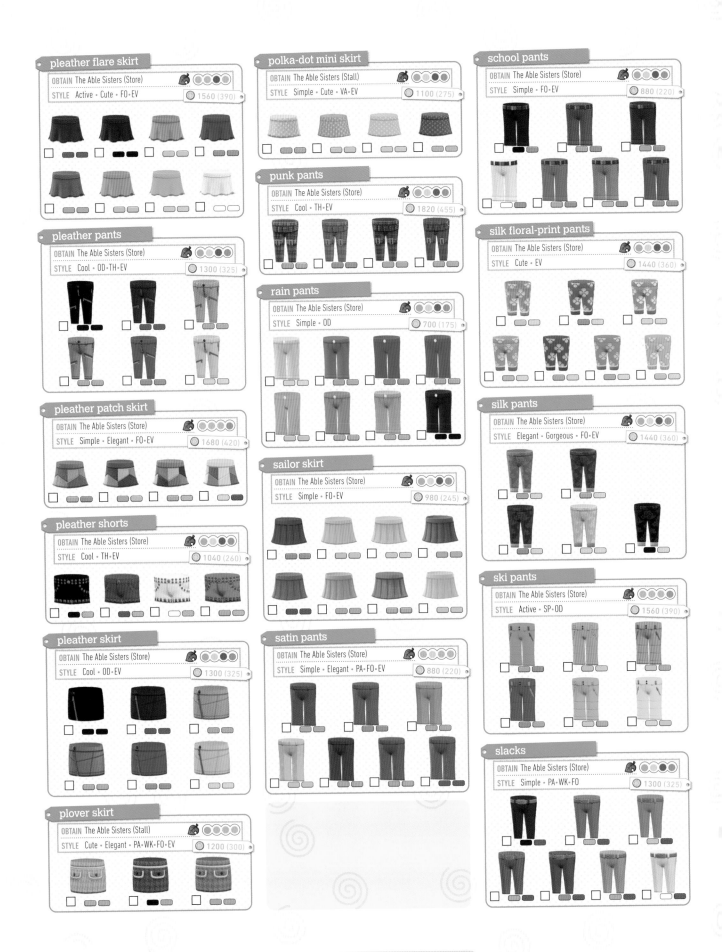

pleather flare skirt
OBTAIN The Able Sisters (Store)
STYLE Active • Cute • FO•EV
1560 (390)

pleather pants
OBTAIN The Able Sisters (Store)
STYLE Cool • OD•TH•EV
1300 (325)

pleather patch skirt
OBTAIN The Able Sisters (Store)
STYLE Simple • Elegant • FO•EV
1680 (420)

pleather shorts
OBTAIN The Able Sisters (Store)
STYLE Cool • TH•EV
1040 (260)

pleather skirt
OBTAIN The Able Sisters (Store)
STYLE Cool • OD•EV
1300 (325)

plover skirt
OBTAIN The Able Sisters (Stall)
STYLE Cute • Elegant • PA•WK•FO•EV
1200 (300)

polka-dot mini skirt
OBTAIN The Able Sisters (Stall)
STYLE Simple • Cute • VA•EV
1100 (275)

punk pants
OBTAIN The Able Sisters (Store)
STYLE Cool • TH•EV
1820 (455)

rain pants
OBTAIN The Able Sisters (Store)
STYLE Simple • OD
700 (175)

sailor skirt
OBTAIN The Able Sisters (Store)
STYLE Simple • FO•EV
980 (245)

satin pants
OBTAIN The Able Sisters (Store)
STYLE Simple • Elegant • PA•FO•EV
880 (220)

school pants
OBTAIN The Able Sisters (Store)
STYLE Simple • FO•EV
880 (220)

silk floral-print pants
OBTAIN The Able Sisters (Store)
STYLE Cute • EV
1440 (360)

silk pants
OBTAIN The Able Sisters (Store)
STYLE Elegant • Gorgeous • FO•EV
1440 (360)

ski pants
OBTAIN The Able Sisters (Store)
STYLE Active • SP•OD
1560 (390)

slacks
OBTAIN The Able Sisters (Store)
STYLE Simple • PA•WK•FO
1300 (325)

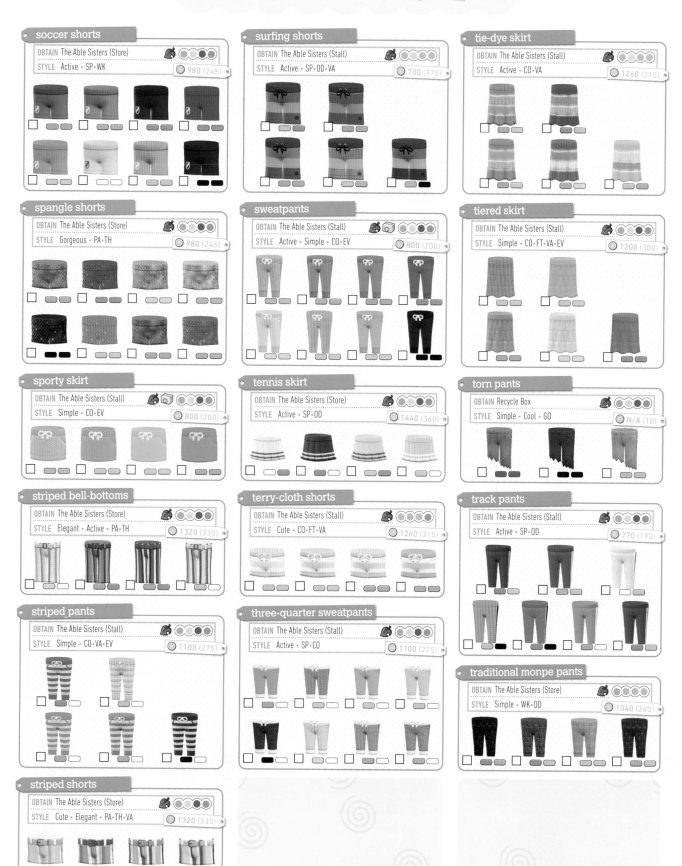

soccer shorts
OBTAIN The Able Sisters (Store)
STYLE Active · SP·WK
980 (245)

surfing shorts
OBTAIN The Able Sisters (Stall)
STYLE Active · SP·OD·VA
700 (175)

tie-dye skirt
OBTAIN The Able Sisters (Stall)
STYLE Active · CO·VA
1260 (315)

spangle shorts
OBTAIN The Able Sisters (Store)
STYLE Gorgeous · PA·TH
980 (245)

sweatpants
OBTAIN The Able Sisters (Stall)
STYLE Active · Simple · CO·EV
800 (200)

tiered skirt
OBTAIN The Able Sisters (Stall)
STYLE Simple · CO·FT·VA·EV
1200 (300)

sporty skirt
OBTAIN The Able Sisters (Stall)
STYLE Simple · CO·EV
800 (200)

tennis skirt
OBTAIN The Able Sisters (Store)
STYLE Active · SP·OD
1440 (360)

torn pants
OBTAIN Recycle Box
STYLE Simple · Cool · GO
N/A (10)

striped bell-bottoms
OBTAIN The Able Sisters (Store)
STYLE Elegant · Active · PA·TH
1320 (330)

terry-cloth shorts
OBTAIN The Able Sisters (Stall)
STYLE Cute · CO·FT·VA
1260 (315)

track pants
OBTAIN The Able Sisters (Stall)
STYLE Active · SP·OD
770 (193)

striped pants
OBTAIN The Able Sisters (Stall)
STYLE Simple · CO·VA·EV
1100 (275)

three-quarter sweatpants
OBTAIN The Able Sisters (Stall)
STYLE Active · SP·CO
1100 (275)

traditional monpe pants
OBTAIN The Able Sisters (Store)
STYLE Simple · WK·OD
1040 (260)

striped shorts
OBTAIN The Able Sisters (Store)
STYLE Cute · Elegant · PA·TH·VA
1320 (330)

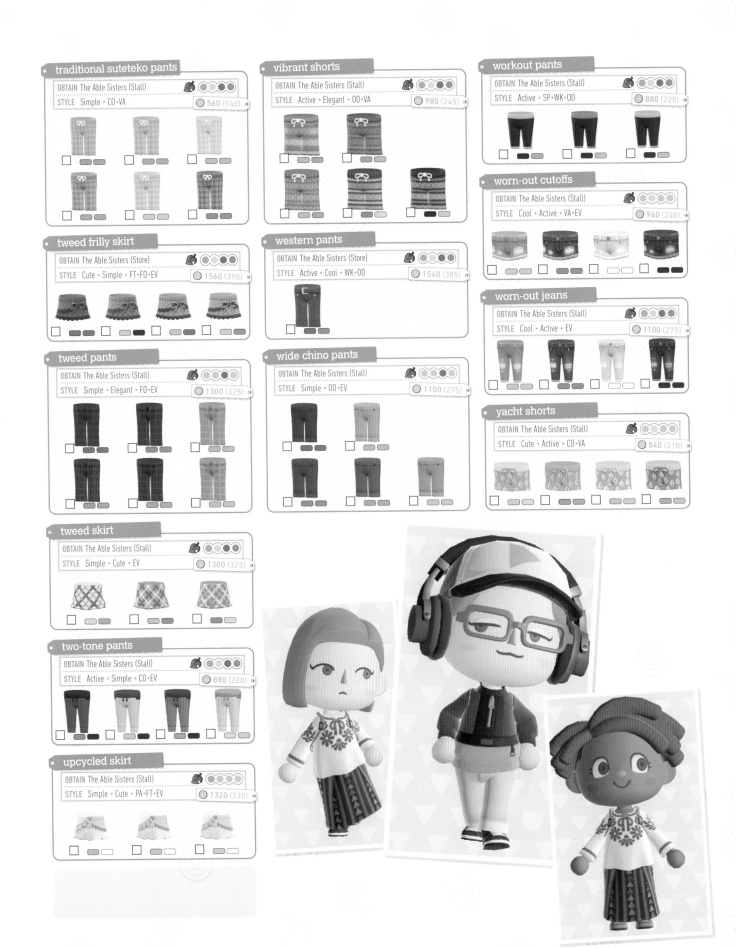

traditional suteteko pants

OBTAIN The Able Sisters (Stall)	
STYLE Simple • CO•VA	560 (140)

tweed frilly skirt

OBTAIN The Able Sisters (Store)	
STYLE Cute • Simple • FT•FO•EV	1560 (390)

tweed pants

OBTAIN The Able Sisters (Stall)	
STYLE Simple • Elegant • FO•EV	1300 (325)

tweed skirt

OBTAIN The Able Sisters (Stall)	
STYLE Simple • Cute • EV	1300 (325)

two-tone pants

OBTAIN The Able Sisters (Stall)	
STYLE Active • Simple • CO•EV	880 (220)

upcycled skirt

OBTAIN The Able Sisters (Stall)	
STYLE Simple • Cute • PA•FT•EV	1320 (330)

vibrant shorts

OBTAIN The Able Sisters (Stall)	
STYLE Active • Elegant • OD•VA	980 (245)

western pants

OBTAIN The Able Sisters (Store)	
STYLE Active • Cool • WK•OD	1540 (385)

wide chino pants

OBTAIN The Able Sisters (Stall)	
STYLE Simple • OD•EV	1100 (275)

workout pants

OBTAIN The Able Sisters (Stall)	
STYLE Active • SP•WK•OD	880 (220)

worn-out cutoffs

OBTAIN The Able Sisters (Stall)	
STYLE Cool • Active • VA•EV	960 (240)

worn-out jeans

OBTAIN The Able Sisters (Stall)	
STYLE Cool • Active • EV	1100 (275)

yacht shorts

OBTAIN The Able Sisters (Stall)	
STYLE Cute • Active • CO•VA	840 (210)

Dresses

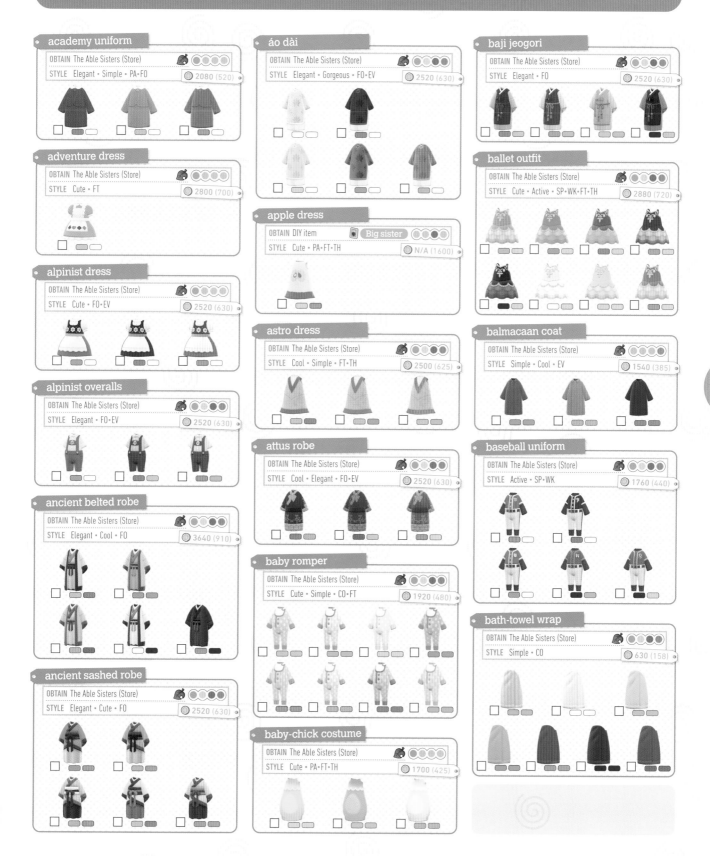

academy uniform
OBTAIN The Able Sisters (Store)
STYLE Elegant • Simple • PA•FO
2080 (520)

adventure dress
OBTAIN The Able Sisters (Store)
STYLE Cute • FT
2800 (700)

alpinist dress
OBTAIN The Able Sisters (Store)
STYLE Cute • FO•EV
2520 (630)

alpinist overalls
OBTAIN The Able Sisters (Store)
STYLE Elegant • FO•EV
2520 (630)

ancient belted robe
OBTAIN The Able Sisters (Store)
STYLE Elegant • Cool • FO
3640 (910)

ancient sashed robe
OBTAIN The Able Sisters (Store)
STYLE Elegant • Cute • FO
2520 (630)

áo dài
OBTAIN The Able Sisters (Store)
STYLE Elegant • Gorgeous • FO•EV
2520 (630)

apple dress
OBTAIN DIY item — Big sister
STYLE Cute • PA•FT•TH
N/A (1600)

astro dress
OBTAIN The Able Sisters (Store)
STYLE Cool • Simple • FT•TH
2500 (625)

attus robe
OBTAIN The Able Sisters (Store)
STYLE Cool • Elegant • FO•EV
2520 (630)

baby romper
OBTAIN The Able Sisters (Store)
STYLE Cute • Simple • CO•FT
1920 (480)

baby-chick costume
OBTAIN The Able Sisters (Store)
STYLE Cute • PA•FT•TH
1700 (425)

baji jeogori
OBTAIN The Able Sisters (Store)
STYLE Elegant • FO
2520 (630)

ballet outfit
OBTAIN The Able Sisters (Store)
STYLE Cute • Active • SP•WK•FT•TH
2880 (720)

balmacaan coat
OBTAIN The Able Sisters (Store)
STYLE Simple • Cool • EV
1540 (385)

baseball uniform
OBTAIN The Able Sisters (Store)
STYLE Active • SP•WK
1760 (440)

bath-towel wrap
OBTAIN The Able Sisters (Store)
STYLE Simple • CO
630 (158)

bathrobe

OBTAIN	The Able Sisters (Store)
STYLE	Simple • Elegant • CO

720 (180)

bear costume

OBTAIN	The Able Sisters (Store)
STYLE	Cute • PA • FT • TH

1700 (425)

bekasab robe

OBTAIN	The Able Sisters (Store)
STYLE	Gorgeous • Elegant • FO • EV

2520 (630)

belted dotted dress

OBTAIN	The Able Sisters (Stall)
STYLE	Cute • Simple • PA • FT • VA

2000 (500)

bingata dress

OBTAIN	The Able Sisters (Store)
STYLE	Elegant • Gorgeous • TH

2520 (630)

blossom dress

OBTAIN	The Able Sisters (Stall)
STYLE	Cute • FT • EV

1500 (375)

blossoming kimono

OBTAIN	The Able Sisters (Store)
STYLE	Elegant • Cute • PA • FO

3220 (805)

boa parka

OBTAIN	The Able Sisters (Stall)
STYLE	Simple • Cute • CO • OD • EV

1800 (450)

Bohemian tunic dress

OBTAIN	The Able Sisters (Stall)
STYLE	Elegant • Cute • CO • VA • EV

1900 (475)

bold muumuu

OBTAIN	The Able Sisters (Stall)
STYLE	Active • Gorgeous • CO • VA

1600 (400)

bolero coat

OBTAIN	The Able Sisters (Store)
STYLE	Cute • CO • FT • EV

2080 (520)

bone costume

OBTAIN	The Able Sisters (Store)
STYLE	Cool • FT • GO

1280 (320)

box-skirt uniform

OBTAIN	The Able Sisters (Store)
STYLE	Simple • Elegant • FO • EV

2300 (575)

bunny dress

OBTAIN	The Able Sisters (Store)
STYLE	Cute • PA • FT

1800 (450)

butterfly visiting kimono

OBTAIN	The Able Sisters (Store)
STYLE	Elegant • Cute • PA • FO

2660 (665)

casual chic dress

OBTAIN	The Able Sisters (Stall)
STYLE	Elegant • Simple • CO • VA • EV

2400 (600)

casual kimono

OBTAIN	The Able Sisters (Store)
STYLE	Cool • Simple • EV

2000 (500)

cat dress

OBTAIN	The Able Sisters (Stall)
STYLE	Cute • PA • FT • TH

1800 (450)

caterpillar costume

OBTAIN	The Able Sisters (Stall)
STYLE	Cute • PA • FT

1700 (425)

caveman tank

OBTAIN	The Able Sisters (Stall)
STYLE	Active • OD

1050 (263)

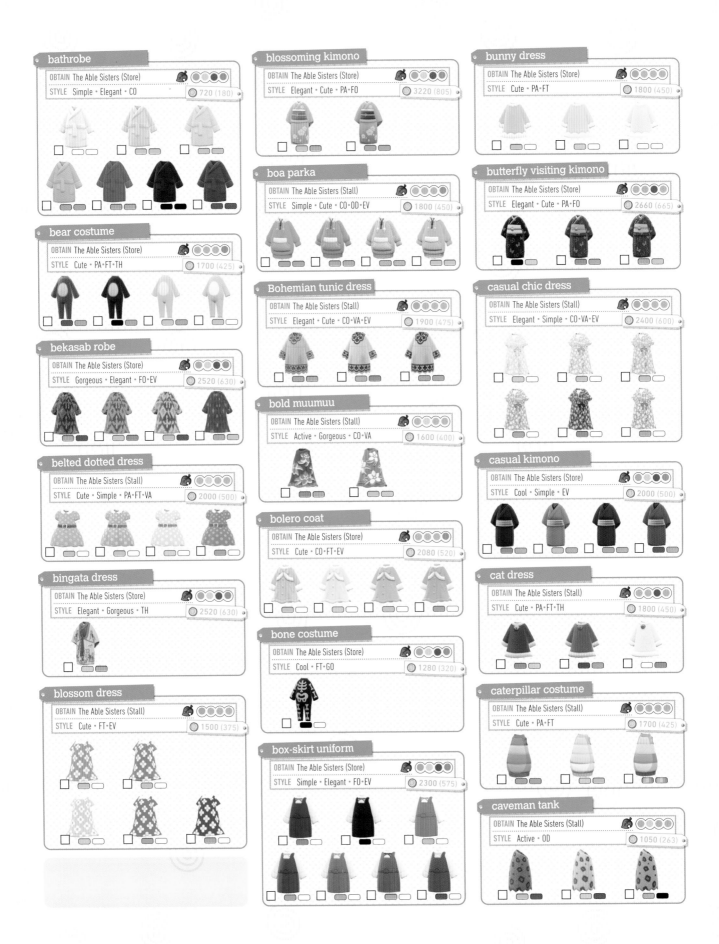

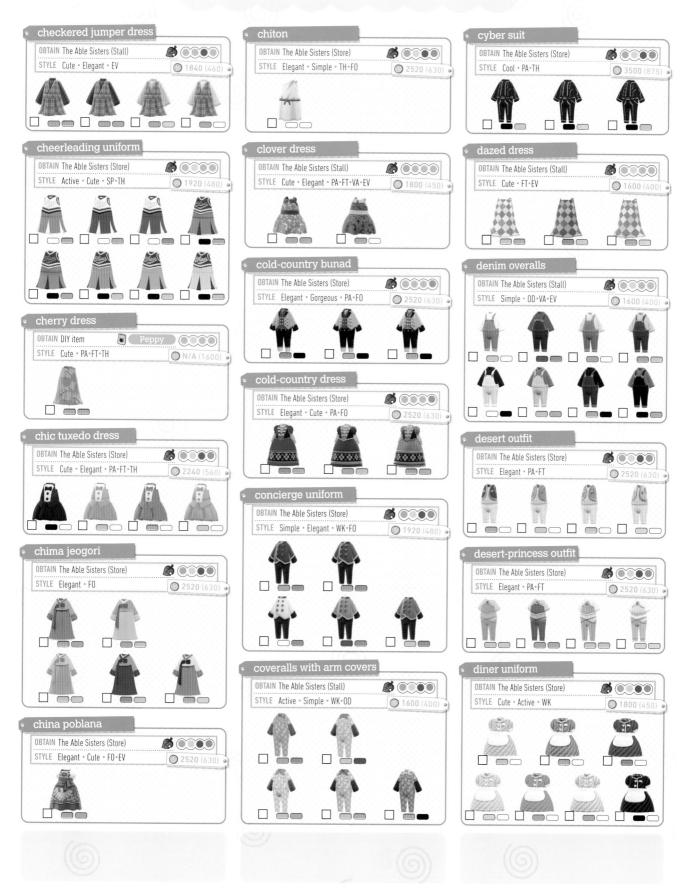

checkered jumper dress
OBTAIN The Able Sisters (Stall)
STYLE Cute • Elegant • EV
1840 (460)

cheerleading uniform
OBTAIN The Able Sisters (Store)
STYLE Active • Cute • SP•TH
1920 (480)

cherry dress
OBTAIN DIY item — Peppy
STYLE Cute • PA•FT•TH
N/A (1600)

chic tuxedo dress
OBTAIN The Able Sisters (Store)
STYLE Cute • Elegant • PA•FT•TH
2240 (560)

chima jeogori
OBTAIN The Able Sisters (Store)
STYLE Elegant • FO
2520 (630)

china poblana
OBTAIN The Able Sisters (Store)
STYLE Elegant • Cute • FO•EV
2520 (630)

chiton
OBTAIN The Able Sisters (Store)
STYLE Elegant • Simple • TH•FO
2520 (630)

clover dress
OBTAIN The Able Sisters (Stall)
STYLE Cute • Elegant • PA•FT•VA•EV
1800 (450)

cold-country bunad
OBTAIN The Able Sisters (Store)
STYLE Elegant • Gorgeous • PA•FO
2520 (630)

cold-country dress
OBTAIN The Able Sisters (Store)
STYLE Elegant • Cute • PA•FO
2520 (630)

concierge uniform
OBTAIN The Able Sisters (Store)
STYLE Simple • Elegant • WK•FO
1920 (480)

coveralls with arm covers
OBTAIN The Able Sisters (Stall)
STYLE Active • Simple • WK•OD
1600 (400)

cyber suit
OBTAIN The Able Sisters (Store)
STYLE Cool • PA•TH
3500 (875)

dazed dress
OBTAIN The Able Sisters (Stall)
STYLE Cute • FT•EV
1600 (400)

denim overalls
OBTAIN The Able Sisters (Stall)
STYLE Simple • OD•VA•EV
1600 (400)

desert outfit
OBTAIN The Able Sisters (Store)
STYLE Elegant • PA•FT
2520 (630)

desert-princess outfit
OBTAIN The Able Sisters (Store)
STYLE Elegant • PA•FT
2520 (630)

diner uniform
OBTAIN The Able Sisters (Store)
STYLE Cute • Active • WK
1800 (450)

7

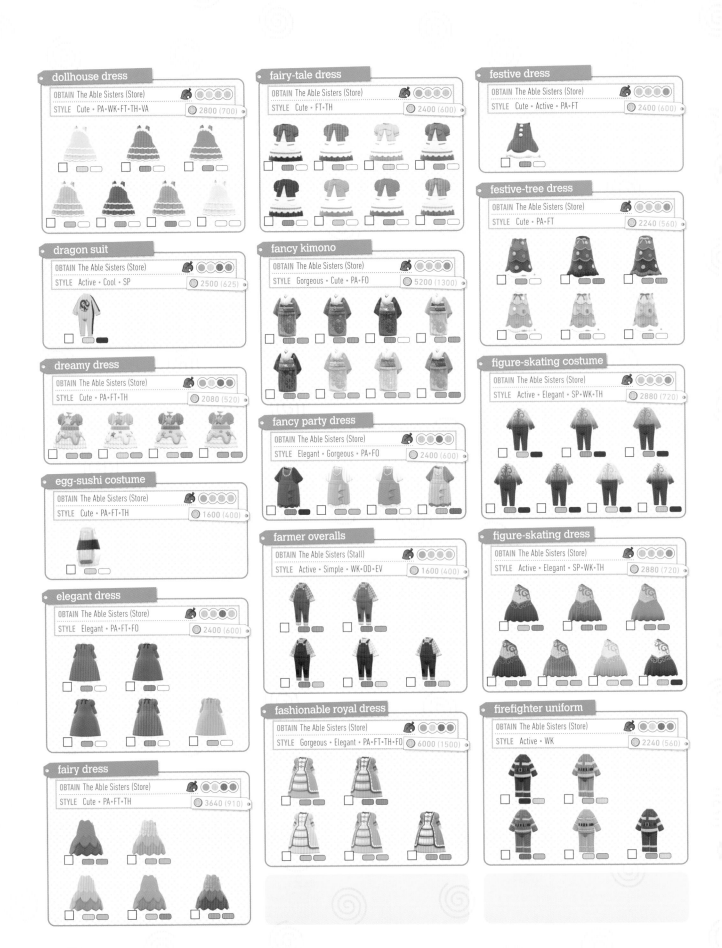

dollhouse dress

OBTAIN The Able Sisters (Store)
STYLE Cute • PA•WK•FT•TH•VA
2800 (700)

dragon suit

OBTAIN The Able Sisters (Store)
STYLE Active • Cool • SP
2500 (625)

dreamy dress

OBTAIN The Able Sisters (Store)
STYLE Cute • PA•FT•TH
2080 (520)

egg-sushi costume

OBTAIN The Able Sisters (Store)
STYLE Cute • PA•FT•TH
1600 (400)

elegant dress

OBTAIN The Able Sisters (Store)
STYLE Elegant • PA•FT•FO
2400 (600)

fairy dress

OBTAIN The Able Sisters (Store)
STYLE Cute • PA•FT•TH
3640 (910)

fairy-tale dress

OBTAIN The Able Sisters (Store)
STYLE Cute • FT•TH
2400 (600)

fancy kimono

OBTAIN The Able Sisters (Store)
STYLE Gorgeous • Cute • PA•FO
5200 (1300)

fancy party dress

OBTAIN The Able Sisters (Store)
STYLE Elegant • Gorgeous • PA•FO
2400 (600)

farmer overalls

OBTAIN The Able Sisters (Stall)
STYLE Active • Simple • WK•OD•EV
1600 (400)

fashionable royal dress

OBTAIN The Able Sisters (Store)
STYLE Gorgeous • Elegant • PA•FT•TH•FO
6000 (1500)

festive dress

OBTAIN The Able Sisters (Store)
STYLE Cute • Active • PA•FT
2400 (600)

festive-tree dress

OBTAIN The Able Sisters (Store)
STYLE Cute • PA•FT
2240 (560)

figure-skating costume

OBTAIN The Able Sisters (Store)
STYLE Active • Elegant • SP•WK•TH
2880 (720)

figure-skating dress

OBTAIN The Able Sisters (Store)
STYLE Active • Elegant • SP•WK•TH
2880 (720)

firefighter uniform

OBTAIN The Able Sisters (Store)
STYLE Active • WK
2240 (560)

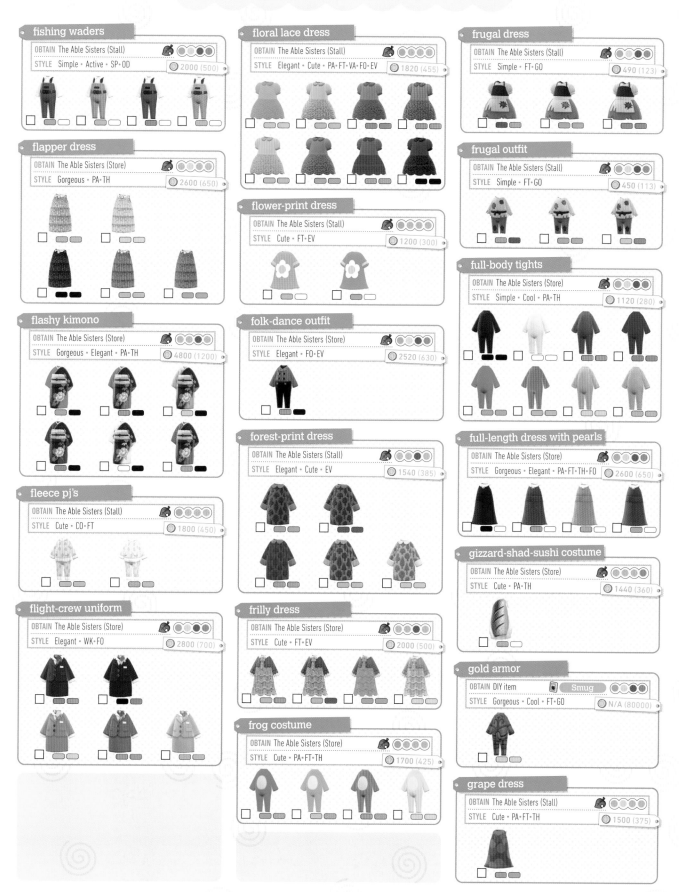

fishing waders
OBTAIN The Able Sisters (Stall)
STYLE Simple • Active • SP•OD
2000 (500)

flapper dress
OBTAIN The Able Sisters (Store)
STYLE Gorgeous • PA•TH
2600 (650)

flashy kimono
OBTAIN The Able Sisters (Store)
STYLE Gorgeous • Elegant • PA•TH
4800 (1200)

fleece pj's
OBTAIN The Able Sisters (Stall)
STYLE Cute • CO•FT
1800 (450)

flight-crew uniform
OBTAIN The Able Sisters (Store)
STYLE Elegant • WK•FO
2800 (700)

floral lace dress
OBTAIN The Able Sisters (Stall)
STYLE Elegant • Cute • PA•FT•VA•FO•EV
1820 (455)

flower-print dress
OBTAIN The Able Sisters (Stall)
STYLE Cute • FT•EV
1200 (300)

folk-dance outfit
OBTAIN The Able Sisters (Store)
STYLE Elegant • FO•EV
2520 (630)

forest-print dress
OBTAIN The Able Sisters (Stall)
STYLE Elegant • Cute • EV
1540 (385)

frilly dress
OBTAIN The Able Sisters (Store)
STYLE Cute • FT•EV
2000 (500)

frog costume
OBTAIN The Able Sisters (Store)
STYLE Cute • PA•FT•TH
1700 (425)

frugal dress
OBTAIN The Able Sisters (Stall)
STYLE Simple • FT•GO
490 (123)

frugal outfit
OBTAIN The Able Sisters (Stall)
STYLE Simple • FT•GO
450 (113)

full-body tights
OBTAIN The Able Sisters (Store)
STYLE Simple • Cool • PA•TH
1120 (280)

full-length dress with pearls
OBTAIN The Able Sisters (Store)
STYLE Gorgeous • Elegant • PA•FT•TH•FO
2600 (650)

gizzard-shad-sushi costume
OBTAIN The Able Sisters (Store)
STYLE Cute • PA•TH
1440 (360)

gold armor
OBTAIN DIY item   Smug
STYLE Gorgeous • Cool • FT•GO
N/A (80000)

grape dress
OBTAIN The Able Sisters (Stall)
STYLE Cute • PA•FT•TH
1500 (375)

gumdrop dress
OBTAIN	The Able Sisters (Stall)
STYLE	Cute • FT•EV

1800 (450)

hakama
OBTAIN	The Able Sisters (Store)
STYLE	Elegant • PA•FO

3180 (795)

hakama with crest
OBTAIN	The Able Sisters (Store)
STYLE	Cool • Elegant • PA•FO

4800 (1200)

hibiscus muumuu
OBTAIN	The Able Sisters (Stall)
STYLE	Cute • Active • CO•VA

1800 (450)

hot-dog costume
OBTAIN	The Able Sisters (Store)
STYLE	Active • Cute • PA•TH

1280 (320)

house-print dress
OBTAIN	The Able Sisters (Stall)
STYLE	Cute • Elegant • FT•EV

1600 (400)

ice-hockey uniform
OBTAIN	The Able Sisters (Stall)
STYLE	Active • SP•WK

2640 (660)

icy dress
OBTAIN	The Able Sisters (Store)
STYLE	Gorgeous • Elegant • PA•FT

5200 (1300)

impish costume
OBTAIN	The Able Sisters (Store)
STYLE	Cool • Cute • FT•GO•TH

2240 (560)

instant-muscles suit
OBTAIN	The Able Sisters (Store)
STYLE	Active • PA•SP•TH

2280 (570)

iron armor
OBTAIN	DIY item	Cranky
STYLE	Cool • Gorgeous • FT•GO	

N/A (6000)

jester costume
OBTAIN	The Able Sisters (Store)
STYLE	Active • Gorgeous • PA•WK•FT•GO•T

2240 (560)

jinbei
OBTAIN	The Able Sisters (Store)
STYLE	Simple • Cool • CO•VA

1820 (455)

jockey uniform
OBTAIN	The Able Sisters (Store)
STYLE	Active • SP•WK

1920 (480)

judogi
OBTAIN	The Able Sisters (Store)
STYLE	Active • SP•WK

1760 (440)

jumper work suit
OBTAIN	The Able Sisters (Stall)
STYLE	Active • Simple • WK•OD

1050 (263)

junihitoe kimono
OBTAIN	The Able Sisters (Store)
STYLE	Gorgeous • PA•TH•FO

7000 (1750)

kabuki-actor yukata
OBTAIN	The Able Sisters (Store)
STYLE	Elegant • Cool • CO•TH•VA

2400 (600)

kandoora
OBTAIN	The Able Sisters (Store)
STYLE	Simple • Elegant • FO•EV

2520 (630)

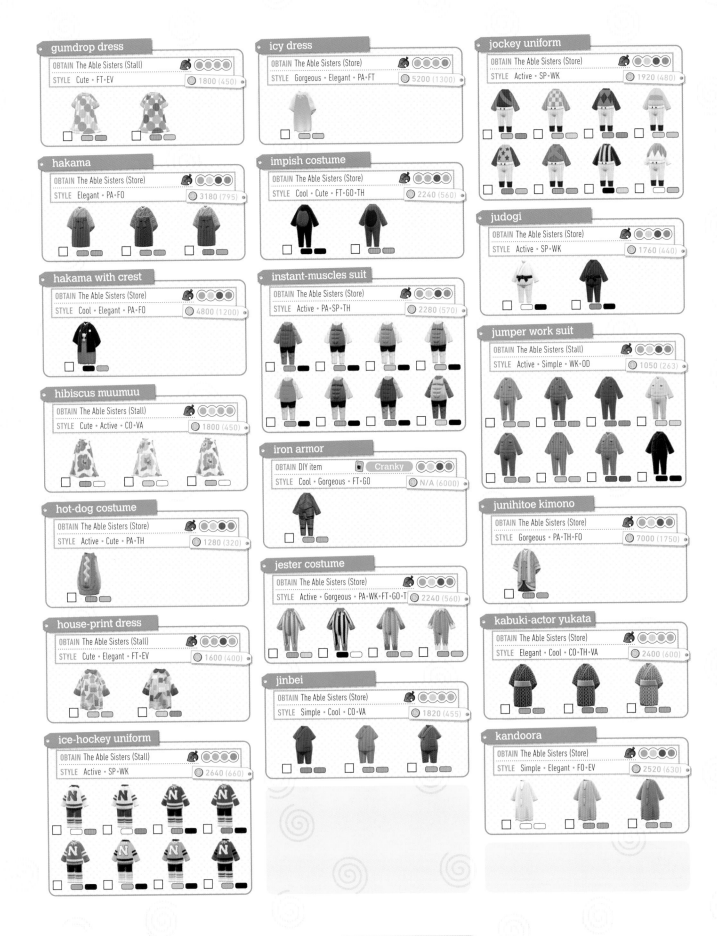

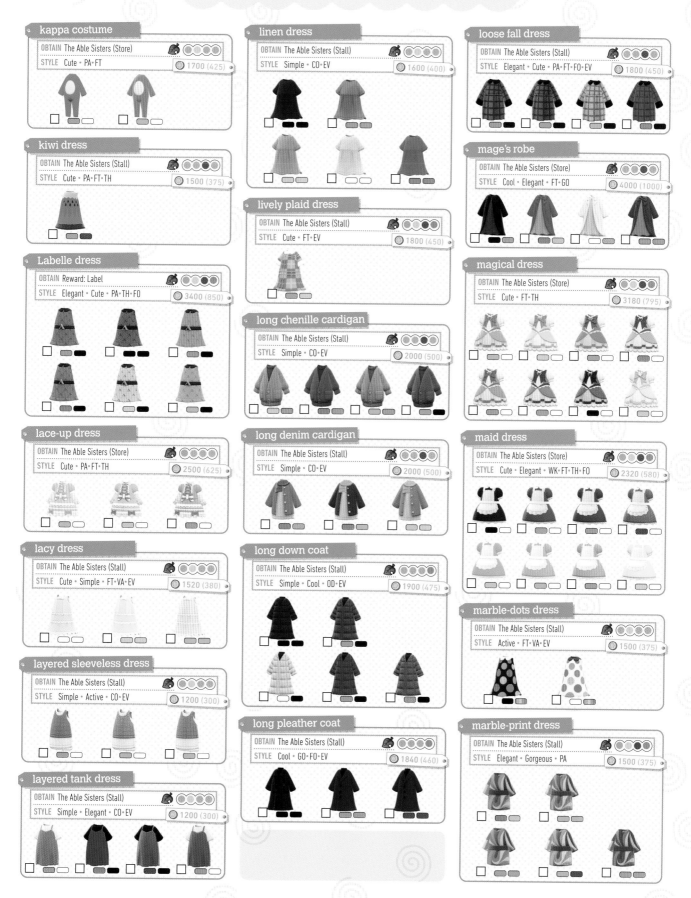

kappa costume
OBTAIN The Able Sisters (Store)
STYLE Cute • PA•FT
1700 (425)

kiwi dress
OBTAIN The Able Sisters (Stall)
STYLE Cute • PA•FT•TH
1500 (375)

Labelle dress
OBTAIN Reward: Label
STYLE Elegant • Cute • PA•TH•FO
3400 (850)

lace-up dress
OBTAIN The Able Sisters (Store)
STYLE Cute • PA•FT•TH
2500 (625)

lacy dress
OBTAIN The Able Sisters (Stall)
STYLE Cute • Simple • FT•VA•EV
1520 (380)

layered sleeveless dress
OBTAIN The Able Sisters (Stall)
STYLE Simple • Active • CO•EV
1200 (300)

layered tank dress
OBTAIN The Able Sisters (Stall)
STYLE Simple • Elegant • CO•EV
1200 (300)

linen dress
OBTAIN The Able Sisters (Stall)
STYLE Simple • CO•EV
1600 (400)

lively plaid dress
OBTAIN The Able Sisters (Stall)
STYLE Cute • FT•EV
1800 (450)

long chenille cardigan
OBTAIN The Able Sisters (Stall)
STYLE Simple • CO•EV
2000 (500)

long denim cardigan
OBTAIN The Able Sisters (Stall)
STYLE Simple • CO•EV
2000 (500)

long down coat
OBTAIN The Able Sisters (Stall)
STYLE Simple • Cool • OD•EV
1900 (475)

long pleather coat
OBTAIN The Able Sisters (Stall)
STYLE Cool • GO•FO•EV
1840 (460)

loose fall dress
OBTAIN The Able Sisters (Stall)
STYLE Elegant • Cute • PA•FT•FO•EV
1800 (450)

mage's robe
OBTAIN The Able Sisters (Store)
STYLE Cool • Elegant • FT•GO
4000 (1000)

magical dress
OBTAIN The Able Sisters (Store)
STYLE Cute • FT•TH
3180 (795)

maid dress
OBTAIN The Able Sisters (Store)
STYLE Cute • Elegant • WK•FT•TH•FO
2320 (580)

marble-dots dress
OBTAIN The Able Sisters (Stall)
STYLE Active • FT•VA•EV
1500 (375)

marble-print dress
OBTAIN The Able Sisters (Stall)
STYLE Elegant • Gorgeous • PA
1500 (375)

7

mariachi clothing

OBTAIN The Able Sisters (Store)

STYLE Elegant • PA•TH•FO 2520 (630)

maxi shirtdress

OBTAIN The Able Sisters (Stall)

STYLE Simple • CO•EV 2000 (500)

miko attire

OBTAIN The Able Sisters (Store)

STYLE Elegant • WK 2240 (560)

milkmaid dress

OBTAIN The Able Sisters (Store)

STYLE Elegant • Cute • FO•EV 2520 (630)

moldy dress

OBTAIN Recycle Box

STYLE Simple • GO N/A (10)

morning-glory yukata

OBTAIN The Able Sisters (Stall)

STYLE Elegant • Cute • CO•FT•VA 2280 (570)

mummy outfit

OBTAIN The Able Sisters (Store)

STYLE Cool • FT•GO 700 (175)

mysterious dress

OBTAIN The Able Sisters (Stall)

STYLE Cool • Elegant • PA•GO 3120 (780)

nightgown

OBTAIN The Able Sisters (Store)

STYLE Elegant • Cute • CO•FT 2100 (525)

ninja costume

OBTAIN The Able Sisters (Store)

STYLE Active • Cool • WK•FT•TH 2240 (560)

noble dress

OBTAIN The Able Sisters (Store)

STYLE Gorgeous • Elegant • PA•FT•TH•FO 5200 (1300)

noble zap suit

OBTAIN The Able Sisters (Store)

STYLE Active • WK•FT•TH 2760 (690)

nurse's dress uniform

OBTAIN The Able Sisters (Store)

STYLE Simple • Active • WK 2200 (550)

office uniform

OBTAIN The Able Sisters (Store)

STYLE Simple • Elegant • WK•FO 1600 (400)

old commoner's kimono

OBTAIN The Able Sisters (Stall)

STYLE Simple • Cute • EV 1920 (480)

orange dress

OBTAIN DIY item Lazy

STYLE Cute • PA•FT•TH N/A (1600)

overall dress

OBTAIN The Able Sisters (Stall)

STYLE Active • Cute • EV 2000 (500)

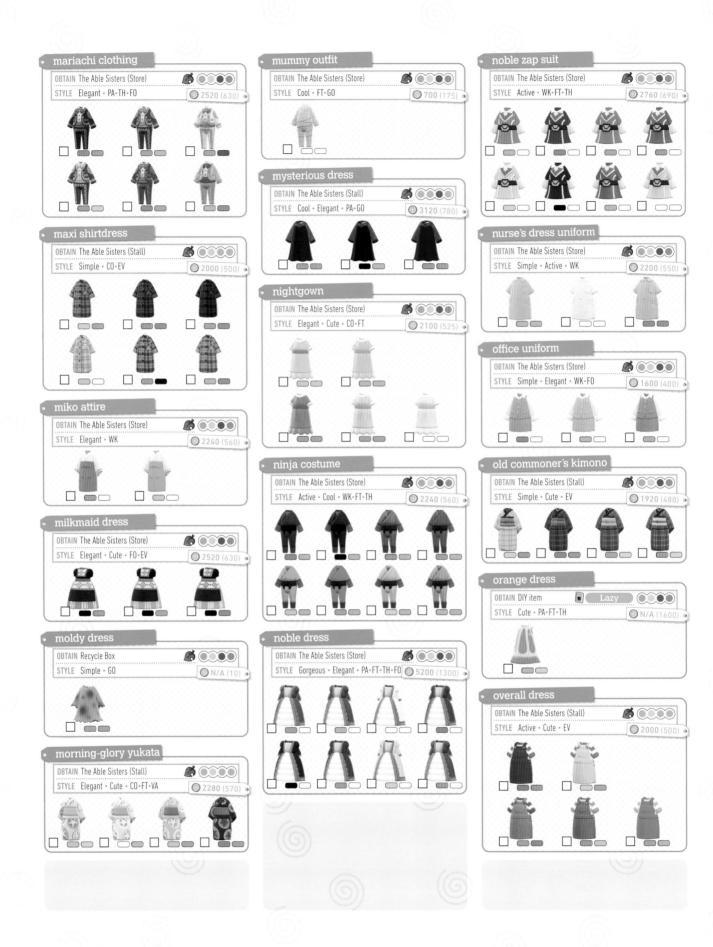

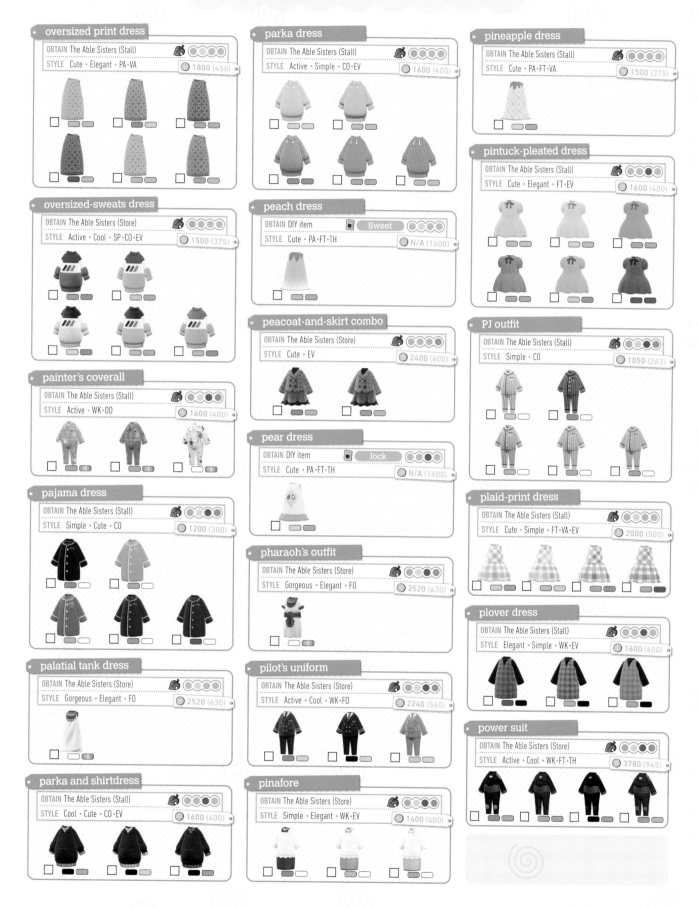

oversized print dress
OBTAIN The Able Sisters (Stall)
STYLE Cute • Elegant • PA•VA
1800 (450)

oversized-sweats dress
OBTAIN The Able Sisters (Store)
STYLE Active • Cool • SP•CO•EV
1500 (375)

painter's coverall
OBTAIN The Able Sisters (Stall)
STYLE Active • WK•OD
1600 (400)

pajama dress
OBTAIN The Able Sisters (Stall)
STYLE Simple • Cute • CO
1200 (300)

palatial tank dress
OBTAIN The Able Sisters (Store)
STYLE Gorgeous • Elegant • FO
2520 (630)

parka and shirtdress
OBTAIN The Able Sisters (Stall)
STYLE Cool • Cute • CO•EV
1600 (400)

parka dress
OBTAIN The Able Sisters (Stall)
STYLE Active • Simple • CO•EV
1600 (400)

peach dress
OBTAIN DIY item — Sweet
STYLE Cute • PA•FT•TH
N/A (1600)

peacoat-and-skirt combo
OBTAIN The Able Sisters (Store)
STYLE Cute • EV
2400 (600)

pear dress
OBTAIN DIY item — Jock
STYLE Cute • PA•FT•TH
N/A (1600)

pharaoh's outfit
OBTAIN The Able Sisters (Store)
STYLE Gorgeous • Elegant • FO
2520 (630)

pilot's uniform
OBTAIN The Able Sisters (Store)
STYLE Active • Cool • WK•FO
2240 (560)

pinafore
OBTAIN The Able Sisters (Store)
STYLE Simple • Elegant • WK•EV
1600 (400)

pineapple dress
OBTAIN The Able Sisters (Stall)
STYLE Cute • PA•FT•VA
1500 (375)

pintuck-pleated dress
OBTAIN The Able Sisters (Stall)
STYLE Cute • Elegant • FT•EV
1600 (400)

PJ outfit
OBTAIN The Able Sisters (Stall)
STYLE Simple • CO
1050 (263)

plaid-print dress
OBTAIN The Able Sisters (Stall)
STYLE Cute • Simple • FT•VA•EV
2000 (500)

plover dress
OBTAIN The Able Sisters (Stall)
STYLE Elegant • Simple • WK•EV
1600 (400)

power suit
OBTAIN The Able Sisters (Store)
STYLE Active • Cool • WK•FT•TH
3780 (945)

7

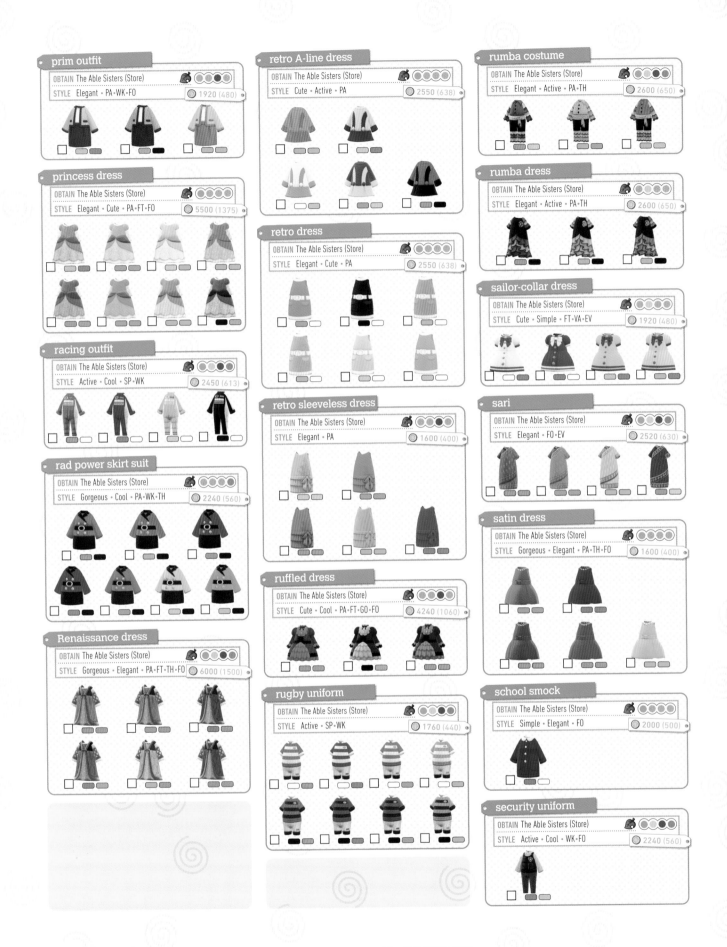

prim outfit

OBTAIN The Able Sisters (Store)
STYLE Elegant • PA•WK•FO
1920 (480)

princess dress

OBTAIN The Able Sisters (Store)
STYLE Elegant • Cute • PA•FT•FO
5500 (1375)

racing outfit

OBTAIN The Able Sisters (Store)
STYLE Active • Cool • SP•WK
2450 (613)

rad power skirt suit

OBTAIN The Able Sisters (Store)
STYLE Gorgeous • Cool • PA•WK•TH
2240 (560)

Renaissance dress

OBTAIN The Able Sisters (Store)
STYLE Gorgeous • Elegant • PA•FT•TH•FO
6000 (1500)

retro A-line dress

OBTAIN The Able Sisters (Store)
STYLE Cute • Active • PA
2550 (638)

retro dress

OBTAIN The Able Sisters (Store)
STYLE Elegant • Cute • PA
2550 (638)

retro sleeveless dress

OBTAIN The Able Sisters (Store)
STYLE Elegant • PA
1600 (400)

ruffled dress

OBTAIN The Able Sisters (Store)
STYLE Cute • Cool • PA•FT•GO•FO
4240 (1060)

rugby uniform

OBTAIN The Able Sisters (Store)
STYLE Active • SP•WK
1760 (440)

rumba costume

OBTAIN The Able Sisters (Store)
STYLE Elegant • Active • PA•TH
2600 (650)

rumba dress

OBTAIN The Able Sisters (Store)
STYLE Elegant • Active • PA•TH
2600 (650)

sailor-collar dress

OBTAIN The Able Sisters (Store)
STYLE Cute • Simple • FT•VA•EV
1920 (480)

sari

OBTAIN The Able Sisters (Store)
STYLE Elegant • FO•EV
2520 (630)

satin dress

OBTAIN The Able Sisters (Store)
STYLE Gorgeous • Elegant • PA•TH•FO
1600 (400)

school smock

OBTAIN The Able Sisters (Store)
STYLE Simple • Elegant • FO
2000 (500)

security uniform

OBTAIN The Able Sisters (Store)
STYLE Active • Cool • WK•FO
2240 (560)

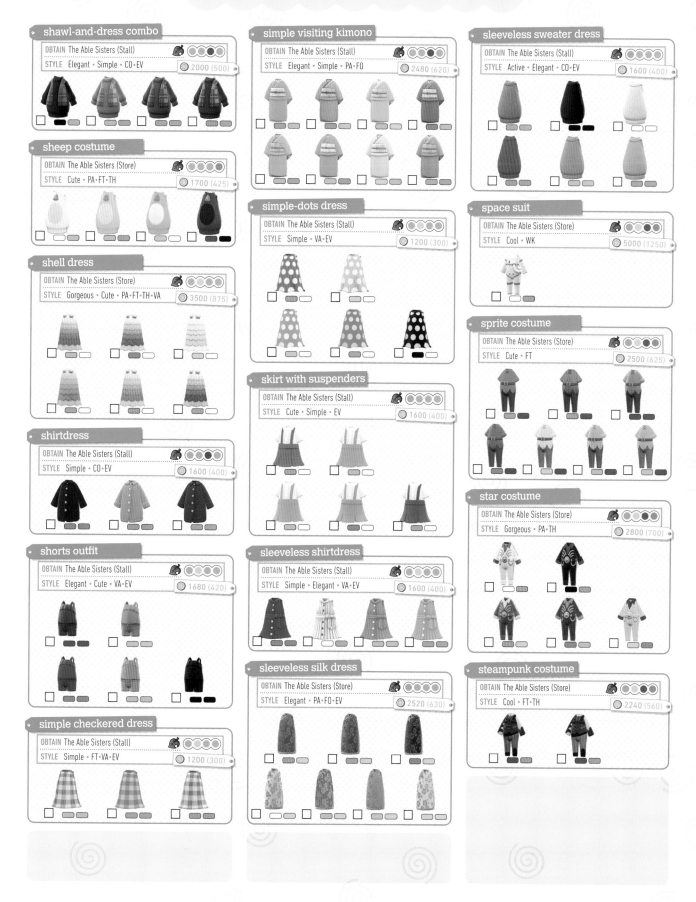

shawl-and-dress combo

OBTAIN	The Able Sisters (Stall)
STYLE	Elegant • Simple • CO•EV

2000 (500)

sheep costume

OBTAIN	The Able Sisters (Store)
STYLE	Cute • PA•FT•TH

1700 (425)

shell dress

OBTAIN	The Able Sisters (Store)
STYLE	Gorgeous • Cute • PA•FT•TH•VA

3500 (875)

shirtdress

OBTAIN	The Able Sisters (Stall)
STYLE	Simple • CO•EV

1600 (400)

shorts outfit

OBTAIN	The Able Sisters (Stall)
STYLE	Elegant • Cute • VA•EV

1680 (420)

simple checkered dress

OBTAIN	The Able Sisters (Stall)
STYLE	Simple • FT•VA•EV

1200 (300)

simple visiting kimono

OBTAIN	The Able Sisters (Stall)
STYLE	Elegant • Simple • PA•FO

2480 (620)

simple-dots dress

OBTAIN	The Able Sisters (Stall)
STYLE	Simple • VA•EV

1200 (300)

skirt with suspenders

OBTAIN	The Able Sisters (Stall)
STYLE	Cute • Simple • EV

1600 (400)

sleeveless shirtdress

OBTAIN	The Able Sisters (Stall)
STYLE	Simple • Elegant • VA•EV

1600 (400)

sleeveless silk dress

OBTAIN	The Able Sisters (Store)
STYLE	Elegant • PA•FO•EV

2520 (630)

sleeveless sweater dress

OBTAIN	The Able Sisters (Stall)
STYLE	Active • Elegant • CO•EV

1600 (400)

space suit

OBTAIN	The Able Sisters (Store)
STYLE	Cool • WK

5000 (1250)

sprite costume

OBTAIN	The Able Sisters (Store)
STYLE	Cute • FT

2500 (625)

star costume

OBTAIN	The Able Sisters (Store)
STYLE	Gorgeous • PA•TH

2800 (700)

steampunk costume

OBTAIN	The Able Sisters (Store)
STYLE	Cool • FT•TH

2240 (560)

7

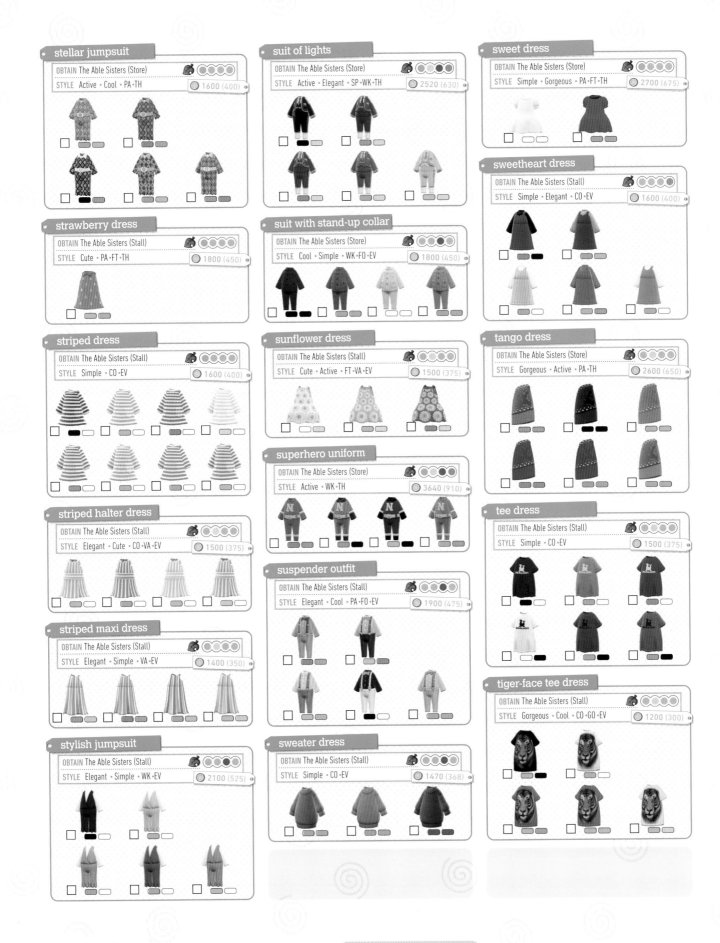

stellar jumpsuit
OBTAIN The Able Sisters (Store)
STYLE Active • Cool • PA • TH
1600 (400)

strawberry dress
OBTAIN The Able Sisters (Stall)
STYLE Cute • PA • FT • TH
1800 (450)

striped dress
OBTAIN The Able Sisters (Stall)
STYLE Simple • CO • EV
1600 (400)

striped halter dress
OBTAIN The Able Sisters (Stall)
STYLE Elegant • Cute • CO • VA • EV
1500 (375)

striped maxi dress
OBTAIN The Able Sisters (Stall)
STYLE Elegant • Simple • VA • EV
1400 (350)

stylish jumpsuit
OBTAIN The Able Sisters (Stall)
STYLE Elegant • Simple • WK • EV
2100 (525)

suit of lights
OBTAIN The Able Sisters (Store)
STYLE Active • Elegant • SP • WK • TH
2520 (630)

suit with stand-up collar
OBTAIN The Able Sisters (Store)
STYLE Cool • Simple • WK • FO • EV
1800 (450)

sunflower dress
OBTAIN The Able Sisters (Stall)
STYLE Cute • Active • FT • VA • EV
1500 (375)

superhero uniform
OBTAIN The Able Sisters (Store)
STYLE Active • WK • TH
3640 (910)

suspender outfit
OBTAIN The Able Sisters (Stall)
STYLE Elegant • Cool • PA • FO • EV
1900 (475)

sweater dress
OBTAIN The Able Sisters (Stall)
STYLE Simple • CO • EV
1470 (368)

sweet dress
OBTAIN The Able Sisters (Store)
STYLE Simple • Gorgeous • PA • FT • TH
2700 (675)

sweetheart dress
OBTAIN The Able Sisters (Stall)
STYLE Simple • Elegant • CO • EV
1600 (400)

tango dress
OBTAIN The Able Sisters (Store)
STYLE Gorgeous • Active • PA • TH
2600 (650)

tee dress
OBTAIN The Able Sisters (Stall)
STYLE Simple • CO • EV
1500 (375)

tiger-face tee dress
OBTAIN The Able Sisters (Stall)
STYLE Gorgeous • Cool • CO • GO • EV
1200 (300)

tight punk outfit

OBTAIN The Able Sisters (Store)
STYLE Cool • TH

1920 (480)

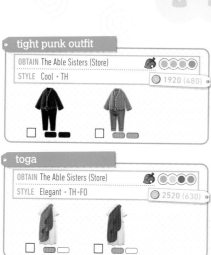

toga

OBTAIN The Able Sisters (Store)
STYLE Elegant • TH • FO

2520 (630)

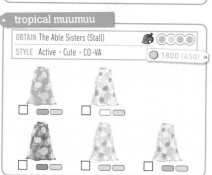

tropical muumuu

OBTAIN The Able Sisters (Stall)
STYLE Active • Cute • CO • VA

1800 (450)

tuna-sushi costume

OBTAIN The Able Sisters (Store)
STYLE Cute • PA • FT • TH

1920 (480)

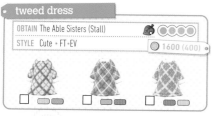

tweed dress

OBTAIN The Able Sisters (Stall)
STYLE Cute • FT • EV

1600 (400)

Victorian dress

OBTAIN The Able Sisters (Store)
STYLE Gorgeous • Elegant • PA • TH • FO

2520 (630)

visual-punk dress

OBTAIN The Able Sisters (Store)
STYLE Cool • PA • WK • TH

2040 (510)

visual-punk outfit

OBTAIN The Able Sisters (Store)
STYLE Cool • PA • WK • TH

2040 (510)

watermelon dress

OBTAIN The Able Sisters (Stall)
STYLE Cute • PA • FT • VA

1500 (375)

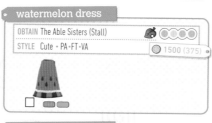

wizard's robe

OBTAIN The Able Sisters (Store)
STYLE Gorgeous • Cute • PA • FT

4000 (1000)

wrestler uniform

OBTAIN The Able Sisters (Store)
STYLE Active • SP • WK • TH

1600 (400)

zap suit

OBTAIN The Able Sisters (Stall)
STYLE Active • WK • FT • TH

2760 (690)

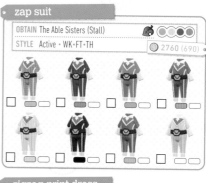

zigzag-print dress

OBTAIN The Able Sisters (Stall)
STYLE Elegant • Active • VA

2000 (500)

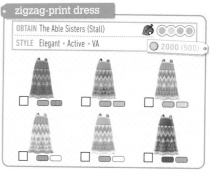

wrestling singlet

OBTAIN The Able Sisters (Store)
STYLE Active • SP • WK

1540 (385)

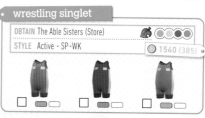

7

Headwear

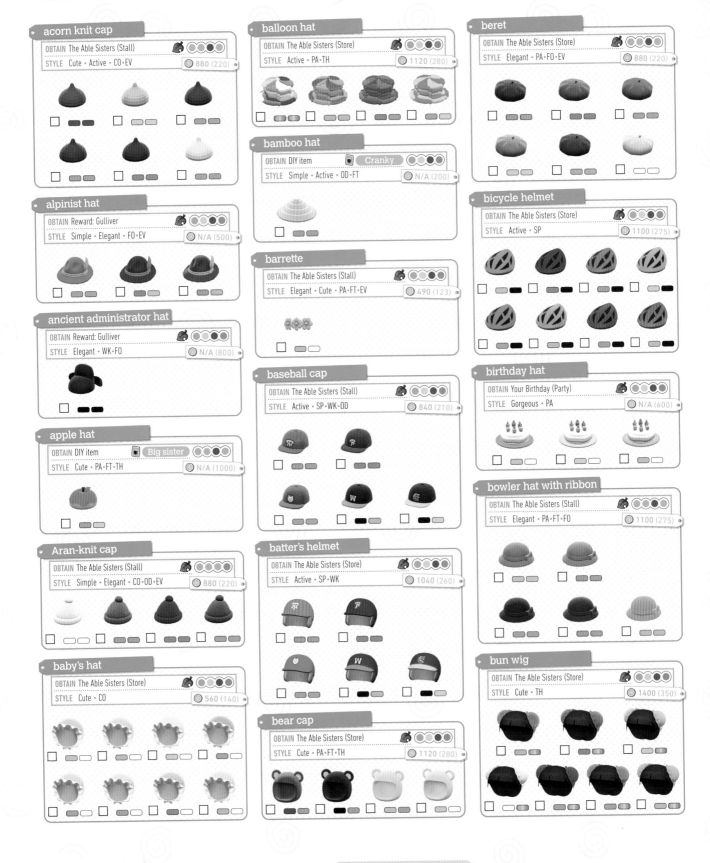

acorn knit cap
OBTAIN The Able Sisters (Stall)
STYLE Cute • Active • CO•EV
880 (220)

alpinist hat
OBTAIN Reward: Gulliver
STYLE Simple • Elegant • FO•EV
N/A (500)

ancient administrator hat
OBTAIN Reward: Gulliver
STYLE Elegant • WK•FO
N/A (800)

apple hat
OBTAIN DIY item — Big sister
STYLE Cute • PA•FT•TH
N/A (1000)

Aran-knit cap
OBTAIN The Able Sisters (Stall)
STYLE Simple • Elegant • CO•OD•EV
880 (220)

baby's hat
OBTAIN The Able Sisters (Store)
STYLE Cute • CO
560 (140)

balloon hat
OBTAIN The Able Sisters (Store)
STYLE Active • PA•TH
1120 (280)

bamboo hat
OBTAIN DIY item — Cranky
STYLE Simple • Active • OD•FT
N/A (200)

barrette
OBTAIN The Able Sisters (Stall)
STYLE Elegant • Cute • PA•FT•EV
490 (123)

baseball cap
OBTAIN The Able Sisters (Stall)
STYLE Active • SP•WK•OD
840 (210)

batter's helmet
OBTAIN The Able Sisters (Store)
STYLE Active • SP•WK
1040 (260)

bear cap
OBTAIN The Able Sisters (Store)
STYLE Cute • PA•FT•TH
1120 (280)

beret
OBTAIN The Able Sisters (Store)
STYLE Elegant • PA•FO•EV
880 (220)

bicycle helmet
OBTAIN The Able Sisters (Store)
STYLE Active • SP
1100 (275)

birthday hat
OBTAIN Your Birthday (Party)
STYLE Gorgeous • PA
N/A (600)

bowler hat with ribbon
OBTAIN The Able Sisters (Stall)
STYLE Elegant • PA•FT•FO
1100 (275)

bun wig
OBTAIN The Able Sisters (Store)
STYLE Cute • TH
1400 (350)

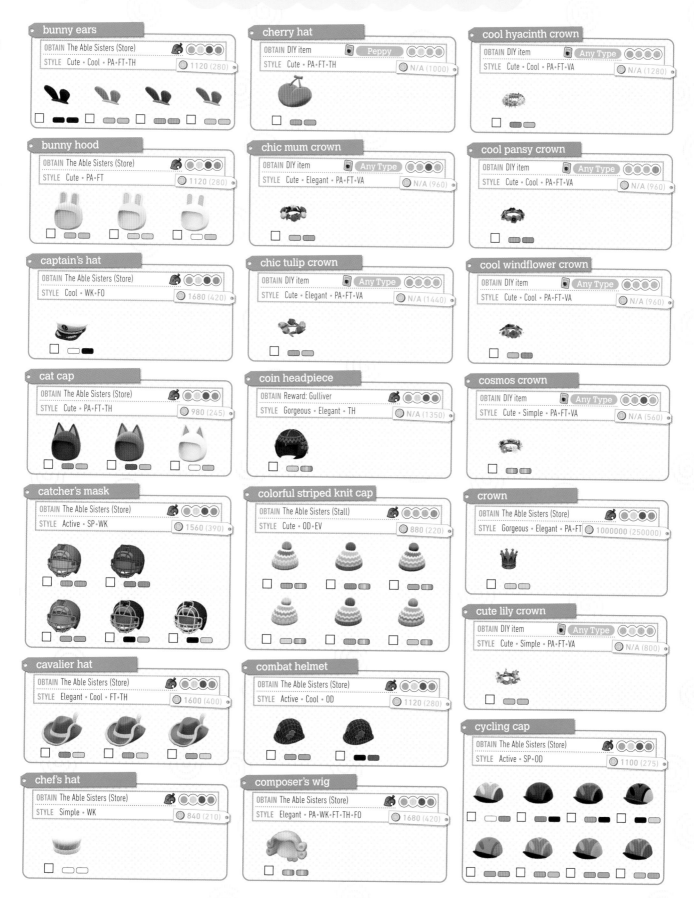

bunny ears

OBTAIN The Able Sisters (Store)
STYLE Cute · Cool · PA·FT·TH
1120 (280)

bunny hood

OBTAIN The Able Sisters (Store)
STYLE Cute · PA·FT
1120 (280)

captain's hat

OBTAIN The Able Sisters (Store)
STYLE Cool · WK·FO
1680 (420)

cat cap

OBTAIN The Able Sisters (Store)
STYLE Cute · PA·FT·TH
980 (245)

catcher's mask

OBTAIN The Able Sisters (Store)
STYLE Active · SP·WK
1560 (390)

cavalier hat

OBTAIN The Able Sisters (Store)
STYLE Elegant · Cool · FT·TH
1600 (400)

chef's hat

OBTAIN The Able Sisters (Store)
STYLE Simple · WK
840 (210)

cherry hat

OBTAIN DIY item — Peppy
STYLE Cute · PA·FT·TH
N/A (1000)

chic mum crown

OBTAIN DIY item — Any Type
STYLE Cute · Elegant · PA·FT·VA
N/A (960)

chic tulip crown

OBTAIN DIY item — Any Type
STYLE Cute · Elegant · PA·FT·VA
N/A (1440)

coin headpiece

OBTAIN Reward: Gulliver
STYLE Gorgeous · Elegant · TH
N/A (1350)

colorful striped knit cap

OBTAIN The Able Sisters (Stall)
STYLE Cute · OD·EV
880 (220)

combat helmet

OBTAIN The Able Sisters (Store)
STYLE Active · Cool · OD
1120 (280)

composer's wig

OBTAIN The Able Sisters (Store)
STYLE Elegant · PA·WK·FT·TH·FO
1680 (420)

cool hyacinth crown

OBTAIN DIY item — Any Type
STYLE Cute · Cool · PA·FT·VA
N/A (1280)

cool pansy crown

OBTAIN DIY item — Any Type
STYLE Cute · Cool · PA·FT·VA
N/A (960)

cool windflower crown

OBTAIN DIY item — Any Type
STYLE Cute · Cool · PA·FT·VA
N/A (960)

cosmos crown

OBTAIN DIY item — Any Type
STYLE Cute · Simple · PA·FT·VA
N/A (560)

crown

OBTAIN The Able Sisters (Store)
STYLE Gorgeous · Elegant · PA·FT
1000000 (250000)

cute lily crown

OBTAIN DIY item — Any Type
STYLE Cute · Simple · PA·FT·VA
N/A (800)

cycling cap

OBTAIN The Able Sisters (Store)
STYLE Active · SP·OD
1100 (275)

7

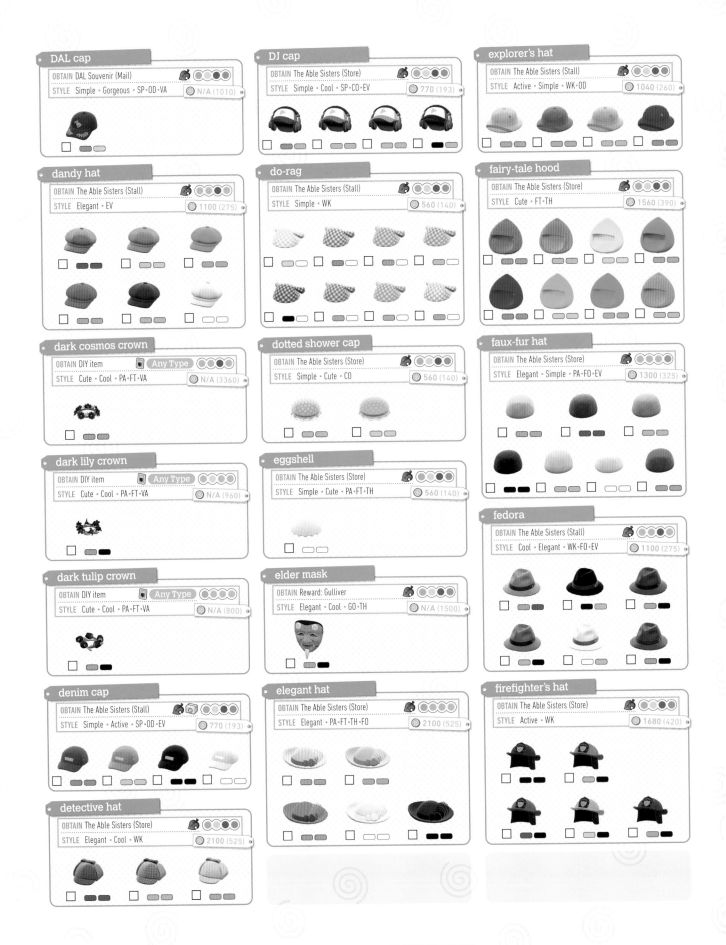

DAL cap

OBTAIN DAL Souvenir (Mail)

STYLE Simple • Gorgeous • SP•OD•VA

N/A (1010)

DJ cap

OBTAIN The Able Sisters (Store)

STYLE Simple • Cool • SP•CO•EV

770 (193)

explorer's hat

OBTAIN The Able Sisters (Stall)

STYLE Active • Simple • WK•OD

1040 (260)

dandy hat

OBTAIN The Able Sisters (Stall)

STYLE Elegant • EV

1100 (275)

do-rag

OBTAIN The Able Sisters (Stall)

STYLE Simple • WK

560 (140)

fairy-tale hood

OBTAIN The Able Sisters (Store)

STYLE Cute • FT•TH

1560 (390)

dark cosmos crown

OBTAIN DIY item — Any Type

STYLE Cute • Cool • PA•FT•VA

N/A (3360)

dotted shower cap

OBTAIN The Able Sisters (Store)

STYLE Simple • Cute • CO

560 (140)

faux-fur hat

OBTAIN The Able Sisters (Store)

STYLE Elegant • Simple • PA•FO•EV

1300 (325)

dark lily crown

OBTAIN DIY item — Any Type

STYLE Cute • Cool • PA•FT•VA

N/A (960)

eggshell

OBTAIN The Able Sisters (Store)

STYLE Simple • Cute • PA•FT•TH

560 (140)

fedora

OBTAIN The Able Sisters (Stall)

STYLE Cool • Elegant • WK•FO•EV

1100 (275)

dark tulip crown

OBTAIN DIY item — Any Type

STYLE Cute • Cool • PA•FT•VA

N/A (800)

elder mask

OBTAIN Reward: Gulliver

STYLE Elegant • Cool • GO•TH

N/A (1500)

denim cap

OBTAIN The Able Sisters (Stall)

STYLE Simple • Active • SP•OD•EV

770 (193)

elegant hat

OBTAIN The Able Sisters (Store)

STYLE Elegant • PA•FT•TH•FO

2100 (525)

firefighter's hat

OBTAIN The Able Sisters (Store)

STYLE Active • WK

1680 (420)

detective hat

OBTAIN The Able Sisters (Store)

STYLE Elegant • Cool • WK

2100 (525)

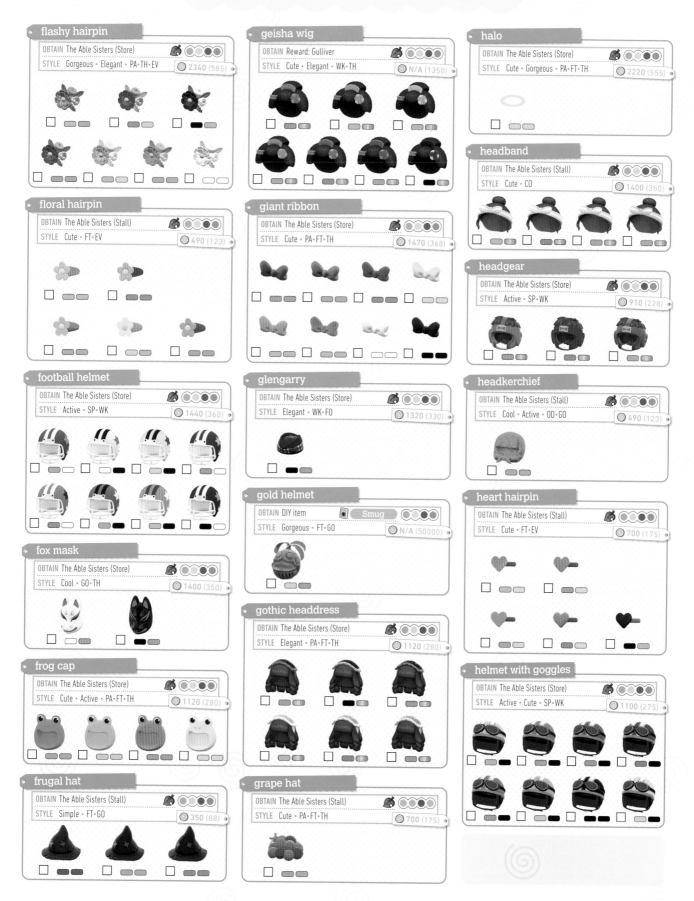

flashy hairpin

OBTAIN The Able Sisters (Store)
STYLE Gorgeous · Elegant · PA·TH·EV
2340 (585)

floral hairpin

OBTAIN The Able Sisters (Stall)
STYLE Cute · FT·EV
490 (123)

football helmet

OBTAIN The Able Sisters (Store)
STYLE Active · SP·WK
1440 (360)

fox mask

OBTAIN The Able Sisters (Store)
STYLE Cool · GO·TH
1400 (350)

frog cap

OBTAIN The Able Sisters (Store)
STYLE Cute · Active · PA·FT·TH
1120 (280)

frugal hat

OBTAIN The Able Sisters (Stall)
STYLE Simple · FT·GO
350 (88)

geisha wig

OBTAIN Reward: Gulliver
STYLE Cute · Elegant · WK·TH
N/A (1350)

giant ribbon

OBTAIN The Able Sisters (Store)
STYLE Cute · PA·FT·TH
1470 (368)

glengarry

OBTAIN The Able Sisters (Store)
STYLE Elegant · WK·FO
1320 (330)

gold helmet

OBTAIN DIY item   Smug
STYLE Gorgeous · FT·GO
N/A (50000)

gothic headdress

OBTAIN The Able Sisters (Store)
STYLE Elegant · PA·FT·TH
1120 (280)

grape hat

OBTAIN The Able Sisters (Stall)
STYLE Cute · PA·FT·TH
700 (175)

halo

OBTAIN The Able Sisters (Store)
STYLE Cute · Gorgeous · PA·FT·TH
2220 (555)

headband

OBTAIN The Able Sisters (Stall)
STYLE Cute · CO
1400 (350)

headgear

OBTAIN The Able Sisters (Store)
STYLE Active · SP·WK
910 (228)

headkerchief

OBTAIN The Able Sisters (Stall)
STYLE Cool · Active · OD·GO
490 (123)

heart hairpin

OBTAIN The Able Sisters (Stall)
STYLE Cute · FT·EV
700 (175)

helmet with goggles

OBTAIN The Able Sisters (Store)
STYLE Active · Cute · SP·WK
1100 (275)

7

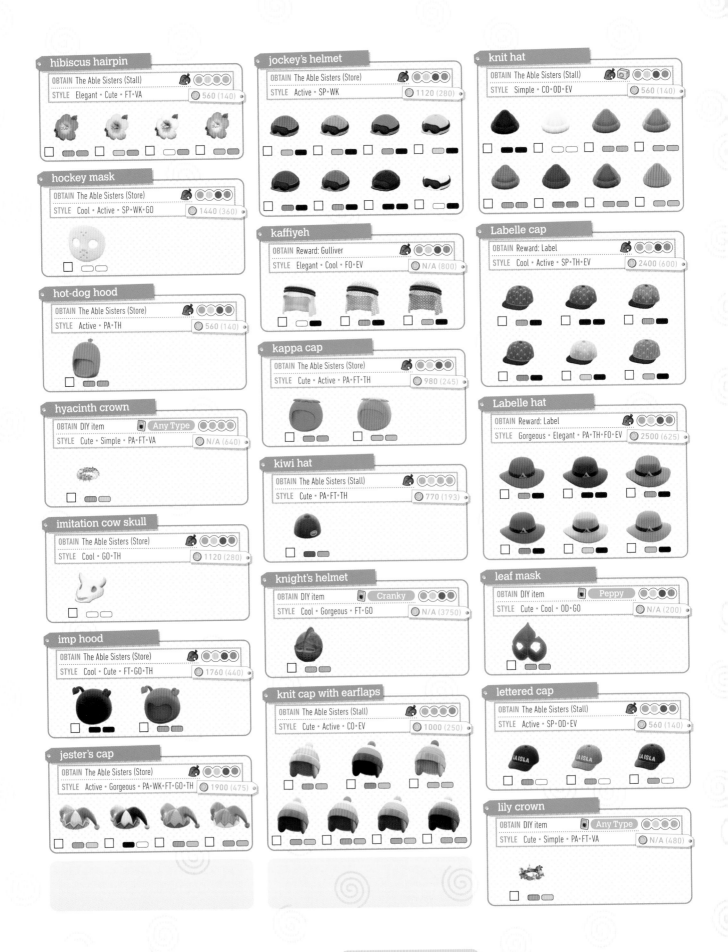

hibiscus hairpin

| OBTAIN | The Able Sisters (Stall) |
| STYLE | Elegant • Cute • FT•VA |

560 (140)

hockey mask

| OBTAIN | The Able Sisters (Store) |
| STYLE | Cool • Active • SP•WK•GO |

1440 (360)

hot-dog hood

| OBTAIN | The Able Sisters (Store) |
| STYLE | Active • PA•TH |

560 (140)

hyacinth crown

| OBTAIN | DIY item — Any Type |
| STYLE | Cute • Simple • PA•FT•VA |

N/A (640)

imitation cow skull

| OBTAIN | The Able Sisters (Store) |
| STYLE | Cool • GO•TH |

1120 (280)

imp hood

| OBTAIN | The Able Sisters (Store) |
| STYLE | Cool • Cute • FT•GO•TH |

1760 (440)

jester's cap

| OBTAIN | The Able Sisters (Store) |
| STYLE | Active • Gorgeous • PA•WK•FT•GO•TH |

1900 (475)

jockey's helmet

| OBTAIN | The Able Sisters (Store) |
| STYLE | Active • SP•WK |

1120 (280)

kaffiyeh

| OBTAIN | Reward: Gulliver |
| STYLE | Elegant • Cool • FO•EV |

N/A (800)

kappa cap

| OBTAIN | The Able Sisters (Store) |
| STYLE | Cute • Active • PA•FT•TH |

980 (245)

kiwi hat

| OBTAIN | The Able Sisters (Stall) |
| STYLE | Cute • PA•FT•TH |

770 (193)

knight's helmet

| OBTAIN | DIY item — Cranky |
| STYLE | Cool • Gorgeous • FT•GO |

N/A (3750)

knit cap with earflaps

| OBTAIN | The Able Sisters (Stall) |
| STYLE | Cute • Active • CO•EV |

1000 (250)

knit hat

| OBTAIN | The Able Sisters (Stall) |
| STYLE | Simple • CO•OD•EV |

560 (140)

Labelle cap

| OBTAIN | Reward: Label |
| STYLE | Cool • Active • SP•TH•EV |

2400 (600)

Labelle hat

| OBTAIN | Reward: Label |
| STYLE | Gorgeous • Elegant • PA•TH•FO•EV |

2500 (625)

leaf mask

| OBTAIN | DIY item — Peppy |
| STYLE | Cute • Cool • OD•GO |

N/A (200)

lettered cap

| OBTAIN | The Able Sisters (Stall) |
| STYLE | Active • SP•OD•EV |

560 (140)

lily crown

| OBTAIN | DIY item — Any Type |
| STYLE | Cute • Simple • PA•FT•VA |

N/A (480)

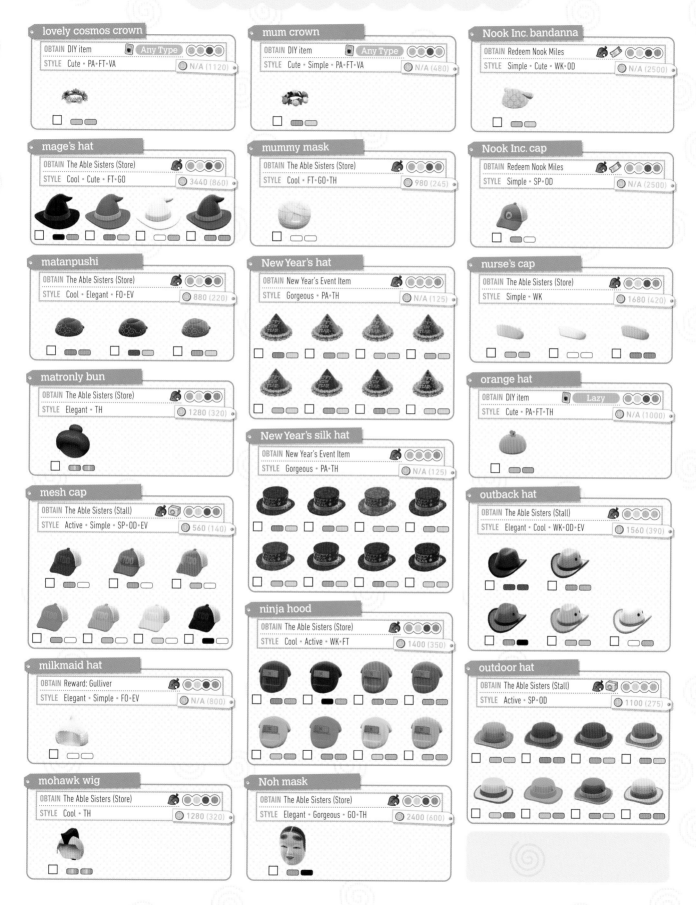

lovely cosmos crown
OBTAIN DIY item — Any Type
STYLE Cute • PA•FT•VA — N/A (1120)

mum crown
OBTAIN DIY item — Any Type
STYLE Cute • Simple • PA•FT•VA — N/A (480)

Nook Inc. bandanna
OBTAIN Redeem Nook Miles
STYLE Simple • Cute • WK•OD — N/A (2500)

mage's hat
OBTAIN The Able Sisters (Store)
STYLE Cool • Cute • FT•GO — 3440 (860)

mummy mask
OBTAIN The Able Sisters (Store)
STYLE Cool • FT•GO•TH — 980 (245)

Nook Inc. cap
OBTAIN Redeem Nook Miles
STYLE Simple • SP•OD — N/A (2500)

matanpushi
OBTAIN The Able Sisters (Store)
STYLE Cool • Elegant • FO•EV — 880 (220)

New Year's hat
OBTAIN New Year's Event Item
STYLE Gorgeous • PA•TH — N/A (125)

nurse's cap
OBTAIN The Able Sisters (Store)
STYLE Simple • WK — 1680 (420)

matronly bun
OBTAIN The Able Sisters (Store)
STYLE Elegant • TH — 1280 (320)

New Year's silk hat
OBTAIN New Year's Event Item
STYLE Gorgeous • PA•TH — N/A (125)

orange hat
OBTAIN DIY item — Lazy
STYLE Cute • PA•FT•TH — N/A (1000)

mesh cap
OBTAIN The Able Sisters (Stall)
STYLE Active • Simple • SP•OD•EV — 560 (140)

outback hat
OBTAIN The Able Sisters (Stall)
STYLE Elegant • Cool • WK•OD•EV — 1560 (390)

ninja hood
OBTAIN The Able Sisters (Store)
STYLE Cool • Active • WK•FT — 1400 (350)

milkmaid hat
OBTAIN Reward: Gulliver
STYLE Elegant • Simple • FO•EV — N/A (800)

outdoor hat
OBTAIN The Able Sisters (Stall)
STYLE Active • SP•OD — 1100 (275)

mohawk wig
OBTAIN The Able Sisters (Store)
STYLE Cool • TH — 1280 (320)

Noh mask
OBTAIN The Able Sisters (Store)
STYLE Elegant • Gorgeous • GO•TH — 2400 (600)

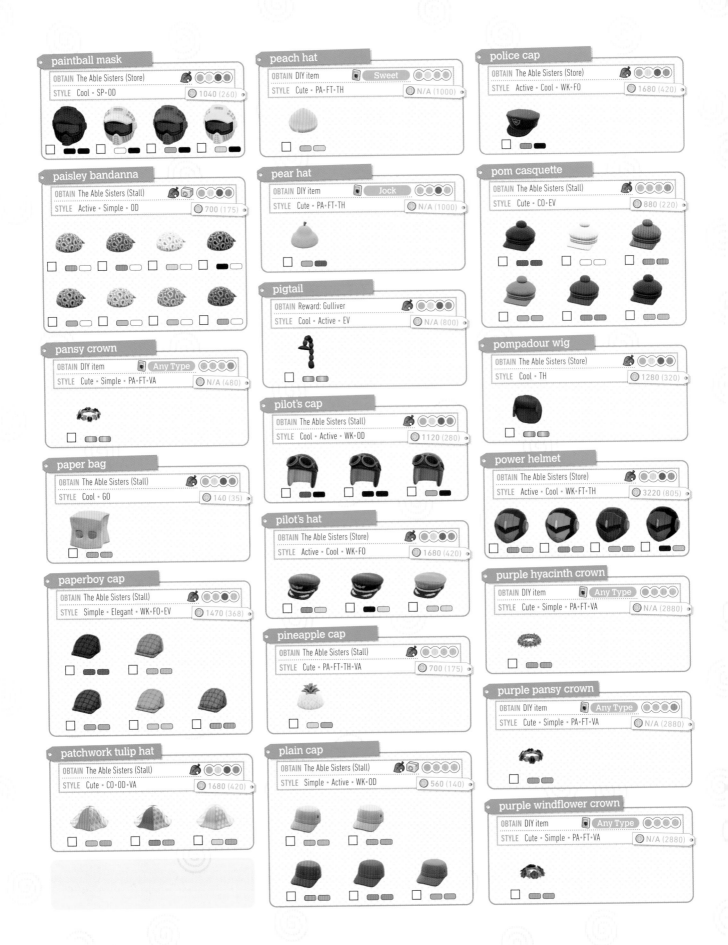

paintball mask
OBTAIN The Able Sisters (Store)
STYLE Cool • SP•OD
1040 (260)

paisley bandanna
OBTAIN The Able Sisters (Stall)
STYLE Active • Simple • OD
700 (175)

pansy crown
OBTAIN DIY item — Any Type
STYLE Cute • Simple • PA•FT•VA
N/A (480)

paper bag
OBTAIN The Able Sisters (Stall)
STYLE Cool • GO
140 (35)

paperboy cap
OBTAIN The Able Sisters (Stall)
STYLE Simple • Elegant • WK•FO•EV
1470 (368)

patchwork tulip hat
OBTAIN The Able Sisters (Stall)
STYLE Cute • CO•OD•VA
1680 (420)

peach hat
OBTAIN DIY item — Sweet
STYLE Cute • PA•FT•TH
N/A (1000)

pear hat
OBTAIN DIY item — Jock
STYLE Cute • PA•FT•TH
N/A (1000)

pigtail
OBTAIN Reward: Gulliver
STYLE Cool • Active • EV
N/A (800)

pilot's cap
OBTAIN The Able Sisters (Stall)
STYLE Cool • Active • WK•OD
1120 (280)

pilot's hat
OBTAIN The Able Sisters (Store)
STYLE Active • Cool • WK•FO
1680 (420)

pineapple cap
OBTAIN The Able Sisters (Stall)
STYLE Cute • PA•FT•TH•VA
700 (175)

plain cap
OBTAIN The Able Sisters (Stall)
STYLE Simple • Active • WK•OD
560 (140)

police cap
OBTAIN The Able Sisters (Store)
STYLE Active • Cool • WK•FO
1680 (420)

pom casquette
OBTAIN The Able Sisters (Stall)
STYLE Cute • CO•EV
880 (220)

pompadour wig
OBTAIN The Able Sisters (Store)
STYLE Cool • TH
1280 (320)

power helmet
OBTAIN The Able Sisters (Store)
STYLE Active • Cool • WK•FT•TH
3220 (805)

purple hyacinth crown
OBTAIN DIY item — Any Type
STYLE Cute • Simple • PA•FT•VA
N/A (2880)

purple pansy crown
OBTAIN DIY item — Any Type
STYLE Cute • Simple • PA•FT•VA
N/A (2880)

purple windflower crown
OBTAIN DIY item — Any Type
STYLE Cute • Simple • PA•FT•VA
N/A (2880)

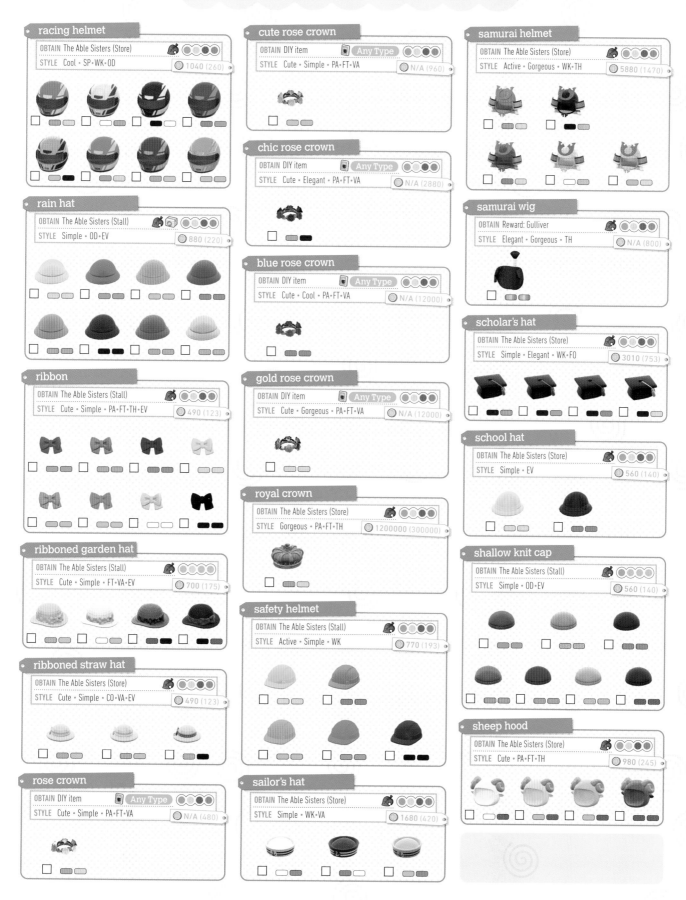

racing helmet
OBTAIN The Able Sisters (Store)
STYLE Cool • SP•WK•OD   1040 (260)

rain hat
OBTAIN The Able Sisters (Stall)
STYLE Simple • OD•EV   880 (220)

ribbon
OBTAIN The Able Sisters (Stall)
STYLE Cute • Simple • PA•FT•TH•EV   490 (123)

ribboned garden hat
OBTAIN The Able Sisters (Stall)
STYLE Cute • Simple • FT•VA•EV   700 (175)

ribboned straw hat
OBTAIN The Able Sisters (Store)
STYLE Cute • Simple • CO•VA•EV   490 (123)

rose crown
OBTAIN DIY item   Any Type
STYLE Cute • Simple • PA•FT•VA   N/A (480)

cute rose crown
OBTAIN DIY item   Any Type
STYLE Cute • Simple • PA•FT•VA   N/A (960)

chic rose crown
OBTAIN DIY item   Any Type
STYLE Cute • Elegant • PA•FT•VA   N/A (2880)

blue rose crown
OBTAIN DIY item   Any Type
STYLE Cute • Cool • PA•FT•VA   N/A (12000)

gold rose crown
OBTAIN DIY item   Any Type
STYLE Cute • Gorgeous • PA•FT•VA   N/A (12000)

royal crown
OBTAIN The Able Sisters (Store)
STYLE Gorgeous • PA•FT•TH   1200000 (300000)

safety helmet
OBTAIN The Able Sisters (Stall)
STYLE Active • Simple • WK   770 (193)

sailor's hat
OBTAIN The Able Sisters (Store)
STYLE Simple • WK•VA   1680 (420)

samurai helmet
OBTAIN The Able Sisters (Store)
STYLE Active • Gorgeous • WK•TH   5880 (1470)

samurai wig
OBTAIN Reward: Gulliver
STYLE Elegant • Gorgeous • TH   N/A (800)

scholar's hat
OBTAIN The Able Sisters (Store)
STYLE Simple • Elegant • WK•FO   3010 (753)

school hat
OBTAIN The Able Sisters (Store)
STYLE Simple • EV   560 (140)

shallow knit cap
OBTAIN The Able Sisters (Stall)
STYLE Simple • OD•EV   560 (140)

sheep hood
OBTAIN The Able Sisters (Store)
STYLE Cute • PA•FT•TH   980 (245)

7

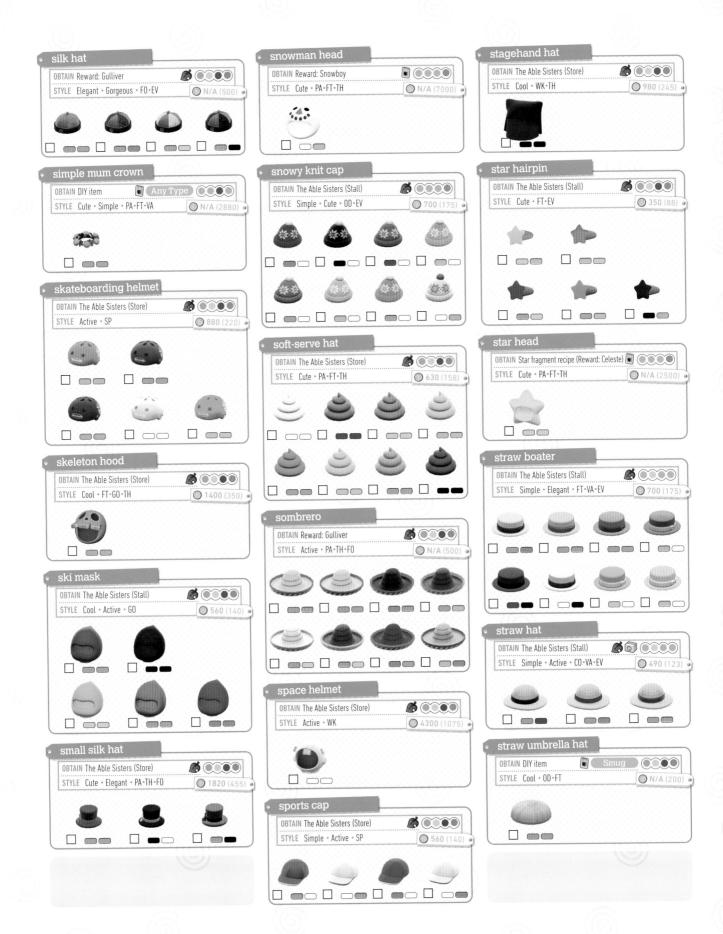

silk hat

OBTAIN Reward: Gulliver
STYLE Elegant • Gorgeous • FO•EV
N/A (500)

simple mum crown

OBTAIN DIY item — Any Type
STYLE Cute • Simple • PA•FT•VA
N/A (2880)

skateboarding helmet

OBTAIN The Able Sisters (Store)
STYLE Active • SP
880 (220)

skeleton hood

OBTAIN The Able Sisters (Store)
STYLE Cool • FT•GO•TH
1400 (350)

ski mask

OBTAIN The Able Sisters (Stall)
STYLE Cool • Active • GO
560 (140)

small silk hat

OBTAIN The Able Sisters (Store)
STYLE Cute • Elegant • PA•TH•FO
1820 (455)

snowman head

OBTAIN Reward: Snowboy
STYLE Cute • PA•FT•TH
N/A (7000)

snowy knit cap

OBTAIN The Able Sisters (Stall)
STYLE Simple • Cute • OD•EV
700 (175)

soft-serve hat

OBTAIN The Able Sisters (Store)
STYLE Cute • PA•FT•TH
630 (158)

sombrero

OBTAIN Reward: Gulliver
STYLE Active • PA•TH•FO
N/A (500)

space helmet

OBTAIN The Able Sisters (Store)
STYLE Active • WK
4300 (1075)

sports cap

OBTAIN The Able Sisters (Store)
STYLE Simple • Active • SP
560 (140)

stagehand hat

OBTAIN The Able Sisters (Store)
STYLE Cool • WK•TH
980 (245)

star hairpin

OBTAIN The Able Sisters (Stall)
STYLE Cute • FT•EV
350 (88)

star head

OBTAIN Star fragment recipe (Reward: Celeste)
STYLE Cute • PA•FT•TH
N/A (2500)

straw boater

OBTAIN The Able Sisters (Stall)
STYLE Simple • Elegant • FT•VA•EV
700 (175)

straw hat

OBTAIN The Able Sisters (Stall)
STYLE Simple • Active • CO•VA•EV
490 (123)

straw umbrella hat

OBTAIN DIY item — Smug
STYLE Cool • OD•FT
N/A (200)

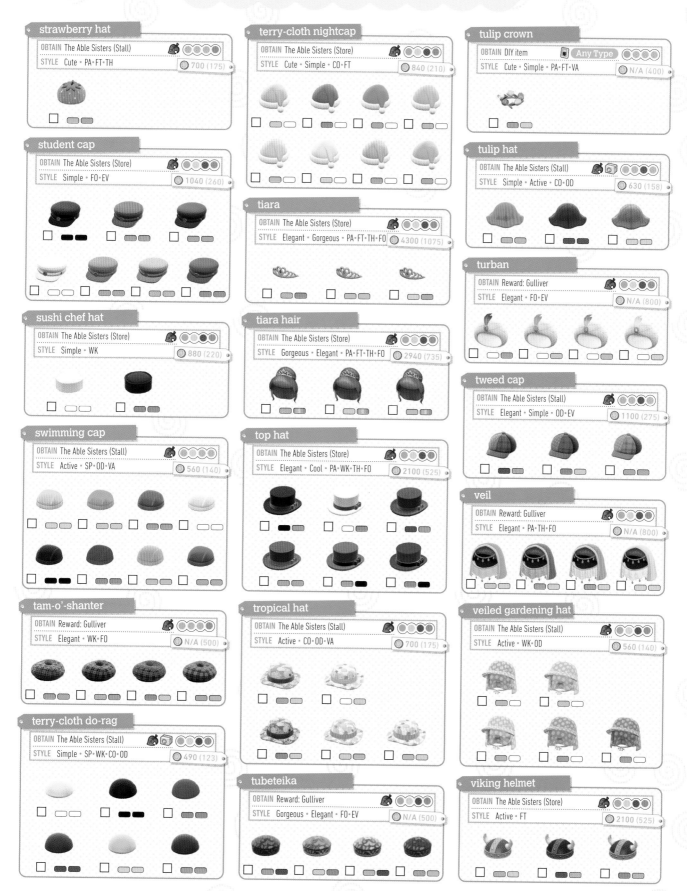

strawberry hat

OBTAIN The Able Sisters (Stall)
STYLE Cute • PA•FT•TH
700 (175)

student cap

OBTAIN The Able Sisters (Store)
STYLE Simple • FO•EV
1040 (260)

sushi chef hat

OBTAIN The Able Sisters (Store)
STYLE Simple • WK
880 (220)

swimming cap

OBTAIN The Able Sisters (Stall)
STYLE Active • SP•OD•VA
560 (140)

tam-o'-shanter

OBTAIN Reward: Gulliver
STYLE Elegant • WK•FO
N/A (500)

terry-cloth do-rag

OBTAIN The Able Sisters (Stall)
STYLE Simple • SP•WK•CO•OD
490 (123)

terry-cloth nightcap

OBTAIN The Able Sisters (Store)
STYLE Cute • Simple • CO•FT
840 (210)

tiara

OBTAIN The Able Sisters (Store)
STYLE Elegant • Gorgeous • PA•FT•TH•FO
4300 (1075)

tiara hair

OBTAIN The Able Sisters (Store)
STYLE Gorgeous • Elegant • PA•FT•TH•FO
2940 (735)

top hat

OBTAIN The Able Sisters (Store)
STYLE Elegant • Cool • PA•WK•TH•FO
2100 (525)

tropical hat

OBTAIN The Able Sisters (Stall)
STYLE Active • CO•OD•VA
700 (175)

tubeteika

OBTAIN Reward: Gulliver
STYLE Gorgeous • Elegant • FO•EV
N/A (500)

tulip crown

OBTAIN DIY item — Any Type
STYLE Cute • Simple • PA•FT•VA
N/A (400)

tulip hat

OBTAIN The Able Sisters (Stall)
STYLE Simple • Active • CO•OD
630 (158)

turban

OBTAIN Reward: Gulliver
STYLE Elegant • FO•EV
N/A (800)

tweed cap

OBTAIN The Able Sisters (Stall)
STYLE Elegant • Simple • OD•EV
1100 (275)

veil

OBTAIN Reward: Gulliver
STYLE Elegant • PA•TH•FO
N/A (800)

veiled gardening hat

OBTAIN The Able Sisters (Stall)
STYLE Active • WK•OD
560 (140)

viking helmet

OBTAIN The Able Sisters (Store)
STYLE Active • FT
2100 (525)

visual-punk wig
OBTAIN	The Able Sisters (Store)
STYLE	Cool · PA·WK·TH

1400 (350)

watermelon hat
OBTAIN	The Able Sisters (Stall)
STYLE	Cute · PA·FT·TH·VA

980 (245)

welding mask
OBTAIN	The Able Sisters (Store)
STYLE	Active · WK·GO

1040 (260)

wide-brim straw hat
OBTAIN	The Able Sisters (Stall)
STYLE	Elegant · PA·VA

1320 (330)

windflower crown
OBTAIN	DIY item — Any Type
STYLE	Cute · Simple · PA·FT·VA

N/A (480)

wizard's cap
OBTAIN	The Able Sisters (Store)
STYLE	Active · Cute · PA·FT

880 (220)

wrestling mask
OBTAIN	The Able Sisters (Store)
STYLE	Active · SP·WK·TH

1120 (280)

zap helmet
OBTAIN	The Able Sisters (Store)
STYLE	Active · WK·FT·TH

1600 (400)

zen hair clip
OBTAIN	The Able Sisters (Store)
STYLE	Cute · Elegant · PA·FO

4300 (1075)

Accessories

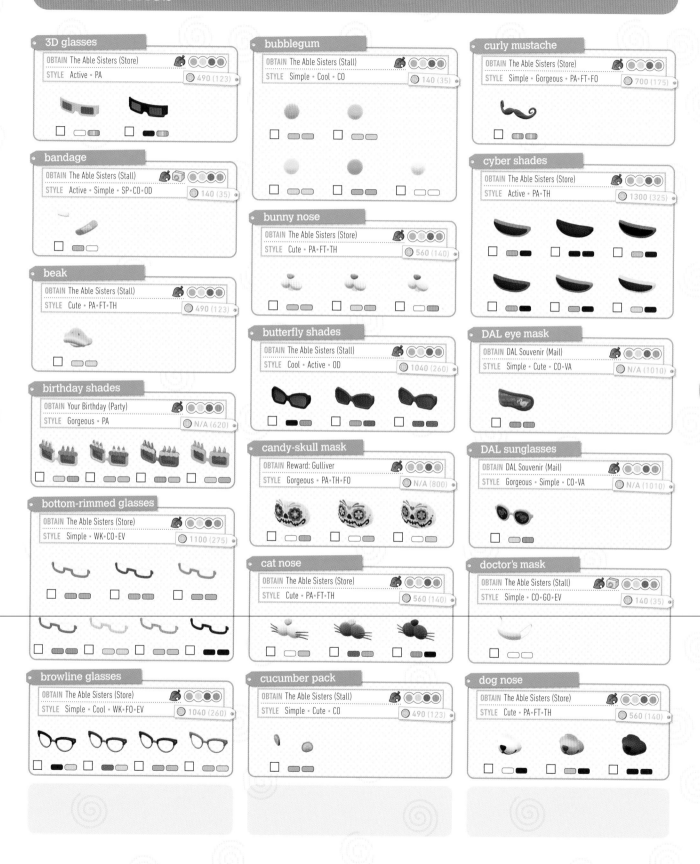

3D glasses
OBTAIN The Able Sisters (Store)
STYLE Active • PA
490 (123)

bandage
OBTAIN The Able Sisters (Stall)
STYLE Active • Simple • SP•CO•OD
140 (35)

beak
OBTAIN The Able Sisters (Stall)
STYLE Cute • PA•FT•TH
490 (123)

birthday shades
OBTAIN Your Birthday (Party)
STYLE Gorgeous • PA
N/A (620)

bottom-rimmed glasses
OBTAIN The Able Sisters (Store)
STYLE Simple • WK•CO•EV
1100 (275)

browline glasses
OBTAIN The Able Sisters (Store)
STYLE Simple • Cool • WK•FO•EV
1040 (260)

bubblegum
OBTAIN The Able Sisters (Stall)
STYLE Simple • Cool • CO
140 (35)

bunny nose
OBTAIN The Able Sisters (Store)
STYLE Cute • PA•FT•TH
560 (140)

butterfly shades
OBTAIN The Able Sisters (Stall)
STYLE Cool • Active • OD
1040 (260)

candy-skull mask
OBTAIN Reward: Gulliver
STYLE Gorgeous • PA•TH•FO
N/A (800)

cat nose
OBTAIN The Able Sisters (Store)
STYLE Cute • PA•FT•TH
560 (140)

cucumber pack
OBTAIN The Able Sisters (Stall)
STYLE Simple • Cute • CO
490 (123)

curly mustache
OBTAIN The Able Sisters (Store)
STYLE Simple • Gorgeous • PA•FT•FO
700 (175)

cyber shades
OBTAIN The Able Sisters (Store)
STYLE Active • PA•TH
1300 (325)

DAL eye mask
OBTAIN DAL Souvenir (Mail)
STYLE Simple • Cute • CO•VA
N/A (1010)

DAL sunglasses
OBTAIN DAL Souvenir (Mail)
STYLE Gorgeous • Simple • CO•VA
N/A (1010)

doctor's mask
OBTAIN The Able Sisters (Stall)
STYLE Simple • CO•GO•EV
140 (35)

dog nose
OBTAIN The Able Sisters (Store)
STYLE Cute • PA•FT•TH
560 (140)

double-bridge glasses
OBTAIN The Able Sisters (Store)
STYLE Elegant • Simple • WK•CO•VA
1100 (275)

drinking-straw glasses
OBTAIN The Able Sisters (Stall)
STYLE Active • Simple • PA
560 (140)

eye mask
OBTAIN The Able Sisters (Stall)
STYLE Simple • CO
560 (140)

eye patch
OBTAIN The Able Sisters (Store)
STYLE Cool • FT•GO
140 (35)

facial mask
OBTAIN The Able Sisters (Store)
STYLE Simple • CO•GO
560 (140)

fake nose
OBTAIN The Able Sisters (Store)
STYLE Cute • PA•FT•TH
490 (123)

flower sunglasses
OBTAIN The Able Sisters (Stall)
STYLE Cute • Active • PA•VA
770 (193)

food mess
OBTAIN The Able Sisters (Stall)
STYLE Simple • Cute • CO
490 (123)

funny glasses
OBTAIN The Able Sisters (Store)
STYLE Cute • PA•FT•TH
1100 (275)

gas mask
OBTAIN The Able Sisters (Store)
STYLE Cool • WK•GO
1100 (275)

glass-bottle glasses
OBTAIN The Able Sisters (Stall)
STYLE Simple • WK•CO
1100 (275)

goatee
OBTAIN The Able Sisters (Store)
STYLE Cool • Simple • CO•TH•EV
980 (245)

goggles
OBTAIN The Able Sisters (Stall)
STYLE Active • SP•OD•VA
560 (140)

handlebar mustache
OBTAIN The Able Sisters (Store)
STYLE Elegant • Gorgeous • FT•TH•FO
1120 (280)

heart shades
OBTAIN The Able Sisters (Stall)
STYLE Cute • Active • PA•VA
1040 (260)

HMD
OBTAIN The Able Sisters (Store)
STYLE Cool • CO
2000 (500)

jester's mask
OBTAIN The Able Sisters (Store)
STYLE Cool • PA•WK•FT•GO•TH
1760 (440)

Labelle sunglasses
OBTAIN Reward: Label
STYLE Gorgeous • Cool • PA•TH•VA•FO•EV
2000 (500)

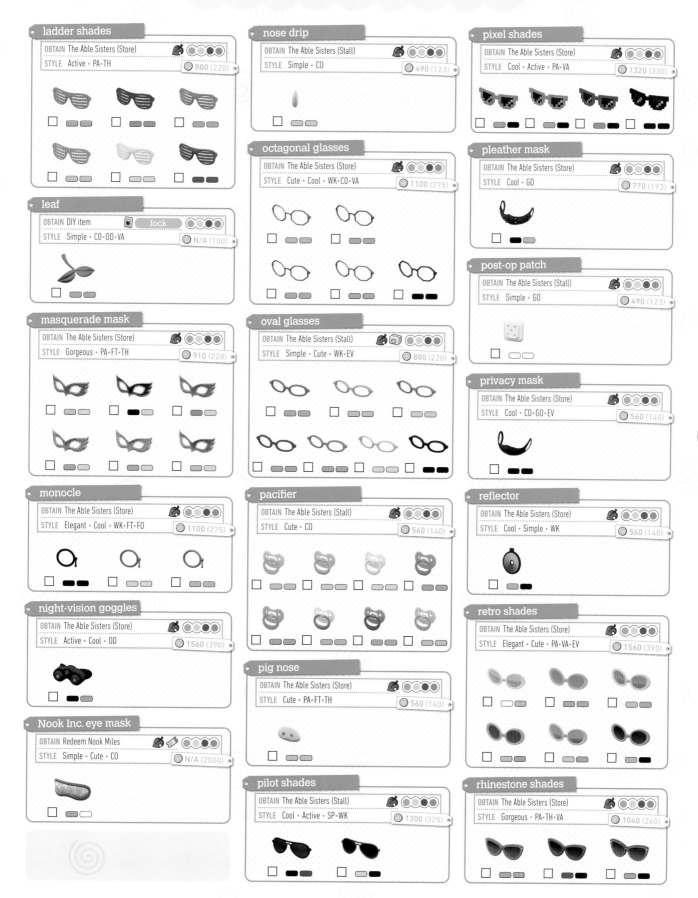

ladder shades
OBTAIN The Able Sisters (Store)
STYLE Active • PA•TH
880 (220)

leaf
OBTAIN DIY item — Jock
STYLE Simple • CO•OD•VA
N/A (100)

masquerade mask
OBTAIN The Able Sisters (Store)
STYLE Gorgeous • PA•FT•TH
910 (228)

monocle
OBTAIN The Able Sisters (Store)
STYLE Elegant • Cool • WK•FT•FO
1100 (275)

night-vision goggles
OBTAIN The Able Sisters (Store)
STYLE Active • Cool • OD
1560 (390)

Nook Inc. eye mask
OBTAIN Redeem Nook Miles
STYLE Simple • Cute • CO
N/A (2000)

nose drip
OBTAIN The Able Sisters (Stall)
STYLE Simple • CO
490 (123)

octagonal glasses
OBTAIN The Able Sisters (Store)
STYLE Cute • Cool • WK•CO•VA
1100 (275)

oval glasses
OBTAIN The Able Sisters (Stall)
STYLE Simple • Cute • WK•EV
880 (220)

pacifier
OBTAIN The Able Sisters (Stall)
STYLE Cute • CO
560 (140)

pig nose
OBTAIN The Able Sisters (Store)
STYLE Cute • PA•FT•TH
560 (140)

pilot shades
OBTAIN The Able Sisters (Stall)
STYLE Cool • Active • SP•WK
1300 (325)

pixel shades
OBTAIN The Able Sisters (Store)
STYLE Cool • Active • PA•VA
1320 (330)

pleather mask
OBTAIN The Able Sisters (Store)
STYLE Cool • GO
770 (193)

post-op patch
OBTAIN The Able Sisters (Stall)
STYLE Simple • GO
490 (123)

privacy mask
OBTAIN The Able Sisters (Store)
STYLE Cool • CO•GO•EV
560 (140)

reflector
OBTAIN The Able Sisters (Store)
STYLE Cool • Simple • WK
560 (140)

retro shades
OBTAIN The Able Sisters (Store)
STYLE Elegant • Cute • PA•VA•EV
1560 (390)

rhinestone shades
OBTAIN The Able Sisters (Store)
STYLE Gorgeous • PA•TH•VA
1040 (260)

7

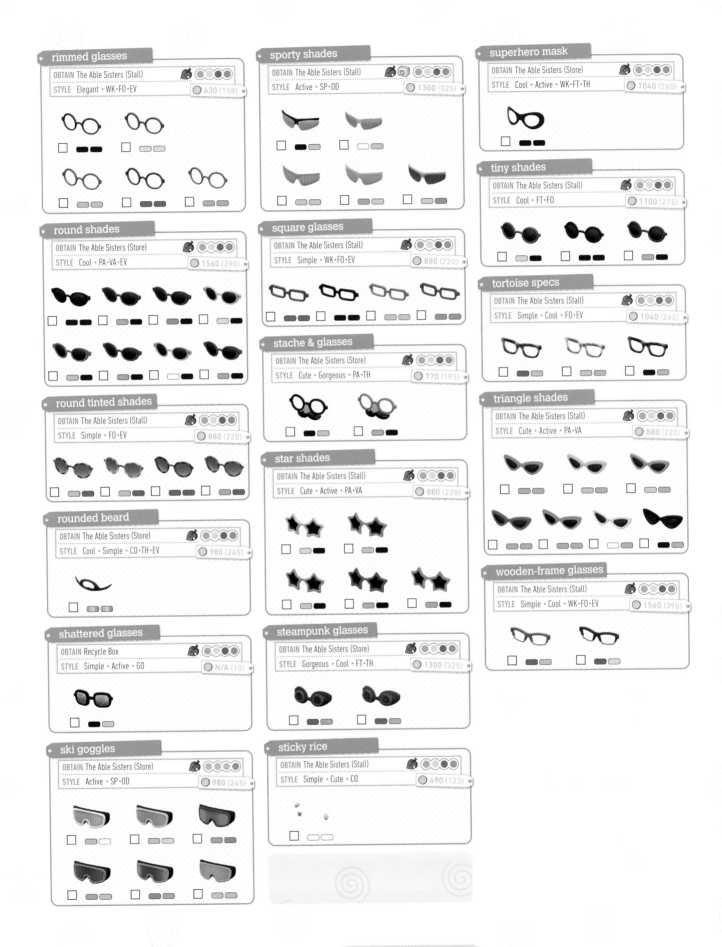

rimmed glasses
OBTAIN The Able Sisters (Stall)
STYLE Elegant • WK•FO•EV
630 (158)

round shades
OBTAIN The Able Sisters (Store)
STYLE Cool • PA•VA•EV
1560 (390)

round tinted shades
OBTAIN The Able Sisters (Stall)
STYLE Simple • FO•EV
880 (220)

rounded beard
OBTAIN The Able Sisters (Store)
STYLE Cool • Simple • CO•TH•EV
980 (245)

shattered glasses
OBTAIN Recycle Box
STYLE Simple • Active • GO
N/A (10)

ski goggles
OBTAIN The Able Sisters (Store)
STYLE Active • SP•OD
980 (245)

sporty shades
OBTAIN The Able Sisters (Stall)
STYLE Active • SP•OD
1300 (325)

square glasses
OBTAIN The Able Sisters (Stall)
STYLE Simple • WK•FO•EV
880 (220)

stache & glasses
OBTAIN The Able Sisters (Store)
STYLE Cute • Gorgeous • PA•TH
770 (193)

star shades
OBTAIN The Able Sisters (Stall)
STYLE Cute • Active • PA•VA
880 (220)

steampunk glasses
OBTAIN The Able Sisters (Store)
STYLE Gorgeous • Cool • FT•TH
1300 (325)

sticky rice
OBTAIN The Able Sisters (Stall)
STYLE Simple • Cute • CO
490 (123)

superhero mask
OBTAIN The Able Sisters (Store)
STYLE Cool • Active • WK•FT•TH
1040 (260)

tiny shades
OBTAIN The Able Sisters (Stall)
STYLE Cool • FT•FO
1100 (275)

tortoise specs
OBTAIN The Able Sisters (Stall)
STYLE Simple • Cool • FO•EV
1040 (260)

triangle shades
OBTAIN The Able Sisters (Stall)
STYLE Cute • Active • PA•VA
880 (220)

wooden-frame glasses
OBTAIN The Able Sisters (Stall)
STYLE Simple • Cool • WK•FO•EV
1560 (390)

Socks

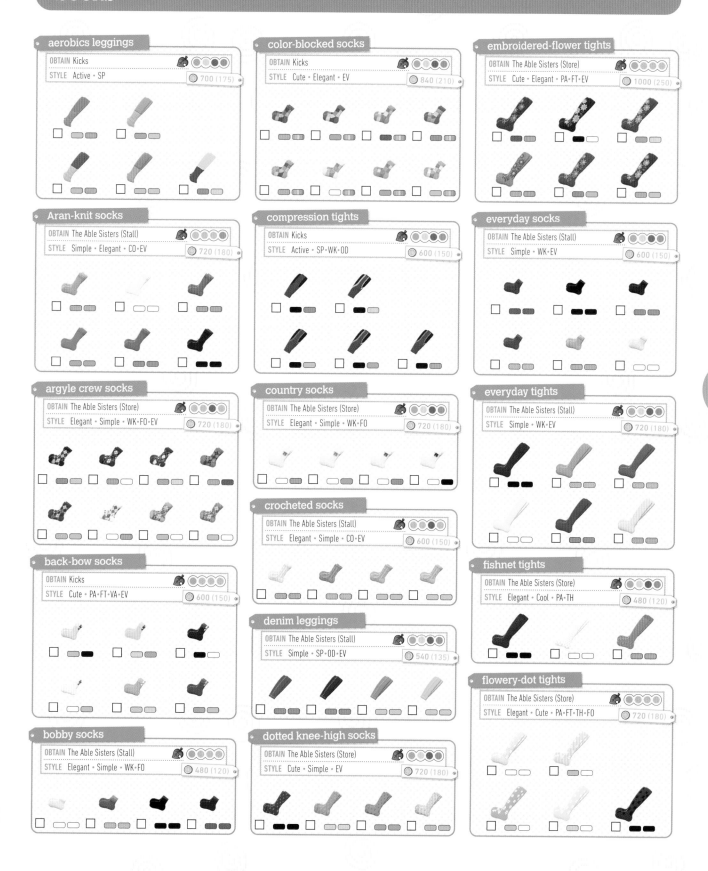

aerobics leggings
OBTAIN Kicks
STYLE Active · SP
700 (175)

color-blocked socks
OBTAIN Kicks
STYLE Cute · Elegant · EV
840 (210)

embroidered-flower tights
OBTAIN The Able Sisters (Store)
STYLE Cute · Elegant · PA·FT·EV
1000 (250)

Aran-knit socks
OBTAIN The Able Sisters (Stall)
STYLE Simple · Elegant · CO·EV
720 (180)

compression tights
OBTAIN Kicks
STYLE Active · SP·WK·OD
600 (150)

everyday socks
OBTAIN The Able Sisters (Stall)
STYLE Simple · WK·EV
600 (150)

argyle crew socks
OBTAIN The Able Sisters (Store)
STYLE Elegant · Simple · WK·FO·EV
720 (180)

country socks
OBTAIN The Able Sisters (Store)
STYLE Elegant · Simple · WK·FO
720 (180)

everyday tights
OBTAIN The Able Sisters (Stall)
STYLE Simple · WK·EV
720 (180)

crocheted socks
OBTAIN The Able Sisters (Stall)
STYLE Elegant · Simple · CO·EV
600 (150)

back-bow socks
OBTAIN Kicks
STYLE Cute · PA·FT·VA·EV
600 (150)

fishnet tights
OBTAIN The Able Sisters (Store)
STYLE Elegant · Cool · PA·TH
480 (120)

denim leggings
OBTAIN The Able Sisters (Stall)
STYLE Simple · SP·OD·EV
540 (135)

flowery-dot tights
OBTAIN The Able Sisters (Store)
STYLE Elegant · Cute · PA·FT·TH·FO
720 (180)

bobby socks
OBTAIN The Able Sisters (Stall)
STYLE Elegant · Simple · WK·FO
480 (120)

dotted knee-high socks
OBTAIN The Able Sisters (Store)
STYLE Cute · Simple · EV
720 (180)

7

frilly knee-high socks

OBTAIN Kicks

STYLE Cute • PA•FT•TH•EV

840 (210)

frilly socks

OBTAIN The Able Sisters (Store)

STYLE Cute • Simple • PA•FT•FO•EV

720 (180)

funny-face socks

OBTAIN Kicks

STYLE Active • Cute • CO•EV

600 (150)

garter socks

OBTAIN Kicks

STYLE Cool • Elegant • PA•TH•FO

980 (245)

geometric-print socks

OBTAIN The Able Sisters (Store)

STYLE Active • Gorgeous • OD

950 (238)

hand-knit socks

OBTAIN The Able Sisters (Stall)

STYLE Simple • Elegant • CO•OD

700 (175)

holey socks

OBTAIN Recycle Box

STYLE Simple • CO•GO

N/A (10)

holey tights

OBTAIN The Able Sisters (Stall)

STYLE Cool • Active • GO•TH•EV

350 (88)

kiddie socks

OBTAIN Kicks

STYLE Cute • Simple • SP•CO•OD•EV

600 (150)

Labelle socks

OBTAIN Reward: Label

STYLE Cool • Simple • SP•TH•FO•EV

940 (235)

Labelle tights

OBTAIN Reward: Label

STYLE Elegant • Cute • PA•TH•FO•EV

1240 (310)

lace socks

OBTAIN The Able Sisters (Store)

STYLE Elegant • Simple • PA•FT•FO•EV

720 (180)

layered socks

OBTAIN The Able Sisters (Store)

STYLE Simple • Active • CO•EV

720 (180)

leg warmers

OBTAIN The Able Sisters (Stall)

STYLE Active • Simple • CO•OD

440 (110)

mixed-tweed socks

OBTAIN The Able Sisters (Stall)

STYLE Simple • Active • CO•EV

800 (200)

neon leggings

OBTAIN The Able Sisters (Stall)
STYLE Active • Simple • PA•OD•TH   540 (135)

neon tights

OBTAIN The Able Sisters (Stall)
STYLE Active • Simple • PA•TH   720 (180)

no-show socks

OBTAIN The Able Sisters (Stall)
STYLE Simple • Active • SP•CO•OD•EV   480 (120)

Nook Inc. socks

OBTAIN Redeem Nook Miles
STYLE Active • Simple • CO•OD•EV   N/A (2000)

nordic socks

OBTAIN The Able Sisters (Stall)
STYLE Elegant • Simple • CO•OD•EV   840 (210)

patterned stockings

OBTAIN The Able Sisters (Store)
STYLE Elegant • Simple • PA•TH•FO•EV   940 (235)

pom-pom socks

OBTAIN The Able Sisters (Store)
STYLE Cute • CO•FT•EV   720 (180)

puckered socks

OBTAIN The Able Sisters (Store)
STYLE Elegant • Simple • EV   600 (150)

running tights

OBTAIN The Able Sisters (Stall)
STYLE Active • SP•WK•OD   550 (138)

semi-opaque socks

OBTAIN The Able Sisters (Store)
STYLE Elegant • Simple • EV   480 (120)

semi-opaque tights

OBTAIN The Able Sisters (Store)
STYLE Elegant • Simple • EV   720 (180)

sequin leggings

OBTAIN Kicks
STYLE Gorgeous • PA•TH   940 (235)

sheer socks

OBTAIN Kicks
STYLE Elegant • Cute • PA•FO•EV   600 (150)

simple knee-high socks

OBTAIN Kicks
STYLE Cute • Simple • EV   600 (150)

simple-accent socks

OBTAIN The Able Sisters (Stall)
STYLE Simple • FO•EV   720 (180)

7

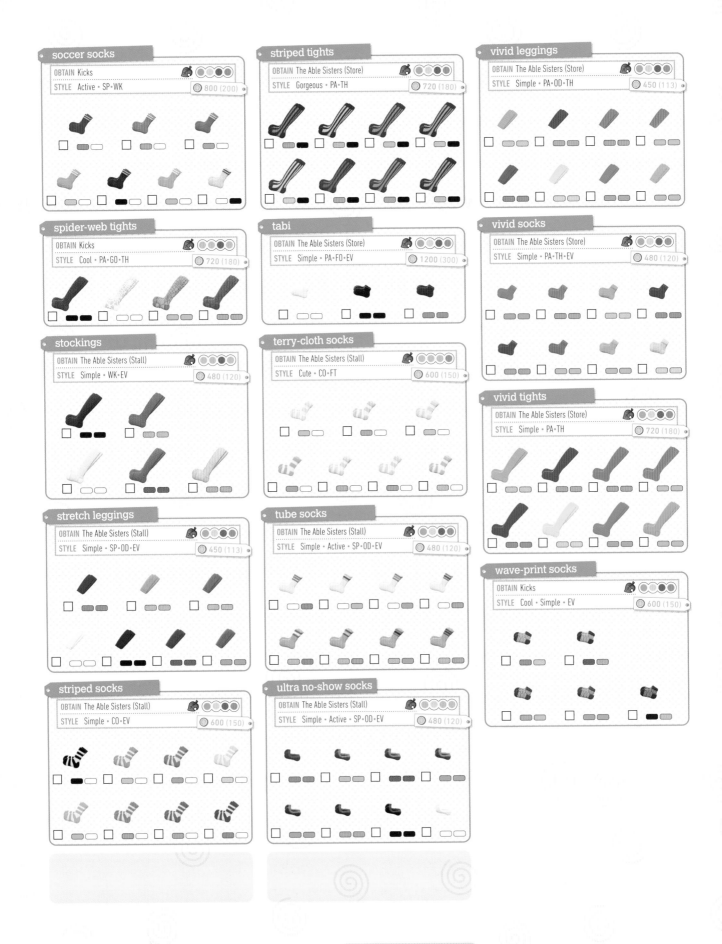

soccer socks
OBTAIN Kicks
STYLE Active • SP•WK
800 (200)

striped tights
OBTAIN The Able Sisters (Store)
STYLE Gorgeous • PA•TH
720 (180)

vivid leggings
OBTAIN The Able Sisters (Store)
STYLE Simple • PA•OD•TH
450 (113)

spider-web tights
OBTAIN Kicks
STYLE Cool • PA•GO•TH
720 (180)

tabi
OBTAIN The Able Sisters (Store)
STYLE Simple • PA•FO•EV
1200 (300)

vivid socks
OBTAIN The Able Sisters (Store)
STYLE Simple • PA•TH•EV
480 (120)

stockings
OBTAIN The Able Sisters (Stall)
STYLE Simple • WK•EV
480 (120)

terry-cloth socks
OBTAIN The Able Sisters (Stall)
STYLE Cute • CO•FT
600 (150)

vivid tights
OBTAIN The Able Sisters (Store)
STYLE Simple • PA•TH
720 (180)

stretch leggings
OBTAIN The Able Sisters (Stall)
STYLE Simple • SP•OD•EV
450 (113)

tube socks
OBTAIN The Able Sisters (Stall)
STYLE Simple • Active • SP•OD•EV
480 (120)

wave-print socks
OBTAIN Kicks
STYLE Cool • Simple • EV
600 (150)

striped socks
OBTAIN The Able Sisters (Stall)
STYLE Simple • CO•EV
600 (150)

ultra no-show socks
OBTAIN The Able Sisters (Stall)
STYLE Simple • Active • SP•OD•EV
480 (120)

Shoes

antique boots
OBTAIN The Able Sisters (Stall)
STYLE Simple • Elegant • FT•EV — 2640 (660)

armor shoes
OBTAIN DIY item — Cranky
STYLE Cool • Gorgeous • FT•GO — N/A (3000)

babouches
OBTAIN Kicks
STYLE Cute • Gorgeous • CO•VA — 560 (140)

ballet slippers
OBTAIN Kicks
STYLE Elegant • Cute • SP•WK•FT•TH — 2200 (550)

basketball shoes
OBTAIN The Able Sisters (Stall)
STYLE Active • SP•WK — 1500 (375)

beaded sandals
OBTAIN The Able Sisters (Stall)
STYLE Gorgeous • CO•VA•EV — 1800 (450)

boots
OBTAIN The Able Sisters (Stall)
STYLE Simple • Active • WK•OD — 560 (140)

business shoes
OBTAIN The Able Sisters (Store)
STYLE Simple • Cool • WK•FO — 1300 (325)

cleats
OBTAIN Kicks
STYLE Active • SP•WK — 1200 (300)

comfy sandals
OBTAIN The Able Sisters (Stall)
STYLE Simple • CO•VA•EV — 1040 (260)

cowboy boots
OBTAIN The Able Sisters (Store)
STYLE Elegant • Active • WK•OD•TH — 2380 (595)

cross-belt sandals
OBTAIN The Able Sisters (Store)
STYLE Elegant • Simple • VA•EV — 1040 (260)

cute sneakers
OBTAIN The Able Sisters (Stall)
STYLE Cute • Active • FT•EV — 1260 (315)

DAL slippers
OBTAIN DAL Souvenir (Mail)
STYLE Simple • CO•VA — N/A (1010)

embroidered shoes
OBTAIN Kicks
STYLE Elegant • Cute • FO•EV — 2100 (525)

faux-fur ankle booties

OBTAIN The Able Sisters (Stall)

STYLE Elegant · Cute · PA·FT·TH·FO·EV 1450 (363)

faux-shearling boots

OBTAIN The Able Sisters (Stall)

STYLE Cute · Active · OD·EV 1600 (400)

faux-suede sneakers

OBTAIN The Able Sisters (Store)

STYLE Simple · Active · SP·OD·EV 1080 (270)

flip-flops

OBTAIN The Able Sisters (Stall)

STYLE Active · SP·CO·OD·VA 350 (88)

flower sandals

OBTAIN The Able Sisters (Store)

STYLE Cute · OD·FT·VA 1200 (300)

ghillie brogues

OBTAIN Kicks

STYLE Gorgeous · Cool · WK·FO 2340 (585)

gladiator sandals

OBTAIN The Able Sisters (Stall)

STYLE Elegant · CO·FT·VA·EV 1800 (450)

gold-armor shoes

OBTAIN DIY item Smug

STYLE Gorgeous · FT·GO N/A (40000)

hi-tech sneakers

OBTAIN The Able Sisters (Store)

STYLE Cool · Active · SP·OD 1260 (315)

high-tops

OBTAIN The Able Sisters (Store)

STYLE Simple · Active · SP·OD·EV 1080 (270)

house slippers

OBTAIN The Able Sisters (Stall)

STYLE Simple · CO·VA 490 (123)

jester's shoes

OBTAIN Kicks

STYLE Active · Gorgeous · PA·WK·FT·GO·TH 1900 (475)

kiddie sneakers

OBTAIN Kicks

STYLE Active · SP·OD·EV 700 (175)

kimono sandals

OBTAIN Kicks

STYLE Simple · Elegant · CO·TH·EV 1600 (400)

kung-fu shoes

OBTAIN Kicks

STYLE Active · Simple · SP·EV 1260 (315)

Labelle pumps

OBTAIN Reward: Label

STYLE Elegant · Gorgeous · PA·WK·TH·FO·EV 3500 (875)

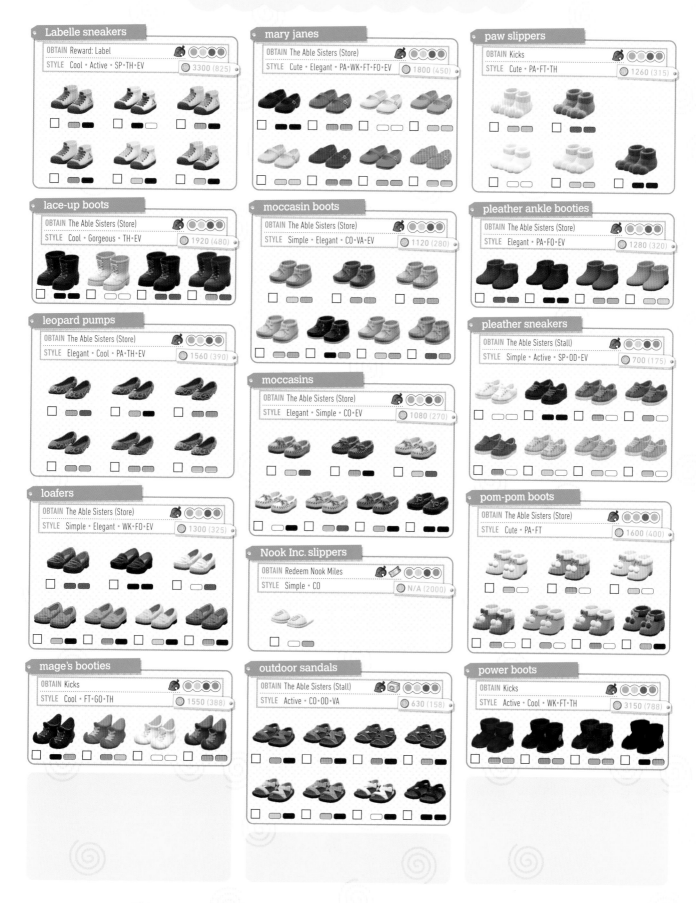

Labelle sneakers

OBTAIN Reward: Label
STYLE Cool • Active • SP•TH•EV
3300 (825)

mary janes

OBTAIN The Able Sisters (Store)
STYLE Cute • Elegant • PA•WK•FT•FO•EV
1800 (450)

paw slippers

OBTAIN Kicks
STYLE Cute • PA•FT•TH
1260 (315)

lace-up boots

OBTAIN The Able Sisters (Store)
STYLE Cool • Gorgeous • TH•EV
1920 (480)

moccasin boots

OBTAIN The Able Sisters (Store)
STYLE Simple • Elegant • CO•VA•EV
1120 (280)

pleather ankle booties

OBTAIN The Able Sisters (Store)
STYLE Elegant • PA•FO•EV
1280 (320)

leopard pumps

OBTAIN The Able Sisters (Store)
STYLE Elegant • Cool • PA•TH•EV
1560 (390)

moccasins

OBTAIN The Able Sisters (Store)
STYLE Elegant • Simple • CO•EV
1080 (270)

pleather sneakers

OBTAIN The Able Sisters (Stall)
STYLE Simple • Active • SP•OD•EV
700 (175)

loafers

OBTAIN The Able Sisters (Store)
STYLE Simple • Elegant • WK•FO•EV
1300 (325)

Nook Inc. slippers

OBTAIN Redeem Nook Miles
STYLE Simple • CO
N/A (2000)

pom-pom boots

OBTAIN The Able Sisters (Store)
STYLE Cute • PA•FT
1600 (400)

mage's booties

OBTAIN Kicks
STYLE Cool • FT•GO•TH
1550 (388)

outdoor sandals

OBTAIN The Able Sisters (Stall)
STYLE Active • CO•OD•VA
630 (158)

power boots

OBTAIN Kicks
STYLE Active • Cool • WK•FT•TH
3150 (788)

7

rain boots
OBTAIN The Able Sisters (Stall)
STYLE Simple · OD·EV
490 (123)

recycled boots
OBTAIN Inspiration: Boot DIY item
STYLE Simple · OD
N/A (40)

restroom slippers
OBTAIN Kicks
STYLE Simple · CO
350 (88)

ribbon sandals
OBTAIN The Able Sisters (Stall)
STYLE Cute · Active · FT·VA·EV
1300 (325)

rubber-toe high tops
OBTAIN The Able Sisters (Store)
STYLE Simple · SP·EV
1260 (315)

rubber-toe sneakers
OBTAIN The Able Sisters (Stall)
STYLE Simple · SP·EV
1080 (270)

samurai greaves
OBTAIN Kicks
STYLE Cool · Gorgeous · WK·TH
4300 (1075)

shiny bow platform shoes
OBTAIN Kicks
STYLE Cute · PA·FT·TH
2400 (600)

shower sandals
OBTAIN The Able Sisters (Stall)
STYLE Active · Simple · CO·OD·VA·EV
350 (88)

ski boots
OBTAIN Kicks
STYLE Active · SP·OD
1800 (450)

slip-on loafers
OBTAIN The Able Sisters (Stall)
STYLE Simple · CO·EV
490 (123)

slip-on sandals
OBTAIN The Able Sisters (Stall)
STYLE Active · Simple · CO·VA
560 (140)

slip-on school shoes
OBTAIN Kicks
STYLE Simple · Active · EV
350 (88)

slippers
OBTAIN Kicks
STYLE Simple · CO·VA·EV
350 (88)

space boots
OBTAIN Kicks
STYLE Active · Simple · WK·FT
4300 (1075)

sporty sandals
OBTAIN The Able Sisters (Store)
STYLE Active · SP·CO·OD·VA
1300 (325)

velour boots
OBTAIN The Able Sisters (Store)
STYLE Elegant · PA·EV
1920 (480)

water shoes
OBTAIN The Able Sisters (Stall)
STYLE Active · SP·OD·VA
900 (225)

steel-toed boots
OBTAIN The Able Sisters (Stall)
STYLE Cool · Elegant · WK·EV
2640 (660)

vinyl round-toed pumps
OBTAIN The Able Sisters (Store)
STYLE Simple · Elegant · PA·WK·FT·TH·FO·EV
1500 (375)

wingtip shoes
OBTAIN The Able Sisters (Store)
STYLE Elegant · Cool · PA·WK·TH·FO·EV
900 (225)

strappy heels
OBTAIN The Able Sisters (Store)
STYLE Gorgeous · PA·TH·FO
1560 (390)

visual-punk boots
OBTAIN Kicks
STYLE Cool · PA·WK·TH
2200 (550)

winklepickers
OBTAIN The Able Sisters (Store)
STYLE Cool · PA·WK·TH
910 (228)

traditional flower shoes
OBTAIN Kicks
STYLE Elegant · Cute · PA·FO
1800 (450)

walking shoes
OBTAIN The Able Sisters (Stall)
STYLE Simple · Active · SP·OD·EV
560 (140)

wooden clogs
OBTAIN Kicks
STYLE Elegant · Cute · EV
1300 (325)

water sandals
OBTAIN The Able Sisters (Stall)
STYLE Cute · Active · CO·OD·VA
1040 (260)

work boots
OBTAIN The Able Sisters (Stall)
STYLE Cool · WK·OD·TH
1920 (480)

trekking shoes
OBTAIN The Able Sisters (Stall)
STYLE Active · SP·OD
1500 (375)

7

wrestling shoes

OBTAIN Kicks
STYLE Active • SP•WK   1080 (270)

zap boots

OBTAIN Kicks
STYLE Active • WK•FT•TH   2640 (660)

zori

OBTAIN The Able Sisters (Store)
STYLE Elegant • Simple • PA•FO•EV   4300 (1075)

Bags

acorn pochette

OBTAIN Seasonal recipe: Acorn/Pinecone
STYLE Cute • FT   N/A (2400)

cherry-blossom pochette

OBTAIN Seasonal recipe: Cherry blossom
STYLE Cute • FT•VA   N/A (2400)

dry bag

OBTAIN Kicks
STYLE Active • SP•OD   1040 (260)

basket pack

OBTAIN Seasonal recipe: Bamboo
STYLE Simple • WK•OD   N/A (2400)

cloth shoulder bag

OBTAIN Kicks
STYLE Simple • EV   1400 (350)

evening bag

OBTAIN Kicks
STYLE Cute • Elegant • PA•FO   1250 (313)

bug cage

OBTAIN Bug-Off
STYLE Active • OD•VA   N/A (123)

crossbody bag

OBTAIN Kicks
STYLE Active • Simple • SP•OD•EV   700 (175)

extra-large backpack

OBTAIN Kicks
STYLE Active • SP•OD   2100 (525)

butterfly backpack

OBTAIN Bug-Off
STYLE Cute • FT•TH•EV   N/A (210)

crossbody boston bag

OBTAIN Kicks
STYLE Simple • Active • SP•OD•EV   1680 (420)

faux-fur bag

OBTAIN Kicks
STYLE Cute • Gorgeous • PA•FO   1400 (350)

canvas backpack

OBTAIN Kicks
STYLE Simple • EV   1300 (325)

DAL backpack

OBTAIN DAL Souvenir (Mail)
STYLE Cool • Active • OD•VA   N/A (1010)

fish pochette

OBTAIN Fishing Tourney
STYLE Cute • VA•EV   N/A (210)

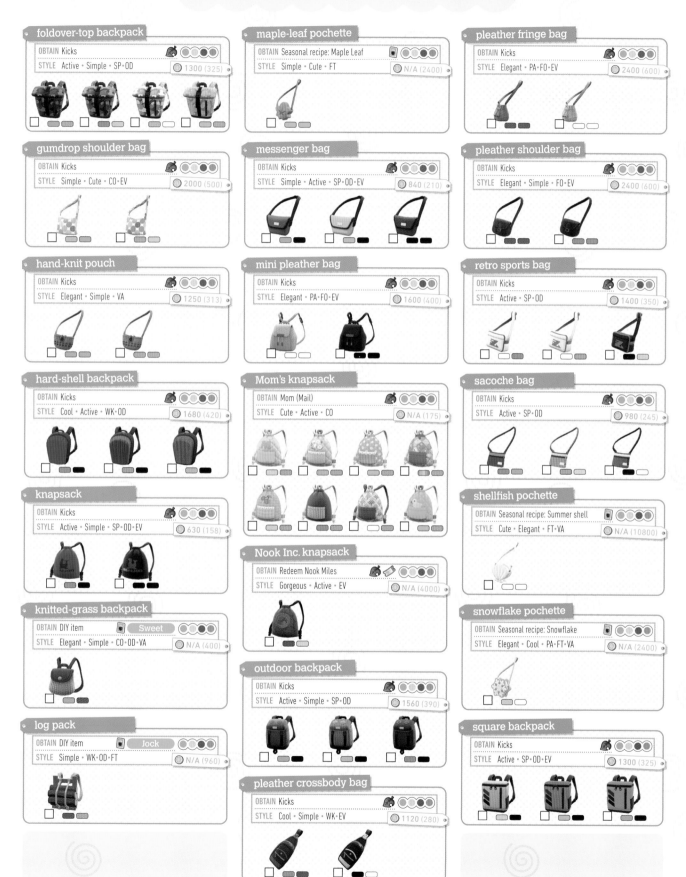

foldover-top backpack

OBTAIN Kicks

STYLE Active • Simple • SP•OD

1300 (325)

gumdrop shoulder bag

OBTAIN Kicks

STYLE Simple • Cute • CO•EV

2000 (500)

hand-knit pouch

OBTAIN Kicks

STYLE Elegant • Simple • VA

1250 (313)

hard-shell backpack

OBTAIN Kicks

STYLE Cool • Active • WK•OD

1680 (420)

knapsack

OBTAIN Kicks

STYLE Active • Simple • SP•OD•EV

630 (158)

knitted-grass backpack

OBTAIN DIY item — Sweet

STYLE Elegant • Simple • CO•OD•VA

N/A (400)

log pack

OBTAIN DIY item — Jock

STYLE Simple • WK•OD•FT

N/A (960)

maple-leaf pochette

OBTAIN Seasonal recipe: Maple Leaf

STYLE Simple • Cute • FT

N/A (2400)

messenger bag

OBTAIN Kicks

STYLE Simple • Active • SP•OD•EV

840 (210)

mini pleather bag

OBTAIN Kicks

STYLE Elegant • PA•FO•EV

1600 (400)

Mom's knapsack

OBTAIN Mom (Mail)

STYLE Cute • Active • CO

N/A (175)

Nook Inc. knapsack

OBTAIN Redeem Nook Miles

STYLE Gorgeous • Active • EV

N/A (4000)

outdoor backpack

OBTAIN Kicks

STYLE Active • Simple • SP•OD

1560 (390)

pleather crossbody bag

OBTAIN Kicks

STYLE Cool • Simple • WK•EV

1120 (280)

pleather fringe bag

OBTAIN Kicks

STYLE Elegant • PA•FO•EV

2400 (600)

pleather shoulder bag

OBTAIN Kicks

STYLE Elegant • Simple • FO•EV

2400 (600)

retro sports bag

OBTAIN Kicks

STYLE Active • SP•OD

1400 (350)

sacoche bag

OBTAIN Kicks

STYLE Active • SP•OD

980 (245)

shellfish pochette

OBTAIN Seasonal recipe: Summer shell

STYLE Cute • Elegant • FT•VA

N/A (10800)

snowflake pochette

OBTAIN Seasonal recipe: Snowflake

STYLE Elegant • Cool • PA•FT•VA

N/A (2400)

square backpack

OBTAIN Kicks

STYLE Active • SP•OD•EV

1300 (325)

7

star pochette
OBTAIN Star fragment recipe (Reward: Celeste)
STYLE Cute • Gorgeous • PA•FT•VA   N/A (3000)

straw pochette
OBTAIN Kicks
STYLE Simple • Elegant • CO•VA   980 (245)

studded backpack
OBTAIN Kicks
STYLE Cool • Cute • GO•EV   1560 (390)

tackle bag
OBTAIN Fishing Tourney
STYLE Active • SP•WK•OD   N/A (175)

tool bag
OBTAIN Kicks
STYLE Active • WK•OD   910 (228)

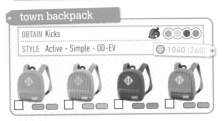

town backpack
OBTAIN Kicks
STYLE Active • Simple • OD•EV   1040 (260)

travel pouch
OBTAIN Kicks
STYLE Active • Simple • OD•EV   840 (210)

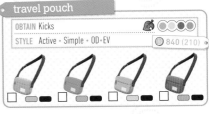

traveler's backpack
OBTAIN Kicks
STYLE Simple • Active • WK•OD•FT   2940 (735)

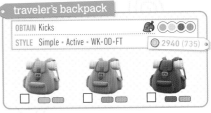

Umbrellas

apple umbrella
OBTAIN DIY item   Big sister
STYLE None   N/A (1400)

bat umbrella
OBTAIN Shop (Cabinet)
STYLE None   840 (210)

beach umbrella
OBTAIN Shop (Cabinet)
STYLE None   770 (193)

bear umbrella
OBTAIN Shop (Expanded Cabinet)
STYLE None   1570 (393)

black chic umbrella
OBTAIN Shop (Expanded Cabinet)
STYLE None   1620 (405)

black lace umbrella
OBTAIN Shop (Cabinet)
STYLE None   750 (188)

blue dot parasol
OBTAIN Shop (Cabinet)
STYLE None   750 (188)

blue shiny-bows parasol
OBTAIN Shop (Expanded Cabinet)
STYLE None   1620 (405)

blue umbrella
OBTAIN Shop (Cabinet)
STYLE None   770 (193)

busted umbrella
OBTAIN Shop (Expanded Cabinet)
STYLE None   1570 (393)

camo umbrella
OBTAIN Shop (Cabinet)
STYLE None   650 (163)

candy umbrella
OBTAIN Shop (Cabinet)
STYLE None   770 (193)

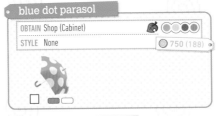
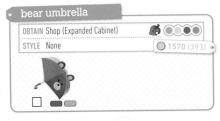

cherry umbrella

OBTAIN DIY item — Peppy

STYLE None — N/A (1400)

cherry-blossom umbrella

OBTAIN Seasonal recipe: Cherry blossom

STYLE None — N/A (2800)

DAL umbrella

OBTAIN DAL Souvenir (Mail)

STYLE None — N/A (1010)

eggy parasol

OBTAIN Shop (Cabinet)

STYLE None — 750 (188)

exquisite parasol

OBTAIN Shop (Expanded Cabinet)

STYLE None — 1670 (418)

fairy-tale umbrella

OBTAIN Shop (Cabinet)

STYLE None — 820 (205)

fish umbrella

OBTAIN Fishing Tourney

STYLE None — N/A (80)

frog umbrella

OBTAIN Shop (Expanded Cabinet)

STYLE None — 1570 (393)

gelato umbrella

OBTAIN Shop (Cabinet)

STYLE None — 750 (188)

ghost umbrella

OBTAIN Shop (Expanded Cabinet)

STYLE None — 1670 (418)

grape umbrella

OBTAIN Shop (Expanded Cabinet)

STYLE None — 1550 (388)

green chic umbrella

OBTAIN Shop (Expanded Cabinet)

STYLE None — 1620 (405)

green umbrella

OBTAIN Shop (Cabinet)

STYLE None — 770 (193)

hydrangea umbrella

OBTAIN Shop (Cabinet)

STYLE None — 750 (188)

kabuki umbrella

OBTAIN Shop (Expanded Cabinet)

STYLE None — 1670 (418)

kiwi umbrella

OBTAIN Shop (Expanded Cabinet)

STYLE None — 1550 (388)

lacy parasol

OBTAIN Shop (Expanded Cabinet)

STYLE None — 1550 (388)

ladybug umbrella

OBTAIN Bug-Off

STYLE None — N/A (80)

leaf umbrella

OBTAIN DIY item — Big sister

STYLE None — N/A (300)

lemon umbrella

OBTAIN Shop (Cabinet)

STYLE None — 770 (193)

logo umbrella

OBTAIN Shop (Cabinet)

STYLE None — 650 (163)

7

maple-leaf umbrella
OBTAIN Seasonal recipe: Maple Leaf
STYLE None
N/A (2800)

melon umbrella
OBTAIN Shop (Cabinet)
STYLE None
770 (193)

mini-flower-print umbrella
OBTAIN Shop (Cabinet)
STYLE None
750 (188)

mint umbrella
OBTAIN Shop (Cabinet)
STYLE None
770 (193)

mush umbrella
OBTAIN Seasonal recipe: Mushroom
STYLE None
N/A (1200)

Nook Inc. umbrella
OBTAIN Redeem Nook Miles
STYLE None
N/A (3500)

orange umbrella
OBTAIN DIY item   Lazy
STYLE None
N/A (1400)

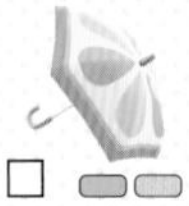

panda umbrella
OBTAIN Shop (Expanded Cabinet)
STYLE None
1570 (393)

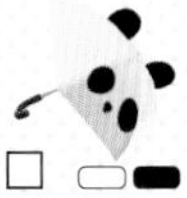

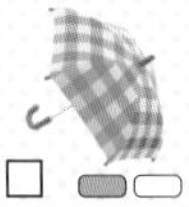

paper parasol
OBTAIN Shop (Cabinet)
STYLE None
870 (218)

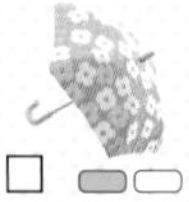

patterned vinyl umbrella
OBTAIN Shop (Cabinet)
STYLE None
750 (188)

peach umbrella
OBTAIN DIY item   Sweet
STYLE None
N/A (1400)

pear umbrella
OBTAIN DIY item   Jock
STYLE None
N/A (1400)

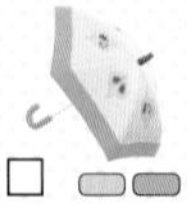

petal parasol
OBTAIN Shop (Expanded Cabinet)
STYLE None
1590 (398)

picnic umbrella
OBTAIN Shop (Cabinet)
STYLE None
770 (193)

pineapple umbrella
OBTAIN Shop (Expanded Cabinet)
STYLE None
1550 (388)

pink shiny-bows parasol
OBTAIN Shop (Expanded Cabinet)
STYLE None
1620 (405)

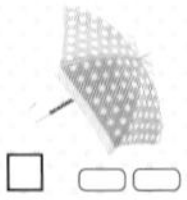

pink umbrella
OBTAIN Shop (Cabinet)
STYLE None
770 (193)

purple chic umbrella
OBTAIN Shop (Expanded Cabinet)
STYLE None
1620 (405)

purple shiny-bows parasol
OBTAIN Shop (Expanded Cabinet)
STYLE None
1620 (405)

rainbow umbrella
OBTAIN Shop (Cabinet)
STYLE None
840 (210)

raindrop umbrella
OBTAIN Shop (Cabinet)
STYLE None
750 (188)

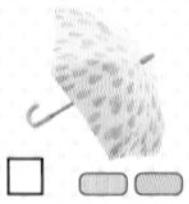

red chic umbrella

OBTAIN	Shop (Expanded Cabinet)
STYLE	None

1620 (405)

red umbrella

OBTAIN	Shop (Cabinet)
STYLE	None

770 (193)

snowflake umbrella

OBTAIN	Shop (Expanded Cabinet)
STYLE	None

1550 (388)

spider umbrella

OBTAIN	Shop (Cabinet)
STYLE	None

840 (210)

strawberry umbrella

OBTAIN	Shop (Expanded Cabinet)
STYLE	None

1550 (388)

striped umbrella

OBTAIN	Shop (Cabinet)
STYLE	None

750 (188)

sunny parasol

OBTAIN	Shop (Cabinet)
STYLE	None

750 (188)

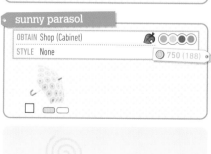

tartan-check umbrella

OBTAIN	Shop (Cabinet)
STYLE	None

750 (188)

Toad parasol

OBTAIN	Shop (Cabinet)
STYLE	None

750 (188)

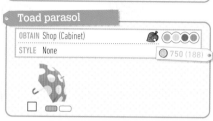

two-tone umbrella

OBTAIN	Shop (Cabinet)
STYLE	None

770 (193)

vinyl umbrella

OBTAIN	Shop (Cabinet)
STYLE	None

770 (193)

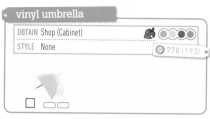

watermelon umbrella

OBTAIN	Shop (Expanded Cabinet)
STYLE	None

1550 (388)

white shiny-bows parasol

OBTAIN	Shop (Expanded Cabinet)
STYLE	None

1620 (405)

7

⑤ Reactions

We covered Reactions in the Meet the Locals chapter on P.77, but here we'll show you exactly what each one looks like. You can acquire 44 Reactions in total—far more than will fit in the Reactions Ring. This means you'll need to register the ones you want easy access to by pressing the Ⓧ Button while the Ring is active and assigning a Reaction to each slot. For convenience, we'll show how to acquire each one again here; remember that to get the ones in red you'll need to be best friends with a resident of a particular personality type!

Access the Reactions Ring by pressing the ZR Button at any time, indoors or outdoors.

Personality	Initial Reaction	Further Reactions Learned				
SWEET		Pleased	Fearful	Sadness	Glee	Daydreaming
PEPPY		Happiness	Aggravation	Sleepy	Curiosity	Mischief
SNOOTY	Joy	Intense	Thought	Sighing	Amazed	Love
BIG SISTER	Greetings	Laughter	Cold Chill	Apologetic	Disagreement	Confident
LAZY	Delight	Bashfulness	Sorrow	Mistaken	Shyness	Pride
JOCK	❗ Surprise!	Encouraging	Sneezing	Distress	Shocked!	Flourish
CRANKY		Agreement	Worry	Sheepish-ness	Bewilderment	Inspiration
SMUG		Smirking	Resignation	Heartbreak	Dozing	Showmanship

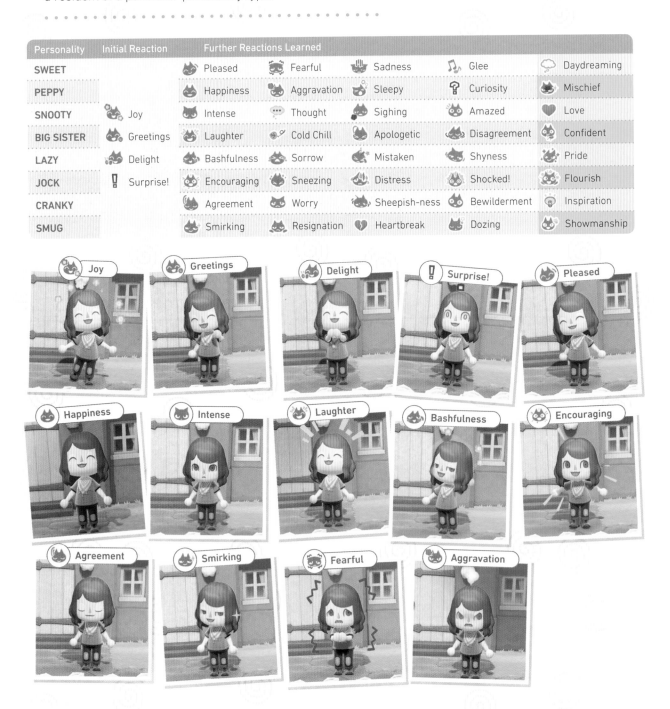

Island Customization

This section of the chapter deals with all of the ways that you can make the island your own. From the way your house looks and the furniture inside it, to the placement and look of bridges, inclines and outdoor decorations, it's all covered here. Put your decorator's scarf on and dive in!

1 Exterior Customization

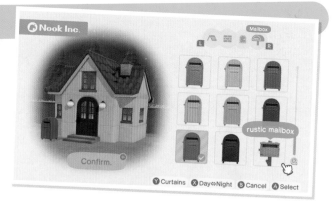

Whether it's inside organizing your furniture or outside landscaping yourself a garden, your house is one of the places where you'll spend much of your time on the island. It's nice to have a home that feels unique, on the inside and out! Thankfully, Tom Nook can provide you with many interesting options that will allow you to make your home truly stand out amongst the rest of the houses on the island. Once you've upgraded your tent into a house, you'll be able to change the exterior of your home, for a single fee of 10,000 Bells. This includes your siding color, roof style, mailbox type, and later on your door. There are many different types of options to choose from, including a large variety of colors. In the customization preview screen, you can see what your home would look like before you commit to any changes. You may also see what it would look like during the day or at night, or with the curtains closed. Try to get that perfect look for your home!

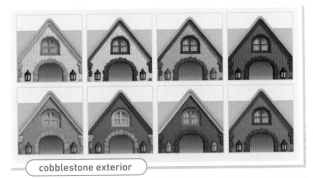

cobblestone exterior

Siding

Siding comes in many colors and styles. Some give a modern feeling, while many of them are more classical and even old-fashioned. Not all styles come in all colors, so you may need to choosing which is more important to you.

pink stucco exterior

chalet exterior

common exterior

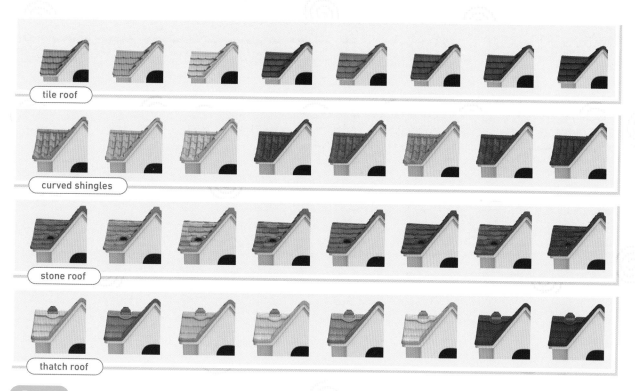

tile roof

curved shingles

stone roof

thatch roof

Roofs

There are 32 roof types to choose from, and most of them are simple color variations. Some have different styles of tiling and some have their own tiny chimneys on top that can even puff out some smoke for an old-fashioned look.

Doors

Once you've upgraded Resident Services to a building and Tom Nook opens the construction consultation counter, changing the way your house looks will become free. The option to change your door is also added at this point, and the selection of possible doors is huge.

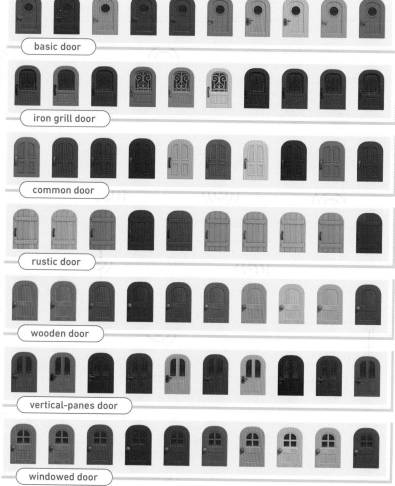

basic door

iron grill door

common door

rustic door

wooden door

vertical-panes door

windowed door

7

fancy door

zen door

iron door

imperial door

metal-accent door

latticework door

simple door

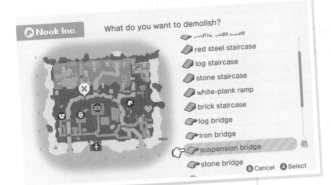

Once you have a lot of bridges and inclines
you'll need to use the map to plan your island.

Moving Your Mailbox

In this version of Animal Crossing, you can put your Mailbox into your inventory by pressing Ⓨ, and then move it wherever you would like. Don't like the default position of your Mailbox? Change it up and collect your mail wherever is most convenient. Of course, having it by your house means it's easy to remember where it is...

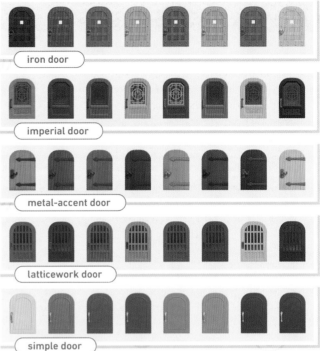

Mailboxes

Mailboxes come in a variety of styles and colors. Unlike siding, almost all style are available in every color, so your choice should be easier—only the rustic mailbox stands alone as the exception to this.

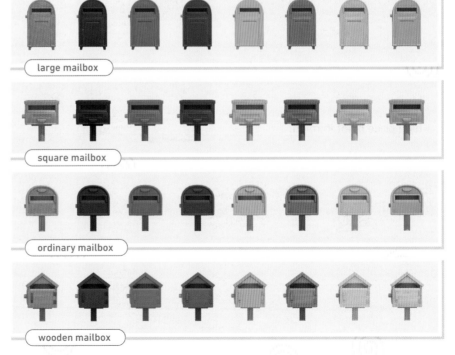

large mailbox

square mailbox

ordinary mailbox

wooden mailbox

rustic mailbox

② Fencing

Fencing recipes cost 1000 Nook Miles each at the Nook Stop. Fences come in all different shapes, materials and sizes. By opening your pockets and selecting the option to build fences, you can place fencing down one at a time on the tiles in front of you by pressing Ⓐ. These can make decorative boundaries in front of your house, intricate mazes, and accentuate important sections of your island.

brick fence

vertical-board fence

bamboo lattice fence

corral fence

country fence

rope fence

imperial fence

straw fence

iron fence

spiky fence

iron-and-stone fence

zen fence

stone fence

barbed-wire fence

simple wooden fence

lattice fence

③ Bridges and Inclines

Aside from practical utility, bridges and inclines can really tie your island together. Inclines come in a wide variety of types, but all take up a 2x3 block of land. Bridges come in many different shapes and materials and can cover up to a 4x3 block of water. If you change your mind about the look or location, bridges can always be demolished and rebuilt, but keep their high price point in mind.

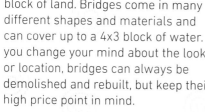
stone bridge
168,000

suspension bridge
129,800

wooden bridge
168,000

brick bridge
198,000

zen bridge
228,000

log bridge
98,000

red zen bridge
228,000

iron bridge
228,000

stone staircase
168,000

red steel staircase
228,000

white-plank ramp
128,000

natural ramp
98,000

log staircase
168,000

blue-plank ramp
128,000

blue steel staircase
228,000

brick staircase
198,000

Whether you've gotten it from Timmy and Tommy, had it fall from a tree or acquired it from a neighbor, there's a lot of furniture to enjoy! This furniture can be used to decorate the inside of your home and also be placed outdoors. It's perfect for every decorator out there, or just anyone who enjoys some comfortable furniture to surround themselves with.

Acquiring Furniture

While you start off with a cozy camping cot, a lamp and a radio, you may find yourself wanting a bit more utility and luxury in your island home. As you continue your stay on your island, you'll find different ways to fill your floors, customize your living space and even deck out your walls. Let's find out how to turn your house into the most fun place to visit!

Furniture can be acquired in numerous ways. You'll purchase most of it from Nook's Cranny once it opens. The Nook Stop also offers furniture through Nook Shopping or the Nook Mileage Program. However, shaking trees, giving gifts, shooting down balloons, or just talking to your island's residents can give you a green, leafy surprise in your pockets.

Decide how you want to theme your rooms and then go after the appropriate items.

Placing Furniture Outdoors

Furniture can be placed indoors or outdoors. and always takes up tiles on your island. Think of each tile as a 1x1 space that you can split your island into, like a grid. Furniture takes up specific spaces on this grid, but can also be placed in increments between tiles as well. In the picture below, the two smallest items take up a 1x1 tile, while the green vending machine take up 1x2, and the bigger grey vending machine takes up 1x3.

These sizes are all listed in the furniture list starting on P.353. You can use them to help see what will fit where.

The easiest way to place down furniture is to face where you want to place it, go into your pockets, select the piece of furniture with the Ⓐ Button, and then select the option to place it down. Its placement can then be adjusted by exiting your pockets menu, facing the piece of furniture and holding Ⓐ. You can then move using the Left Stick to make small adjustments to its placement by pushing or pulling the piece of furniture, moving a piece one half-tile at a time. Furniture that is placed on top of another piece of furniture can't be dragged, so position yourself accordingly.

Placing Furniture Indoors

Placing furniture inside is much simpler. Once inside your house, pressing Right on the Directional Pad allows you to view furniture you've placed in your storage and move pieces back into your pockets. Pressing Down on the Directional Pad lets you to shift into decoration mode. This mode offers a myriad of features to help you decorate your house perfectly. Once in decoration mode you can press ✛ to toggle between floor and wall placement modes.

In decoration mode, you can still grab any piece of furniture from your storage by pressing Right on the Directional Pad or access your pockets with the Ⓧ Button, but now you have the option to see a guide when placing things. You'll also gain more control of the camera. This allows you to look at your room from different angles using the Right Stick, which can be really useful if you want to be sure your house looks good from all sides.

You can drag and drop furniture by hovering the cursor over it and then pressing and holding Ⓐ. Let go again to plop it down right where you want it. Pressing Ⓐ quickly will allow you to rotate the item. Pressing Ⓨ while hovering over an item will place the piece back into your storage. Holding the Ⓡ Button will allow you to select multiple pieces of furniture and move them all at once.

Wall furniture really makes a difference in your house! When decorating your house, try different positions to see where exactly on the wall these pieces look best.

Think of each square in this room as a tile. Objects can be shifted in half-tile increments. Some smaller objects can be placed either on top of or underneath other objects. In these case, as with the lamp above, press Ⓛ to choose.

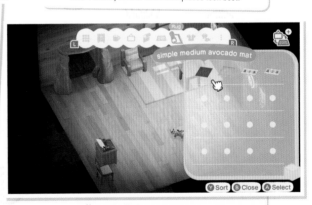

You can walk under some furniture, which makes pieces like this one great for doorways.

Special Furniture

Not all furniture acts the same. Some pieces will animate, either automatically, like the fan on the wall here, or when interacted with. Certain pieces can be interacted with, like chairs or electronics, and can sometimes have unusual functions. When placing these types of item, be mindful that your character will need to be able to get close to them in order to interact with them.

Don't like the look of certain furniture? No problem. Once you've completed Tom Nook's Customization Workshop, you can take your furniture to a DIY Bench and change how it looks. Select the "Customize Something" option and then select your furniture item to get started.

Only items with the small box and paintbrush icon can be customized at a workbench.

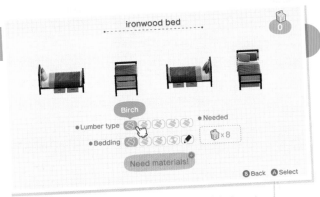

Some furniture can have only the body or fabric changed, while others allow both This bed, for example, can have the lumber (body) or the bedding (fabric) changed.

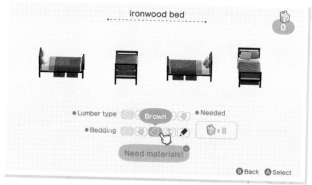

On items that let you change the body and fabric, you can change both at once for the same cost in customization kits.

Most items of furniture that can be customized will let you change their body style and fabric pattern. Each will have its own options and some will have more possibilities than others. Some will let you use a pattern or a custom design for the fabric, and some will even let you add a design of your own to the body. When a custom design can be used, it can be selected by using the pencil icon at the end of the list.

Customization Kits

Customization kits can be bought from Nook's Cranny after you've completed Tom Nook's customization workshop. These kits can be used to change the colors of a piece of furniture. You can even decorate some furniture using your custom designs. The amount of kits you'll need varies depending on the item, but you want to customize multiple items then we suggest buying them in bulk—Nook's Cranny can sell you five at a time.

It's always worth checking which customization options an item has, since you'll often be surprised at what's possible. The body customization can mean vastly different things depending on the item you're working with; while it changes the type of wood used on the frame of the bed in the examples above, it may change the basic structure of an item in other cases, especially smaller objects such as picture frames and lamps.

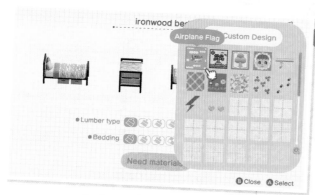

Not all custom designs will work equally well on fabric, but if you experiment you can come up with some that fit perfectly!

Sable's Patterns

For a wider selection of options, you'll need to befriend Sable, who will give you the option to use her patterns after you've spoken to her for 11 days in a row. She'll then give you a new pattern set each day. Eventually, you'll get 10 different categories of pattern to liven up any piece of furniture that allows fabric patterns. When patterns are available to use, they'll show up in the fabric list as a small checked cloth icon after the paintbrush icons. This feature allows you to let your own creativity shine and quickly build an entire set of furniture that is incredibly unique.

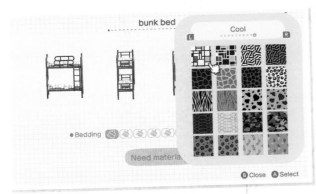

Once you've got access to Sable's full selection it's easy to customize bigger pieces of furniture to create matching sets.

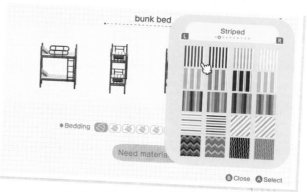

Often the most basic patterns will lead to the most striking results, so don't rule them out.

⑥ Furniture List

An empty home is a sad home. Luckily, on your island you can build, buy and discover tons of furniture. Furniture comes in various sizes and types: some can act as a chair, some can go on top of other pieces of furniture, and others hold practical uses like changing your appearance. You can even use furniture to decorate your walls. Here, we'll go over every piece of furniture you can obtain and provide everything you'd want to know about them. Note that entries with orange name backgrounds are those that can be customized, and will have additional customization information.

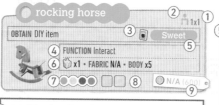

① **SIZE** This value tells you how many tiles the item takes up. Furniture will usually be placed on the floor, but if it can go on a wall, you'll see a W.

② **ARRANGEMENT** This icon will be highlighted differently depending on how the item can be placed. If the lower part is orange, then it can be used as a table or platform. If the upper part is orange, then it can be placed on/under a table/platform. Some items be be used in both ways, in which case both parts will be orange.

③ **OBTAIN** This tells you how to acquire the item. Depending on how you receive the item, at least one of the following icons will be shown:

 This means you'll receive it as an item.

 This means you'll receive it as a DIY recipe and must then craft it.

 This means you'll receive it via mail.

 This means you'll need to acquire it by redeeming Nook Miles at the Nook Stop.

④ **FUNCTION** This tells you if the item has any specific or unusual function, or if it can be interacted with using the Ⓐ Button.

⑤ **PERSONALITY** This appears when the item can be obtained as a DIY recipe by talking to a resident, and means that the resident must be of the listed personality type. If there's a number in parenthesis before this label, it means you must have that many DIY recipes unlocked in order for a resident to give you this one.

⑥ **CUSTOMIZATION** This box tells you how many customization kits are required, and how many body and fabric parts can be changed, and in what way.

⑦ **SEASON** These circles are highlighted to indicate the seasons the item is available in. If all are highlighted then it's available all year round.
   - ● Spring   ○ Summer
   - ● Autumn   ● Winter

⑧ **COLORS** These are the item's system colors, which can affect resident conversations and HHA grading (if you place the item in your house as furniture).

⑨ **PRICE** This shows you how much the item costs in Bells. The number in parenthesis tells you how much it will sell for to Timmy and Tommy.

Furniture

acoustic guitar
1x1
OBTAIN DIY item — Smug
FUNCTION Musical Instrument
x5 • FABRIC N/A • BODY x7
N/A (3210)

air circulator
1x1
OBTAIN Shop (Small Item)
FUNCTION Animates (Fades out)
not customizable; purchasable in 5 colors
1100 (275)

alto saxophone
1x1
OBTAIN Shop (Large Item)
FUNCTION Musical Instrument
not customizable
3400 (850)

anatomical model
1x1
OBTAIN Shop (Small Item)
FUNCTION None
not customizable
3500 (875)

anchor statue
1x1
OBTAIN Fishing Tourney
FUNCTION None
x2 • FABRIC N/A • BODY x6 Custom
N/A (1400)

angled signpost
1x1
OBTAIN DIY item — (100) Lazy
FUNCTION None
x1 • FABRIC N/A • BODY x8
N/A (600)

antique bed
2x2
OBTAIN Shop (Luxury Item)
FUNCTION Bed: Normal
not customizable; purchasable in 3 colors
28,000 (7000)

antique bureau
1x1
OBTAIN Shop (Luxury Item)
FUNCTION Interact (On/Off)
not customizable; purchasable in 3 colors
20,000 (5000)

antique chair
1x1
OBTAIN Shop (Luxury Item)
FUNCTION Chair: SP
not customizable; purchasable in 3 colors
10,000 (2500)

antique clock
1x1
OBTAIN Shop (Luxury Item)
FUNCTION Clock: Pendulum
not customizable; purchasable in 3 colors
44,000 (11,000)

antique console table
2x1
OBTAIN Shop (Luxury Item)
FUNCTION None
not customizable; purchasable in 3 colors
17,000 (4250)

antique mini table
1x1
OBTAIN Shop (Luxury Item)
FUNCTION None
not customizable; purchasable in tt
6700 (1675)

antique table
2x2
OBTAIN Shop (Luxury Item)
FUNCTION None
not customizable; purchasable in 3 colors
25,000 (6250)

antique vanity
2x1
OBTAIN Shop (Luxury Item)
FUNCTION Mirror
not customizable; purchasable in 3 colors
31,000 (7750)

antique wardrobe
2x1
OBTAIN Shop (Luxury Item)
FUNCTION Dresser
not customizable; purchasable in 3 colors
37,000 (9250)

apple chair
1x1
OBTAIN DIY item — (100) Big sister
FUNCTION Chair: SP
x4 • FABRIC N/A • BODY x2
N/A (2480)

Aquarius urn
1x1
OBTAIN Zodiac recipe (Reward: Celeste)
FUNCTION None
not customizable
N/A (22,125)

arcade combat game
1x1
OBTAIN Shop (Luxury Item)
FUNCTION Animates (Loop)
not customizable
64,000 (16,000)

arcade fighting game
1x1
OBTAIN Shop (Luxury Item)
FUNCTION Animates (Loop)
not customizable
64,000 (16,000)

arcade mahjong game
1x1
OBTAIN Shop (Luxury Item)
FUNCTION Animates (Loop)
not customizable
64,000 (16,000)

arcade seat
1x1
OBTAIN Shop (Large Item)
FUNCTION Chair: Stool
not customizable; purchasable in 3 colors
1300 (325)

Aries rocking chair
1x1
OBTAIN Zodiac recipe (Reward: Celeste)
FUNCTION Interact (Start/Stop)
not customizable
N/A (12,125)

artisanal bug cage
2x1
OBTAIN Bug-Off
FUNCTION Closet: Flip
not customizable
N/A (450)

asteroid
1x1
OBTAIN Star fragment recipe (Reward: Celeste)
FUNCTION Animates (Loop)
not customizable
N/A (4000)

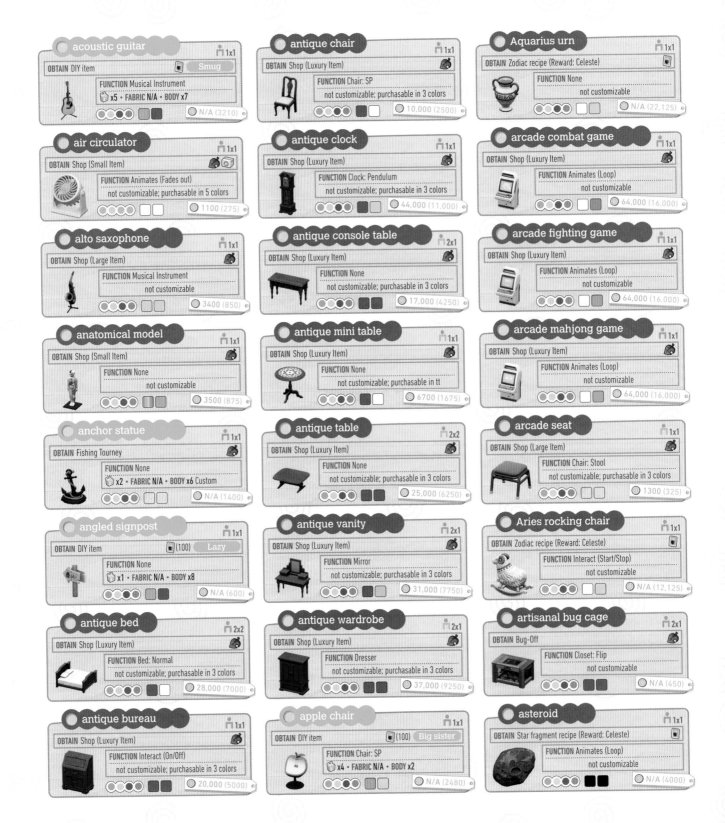

astronaut suit
1x1
OBTAIN Star fragment recipe (Reward: Celeste)
FUNCTION None
not customizable
N/A (6250)

automatic washer
1x1
OBTAIN Shop (Large Item)
FUNCTION Interact (On/Off)
not customizable; purchasable in 6 colors
4500 (1125)

baby chair
1x1
OBTAIN Shop (Small Item)
FUNCTION Chair: Normal
x1 • FABRIC x4 Generic/Custom • BODY x7
1200 (300)

bamboo basket
1x1
OBTAIN DIY item (50) Snooty
FUNCTION None
x2 • FABRIC N/A • BODY x3
N/A (1120)

bamboo bench
2x1
OBTAIN DIY item (50) Sweet
FUNCTION Chair: Stool
x2 • FABRIC N/A • BODY x3
N/A (1280)

bamboo doll
1x1
OBTAIN Seasonal recipe: Bamboo
FUNCTION Interact (Loop On/Off)
not customizable
N/A (2400)

bamboo floor lamp
1x1
OBTAIN DIY item (50) Sweet
FUNCTION Interact (On/Off)
x2 • FABRIC N/A • BODY x3
N/A (1280)

bamboo noodle slide
3x1
OBTAIN Seasonal recipe: Bamboo
FUNCTION Interact (Start/Stop)
not customizable
N/A (3160)

bamboo partition
2x0.5
OBTAIN DIY item (50) Cranky
FUNCTION None
x3 • FABRIC N/A • BODY x3
N/A (2020)

bamboo shelf
2x1
OBTAIN DIY item (50) Snooty
FUNCTION None
x4 • FABRIC N/A • BODY x3
N/A (2400)

bamboo speaker
1x1
OBTAIN DIY item (50) Snooty
FUNCTION Audio
x2 • FABRIC N/A • BODY x3
N/A (1230)

bamboo stool
1x1
OBTAIN DIY item (50) Snooty
FUNCTION Chair: Stool
x2 • FABRIC N/A • BODY x3
N/A (800)

bamboo stopblock
1x0.5
OBTAIN DIY item (50) Jock
FUNCTION None
x1 • FABRIC N/A • BODY x3
N/A (480)

barbecue
1x1
OBTAIN Shop (All)
FUNCTION Animates (Loop)
not customizable; purchasable in 5 colors
2500 (625)

barbell
2x1
OBTAIN DIY item Jock
FUNCTION None
x7 • FABRIC N/A • BODY x4
N/A (7500)

barrel
1x1
OBTAIN Tom Nook ("Three New Plots" quest) Cranky
FUNCTION None
not customizable
N/A (2100)

basic teacher's desk
2x1
OBTAIN Shop (Large Item)
FUNCTION None
not customizable; purchasable in 3 colors
2000 (500)

basketball hoop
2x2
OBTAIN Shop (Large Item)
FUNCTION None
not customizable; purchasable in 3 colors
11,000 (2750)

bathroom sink
1x1
OBTAIN Shop (Small Item)
FUNCTION Interact (On/Off)
not customizable; purchasable in 3 colors
3300 (825)

beach chair
2x1
OBTAIN Shop (Small Item)
FUNCTION Bed: Normal
not customizable; purchasable in 6 colors
920 (230)

beach towel
2x1
OBTAIN Shop (All)
FUNCTION Bed: Normal
x1 • FABRIC x6 Generic/Custom • BODY x7
380 (95)

beekeeper's hive
1x1
OBTAIN DIY item Jock
FUNCTION None
x4 • FABRIC N/A • BODY x5
N/A (2400)

bidet
1x1
OBTAIN Shop (Large Item)
FUNCTION Chair: SP
not customizable
1800 (450)

big festive tree
2x2
OBTAIN Seasonal recipe: Ornament
FUNCTION Interact (Loop On/Off)
x5 • FABRIC N/A • BODY x6
N/A (3200)

billiard table
2x1
OBTAIN Shop (Luxury Item)
FUNCTION None
not customizable; purchasable in 3 colors
77,000 (19,250)

birdbath
1x1
OBTAIN Tom Nook ("Three New Plots" quest) Snooty
FUNCTION None
x2 • FABRIC N/A • BODY x4
N/A (900)

birdcage
1x1
OBTAIN DIY item Big sister
FUNCTION Animates (Loop)
x2 • FABRIC N/A • BODY x5
N/A (960)

7

birdhouse
🏠 1x1
OBTAIN Reward: Give Tom Nook 2nd creature 🐾 Peppy
FUNCTION None
🍎 x2 • FABRIC N/A • BODY x6
⚫⚪⚪⚪ ⬛⬜ N/A (840)

brick oven
🏠 1.5x1.5
OBTAIN Wildest Dreams DIY: Shop (Cabinet)
FUNCTION Interact (On/Off)
🍎 x6 • FABRIC N/A • BODY x4
⚫⚪⚪⚪ ⬛⬜ N/A (3820)

candy machine
🏠 1x1
OBTAIN Shop (Small Item)
FUNCTION Interact (Start/Stop)
not customizable; purchasable in 4 colors
⚫⚪⚪⚪ ⬜⬜ 2800 (700)

birthday sign
🏠 2x1
OBTAIN Your Birthday
FUNCTION None
🍎 x1 • FABRIC N/A • BODY x6 Custom
⚫⚪⚪⚪ ⬜⬜ N/A (300)

brick well
🏠 1.5x1.5
OBTAIN Redeem Nook Miles (2000 miles)
FUNCTION None
🍎 x4 • FABRIC N/A • BODY x3
⚫⚪⚪⚪ ⬛⬜ N/A (2800)

Capricorn ornament
🏠 2x1
OBTAIN Zodiac recipe (Reward: Celeste)
FUNCTION Dresser
not customizable
⚫⚪⚪⚪ ⬜⬜ N/A (22,650)

birthday table
🏠 2x2
OBTAIN Your Birthday
FUNCTION Interact (Loop On/Off)
🍎 x1 • FABRIC N/A • BODY x6 Custom
⚫⚪⚪⚪ ⬜⬜ N/A (300)

bunk bed
🏠 2x1
OBTAIN Shop (Small Item)
FUNCTION Bed: Normal
🍎 x2 • FABRIC x4 Generic/Custom • BODY x7
⚫⚪⚪⚪ 5000 (1250)

cardboard bed
🏠 2x1
OBTAIN DIY item 🔲 Lazy
FUNCTION Bed: Normal
🍎 x1 • FABRIC N/A • BODY x2
⚫⚪⚪⚪ N/A (240)

blossom-viewing lantern
🏠 1x1
OBTAIN Seasonal recipe: Cherry blossom
FUNCTION Interact (On/Off)
🍎 x4 • FABRIC N/A • BODY x2
⚫⚪⚪⚪ ⬛⬜ N/A (2880)

butter churn
🏠 1x1
OBTAIN DIY item 🔲 Snooty
FUNCTION None
🍎 x3 • FABRIC N/A • BODY x2
⚫⚪⚪⚪ ⬜⬜ N/A (1980)

cardboard chair
🏠 1x1
OBTAIN DIY item 🔲 Lazy
FUNCTION Chair: SP
🍎 x1 • FABRIC N/A • BODY x2
⚫⚪⚪⚪ N/A (60)

blue corner
🏠 2x2
OBTAIN Shop (Large Item)
FUNCTION Bed: Normal
🍎 x3 • FABRIC x4 Custom • BODY N/A
⚫⚪⚪⚪ ⬜⬜ 6100 (1525)

cacao tree
🏠 1x1
OBTAIN Shop (Large Item)
FUNCTION None
not customizable
⚫⚪⚪⚪ ⬛⬛ 2300 (575)

cardboard sofa
🏠 2x1
OBTAIN DIY item 🔲 Peppy
FUNCTION Chair: Normal
🍎 x1 • FABRIC N/A • BODY x2
⚫⚪⚪⚪ N/A (120)

bonfire
🏠 2x2
OBTAIN Reward: Give Tom Nook 2nd creature 🐾 Cranky
FUNCTION Interact (Loop On/Off)
not customizable
⚫⚪⚪⚪ ⬛⬜ N/A (1230)

campfire
🏠 1x1
OBTAIN Reward: DIY Workshop
FUNCTION Interact (Loop On/Off)
not customizable
⚫⚪⚪⚪ ⬛⬜ N/A (30)

cardboard table
🏠 2x2
OBTAIN DIY item 🔲 Peppy
FUNCTION None
🍎 x1 • FABRIC N/A • BODY x2
⚫⚪⚪⚪ ⬜⬜ N/A (240)

bonsai shelf
🏠 2x1
OBTAIN DIY item 🔲 (100) Cranky
FUNCTION None
not customizable
⚫⚪⚪⚪ ⬛⬜ N/A (8460)

campfire cookware
🏠 1x1
OBTAIN Shop (All)
FUNCTION Interact (Loop On/Off)
not customizable
⚫⚪⚪⚪ ⬛⬛ 900 (225)

cat tower
🏠 1x1
OBTAIN Shop (Small Item)
FUNCTION Interact (Stop)
not customizable; purchasable in 6 colors
⚫⚪⚪⚪ 3000 (750)

box corner sofa
🏠 1x1
OBTAIN Shop (Large Item)
FUNCTION Chair: Front/Left
not customizable; purchasable in 8 colors
⚫⚪⚪⚪ ⬜⬛ 2700 (675)

camping cot
🏠 2x1
OBTAIN Default Furniture
FUNCTION Bed: Normal
not customizable; purchasable in 8 colors
⚫⚪⚪⚪ ⬜⬜ 1800 (450)

cello
🏠 1x1
OBTAIN Shop (Luxury Item)
FUNCTION Musical Instrument
not customizable; purchasable in 3 colors
⚫⚪⚪⚪ ⬜⬜ 130,000 (32,500)

box sofa
🏠 1x1
OBTAIN Shop (Large Item)
FUNCTION Chair: SP
not customizable; purchasable in 8 colors
⚫⚪⚪⚪ ⬜⬛ 2700 (675)

Cancer table
🏠 1x1
OBTAIN Zodiac recipe (Reward: Celeste)
FUNCTION None
not customizable
⚫⚪⚪⚪ ⬜⬜ N/A (21,975)

chalkboard
🏠 2x1
OBTAIN Shop (Large Item)
FUNCTION None
not customizable; purchasable in 7 colors
⚫⚪⚪⚪ ⬜⬜ 2600 (650)

champion's pennant — 1x1
OBTAIN Shop (Large Item)
FUNCTION None
not customizable; purchasable in 4 colors
3900 (975)

clothes closet — 1x1
OBTAIN Shop (Small Item)
FUNCTION Closet: Flip
not customizable; purchasable in 6 colors
3100 (775)

crewed spaceship — 2x2
OBTAIN Star fragment recipe (Reward: Celeste)
FUNCTION Animates (Loop)
not customizable
N/A (20,000)

changing room — 1x1
OBTAIN Shop (Large Item)
FUNCTION Closet: Flip
x2 • FABRIC x7 Generic/Custom • BODY x8
3700 (925)

clothesline — 2x0.5
OBTAIN Tom Nook ("Three New Plots" quest) — Cranky
FUNCTION None
x2 • FABRIC x4 Generic/Custom • BODY N/A
N/A (100)

cute bed — 2x2
OBTAIN Shop (Large Item)
FUNCTION Bed: Normal
not customizable; purchasable in 5 colors
12,000 (3000)

cherry-blossom branches — 1.5x1.5
OBTAIN Seasonal recipe: Cherry blossom
FUNCTION Interact (Start/Stop)
not customizable
N/A (4240)

clothesline pole — 2x0.5
OBTAIN Shop (Small Item)
FUNCTION None
x1 • FABRIC x3 Generic/Custom • BODY x2
1100 (275)

cute chair — 1x1
OBTAIN Shop (Large Item)
FUNCTION Chair: SP
not customizable; purchasable in 5 colors
4300 (1075)

cherry-blossom pond stone — 2x1
OBTAIN Seasonal recipe: Cherry blossom
FUNCTION None
not customizable
N/A (2700)

colorful wheel — 2x1
OBTAIN Shop (Large Item)
FUNCTION Animates (Fades out)
not customizable; purchasable in 5 colors
2900 (725)

cute DIY table — 2x1
OBTAIN Shop (Large Item)
FUNCTION Workbench
not customizable; purchasable in 5 colors
7000 (1750)

cherry-blossom-petal pile — 1x1
OBTAIN Seasonal recipe: Cherry blossom
FUNCTION Walk over/Pass through
not customizable
N/A (2000)

cone — 1x1
OBTAIN Shop (Small Item)
FUNCTION None
not customizable; purchasable in 8 colors
630 (157)

cute floor lamp — 1x1
OBTAIN Shop (Large Item)
FUNCTION Interact (On/Off)
not customizable; purchasable in 5 colors
3500 (875)

clackercart — 1x1
OBTAIN DIY item — Lazy
FUNCTION None
x2 • FABRIC N/A • BODY x6
N/A (960)

construction sign — 1x1
OBTAIN Redeem Nook Miles (1000 miles)
FUNCTION None
not customizable; purchasable in 5 colors
N/A (5000)

cute sofa — 2x1
OBTAIN Shop (Large Item)
FUNCTION Chair: Normal
not customizable; purchasable in 5 colors
9600 (2400)

claw-foot tub — 2x1
OBTAIN Shop (Luxury Item)
FUNCTION None
not customizable; purchasable in 6 colors
63,000 (15,750)

cosmos shower — 1x1
OBTAIN DIY item — (50) Snooty
FUNCTION Interact (Loop On/Off)
x5 • FABRIC N/A • BODY x3
N/A (3050)

cute tea table — 1x1
OBTAIN Shop (Large Item)
FUNCTION None
not customizable; purchasable in 5 colors
3000 (750)

clay furnace — 2x1
OBTAIN Shop (Small Item)
FUNCTION Animates (Loop)
not customizable
3300 (825)

cotton-candy stall — 2x1
OBTAIN Redeem Nook Miles (3000 miles)
FUNCTION Animates (Fades out)
not customizable; purchasable in 3 colors
N/A (15,000)

cute vanity — 1x1
OBTAIN Shop (Large Item)
FUNCTION Mirror
not customizable; purchasable in 5 colors
5400 (1350)

climbing wall — 2x0.5
OBTAIN Shop (Large Item)
FUNCTION None
not customizable; purchasable in 4 colors
4300 (1075)

crescent-moon chair — 2x1
OBTAIN Star fragment recipe (Reward: Celeste)
FUNCTION Chair: Front and Back (Left half)
x7 • FABRIC N/A • BODY x7
N/A (8500)

cute wardrobe — 1x1
OBTAIN Shop (Large Item)
FUNCTION Closet: Double Door
not customizable; purchasable in 5 colors
7300 (1825)

cypress bathtub
2x2
OBTAIN Shop (Large Item)
FUNCTION None
not customizable; purchasable in 3 colors
13,000 (3250)

cypress plant
1x1
OBTAIN Shop (Small Item)
FUNCTION None
not customizable; purchasable in 5 colors
1000 (250)

dartboard
1x1
OBTAIN Shop (Large Item)
FUNCTION Interact (Start/Stop)
not customizable
5200 (1300)

deer scare
1x1
OBTAIN DIY item (50) Cranky
FUNCTION Animates (Loop)
x3 • FABRIC N/A • BODY x3
N/A (1740)

deluxe washer
1x1
OBTAIN Shop (Luxury Item)
FUNCTION Interact (On/Off)
not customizable; purchasable in 6 colors
76,000 (19,000)

den chair
1x1
OBTAIN Shop (Large Item)
FUNCTION Chair: Normal
not customizable; purchasable in 6 colors
8700 (2175)

den desk
2x1
OBTAIN Shop (Large Item)
FUNCTION None
not customizable; purchasable in 5 colors
10,000 (2500)

destinations signpost
1.5x1.5
OBTAIN Redeem Nook Miles (1500 miles)
FUNCTION None
x2 • FABRIC N/A • BODY x6
N/A (1440)

digital scale
1x1
OBTAIN Shop (Small Item)
FUNCTION None
x1 • FABRIC x4 Generic/Custom • BODY x7
930 (232)

diner chair
1x1
OBTAIN Shop (Large Item)
FUNCTION Chair: SP
not customizable; purchasable in 7 colors
1600 (400)

diner counter chair
1x1
OBTAIN Shop (Large Item)
FUNCTION Chair: Stool
not customizable; purchasable in 7 colors
1100 (275)

diner counter table
2x1
OBTAIN Shop (Large Item)
FUNCTION None
not customizable; purchasable in 7 colors
6000 (1500)

diner dining table
2x2
OBTAIN Shop (Large Item)
FUNCTION None
not customizable; purchasable in 7 colors
6400 (1600)

diner mini table
1x1
OBTAIN Shop (Large Item)
FUNCTION None
not customizable; purchasable in 7 colors
1600 (400)

diner neon sign
2x1
OBTAIN Shop (Large Item)
FUNCTION Interact (Loop On/Off)
not customizable; purchasable in 5 colors
3900 (975)

diner sofa
2x1
OBTAIN Shop (Large Item)
FUNCTION Chair: SP
not customizable; purchasable in 7 colors
3500 (875)

director's chair
1x1
OBTAIN Shop (All)
FUNCTION Chair: Normal
x1 • FABRIC x2 Generic/Custom • BODY x4
1600 (400)

DIY workbench
2x1
OBTAIN DIY item (100) Big sister
FUNCTION Workbench
x7 • FABRIC N/A • BODY x8
N/A (6630)

DJ's turntable
2x1
OBTAIN Shop (Large Item)
FUNCTION Audio
x4 • FABRIC x7 Generic/Custom • BODY x4
9300 (2325)

doghouse
1x1
OBTAIN DIY item Jock
FUNCTION Interact (Start/Stop)
x3 • FABRIC N/A • BODY x5
N/A (2040)

double sofa
2x1
OBTAIN Shop (Small Item)
FUNCTION Chair: Normal
not customizable; purchasable in 8 colors
4300 (1075)

double-door refrigerator
1x1
OBTAIN Shop (Luxury Item)
FUNCTION Closet: Double Door
not customizable; purchasable in 4 colors
60,000 (15,000)

drink machine
1x1
OBTAIN Redeem Nook Miles (2000 miles)
FUNCTION Interact (Start/Stop)
x7 • FABRIC x3 Custom • BODY x6
N/A (10,000)

drinking fountain
1x1
OBTAIN Redeem Nook Miles (800 miles)
FUNCTION Interact (On/Off)
x4 • FABRIC N/A • BODY x4
N/A (2700)

drum set
2x2
OBTAIN Shop (Large Item)
FUNCTION Musical Instrument
x2 • FABRIC x5 Custom • BODY x8
5600 (1400)

drying rack
2x1
OBTAIN Shop (Small Item)
FUNCTION None
not customizable; purchasable in 4 colors
2700 (675)

effects rack
1x1
OBTAIN Shop (Large Item)
FUNCTION None
x3 • FABRIC x7 Custom • BODY x6
6800 (1700)

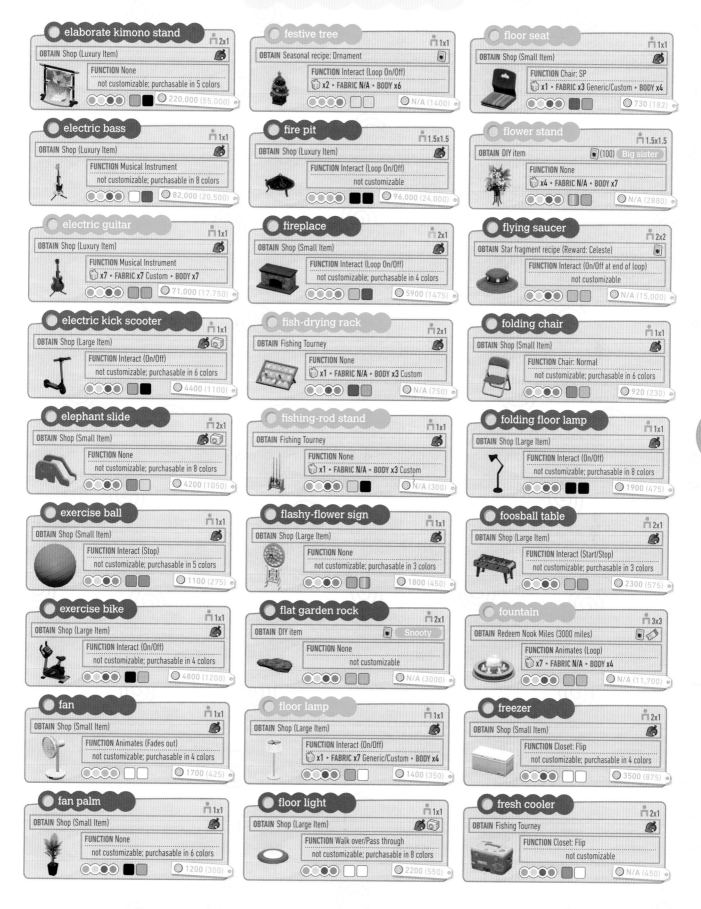

elaborate kimono stand 2x1
OBTAIN Shop (Luxury Item)
FUNCTION None
not customizable; purchasable in 5 colors
220,000 (55,000)

electric bass 1x1
OBTAIN Shop (Luxury Item)
FUNCTION Musical Instrument
not customizable; purchasable in 8 colors
82,000 (20,500)

electric guitar 1x1
OBTAIN Shop (Luxury Item)
FUNCTION Musical Instrument
x7 • FABRIC x7 Custom • BODY x7
71,000 (17,750)

electric kick scooter 1x1
OBTAIN Shop (Large Item)
FUNCTION Interact (On/Off)
not customizable; purchasable in 6 colors
4400 (1100)

elephant slide 2x1
OBTAIN Shop (Small Item)
FUNCTION None
not customizable; purchasable in 8 colors
4200 (1050)

exercise ball 1x1
OBTAIN Shop (Small Item)
FUNCTION Interact (Stop)
not customizable; purchasable in 5 colors
1100 (275)

exercise bike 1x1
OBTAIN Shop (Large Item)
FUNCTION Interact (On/Off)
not customizable; purchasable in 4 colors
4800 (1200)

fan 1x1
OBTAIN Shop (Small Item)
FUNCTION Animates (Fades out)
not customizable; purchasable in 4 colors
1700 (425)

fan palm 1x1
OBTAIN Shop (Small Item)
FUNCTION None
not customizable; purchasable in 6 colors
1200 (300)

festive tree 1x1
OBTAIN Seasonal recipe: Ornament
FUNCTION Interact (Loop On/Off)
x2 • FABRIC N/A • BODY x6
N/A (1400)

fire pit 1.5x1.5
OBTAIN Shop (Luxury Item)
FUNCTION Interact (Loop On/Off)
not customizable
96,000 (24,000)

fireplace 2x1
OBTAIN Shop (Small Item)
FUNCTION Interact (Loop On/Off)
not customizable; purchasable in 4 colors
5900 (1475)

fish-drying rack 2x1
OBTAIN Fishing Tourney
FUNCTION None
x1 • FABRIC N/A • BODY x3 Custom
N/A (750)

fishing-rod stand 1x1
OBTAIN Fishing Tourney
FUNCTION None
x1 • FABRIC N/A • BODY x3 Custom
N/A (300)

flashy-flower sign 1x1
OBTAIN Shop (Large Item)
FUNCTION None
not customizable; purchasable in 3 colors
1800 (450)

flat garden rock 2x1
OBTAIN DIY item — Snooty
FUNCTION None
not customizable
N/A (3000)

floor lamp 1x1
OBTAIN Shop (Large Item)
FUNCTION Interact (On/Off)
x1 • FABRIC x7 Generic/Custom • BODY x4
1400 (350)

floor light 1x1
OBTAIN Shop (Large Item)
FUNCTION Walk over/Pass through
not customizable; purchasable in 8 colors
2200 (550)

floor seat 1x1
OBTAIN Shop (Small Item)
FUNCTION Chair: SP
x1 • FABRIC x3 Generic/Custom • BODY x4
730 (182)

flower stand 1.5x1.5
OBTAIN DIY item — (100) Big sister
FUNCTION None
x4 • FABRIC N/A • BODY x7
N/A (2880)

flying saucer 2x2
OBTAIN Star fragment recipe (Reward: Celeste)
FUNCTION Interact (On/Off at end of loop)
not customizable
N/A (15,000)

folding chair 1x1
OBTAIN Shop (Small Item)
FUNCTION Chair: Normal
not customizable; purchasable in 6 colors
920 (230)

folding floor lamp 1x1
OBTAIN Shop (Large Item)
FUNCTION Interact (On/Off)
not customizable; purchasable in 8 colors
1900 (475)

foosball table 2x1
OBTAIN Shop (Large Item)
FUNCTION Interact (Start/Stop)
not customizable; purchasable in 3 colors
2300 (575)

fountain 3x3
OBTAIN Redeem Nook Miles (3000 miles)
FUNCTION Animates (Loop)
x7 • FABRIC N/A • BODY x4
N/A (11,700)

freezer 2x1
OBTAIN Shop (Small Item)
FUNCTION Closet: Flip
not customizable; purchasable in 4 colors
3500 (875)

fresh cooler 2x1
OBTAIN Fishing Tourney
FUNCTION Closet: Flip
not customizable
N/A (450)

frozen arch
3x1
OBTAIN Reward: Snowboy
FUNCTION None
x7 • FABRIC N/A • BODY x7
N/A (9000)

futon
2x1
OBTAIN Shop (Small Item)
FUNCTION Bed: Normal
x1 • FABRIC x3 Generic/Custom • BODY N/A
1600 (400)

gas range
1x1
OBTAIN Shop (Small Item)
FUNCTION Interact (On/Off)
not customizable; purchasable in 5 colors
3500 (875)

frozen bed
2x2
OBTAIN Reward: Snowboy
FUNCTION Bed: Normal
x8 • FABRIC x3 • BODY x7
N/A (9000)

garbage bin
1x1
OBTAIN Shop (Small Item)
FUNCTION Trash Bin
not customizable; purchasable in 7 colors
1000 (250)

Gemini closet
1x1
OBTAIN Zodiac recipe (Reward: Celeste)
FUNCTION Closet: Double Door
not customizable
N/A (22,200)

frozen chair
1x1
OBTAIN Reward: Snowboy
FUNCTION Chair: Normal
x7 • FABRIC N/A • BODY x7
N/A (6200)

garbage can
1x1
OBTAIN Shop (Small Item)
FUNCTION Trash Bin
not customizable
960 (240)

giant teddy bear
3x3
OBTAIN DIY item (100) Peppy
FUNCTION None
x8 • FABRIC x3 Generic/Custom • BODY x6
N/A (6300)

frozen counter
2x1
OBTAIN Reward: Snowboy
FUNCTION None
x7 • FABRIC N/A • BODY x7
N/A (7000)

garbage pail
1x1
OBTAIN Shop (Small Item)
FUNCTION Trash Bin
not customizable
1000 (250)

go board
1x1
OBTAIN Shop (Small Item)
FUNCTION None
not customizable
1800 (450)

frozen partition
2x0.5
OBTAIN Reward: Snowboy
FUNCTION None
x7 • FABRIC N/A • BODY x7
N/A (7400)

garden bench
2x1
OBTAIN DIY item Snooty
FUNCTION Chair: Normal
x6 • FABRIC N/A • BODY x6
N/A (4440)

golden casket
2x1
OBTAIN DIY item (200) Smug
FUNCTION None
not customizable
N/A (80,000)

frozen pillar
1x1
OBTAIN Reward: Snowboy
FUNCTION None
x7 • FABRIC N/A • BODY x7
N/A (6200)

garden faucet
1x1
OBTAIN Shop (Small Item)
FUNCTION Interact (On/Off)
not customizable; purchasable in 5 colors
1900 (475)

golden seat
2x1
OBTAIN DIY item (200) Snooty
FUNCTION Chair: Normal
not customizable
N/A (50,000)

frozen sculpture
1.5x1.5
OBTAIN Reward: Snowboy
FUNCTION None
x7 • FABRIC N/A • BODY x7
N/A (6600)

garden lantern
1x1
OBTAIN Shop (Small Item)
FUNCTION Outdoor Light (Brightness Sensor)
not customizable; purchasable in 3 colors
1400 (350)

golden toilet
1x1
OBTAIN DIY item (200) Snooty
FUNCTION Chair: SP
not customizable
N/A (60,000)

frozen table
2x2
OBTAIN Reward: Snowboy
FUNCTION None
x7 • FABRIC N/A • BODY x7
N/A (8200)

garden rock
1x1
OBTAIN DIY item Lazy
FUNCTION None
not customizable
N/A (2250)

golf bag
1x1
OBTAIN Shop (Luxury Item)
FUNCTION None
not customizable; purchasable in 6 colors
54,000 (13,500)

frozen tree
2x2
OBTAIN Reward: Snowboy
FUNCTION None
x7 • FABRIC N/A • BODY x7
N/A (8200)

garden wagon
2x1
OBTAIN DIY item Peppy
FUNCTION None
x5 • FABRIC N/A • BODY x4
N/A (3180)

gong
2x1
OBTAIN DIY item Cranky
FUNCTION Musical Instrument
x7 • FABRIC N/A • BODY x2
N/A (5100)

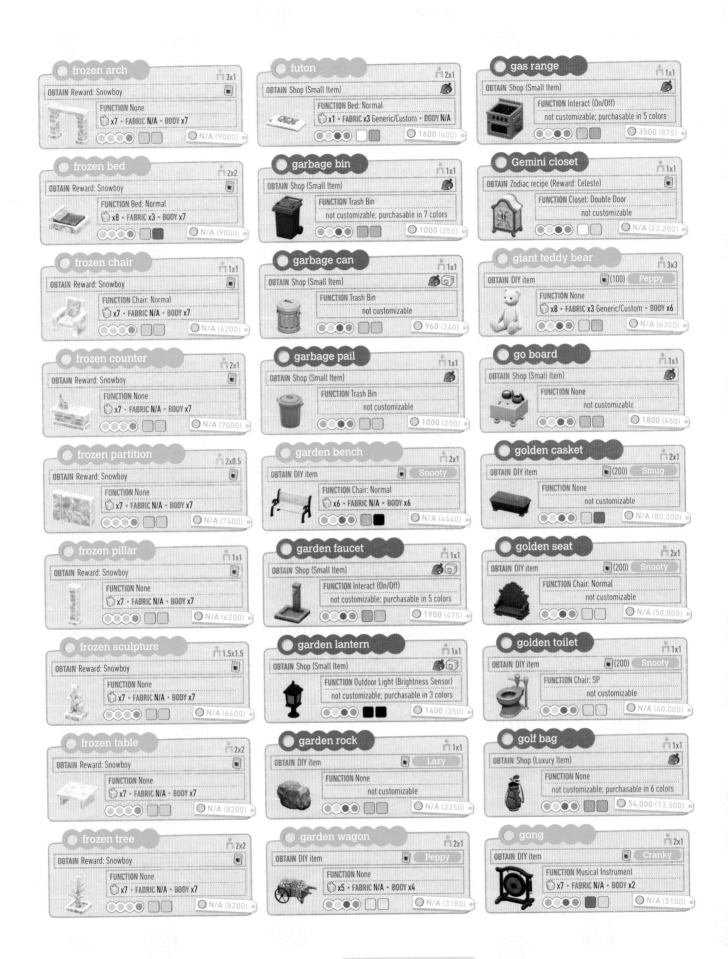

grand piano 🏠2x2
OBTAIN Shop (Luxury Item)
FUNCTION Musical Instrument
not customizable; purchasable in 4 colors
260,000 (65,000)

grass standee 🏠1x0.5
OBTAIN DIY item — Sweet
FUNCTION None
x1 · FABRIC N/A · BODY x4
N/A (480)

green-leaf pile 🏠1.5x1.5
OBTAIN Seasonal recipe: Bamboo
FUNCTION Walk over/Pass through
not customizable
N/A (600)

hammock 🏠2x1
OBTAIN Shop (All)
FUNCTION Bed: Normal
x1 · FABRIC x3 Generic/Custom · BODY x7
1300 (325)

handcart 🏠1x1
OBTAIN Shop (Small Item)
FUNCTION None
not customizable; purchasable in 6 colors
1900 (475)

harp 🏠1x1
OBTAIN Shop (Luxury Item)
FUNCTION Musical Instrument
not customizable; purchasable in 5 colors
130,000 (32,500)

hay bed 🏠2x1
OBTAIN DIY for Beginners: Shop (Cabinet)
FUNCTION Bed: Normal
x1 · FABRIC N/A · BODY x3
N/A (400)

hearth 🏠2x2
OBTAIN Wildest Dreams DIY: Shop (Cabinet)
FUNCTION Animates (Loop)
not customizable
N/A (5470)

hedge standee 🏠1x0.5
OBTAIN DIY item — Sweet
FUNCTION None
x1 · FABRIC N/A · BODY x7
N/A (600)

hi-fi stereo 🏠2x1
OBTAIN Shop (Luxury Item)
FUNCTION Audio
not customizable
82,000 (20,500)

high-end stereo 🏠2x1
OBTAIN Shop (Small Item)
FUNCTION Audio
not customizable
10,000 (2500)

hose reel 🏠1x1
OBTAIN Shop (Small Item)
FUNCTION None
not customizable; purchasable in 6 colors
1400 (350)

illuminated present 🏠1x1
OBTAIN Seasonal recipe: Ornament
FUNCTION Outdoor Light (Brightness Sensor)
x4 · FABRIC N/A · BODY x4
N/A (2950)

illuminated reindeer 🏠2x1
OBTAIN Seasonal recipe: Ornament
FUNCTION Outdoor Light (Brightness Sensor)
x6 · FABRIC N/A · BODY x5
N/A (4350)

illuminated snowflakes 🏠2x1
OBTAIN Seasonal recipe: Ornament
FUNCTION Outdoor Light (Brightness Sensor)
x5 · FABRIC N/A · BODY x4
N/A (3150)

illuminated tree 🏠2x2
OBTAIN Seasonal recipe: Ornament
FUNCTION Outdoor Light (Brightness Sensor)
x7 · FABRIC N/A · BODY x6
N/A (6700)

imperial bed 🏠2x2
OBTAIN Shop (Large Item)
FUNCTION Bed: Normal
not customizable; purchasable in 4 colors
23,000 (5750)

imperial chest 🏠2x1
OBTAIN Shop (Large Item)
FUNCTION Closet: Double Door
not customizable; purchasable in 4 colors
9300 (2325)

imperial dining chair 🏠1x1
OBTAIN Shop (Luxury Item)
FUNCTION Chair: SP
not customizable; purchasable in 2 colors
29,000 (7250)

imperial dining table 🏠2x2
OBTAIN Shop (Luxury Item)
FUNCTION Interact (On/Off)
not customizable; purchasable in 2 colors
73,000 (18,250)

imperial low table 🏠2x1
OBTAIN Shop (Large Item)
FUNCTION None
not customizable; purchasable in 4 colors
3700 (925)

imperial partition 🏠2x1
OBTAIN Shop (Large Item)
FUNCTION None
not customizable; purchasable in 4 colors
5000 (1250)

inflatable sofa 🏠2x1
OBTAIN Shop (All)
FUNCTION Bed: Normal
not customizable; purchasable in 8 colors
1100 (275)

iron closet 🏠1x1
OBTAIN DIY item — Big sister
FUNCTION Closet: Double Door
x7 · FABRIC N/A · BODY x2
N/A (9000)

iron frame 🏠2x1
OBTAIN DIY item — Jock
FUNCTION None
x7 · FABRIC N/A · BODY x3
N/A (15,000)

iron garden bench 🏠2x1
OBTAIN DIY item — Big sister
FUNCTION Chair: SP
x7 · FABRIC N/A · BODY x5
N/A (6000)

iron garden chair 🏠1x1
OBTAIN Tom Nook ("Three New Plots" quest) — Big sister
FUNCTION Chair: SP
x3 · FABRIC N/A · BODY x5
N/A (2250)

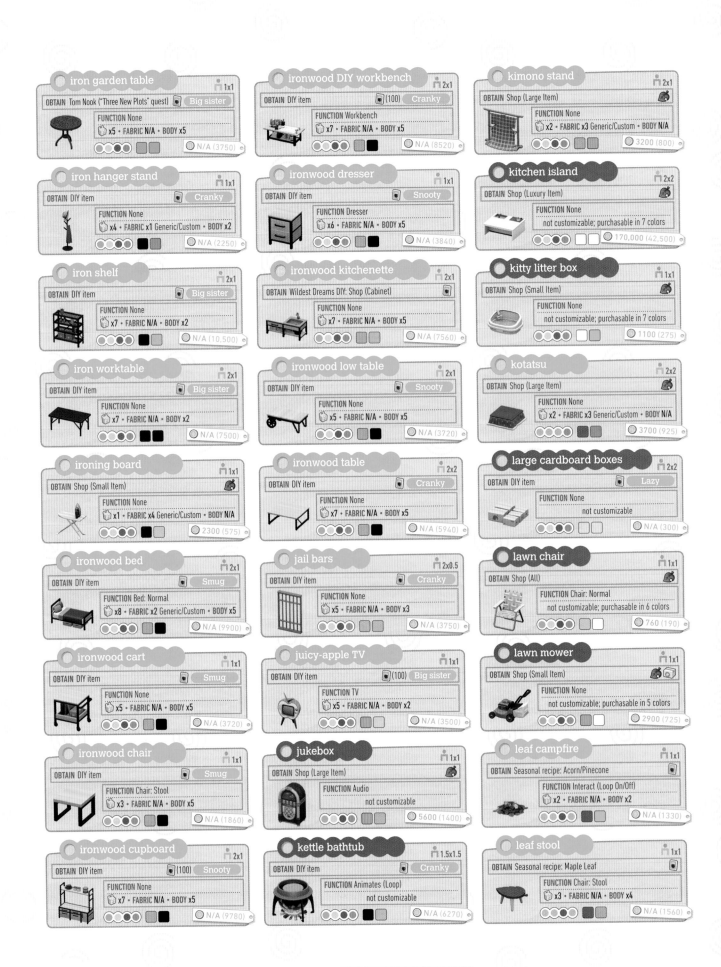

iron garden table
1x1
OBTAIN Tom Nook ("Three New Plots" quest) — Big sister
FUNCTION None
x5 • FABRIC N/A • BODY x5
N/A (3750)

ironwood DIY workbench
2x1
OBTAIN DIY item — (100) Cranky
FUNCTION Workbench
x7 • FABRIC N/A • BODY x5
N/A (8520)

kimono stand
2x1
OBTAIN Shop (Large Item)
FUNCTION None
x2 • FABRIC x3 Generic/Custom • BODY N/A
3200 (800)

iron hanger stand
1x1
OBTAIN DIY item — Cranky
FUNCTION None
x4 • FABRIC x1 Generic/Custom • BODY x2
N/A (2250)

ironwood dresser
1x1
OBTAIN DIY item — Snooty
FUNCTION Dresser
x6 • FABRIC N/A • BODY x5
N/A (3840)

kitchen island
2x2
OBTAIN Shop (Luxury Item)
FUNCTION None
not customizable; purchasable in 7 colors
170,000 (42,500)

iron shelf
2x1
OBTAIN DIY item — Big sister
FUNCTION None
x7 • FABRIC N/A • BODY x2
N/A (10,500)

ironwood kitchenette
2x1
OBTAIN Wildest Dreams DIY: Shop (Cabinet)
FUNCTION None
x7 • FABRIC N/A • BODY x5
N/A (7560)

kitty litter box
1x1
OBTAIN Shop (Small Item)
FUNCTION None
not customizable; purchasable in 7 colors
1100 (275)

iron worktable
2x1
OBTAIN DIY item — Big sister
FUNCTION None
x7 • FABRIC N/A • BODY x2
N/A (7500)

ironwood low table
2x1
OBTAIN DIY item — Snooty
FUNCTION None
x5 • FABRIC N/A • BODY x5
N/A (3720)

kotatsu
2x2
OBTAIN Shop (Large Item)
FUNCTION None
x2 • FABRIC x3 Generic/Custom • BODY N/A
3700 (925)

ironing board
1x1
OBTAIN Shop (Small Item)
FUNCTION None
x1 • FABRIC x4 Generic/Custom • BODY N/A
2300 (575)

ironwood table
2x2
OBTAIN DIY item — Cranky
FUNCTION None
x7 • FABRIC N/A • BODY x5
N/A (5940)

large cardboard boxes
2x2
OBTAIN DIY item — Lazy
FUNCTION None
not customizable
N/A (300)

ironwood bed
2x1
OBTAIN DIY item — Smug
FUNCTION Bed: Normal
x8 • FABRIC x2 Generic/Custom • BODY x5
N/A (9900)

jail bars
2x0.5
OBTAIN DIY item — Cranky
FUNCTION None
x5 • FABRIC N/A • BODY x3
N/A (3750)

lawn chair
1x1
OBTAIN Shop (All)
FUNCTION Chair: Normal
not customizable; purchasable in 6 colors
760 (190)

ironwood cart
1x1
OBTAIN DIY item — Smug
FUNCTION None
x5 • FABRIC N/A • BODY x5
N/A (3720)

juicy-apple TV
1x1
OBTAIN DIY item — (100) Big sister
FUNCTION TV
x5 • FABRIC N/A • BODY x2
N/A (3500)

lawn mower
1x1
OBTAIN Shop (Small Item)
FUNCTION None
not customizable; purchasable in 5 colors
2900 (725)

ironwood chair
1x1
OBTAIN DIY item — Smug
FUNCTION Chair: Stool
x3 • FABRIC N/A • BODY x5
N/A (1860)

jukebox
1x1
OBTAIN Shop (Large Item)
FUNCTION Audio
not customizable
5600 (1400)

leaf campfire
1x1
OBTAIN Seasonal recipe: Acorn/Pinecone
FUNCTION Interact (Loop On/Off)
x2 • FABRIC N/A • BODY x2
N/A (1330)

ironwood cupboard
2x1
OBTAIN DIY item — (100) Snooty
FUNCTION None
x7 • FABRIC N/A • BODY x5
N/A (9780)

kettle bathtub
1.5x1.5
OBTAIN DIY item — Cranky
FUNCTION Animates (Loop)
not customizable
N/A (6270)

leaf stool
1x1
OBTAIN Seasonal recipe: Maple Leaf
FUNCTION Chair: Stool
x3 • FABRIC N/A • BODY x4
N/A (1560)

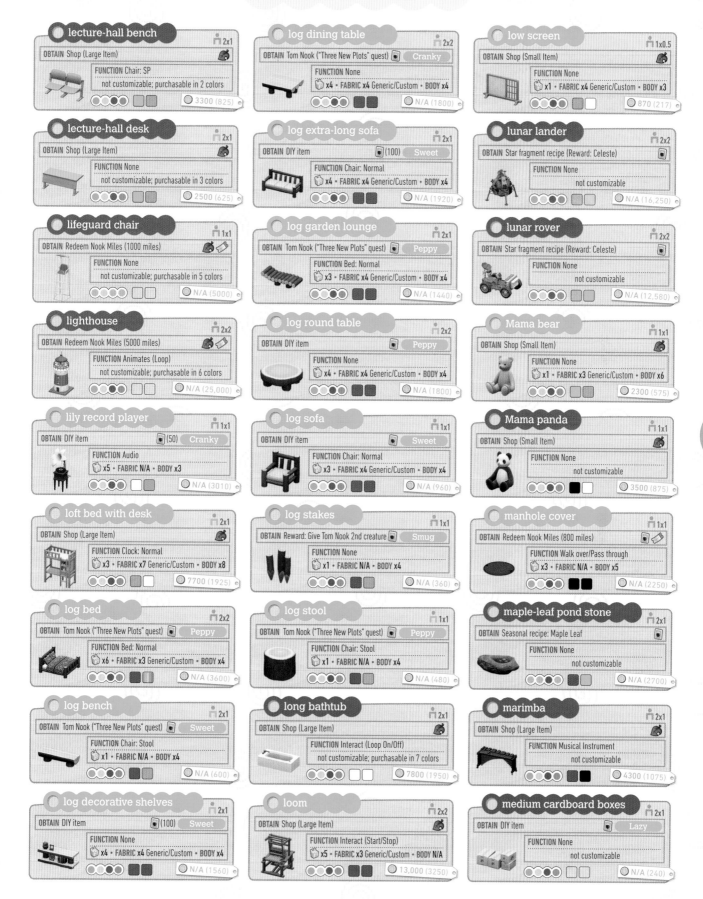

lecture-hall bench 2x1
OBTAIN Shop (Large Item)
FUNCTION Chair: SP
not customizable; purchasable in 2 colors
3300 (825)

lecture-hall desk 2x1
OBTAIN Shop (Large Item)
FUNCTION None
not customizable; purchasable in 3 colors
2500 (625)

lifeguard chair 1x1
OBTAIN Redeem Nook Miles (1000 miles)
FUNCTION None
not customizable; purchasable in 5 colors
N/A (5000)

lighthouse 2x2
OBTAIN Redeem Nook Miles (5000 miles)
FUNCTION Animates (Loop)
not customizable; purchasable in 6 colors
N/A (25,000)

lily record player 1x1
OBTAIN DIY item (50) Cranky
FUNCTION Audio
x5 • FABRIC N/A • BODY x3
N/A (3010)

loft bed with desk 2x1
OBTAIN Shop (Large Item)
FUNCTION Clock: Normal
x3 • FABRIC x7 Generic/Custom • BODY x8
7700 (1925)

log bed 2x2
OBTAIN Tom Nook ("Three New Plots" quest) Peppy
FUNCTION Bed: Normal
x6 • FABRIC x3 Generic/Custom • BODY x4
N/A (3600)

log bench 2x1
OBTAIN Tom Nook ("Three New Plots" quest) Sweet
FUNCTION Chair: Stool
x1 • FABRIC N/A • BODY x4
N/A (600)

log decorative shelves 2x1
OBTAIN DIY item (100) Sweet
FUNCTION None
x4 • FABRIC x4 Generic/Custom • BODY x4
N/A (1560)

log dining table 2x2
OBTAIN Tom Nook ("Three New Plots" quest) Cranky
FUNCTION None
x4 • FABRIC x4 Generic/Custom • BODY x4
N/A (1800)

log extra-long sofa 2x1
OBTAIN DIY item (100) Sweet
FUNCTION Chair: Normal
x4 • FABRIC x4 Generic/Custom • BODY x4
N/A (1920)

log garden lounge 2x1
OBTAIN Tom Nook ("Three New Plots" quest) Peppy
FUNCTION Bed: Normal
x3 • FABRIC x4 Generic/Custom • BODY x4
N/A (1440)

log round table 2x2
OBTAIN DIY item Peppy
FUNCTION None
x4 • FABRIC x4 Generic/Custom • BODY x4
N/A (1800)

log sofa 1x1
OBTAIN DIY item Sweet
FUNCTION Chair: Normal
x3 • FABRIC x4 Generic/Custom • BODY x4
N/A (960)

log stakes 1x1
OBTAIN Reward: Give Tom Nook 2nd creature Smug
FUNCTION None
x1 • FABRIC N/A • BODY x4
N/A (360)

log stool 1x1
OBTAIN Tom Nook ("Three New Plots" quest) Peppy
FUNCTION Chair: Stool
x1 • FABRIC N/A • BODY x4
N/A (480)

long bathtub 2x1
OBTAIN Shop (Large Item)
FUNCTION Interact (Loop On/Off)
not customizable; purchasable in 7 colors
7800 (1950)

loom 2x2
OBTAIN Shop (Large Item)
FUNCTION Interact (Start/Stop)
x5 • FABRIC x3 Generic/Custom • BODY N/A
13,000 (3250)

low screen 1x0.5
OBTAIN Shop (Small Item)
FUNCTION None
x1 • FABRIC x4 Generic/Custom • BODY x3
870 (217)

lunar lander 2x2
OBTAIN Star fragment recipe (Reward: Celeste)
FUNCTION None
not customizable
N/A (16,250)

lunar rover 2x2
OBTAIN Star fragment recipe (Reward: Celeste)
FUNCTION None
not customizable
N/A (12,580)

Mama bear 1x1
OBTAIN Shop (Small Item)
FUNCTION None
x1 • FABRIC x3 Generic/Custom • BODY x6
2300 (575)

Mama panda 1x1
OBTAIN Shop (Small Item)
FUNCTION None
not customizable
3500 (875)

manhole cover 1x1
OBTAIN Redeem Nook Miles (800 miles)
FUNCTION Walk over/Pass through
x3 • FABRIC N/A • BODY x5
N/A (2250)

maple-leaf pond stone 2x1
OBTAIN Seasonal recipe: Maple Leaf
FUNCTION None
not customizable
N/A (2700)

marimba 2x1
OBTAIN Shop (Large Item)
FUNCTION Musical Instrument
not customizable
4300 (1075)

medium cardboard boxes 2x1
OBTAIN DIY item Lazy
FUNCTION None
not customizable
N/A (240)

7

menu chalkboard
🔲 1x1
OBTAIN Shop (Small Item) 🛍️
FUNCTION None
not customizable; purchasable in 5 colors
🔵 1800 (450)

mic stand
🔲 1x1
OBTAIN Shop (Large Item) 🛍️
FUNCTION None
not customizable
🔵 1000 (250)

mini DIY workbench
🔲 1x1
OBTAIN Test Your DIY Skills; Shop (Cabinet) 📦
FUNCTION Workbench
🪵 x4 • FABRIC N/A • BODY x8
🔵 N/A (2580)

mini fridge
🔲 1x1
OBTAIN Shop (Large Item) 🛍️
FUNCTION Closet: Single Door
not customizable; purchasable in 8 colors
🔵 1300 (325)

moai statue
🔲 2x2
OBTAIN Reward: Gulliver 🛍️
FUNCTION None
not customizable
🔵 N/A (1900)

modern office chair
🔲 1x1
OBTAIN Shop (Large Item) 🛍️
FUNCTION Chair: Normal
not customizable; purchasable in 7 colors
🔵 2200 (550)

monster statue
🔲 3x3
OBTAIN Redeem Nook Miles (5000 miles) 🛍️📋
FUNCTION Interact (Start/Stop)
not customizable; purchasable in 4 colors
🔵 N/A (25,000)

monstera
🔲 1x1
OBTAIN Shop (Small Item) 🍎
FUNCTION None
not customizable; purchasable in 6 colors
🔵 1700 (425)

moon
🔲 2x2
OBTAIN Star fragment recipe (Reward: Celeste) 📦
FUNCTION Animates (Loop)
not customizable
🔵 N/A (12,500)

mossy garden rock
🔲 1x1
OBTAIN DIY item 📦 **Lazy**
FUNCTION None
not customizable
🔵 N/A (2550)

mountain bike
🔲 2x1
OBTAIN Shop (Small Item) 🛍️📦
FUNCTION None
not customizable; purchasable in 6 colors
🔵 5100 (1275)

mountain standee
🔲 2x1
OBTAIN DIY item 📦 **Jock**
FUNCTION None
🪵 x2 • FABRIC N/A • BODY x6
🔵 N/A (1080)

Mr. Flamingo
🔲 1x1
OBTAIN Shop (Small Item) 🛍️📦
FUNCTION None
not customizable; purchasable in 2 colors
🔵 3000 (750)

Mrs. Flamingo
🔲 1x1
OBTAIN Shop (Small Item) 🛍️📦
FUNCTION None
not customizable; purchasable in 2 colors
🔵 3000 (750)

mum cushion
🔲 1x1
OBTAIN DIY item 📦 (50) **Peppy**
FUNCTION Chair: Stool
🌼 x1 • FABRIC N/A • BODY x3
🔵 N/A (440)

mush lamp
🔲 1x1
OBTAIN Seasonal recipe: Mushroom 📦
FUNCTION Interact (On/Off)
🍄 x3 • FABRIC N/A • BODY x5
🔵 N/A (1600)

mush log
🔲 1x1
OBTAIN Seasonal recipe: Mushroom 📦
FUNCTION None
🍄 x3 • FABRIC N/A • BODY x5
🔵 N/A (1680)

mush low stool
🔲 1x1
OBTAIN Seasonal recipe: Mushroom 📦
FUNCTION Chair: Stool
🍄 x2 • FABRIC N/A • BODY x5
🔵 N/A (800)

mush parasol
🔲 2x2
OBTAIN Seasonal recipe: Mushroom 📦
FUNCTION None
🍄 x2 • FABRIC N/A • BODY x5
🔵 N/A (1200)

mush partition
🔲 2x1
OBTAIN Seasonal recipe: Mushroom 📦
FUNCTION None
🍄 x3 • FABRIC N/A • BODY x5
🔵 N/A (1800)

mush table
🔲 2x2
OBTAIN Seasonal recipe: Mushroom 📦
FUNCTION None
🍄 x3 • FABRIC N/A • BODY x5
🔵 N/A (1520)

music stand
🔲 1x1
OBTAIN DIY item 📦 **Lazy**
FUNCTION None
🪵 x2 • FABRIC N/A • BODY x4
🔵 N/A (960)

natural garden chair
🔲 1x1
OBTAIN Tom Nook ("Three New Plots" quest) 📦 **Peppy**
FUNCTION Chair: SP
🪵 x3 • FABRIC N/A • BODY x3
🔵 N/A (2220)

natural garden table
🔲 2x2
OBTAIN Tom Nook ("Three New Plots" quest) 📦 **Sweet**
FUNCTION None
🪵 x5 • FABRIC N/A • BODY x3
🔵 N/A (3330)

natural square table
🔲 1x1
OBTAIN DIY item 📦 **Sweet**
FUNCTION None
🪵 x3 • FABRIC N/A • BODY x3
🔵 N/A (1980)

neutral corner
🔲 2x2
OBTAIN Shop (Large Item) 🍎
FUNCTION Bed: Normal
🪵 x3 • FABRIC x4 Custom • BODY N/A
🔵 6100 (1525)

office desk
🔲 2x1
OBTAIN Shop (Large Item) 🍎
FUNCTION None
not customizable; purchasable in 4 colors
🔵 3600 (900)

oil barrel — 1x1
OBTAIN Shop (All)
FUNCTION None
not customizable; purchasable in 8 colors
650 (162)

outdoor picnic set — 1.5x1.5
OBTAIN Seasonal recipe: Cherry blossom
FUNCTION None
not customizable
N/A (4000)

parabolic antenna — 3x3
OBTAIN Redeem Nook Miles (4000 miles)
FUNCTION Animates (Fades out)
not customizable; purchasable in 3 colors
N/A (20,000)

oil-barrel bathtub — 1x1
OBTAIN DIY item — (100) Jock
FUNCTION Animates (Loop)
x1 • FABRIC N/A • BODY x6
N/A (655)

outdoor table — 2x1
OBTAIN Shop (Small Item)
FUNCTION None
x1 • FABRIC x6 Generic/Custom • BODY x5
2200 (550)

park clock — 1x1
OBTAIN Redeem Nook Miles (2400 miles)
FUNCTION Clock: Normal
not customizable; purchasable in 4 colors
N/A (12,000)

old sewing machine — 2x1
OBTAIN Shop (Small Item)
FUNCTION Interact (Loop On/Off)
not customizable; purchasable in 3 colors
2200 (550)

pagoda — 1.5x1.5
OBTAIN Reward: Gulliver
FUNCTION None
x3 • FABRIC N/A • BODY x3 Custom
N/A (2030)

peach chair — 1x1
OBTAIN DIY item — (100) Sweet
FUNCTION Chair: Normal
x4 • FABRIC N/A • BODY x2
N/A (2600)

open-frame kitchen — 2x1
OBTAIN Shop (Luxury Item)
FUNCTION Interact (Loop On/Off)
not customizable
140,000 (35,000)

palm-tree lamp — 1.5x1.5
OBTAIN DIY item — Snooty
FUNCTION Interact (On/Off)
x5 • FABRIC N/A • BODY x4
N/A (3280)

pear bed — 2x1
OBTAIN DIY item — (100) Jock
FUNCTION Bed: Normal
x4 • FABRIC N/A • BODY x2
N/A (2720)

orange end table — 1x1
OBTAIN DIY item — (100) Lazy
FUNCTION None
x4 • FABRIC N/A • BODY x2
N/A (2480)

pansy table — 1x1
OBTAIN DIY item — (50) Sweet
FUNCTION None
x2 • FABRIC N/A • BODY x3
N/A (760)

pear wardrobe — 1x1
OBTAIN DIY item — (100) Jock
FUNCTION Closet: Double Door
x4 • FABRIC N/A • BODY x2
N/A (2600)

outdoor air conditioner — 1x1
OBTAIN Shop (Small Item)
FUNCTION Animates (Fades out)
not customizable
2200 (550)

pants press — 1x1
OBTAIN Shop (Large Item)
FUNCTION Interact (Start/Stop)
not customizable; purchasable in 3 colors
1900 (475)

pet bed — 1x1
OBTAIN Shop (Small Item)
FUNCTION Chair: Normal
x1 • FABRIC x4 Generic/Custom • BODY x3
1100 (275)

outdoor bath — 3x3
OBTAIN Redeem Nook Miles (3000 miles)
FUNCTION Outdoor Light (Brightness Sensor)
x6 • FABRIC N/A • BODY x4
N/A (4350)

Papa bear — 2x2
OBTAIN Shop (Large Item)
FUNCTION None
x3 • FABRIC x3 Generic/Custom • BODY x6
8500 (2125)

phone box — 1x1
OBTAIN Redeem Nook Miles (2400 miles)
FUNCTION Outdoor Light (Brightness Sensor)
not customizable; purchasable in 8 colors
N/A (12,000)

outdoor bench — 2x1
OBTAIN Shop (Small Item)
FUNCTION Chair: Stool
x1 • FABRIC x6 Generic/Custom • BODY x5
1300 (325)

Papa panda — 2x2
OBTAIN Shop (Large Item)
FUNCTION None
not customizable
8500 (2125)

piano bench — 1x1
OBTAIN Shop (Small Item)
FUNCTION Chair: Stool
not customizable; purchasable in 8 colors
990 (247)

outdoor generator — 1x1
OBTAIN Shop (All)
FUNCTION Interact (Loop On/Off)
not customizable; purchasable in 6 colors
4900 (1225)

paper lantern — 1x1
OBTAIN Shop (Small Item)
FUNCTION Interact (Loop On/Off)
x1 • FABRIC x4 Generic/Custom • BODY x3
780 (195)

pile of leaves — 1.5x1.5
OBTAIN Seasonal recipe: Acorn/Pinecone
FUNCTION Walk over/Pass through
not customizable
N/A (1300)

pile of zen cushions
1x1
OBTAIN DIY item · (100) · Cranky
FUNCTION Chair: Stool
x2 · FABRIC x6 Generic/Custom · BODY N/A
N/A (750)

pinball machine
1x1
OBTAIN Shop (Large Item)
FUNCTION Interact (Start/Stop)
not customizable; purchasable in 5 colors
2700 (675)

Pisces lamp
1x1
OBTAIN Zodiac recipe (Reward: Celeste)
FUNCTION Interact (On/Off)
not customizable
N/A (22,050)

plain sink
1x1
OBTAIN Wildest Dreams DIY: Shop (Cabinet)
FUNCTION Interact (On/Off)
x4 · FABRIC N/A · BODY x6
N/A (2270)

plain wooden shop sign
1x1
OBTAIN DIY item · Jock
FUNCTION None
x2 · FABRIC x3 Custom · BODY x3
N/A (720)

plastic pool
2x2
OBTAIN Shop (Large Item)
FUNCTION Interact (Stop)
not customizable; purchasable in 6 colors
3100 (775)

playground gym
2x2
OBTAIN Redeem Nook Miles (3000 miles)
FUNCTION Chair: Front (Center Only)
not customizable; purchasable in 5 colors
N/A (15,000)

podium
1x1
OBTAIN Shop (Large Item)
FUNCTION None
not customizable
3400 (850)

pond stone
2x1
OBTAIN DIY item · Snooty
FUNCTION None
x2 · FABRIC N/A · BODY x2
N/A (1500)

pool
3x3
OBTAIN Redeem Nook Miles (5000 miles)
FUNCTION None
not customizable; purchasable in 3 colors
N/A (25,000)

poolside bed
2x1
OBTAIN Shop (Large Item)
FUNCTION Bed: Normal
x2 · FABRIC x4 Generic/Custom · BODY x3
3400 (850)

popcorn machine
1x1
OBTAIN Shop (Small Item)
FUNCTION Interact (Loop On/Off)
not customizable; purchasable in 5 colors
4900 (1225)

portable toilet
1x1
OBTAIN Redeem Nook Miles (1000 miles)
FUNCTION None
not customizable; purchasable in 5 colors
N/A (5000)

public bench
2x1
OBTAIN Redeem Nook Miles (2000 miles)
FUNCTION Chair: SP
not customizable; purchasable in 8 colors
N/A (10,000)

pull-up-bar stand
1x1
OBTAIN Shop (Large Item)
FUNCTION None
not customizable; purchasable in 4 colors
4800 (1200)

punching bag
1x1
OBTAIN Shop (Small Item)
FUNCTION Interact (Stop)
not customizable; purchasable in 3 colors
3800 (950)

pyramid
3x3
OBTAIN Reward: Gulliver
FUNCTION None
not customizable
N/A (2300)

raccoon figurine
1x1
OBTAIN DIY item · Cranky
FUNCTION None
not customizable
N/A (1200)

rattan armchair
1x1
OBTAIN Shop (Large Item)
FUNCTION Chair: Normal
not customizable; purchasable in 6 colors
3200 (800)

rattan bed
2x2
OBTAIN Shop (Large Item)
FUNCTION Bed: Normal
not customizable; purchasable in 6 colors
7200 (1800)

rattan end table
1x1
OBTAIN Shop (Large Item)
FUNCTION None
not customizable; purchasable in 6 colors
4300 (1075)

rattan low table
2x1
OBTAIN Shop (Large Item)
FUNCTION None
not customizable; purchasable in 6 colors
2900 (725)

rattan stool
1x1
OBTAIN Shop (Large Item)
FUNCTION Chair: Stool
not customizable; purchasable in 6 colors
2900 (725)

rattan vanity
1x1
OBTAIN Shop (Large Item)
FUNCTION Mirror
not customizable; purchasable in 6 colors
5900 (1475)

rattan wardrobe
1x1
OBTAIN Shop (Large Item)
FUNCTION Closet: Double Door
not customizable; purchasable in 6 colors
6900 (1725)

rattan waste bin
1x1
OBTAIN Shop (Large Item)
FUNCTION Trash Bin
not customizable; purchasable in 6 colors
1000 (250)

red corner
2x2
OBTAIN Shop (Large Item)
FUNCTION Bed: Normal
x3 · FABRIC x4 Custom · BODY N/A
6100 (1525)

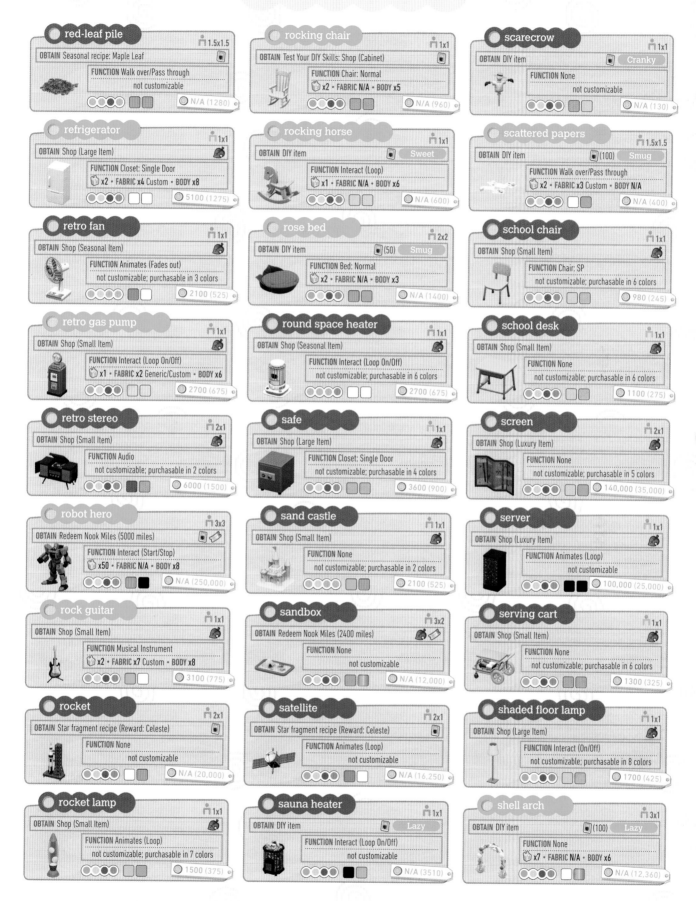

red-leaf pile
1.5x1.5
OBTAIN Seasonal recipe: Maple Leaf
FUNCTION Walk over/Pass through
not customizable
N/A (1280)

rocking chair
1x1
OBTAIN Test Your DIY Skills: Shop (Cabinet)
FUNCTION Chair: Normal
x2 • FABRIC N/A • BODY x5
N/A (960)

scarecrow
1x1
OBTAIN DIY item — Cranky
FUNCTION None
not customizable
N/A (130)

refrigerator
1x1
OBTAIN Shop (Large Item)
FUNCTION Closet: Single Door
x2 • FABRIC x4 Custom • BODY x8
5100 (1275)

rocking horse
1x1
OBTAIN DIY item — Sweet
FUNCTION Interact (Loop)
x1 • FABRIC N/A • BODY x6
N/A (600)

scattered papers
1.5x1.5
OBTAIN DIY item — (100) Smug
FUNCTION Walk over/Pass through
x2 • FABRIC x3 Custom • BODY N/A
N/A (400)

retro fan
1x1
OBTAIN Shop (Seasonal Item)
FUNCTION Animates (Fades out)
not customizable; purchasable in 3 colors
2100 (525)

rose bed
2x2
OBTAIN DIY item — (50) Smug
FUNCTION Bed: Normal
x2 • FABRIC N/A • BODY x3
N/A (1400)

school chair
1x1
OBTAIN Shop (Small Item)
FUNCTION Chair: SP
not customizable; purchasable in 6 colors
980 (245)

retro gas pump
1x1
OBTAIN Shop (Small Item)
FUNCTION Interact (Loop On/Off)
x1 • FABRIC x2 Generic/Custom • BODY x6
2700 (675)

round space heater
1x1
OBTAIN Shop (Seasonal Item)
FUNCTION Interact (Loop On/Off)
not customizable; purchasable in 6 colors
2700 (675)

school desk
1x1
OBTAIN Shop (Small Item)
FUNCTION None
not customizable; purchasable in 6 colors
1100 (275)

retro stereo
2x1
OBTAIN Shop (Small Item)
FUNCTION Audio
not customizable; purchasable in 2 colors
6000 (1500)

safe
1x1
OBTAIN Shop (Large Item)
FUNCTION Closet: Single Door
not customizable; purchasable in 4 colors
3600 (900)

screen
2x1
OBTAIN Shop (Luxury Item)
FUNCTION None
not customizable; purchasable in 5 colors
140,000 (35,000)

robot hero
3x3
OBTAIN Redeem Nook Miles (5000 miles)
FUNCTION Interact (Start/Stop)
x50 • FABRIC N/A • BODY x8
N/A (250,000)

sand castle
1x1
OBTAIN Shop (Small Item)
FUNCTION None
not customizable; purchasable in 2 colors
2100 (525)

server
1x1
OBTAIN Shop (Luxury Item)
FUNCTION Animates (Loop)
not customizable
100,000 (25,000)

rock guitar
1x1
OBTAIN Shop (Small Item)
FUNCTION Musical Instrument
x2 • FABRIC x7 Custom • BODY x8
3100 (775)

sandbox
3x2
OBTAIN Redeem Nook Miles (2400 miles)
FUNCTION None
not customizable
N/A (12,000)

serving cart
1x1
OBTAIN Shop (Small Item)
FUNCTION None
not customizable; purchasable in 6 colors
1300 (325)

rocket
2x1
OBTAIN Star fragment recipe (Reward: Celeste)
FUNCTION None
not customizable
N/A (20,000)

satellite
2x1
OBTAIN Star fragment recipe (Reward: Celeste)
FUNCTION Animates (Loop)
not customizable
N/A (16,250)

shaded floor lamp
1x1
OBTAIN Shop (Large Item)
FUNCTION Interact (On/Off)
not customizable; purchasable in 8 colors
1700 (425)

rocket lamp
1x1
OBTAIN Shop (Small Item)
FUNCTION Animates (Loop)
not customizable; purchasable in 7 colors
1500 (375)

sauna heater
1x1
OBTAIN DIY item — Lazy
FUNCTION Interact (Loop On/Off)
not customizable
N/A (3510)

shell arch
3x1
OBTAIN DIY item — (100) Lazy
FUNCTION None
x7 • FABRIC N/A • BODY x6
N/A (12,360)

shell bed
2x2
OBTAIN DIY item · Peppy
FUNCTION Bed: Normal
x7 · FABRIC N/A · BODY x6
N/A (10,200)

shell fountain
1.5x1.5
OBTAIN DIY item · Lazy
FUNCTION Animates (Loop)
x7 · FABRIC N/A · BODY x6
N/A (9450)

shell partition
2x1
OBTAIN DIY item · Big sister
FUNCTION None
x7 · FABRIC N/A · BODY x6
N/A (8000)

shell stool
1x1
OBTAIN DIY item · Big sister
FUNCTION Chair: Stool
x1 · FABRIC N/A · BODY x6
N/A (600)

shell table
2x2
OBTAIN DIY item · Peppy
FUNCTION None
x4 · FABRIC N/A · BODY x6
N/A (2280)

shower booth
1.5x1.5
OBTAIN Shop (Luxury Item)
FUNCTION None
not customizable; purchasable in 4 colors
110,000 (27,500)

signpost
1x1
OBTAIN DIY item (100) · Lazy
FUNCTION None
x1 · FABRIC N/A · BODY x8
N/A (600)

silo
2x2
OBTAIN Redeem Nook Miles (3000 miles)
FUNCTION None
x7 · FABRIC N/A · BODY x5
N/A (13,920)

silver mic
1x1
OBTAIN Shop (Small Item)
FUNCTION None
not customizable
1800 (450)

simple DIY workbench
1.5x1.5
OBTAIN DIY item · Jock
FUNCTION Workbench
not customizable
N/A (1350)

simple panel
1x0.5
OBTAIN Shop (Small Item)
FUNCTION None
x1 · FABRIC x7 Generic/Custom · BODY x8
810 (202)

simple well
2x2
OBTAIN Redeem Nook Miles (2000 miles)
FUNCTION None
not customizable
N/A (2850)

skeleton
1x1
OBTAIN Shop (Small Item)
FUNCTION Interact (Stop)
not customizable
3900 (975)

sleeping bag
2x1
OBTAIN Shop (All)
FUNCTION Bed: Normal
not customizable; purchasable in 8 colors
1400 (350)

sleigh
2x1
OBTAIN DIY item · Cranky
FUNCTION Chair: Front and Back (Left half)
x2 · FABRIC N/A · BODY x4
N/A (960)

small cardboard boxes
1x1
OBTAIN DIY item · Peppy
FUNCTION None
not customizable
N/A (120)

smoker
1x1
OBTAIN Shop (All)
FUNCTION Interact (Loop On/Off)
not customizable; purchasable in 3 colors
5500 (1375)

snack machine
2x1
OBTAIN Redeem Nook Miles (2000 miles)
FUNCTION Interact (Start/Stop)
not customizable; purchasable in 4 colors
N/A (10,000)

soccer goal
3x2
OBTAIN Redeem Nook Miles (4000 miles)
FUNCTION None
not customizable
N/A (20,000)

soft-serve lamp
1x1
OBTAIN Shop (Large Item)
FUNCTION Interact (On/Off)
not customizable; purchasable in 8 colors
3000 (750)

solar panel
3x2
OBTAIN Redeem Nook Miles (4000 miles)
FUNCTION None
not customizable; purchasable in 2 colors
N/A (20,000)

South Pole
1x1
OBTAIN Reward: Gulliver
FUNCTION None
not customizable
N/A (1050)

space shuttle
2x1
OBTAIN Star fragment recipe (Reward: Celeste)
FUNCTION Interact (On/Off)
not customizable
N/A (10,000)

speed bag
1x1
OBTAIN Shop (Small Item)
FUNCTION Interact (Stop)
not customizable; purchasable in 3 colors
3500 (875)

sphinx
3x1
OBTAIN Reward: Gulliver
FUNCTION None
not customizable
N/A (2100)

spinning wheel
1x1
OBTAIN Shop (Small Item)
FUNCTION Interact (Start/Stop)
not customizable
970 (242)

springy ride-on
1x1
OBTAIN Redeem Nook Miles (2000 miles)
FUNCTION Interact (Stop)
not customizable; purchasable in 7 colors
N/A (10,000)

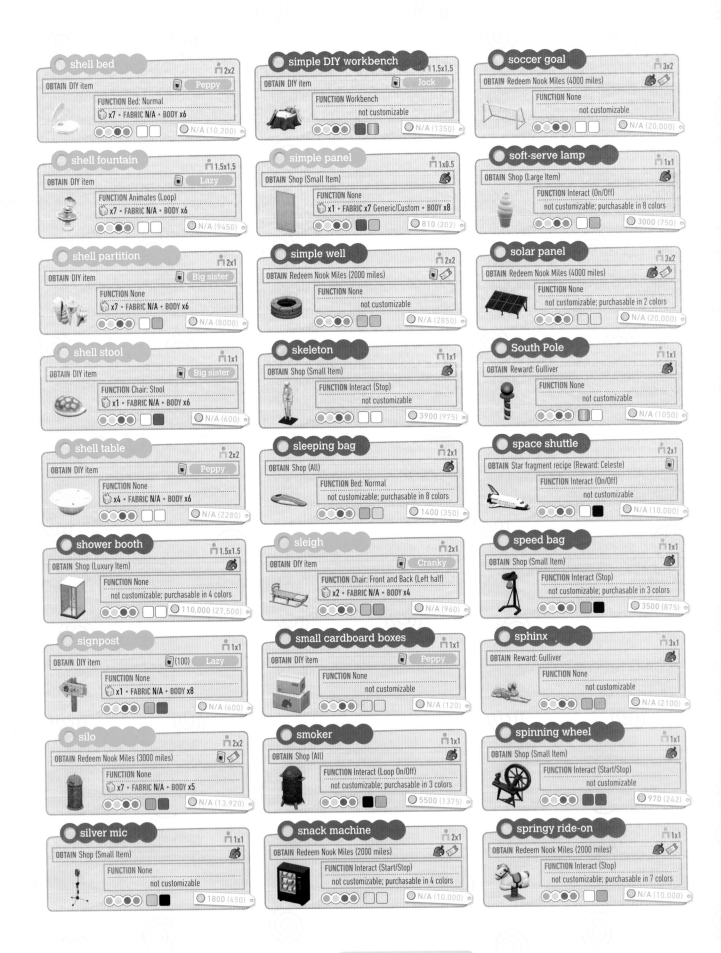

squat toilet
1x1
OBTAIN Shop (Small Item)
FUNCTION Interact (Start/Stop)
not customizable
1500 (375)

stone table
2x2
OBTAIN Tom Nook ("Three New Plots" quest) Lazy
FUNCTION None
not customizable
N/A (1200)

synthesizer
2x1
OBTAIN Shop (Luxury Item)
FUNCTION Musical Instrument
not customizable; purchasable in 6 colors
66,000 (16,500)

stadiometer
1x1
OBTAIN Shop (Small Item)
FUNCTION None
not customizable; purchasable in 3 colors
2100 (525)

stone tablet
1x1
OBTAIN Redeem Nook Miles (800 miles)
FUNCTION None
x3 • FABRIC N/A • BODY x2
N/A (1800)

system kitchen
2x1
OBTAIN Shop (Luxury Item)
FUNCTION None
not customizable; purchasable in 8 colors
130,000 (32,500)

stall
2x1
OBTAIN Redeem Nook Miles (2000 miles)
FUNCTION None
x3 • FABRIC x4 Generic/Custom • BODY x8
N/A (1440)

Stonehenge
3x3
OBTAIN Reward: Gulliver
FUNCTION None
not customizable
N/A (2300)

table with cloth
2x2
OBTAIN Shop (Large Item)
FUNCTION None
x2 • FABRIC x7 Generic/Custom • BODY N/A
5100 (1275)

standard umbrella stand
1x1
OBTAIN DIY item Cranky
FUNCTION None
x4 • FABRIC x3 Generic/Custom • BODY x4
N/A (2250)

street organ
1x1
OBTAIN Shop (Large Item)
FUNCTION Interact (Hold Ⓐ at end of loop)
not customizable; purchasable in 4 colors
5000 (1250)

tall garden rock
1x1
OBTAIN DIY item Snooty
FUNCTION None
not customizable
N/A (9000)

standing toilet
1x1
OBTAIN Shop (Small Item)
FUNCTION Interact (Start/Stop)
not customizable
1900 (475)

street piano
2x1
OBTAIN DIY item (100) Big sister
FUNCTION Musical Instrument
x7 • FABRIC N/A • BODY x2
N/A (26,755)

tall lantern
1x1
OBTAIN DIY item (100) Smug
FUNCTION Interact (Loop On/Off)
x4 • FABRIC N/A • BODY x3
N/A (2700)

Statue of Liberty
1x1
OBTAIN Reward: Gulliver
FUNCTION Outdoor Light (Brightness Sensor)
not customizable
N/A (2300)

streetlamp
1x1
OBTAIN Redeem Nook Miles (1000 miles)
FUNCTION Outdoor Light (Brightness Sensor)
not customizable; purchasable in 4 colors
N/A (5000)

tankless toilet
1x1
OBTAIN Shop (Large Item)
FUNCTION Chair: SP (Interact: On/Off)
not customizable; purchasable in 5 colors
4100 (1025)

stone arch
3x1
OBTAIN Redeem Nook Miles (2000 miles)
FUNCTION None
x7 • FABRIC N/A • BODY x2
N/A (13,500)

studio spotlight
1x1
OBTAIN Shop (Small Item)
FUNCTION Interact (On/Off)
not customizable; purchasable in 8 colors
2100 (525)

tatami bed
2x1
OBTAIN Shop (Small Item)
FUNCTION Bed: Normal
not customizable; purchasable in 4 colors
2800 (700)

stone lion-dog
1x1
OBTAIN DIY item (100) Smug
FUNCTION None
x5 • FABRIC N/A • BODY x3
N/A (3600)

surfboard
1x1
OBTAIN Shop (Seasonal Item)
FUNCTION None
not customizable; purchasable in 6 colors
4100 (1025)

Taurus bathtub
2x1
OBTAIN Zodiac recipe (Reward: Celeste)
FUNCTION None
not customizable
N/A (12,350)

stone stool
1x1
OBTAIN DIY for Beginners: Shop (Cabinet)
FUNCTION Chair: Stool
not customizable
N/A (450)

swinging bench
2x1
OBTAIN Test Your DIY Skills: Shop (Cabinet)
FUNCTION Chair: Normal
x2 • FABRIC N/A • BODY x5
N/A (1440)

tea table
2x2
OBTAIN DIY item Cranky
FUNCTION None
x2 • FABRIC N/A • BODY x5
N/A (1440)

7

teacup ride
3x3
OBTAIN Redeem Nook Miles (5000 miles)
FUNCTION Animates (Fades out)
not customizable; purchasable in 4 colors
N/A (25,000)

throwback rocket
1x1
OBTAIN Shop (Large Item)
FUNCTION Closet: Single Door
not customizable; purchasable in 6 colors
5900 (1475)

tourist telescope
1x1
OBTAIN Redeem Nook Miles (2000 miles)
FUNCTION None
not customizable; purchasable in 5 colors
N/A (10,000)

telescope
1x1
OBTAIN Shop (Small Item)
FUNCTION None
not customizable
5600 (1400)

tiki torch
1x1
OBTAIN Reward: Give Tom Nook 2nd creature · Cranky
FUNCTION Interact (Loop On/Off)
not customizable
N/A (650)

Tower of Pisa
1x1
OBTAIN Reward: Gulliver
FUNCTION None
not customizable
N/A (2300)

tennis table
2x1
OBTAIN Shop (Luxury Item)
FUNCTION None
not customizable
44,000 (11,000)

tiny library
1x1
OBTAIN DIY item · (100) Sweet
FUNCTION None
x2 · FABRIC N/A · BODY x6
N/A (1035)

train set
2x2
OBTAIN Shop (Large Item)
FUNCTION Animates (Fades out)
not customizable; purchasable in 4 colors
7900 (1975)

termite mound
1x1
OBTAIN Bug-Off
FUNCTION None
not customizable
N/A (550)

tire stack
1x1
OBTAIN Inspiration: Old tire
FUNCTION None
x1 · FABRIC N/A · BODY x4
N/A (60)

treadmill
2x1
OBTAIN Shop (Luxury Item)
FUNCTION Interact (On/Off at end of loop)
not customizable; purchasable in 4 colors
64,000 (16,000)

three-tiered snowman
1x1
OBTAIN Reward: Snowboy
FUNCTION None
x7 · FABRIC N/A · BODY x4
N/A (7420)

tire toy
1x1
OBTAIN Inspiration: Old tire
FUNCTION Chair: Stool
x1 · FABRIC N/A · BODY x6
N/A (20)

tree standee
2x1
OBTAIN DIY item · Jock
FUNCTION None
x3 · FABRIC N/A · BODY x5
N/A (1560)

throwback dino screen
2x0.5
OBTAIN Shop (Large Item)
FUNCTION None
not customizable
3600 (900)

toilet
1x1
OBTAIN Shop (Large Item)
FUNCTION Chair: SP
not customizable; purchasable in 3 colors
4400 (1100)

tree's bounty arch
3x1
OBTAIN Seasonal recipe: Maple Leaf
FUNCTION None
x7 · FABRIC N/A · BODY x2
N/A (5750)

throwback hat table
2x2
OBTAIN Shop (Large Item)
FUNCTION None
not customizable; purchasable in 8 colors
3800 (950)

toilet-cleaning set
1x1
OBTAIN Shop (Small Item)
FUNCTION None
not customizable; purchasable in 2 colors
670 (167)

tree's bounty big tree
1x1
OBTAIN Seasonal recipe: Maple Leaf
FUNCTION None
x7 · FABRIC N/A · BODY x2
N/A (6080)

throwback mitt chair
1x1
OBTAIN Shop (Large Item)
FUNCTION Chair: Normal
not customizable; purchasable in 6 colors
1400 (350)

tool cart
1x1
OBTAIN Shop (Small Item)
FUNCTION None
not customizable; purchasable in 8 colors
2400 (600)

tricycle
1x1
OBTAIN Shop (Small Item)
FUNCTION None
not customizable; purchasable in 5 colors
1600 (400)

throwback race-car bed
2x1
OBTAIN Shop (Large Item)
FUNCTION Bed: Switch
not customizable; purchasable in 7 colors
3800 (950)

tool shelf
2x1
OBTAIN Shop (Small Item)
FUNCTION None
not customizable; purchasable in 4 colors
7300 (1825)

trophy case
2x1
OBTAIN DIY item · (100) Jock
FUNCTION None
not customizable
N/A (33,690)

tulip surprise box — 1x1
OBTAIN DIY item — (50) Jock
FUNCTION Interact (Start/Stop)
x2 • FABRIC N/A • BODY x3
N/A (760)

TV camera — 1x1
OBTAIN Shop (Luxury Item)
FUNCTION Interact (On/Off)
not customizable; purchasable in 2 colors
14,000 (3500)

upright locker — 1x1
OBTAIN Shop (Small Item)
FUNCTION Closet: Single Door
x2 • FABRIC x4 Custom • BODY x7
3700 (925)

upright piano — 2x1
OBTAIN Shop (Luxury Item)
FUNCTION Musical Instrument
not customizable; purchasable in 4 colors
53,000 (13,250)

upright vacuum — 1x1
OBTAIN Shop (Large Item)
FUNCTION Interact (On/Off)
not customizable; purchasable in 7 colors
2500 (625)

utility pole — 1x1
OBTAIN Redeem Nook Miles (1000 miles)
FUNCTION None
not customizable; purchasable in 2 colors
N/A (5000)

utility sink — 1x1
OBTAIN Shop (Small Item)
FUNCTION Interact (On/Off)
not customizable
3500 (875)

vacuum cleaner — 1x1
OBTAIN Shop (Small Item)
FUNCTION Interact (On/Off)
not customizable; purchasable in 5 colors
3800 (950)

velvet stool — 1x1
OBTAIN Shop (Small Item)
FUNCTION Chair: Stool
not customizable
1000 (250)

video camera — 1x1
OBTAIN Shop (Luxury Item)
FUNCTION Interact (On/Off)
not customizable; purchasable in 3 colors
32,000 (8000)

vintage TV tray — 1x1
OBTAIN Shop (Small Item)
FUNCTION None
x1 • FABRIC x3 Generic/Custom • BODY x4
1200 (300)

Virgo harp — 1x1
OBTAIN Zodiac recipe (Reward: Celeste)
FUNCTION Musical Instrument
not customizable
N/A (22,050)

water cooler — 1x1
OBTAIN Shop (Small Item)
FUNCTION Interact (Start/Stop)
not customizable; purchasable in 2 colors
3400 (850)

water pump — 1x1
OBTAIN Tom Nook ("Three New Plots" quest) — Lazy
FUNCTION Interact (Start/Stop)
x4 • FABRIC N/A • BODY x4
N/A (2700)

wave breaker — 2x2
OBTAIN Redeem Nook Miles (1500 miles)
FUNCTION None
not customizable
N/A (3500)

weight bench — 2x1
OBTAIN Shop (Large Item)
FUNCTION Bed: Normal
not customizable
5400 (1350)

western-style stone — 2x1
OBTAIN DIY item — (100) Sweet
FUNCTION None
x6 • FABRIC N/A • BODY x5
N/A (4500)

wheelchair — 1x1
OBTAIN Shop (Small Item)
FUNCTION Chair: Normal
x1 • FABRIC x4 Generic/Custom • BODY N/A
2700 (675)

whirlpool bath — 2x2
OBTAIN Shop (Luxury Item)
FUNCTION Interact (On/Off)
not customizable; purchasable in 2 colors
130,000 (32,500)

whiteboard — 2x1
OBTAIN Shop (Large Item)
FUNCTION None
not customizable; purchasable in 7 colors
2600 (650)

wild log bench — 2x1
OBTAIN DIY item — Jock
FUNCTION Chair: Stool
x2 • FABRIC N/A • BODY x4
N/A (960)

wind turbine — 2x1
OBTAIN Redeem Nook Miles (4000 miles)
FUNCTION None
not customizable; purchasable in 2 colors
N/A (20,000)

wood-burning stove — 1x1
OBTAIN Shop (Large Item)
FUNCTION Animates (Loop)
not customizable
2100 (525)

wooden bookshelf — 2x0.5
OBTAIN DIY item — (100) Lazy
FUNCTION None
x3 • FABRIC N/A • BODY x4
N/A (1925)

wooden bucket — 1x1
OBTAIN Tom Nook ("Three New Plots" quest) — Smug
FUNCTION None
not customizable
N/A (1110)

wooden chair — 1x1
OBTAIN Tom Nook ("Three New Plots" quest) — Snooty
FUNCTION Chair: SP
x1 • FABRIC N/A • BODY x8
N/A (720)

wooden chest — 2x1
OBTAIN DIY item — Lazy
FUNCTION Dresser
x3 • FABRIC N/A • BODY x8
N/A (1920)

Item	Size	Obtain	Function	Materials	Price
wooden double bed	2x2	DIY item — Smug	Bed: Normal	x6 · FABRIC x3 Generic/Custom · BODY x8	N/A (3600)
wooden end table	1x1	DIY item — Snooty	None	x2 · FABRIC N/A · BODY x8	N/A (960)
wooden full-length mirror	1x1	DIY item — Peppy	Dresser	x2 · FABRIC N/A · BODY x8	N/A (1350)
wooden low table	2x1	DIY item — Smug	None	x2 · FABRIC N/A · BODY x8	N/A (1200)
wooden mini table	1x1	DIY item — Big sister	None	x2 · FABRIC x4 Generic/Custom · BODY x8	N/A (720)
wooden simple bed	2x1	Tom Nook ("Three New Plots" quest) — Lazy	Bed: Normal	x4 · FABRIC x3 Generic/Custom · BODY x8	N/A (2160)
wooden stool	1x1	DIY item — Peppy	Chair: Stool	x2 · FABRIC x4 Generic/Custom · BODY x8	N/A (480)
wooden table	2x2	DIY item — Big sister	None	x4 · FABRIC x4 Generic/Custom · BODY x8	N/A (1800)
wooden wardrobe	1x1	Reward: Customization Workshop	Closet: Double Door	x2 · FABRIC N/A · BODY x8	N/A (1440)
wooden waste bin	1x1	DIY item — Big sister	Trash Bin	x1 · FABRIC N/A · BODY x6	N/A (480)
wooden-block bed	2x1	DIY item — Sweet	Bed: Normal	x4 · FABRIC N/A · BODY x5	N/A (2400)
wooden-block bench	2x1	DIY item — Big sister	Chair: Front and Back	x2 · FABRIC N/A · BODY x5	N/A (840)
wooden-block bookshelf	1x1	Test Your DIY Skills: Shop (Cabinet)	None	x1 · FABRIC N/A · BODY x5	N/A (720)
wooden-block chair	1x1	Test Your DIY Skills: Shop (Cabinet)	Chair: SP	x1 · FABRIC N/A · BODY x5	N/A (720)
wooden-block chest	2x1	DIY item — Sweet	Dresser	x3 · FABRIC N/A · BODY x5	N/A (1800)
wooden-block stereo	2x1	Test Your DIY Skills: Shop (Cabinet)	Audio	x4 · FABRIC N/A · BODY x5	N/A (2460)
wooden-block stool	1x1	DIY item — Peppy	Chair: Stool	x1 · FABRIC N/A · BODY x5	N/A (600)
wooden-block table	2x2	Tom Nook ("Three New Plots" quest) — Big sister	None	x2 · FABRIC N/A · BODY x5	N/A (1320)
writing chair	1x1	Shop (Small Item)	Chair: SP	x1 · FABRIC x2 Generic/Custom · BODY x4	1700 (425)
writing desk	2x1	Shop (Small Item)	Interact (On/Off) — not customizable; purchasable in 4 colors		7100 (1775)
yellow-leaf pile	1.5x1.5	Seasonal recipe: Acorn/Pinecone	Walk over/Pass through — not customizable		N/A (1300)
yucca	1x1	Shop (Small Item)	None — not customizable; purchasable in 5 colors		2100 (525)
zen cushion	1x1	Shop (Small Item)	Chair: Stool	x1 · FABRIC x6 Generic/Custom · BODY N/A	500 (125)
zen-style stone	1x1	DIY item (100) — Lazy	None	x6 · FABRIC N/A · BODY x5	N/A (4500)

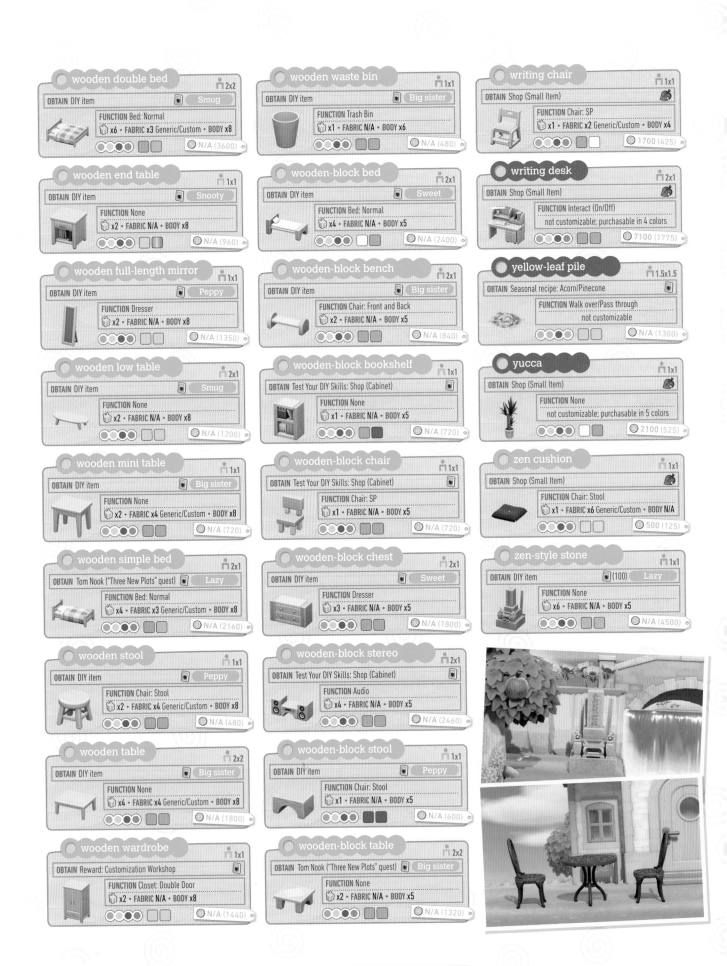

Accessories

bingo wheel 1x1
OBTAIN Shop (Small item)
FUNCTION Interact (Start/Stop)
not customizable
1000 (250)

accessories stand 1x1
OBTAIN Shop (Small item)
FUNCTION None
not customizable; purchasable in 5 colors
1500 (375)

Baby panda 1x1
OBTAIN Shop (Small item)
FUNCTION None
not customizable
1800 (450)

birthday cake 1x1
OBTAIN Your Birthday
FUNCTION Interact (On/Off)
x1 • FABRIC N/A • BODY x3 Custom
N/A (100)

aluminum briefcase 1x1
OBTAIN Shop (Luxury Item)
FUNCTION Interact (On/Off)
not customizable; purchasable in 2 colors
100,000 (25,000)

ball 1x1
OBTAIN Shop (Small item)
FUNCTION Interact (Stop)
not customizable; purchasable in 4 colors
520 (130)

birthday candles 1x1
OBTAIN Your Birthday
FUNCTION Interact (Loop On/Off)
x1 • FABRIC N/A • BODY x6 Custom
N/A (300)

amp 1x1
OBTAIN Shop (Small item)
FUNCTION None
not customizable; purchasable in 7 colors
5100 (1275)

bamboo candleholder 1x1
OBTAIN DIY item (50) Snooty
FUNCTION Interact (Loop On/Off)
x2 • FABRIC N/A • BODY x3
N/A (880)

board game 1x1
OBTAIN Shop (Small item)
FUNCTION Interact (Start/Stop)
not customizable; purchasable in 3 colors
1300 (325)

analog kitchen scale 1x1
OBTAIN Shop (Small item)
FUNCTION Interact (Stop)
not customizable; purchasable in 8 colors
1100 (275)

bamboo drum 1x1
OBTAIN DIY item (50) Jock
FUNCTION Musical Instrument
x1 • FABRIC N/A • BODY x3
N/A (720)

book 1x1
OBTAIN Shop (Small item)
FUNCTION None
not customizable; purchasable in 4 colors
290 (72)

ant farm 1x1
OBTAIN Shop (Large Item)
FUNCTION None
not customizable
1400 (350)

bamboo lunch box 1x1
OBTAIN DIY item (50) Snooty
FUNCTION None
x1 • FABRIC N/A • BODY x3
N/A (640)

book stands 1x1
OBTAIN Shop (Small item)
FUNCTION None
not customizable; purchasable in 4 colors
1100 (275)

anthurium plant 1x1
OBTAIN Shop (Small item)
FUNCTION None
not customizable; purchasable in 5 colors
990 (247)

bamboo sphere 1x1
OBTAIN DIY item (50) Sweet
FUNCTION None
x1 • FABRIC N/A • BODY x3
N/A (480)

bottled ship 1x1
OBTAIN Shop (Small item)
FUNCTION None
not customizable; purchasable in 3 colors
1800 (450)

aroma pot 1x1
OBTAIN DIY item Snooty
FUNCTION Interact (Loop On/Off)
x1 • FABRIC N/A • BODY x6
N/A (600)

bamboo-shoot lamp 1x1
OBTAIN Seasonal recipe: Bamboo
FUNCTION Interact (On/Off)
not customizable
N/A (4900)

brine-shrimp aquarium 1x1
OBTAIN Shop (Large Item)
FUNCTION Animates (Loop)
not customizable
1400 (350)

Baby bear 1x1
OBTAIN Shop (Small item)
FUNCTION None
x1 • FABRIC x3 Generic/Custom • BODY x6
1800 (450)

beach ball 1x1
OBTAIN Shop (All)
FUNCTION Interact (Stop)
not customizable; purchasable in 4 colors
430 (107)

bronze bug trophy 1x1
OBTAIN Fishing Tourney/Bug-Off
FUNCTION None
not customizable
N/A (400)

bronze fish trophy

1x1

OBTAIN Fishing Tourney/Bug-Off

FUNCTION None
not customizable

N/A (400)

bronze HHA trophy

1x1

OBTAIN HHA Reward (Mail)

FUNCTION None
not customizable

N/A (400)

camp stove

1x1

OBTAIN Shop (All)

FUNCTION Interact (Loop On/Off)
not customizable; purchasable in 6 colors

1300 (325)

candle

1x1

OBTAIN Shop (All)

FUNCTION Interact (On/Off)
not customizable; purchasable in 5 colors

600 (150)

cardboard box

1x1

OBTAIN Shop (All)

FUNCTION None
not customizable; purchasable in 7 colors

120 (30)

cartoonist's set

1x1

OBTAIN Shop (Small item)

FUNCTION Interact (On/Off)
x1 • FABRIC x2 Custom • BODY x4

1200 (300)

cassette player

1x1

OBTAIN Shop (Small item)

FUNCTION Audio
not customizable; purchasable in 8 colors

2000 (500)

cat grass

1x1

OBTAIN Shop (Small item)

FUNCTION None
not customizable; purchasable in 5 colors

570 (142)

celebratory candles

1x1

OBTAIN Shop (Seasonal Item)

FUNCTION Interact (Loop On/Off)
not customizable; purchasable in 5 colors

1500 (375)

cherry speakers

1x1

OBTAIN DIY item   (100) Peppy

FUNCTION Audio
x5 • FABRIC N/A • BODY x2

N/A (3500)

cherry-blossom bonsai

1x1

OBTAIN Seasonal recipe: Cherry blossom

FUNCTION None
not customizable

N/A (3300)

chessboard

1x1

OBTAIN Shop (Luxury Item)

FUNCTION None
not customizable; purchasable in 2 colors

95,000 (23,750)

classic pitcher

1x1

OBTAIN Tom Nook ("Three New Plots" quest)   Snooty

FUNCTION None
x2 • FABRIC N/A • BODY x6

N/A (800)

coconut juice

1x1

OBTAIN DIY item   Snooty

FUNCTION None
not customizable

N/A (500)

coffee cup

1x1

OBTAIN Shop (Small item)

FUNCTION None
not customizable; purchasable in 6 colors

270 (67)

coffee grinder

1x1

OBTAIN Shop (Small item)

FUNCTION Interact (Hold Ⓐ at end of loop)
not customizable

2200 (550)

cooler box

1x1

OBTAIN Shop (All)

FUNCTION Closet: Flip
not customizable; purchasable in 4 colors

1700 (425)

cordless phone

1x1

OBTAIN Shop (Small item)

FUNCTION Interact (Start/Stop)
not customizable; purchasable in 7 colors

1600 (400)

cream and sugar

1x1

OBTAIN Shop (Small item)

FUNCTION None
not customizable; purchasable in 4 colors

500 (125)

cushion

1x1

OBTAIN Shop (Small item)

FUNCTION Chair: Stool
x1 • FABRIC x5 Generic/Custom • BODY N/A

300 (75)

cute music player

1x1

OBTAIN Shop (Small item)

FUNCTION Audio
not customizable; purchasable in 5 colors

2600 (650)

cutting board

1x1

OBTAIN DIY item   Sweet

FUNCTION None
x3 • FABRIC x2 Generic/Custom • BODY x4

N/A (990)

DAL model plane

1x1

OBTAIN DAL Souvenir (Mail)

FUNCTION None
x2 • FABRIC N/A • BODY x4 Custom

N/A (1010)

DAL mug

1x1

OBTAIN DAL Souvenir (Mail)

FUNCTION None
not customizable

N/A (1010)

Dala horse

1x1

OBTAIN Reward: Gulliver

FUNCTION None
x2 • FABRIC N/A • BODY x3 Custom

N/A (1300)

decoy duck

1x1

OBTAIN DIY item   Smug

FUNCTION None
x1 • FABRIC N/A • BODY x7

N/A (480)

desk mirror

1x1

OBTAIN Shop (Small item)

FUNCTION Dresser
not customizable; purchasable in 6 colors

1600 (400)

desktop computer 🏠1x1
OBTAIN Shop (Luxury Item)
FUNCTION Interact (On/Off)
🔨 x7 • FABRIC x6 Generic/Custom • BODY x4
100,000 (25,000)

digital alarm clock 🏠1x1
OBTAIN Shop (Small item)
FUNCTION Clock: Digital
not customizable; purchasable in 8 colors
1600 (400)

dinnerware 🏠1x1
OBTAIN Shop (Small item)
FUNCTION None
not customizable
930 (232)

dish-drying rack 🏠1x1
OBTAIN Shop (Small item)
FUNCTION None
not customizable; purchasable in 6 colors
530 (132)

document stack 🏠1x1
OBTAIN Shop (Small item) (100) Smug
FUNCTION None
🔨 x2 • FABRIC x3 Custom • BODY N/A
1600 (400)

dolly 🏠1x1
OBTAIN Shop (Small item)
FUNCTION None
not customizable; purchasable in 6 colors
1600 (400)

electronics kit 🏠1x1
OBTAIN Shop (Small item)
FUNCTION Interact (On/Off)
not customizable; purchasable in 2 colors
1300 (325)

espresso maker 🏠1x1
OBTAIN Shop (Small item)
FUNCTION Interact (Start/Stop)
not customizable; purchasable in 7 colors
5600 (1400)

essay set 🏠1x1
OBTAIN Shop (Small item)
FUNCTION None
not customizable; purchasable in 4 colors
650 (162)

fancy violin 🏠1x1
OBTAIN Shop (Luxury Item)
FUNCTION Musical Instrument
not customizable; purchasable in 3 colors
140,000 (35,000)

fax machine 🏠1x1
OBTAIN Shop (Small item)
FUNCTION Interact (Start/Stop)
🔨 x1 • FABRIC x3 Custom • BODY x4
1500 (375)

festive top set 🏠1x1
OBTAIN Seasonal recipe: Ornament
FUNCTION None
not customizable
N/A (320)

film projector 🏠1x1
OBTAIN Shop (Small item)
FUNCTION Interact (On/Off at end of loop)
not customizable
2400 (600)

firewood 🏠1x1
OBTAIN DIY item Jock
FUNCTION None
not customizable
N/A (960)

floating-biotope planter 🏠1x1
OBTAIN Shop (Small Item)
FUNCTION None
not customizable; purchasable in 4 colors
1600 (400)

floor sign 🏠1x1
OBTAIN Shop (Small Item)
FUNCTION None
not customizable; purchasable in 5 colors
890 (222)

football 🏠1x1
OBTAIN Shop (Small item)
FUNCTION None
not customizable
400 (100)

fortune-telling set 🏠1x1
OBTAIN Shop (Small item)
FUNCTION Interact (On/Off)
not customizable; purchasable in 2 colors
1000 (250)

fragrance diffuser 🏠1x1
OBTAIN Shop (Small item)
FUNCTION Interact (On/Off)
not customizable; purchasable in 5 colors
1400 (350)

fragrance sticks 🏠1x1
OBTAIN Shop (Small item)
FUNCTION None
not customizable; purchasable in 4 colors
830 (207)

frozen-treat set 🏠1x1
OBTAIN Reward: Snowboy
FUNCTION None
🔨 x7 • FABRIC N/A • BODY x6
N/A (5400)

fruit basket 🏠1x1
OBTAIN DIY item (100) Cranky
FUNCTION None
not customizable
N/A (1000)

frying pan 🏠1x1
OBTAIN DIY for Beginners: Shop (Cabinet)
FUNCTION None
🔨 x2 • FABRIC N/A • BODY x6
N/A (1500)

garden gnome 🏠1x1
OBTAIN Shop (Small Item)
FUNCTION None
not customizable; purchasable in 8 colors
1900 (475)

glass holder with candle 🏠1x1
OBTAIN Shop (Small item)
FUNCTION Interact (Loop On/Off)
not customizable; purchasable in 6 colors
350 (87)

globe 🏠1x1
OBTAIN Shop (Small item)
FUNCTION Interact (Stop)
not customizable; purchasable in 3 colors
1800 (450)

gold bars 🏠1x1
OBTAIN DIY item (100) Snooty
FUNCTION None
not customizable
N/A (30,000)

7

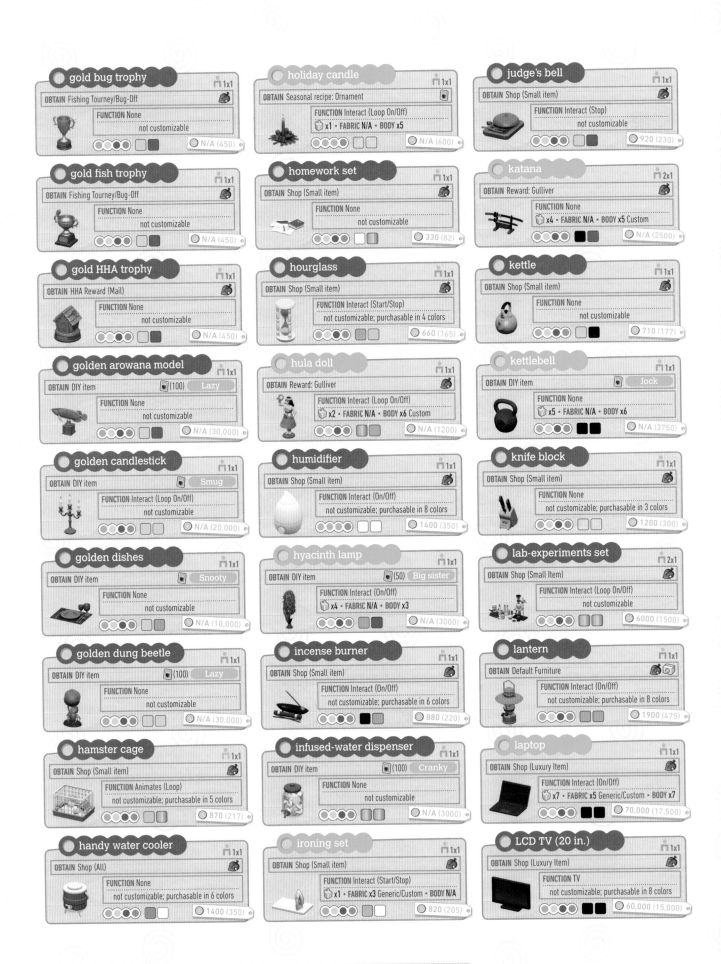

gold bug trophy ⌂1x1
OBTAIN Fishing Tourney/Bug-Off
FUNCTION None
not customizable
N/A (450)

gold fish trophy ⌂1x1
OBTAIN Fishing Tourney/Bug-Off
FUNCTION None
not customizable
N/A (450)

gold HHA trophy ⌂1x1
OBTAIN HHA Reward (Mail)
FUNCTION None
not customizable
N/A (450)

golden arowana model ⌂1x1
OBTAIN DIY item (100) Lazy
FUNCTION None
not customizable
N/A (30,000)

golden candlestick ⌂1x1
OBTAIN DIY item Smug
FUNCTION Interact (Loop On/Off)
not customizable
N/A (20,000)

golden dishes ⌂1x1
OBTAIN DIY item Snooty
FUNCTION None
not customizable
N/A (10,000)

golden dung beetle ⌂1x1
OBTAIN DIY item (100) Lazy
FUNCTION None
not customizable
N/A (30,000)

hamster cage ⌂1x1
OBTAIN Shop (Small item)
FUNCTION Animates (Loop)
not customizable; purchasable in 5 colors
870 (217)

handy water cooler ⌂1x1
OBTAIN Shop (All)
FUNCTION None
not customizable; purchasable in 6 colors
1400 (350)

holiday candle ⌂1x1
OBTAIN Seasonal recipe: Ornament
FUNCTION Interact (Loop On/Off)
x1 • FABRIC N/A • BODY x5
N/A (600)

homework set ⌂1x1
OBTAIN Shop (Small item)
FUNCTION None
not customizable
330 (82)

hourglass ⌂1x1
OBTAIN Shop (Small item)
FUNCTION Interact (Start/Stop)
not customizable; purchasable in 4 colors
660 (165)

hula doll ⌂1x1
OBTAIN Reward: Gulliver
FUNCTION Interact (Loop On/Off)
x2 • FABRIC N/A • BODY x6 Custom
N/A (1200)

humidifier ⌂1x1
OBTAIN Shop (Small item)
FUNCTION Interact (On/Off)
not customizable; purchasable in 8 colors
1400 (350)

hyacinth lamp ⌂1x1
OBTAIN DIY item (50) Big sister
FUNCTION Interact (On/Off)
x4 • FABRIC N/A • BODY x3
N/A (3000)

incense burner ⌂1x1
OBTAIN Shop (Small item)
FUNCTION Interact (On/Off)
not customizable; purchasable in 6 colors
880 (220)

infused-water dispenser ⌂1x1
OBTAIN DIY item (100) Cranky
FUNCTION None
not customizable
N/A (3000)

ironing set ⌂1x1
OBTAIN Shop (Small item)
FUNCTION Interact (Start/Stop)
x1 • FABRIC x3 Generic/Custom • BODY N/A
820 (205)

judge's bell ⌂1x1
OBTAIN Shop (Small item)
FUNCTION Interact (Stop)
not customizable
920 (230)

katana ⌂2x1
OBTAIN Reward: Gulliver
FUNCTION None
x4 • FABRIC N/A • BODY x5 Custom
N/A (2500)

kettle ⌂1x1
OBTAIN Shop (Small item)
FUNCTION None
not customizable
710 (177)

kettlebell ⌂1x1
OBTAIN DIY item Jock
FUNCTION None
x5 • FABRIC N/A • BODY x6
N/A (3750)

knife block ⌂1x1
OBTAIN Shop (Small item)
FUNCTION None
not customizable; purchasable in 3 colors
1200 (300)

lab-experiments set ⌂2x1
OBTAIN Shop (Small Item)
FUNCTION Interact (Loop On/Off)
not customizable
6000 (1500)

lantern ⌂1x1
OBTAIN Default Furniture
FUNCTION Interact (On/Off)
not customizable; purchasable in 8 colors
1900 (475)

laptop ⌂1x1
OBTAIN Shop (Luxury Item)
FUNCTION Interact (On/Off)
x7 • FABRIC x5 Generic/Custom • BODY x7
70,000 (17,500)

LCD TV (20 in.) ⌂1x1
OBTAIN Shop (Luxury Item)
FUNCTION TV
not customizable; purchasable in 8 colors
60,000 (15,000)

LCD TV (50 in.)
2x1
OBTAIN Shop (Luxury Item)
FUNCTION TV
not customizable; purchasable in 5 colors
99,000 (24,750)

Libra scale
1x1
OBTAIN Zodiac recipe (Reward: Celeste)
FUNCTION Interact (Stop)
not customizable
N/A (21,750)

life ring
1x1
OBTAIN Shop (All)
FUNCTION Chair: Stool
not customizable; purchasable in 4 colors
360 (90)

lucky cat
1x1
OBTAIN Reward: Gulliver
FUNCTION None
x3 • FABRIC N/A • BODY x2 Custom
N/A (1675)

lucky gold cat
1x1
OBTAIN DIY item (100) Snooty
FUNCTION None
not customizable
N/A (21,675)

magazine
1x1
OBTAIN Shop (Small item)
FUNCTION None
x1 • FABRIC x6 Custom • BODY N/A
210 (52)

magazine rack
1x1
OBTAIN DIY item (100) Peppy
FUNCTION None
x2 • FABRIC x6 Custom • BODY x8
N/A (690)

magic kit
1x1
OBTAIN Shop (Small item)
FUNCTION Interact (Start/Stop)
not customizable; purchasable in 2 colors
980 (245)

matryoshka
1x1
OBTAIN DIY item Lazy
FUNCTION Interact (On/Off)
x1 • FABRIC N/A • BODY x5
N/A (600)

metal can
1x1
OBTAIN Shop (Small item)
FUNCTION None
not customizable
600 (150)

metronome
1x1
OBTAIN Shop (Small item)
FUNCTION Interact (On/Off at end of loop)
not customizable; purchasable in 5 colors
1300 (325)

microscope
1x1
OBTAIN Shop (Small item)
FUNCTION None
not customizable; purchasable in 3 colors
3100 (775)

microwave
1x1
OBTAIN Shop (Small item)
FUNCTION Interact (Start/Stop)
not customizable; purchasable in 4 colors
3000 (750)

mini-cactus set
1x1
OBTAIN Shop (Small item)
FUNCTION None
not customizable
400 (100)

mixer
1x1
OBTAIN Shop (Small item)
FUNCTION Interact (Loop On/Off)
not customizable; purchasable in 8 colors
1400 (350)

modeling clay
1x1
OBTAIN DIY item Cranky
FUNCTION None
x1 • FABRIC N/A • BODY x7
N/A (400)

Mom's candle set
1x1
OBTAIN Mom (Mail)
FUNCTION Interact (On/Off)
x1 • FABRIC N/A • BODY x6 Custom
N/A (88)

Mom's cushion
1x1
OBTAIN Mom (Mail)
FUNCTION Chair: Stool
x1 • FABRIC N/A • BODY x6 Custom
N/A (88)

Mom's homemade cake
1x1
OBTAIN Mom (Mail)
FUNCTION None
x1 • FABRIC N/A • BODY x6 Custom
N/A (88)

Mom's pen stand
1x1
OBTAIN Mom (Mail)
FUNCTION None
x1 • FABRIC N/A • BODY x6 Custom
N/A (88)

Mom's plushie
1x1
OBTAIN Mom (Mail)
FUNCTION None
x1 • FABRIC N/A • BODY x6 Custom
N/A (88)

Mom's tea cozy
1x1
OBTAIN Mom (Mail)
FUNCTION None
x1 • FABRIC N/A • BODY x6 Custom
N/A (88)

Mom's tissue box
1x1
OBTAIN Mom (Mail)
FUNCTION None
x1 • FABRIC N/A • BODY x6 Custom
N/A (88)

moss ball
1x1
OBTAIN Shop (Small item)
FUNCTION None
not customizable
720 (180)

mug
1x1
OBTAIN Shop (Small item)
FUNCTION None
x1 • FABRIC x5 Generic/Custom • BODY x8
460 (115)

nail-art set
1x1
OBTAIN Shop (Small item)
FUNCTION Interact (On/Off)
not customizable; purchasable in 2 colors
1000 (250)

Newton's cradle
1x1
OBTAIN Shop (Small item)
FUNCTION Interact (On/Off at end of loop)
not customizable
1300 (325)

7

nova light
1x1
OBTAIN Star fragment recipe (Reward: Celeste)
FUNCTION Interact (On/Off)
x4 • FABRIC N/A • BODY x7
N/A (2500)

pet food bowl
1x1
OBTAIN Shop (Small item)
FUNCTION None
not customizable; purchasable in 5 colors
830 (207)

pot
1x1
OBTAIN Tom Nook ("Three New Plots" quest) — Cranky
FUNCTION None
x2 • FABRIC N/A • BODY x5
N/A (1000)

nutcracker
1x1
OBTAIN Reward: Gulliver
FUNCTION Interact (Start/Stop)
x2 • FABRIC N/A • BODY x2 Custom
N/A (1200)

phonograph
1x1
OBTAIN Shop (Luxury Item)
FUNCTION Audio
not customizable
53,000 (13,250)

pro tape recorder
1x1
OBTAIN Shop (Small item)
FUNCTION Audio
not customizable; purchasable in 3 colors
5400 (1350)

oil lamp
1x1
OBTAIN Shop (Small item)
FUNCTION Interact (Loop On/Off)
not customizable
400 (100)

picnic basket
1x1
OBTAIN Shop (All)
FUNCTION None
not customizable; purchasable in 6 colors
1300 (325)

protein shaker bottle
1x1
OBTAIN Shop (Small item)
FUNCTION None
not customizable; purchasable in 4 colors
1400 (350)

old-fashioned alarm clock
1x1
OBTAIN Shop (Small item)
FUNCTION Clock: Normal
not customizable; purchasable in 8 colors
1200 (300)

pine bonsai tree
1x1
OBTAIN Seasonal recipe: Acorn/Pinecone
FUNCTION None
not customizable
N/A (4200)

rattan table lamp
1x1
OBTAIN Shop (Large Item)
FUNCTION Interact (On/Off)
not customizable; purchasable in 6 colors
1500 (375)

old-fashioned washtub
1x1
OBTAIN DIY for Beginners: Shop (Cabinet)
FUNCTION None
not customizable
N/A (360)

plasma ball
1x1
OBTAIN Shop (Small item)
FUNCTION Interact (On/Off)
not customizable
2600 (650)

rattan towel basket
1x1
OBTAIN Shop (Large Item)
FUNCTION None
not customizable; purchasable in 6 colors
1800 (450)

painting set
1x1
OBTAIN Shop (Small item)
FUNCTION None
x1 • FABRIC x3 Custom • BODY x4
510 (127)

plastic canister
1x1
OBTAIN Shop (All)
FUNCTION None
not customizable; purchasable in 5 colors
680 (170)

record box
1x1
OBTAIN Shop (Small item)
FUNCTION None
x1 • FABRIC x3 Custom • BODY x8
2600 (650)

paper tiger
1x1
OBTAIN Shop (Small item)
FUNCTION Interact (Stop)
not customizable
1500 (375)

pop-up toaster
1x1
OBTAIN Shop (Small item)
FUNCTION Interact (Start/Stop)
not customizable; purchasable in 6 colors
2300 (575)

recycled-can thumb piano
1x1
OBTAIN Inspiration: Empty can
FUNCTION Musical Instrument
x2 • FABRIC N/A • BODY x6
N/A (890)

peach surprise box
1x1
OBTAIN DIY item (100) — Sweet
FUNCTION Interact (On/Off)
x4 • FABRIC N/A • BODY x2
N/A (2480)

portable radio
1x1
OBTAIN Default Furniture
FUNCTION Radio
not customizable; purchasable in 8 colors
1500 (375)

revolving spice rack
1x1
OBTAIN Shop (Small item)
FUNCTION None
not customizable; purchasable in 3 colors
1400 (350)

pedal board
1x1
OBTAIN Shop (Small item)
FUNCTION Animates (Loop)
not customizable; purchasable in 3 colors
1400 (350)

portable record player
1x1
OBTAIN Shop (Small item)
FUNCTION Audio
not customizable; purchasable in 7 colors
4000 (1000)

rice cooker
1x1
OBTAIN Shop (Small item)
FUNCTION Interact (On/Off)
not customizable; purchasable in 5 colors
2500 (625)

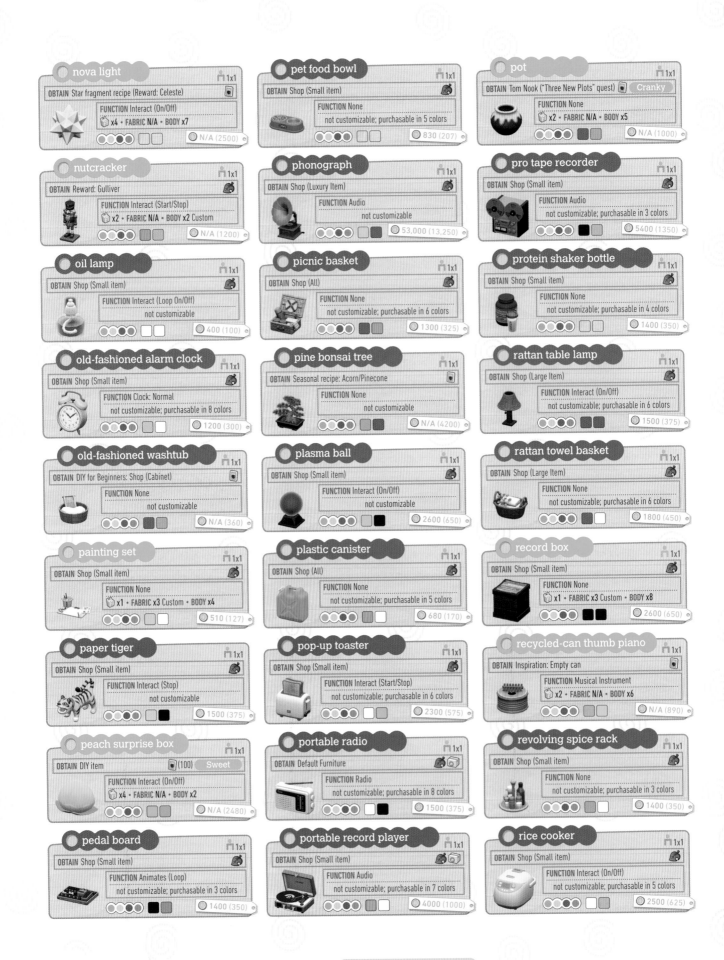

ring
OBTAIN Shop (Luxury Item)
FUNCTION Interact (On/Off)
not customizable; purchasable in 8 colors
69,000 (17,250)
1x1

ringtoss
OBTAIN Test Your DIY Skills: Shop (Cabinet)
FUNCTION None
x1 • FABRIC N/A • BODY x4
N/A (480)
1x1

rotary phone
OBTAIN Shop (Small item)
FUNCTION None
not customizable; purchasable in 8 colors
640 (160)
1x1

Scorpio lamp
OBTAIN Zodiac recipe (Reward: Celeste)
FUNCTION Interact (On/Off)
not customizable
N/A (22,125)
1x1

sea globe
OBTAIN Shop (Small item)
FUNCTION Interact (Loop On/Off)
not customizable
1200 (300)
1x1

sewing machine
OBTAIN Shop (Small item)
FUNCTION Interact (Loop On/Off)
not customizable; purchasable in 7 colors
2100 (525)
1x1

sewing project
OBTAIN Shop (Small item)
FUNCTION None
not customizable; purchasable in 6 colors
430 (107)
1x1

shaved-ice maker
OBTAIN Shop (Small item)
FUNCTION Interact (Hold Ⓐ at end of loop)
not customizable; purchasable in 2 colors
1400 (350)
1x1

shell lamp
OBTAIN DIY item — Big sister
FUNCTION Interact (On/Off)
x6 • FABRIC N/A • BODY x6
N/A (4200)
1x1

shell speaker
OBTAIN DIY item — Big sister
FUNCTION Audio
x7 • FABRIC N/A • BODY x6
N/A (5700)
1x1

silver bug trophy
OBTAIN Fishing Tourney/Bug-Off
FUNCTION None
not customizable
N/A (425)
1x1

silver fish trophy
OBTAIN Fishing Tourney/Bug-Off
FUNCTION None
not customizable
N/A (425)
1x1

silver HHA trophy
OBTAIN HHA Reward (Mail)
FUNCTION None
not customizable
N/A (425)
1x1

simple kettle
OBTAIN Shop (Small item)
FUNCTION None
not customizable; purchasable in 7 colors
1300 (325)
1x1

snow globe
OBTAIN Shop (Small item)
FUNCTION Interact (Start/Stop)
not customizable
1300 (325)
1x1

soup kettle
OBTAIN Shop (Small item)
FUNCTION None
not customizable; purchasable in 8 colors
3300 (825)
1x1

stack of books
OBTAIN DIY item (100) — Lazy
FUNCTION None
x1 • FABRIC N/A • BODY x4
N/A (725)
1x1

stacked magazines
OBTAIN DIY item (100) — Peppy
FUNCTION None
x2 • FABRIC x6 Custom • BODY N/A
N/A (630)
1x1

stand mixer
OBTAIN Shop (Small item)
FUNCTION Animates (Fades out)
not customizable; purchasable in 6 colors
1400 (350)
1x1

star clock
OBTAIN Star fragment recipe (Reward: Celeste)
FUNCTION Clock: Normal
x3 • FABRIC N/A • BODY x7
N/A (2250)
1x1

steamer-basket set
OBTAIN Seasonal recipe: Bamboo
FUNCTION None
not customizable
N/A (2400)
1x1

stovetop espresso maker
OBTAIN Shop (Small item)
FUNCTION None
not customizable; purchasable in 3 colors
1700 (425)
1x1

sturdy sewing box
OBTAIN Shop (Small item)
FUNCTION Interact (On/Off)
not customizable; purchasable in 6 colors
1000 (250)
1x1

succulent plant
OBTAIN Inspiration: Clump of weeds
FUNCTION None
not customizable
N/A (220)
1x1

table lamp
OBTAIN Shop (Small item)
FUNCTION Interact (On/Off)
x1 • FABRIC x6 Generic/Custom • BODY N/A
1100 (275)
1x1

table setting
OBTAIN Shop (Large Item)
FUNCTION None
x1 • FABRIC x4 Generic/Custom • BODY x5
720 (180)
1x1

tabletop festive tree
OBTAIN Seasonal recipe: Ornament
FUNCTION Interact (On/Off)
x2 • FABRIC N/A • BODY x6
N/A (930)
1x1

7

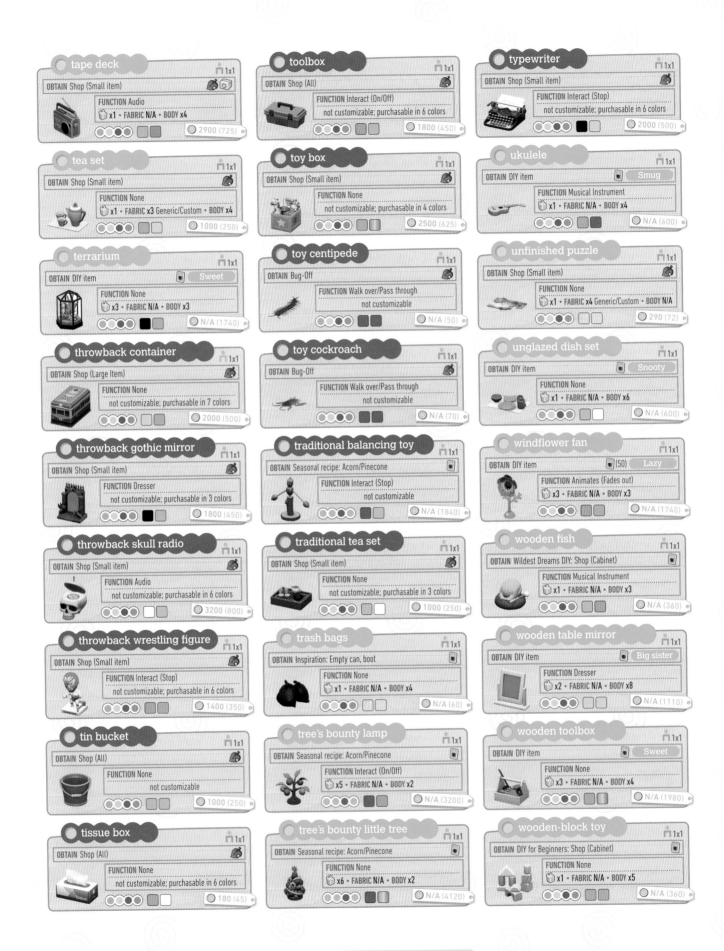

tape deck — 1x1
OBTAIN Shop (Small item)
FUNCTION Audio
x1 • FABRIC N/A • BODY x4
2900 (725)

toolbox — 1x1
OBTAIN Shop (All)
FUNCTION Interact (On/Off)
not customizable; purchasable in 6 colors
1800 (450)

typewriter — 1x1
OBTAIN Shop (Small item)
FUNCTION Interact (Stop)
not customizable; purchasable in 6 colors
2000 (500)

tea set — 1x1
OBTAIN Shop (Small item)
FUNCTION None
x1 • FABRIC x3 Generic/Custom • BODY x4
1000 (250)

toy box — 1x1
OBTAIN Shop (Small item)
FUNCTION None
not customizable; purchasable in 4 colors
2500 (625)

ukulele — 1x1
OBTAIN DIY item — Smug
FUNCTION Musical Instrument
x1 • FABRIC N/A • BODY x4
N/A (600)

terrarium — 1x1
OBTAIN DIY item — Sweet
FUNCTION None
x3 • FABRIC N/A • BODY x3
N/A (1740)

toy centipede — 1x1
OBTAIN Bug-Off
FUNCTION Walk over/Pass through
not customizable
N/A (50)

unfinished puzzle — 1x1
OBTAIN Shop (Small item)
FUNCTION None
x1 • FABRIC x4 Generic/Custom • BODY N/A
290 (72)

throwback container — 1x1
OBTAIN Shop (Large Item)
FUNCTION None
not customizable; purchasable in 7 colors
2000 (500)

toy cockroach — 1x1
OBTAIN Bug-Off
FUNCTION Walk over/Pass through
not customizable
N/A (70)

unglazed dish set — 1x1
OBTAIN DIY item — Snooty
FUNCTION None
x1 • FABRIC N/A • BODY x6
N/A (600)

throwback gothic mirror — 1x1
OBTAIN Shop (Small item)
FUNCTION Dresser
not customizable; purchasable in 3 colors
1800 (450)

traditional balancing toy — 1x1
OBTAIN Seasonal recipe: Acorn/Pinecone
FUNCTION Interact (Stop)
not customizable
N/A (1840)

windflower fan — 1x1
OBTAIN DIY item — (50) Lazy
FUNCTION Animates (Fades out)
x3 • FABRIC N/A • BODY x3
N/A (1740)

throwback skull radio — 1x1
OBTAIN Shop (Small item)
FUNCTION Audio
not customizable; purchasable in 6 colors
3200 (800)

traditional tea set — 1x1
OBTAIN Shop (Small item)
FUNCTION None
not customizable; purchasable in 3 colors
1000 (250)

wooden fish — 1x1
OBTAIN Wildest Dreams DIY: Shop (Cabinet)
FUNCTION Musical Instrument
x1 • FABRIC N/A • BODY x3
N/A (360)

throwback wrestling figure — 1x1
OBTAIN Shop (Small item)
FUNCTION Interact (Stop)
not customizable; purchasable in 6 colors
1400 (350)

trash bags — 1x1
OBTAIN Inspiration: Empty can, boot
FUNCTION None
x1 • FABRIC N/A • BODY x4
N/A (60)

wooden table mirror — 1x1
OBTAIN DIY item — Big sister
FUNCTION Dresser
x2 • FABRIC N/A • BODY x8
N/A (1110)

tin bucket — 1x1
OBTAIN Shop (All)
FUNCTION None
not customizable
1000 (250)

tree's bounty lamp — 1x1
OBTAIN Seasonal recipe: Acorn/Pinecone
FUNCTION Interact (On/Off)
x5 • FABRIC N/A • BODY x2
N/A (3200)

wooden toolbox — 1x1
OBTAIN DIY item — Sweet
FUNCTION None
x3 • FABRIC N/A • BODY x4
N/A (1980)

tissue box — 1x1
OBTAIN Shop (All)
FUNCTION None
not customizable; purchasable in 6 colors
180 (45)

tree's bounty little tree — 1x1
OBTAIN Seasonal recipe: Acorn/Pinecone
FUNCTION None
x6 • FABRIC N/A • BODY x2
N/A (4120)

wooden-block toy — 1x1
OBTAIN DIY for Beginners: Shop (Cabinet)
FUNCTION None
x1 • FABRIC N/A • BODY x5
N/A (360)

Wall decorations

deer decoration
🏠 1x1.5 W
OBTAIN DIY item · 🔲(50) · Lazy
FUNCTION None
🔲 x2 · FABRIC N/A · BODY x5
N/A (960)

air conditioner
🏠 2x1W
OBTAIN Shop (Luxury Item)
FUNCTION Interact (On/Off)
not customizable; purchasable in 6 colors
63,000 (15,750)

broom and dustpan
🏠 1x1.5 W
OBTAIN Shop (Small Item)
FUNCTION None
not customizable; purchasable in 4 colors
910 (227)

diner neon clock
🏠 1x1W
OBTAIN Shop (Large Item)
FUNCTION Clock: Switch
🔲 x1 · FABRIC x2 Generic/Custom · BODY x7
1500 (375)

antique phone
🏠 1x1W
OBTAIN Shop (Luxury Item)
FUNCTION None
not customizable; purchasable in 3 colors
16,000 (4000)

butterfly-fish model
🏠 1x1W
OBTAIN Shop (Large Item)
FUNCTION None
not customizable
1300 (325)

double-sided wall clock
🏠 0.5x1W
OBTAIN Shop (Large Item)
FUNCTION Clock: Normal
not customizable; purchasable in 6 colors
1100 (275)

autograph cards
🏠 2x1W
OBTAIN Shop (Large Item)
FUNCTION None
🔲 x1 · FABRIC x1 Custom · BODY x4
1400 (350)

cherry lamp
🏠 1x1W
OBTAIN DIY item · 🔲(100) · Peppy
FUNCTION Interact (Loop On/Off)
🔲 x4 · FABRIC N/A · BODY x2
N/A (2400)

exit sign
🏠 1x0.5W
OBTAIN Shop (Small Item)
FUNCTION Interact (Loop On/Off)
not customizable; purchasable in 4 colors
810 (202)

bamboo wall decoration
🏠 0.5x1W
OBTAIN DIY (Bamboo Recipe) · 🔲(50) · Jock
FUNCTION None
🔲 x1 · FABRIC N/A · BODY x3
N/A (160)

cherry-blossom clock
🏠 1x1W
OBTAIN Seasonal recipe: Cherry blossom
FUNCTION Clock: Normal
🔲 x4 · FABRIC N/A · BODY x2
N/A (2750)

fish print
🏠 2x1W
OBTAIN Fishing Tourney
FUNCTION None
🔲 x1 · FABRIC N/A · BODY x7 Custom
N/A (700)

bathroom towel rack
🏠 1x1W
OBTAIN Shop (Small Item)
FUNCTION None
not customizable; purchasable in 4 colors
1400 (350)

coconut wall planter
🏠 1x1.5 W
OBTAIN DIY item · 🔲(50) · Snooty
FUNCTION None
not customizable
N/A (600)

fishing-boat flag
🏠 2x1.5 W
OBTAIN Shop (Small Item)
FUNCTION None
not customizable; purchasable in 4 colors
2200 (550)

boomerang
🏠 1x0.5W
OBTAIN DIY item · 🔲(50) · Lazy
FUNCTION None
🔲 x1 · FABRIC N/A · BODY x5
N/A (360)

corkboard
🏠 2x1W
OBTAIN Shop (Small Item)
FUNCTION None
🔲 x1 · FABRIC x2 Generic/Custom · BODY x3
1400 (350)

floral swag
🏠 1x1W
OBTAIN DIY item · 🔲(50) · Sweet
FUNCTION None
🔲 x1 · FABRIC N/A · BODY x5
N/A (200)

breaker
🏠 1x1W
OBTAIN Shop (Large Item)
FUNCTION None
not customizable
820 (205)

cuckoo clock
🏠 1x1.5 W
OBTAIN Shop (Small Item)
FUNCTION Clock: Cuckoo
not customizable; purchasable in 7 colors
3200 (800)

formal paper
🏠 1x1W
OBTAIN Shop (Small Item)
FUNCTION None
not customizable; purchasable in 3 colors
620 (155)

bronze HHA plaque
🏠 1x1W
OBTAIN HHA Reward (Mail)
FUNCTION None
not customizable
N/A (400)

cute wall-mounted clock
🏠 1x1W
OBTAIN Shop (Large Item)
FUNCTION Clock: Normal
not customizable; purchasable in 5 colors
1200 (300)

gears
🏠 2x1W
OBTAIN Shop (Large Item)
FUNCTION Animates (Fades out)
not customizable; purchasable in 5 colors
1500 (375)

7

gold HHA plaque
1x1W

OBTAIN HHA Reward (Mail)

FUNCTION None
not customizable

N/A (450)

golden gears
2x1W

OBTAIN DIY item ● (50) Smug

FUNCTION Animates (Fades out)
not customizable

N/A (11,125)

grasshopper-head model
1x1W

OBTAIN Shop (Large Item)

FUNCTION None
not customizable

1400 (350)

hanging scroll
1x2W

OBTAIN Shop (Luxury Item)

FUNCTION None
x7 • FABRIC x4 Custom • BODY x5

140,000 (35,000)

hanging terrarium
1x1.5 W

OBTAIN DIY item ● (50) Peppy

FUNCTION None
x5 • FABRIC N/A • BODY x3

N/A (3240)

HHA pennant
1x1.5 W

OBTAIN HHA Reward (Mail)

FUNCTION None
not customizable

N/A (375)

imperial decorative shelves
2x1.5 W

OBTAIN Shop (Large Item)

FUNCTION None
not customizable; purchasable in 4 colors

8500 (2125)

imperial dining lantern
1x1.5 W

OBTAIN Shop (Luxury Item)

FUNCTION Interact (On/Off)
not customizable; purchasable in 4 colors

19,000 (4750)

intercom monitor
1x1W

OBTAIN Shop (Large Item)

FUNCTION Interact (Start/Stop)
not customizable

860 (215)

iron wall lamp
1x1W

OBTAIN Wildest Dreams DIY: Shop (Cabinet)

FUNCTION Interact (On/Off)
x5 • FABRIC N/A • BODY x2

N/A (3400)

iron wall rack
1x1W

OBTAIN DIY item ● (50) Smug

FUNCTION None
x4 • FABRIC N/A • BODY x2

N/A (2450)

ironwood clock
1x1W

OBTAIN DIY item ● (50) Smug

FUNCTION Clock: Normal
x3 • FABRIC N/A • BODY x5

N/A (1740)

key holder
1x1W

OBTAIN DIY item ● (50) Big sister

FUNCTION None
x2 • FABRIC N/A • BODY x4

N/A (1110)

Leo sculpture
1x1W

OBTAIN Zodiac recipe (Reward: Celeste)

FUNCTION None
not customizable

N/A (21,975)

log wall-mounted clock
1x1W

OBTAIN DIY item ● (50) Lazy

FUNCTION Clock: Normal
x2 • FABRIC N/A • BODY x4

N/A (990)

macrame tapestry
1x1.5 W

OBTAIN Shop (Small Item)

FUNCTION None
not customizable; purchasable in 4 colors

840 (210)

magnetic knife rack
1x1W

OBTAIN Shop (Small Item)

FUNCTION None
not customizable; purchasable in 3 colors

1400 (350)

mantis-head model
1x1W

OBTAIN Shop (Large Item)

FUNCTION None
not customizable

1500 (375)

mobile
1x1.5 W

OBTAIN Shop (Small Item)

FUNCTION Animates (Loop)
not customizable; purchasable in 5 colors

780 (195)

Mom's art
1x1W

OBTAIN Mom (Mail)

FUNCTION None
x1 • FABRIC N/A • BODY x8 Custom

N/A (88)

Mom's embroidery
1x1W

OBTAIN Mom (Mail)

FUNCTION None
x1 • FABRIC N/A • BODY x6 Custom

N/A (88)

mounted black bass
1x0.5W

OBTAIN Shop (Large Item)

FUNCTION None
not customizable

1300 (325)

mounted blue marlin
2x1W

OBTAIN Shop (Large Item)

FUNCTION None
not customizable

5000 (1250)

orange wall-mounted clock
1x1W

OBTAIN DIY item ● (100) Lazy

FUNCTION Clock: Normal
x3 • FABRIC N/A • BODY x2

N/A (2240)

ornament mobile
1x1W

OBTAIN Seasonal recipe: Ornament

FUNCTION Animates (Loop)
x1 • FABRIC N/A • BODY x6

N/A (340)

party garland
2x1W

OBTAIN Shop (Small Item)

FUNCTION None
not customizable; purchasable in 6 colors

650 (162)

pendulum clock
1x1W

OBTAIN Shop (Small Item)

FUNCTION Clock: Pendulum
not customizable

1900 (475)

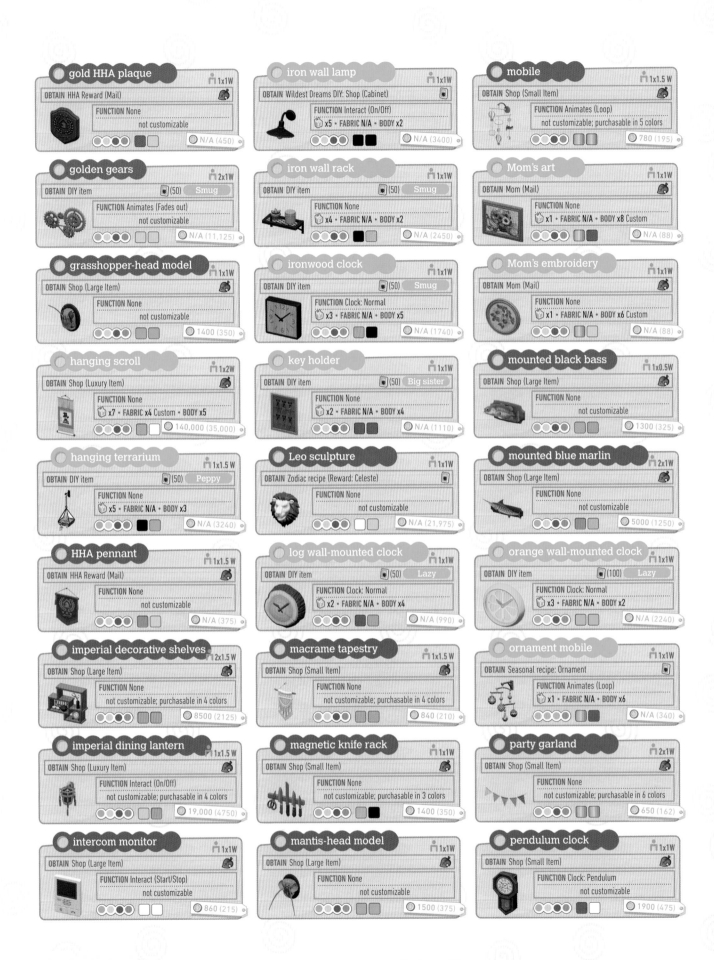

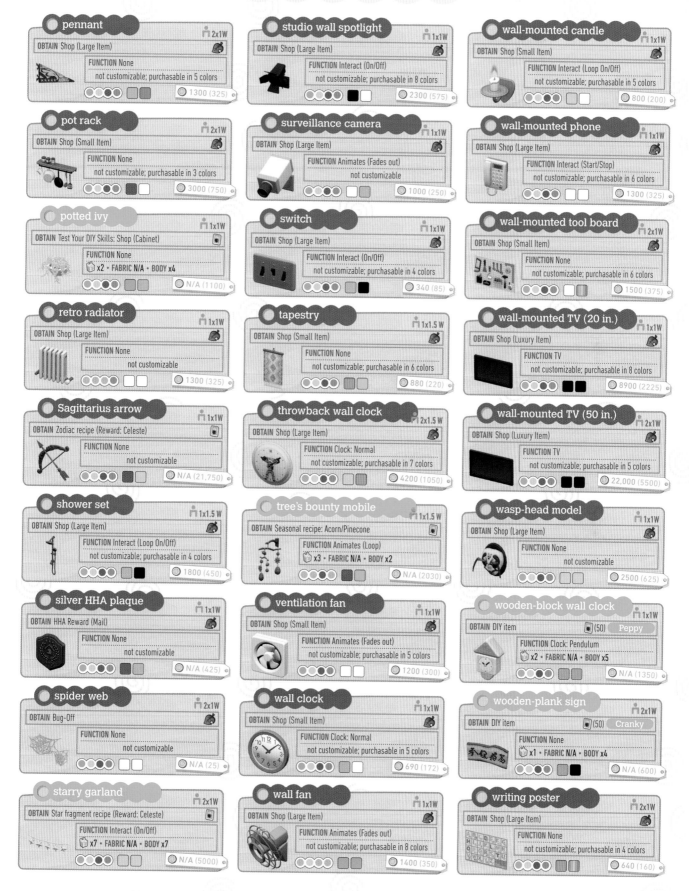

pennant
🏠 2x1W
OBTAIN Shop (Large Item)
FUNCTION None
not customizable; purchasable in 5 colors
1300 (325)

pot rack
🏠 2x1W
OBTAIN Shop (Small Item)
FUNCTION None
not customizable; purchasable in 3 colors
3000 (750)

potted ivy
🏠 1x1W
OBTAIN Test Your DIY Skills: Shop (Cabinet)
FUNCTION None
x2 • FABRIC N/A • BODY x4
N/A (1100)

retro radiator
🏠 1x1W
OBTAIN Shop (Large Item)
FUNCTION None
not customizable
1300 (325)

Sagittarius arrow
🏠 1x1W
OBTAIN Zodiac recipe (Reward: Celeste)
FUNCTION None
not customizable
N/A (21,750)

shower set
🏠 1x1.5 W
OBTAIN Shop (Large Item)
FUNCTION Interact (Loop On/Off)
not customizable; purchasable in 4 colors
1800 (450)

silver HHA plaque
🏠 1x1W
OBTAIN HHA Reward (Mail)
FUNCTION None
not customizable
N/A (425)

spider web
🏠 2x1W
OBTAIN Bug-Off
FUNCTION None
not customizable
N/A (25)

starry garland
🏠 2x1W
OBTAIN Star fragment recipe (Reward: Celeste)
FUNCTION Interact (On/Off)
x7 • FABRIC N/A • BODY x7
N/A (5000)

studio wall spotlight
🏠 1x1W
OBTAIN Shop (Large Item)
FUNCTION Interact (On/Off)
not customizable; purchasable in 8 colors
2300 (575)

surveillance camera
🏠 1x1W
OBTAIN Shop (Large Item)
FUNCTION Animates (Fades out)
not customizable
1000 (250)

switch
🏠 1x1W
OBTAIN Shop (Large Item)
FUNCTION Interact (On/Off)
not customizable; purchasable in 4 colors
340 (85)

tapestry
🏠 1x1.5 W
OBTAIN Shop (Small Item)
FUNCTION None
not customizable; purchasable in 6 colors
880 (220)

throwback wall clock
🏠 2x1.5 W
OBTAIN Shop (Large Item)
FUNCTION Clock: Normal
not customizable; purchasable in 7 colors
4200 (1050)

tree's bounty mobile
🏠 1x1.5 W
OBTAIN Seasonal recipe: Acorn/Pinecone
FUNCTION Animates (Loop)
x3 • FABRIC N/A • BODY x2
N/A (2030)

ventilation fan
🏠 1x1W
OBTAIN Shop (Small Item)
FUNCTION Animates (Fades out)
not customizable; purchasable in 5 colors
1200 (300)

wall clock
🏠 1x1W
OBTAIN Shop (Small Item)
FUNCTION Clock: Normal
not customizable; purchasable in 5 colors
690 (172)

wall fan
🏠 1x1W
OBTAIN Shop (Large Item)
FUNCTION Animates (Fades out)
not customizable; purchasable in 8 colors
1400 (350)

wall-mounted candle
🏠 1x1W
OBTAIN Shop (Small Item)
FUNCTION Interact (Loop On/Off)
not customizable; purchasable in 5 colors
800 (200)

wall-mounted phone
🏠 1x1W
OBTAIN Shop (Large Item)
FUNCTION Interact (Start/Stop)
not customizable; purchasable in 6 colors
1300 (325)

wall-mounted tool board
🏠 2x1W
OBTAIN Shop (Small Item)
FUNCTION None
not customizable; purchasable in 6 colors
1500 (375)

wall-mounted TV (20 in.)
🏠 1x1W
OBTAIN Shop (Luxury Item)
FUNCTION TV
not customizable; purchasable in 8 colors
8900 (2225)

wall-mounted TV (50 in.)
🏠 2x1W
OBTAIN Shop (Luxury Item)
FUNCTION TV
not customizable; purchasable in 5 colors
22,000 (5500)

wasp-head model
🏠 1x1W
OBTAIN Shop (Large Item)
FUNCTION None
not customizable
2500 (625)

wooden-block wall clock
🏠 1x1W
OBTAIN DIY item (50) Peppy
FUNCTION Clock: Pendulum
x2 • FABRIC N/A • BODY x5
N/A (1350)

wooden-plank sign
🏠 2x1W
OBTAIN DIY item (50) Cranky
FUNCTION None
x1 • FABRIC N/A • BODY x4
N/A (600)

writing poster
🏠 2x1W
OBTAIN Shop (Large Item)
FUNCTION None
not customizable; purchasable in 4 colors
640 (160)

Door decorations

blue rose wreath 1x1W
OBTAIN DIY item — (200) Any Type
FUNCTION None
not customizable
N/A (20,000)

crest doorplate 1x1W
OBTAIN DIY item — (50) Smug
FUNCTION None
x1 • FABRIC N/A • BODY x6
N/A (3000)

fossil doorplate 1x1W
OBTAIN DIY item — (50) Jock
FUNCTION None
x1 • FABRIC N/A • BODY x2
N/A (500)

bone doorplate 1x1W
OBTAIN DIY item — (50) Lazy
FUNCTION None
WELCOME x1 • FABRIC N/A • BODY x8
N/A (360)

dark lily wreath 1x1W
OBTAIN DIY item — (200) Any Type
FUNCTION None
not customizable
N/A (1600)

fruit wreath 1x1W
OBTAIN DIY item — (100) Cranky
FUNCTION None
not customizable
N/A (2000)

chic cosmos wreath 1x1W
OBTAIN DIY item — (200) Any Type
FUNCTION None
not customizable
N/A (4800)

dark rose wreath 1x1W
OBTAIN DIY item — (200) Any Type
FUNCTION None
not customizable
N/A (4320)

gold rose wreath 1x1W
OBTAIN DIY item — (200) Any Type
FUNCTION None
not customizable
N/A (20,000)

chic windflower wreath 1x1W
OBTAIN DIY item — (200) Any Type
FUNCTION None
not customizable
N/A (4800)

dark tulip wreath 1x1W
OBTAIN DIY item — (200) Any Type
FUNCTION None
not customizable
N/A (1600)

heart doorplate 1x1W
OBTAIN Shop (Small Item)
FUNCTION None
not customizable; purchasable in 8 colors
600 (150)

cool hyacinth wreath 1x1W
OBTAIN DIY item — (100) Any Type
FUNCTION None
not customizable
N/A (1440)

fancy lily wreath 1x1W
OBTAIN DIY item — (100) Any Type
FUNCTION None
not customizable
N/A (1200)

hyacinth wreath 1x1W
OBTAIN DIY item — (50) Any Type
FUNCTION None
not customizable
N/A (720)

cool pansy wreath 1x1W
OBTAIN DIY item — (200) Any Type
FUNCTION None
not customizable
N/A (4800)

fancy mum wreath 1x1W
OBTAIN DIY item — (100) Any Type
FUNCTION None
not customizable
N/A (1200)

iron doorplate 1x1W
OBTAIN DIY item — (50) Big sister
FUNCTION None
x1 • FABRIC N/A • BODY x8
N/A (1500)

cool windflower wreath 1x1W
OBTAIN DIY item — (100) Any Type
FUNCTION None
not customizable
N/A (1200)

fancy rose wreath 1x1W
OBTAIN DIY item — (100) Any Type
FUNCTION None
not customizable
N/A (1200)

lily wreath 1x1W
OBTAIN DIY item — (50) Any Type
FUNCTION None
not customizable
N/A (720)

cosmos wreath 1x1W
OBTAIN DIY item — (50) Any Type
FUNCTION None
not customizable
N/A (720)

fish doorplate 1x1W
OBTAIN Fishing Tourney
FUNCTION None
x1 • FABRIC N/A • BODY x8 Custom
N/A (90)

mum wreath 1x1W
OBTAIN DIY item — (50) Any Type
FUNCTION None
not customizable
N/A (720)

mushroom wreath 1x1W
OBTAIN Seasonal recipe: Mushroom
FUNCTION None
not customizable
N/A (1500)

pretty tulip wreath 1x1W
OBTAIN DIY item (100) Any Type
FUNCTION None
not customizable
N/A (2400)

snowflake wreath 1x1W
OBTAIN Seasonal recipe: Snowflake
FUNCTION None
not customizable
N/A (1600)

natural mum wreath 1x1W
OBTAIN DIY item (200) Any Type
FUNCTION None
not customizable
N/A (4800)

purple hyacinth wreath 1x1W
OBTAIN DIY item (200) Any Type
FUNCTION None
not customizable
N/A (4800)

spider doorplate 1x1W
OBTAIN Bug-Off
FUNCTION None
x1 • FABRIC N/A • BODY x8 Custom
N/A (90)

ornament wreath 1x1W
OBTAIN Seasonal recipe: Ornament
FUNCTION None
x1 • FABRIC N/A • BODY x8
N/A (800)

rose wreath 1x1W
OBTAIN DIY item (50) Any Type
FUNCTION None
not customizable
N/A (720)

timber doorplate 1x1W
OBTAIN DIY item (50) Snooty
FUNCTION None
x1 • FABRIC N/A • BODY x8
N/A (400)

pansy wreath 1x1W
OBTAIN DIY item (50) Any Type
FUNCTION None
not customizable
N/A (720)

shell wreath 1x1W
OBTAIN Seasonal recipe: Summer shell
FUNCTION None
not customizable
N/A (4720)

tree branch wreath 1x1W
OBTAIN DIY item (50) Big sister
FUNCTION None
not customizable
N/A (100)

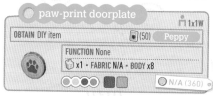
paw-print doorplate 1x1W
OBTAIN DIY item (50) Peppy
FUNCTION None
x1 • FABRIC N/A • BODY x8
N/A (360)

skull doorplate 1x1W
OBTAIN Shop (Small Item)
FUNCTION None
not customizable; purchasable in 2 colors
540 (135)

tulip wreath 1x1W
OBTAIN DIY item (50) Any Type
FUNCTION None
not customizable
N/A (720)

pretty cosmos wreath 1x1W
OBTAIN DIY item (100) Any Type
FUNCTION None
not customizable
N/A (1200)

snazzy pansy wreath 1x1W
OBTAIN DIY item (100) Any Type
FUNCTION None
not customizable
N/A (1200)

windflower wreath 1x1W
OBTAIN DIY item (50) Any Type
FUNCTION None
not customizable
N/A (720)

7

Wallpapers

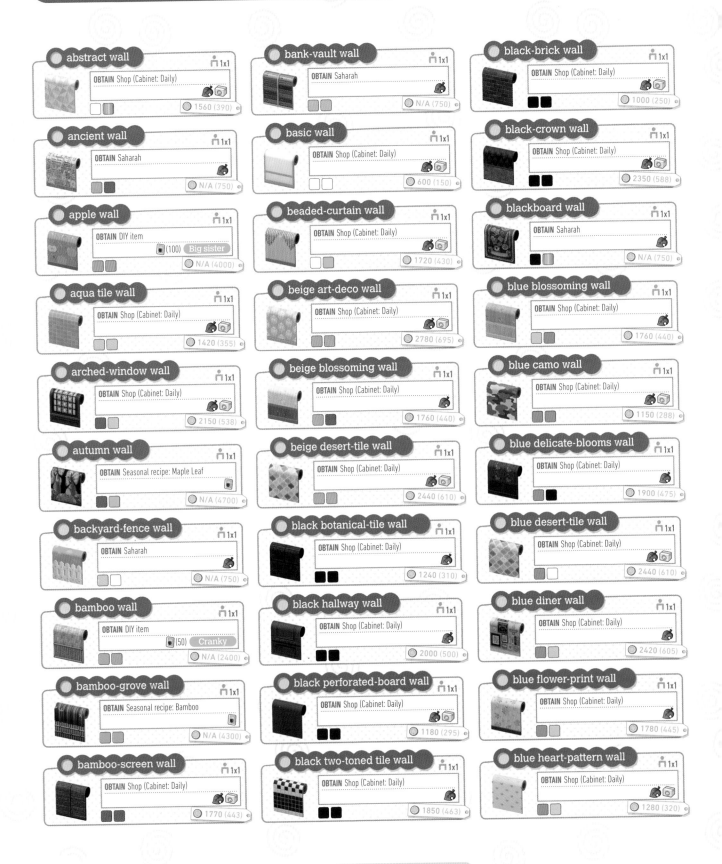

abstract wall 🏠1x1
OBTAIN Shop (Cabinet: Daily)
🔔 1560 (390)

ancient wall 🏠1x1
OBTAIN Saharah
🔔 N/A (750)

apple wall 🏠1x1
OBTAIN DIY item
(100) Big sister
🔔 N/A (4000)

aqua tile wall 🏠1x1
OBTAIN Shop (Cabinet: Daily)
🔔 1420 (355)

arched-window wall 🏠1x1
OBTAIN Shop (Cabinet: Daily)
🔔 2150 (538)

autumn wall 🏠1x1
OBTAIN Seasonal recipe: Maple Leaf
🔔 N/A (4700)

backyard-fence wall 🏠1x1
OBTAIN Saharah
🔔 N/A (750)

bamboo wall 🏠1x1
OBTAIN DIY item
(50) Cranky
🔔 N/A (2400)

bamboo-grove wall 🏠1x1
OBTAIN Seasonal recipe: Bamboo
🔔 N/A (4300)

bamboo-screen wall 🏠1x1
OBTAIN Shop (Cabinet: Daily)
🔔 1770 (443)

bank-vault wall 🏠1x1
OBTAIN Saharah
🔔 N/A (750)

basic wall 🏠1x1
OBTAIN Shop (Cabinet: Daily)
🔔 600 (150)

beaded-curtain wall 🏠1x1
OBTAIN Shop (Cabinet: Daily)
🔔 1720 (430)

beige art-deco wall 🏠1x1
OBTAIN Shop (Cabinet: Daily)
🔔 2780 (695)

beige blossoming wall 🏠1x1
OBTAIN Shop (Cabinet: Daily)
🔔 1760 (440)

beige desert-tile wall 🏠1x1
OBTAIN Shop (Cabinet: Daily)
🔔 2440 (610)

black botanical-tile wall 🏠1x1
OBTAIN Shop (Cabinet: Daily)
🔔 1240 (310)

black hallway wall 🏠1x1
OBTAIN Shop (Cabinet: Daily)
🔔 2000 (500)

black perforated-board wall 🏠1x1
OBTAIN Shop (Cabinet: Daily)
🔔 1180 (295)

black two-toned tile wall 🏠1x1
OBTAIN Shop (Cabinet: Daily)
🔔 1850 (463)

black-brick wall 🏠1x1
OBTAIN Shop (Cabinet: Daily)
🔔 1000 (250)

black-crown wall 🏠1x1
OBTAIN Shop (Cabinet: Daily)
🔔 2350 (588)

blackboard wall 🏠1x1
OBTAIN Saharah
🔔 N/A (750)

blue blossoming wall 🏠1x1
OBTAIN Shop (Cabinet: Daily)
🔔 1760 (440)

blue camo wall 🏠1x1
OBTAIN Shop (Cabinet: Daily)
🔔 1150 (288)

blue delicate-blooms wall 🏠1x1
OBTAIN Shop (Cabinet: Daily)
🔔 1900 (475)

blue desert-tile wall 🏠1x1
OBTAIN Shop (Cabinet: Daily)
🔔 2440 (610)

blue diner wall 🏠1x1
OBTAIN Shop (Cabinet: Daily)
🔔 2420 (605)

blue flower-print wall 🏠1x1
OBTAIN Shop (Cabinet: Daily)
🔔 1780 (445)

blue heart-pattern wall 🏠1x1
OBTAIN Shop (Cabinet: Daily)
🔔 1280 (320)

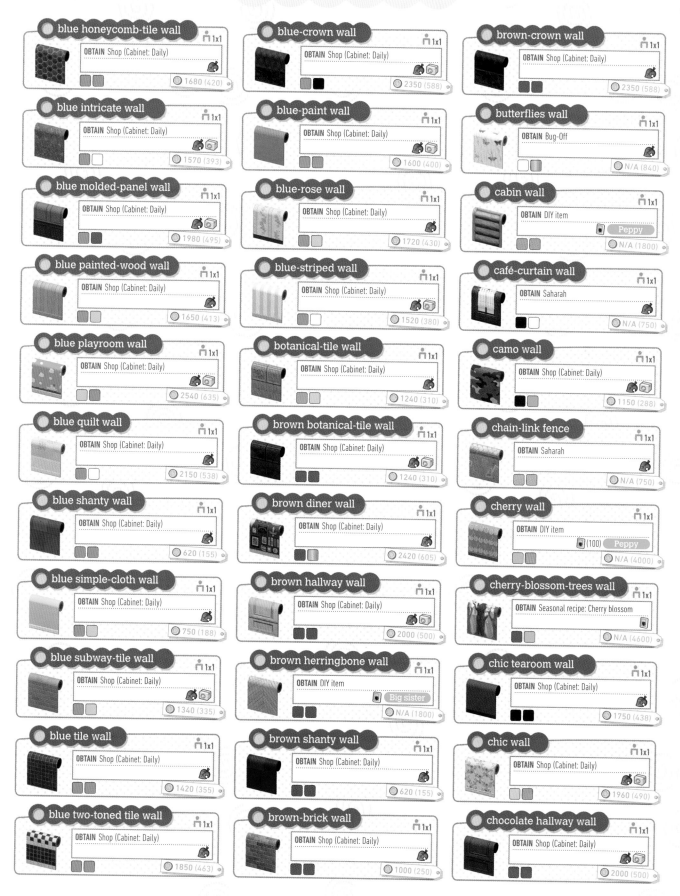

blue honeycomb-tile wall 1x1
OBTAIN Shop (Cabinet: Daily)
1680 (420)

blue-crown wall 1x1
OBTAIN Shop (Cabinet: Daily)
2350 (588)

brown-crown wall 1x1
OBTAIN Shop (Cabinet: Daily)
2350 (588)

blue intricate wall 1x1
OBTAIN Shop (Cabinet: Daily)
1570 (393)

blue-paint wall 1x1
OBTAIN Shop (Cabinet: Daily)
1600 (400)

butterflies wall 1x1
OBTAIN Bug-Off
N/A (840)

blue molded-panel wall 1x1
OBTAIN Shop (Cabinet: Daily)
1980 (495)

blue-rose wall 1x1
OBTAIN Shop (Cabinet: Daily)
1720 (430)

cabin wall 1x1
OBTAIN DIY item
Peppy
N/A (1800)

blue painted-wood wall 1x1
OBTAIN Shop (Cabinet: Daily)
1650 (413)

blue-striped wall 1x1
OBTAIN Shop (Cabinet: Daily)
1520 (380)

café-curtain wall 1x1
OBTAIN Saharah
N/A (750)

blue playroom wall 1x1
OBTAIN Shop (Cabinet: Daily)
2540 (635)

botanical-tile wall 1x1
OBTAIN Shop (Cabinet: Daily)
1240 (310)

camo wall 1x1
OBTAIN Shop (Cabinet: Daily)
1150 (288)

blue quilt wall 1x1
OBTAIN Shop (Cabinet: Daily)
2150 (538)

brown botanical-tile wall 1x1
OBTAIN Shop (Cabinet: Daily)
1240 (310)

chain-link fence 1x1
OBTAIN Saharah
N/A (750)

blue shanty wall 1x1
OBTAIN Shop (Cabinet: Daily)
620 (155)

brown diner wall 1x1
OBTAIN Shop (Cabinet: Daily)
2420 (605)

cherry wall 1x1
OBTAIN DIY item
(100) Peppy
N/A (4000)

blue simple-cloth wall 1x1
OBTAIN Shop (Cabinet: Daily)
750 (188)

brown hallway wall 1x1
OBTAIN Shop (Cabinet: Daily)
2000 (500)

cherry-blossom-trees wall 1x1
OBTAIN Seasonal recipe: Cherry blossom
N/A (4600)

blue subway-tile wall 1x1
OBTAIN Shop (Cabinet: Daily)
1340 (335)

brown herringbone wall 1x1
OBTAIN DIY item
Big sister
N/A (1800)

chic tearoom wall 1x1
OBTAIN Shop (Cabinet: Daily)
1750 (438)

blue tile wall 1x1
OBTAIN Shop (Cabinet: Daily)
1420 (355)

brown shanty wall 1x1
OBTAIN Shop (Cabinet: Daily)
620 (155)

chic wall 1x1
OBTAIN Shop (Cabinet: Daily)
1960 (490)

blue two-toned tile wall 1x1
OBTAIN Shop (Cabinet: Daily)
1850 (463)

brown-brick wall 1x1
OBTAIN Shop (Cabinet: Daily)
1000 (250)

chocolate hallway wall 1x1
OBTAIN Shop (Cabinet: Daily)
2000 (500)

chocolate herringbone wall 1x1
OBTAIN DIY item — Smug
N/A (1800)

circuit-board wall 1x1
OBTAIN Saharah
N/A (750)

cityscape wall 1x1
OBTAIN Saharah
N/A (750)

classic-library wall 1x1
OBTAIN DIY item — (100) Sweet
N/A (1450)

colorful puzzle wall 1x1
OBTAIN Shop (Cabinet: Daily)
1540 (385)

colorful-tile wall 1x1
OBTAIN Shop (Cabinet: Daily)
1420 (355)

common wall 1x1
OBTAIN Shop (Cabinet: Daily)
800 (200)

concrete wall 1x1
OBTAIN Shop (Cabinet: Daily)
940 (235)

construction-site wall 1x1
OBTAIN Saharah
N/A (750)

crepe-design wall 1x1
OBTAIN Shop (Cabinet: Daily)
1550 (388)

cute blue wall 1x1
OBTAIN Shop (Cabinet: Daily)
1880 (470)

cute red wall 1x1
OBTAIN Shop (Cabinet: Daily)
1880 (470)

cute white wall 1x1
OBTAIN Shop (Cabinet: Daily)
1880 (470)

cute yellow wall 1x1
OBTAIN Shop (Cabinet: Daily)
1880 (470)

dark wooden-mosaic wall 1x1
OBTAIN DIY item — Big sister
N/A (1800)

dark-chocolate wall 1x1
OBTAIN Saharah
N/A (750)

desert vista 1x1
OBTAIN Saharah
N/A (750)

dig-site wall 1x1
OBTAIN Saharah
N/A (750)

dirt-clod wall 1x1
OBTAIN Shop (Cabinet: Daily)
200 (50)

dojo wall 1x1
OBTAIN Saharah
N/A (750)

dungeon wall 1x1
OBTAIN Saharah
N/A (750)

exquisite wall 1x1
OBTAIN Saharah
N/A (750)

forest wall 1x1
OBTAIN Seasonal recipe: Mushroom
N/A (44,000)

future-tech wall 1x1
OBTAIN Saharah
N/A (750)

garbage-heap wall 1x1
OBTAIN Inspiration: Empty can
N/A (120)

gold-screen wall 1x1
OBTAIN DIY item — (100) Smug
N/A (20,750)

golden wall 1x1
OBTAIN DIY item — (100) Smug
N/A (40,000)

gray diner wall 1x1
OBTAIN Shop (Cabinet: Daily)
2420 (605)

gray molded-panel wall 1x1
OBTAIN Shop (Cabinet: Daily)
1980 (495)

gray shanty wall 1x1
OBTAIN Shop (Cabinet: Daily)
620 (155)

gray-striped wall 1x1
OBTAIN Shop (Cabinet: Daily)
1520 (380)

green blossoming wall 1x1
OBTAIN Shop (Cabinet: Daily)
1760 (440)

green delicate-blooms wall 1x1
OBTAIN Shop (Cabinet: Daily)
1900 (475)

green flower-print wall — 1x1
OBTAIN Shop (Cabinet: Daily)
1780 (445)

honeycomb-tile wall — 1x1
OBTAIN Shop (Cabinet: Daily)
1680 (420)

magma-cavern wall — 1x1
OBTAIN Saharah
N/A (750)

green honeycomb-tile wall — 1x1
OBTAIN Shop (Cabinet: Daily)
1680 (420)

ice wall — 1x1
OBTAIN Reward: Snowboy
N/A (8200)

manga-library wall — 1x1
OBTAIN DIY item
(100) Peppy
N/A (1050)

green intricate wall — 1x1
OBTAIN Shop (Cabinet: Daily)
1570 (393)

iceberg wall — 1x1
OBTAIN Seasonal recipe: Snowflake
N/A (4000)

mangrove wall — 1x1
OBTAIN Saharah
N/A (750)

green molded-panel wall — 1x1
OBTAIN Shop (Cabinet: Daily)
1980 (495)

imperial wall — 1x1
OBTAIN Saharah
N/A (750)

marine pop wall — 1x1
OBTAIN Fishing Tourney
N/A (805)

green painted-wood wall — 1x1
OBTAIN Shop (Cabinet: Daily)
1650 (413)

industrial wall — 1x1
OBTAIN Saharah
N/A (750)

meadow vista — 1x1
OBTAIN Saharah
N/A (750)

green playroom wall — 1x1
OBTAIN Shop (Cabinet: Daily)
2540 (635)

ivy wall — 1x1
OBTAIN Saharah
N/A (750)

misty-garden wall — 1x1
OBTAIN Saharah
N/A (585)

green-paint wall — 1x1
OBTAIN Shop (Cabinet: Daily)
1600 (400)

Jingle wall — 1x1
OBTAIN Seasonal recipe: Ornament
N/A (2500)

mod wall — 1x1
OBTAIN Shop (Cabinet: Daily)
1220 (305)

groovy wall — 1x1
OBTAIN Shop (Cabinet: Daily)
1280 (320)

jungle wall — 1x1
OBTAIN DIY item
Jock
N/A (1380)

modern shoji-screen wall — 1x1
OBTAIN Shop (Cabinet: Daily)
1150 (288)

harmonious wall — 1x1
OBTAIN Shop (Cabinet: Daily)
1780 (445)

kisses wall — 1x1
OBTAIN Saharah
N/A (750)

modern tearoom wall — 1x1
OBTAIN Shop (Cabinet: Daily)
1750 (438)

heavy-curtain wall — 1x1
OBTAIN Saharah
N/A (750)

laboratory wall — 1x1
OBTAIN Saharah
N/A (750)

modern wood wall — 1x1
OBTAIN DIY item
Snooty
N/A (1800)

honeycomb wall — 1x1
OBTAIN DIY item
Jock
N/A (3600)

lattice wall — 1x1
OBTAIN Shop (Cabinet: Daily)
1780 (445)

monochromatic dotted wall — 1x1
OBTAIN Shop (Cabinet: Daily)
1100 (275)

monochromatic-tile wall
1x1
OBTAIN Shop (Cabinet: Daily)
1420 (355)

mortar wall
1x1
OBTAIN Saharah
N/A (750)

mosaic-tile wall
1x1
OBTAIN Shop (Cabinet: Daily)
1450 (363)

mossy-garden wall
1x1
OBTAIN Saharah
N/A (750)

mush wall
1x1
OBTAIN Seasonal recipe: Mushroom
N/A (21,400)

Nook Inc. wall
1x1
OBTAIN Redeem Nook Miles
N/A (6000)

ocean-horizon wall
1x1
OBTAIN Saharah
N/A (750)

office wall
1x1
OBTAIN Saharah
N/A (750)

old wallpaper
1x1
OBTAIN Shop (Cabinet: Daily)
200 (50)

olive desert-tile wall
1x1
OBTAIN Shop (Cabinet: Daily)
2440 (610)

orange camo wall
1x1
OBTAIN Shop (Cabinet: Daily)
1150 (288)

orange molded-panel wall
1x1
OBTAIN Shop (Cabinet: Daily)
1980 (495)

orange wall
1x1
OBTAIN DIY item
(100) Lazy
N/A (4000)

orange-paint wall
1x1
OBTAIN Shop (Cabinet: Daily)
1600 (400)

paintball wall
1x1
OBTAIN Saharah
N/A (750)

palace wall
1x1
OBTAIN Saharah
N/A (750)

party wall
1x1
OBTAIN Your Birthday
N/A (370)

pastel dotted wall
1x1
OBTAIN Shop (Cabinet: Daily)
1100 (275)

pastel puzzle wall
1x1
OBTAIN Shop (Cabinet: Daily)
1540 (385)

peach two-toned tile wall
1x1
OBTAIN Shop (Cabinet: Daily)
1850 (463)

peach wall
1x1
OBTAIN DIY item
(100) Sweet
N/A (4000)

pear wall
1x1
OBTAIN DIY item
(100) Jock
N/A (4000)

perforated-board wall
1x1
OBTAIN Shop (Cabinet: Daily)
1180 (295)

pink blossoming wall
1x1
OBTAIN Shop (Cabinet: Daily)
1760 (440)

pink diner wall
1x1
OBTAIN Shop (Cabinet: Daily)
2420 (605)

pink flower-print wall
1x1
OBTAIN Shop (Cabinet: Daily)
1780 (445)

pink heart-pattern wall
1x1
OBTAIN Shop (Cabinet: Daily)
1280 (320)

pink painted-wood wall
1x1
OBTAIN Shop (Cabinet: Daily)
1650 (413)

pink playroom wall
1x1
OBTAIN Shop (Cabinet: Daily)
2540 (635)

pink quilt wall
1x1
OBTAIN Shop (Cabinet: Daily)
2150 (538)

pink shanty wall
1x1
OBTAIN Shop (Cabinet: Daily)
620 (155)

pink simple-cloth wall
1x1
OBTAIN Shop (Cabinet: Daily)
750 (188)

pink-crown wall
1x1
OBTAIN Shop (Cabinet: Daily)
2350 (588)

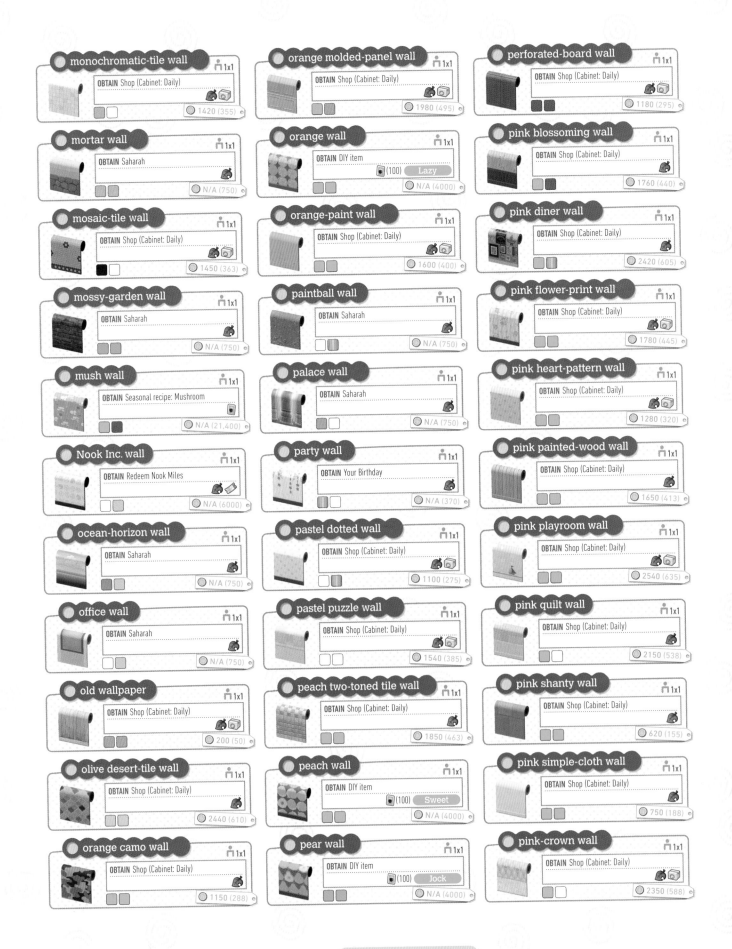

pink-striped wall
1x1
OBTAIN Shop (Cabinet: Daily)
1520 (380)

purple camo wall
1x1
OBTAIN Shop (Cabinet: Daily)
1150 (288)

purple desert-tile wall
1x1
OBTAIN Shop (Cabinet: Daily)
2440 (610)

purple dotted wall
1x1
OBTAIN Shop (Cabinet: Daily)
1100 (275)

purple puzzle wall
1x1
OBTAIN Shop (Cabinet: Daily)
1540 (385)

purple quilt wall
1x1
OBTAIN Shop (Cabinet: Daily)
2150 (538)

purple-rose wall
1x1
OBTAIN Shop (Cabinet: Daily)
1720 (430)

rammed-earth wall
1x1
OBTAIN Shop (Cabinet: Daily)
1800 (450)

ramshackle wall
1x1
OBTAIN Saharah
N/A (750)

red art-deco wall
1x1
OBTAIN Shop (Cabinet: Daily)
2780 (695)

red delicate-blooms wall
1x1
OBTAIN Shop (Cabinet: Daily)
1900 (475)

red dotted wall
1x1
OBTAIN Shop (Cabinet: Daily)
1100 (275)

red heart-pattern wall
1x1
OBTAIN Shop (Cabinet: Daily)
1280 (320)

red intricate wall
1x1
OBTAIN Shop (Cabinet: Daily)
1570 (393)

red perforated-board wall
1x1
OBTAIN Shop (Cabinet: Daily)
1180 (295)

red two-toned tile wall
1x1
OBTAIN Shop (Cabinet: Daily)
1850 (463)

red-brick wall
1x1
OBTAIN Shop (Cabinet: Daily)
1000 (250)

retro flower-print wall
1x1
OBTAIN Shop (Cabinet: Daily)
1660 (415)

rice-paddy wall
1x1
OBTAIN Saharah
N/A (750)

ringside seating
1x1
OBTAIN Saharah
N/A (750)

rock-climbing wall
1x1
OBTAIN Saharah
N/A (750)

rose wall
1x1
OBTAIN Shop (Cabinet: Daily)
1720 (430)

ruins wall
1x1
OBTAIN Saharah
N/A (750)

rustic-stone wall
1x1
OBTAIN DIY item
Snooty
N/A (1750)

sakura-wood wall
1x1
OBTAIN Seasonal recipe: Cherry blossom
N/A (3200)

sci-fi wall
1x1
OBTAIN Star fragment recipe (Reward: Celeste)
N/A (7500)

screen wall
1x1
OBTAIN Shop (Cabinet: Daily)
3000 (750)

sea view
1x1
OBTAIN Saharah
N/A (750)

security-monitors wall
1x1
OBTAIN Saharah
N/A (750)

sepia puzzle wall
1x1
OBTAIN Shop (Cabinet: Daily)
1540 (385)

server-room wall
1x1
OBTAIN Saharah
N/A (750)

shoji screen
1x1
OBTAIN Shop (Cabinet: Daily)
1880 (470)

shutter wall
1x1
OBTAIN Saharah
N/A (750)

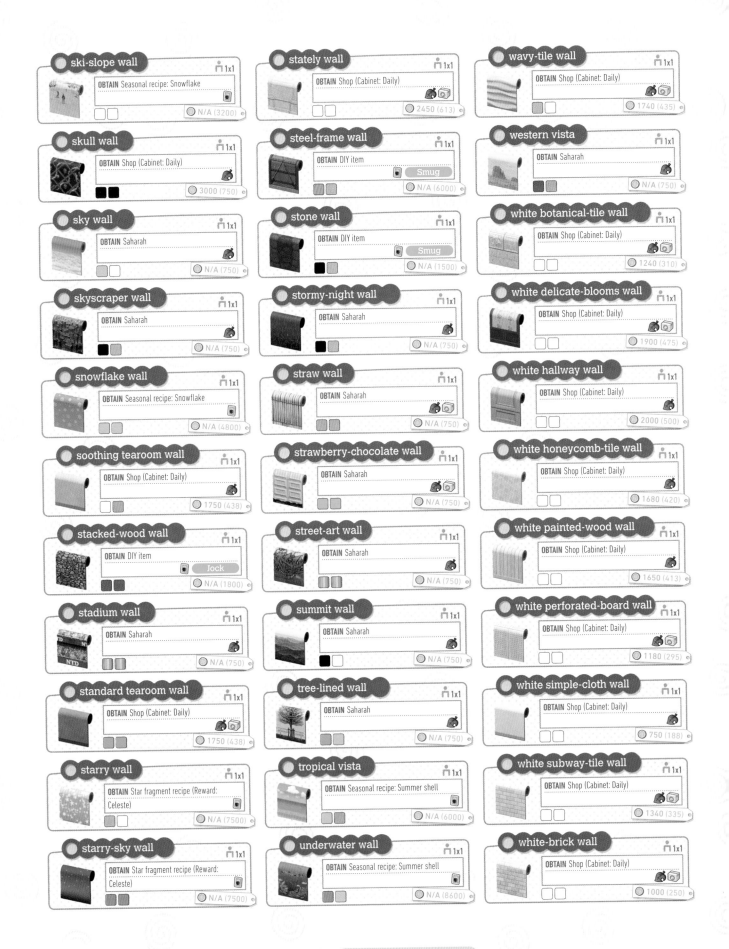

ski-slope wall 1x1
OBTAIN Seasonal recipe: Snowflake
N/A (3200)

skull wall 1x1
OBTAIN Shop (Cabinet: Daily)
3000 (750)

sky wall 1x1
OBTAIN Saharah
N/A (750)

skyscraper wall 1x1
OBTAIN Saharah
N/A (750)

snowflake wall 1x1
OBTAIN Seasonal recipe: Snowflake
N/A (4800)

soothing tearoom wall 1x1
OBTAIN Shop (Cabinet: Daily)
1750 (438)

stacked-wood wall 1x1
OBTAIN DIY item
Jock
N/A (1800)

stadium wall 1x1
OBTAIN Saharah
N/A (750)

standard tearoom wall 1x1
OBTAIN Shop (Cabinet: Daily)
1750 (438)

starry wall 1x1
OBTAIN Star fragment recipe (Reward: Celeste)
N/A (7500)

starry-sky wall 1x1
OBTAIN Star fragment recipe (Reward: Celeste)
N/A (7500)

stately wall 1x1
OBTAIN Shop (Cabinet: Daily)
2450 (613)

steel-frame wall 1x1
OBTAIN DIY item
Smug
N/A (6000)

stone wall 1x1
OBTAIN DIY item
Smug
N/A (1500)

stormy-night wall 1x1
OBTAIN Saharah
N/A (750)

straw wall 1x1
OBTAIN Saharah
N/A (750)

strawberry-chocolate wall 1x1
OBTAIN Saharah
N/A (750)

street-art wall 1x1
OBTAIN Saharah
N/A (750)

summit wall 1x1
OBTAIN Saharah
N/A (750)

tree-lined wall 1x1
OBTAIN Saharah
N/A (750)

tropical vista 1x1
OBTAIN Seasonal recipe: Summer shell
N/A (6000)

underwater wall 1x1
OBTAIN Seasonal recipe: Summer shell
N/A (8600)

wavy-tile wall 1x1
OBTAIN Shop (Cabinet: Daily)
1740 (435)

western vista 1x1
OBTAIN Saharah
N/A (750)

white botanical-tile wall 1x1
OBTAIN Shop (Cabinet: Daily)
1240 (310)

white delicate-blooms wall 1x1
OBTAIN Shop (Cabinet: Daily)
1900 (475)

white hallway wall 1x1
OBTAIN Shop (Cabinet: Daily)
2000 (500)

white honeycomb-tile wall 1x1
OBTAIN Shop (Cabinet: Daily)
1680 (420)

white painted-wood wall 1x1
OBTAIN Shop (Cabinet: Daily)
1650 (413)

white perforated-board wall 1x1
OBTAIN Shop (Cabinet: Daily)
1180 (295)

white simple-cloth wall 1x1
OBTAIN Shop (Cabinet: Daily)
750 (188)

white subway-tile wall 1x1
OBTAIN Shop (Cabinet: Daily)
1340 (335)

white-brick wall 1x1
OBTAIN Shop (Cabinet: Daily)
1000 (250)

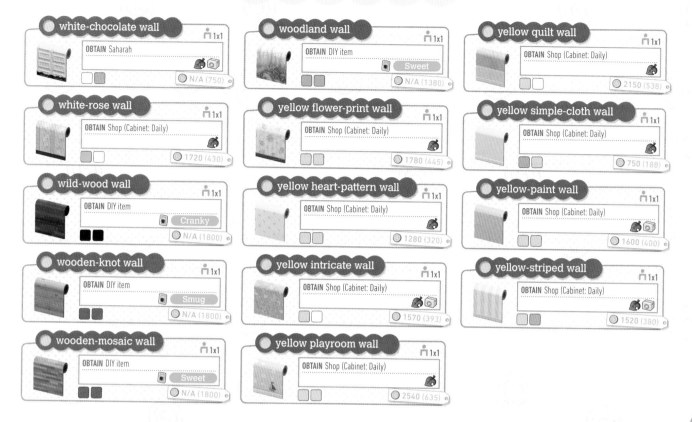

white-chocolate wall
1x1
OBTAIN Saharah
N/A (750)

woodland wall
1x1
OBTAIN DIY item
Sweet
N/A (1380)

yellow quilt wall
1x1
OBTAIN Shop (Cabinet: Daily)
2150 (538)

white-rose wall
1x1
OBTAIN Shop (Cabinet: Daily)
1720 (430)

yellow flower-print wall
1x1
OBTAIN Shop (Cabinet: Daily)
1780 (445)

yellow simple-cloth wall
1x1
OBTAIN Shop (Cabinet: Daily)
750 (188)

wild-wood wall
1x1
OBTAIN DIY item
Cranky
N/A (1800)

yellow heart-pattern wall
1x1
OBTAIN Shop (Cabinet: Daily)
1280 (320)

yellow-paint wall
1x1
OBTAIN Shop (Cabinet: Daily)
1600 (400)

wooden-knot wall
1x1
OBTAIN DIY item
Smug
N/A (1800)

yellow intricate wall
1x1
OBTAIN Shop (Cabinet: Daily)
1570 (393)

yellow-striped wall
1x1
OBTAIN Shop (Cabinet: Daily)
1520 (380)

wooden-mosaic wall
1x1
OBTAIN DIY item
Sweet
N/A (1800)

yellow playroom wall
1x1
OBTAIN Shop (Cabinet: Daily)
2540 (635)

Rugs

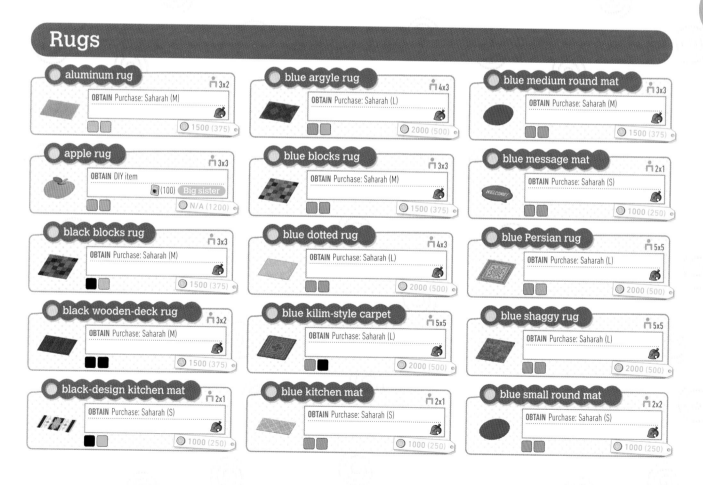

aluminum rug
3x2
OBTAIN Purchase: Saharah (M)
1500 (375)

blue argyle rug
4x3
OBTAIN Purchase: Saharah (L)
2000 (500)

blue medium round mat
3x3
OBTAIN Purchase: Saharah (M)
1500 (375)

apple rug
3x3
OBTAIN DIY item
(100) Big sister
N/A (1200)

blue blocks rug
3x3
OBTAIN Purchase: Saharah (M)
1500 (375)

blue message mat
2x1
OBTAIN Purchase: Saharah (S)
1000 (250)

black blocks rug
3x3
OBTAIN Purchase: Saharah (M)
1500 (375)

blue dotted rug
4x3
OBTAIN Purchase: Saharah (L)
2000 (500)

blue Persian rug
5x5
OBTAIN Purchase: Saharah (L)
2000 (500)

black wooden-deck rug
3x2
OBTAIN Purchase: Saharah (M)
1500 (375)

blue kilim-style carpet
5x5
OBTAIN Purchase: Saharah (L)
2000 (500)

blue shaggy rug
5x5
OBTAIN Purchase: Saharah (L)
2000 (500)

black-design kitchen mat
2x1
OBTAIN Purchase: Saharah (S)
1000 (250)

blue kitchen mat
2x1
OBTAIN Purchase: Saharah (S)
1000 (250)

blue small round mat
2x2
OBTAIN Purchase: Saharah (S)
1000 (250)

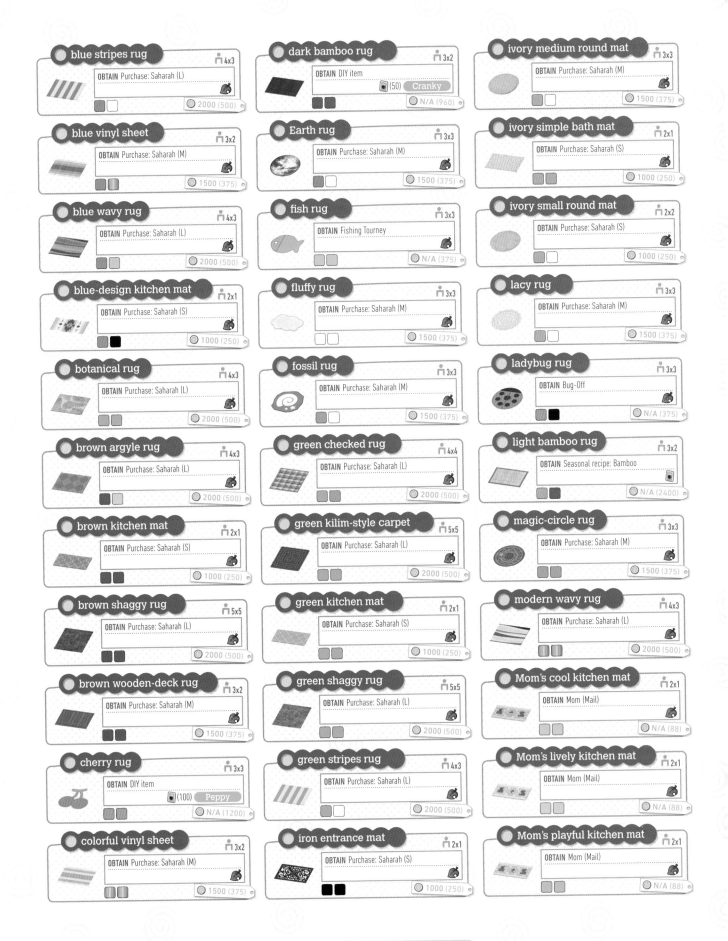

blue stripes rug
🛏 4x3
OBTAIN Purchase: Saharah (L)
🔔 2000 (500)

blue vinyl sheet
🛏 3x2
OBTAIN Purchase: Saharah (M)
🔔 1500 (375)

blue wavy rug
🛏 4x3
OBTAIN Purchase: Saharah (L)
🔔 2000 (500)

blue-design kitchen mat
🛏 2x1
OBTAIN Purchase: Saharah (S)
🔔 1000 (250)

botanical rug
🛏 4x3
OBTAIN Purchase: Saharah (L)
🔔 2000 (500)

brown argyle rug
🛏 4x3
OBTAIN Purchase: Saharah (L)
🔔 2000 (500)

brown kitchen mat
🛏 2x1
OBTAIN Purchase: Saharah (S)
🔔 1000 (250)

brown shaggy rug
🛏 5x5
OBTAIN Purchase: Saharah (L)
🔔 2000 (500)

brown wooden-deck rug
🛏 3x2
OBTAIN Purchase: Saharah (M)
🔔 1500 (375)

cherry rug
🛏 3x3
OBTAIN DIY item
🍒(100) Peppy
🔔 N/A (1200)

colorful vinyl sheet
🛏 3x2
OBTAIN Purchase: Saharah (M)
🔔 1500 (375)

dark bamboo rug
🛏 3x2
OBTAIN DIY item
🗒(50) Cranky
🔔 N/A (960)

Earth rug
🛏 3x3
OBTAIN Purchase: Saharah (M)
🔔 1500 (375)

fish rug
🛏 3x3
OBTAIN Fishing Tourney
🔔 N/A (375)

fluffy rug
🛏 3x3
OBTAIN Purchase: Saharah (M)
🔔 1500 (375)

fossil rug
🛏 3x3
OBTAIN Purchase: Saharah (M)
🔔 1500 (375)

green checked rug
🛏 4x4
OBTAIN Purchase: Saharah (L)
🔔 2000 (500)

green kilim-style carpet
🛏 5x5
OBTAIN Purchase: Saharah (L)
🔔 2000 (500)

green kitchen mat
🛏 2x1
OBTAIN Purchase: Saharah (S)
🔔 1000 (250)

green shaggy rug
🛏 5x5
OBTAIN Purchase: Saharah (L)
🔔 2000 (500)

green stripes rug
🛏 4x3
OBTAIN Purchase: Saharah (L)
🔔 2000 (500)

iron entrance mat
🛏 2x1
OBTAIN Purchase: Saharah (S)
🔔 1000 (250)

ivory medium round mat
🛏 3x3
OBTAIN Purchase: Saharah (M)
🔔 1500 (375)

ivory simple bath mat
🛏 2x1
OBTAIN Purchase: Saharah (S)
🔔 1000 (250)

ivory small round mat
🛏 2x2
OBTAIN Purchase: Saharah (S)
🔔 1000 (250)

lacy rug
🛏 3x3
OBTAIN Purchase: Saharah (M)
🔔 1500 (375)

ladybug rug
🛏 3x3
OBTAIN Bug-Off
🔔 N/A (375)

light bamboo rug
🛏 3x2
OBTAIN Seasonal recipe: Bamboo
🔔 N/A (2400)

magic-circle rug
🛏 3x3
OBTAIN Purchase: Saharah (M)
🔔 1500 (375)

modern wavy rug
🛏 4x3
OBTAIN Purchase: Saharah (L)
🔔 2000 (500)

Mom's cool kitchen mat
🛏 2x1
OBTAIN Mom (Mail)
🔔 N/A (88)

Mom's lively kitchen mat
🛏 2x1
OBTAIN Mom (Mail)
🔔 N/A (88)

Mom's playful kitchen mat
🛏 2x1
OBTAIN Mom (Mail)
🔔 N/A (88)

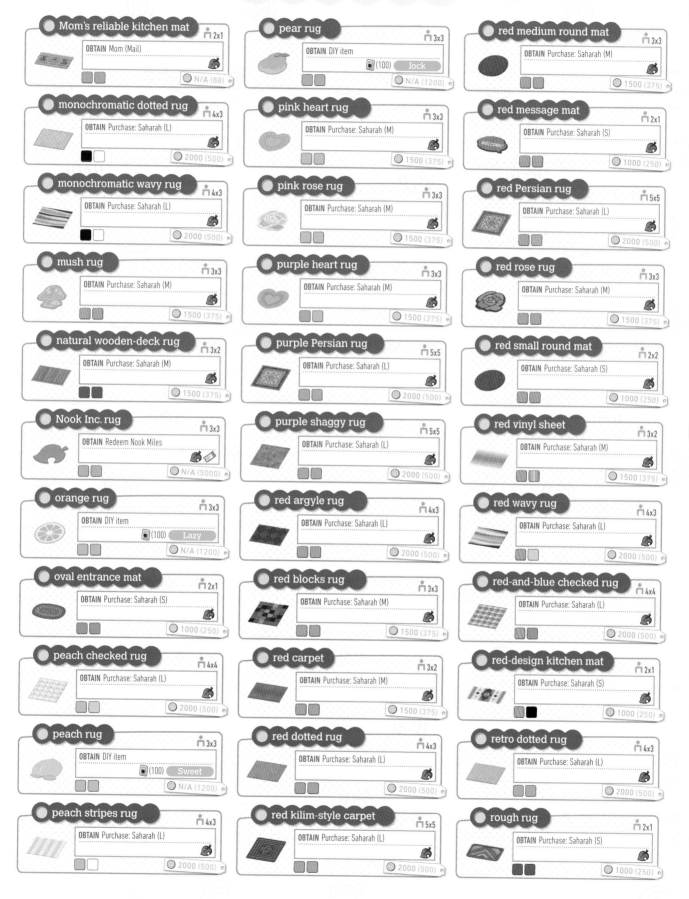

Mom's reliable kitchen mat 2x1
OBTAIN Mom (Mail)
N/A (88)

monochromatic dotted rug 4x3
OBTAIN Purchase: Saharah (L)
2000 (500)

monochromatic wavy rug 4x3
OBTAIN Purchase: Saharah (L)
2000 (500)

mush rug 3x3
OBTAIN Purchase: Saharah (M)
1500 (375)

natural wooden-deck rug 3x2
OBTAIN Purchase: Saharah (M)
1500 (375)

Nook Inc. rug 3x3
OBTAIN Redeem Nook Miles
N/A (5000)

orange rug 3x3
OBTAIN DIY item
(100) Lazy
N/A (1200)

oval entrance mat 2x1
OBTAIN Purchase: Saharah (S)
1000 (250)

peach checked rug 4x4
OBTAIN Purchase: Saharah (L)
2000 (500)

peach rug 3x3
OBTAIN DIY item
(100) Sweet
N/A (1200)

peach stripes rug 4x3
OBTAIN Purchase: Saharah (L)
2000 (500)

pear rug 3x3
OBTAIN DIY item
(100) Jock
N/A (1200)

pink heart rug 3x3
OBTAIN Purchase: Saharah (M)
1500 (375)

pink rose rug 3x3
OBTAIN Purchase: Saharah (M)
1500 (375)

purple heart rug 3x3
OBTAIN Purchase: Saharah (M)
1500 (375)

purple Persian rug 5x5
OBTAIN Purchase: Saharah (L)
2000 (500)

purple shaggy rug 5x5
OBTAIN Purchase: Saharah (L)
2000 (500)

red argyle rug 4x3
OBTAIN Purchase: Saharah (L)
2000 (500)

red blocks rug 3x3
OBTAIN Purchase: Saharah (M)
1500 (375)

red carpet 3x2
OBTAIN Purchase: Saharah (M)
1500 (375)

red dotted rug 4x3
OBTAIN Purchase: Saharah (L)
2000 (500)

red kilim-style carpet 5x5
OBTAIN Purchase: Saharah (L)
2000 (500)

red medium round mat 3x3
OBTAIN Purchase: Saharah (M)
1500 (375)

red message mat 2x1
OBTAIN Purchase: Saharah (S)
1000 (250)

red Persian rug 5x5
OBTAIN Purchase: Saharah (L)
2000 (500)

red rose rug 3x3
OBTAIN Purchase: Saharah (M)
1500 (375)

red small round mat 2x2
OBTAIN Purchase: Saharah (S)
1000 (250)

red vinyl sheet 3x2
OBTAIN Purchase: Saharah (M)
1500 (375)

red wavy rug 4x3
OBTAIN Purchase: Saharah (L)
2000 (500)

red-and-blue checked rug 4x4
OBTAIN Purchase: Saharah (L)
2000 (500)

red-design kitchen mat 2x1
OBTAIN Purchase: Saharah (S)
1000 (250)

retro dotted rug 4x3
OBTAIN Purchase: Saharah (L)
2000 (500)

rough rug 2x1
OBTAIN Purchase: Saharah (S)
1000 (250)

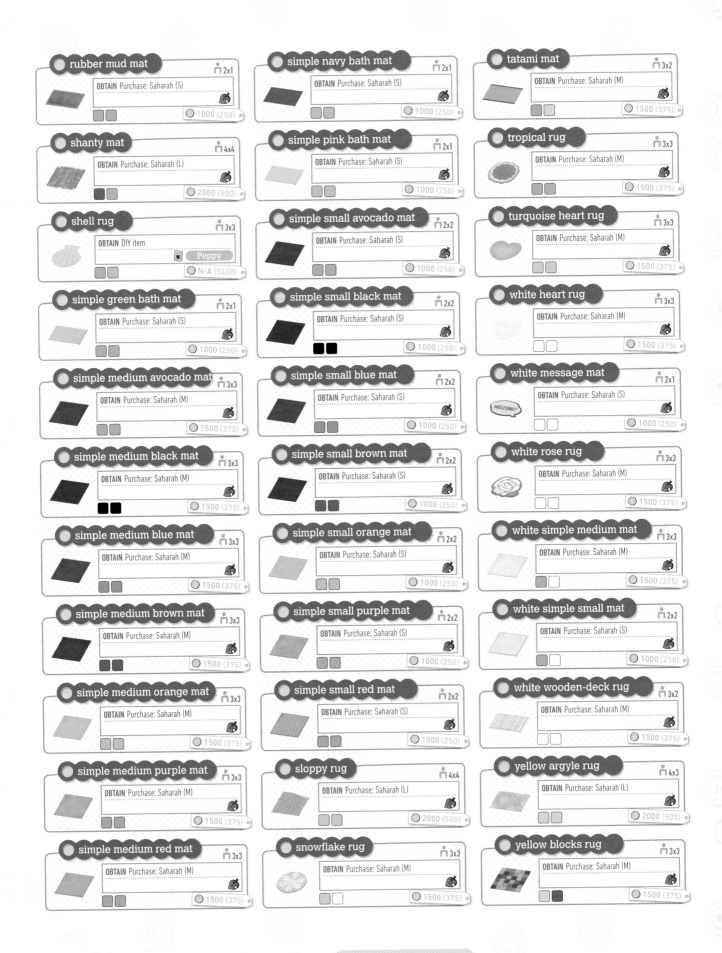

rubber mud mat
🏠 2x1
OBTAIN Purchase: Saharah (S)
🔔 1000 (250)

shanty mat
🏠 4x4
OBTAIN Purchase: Saharah (L)
🔔 2000 (500)

shell rug
🏠 3x3
OBTAIN DIY item
Peppy
N/A (5400)

simple green bath mat
🏠 2x1
OBTAIN Purchase: Saharah (S)
🔔 1000 (250)

simple medium avocado mat
🏠 3x3
OBTAIN Purchase: Saharah (M)
🔔 1500 (375)

simple medium black mat
🏠 3x3
OBTAIN Purchase: Saharah (M)
🔔 1500 (375)

simple medium blue mat
🏠 3x3
OBTAIN Purchase: Saharah (M)
🔔 1500 (375)

simple medium brown mat
🏠 3x3
OBTAIN Purchase: Saharah (M)
🔔 1500 (375)

simple medium orange mat
🏠 3x3
OBTAIN Purchase: Saharah (M)
🔔 1500 (375)

simple medium purple mat
🏠 3x3
OBTAIN Purchase: Saharah (M)
🔔 1500 (375)

simple medium red mat
🏠 3x3
OBTAIN Purchase: Saharah (M)
🔔 1500 (375)

simple navy bath mat
🏠 2x1
OBTAIN Purchase: Saharah (S)
🔔 1000 (250)

simple pink bath mat
🏠 2x1
OBTAIN Purchase: Saharah (S)
🔔 1000 (250)

simple small avocado mat
🏠 2x2
OBTAIN Purchase: Saharah (S)
🔔 1000 (250)

simple small black mat
🏠 2x2
OBTAIN Purchase: Saharah (S)
🔔 1000 (250)

simple small blue mat
🏠 2x2
OBTAIN Purchase: Saharah (S)
🔔 1000 (250)

simple small brown mat
🏠 2x2
OBTAIN Purchase: Saharah (S)
🔔 1000 (250)

simple small orange mat
🏠 2x2
OBTAIN Purchase: Saharah (S)
🔔 1000 (250)

simple small purple mat
🏠 2x2
OBTAIN Purchase: Saharah (S)
🔔 1000 (250)

simple small red mat
🏠 2x2
OBTAIN Purchase: Saharah (S)
🔔 1000 (250)

sloppy rug
🏠 4x4
OBTAIN Purchase: Saharah (L)
🔔 2000 (500)

snowflake rug
🏠 3x3
OBTAIN Purchase: Saharah (M)
🔔 1500 (375)

tatami mat
🏠 3x2
OBTAIN Purchase: Saharah (M)
🔔 1500 (375)

tropical rug
🏠 3x3
OBTAIN Purchase: Saharah (M)
🔔 1500 (375)

turquoise heart rug
🏠 3x3
OBTAIN Purchase: Saharah (M)
🔔 1500 (375)

white heart rug
🏠 3x3
OBTAIN Purchase: Saharah (M)
🔔 1500 (375)

white message mat
🏠 2x1
OBTAIN Purchase: Saharah (S)
🔔 1000 (250)

white rose rug
🏠 3x3
OBTAIN Purchase: Saharah (M)
🔔 1500 (375)

white simple medium mat
🏠 3x3
OBTAIN Purchase: Saharah (M)
🔔 1500 (375)

white simple small mat
🏠 2x2
OBTAIN Purchase: Saharah (S)
🔔 1000 (250)

white wooden-deck rug
🏠 3x2
OBTAIN Purchase: Saharah (M)
🔔 1500 (375)

yellow argyle rug
🏠 4x3
OBTAIN Purchase: Saharah (L)
🔔 2000 (500)

yellow blocks rug
🏠 3x3
OBTAIN Purchase: Saharah (M)
🔔 1500 (375)

yellow checked rug
4x4
OBTAIN Purchase: Saharah (L)
2000 (500)

yellow message mat
2x1
OBTAIN Purchase: Saharah (S)
1000 (250)

yellow stripes rug
4x3
OBTAIN Purchase: Saharah (L)
2000 (500)

yellow kilim-style carpet
5x5
OBTAIN Purchase: Saharah (L)
2000 (500)

yellow Persian rug
5x5
OBTAIN Purchase: Saharah (L)
2000 (500)

yellow vinyl sheet
3x2
OBTAIN Purchase: Saharah (M)
1500 (375)

yellow kitchen mat
2x1
OBTAIN Purchase: Saharah (S)
1000 (250)

yellow rose rug
3x3
OBTAIN Purchase: Saharah (M)
1500 (375)

yellow-design kitchen mat
2x1
OBTAIN Purchase: Saharah (S)
1000 (250)

yellow medium round mat
3x3
OBTAIN Purchase: Saharah (M)
1500 (375)

yellow small round mat
2x2
OBTAIN Purchase: Saharah (S)
1000 (250)

Flooring

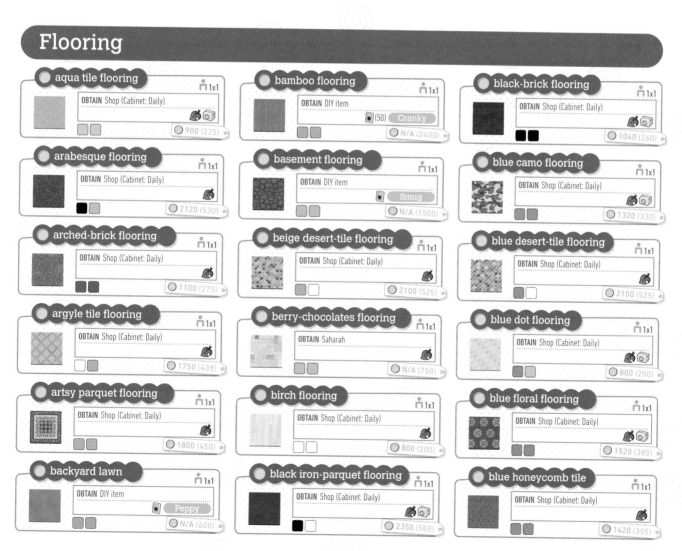

aqua tile flooring
1x1
OBTAIN Shop (Cabinet: Daily)
900 (225)

bamboo flooring
1x1
OBTAIN DIY item
(50) Cranky
N/A (2400)

black-brick flooring
1x1
OBTAIN Shop (Cabinet: Daily)
1040 (260)

arabesque flooring
1x1
OBTAIN Shop (Cabinet: Daily)
2120 (530)

basement flooring
1x1
OBTAIN DIY item
Smug
N/A (1500)

blue camo flooring
1x1
OBTAIN Shop (Cabinet: Daily)
1320 (330)

arched-brick flooring
1x1
OBTAIN Shop (Cabinet: Daily)
1100 (275)

beige desert-tile flooring
1x1
OBTAIN Shop (Cabinet: Daily)
2100 (525)

blue desert-tile flooring
1x1
OBTAIN Shop (Cabinet: Daily)
2100 (525)

argyle tile flooring
1x1
OBTAIN Shop (Cabinet: Daily)
1750 (438)

berry-chocolates flooring
1x1
OBTAIN Saharah
N/A (750)

blue dot flooring
1x1
OBTAIN Shop (Cabinet: Daily)
800 (200)

artsy parquet flooring
1x1
OBTAIN Shop (Cabinet: Daily)
1800 (450)

birch flooring
1x1
OBTAIN Shop (Cabinet: Daily)
800 (200)

blue floral flooring
1x1
OBTAIN Shop (Cabinet: Daily)
1520 (380)

backyard lawn
1x1
OBTAIN DIY item
Peppy
N/A (600)

black iron-parquet flooring
1x1
OBTAIN Shop (Cabinet: Daily)
2350 (588)

blue honeycomb tile
1x1
OBTAIN Shop (Cabinet: Daily)
1420 (355)

7

blue mosaic-tile flooring 🏠 1x1
OBTAIN Shop (Cabinet: Daily)
900 (225)

blue rubber flooring 🏠 1x1
OBTAIN Shop (Cabinet: Daily)
850 (213)

blue-paint flooring 🏠 1x1
OBTAIN Shop (Cabinet: Daily)
1040 (260)

boxing-ring mat 🏠 1x1
OBTAIN Saharah
N/A (750)

brown argyle-tile flooring 🏠 1x1
OBTAIN Shop (Cabinet: Daily)
1440 (360)

brown floral flooring 🏠 1x1
OBTAIN Shop (Cabinet: Daily)
1520 (380)

brown honeycomb tile 🏠 1x1
OBTAIN Shop (Cabinet: Daily)
1420 (355)

brown iron-parquet flooring 🏠 1x1
OBTAIN Shop (Cabinet: Daily)
2350 (588)

brown-brick flooring 🏠 1x1
OBTAIN Shop (Cabinet: Daily)
1040 (260)

camo flooring 🏠 1x1
OBTAIN Shop (Cabinet: Daily)
1320 (330)

cherry-blossom flooring 🏠 1x1
OBTAIN Seasonal recipe: Cherry blossom
N/A (4400)

circuit-board flooring 🏠 1x1
OBTAIN Saharah
N/A (750)

cloud flooring 🏠 1x1
OBTAIN Saharah
N/A (750)

colored-leaves flooring 🏠 1x1
OBTAIN Seasonal recipe: Maple Leaf
N/A (4300)

colorful mosaic-tile flooring 🏠 1x1
OBTAIN Shop (Cabinet: Daily)
900 (225)

colorful puzzle flooring 🏠 1x1
OBTAIN Shop (Cabinet: Daily)
1450 (363)

colorful tile flooring 🏠 1x1
OBTAIN Shop (Cabinet: Daily)
1620 (405)

common flooring 🏠 1x1
OBTAIN Shop (Cabinet: Daily)
720 (180)

concrete flooring 🏠 1x1
OBTAIN Shop (Cabinet: Daily)
820 (205)

construction-site flooring 🏠 1x1
OBTAIN Saharah
N/A (750)

cool vinyl flooring 🏠 1x1
OBTAIN Shop (Cabinet: Daily)
1150 (288)

cool-paint flooring 🏠 1x1
OBTAIN Shop (Cabinet: Daily)
2200 (550)

cork flooring 🏠 1x1
OBTAIN Shop (Cabinet: Daily)
1500 (375)

crop-circles flooring 🏠 1x1
OBTAIN Saharah
N/A (750)

crosswalk flooring 🏠 1x1
OBTAIN Saharah
N/A (750)

cubic parquet flooring 🏠 1x1
OBTAIN Shop (Cabinet: Daily)
1500 (375)

cute blue-tile flooring 🏠 1x1
OBTAIN Shop (Cabinet: Daily)
780 (195)

cute red-tile flooring 🏠 1x1
OBTAIN Shop (Cabinet: Daily)
780 (195)

cute white-tile flooring 🏠 1x1
OBTAIN Shop (Cabinet: Daily)
780 (195)

cute yellow-tile flooring 🏠 1x1
OBTAIN Shop (Cabinet: Daily)
780 (195)

cute-paint flooring 🏠 1x1
OBTAIN Shop (Cabinet: Daily)
2200 (550)

daisy meadow 🏠 1x1
OBTAIN Saharah
N/A (750)

dark herringbone flooring 🏠 1x1
OBTAIN Shop (Cabinet: Daily)
1200 (300)

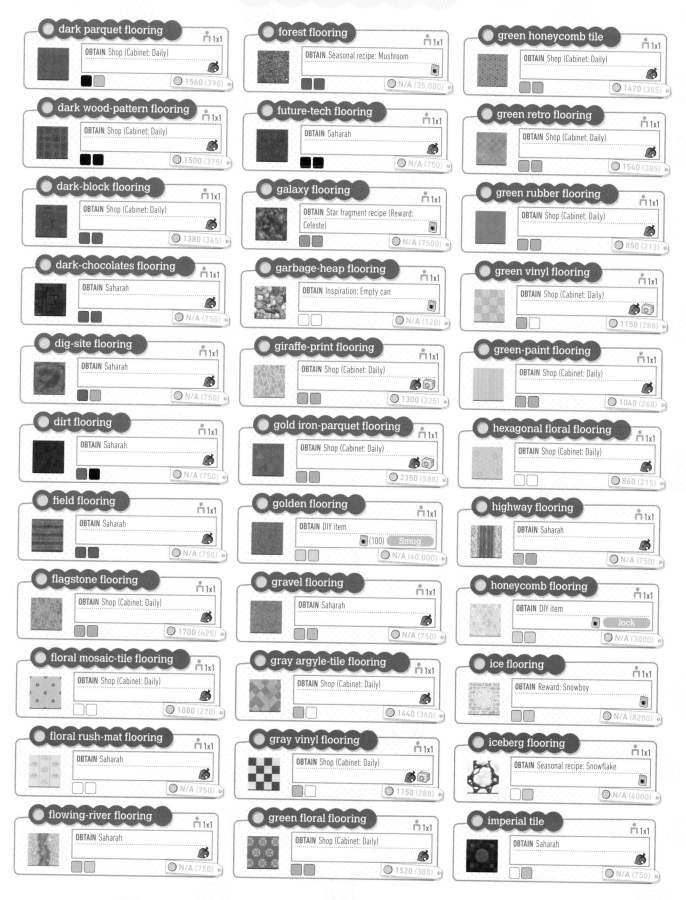

dark parquet flooring — 1x1
OBTAIN Shop (Cabinet: Daily)
1560 (390)

forest flooring — 1x1
OBTAIN Seasonal recipe: Mushroom
N/A (35,000)

green honeycomb tile — 1x1
OBTAIN Shop (Cabinet: Daily)
1420 (355)

dark wood-pattern flooring — 1x1
OBTAIN Shop (Cabinet: Daily)
1500 (375)

future-tech flooring — 1x1
OBTAIN Saharah
N/A (750)

green retro flooring — 1x1
OBTAIN Shop (Cabinet: Daily)
1540 (385)

dark-block flooring — 1x1
OBTAIN Shop (Cabinet: Daily)
1380 (345)

galaxy flooring — 1x1
OBTAIN Star fragment recipe (Reward: Celeste)
N/A (7500)

green rubber flooring — 1x1
OBTAIN Shop (Cabinet: Daily)
850 (213)

dark-chocolates flooring — 1x1
OBTAIN Saharah
N/A (750)

garbage-heap flooring — 1x1
OBTAIN Inspiration: Empty can
N/A (120)

green vinyl flooring — 1x1
OBTAIN Shop (Cabinet: Daily)
1150 (288)

dig-site flooring — 1x1
OBTAIN Saharah
N/A (750)

giraffe-print flooring — 1x1
OBTAIN Shop (Cabinet: Daily)
1300 (325)

green-paint flooring — 1x1
OBTAIN Shop (Cabinet: Daily)
1040 (260)

dirt flooring — 1x1
OBTAIN Saharah
N/A (750)

gold iron-parquet flooring — 1x1
OBTAIN Shop (Cabinet: Daily)
2350 (588)

hexagonal floral flooring — 1x1
OBTAIN Shop (Cabinet: Daily)
860 (215)

field flooring — 1x1
OBTAIN Saharah
N/A (750)

golden flooring — 1x1
OBTAIN DIY item
(100) Smug
N/A (40,000)

highway flooring — 1x1
OBTAIN Saharah
N/A (750)

flagstone flooring — 1x1
OBTAIN Shop (Cabinet: Daily)
1700 (425)

gravel flooring — 1x1
OBTAIN Saharah
N/A (750)

honeycomb flooring — 1x1
OBTAIN DIY item
Jock
N/A (3000)

floral mosaic-tile flooring — 1x1
OBTAIN Shop (Cabinet: Daily)
1080 (270)

gray argyle-tile flooring — 1x1
OBTAIN Shop (Cabinet: Daily)
1440 (360)

ice flooring — 1x1
OBTAIN Reward: Snowboy
N/A (8200)

floral rush-mat flooring — 1x1
OBTAIN Saharah
N/A (750)

gray vinyl flooring — 1x1
OBTAIN Shop (Cabinet: Daily)
1150 (288)

iceberg flooring — 1x1
OBTAIN Seasonal recipe: Snowflake
N/A (4000)

flowing-river flooring — 1x1
OBTAIN Saharah
N/A (750)

green floral flooring — 1x1
OBTAIN Shop (Cabinet: Daily)
1520 (380)

imperial tile — 1x1
OBTAIN Saharah
N/A (750)

7

jointed-mat flooring
1x1
OBTAIN Shop (Cabinet: Daily)
1050 (263)

jungle flooring
1x1
OBTAIN DIY item
Jock
N/A (2200)

kitschy tile
1x1
OBTAIN Shop (Cabinet: Daily)
1280 (320)

lava flooring
1x1
OBTAIN Saharah
N/A (750)

leopard-print flooring
1x1
OBTAIN Shop (Cabinet: Daily)
1300 (325)

light herringbone flooring
1x1
OBTAIN Shop (Cabinet: Daily)
1200 (300)

light parquet flooring
1x1
OBTAIN Shop (Cabinet: Daily)
1560 (390)

light wood-pattern flooring
1x1
OBTAIN Shop (Cabinet: Daily)
1500 (375)

lobby flooring
1x1
OBTAIN Saharah
N/A (750)

lunar surface
1x1
OBTAIN Star fragment recipe (Reward: Celeste)
N/A (7500)

marine pop flooring
1x1
OBTAIN Shop (Cabinet: Daily)
2020 (505)

mint dot flooring
1x1
OBTAIN Shop (Cabinet: Daily)
800 (200)

modern wood flooring
1x1
OBTAIN Shop (Cabinet: Daily)
1280 (320)

money flooring
1x1
OBTAIN DIY item
(100) Snooty
N/A (25,000)

monochromatic dot flooring
1x1
OBTAIN Shop (Cabinet: Daily)
800 (200)

monochromatic tile flooring
1x1
OBTAIN Shop (Cabinet: Daily)
1620 (405)

mossy-garden flooring
1x1
OBTAIN Saharah
N/A (750)

natural-block flooring
1x1
OBTAIN Shop (Cabinet: Daily)
1380 (345)

Nook Inc. flooring
1x1
OBTAIN Redeem Nook Miles
N/A (6000)

oasis flooring
1x1
OBTAIN Saharah
N/A (750)

olive desert-tile flooring
1x1
OBTAIN Shop (Cabinet: Daily)
2100 (525)

orange camo flooring
1x1
OBTAIN Shop (Cabinet: Daily)
1320 (330)

orange retro flooring
1x1
OBTAIN Shop (Cabinet: Daily)
1540 (385)

paintball flooring
1x1
OBTAIN Saharah
N/A (750)

palace tile
1x1
OBTAIN Saharah
N/A (750)

parking flooring
1x1
OBTAIN Saharah
N/A (750)

party flooring
1x1
OBTAIN Your Birthday
N/A (370)

pastel puzzle flooring
1x1
OBTAIN Shop (Cabinet: Daily)
1450 (363)

patchwork-tile flooring
1x1
OBTAIN Shop (Cabinet: Daily)
2100 (525)

pine-board flooring
1x1
OBTAIN Shop (Cabinet: Daily)
2500 (625)

pink-paint flooring
1x1
OBTAIN Shop (Cabinet: Daily)
1040 (260)

purple camo flooring
1x1
OBTAIN Shop (Cabinet: Daily)
1320 (330)

purple desert-tile flooring
1x1
OBTAIN Shop (Cabinet: Daily)
2100 (525)

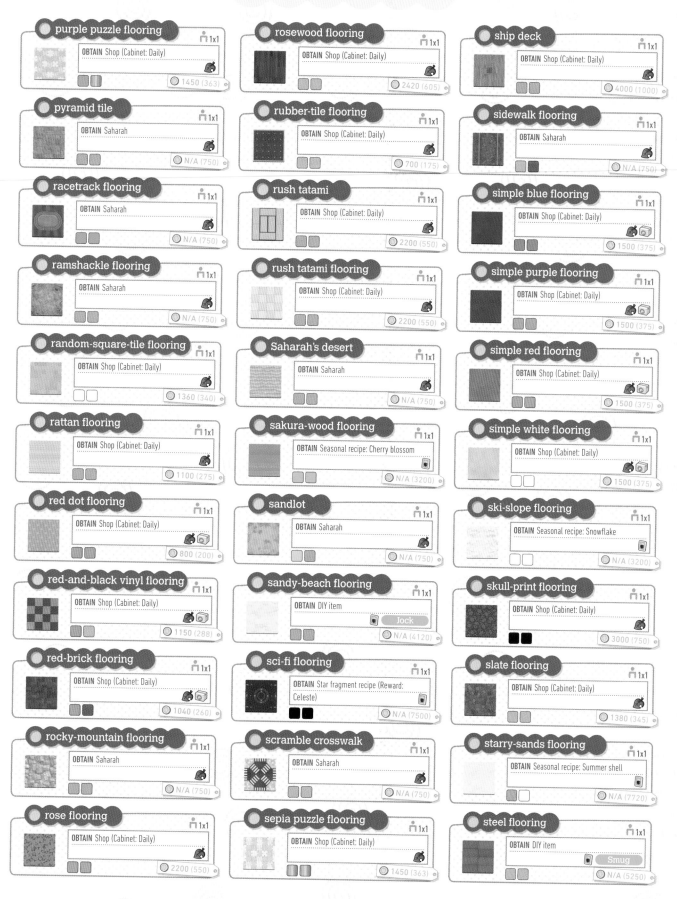

purple puzzle flooring 1x1
OBTAIN Shop (Cabinet: Daily)
1450 (363)

pyramid tile 1x1
OBTAIN Saharah
N/A (750)

racetrack flooring 1x1
OBTAIN Saharah
N/A (750)

ramshackle flooring 1x1
OBTAIN Saharah
N/A (750)

random-square-tile flooring 1x1
OBTAIN Shop (Cabinet: Daily)
1360 (340)

rattan flooring 1x1
OBTAIN Shop (Cabinet: Daily)
1100 (275)

red dot flooring 1x1
OBTAIN Shop (Cabinet: Daily)
800 (200)

red-and-black vinyl flooring 1x1
OBTAIN Shop (Cabinet: Daily)
1150 (288)

red-brick flooring 1x1
OBTAIN Shop (Cabinet: Daily)
1040 (260)

rocky-mountain flooring 1x1
OBTAIN Saharah
N/A (750)

rose flooring 1x1
OBTAIN Shop (Cabinet: Daily)
2200 (550)

rosewood flooring 1x1
OBTAIN Shop (Cabinet: Daily)
2420 (605)

rubber-tile flooring 1x1
OBTAIN Shop (Cabinet: Daily)
700 (175)

rush tatami 1x1
OBTAIN Shop (Cabinet: Daily)
2200 (550)

rush tatami flooring 1x1
OBTAIN Shop (Cabinet: Daily)
2200 (550)

Saharah's desert 1x1
OBTAIN Saharah
N/A (750)

sakura-wood flooring 1x1
OBTAIN Seasonal recipe: Cherry blossom
N/A (3200)

sandlot 1x1
OBTAIN Saharah
N/A (750)

sandy-beach flooring 1x1
OBTAIN DIY item
Jock
N/A (4120)

sci-fi flooring 1x1
OBTAIN Star fragment recipe (Reward: Celeste)
N/A (7500)

scramble crosswalk 1x1
OBTAIN Saharah
N/A (750)

sepia puzzle flooring 1x1
OBTAIN Shop (Cabinet: Daily)
1450 (363)

ship deck 1x1
OBTAIN Shop (Cabinet: Daily)
4000 (1000)

sidewalk flooring 1x1
OBTAIN Saharah
N/A (750)

simple blue flooring 1x1
OBTAIN Shop (Cabinet: Daily)
1500 (375)

simple purple flooring 1x1
OBTAIN Shop (Cabinet: Daily)
1500 (375)

simple red flooring 1x1
OBTAIN Shop (Cabinet: Daily)
1500 (375)

simple white flooring 1x1
OBTAIN Shop (Cabinet: Daily)
1500 (375)

ski-slope flooring 1x1
OBTAIN Seasonal recipe: Snowflake
N/A (3200)

skull-print flooring 1x1
OBTAIN Shop (Cabinet: Daily)
3000 (750)

slate flooring 1x1
OBTAIN Shop (Cabinet: Daily)
1380 (345)

starry-sands flooring 1x1
OBTAIN Seasonal recipe: Summer shell
N/A (7720)

steel flooring 1x1
OBTAIN DIY item
Smug
N/A (5250)

stone tile 1x1
OBTAIN Shop (Cabinet: Daily)
3000 (750)

tiger-print flooring 1x1
OBTAIN Shop (Cabinet: Daily)
1300 (325)

white mosaic-tile flooring 1x1
OBTAIN Shop (Cabinet: Daily)
900 (225)

stripe flooring 1x1
OBTAIN Shop (Cabinet: Daily)
1200 (300)

train-station flooring 1x1
OBTAIN Saharah
N/A (750)

white-brick flooring 1x1
OBTAIN Shop (Cabinet: Daily)
1040 (260)

sumo ring 1x1
OBTAIN Saharah
N/A (750)

underwater flooring 1x1
OBTAIN Seasonal recipe: Summer shell
N/A (6600)

white-chocolates flooring 1x1
OBTAIN Saharah
N/A (750)

swamp flooring 1x1
OBTAIN Saharah
N/A (750)

water flooring 1x1
OBTAIN Seasonal recipe: Summer shell
N/A (7200)

white-paint flooring 1x1
OBTAIN Shop (Cabinet: Daily)
1040 (260)

tatami 1x1
OBTAIN Shop (Cabinet: Daily)
2200 (550)

western desert 1x1
OBTAIN Saharah
N/A (750)

wildflower meadow 1x1
OBTAIN Saharah
N/A (750)

tatami flooring 1x1
OBTAIN Shop (Cabinet: Daily)
2200 (550)

white honeycomb tile 1x1
OBTAIN Shop (Cabinet: Daily)
1420 (355)

wooden-knot flooring 1x1
OBTAIN Shop (Cabinet: Daily)
780 (195)

terra-cotta flooring 1x1
OBTAIN Shop (Cabinet: Daily)
1800 (450)

white iron-parquet flooring 1x1
OBTAIN Shop (Cabinet: Daily)
2350 (588)

yellow floral flooring 1x1
OBTAIN Shop (Cabinet: Daily)
1520 (380)

zebra-print flooring 1x1
OBTAIN Shop (Cabinet: Daily)
1300 (325)

Flowers and Trees

The lists here show you every growth stage of each tree and flower, along with their sell price. Mature flowers aren't covered; to see the sell prices and breeding details for mature flowers, flip back to P.171. The list here lets you see which ones have seed bags for purchase (for 240 Bells) from Nook's Cranny. Remember that Nook's Cranny will only sell seeds for your island's native flower. They will initially sell two colors, but will sell all colors once the shop has been upgraded. In addition to this, Nook's Cranny will also sell all colors of the current seasonal flower (as long as it's not your native one). You can also buy the hardwood sapling and cedar sapling for 640 Bells a piece. Finally, there's the rare lily-of-the-valley flower, which you can't buy, but can sell to Timmy and Tommy for 222 Bells. For more on this, check out P.234.

Trees & saplings

	Trees & saplings	Sell
apple	nursery apple	100
	small young apple	150
	medium young apple	200
	large young apple	250
	apple tree	300
bamboo	bamboo shoot	250
	nursery bamboo	750
	small young bamboo	938
	medium young bamboo	1125
	large young bamboo	1313
	bamboo tree	1500
cherry	nursery cherry	100
	small young cherry	150
	medium young cherry	200
	large young cherry	250
	cherry tree	300
cedar	cedar sapling	160
	nursery cedar	160
	small young cedar	180
	medium young cedar	200
	large young cedar	220
	cedar tree	240
coconut	nursery coconut	250
	small young coconut	313
	medium young coconut	375
	large young coconut	438
	coconut tree	500
hardwood	sapling	160
	nursery hardwood	160
	small young hardwood	180
	medium young hardwood	200
	large young hardwood	220
	hardwood tree	240
money	nursery money tree	160
	small young money tree	180
	medium young money tree	200
	large young money tree	220
	money tree	240
orange	nursery orange	100
	small young orange	150
	medium young orange	200
	large young orange	250
	orange tree	300
peach	nursery peach	100
	small young peach	150
	medium young peach	200
	large young peach	250
	peach tree	300
pear	nursery pear	100
	small young pear	150
	medium young pear	200
	large young pear	250
	pear tree	300

Flower stems, buds, strains

Flower stems, buds, strains	Sell
red-rose bag	60
red-rose sprouts	40
red-rose stems	40
red-rose buds	40
red-rose plant	40
yellow-rose bag	60
yellow-rose sprouts	40
yellow-rose stems	40
yellow-rose buds	40
yellow-rose plant	40

Flower	Sell
orange-rose stems	80
orange-rose buds	80
orange-rose plant	80
white-rose bag	60
white-rose sprouts	40
white-rose stems	40
white-rose buds	40
white-rose plant	40
pink-rose stems	80
pink-rose buds	80
pink-rose plant	80
blue-rose stems	1000
blue-rose buds	1000
blue-rose plant	1000
purple-rose stems	240
purple-rose buds	240
purple-rose plant	240
black-rose stems	240
black-rose buds	240
black-rose plant	240
gold-rose stems	1000
gold-rose buds	1000
gold-rose plant	1000
red-tulip bag	60
red-tulip sprouts	40
red-tulip stems	40
red-tulip buds	40
red-tulip plant	40
orange-tulip stems	80
orange-tulip buds	80
orange-tulip plant	80
yellow-tulip bag	60
yellow-tulip sprouts	40
yellow-tulip stems	40
yellow-tulip buds	40
yellow-tulip plant	40
white-tulip bag	60
white-tulip sprouts	40
white-tulip stems	40
white-tulip buds	40
white-tulip plant	40
pink-tulip stems	80
pink-tulip buds	80
pink-tulip plant	80
purple-tulip stems	240
purple-tulip buds	240
purple-tulip plant	240
black-tulip stems	80
black-tulip buds	80
black-tulip plant	80
red-cosmos bag	60
red-cosmos sprouts	40
red-cosmos stems	40
red-cosmos buds	40
red-cosmos plant	40
yellow-cosmos bag	60
yellow-cosmos sprouts	40
yellow-cosmos stems	40
yellow-cosmos buds	40
yellow-cosmos plant	40
orange-cosmos stems	80
orange-cosmos buds	80
orange-cosmos plant	80
pink-cosmos stems	80
pink-cosmos buds	80
pink-cosmos plant	80

Flower	Sell
black-cosmos stems	240
black-cosmos buds	240
black-cosmos plant	240
red-pansy bag	60
red-pansy sprouts	40
red-pansy stems	40
red-pansy buds	40
red-pansy plant	40
orange-pansy stems	80
orange-pansy buds	80
orange-pansy plant	80
yellow-pansy bag	60
yellow-pansy sprouts	40
yellow-pansy stems	40
yellow-pansy buds	40
yellow-pansy plant	40
white-pansy bag	60
white-pansy sprouts	40
white-pansy stems	40
white-pansy buds	40
white-pansy plant	40
blue-pansy stems	80
blue-pansy buds	80
blue-pansy plant	80
purple-pansy stems	240
purple-pansy buds	240
purple-pansy plant	240
red-hyacinth bag	60
red-hyacinth sprouts	40
red-hyacinth stems	40
red-hyacinth buds	40
red-hyacinth plant	40
orange-hyacinth stems	80
orange-hyacinth buds	80
orange-hyacinth plant	80
yellow-hyacinth bag	60
yellow-hyacinth sprouts	40
yellow-hyacinth stems	40
yellow-hyacinth buds	40
yellow-hyacinth plant	40
white-hyacinth bag	60
white-hyacinth sprouts	40
white-hyacinth stems	40
white-hyacinth buds	40
white-hyacinth plant	40
pink-hyacinth stems	80
pink-hyacinth buds	80
pink-hyacinth plant	80
blue-hyacinth stems	80
blue-hyacinth buds	80
blue-hyacinth plant	80
purple-hyacinth stems	240
purple-hyacinth buds	240
purple-hyacinth plant	240
red-windflower bag	60
red-windflower sprouts	40
red-windflower stems	40
red-windflower buds	40
red-windflower plant	40
orange-windflower bag	60
orange-windflower sprouts	40
orange-windflower stems	40
orange-windflower buds	40
orange-windflower plant	40

Flower	Sell
white-windflower bag	60
white-windflower sprouts	40
white-windflower stems	40
white-windflower buds	40
white-windflower plant	40
pink-windflower stems	80
pink-windflower buds	80
pink-windflower plant	80
blue-windflower stems	80
blue-windflower buds	80
blue-windflower plant	80
purple-windflower stems	240
purple-windflower buds	240
purple-windflower plant	240
red-lily bag	60
red-lily sprouts	40
red-lily stems	40
red-lily buds	40
red-lily plant	40
orange-lily stems	80
orange-lily buds	80
orange-lily plant	80
yellow-lily bag	60
yellow-lily sprouts	40
yellow-lily stems	40
yellow-lily buds	40
yellow-lily plant	40
white-lily bag	60
white-lily sprouts	40
white-lily stems	40
white-lily buds	40
white-lily plant	40
pink-lily stems	80
pink-lily buds	80
pink-lily plant	80
black-lily stems	80
black-lily buds	80
black-lily plant	80
red-mum bag	60
red-mum sprouts	40
red-mum stems	40
red-mum buds	40
red-mum plant	40
yellow-mum bag	60
yellow-mum sprouts	40
yellow-mum stems	40
yellow-mum buds	40
yellow-mum plant	40
white-mum bag	60
white-mum sprouts	40
white-mum stems	40
white-mum buds	40
white-mum plant	40
pink-mum stems	80
pink-mum buds	80
pink-mum plant	80
purple-mum stems	80
purple-mum buds	80
purple-mum plant	80
green-mum stems	240
green-mum buds	240
green-mum plant	240

7

Fish models

anchovy

1x1
600

blue marlin
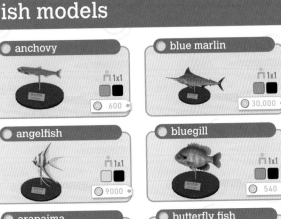
1x1
30,000

crucian carp
1x1
480

golden trout

1x1
45,000

angelfish
1x1
9000

bluegill
1x1
540

dab

1x1
900

goldfish

1x1
3900

arapaima
2x1
30,000

butterfly fish
1x1
3000

dace
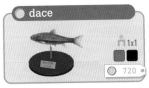
1x1
720

great white shark

2x1
45,000

arowana
1x1
30,000

carp

1x1
900

dorado

1x1
45,000

guppy

1x1
3900

barred knifejaw
1x1
15,000

catfish

1x1
2400

football fish
1x1
7500

hammerhead shark

1x1
24,000

barreleye
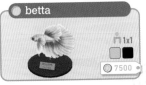
1x1
45,000

char

1x1
11,400

freshwater goby

1x1
1200

horse mackerel

1x1
450

betta

1x1
7500

cherry salmon

1x1
3000

frog

1x1
360

killifish

1x1
900

bitterling

1x1
2700

clown fish

1x1
1950

gar

1x1
18,000

king salmon

1x1
5400

black bass

1x1
1200

coelacanth

1x1
18,000

giant snakehead

1x1
16,500

koi

1x1
12,000

blowfish

1x1
15,000

crawfish

1x1
600

giant trevally

1x1
13,500

loach

1x1
1200

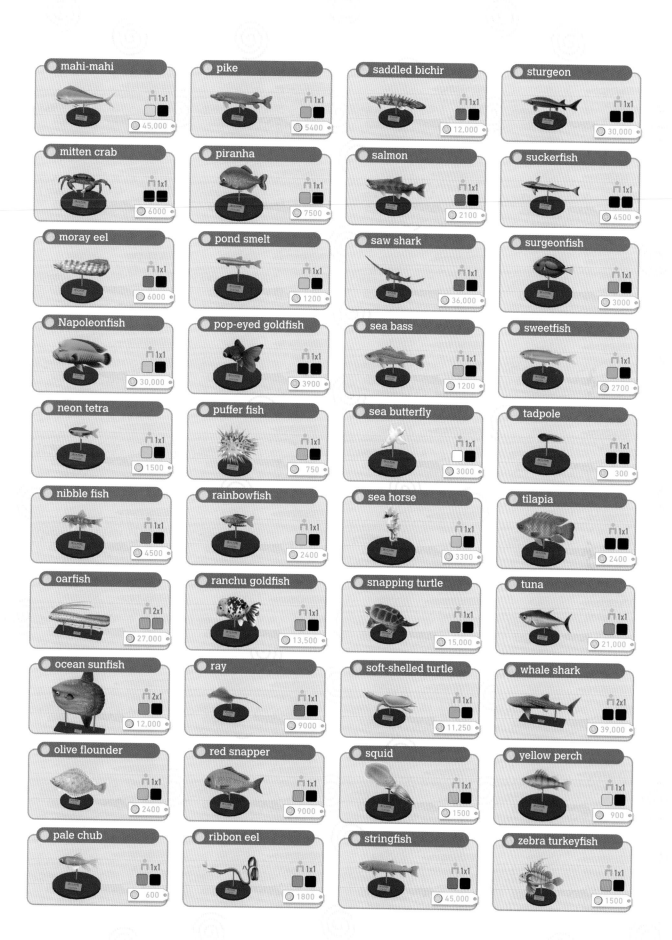

mahi-mahi	1x1	45,000
pike	1x1	5400
saddled bichir	1x1	12,000
sturgeon	1x1	30,000
mitten crab	1x1	6000
piranha	1x1	7500
salmon	1x1	2100
suckerfish	1x1	4500
moray eel	1x1	6000
pond smelt	1x1	1200
saw shark	1x1	36,000
surgeonfish	1x1	3000
Napoleonfish	1x1	30,000
pop-eyed goldfish	1x1	3900
sea bass	1x1	1200
sweetfish	1x1	2700
neon tetra	1x1	1500
puffer fish	1x1	750
sea butterfly	1x1	3000
tadpole	1x1	300
nibble fish	1x1	4500
rainbowfish	1x1	2400
sea horse	1x1	3300
tilapia	1x1	2400
oarfish	2x1	27,000
ranchu goldfish	1x1	13,500
snapping turtle	1x1	15,000
tuna	1x1	21,000
ocean sunfish	2x1	12,000
ray	1x1	9000
soft-shelled turtle	1x1	11,250
whale shark	2x1	39,000
olive flounder	1x1	2400
red snapper	1x1	9000
squid	1x1	1500
yellow perch	1x1	900
pale chub	1x1	600
ribbon eel	1x1	1800
stringfish	1x1	45,000
zebra turkeyfish	1x1	1500

7

Insect models

saw stag

1x1
6000

R. Brooke's birdwing

1x1
7500

grand goliath beetle

2x1
24,000

stinkbug

1x1
360

grand h. hercules

2x1
36,000

red dragonfly

1x1
540

fly

1x1
180

citrus long-horned b.
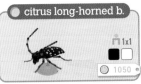
1x1
1050

wasp
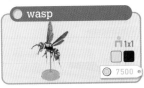
1x1
7500

grand Q. A. birdwing

2x2
12,000

orchid mantis

1x1
7200

peacock butterfly

1x1
7500

honeybee

1x1
600

pondskater

1x1
390

tiger beetle

1x1
4500

snail

1x1
750

scarab beetle
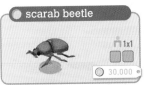
1x1
30,000

ant
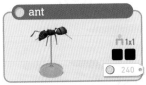
1x1
240

evening cicada

1x1
1650

grasshopper

1x1
480

flea

1x1
210

pill bug

1x1
750

cyclommatus stag
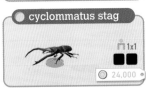
1x1
24,000

earth-boring dung b.

1x1
900

mosquito
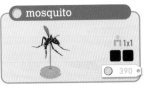
1x1
390

wharf roach
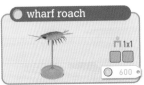
1x1
600

firefly

1x1
900

horned atlas

1x1
24,000

horned dynastid

1x1
4050

moth
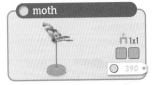
1x1
390

dung beetle

1x1
9000

walking leaf

1x1
1800

tiger butterfly

1x1
720

diving beetle

1x1
2400

rice grasshopper

1x1
1200

cricket

1x1
390

brown cicada

1x1
750

darner dragonfly

1x1
690

mantis
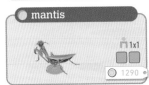
1x1
1290

giant cicada

1x1
1500

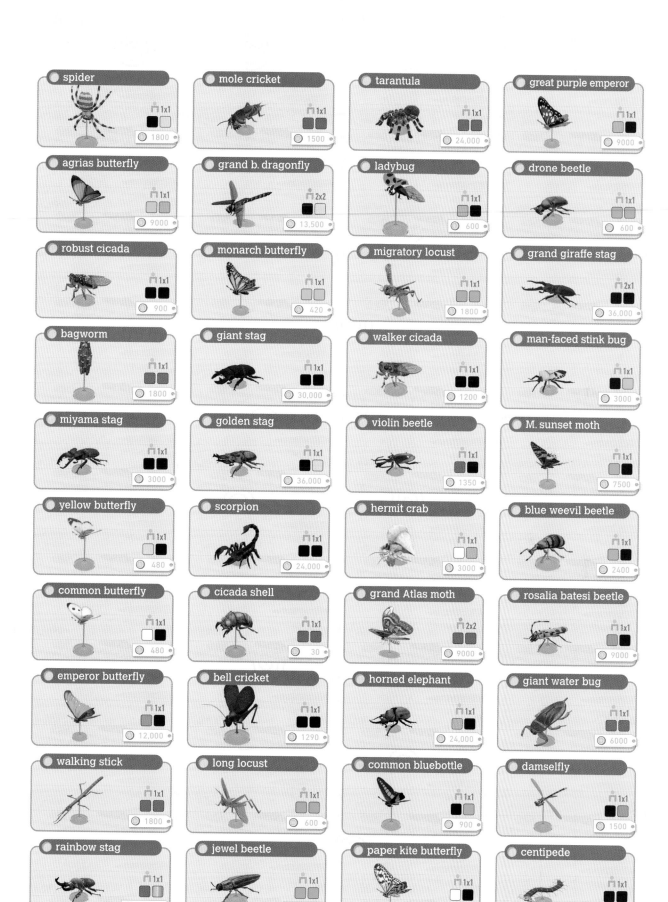

spider — 1x1 — 1800	mole cricket — 1x1 — 1500	tarantula — 1x1 — 24,000	great purple emperor — 1x1 — 9000
agrias butterfly — 1x1 — 9000	grand b. dragonfly — 2x2 — 13,500	ladybug — 1x1 — 600	drone beetle — 1x1 — 600
robust cicada — 1x1 — 900	monarch butterfly — 1x1 — 420	migratory locust — 1x1 — 1800	grand giraffe stag — 2x1 — 36,000
bagworm — 1x1 — 1800	giant stag — 1x1 — 30,000	walker cicada — 1x1 — 1200	man-faced stink bug — 1x1 — 3000
miyama stag — 1x1 — 3000	golden stag — 1x1 — 36,000	violin beetle — 1x1 — 1350	M. sunset moth — 1x1 — 7500
yellow butterfly — 1x1 — 480	scorpion — 1x1 — 24,000	hermit crab — 1x1 — 3000	blue weevil beetle — 1x1 — 2400
common butterfly — 1x1 — 480	cicada shell — 1x1 — 30	grand Atlas moth — 2x2 — 9000	rosalia batesi beetle — 1x1 — 9000
emperor butterfly — 1x1 — 12,000	bell cricket — 1x1 — 1290	horned elephant — 1x1 — 24,000	giant water bug — 1x1 — 6000
walking stick — 1x1 — 1800	long locust — 1x1 — 600	common bluebottle — 1x1 — 900	damselfly — 1x1 — 1500
rainbow stag — 1x1 — 18,000	jewel beetle — 1x1 — 7200	paper kite butterfly — 1x1 — 3000	centipede — 1x1 — 900

Bonus Lists

This section covers a few important things that true collectors will care about that aren't already listed elsewhere in the book.

1 Music

You've met K.K. Slider in the Meet the Locals chapter. Next up in our big lists of lists is his entire available catalogue, complete with record covers for you to admire! If you're looking to complete your collection of songs, remember that when requesting that you must type the title of the song as accurately as possible. K.K. Slider might get confused and not play you what you asked for if you don't give him the exact title of the song you want him to perform.

You can also buy vinyls of his tracks from the Nook Shopping catalogue, at a cost of 3200 Bells each. Once you've obtained a particular song, you can 'Register' it at any music player. This permanently adds it to your song collection, which can then be accessed using any music player, stereo or turntable (and it can appear on radio broadcasts).

Mood: Good!	Mood: Grumpy	Mood: Lazy	Mood: A little sad	Mood: Hard to Say
1 Mountain Song	20 K.K. Cruisin'	38 Aloha K.K.	59 Two Days Ago	76 Hypno K.K.
2 Bubblegum K.K.	21 Lucky K.K.	39 K.K. Stroll	60 Only Me	77 K.K. Rally
3 K.K. Calypso	22 Surfin' K.K.	40 Pondering	61 K.K. Western	78 K.K. Marathon
4 K.K. Country	23 K.K. Safari	41 Soulful K.K.	62 K.K. Lament	79 Agent K.K.
5 K.K. Groove	24 K.K. Jongara	42 K.K. Jazz	63 K.K. Chorale	80 K.K. Soul
6 K.K. Salsa	25 K.K. Tango	43 K.K. Swing	64 King K.K.	81 K.K. Song
7 K.K. Samba	26 Imperial K.K.	44 Mr. K.K.	65 K.K. Étude	82 The K. Funk
8 K.K. Ska	27 Rockin' K.K.	45 K.K. Synth	66 K.K. Sonata	83 K.K. Blues
9 K.K. Dixie	28 K.K. House	46 K.K. Fusion	67 K.K. Milonga	84 K.K. Oasis
10 K.K. Disco	29 K.K. Adventure	47 K.K. Bossa	68 K.K. Ballad	85 K.K. Folk
11 Café K.K.	30 K.K. Flamenco	48 K.K. Moody	69 K.K. Lullaby	86 K.K. Technopop
12 K.K. Parade	31 K.K. Metal	49 K.K. Aria	70 K.K. Waltz	87 K.K. D&B
13 K.K. Rockabilly	32 K.K. Rock	50 K.K. Love Song	71 K.K. Dirge	88 To the Edge
14 K.K. March	33 K.K. Bazaar	51 K.K. Reggae	72 Comrade K.K.	89 K.K. Gumbo
15 K.K. Mambo	34 K.K. Steppe	52 I Love You	73 Steep Hill	90 Space K.K.
16 K.K. Mariachi	35 K.K. Casbah	53 K.K. Island	74 Stale Cupcakes	
17 Neapolitan	36 DJ K.K.	54 K.K. Faire	75 K.K. Condor	
18 Spring Blossoms	37 Go K.K. Rider	55 Marine Song 2001		
19 K.K. Ragtime		56 Wandering		
		57 My Place		
		58 Forest Life		

Special Songs	Hidden Songs
91 K.K. Birthday	93 Animal City
92 Welcome Horizons	94 Farewell
	95 Drivin'

② TV Guide

Most TVs are luxury items sold at Nook's Cranny, but if you really want one, you can save money by getting the recipe for the juicy-apple TV. Set it up wherever you want and tune in for some riveting viewing. TVs come in two types: 4:3 and 16:9 (widescreen) and broadcasts on your island offer a range of programming with daily schedules. Each day of the week has its own programs, but every day you'll be able to catch the news and three weather forecasts. Forecasts after 6:30PM will show you tomorrow's weather, which can be worth keeping an eye out for if you're waiting for meteor showers. Here you'll find the full weekly programming schedule.

Monday

Time	Program	Time	Program	Time	Program	Time	Program
00:00	Variety Show	09:20	Documentary	14:00	Variety Show	19:29	Seasonal Commercial
00:57	Shopping Commercial	09:59	Shopping Commercial	14:29	Fruit Commercial	19:30	Variety Show
01:00	Documentary	10:00	Kid's Show	14:30	Variety Show	19:59	Snack Commercial
02:45	Shopping Commercial	10:29	Fruit Commercial	14:59	Shopping Commercial	20:00	Quiz Show
03:00	Color Bars	10:30	Kid's Show	15:00	Exercise	20:29	Fruit Commercial
04:00	Static	10:59	Corporate Commercial	15:29	Corporate Commercial	20:30	Quiz Show
05:00	Color Bars	11:00	Cooking Show	15:30	Exercise	20:57	Fruit Commercial
05:55	Snack Commercial	11:29	Fruit Commercial	15:59	Seasonal Commercial	20:58	Seasonal Commercial
06:00	News	11:30	News	16:00	Cartoon	20:59	Corporate Commercial
06:15	Weather Forecast	11:45	Weather Forecast	16:29	Snack Commercial	21:00	Drama
06:30	Exercise	11:59	Seasonal Commercial	16:30	Cartoon	21:29	Seasonal Commercial
06:59	Shopping Commercial	12:00	Variety Show	16:59	Corporate Commercial	21:30	Drama
07:00	News	12:29	Fruit Commercial	17:00	Variety Show	21:59	Fruit Commercial
07:45	Weather Forecast	12:30	Variety Show	17:29	Seasonal Commercial	22:00	News
07:59	Shopping Commercial	12:59	Shopping Commercial	17:30	Variety Show	22:45	Weather Forecast
08:00	Drama	13:00	Drama	17:59	Fruit Commercial	22:59	Shopping Commercial
08:29	Shopping Commercial	13:29	Corporate Commercial	18:00	News	23:00	Variety Show
08:30	Documentary	13:30	Talk Show	18:30	Weather Forecast	23:29	Corporate Commercial
09:18	Seasonal Commercial	13:58	Fruit Commercial	18:59	Corporate Commercial	23:30	Variety Show
09:19	Fruit Commercial	13:59	Snack Commercial	19:00	Variety Show	23:55	Shopping Commercial

Secret Visitors?

For those who like to stay up late, tune in to your TV at exactly 3:33AM on a Saturday and you might catch an unscheduled broadcast... Are otherworldly visitors showing an interest in your island? What's going on?

Tuesday

00:00	Talk Show
00:57	Shopping Commercial
01:00	Movie
02:45	Shopping Commercial
03:00	Color Bars
04:00	Static
05:00	Color Bars
05:55	Corporate Commercial
06:00	News
06:15	Weather Forecast
06:30	Exercise
06:59	Fruit Commercial
07:00	News
07:45	Weather Forecast
07:59	Shopping Commercial
08:00	Drama
08:29	Shopping Commercial
08:30	Documentary
09:18	Seasonal Commercial
09:19	Fruit Commercial
09:20	Documentary
09:59	Shopping Commercial
10:00	Cartoon
10:29	Fruit Commercial
10:30	Cartoon
10:59	Corporate Commercial
11:00	Cooking Show
11:29	Seasonal Commercial
11:30	News
11:45	Weather Forecast
11:59	Shopping Commercial
12:00	Variety Show
12:29	Fruit Commercial
12:30	Variety Show
12:59	Shopping Commercial
13:00	Drama
13:29	Corporate Commercial
13:30	Talk Show
13:59	Corporate Commercial
14:00	Documentary
14:29	Seasonal Commercial
14:30	Documentary
14:59	Shopping Commercial
15:00	Exercise
15:29	Snack Commercial
15:30	Exercise
15:59	Seasonal Commercial
16:00	Kid's Show
16:29	Snack Commercial
16:30	Cooking Show
16:59	Corporate Commercial
17:00	Variety Show
17:29	Snack Commercial
17:30	Variety Show
17:59	Fruit Commercial
18:00	News
18:30	Weather Forecast
18:59	Corporate Commercial
19:00	Sports
19:50	Corporate Commercial
19:51	Sports
20:57	Fruit Commercial
20:58	Shopping Commercial
20:59	Seasonal Commercial
21:00	Talk Show
21:29	Corporate Commercial
21:30	Talk Show
21:59	Snack Commercial
22:00	News
22:45	Weather Forecast
22:59	Seasonal Commercial
23:00	Documentary
23:29	Corporate Commercial
23:30	Documentary
23:55	Shopping Commercial

Wednesday

00:00	Documentary
00:57	Shopping Commercial
01:00	Documentary
02:45	Shopping Commercial
03:00	Color Bars
04:00	Static
05:00	Color Bars
05:55	Snack Commercial
06:00	News
06:15	Weather Forecast
06:30	Exercise
06:59	Seasonal Commercial
07:00	News
07:45	Weather Forecast
07:59	Shopping Commercial
08:00	Drama
08:29	Shopping Commercial
08:30	Documentary
09:18	Seasonal Commercial
09:19	Fruit Commercial
09:20	Documentary
09:59	Shopping Commercial
10:00	Kid's Show
10:29	Snack Commercial
10:30	Kid's Show
10:59	Corporate Commercial
11:00	Cooking Show
11:29	Fruit Commercial
11:30	News
11:45	Weather Forecast
11:59	Seasonal Commercial
12:00	Variety Show
12:29	Fruit Commercial
12:30	Variety Show
12:59	Shopping Commercial
13:00	Drama
13:29	Corporate Commercial
13:30	Talk Show
13:59	Corporate Commercial
14:00	Variety Show
14:29	Fruit Commercial
14:30	Variety Show
14:58	Seasonal Commercial
15:00	Exercise
15:29	Fruit Commercial
15:30	Exercise
15:59	Seasonal Commercial
16:00	Cartoon
16:29	Snack Commercial
16:30	Cartoon
16:59	Corporate Commercial
17:00	Variety Show
17:29	Fruit Commercial
17:30	Variety Show
17:59	Seasonal Commercial
18:00	News
18:30	Weather Forecast
18:59	Corporate Commercial
19:00	Cooking Show
19:29	Seasonal Commercial
19:30	Cooking Show
19:59	Snack Commercial
20:00	Music Program
20:29	Seasonal Commercial
20:30	Music Program
20:57	Snack Commercial
20:58	Corporate Commercial
20:59	Shopping Commercial
21:00	Drama
21:29	Seasonal Commercial
21:30	Drama
21:59	Snack Commercial
22:00	News
22:45	Weather Forecast
22:59	Shopping Commercial
23:00	Quiz Show
23:29	Corporate Commercial
23:30	Quiz Show
23:55	Shopping Commercial

Thursday

00:00	Variety Show
00:57	Shopping Commercial
01:00	Sports
02:45	Shopping Commercial
03:00	Color Bars
04:00	Static
05:00	Color Bars
05:55	Snack Commercial
06:00	News
06:15	Weather Forecast
06:30	Exercise
06:59	Shopping Commercial
07:00	News
07:45	Weather Forecast
07:59	Shopping Commercial
08:00	Drama
08:29	Shopping Commercial
08:30	Documentary
09:18	Seasonal Commercial
09:19	Fruit Commercial
09:20	Documentary
09:59	Shopping Commercial
10:00	Kid's Show
10:29	Snack Commercial
10:30	Kid's Show
10:59	Corporate Commercial
11:00	Cooking Show
11:29	Seasonal Commercial
11:30	News
11:45	Weather Forecast
11:59	Shopping Commercial
12:00	Variety Show
12:29	Fruit Commercial
12:30	Variety Show
12:59	Shopping Commercial
13:00	Drama
13:29	Corporate Commercial
13:30	Talk Show
13:59	Corporate Commercial
14:00	Variety Show
14:29	Fruit Commercial
14:30	Variety Show
14:59	Shopping Commercial
15:00	Exercise
15:29	Snack Commercial
15:30	Exercise
15:59	Seasonal Commercial
16:00	Kid's Show
16:29	Snack Commercial
16:30	Kid's Show
16:59	Corporate Commercial
17:00	Variety Show
17:29	Snack Commercial
17:30	Variety Show
17:59	Fruit Commercial
18:00	News
18:30	Weather Forecast
18:59	Corporate Commercial
19:00	Cartoon
19:29	Seasonal Commercial
19:30	Cartoon
19:59	Snack Commercial
20:00	Documentary
20:29	Seasonal Commercial
20:30	Documentary
20:57	Snack Commercial
20:58	Corporate Commercial
20:59	Shopping Commercial
21:00	Drama
21:29	Seasonal Commercial
21:30	Drama
21:59	Corporate Commercial
22:00	News
22:45	Weather Forecast
22:59	Seasonal Commercial
23:00	Variety Show
23:29	Snack Commercial
23:30	Variety Show
23:55	Shopping Commercial

Friday

Time	Program	Time	Program	Time	Program	Time	Program
00:00	Variety Show	09:20	Documentary	14:00	Talk Show	19:00	Sports
00:57	Shopping Commercial	09:59	Shopping Commercial	14:29	Snack Commercial	19:57	Shopping Commercial
01:00	Documentary	10:00	Cartoon	14:30	Talk Show	20:00	Sports
02:45	Shopping Commercial	10:29	Snack Commercial	14:59	Seasonal Commercial	20:57	Corporate Commercial
03:00	Color Bars	10:30	Cartoon	15:00	Exercise	20:58	Snack Commercial
04:00	Static	10:59	Corporate Commercial	15:29	Fruit Commercial	20:59	Seasonal Commercial
05:00	Color Bars	11:00	Cooking Show	15:30	Exercise	21:00	Music Program
05:55	Corporate Commercial	11:29	Fruit Commercial	15:59	Seasonal Commercial	21:29	Corporate Commercial
06:00	News	11:30	News	16:00	Kid's Show	21:30	Music Program
06:15	Weather Forecast	11:45	Weather Forecast	16:29	Snack Commercial	21:59	Fruit Commercial
06:30	Exercise	11:59	Seasonal Commercial	16:30	Kid's Show	22:00	News
06:59	Fruit Commercial	12:00	Variety Show	16:59	Corporate Commercial	22:45	Weather Forecast
07:00	News	12:29	Fruit Commercial	17:00	Variety Show	22:59	Seasonal Commercial
07:45	Weather Forecast	12:30	Variety Show	17:29	Snack Commercial	23:00	Quiz Show
07:59	Shopping Commercial	12:59	Shopping Commercial	17:30	Variety Show	23:29	Fruit Commercial
08:00	Drama	13:00	Drama	17:58	Fruit Commercial	23:30	Quiz Show
08:29	Shopping Commercial	13:29	Corporate Commercial	17:59	Seasonal Commercial	23:55	Corporate Commercial
08:30	Documentary	13:30	Drama	18:00	News		
09:18	Seasonal Commercial	13:58	Fruit Commercial	18:30	Weather Forecast		
09:19	Fruit Commercial	13:59	Corporate Commercial	18:59	Corporate Commercial		

Saturday

Time	Program	Time	Program	Time	Program	Time	Program
00:00	Color Bars	09:00	Documentary	14:00	Documentary	19:30	Quiz Show
01:00	Static	09:29	Shopping Commercial	14:29	Snack Commercial	19:59	Snack Commercial
03:33	(Secret Program)	09:30	Documentary	14:30	Documentary	20:00	Variety Show
03:34	Static	09:59	Shopping Commercial	14:59	Seasonal Commercial	20:57	Fruit Commercial
05:00	Color Bars	10:00	Kid's Show	15:00	Sports	20:58	Seasonal Commercial
05:55	Snack Commercial	10:29	Fruit Commercial	15:50	Snack Commercial	20:59	Snack Commercial
06:00	News	10:30	Kid's Show	15:51	Sports	21:00	Movie
06:15	Weather Forecast	10:59	Corporate Commercial	16:59	Seasonal Commercial	21:54	Corporate Commercial
06:30	Exercise	11:00	News	17:00	Variety Show	21:55	Movie
06:59	Seasonal Commercial	11:45	Weather Forecast	17:29	Snack Commercial	22:44	Seasonal Commercial
07:00	News	11:59	Shopping Commercial	17:30	Variety Show	22:45	Weather Forecast
07:45	Weather Forecast	12:00	Variety Show	17:59	Corporate Commercial	23:00	News
07:59	Seasonal Commercial	12:29	Fruit Commercial	18:00	News	23:29	Shopping Commercial
08:00	Variety Show	12:30	Variety Show	18:45	Weather Forecast	23:30	Cooking Show
08:29	Corporate Commercial	12:59	Shopping Commercial	18:59	Corporate Commercial	23:55	Corporate Commercial
08:30	Variety Show	13:00	Talk Show	19:00	Quiz Show		
08:59	Snack Commercial	13:59	Corporate Commercial	19:29	Seasonal Commercial		

Sunday

Time	Program	Time	Program	Time	Program	Time	Program
00:00	Music Program	08:30	Cartoon	13:29	Shopping Commercial	18:59	Corporate Commercial
00:57	Shopping Commercial	08:59	Snack Commercial	13:30	Sports	19:00	Sports
01:00	Documentary	09:00	Quiz Show	14:59	Seasonal Commercial	19:50	Seasonal Commercial
02:45	Shopping Commercial	09:29	Shopping Commercial	15:00	Quiz Show	19:51	Sports
03:00	Color Bars	09:30	Quiz Show	15:29	Snack Commercial	20:57	Corporate Commercial
04:00	Static	09:59	Snack Commercial	15:30	Quiz Show	20:58	Snack Commercial
05:00	Color Bars	10:00	Variety Show	15:59	Seasonal Commercial	20:59	Seasonal Commercial
05:55	Corporate Commercial	10:29	Snack Commercial	16:00	Cooking Show	21:00	Movie
06:00	News	10:30	Variety Show	16:29	Snack Commercial	21:53	Snack Commercial
06:15	Weather Forecast	10:59	Corporate Commercial	16:30	Cooking Show	21:54	Corporate Commercial
06:30	Exercise	11:00	News	16:59	Fruit Commercial	21:55	Movie
06:59	Fruit Commercial	11:45	Weather Forecast	17:00	Variety Show	22:44	Snack Commercial
07:00	Kid's Show	11:59	Shopping Commercial	17:29	Seasonal Commercial	22:45	Weather Forecast
07:29	Fruit Commercial	12:00	Talk Show	17:30	Variety Show	23:00	News
07:30	Kid's Show	12:29	Snack Commercial	17:59	Corporate Commercial	23:55	Seasonal Commercial
07:59	Snack Commercial	12:30	Talk Show	18:00	Cartoon		
08:00	Cartoon	12:59	Shopping Commercial	18:29	Fruit Commercial		
08:29	Seasonal Commercial	13:00	Sports	18:30	Cartoon		

3 Postcards

For just 200 Bells, you can send a postcard to any resident on your island. Or yourself, in the future. Some of these postcards are limited edition prints and can only be bought during short periods of the year. Try to see if you can send a letter on each and every one!

Orville

Oh! And we've also got a mail service at this airport! Sometimes a letter's just better, you know?

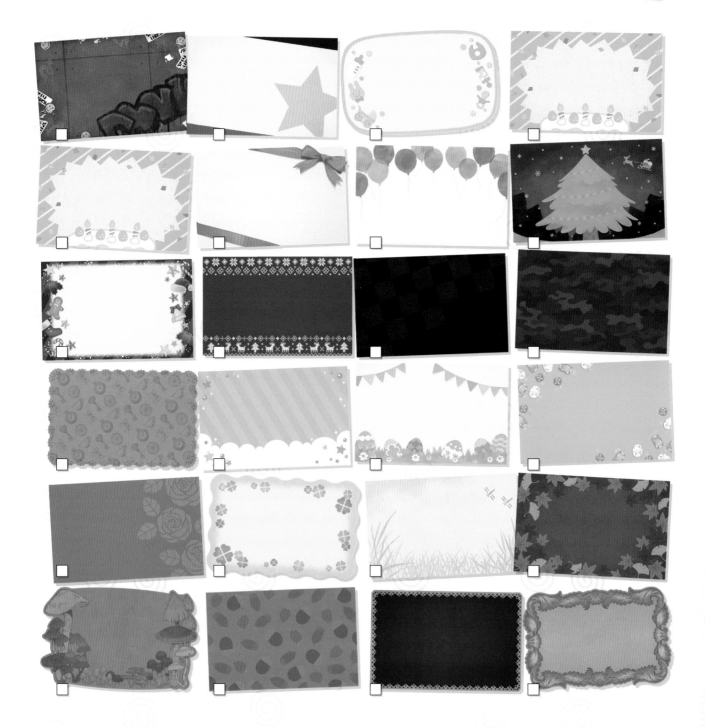

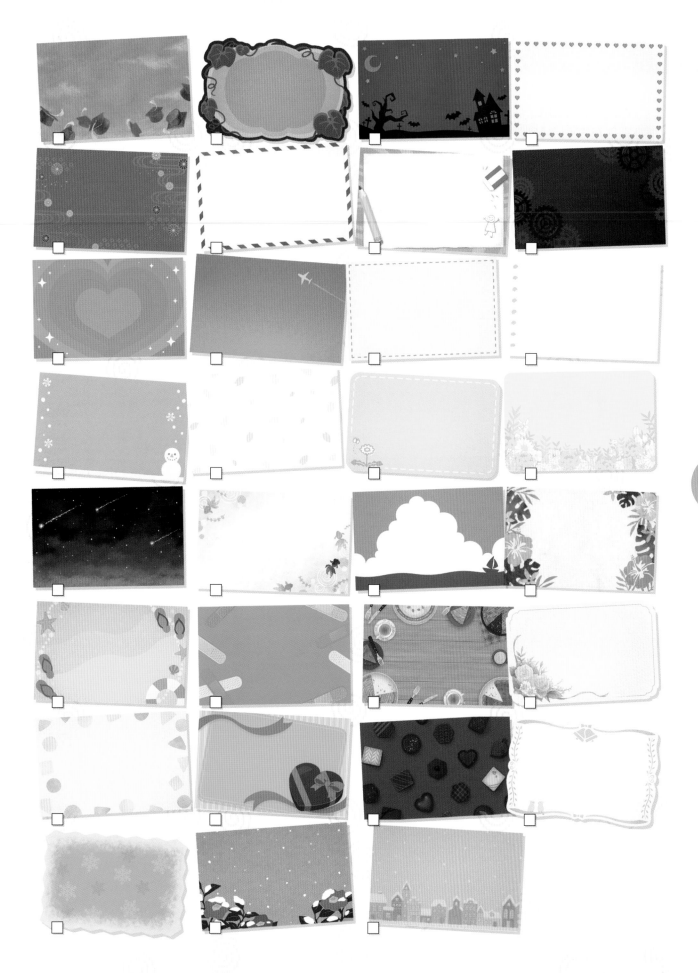

Are you a collector of Animal Crossing amiibo cards or figures? You're in for a treat—Animal Crossing amiibo cards are of course compatible with Animal Crossing: New Horizons. Use your cards to summon whichever resident you'd like to have move into the island via Resident Services. P.30 has all the details about this process; here, we'll list all of the currently available amiibo cards you can use to bring residents onto the island. All cards and figures listed here can be read by the game; any not listed will not work with Animal Crossing: New Horizons.

① amiibo series ② specific amiibo
③ Nook Stop – Can you call them?
④ Nook Stop – Can you invite them to the Campsite?
⑤ Can you invite them to Photopia?

Really Special Characters

You can talk to the character (if you've met them in person at least once), but they won't be able to come to the campsite. These characters can appear at Photopia, however, and you'll obtain a poster if you invite them there.

Blathers	Mabel
Celeste	Sable
Gulliver	Saharah
Isabelle	Timmy
K.K.	Timmy & Tommy
Kicks	Tom Nook
Labelle	Tommy

Special Characters

Inviting the to the campsite triggers a message that claiming a technical error. You'll receive a message that the character cannot be called, so you cannot invite them to Photopia. You'll get a poster for attempting to call them.

Blanca	Don	Kapp'n	Lyle	Porter
Booker	Franklin	Katie	Nat	Redd
Brewster	Gracie	Katrina	Pascal	Reese
Chip	Grams	Leif	Pavé	Resetti
Copper	Harriet	Leila	Pelly	Rover
Cyrus	Jack	Leilani	Pete	Shrunk
Digby	Jingle	Lottie	Phineas	Tortimer
DJ KK	Joan	Luna	Phyllis	Wendell
				Zipper

Residents (Sanrio Set)

You cannot invite them to the campsite; you'll get an error message if you try. You can invite them to photopia, but they won't accept. You will get a poster for inviting them, however it'll be of the corresponding Sanrio character and not the resident themselves.

| Chai | Étoile | Rilla |
| Chelsea | Marty | Toby |

Super Smash Bros. Series

You cannot invite them to the campsite; you'll get an error message if you try. You can invite them to Photopia, but they won't accept. You will get a poster for inviting them, though.

| Villager |

amiibo type: card

①	②	③	④	⑤
Animal Crossing amiibo Cards (Series 1-4)	Potential Residents (All 333)**	✓	✓*	✓
	Really Special Characters	✓	✗	✓
	Special Characters	✗	✗	✗
New Leaf Series	Camper amiibo	✓	✓*	✓
	Residents (50)**	✓	✓	✓
New Leaf Series*	Sanrio collection	●	✗	✗

*Sanrio Characters
**Excluding current island residents
● "Out of Service" error.

amiibo type: figure

	②	③	④	⑤
Animal Crossing	Summer Isabelle	✓	✗	✓
	Kappn	●	-	✗
	Timmy and Tommy	✓	✗	✓
	Rover	●	-	✗
	Blathers	✓	✗	✓
	Celeste	✓	✗	✓
	Resetti	●	-	✗
	Kicks	✓	✗	✓
	Winter Isabelle	✓	✗	✓
	KK Slider	✓	✗	✓
	Mabel	✓	✗	✓
	Tom Nook	✓	✗	✓
	Digby	●	-	✗
	Lottie	●	-	✗
	Reese	●	-	✗
	Cyrus	●	-	✗
Super Smash Bros. Series	Villager	●	-	✗
	New Isabelle	✓	✗	✓

Bob

Nǐn hǎo! Ahlan! Guten Tag! Anyoung! Konnichiwa! Zdravstvuyte! Saluton! Namaste! Shikamoo! And, umm

Bob

The **wooden simple bed** ya made me is real nice. Real nice! Thanks, pthhpth.

Potential Residents

You can invite them to the campsite, and you can also invite them to Photopia. If you invite them to Photopia, you'll get a poster.

1st fan	Bill	Chief	Elise	Hamlet
2nd fan	Billy	Chops	Ellie	Hamphrey
3rd fan	Biskit	Chow	Elmer	Hans
4th fan	Bitty	Chrissy	Eloise	Harry
Admiral	Blaire	Claude	Elvis	Hazel
Agnes	Blanche	Claudia	Erik	Henry
Al	Bluebear	Clay	Eugene	Hippeux
Alfonso	Bob	Cleo	Eunice	Hopkins
Alice	Bonbon	Clyde	Fang	Hopper
Alli	Bones	Coach	Fauna	Hornsby
Amelia	Boomer	Cobb	Felicity	Huck
Anabelle	Boone	Coco	Filbert	Hugh
Anchovy	Boots	Cole	Flip	Iggly
Angus	Boris	Colton	Flo	Ike
Anicotti	Boyd	Cookie	Flora	Jacob
Ankha	Bree	Cousteau	Flurry	Jacques
Annalisa	Broccolo	Cranston	Francine	Jambette
Annalise	Broffina	Croque	Frank	Jay
Antonio	Bruce	Cube	Freckles	Jeremiah
Apollo	Bubbles	Curlos	Freya	Jitters
Apple	Buck	Curly	Friga	Joey
Astrid	Bud	Curt	Frita	Julia
Aurora	Bunnie	Cyrano	Frobert	Julian
Ava	Butch	Daisy	Fuchsia	June
Avery	Buzz	Deena	Gabi	Kabuki
Axel	Cally	Deirdre	Gala	Katt
Baabara	Camofrog	Del	Gaston	Keaton
Bam	Canberra	Deli	Gayle	Ken
Bangle	Candi	Derwin	Genji	Ketchup
Barold	Carmen	Diana	Gigi	Kevin
Bea	Caroline	Diva	Gladys	Kidd
Beardo	Carrie	Dizzy	Gloria	Kiki
Beau	Cashmere	Dobie	Goldie	Kitt
Becky	Celia	Doc	Gonzo	Kitty
Bella	Cesar	Dora	Goose	Klaus
Benedict	Chadder	Dotty	Graham	Knox
Benjamin	Charlise	Drago	Greta	Kody
Bertha	Cheri	Drake	Grizzly	Kyle
Bettina	Cherry	Drift	Groucho	Leonardo
Bianca	Chester	Ed	Gruff	Leopold
Biff	Chevre	Egbert	Gwen	Lily

Limberg	Octavian	Rex	Sylvana
Lionel	Olaf	Rhonda	Sylvia
Lobo	Olive	Ribbot	T-Bone
Lolly	Olivia	Ricky	Tabby
Lopez	Opal	Rizzo	Tad
Louie	Ozzie	Roald	Tammi
Lucha	Pancetti	Robin	Tammy
Lucky	Pango	Rocco	Tangy
Lucy	Paolo	Rod	Tank
Lyman	Papi	Rodeo	Tasha
Mac	Pashmina	Rodney	Teddy
Maddie	Pate	Rolf	Tex
Maelle	Patty	Rooney	Tia
Maggie	Paula	Rory	Tiffany
Mallary	Peaches	Roscoe	Timbra
Maple	Peanut	Rosie	Tipper
Marcel	Pecan	Rowan	Tom
Marcie	Peck	Ruby	Truffles
Margie	Peewee	Rudy	Tucker
Marina	Peggy	Sally	Tutu
Marshal	Pekoe	Samson	Twiggy
Mathilda	Penelope	Sandy	Tybalt
Melba	Phil	Savannah	Ursala
Merengue	Phoebe	Scoot	Velma
Merry	Pierce	Shari	Vesta
Midge	Pietro	Sheldon	Vic
Mint	Pinky	Shep	Victoria
Mira	Piper	Simon	Violet
Miranda	Pippy	Skye	Vivian
Mitzi	Plucky	Sly	Vladimir
Moe	Pompom	Snake	Wade
Molly	Poncho	Snooty	Walker
Monique	Poppy	Soleil	Walt
Monty	Portia	Sparro	Wart Jr.
Moose	Prince	Spike	Weber
Mott	Puck	Spork	Wendy
Muffy	Puddles	Sprinkle	Whitney
Murphy	Pudge	Sprocket	Willow
Nan	Punchy	Static	Winnie
Nana	Purrl	Stella	Wolfgang
Naomi	Queenie	Sterling	Yuka
Nate	Quillson	Stinky	Zell
Nibbles	Raddle	Stitches	Zucker
Norma	Rasher	Stu	
O'Hare	Renée	Sydney	

7

⑤ Photos and Posters

What's the best way to decorate your home? Pictures of your friends, of course! There are two different kinds of pictures you can acquire. You can get posters of residents and special characters by inviting them to "Photopia" on Harv's Island. Their poster will then become available for purchase from the Nook Shopping catalog for 1000 Bells each. Or, if you like something smaller and a bit more personal, becoming best friends with a villager and then completing a request for them gives you a chance to be gifted an adorable, framed photo.

Big sister

Agnes	Diva	Katt	Phoebe	Shari
Canberra	Flo	Mira	Plucky	Sylvia
Charlise	Frita	Muffy	Renée	Tammy
Cherry	Fuchsia	Pashmina	Reneigh	Ursala
Deirdre	Hazel	Paula	Rocket	

Jock

Antonio	Buck	Flip	Kevin	Mott
Axel	Bud	Frobert	Kid Cat	Peck
Bam	Coach	Genji	Kody	Pierce
Biff	Cobb	Goose	Leonardo	Poncho
Bill	Cousteau	Hamlet	Louie	Ribbot
Billy	Curly	Iggly	Lyman	Roald
Boone	Dom	Jay	Mac	Rod
Boots	Drift	Jitters	Moose	Rory

7

Rowan
Scoot
Snake
Sterling
Tank

Rudy
Sheldon
Sparro
Stinky
Teddy

Samson
Sly
Sprocket
Tad
Tybalt

Peppy

Agent S
Bangle
Bubbles
Chrissy
Freckles

Anabelle
Bella
Bunnie
Cookie
Gabi

Anicotti
Bianca
Candi
Dotty
Ketchup

Apple
Bluebear
Carmen
Felicity
Maddie

Audie
Bonbon
Cheri
Flora
Merry

- Nibbles
- Peggy
- Pompom
- Tabby
- Twiggy
- Pango
- Penelope
- Puddles
- Tammi
- Victoria
- Pate
- Pinky
- Rosie
- Tangy
- Wendy
- Patty
- Piper
- Ruby
- Truffles
- Winnie
- Peanut
- Pippy
- Sprinkle
- Tutu

Smug

- Beardo
- Colton
- Eugene
- Henry
- Jacques
- Chadder
- Curlos
- Graham
- Hippeux
- Julian
- Chops
- Ed
- Hans
- Huck
- Keaton

Ken · Leopold · Marshal · Pietro · Shep
Kidd · Lionel · O'Hare · Quillson · Tex
Klaus · Lopez · Olaf · Raymond · Zell
Kyle · Lucha · Phil · Rodney

Snooty

Alli · Astrid · Blaire · Cashmere · Elise
Amelia · Baabara · Blanche · Claudia · Eloise
Ankha · Becky · Bree · Cleo · Francine
Annalise · Bitty · Broffina · Diana · Freya

Friga	Kitty	Naomi	Queenie	Tipper
Gigi	Maelle	Olivia	Robin	Velma
Gloria	Mallary	Opal	Snooty	Violet
Greta	Mathilda	Pancetti	Soleil	Vivian
Gwen	Mint	Pecan	Tasha	Whitney
Judy	Miranda	Portia	Tiffany	Willow
Julia	Monique	Purrl	Timbra	Yuka

Cranky

| Admiral | Angus | Apollo | Avery | Boris |

Boyd	Curt	Gonzo	Knox	Rizzo
Bruce	Cyd	Grizzly	Limberg	Rocco
Butch	Cyrano	Groucho	Lobo	Rolf
Buzz	Del	Gruff	Monty	Rooney
Camofrog	Dobie	Hamphrey	Murphy	Roscoe
Cesar	Elvis	Harry	Octavian	Spike
Chief	Fang	Hopper	Peewee	Static
Chow	Frank	Ike	Rasher	T-Bone
Croque	Gaston	Kabuki	Ricky	Tom

 Vic
 Vladimir
 Walt
 Wart Jr.
 Wolfgang

Sweet

Alice	Cally	Deena
Annalisa	Caroline	Dora
Aurora	Carrie	Ellie
Ava	Celia	Eunice
Bea	Chevre	Fauna
Bertha	Coco	Flurry
Bettina	Daisy	Gala

Gayle, Lily
Gladys, Lolly
Goldie, Lucy
Jambette, Maggie
June, Maple
Kiki, Marcie
Kitt, Margie

7

Marina | Mitzi | Olive | Sally | Sydney

Megan | Molly | Peaches | Sandy | Sylvana

Melba | Nan | Pekoe | Savannah | Tia

Merengue | Nana | Poppy | Skye | Vesta

Midge | Norma | Rhonda | Stella

Lazy

Al | Barold | Benjamin | Bob | Broccolo

Alfonso | Beau | Big Top | Bones | Chester

Anchovy | Benedict | Biskit | Boomer | Claude

Clay
Drago
Jacob
Papi
Simon

Clyde
Drake
Jeremiah
Prince
Spork

Cole
Egbert
Joey
Puck
Stitches

Cranston
Elmer
Lucky
Pudge
Stu

Cube
Erik
Marcel
Punchy
Tucker

Deli
Filbert
Moe
Raddle
Wade

Derwin
Hopkins
Nate
Rex
Walker

Dizzy
Hornsby
Ozzie
Rodeo
Weber

Doc
Hugh
Paolo
Sherb
Zucker

7

Special Characters Posters

Blanca

Blathers

Booker

Brewster

Celeste

Chip

Copper

Cyrus

Digby

DJ KK

Don

Franklin

Gracie

Grams

Gulliver

Harriet

Isabelle

Jack

Jingle

Joan

K.K.

Kapp'n

Katie

Katrina

Kicks

Label

Leif

Leila

Leilani

Lottie

Luna

Lyle

Mabel

Nat

Pascal

Pavé

Pelly

Pete

Phineas

Phyllis

Porter

Redd

Reese

Resetti

Rover

Sable

Saharah

Shrunk

Timmy

Tommy

Tom Nook

Tortimer

Villager

Wendell

Zipper

Sanrio Special Posters

Cinnamoroll

Hello Kitty

Kerokerokeroppi

Kiki & Lala

My Melody

Pompompurin

New Years' Eve

New Years can be quite a big event in the real world, and this is no exception in Animal Crossing. In every game, there has been a New Year's celebration, and there's one taking place on your island as well! Resident Services will close on December 31st so Tom Nook and Isabelle can set up their display outside. Don't worry—other buildings in town will still operate per their usual hours.

The pair can be seen wearing tuxedos and party hats—very chic. You will also notice a big countdown clock outside, just waiting for 12AM. Speak to Tom Nook and he will give you a Party Popper, a great way to kick off celebrations with a bang. When you talk with Isabelle, she will give you a Light Stick! This item is sure to light the way for the new year. For even more festive goodies, speak with Tom Nook again and you will have the option to buy a New Year's Hat for 500 Bells and a set of 5 Party Poppers for 300 Bells.

With 1 hour remaining until the New Year, all of the island's residents will gather outside of Resident Services in preparation for the fireworks display. When there are less than 5 minutes to go, your residents will get their own Light Sticks out. What a colorful display! The clock will then begin to countdown. Once it hits 0, Happy New Years! The fireworks show will begin and last until 2AM on January 1st. Be sure to talk with your fellow residents to celebrate the new year with them.

New Years' Hat

The New Year's Hat is available in four colors: yellow, pink, green and aqua. It's possible to purchase all four colors provided that you've got enough Bells; collectors should consider buying each color, since they're only available once a year!

A List of Lists

A full index for a game with as many different items as Animal Crossing: New Horizons would take up a lot of pages and hardly be more practical than simply listing the starting page of the relevant, alphabetically-organized list that each item appears in. So that's what we've decided to do! No matter what you're looking for, you're very likely to find it in one of the categories here.

5 Island Customization

7 Nature & Tools

6 Characters & Story

8 Residents

OFFICIAL COMPANION GUIDE

A sincere **THANK YOU** to the teams at Nintendo for your great support and treating us like family! It was a pleasure working with you—we can't wait to work with you again!

We would like to thank the following people in particular for their untiring support throughout this project:

NINTENDO OF AMERICA INC.

Melena Anderson	Riley Scott
Taylor Stockton	Zaher Khan
Rob Dietrick	Caleb Pauley
Ai Nakamura	Victoria Arvisais
Emiko Ohmori	Sam Barrett-Farris
Nancy Storment	Emmanuel Bisson
Hugo Cordero	Dynah Bodvel
Jadyn Rosario	Patrick Brady
Karyn Culbert	Gatlin Brown
Emily Mansell	Brynne Caudill
Erin Colwill	Kindre Combs
Allen Perez	Tristan Conley
Michael Keough	Geoffrey Cox
James Sakshaug	Cameron Hamad
Lindsey Newman	Matt Hunziker
Noriko Kaji	Scott Kim
Bill Hutchens	William Mashburn
Kristen Copeland	Riley Murphy
Rob Heiret	Christopher Ogawa
Billy Berghammer	Blake Radcliffe
Sebastian Galloway	Pascal Ramirez
Brette Levitan	

ANIMAL CROSSING™: NEW HORIZONS OFFICIAL COMPANION GUIDE

created and published by

FUTURE PRESS
Verlag & Marketing GmbH
Mansteinstr. 52, 20253 Hamburg, Germany

Managing Directors	Frank Glaser
	Jörg Kraut
Editor-in-chief	Wil Murray
Creative Director	Jörg Kraut
Authors	Jade Bacalso
	Jonathan Gagné
	Ryan Seals
	Ben Blackman
Editorial Support	Bruce Byrne
Screenshot Editor	Ryan Seals
Assets Translator	Claire Newhard
	Takayuki Donald Yokota
	Hirofumi Yamada
Assistant Translator	Nozomi Payton
Layout	Jörg Kraut
	Wil Murray
Coordinator	Ryan Payton
Stay in touch	www.future-press.com
	facebook/futurepress
	Twitter@futurepress

Thanks to our friends & families

Wayne Norwood, Bailey Strauss, David Waybright, Saurian Dash, Nick Suttner, Anwar Hassan, Mary Bacalso, Jeremy Venable, Fran Smyth, Lyne & Serge Gagné, Crystal Moutoussamy, Jezzie Bacalso, Annette & Patrick Byrne, Kathleen & Patrick Murray, Ulrike, Jim & Caitlin Murray, Grit, Jil & Emmie Preuss, Alex, Lea & Katja Glaser